W9-ACG-264

KENNETH L. KNICKERBOCKER

University of Tennessee

～ *IDEAS*

FOR WRITING

Readings for College Composition

REVISED

SALEM COLLEGE LIBRARY
WINSTON-SALEM, N. C.

HOLT, RINEHART AND WINSTON, INC.

NEW YORK

Copyright © 1956

By Holt, Rinehart and Winston, Inc.

Library of Congress Catalog Card Number 56-6065

June, 1960

810.8
K 74

24994-0316

Printed in the United States of America

This book is respectfully dedicated to those with whom I have been associated, closely or remotely, for the past twenty-five years—the teachers of composition and communication in the colleges and universities of America.

OCT 4 '52

61832

Preface to the Revised Edition

THE ORIGINAL PURPOSE of the first edition of this book has been maintained in the present revision. Indeed, all changes have been adopted as means of strengthening the usefulness of the selections in stimulating thoughtful responses from freshman students, responses which may be translated into papers with college-level content.

A number of selections—about one-third of those in the original edition—have been eliminated. Over fifty new selections have been added. The new selections have been chosen for various reasons. Some of them are simpler than the selections which they replace. For example, "The Tenets of Communism" by Salvadori gives a clearer notion of the nature of communism than did the excerpt from Marx and Engels. Many of the new selections, athletics and advertising, for example, bring topics up-to-date. Whenever possible, new selections have been found to sharpen differences in points of view. Over half the sections now offer two sides to the question being considered.

The emphasis on social and political issues has been reduced by merging chapters and by eliminating some of the less stimulating selections. Four completely new topics have been added: "Focus on English," "Stories and Ideas," "Writing about Books," and a sub-section in a chapter now called "Two College Problems: Athletics and Fraternities."

The editorial materials follow the same plan as that used in the first edition. Although there are now twenty-one instead of twenty-eight chapters, the number of suggestions for papers has been increased.

I owe a considerable debt to a great many persons. The teachers of freshman English at several institutions have given concerted, vigorous, and constructive attention to the problem of revising the first edition. I have read with care and have in various ways profited by the staff criticisms which have come to me from Professor Sharon Brown of Brown University, from Professor H. Willard Reninger of

Iowa State Teachers College, from Professor Albert Kitzhaber of the University of Kansas, and from Professor C. R. Petty of the College of San Mateo, California. Professor Kitzhaber's thoughtful suggestions were particularly useful to me.

For the past five years the staff here at the University of Tennessee has kept me aware of the good and bad features of the first edition of *Ideas for Writing*. For providing me with specific, usable suggestions, I am particularly grateful to Professors Adams, Lee, Miller, and Stewart and to Dr. da Ponte, Dr. Markman, Mr. Hardison, and Mr. Park.

To that veteran of many battles with books, my wife, I owe my persistent survival.

K.L.K.

Knoxville, Tennessee
March 1, 1956

To the Instructor

THE IDEA IS THE THING! A student paper undisturbed by an idea is a clod and, no matter how precise the grammar, need not have been written. College freshmen are neither too young nor too inexperienced to have ideas. Through their minds, one may be sure, pass thoughts on many subjects, bright thoughts and dull, but all in need of winnowing and organizing before they can be acceptably communicated. Both winnowing and organizing, however, involve choice—the selection of the relevant and the rejection of the irrelevant. Choice requires the kind of mental effort from which everyone, including students, shrinks. When, therefore, the English instructor asks the student to show a sample of his mental wares, the reply is too often: "Indeed, I haven't any." It does not help matters that the student feels unabashed by his blankness. Nor does it seem to be the height of justice—though it may be the height of something—for the student with a shrug to shift the blame to his instructor!

The chief aim of this book is to remove the student's feeling that he has nothing to say. If the selections and the editorial matter succeed in carrying out this single purpose, then the end result of a composition course—the student paper—should be a more thoughtful and, therefore, a more satisfactory performance.

Some of the selections present controversial material. No reader will be able to agree with all the opinions set forth in this book for the simple reason that opposing ideas have been represented whenever possible. I have deliberately included statements of points of view with which I am personally in partial or total disagreement. These statements are the devil's advocates, so to speak, and it will be my duty—and pleasure!—to confound them in the classroom. The excerpt concerning communism, for example, presents a theory which can be refuted on strictly logical grounds. Students, I am confident, can pick out the flaws in the communist argument; they can see, for one thing, that a class struggle requires sharply defined classes and that a capitalistic society tends to keep fluid the imagined boundaries between classes. Teachers and students together can find much more that is wrong with the Marxian doctrine. They can combine further to examine the atheistic argument in Professor Stace's "Man against Darkness." I have referred frequently to this article because it represents a strong statement of an extreme point of view. That I disagree with it—that others will surely and perhaps violently disagree with it—is the best reason for including it. From class discussions of controversial issues will come some wisdom; out of the wisdom will come better writing.

There are, of course, numerous books of readings for college freshmen. They are organized in a variety of ways: by types (short stories, essays, drama, poetry), by forms (exposition, narration, description, argumentation), by broad topics (Conflicts in Social Thought, Modern Problems, The World of the Future, and the like). Some texts provide two or more tables of contents to show how the same materials can be fitted into different patterns. Each kind of organization has certain advantages and, perhaps, certain disadvantages.

The organization of this text is based upon ideas. Each selection contributes to the chapter idea so that, in effect, every chapter is a tiny anthology of material on a restricted topic. This arrangement offers several advantages: (1) it enables the reader to look at the idea from two or more points of view; (2) through repetition with a difference, it tends to make clear what may be obscure in a single statement; (3) it demonstrates that exposition in its broad sense includes all the types and forms of writing, even poetry.

A word of explanation is necessary about the inclusion of poetry. Many anthologies for freshmen provide a section devoted entirely to poems. When the time comes for studying that section, the average student groans. He may not care greatly for other types of writing, but he is sure that poetry is difficult and that he does not like it. If, however, poems are used with prose selections as part of the exposition of an idea, some of the prejudice may be removed. A colleague has described this procedure as slipping up on the students' blind side. All is fair in love, war, and the teaching of poetry!

All selections, prose and poetry, were chosen for their clear statement of an idea. The quality of the writing ranges from good to excellent. On the average the selections are relatively short, with the longest running to about six thousand words. Since student papers are normally brief, it has seemed useful to provide examples of brevity in the treatment of a topic.

Because many teachers prefer to require two papers on a single chapter (the second paper almost invariably is better than the first), material in many chapters has been augmented for this edition. Although it is not necessary to assign the whole chapter at once, there is an obvious advantage in reading, whether in one assignment or more, all the materials which make up the chapter.

Editorial aids are of three kinds: (1) a brief introduction to each chapter; (2) study aids at the end of each selection; (3) suggestions for papers at the end of each chapter. The chapter introductions brief the reader on the chapter idea. They provide, in the first paragraph, a preliminary view of the idea as a whole and attempt to start and direct the reader's thinking on the chapter theme. After this orientation paragraph come explanatory comments on each selection. For the most part these comments vary in length according to the difficulty of the selection. It is the intention of the introductions to encourage thoughtfulness by offering the kind of help that the average college freshman may reasonably be expected to need.

The study aids at the end of each selection are intended to serve three purposes: (1) to test the care with which the selection has been read; (2) to call attention to relationships of facts and ideas within the selection; (3) to remind the reader of facts and ideas in previous selections which bear upon the selection being read. In addition, the reader is frequently asked to explain or to discuss a point in the light of his own experience. If the student answers all the questions and follows all the directions at the end of each selection, he should be adequately prepared to cope with the writing assignments at the end of each chapter.

The suggestions for papers at the end of each chapter are preceded by a short paragraph which reviews the chapter idea and indicates in general terms what *any* paper on this idea will be like. Following this are two lists of suggestions for specific papers. The first is made up of fairly detailed questions and directions which demand a thoughtful approach to the chapter theme. After the student has jotted down the answers to the questions and has followed the directions, he will have the materials for a paper. In some instances, the organization of the paper is suggested, but for the most part the student must do his own organizing and must provide the title for his paper. The second list consists of titles for papers. Each title is intended to suggest a definite approach to the chapter theme. Although there are approximately thirty suggestions for papers at the end of each chapter and more than eight hundred such suggestions in the whole book, instructors and students will doubtless find still other suitable approaches to the chapter ideas.

The best way to use this book will be determined, of course, by the instructor acting on his own initiative or by the instructor acting in accordance with a departmental plan. I would, however, offer this suggestion. If the class meets three times a week on the normal Monday, Wednesday and Friday or Tuesday, Thursday and Saturday pattern, and if there is to be a paper each week, the following scheme is effective: (1) at the first class meeting of the week discuss the chapter which was assigned at the previous class meeting and assign a paper to be written in accordance with the suggestions at the end of the chapter or with the instructor's directions; (2) at the second class meeting of the week, receive the papers; (3) at the third class meeting, return the papers and assign another chapter.

In assigning a chapter, the instructor may wish to emphasize that the chapter introduction, the questions and directions at the end of each selection, and the suggestions for papers are an integral part of the assignment. He probably will add his own briefing on what the students should look for while reading the selections. A practical pattern for class discussion of the assigned chapter is provided by the questions on the selections. All parts of the discussion should be focused on the writing assignment. If this focus is maintained, the question of what to write about will be at least partially solved by the time the class discussion ends.

At this point one must assume that the student, during the time which he has set aside for the purpose, will review the material which bears on his topic. If he is well advised, he will write his first draft no later than the night of the day on which the class discussion took place. This practice will not allow his idea to cool but will allow the first draft to do so. The paper may be put into final shape the following night.

At the third class period of the week, the instructor has the opportunity to prepare the way for the next paper by comments on the best and worst features of the papers being returned. With the assignment of the next chapter, the process begins all over again.

Newman once observed that there are "few, indeed . . . who can dispense with the stimulus and support of instructors, or will do anything at all, if left to themselves." This text makes no pretense of substituting for the instructor, but it offers him some practical help toward stimulating a disciplined flow of thought from his students.

To the Student

THE THEORY OF THIS BOOK is that, in spite of protests to the contrary, you, the college student, have something to say. You may not like to write themes, but you certainly like to air your ideas. College is a place for doing this and for testing the worth of one's ideas. You will be given numerous opportunities to say what you want to say and to have what you say read with sympathetic, expert care. If you write each paper with sincerity, you will have at the end of the course a record of your best thinking on a variety of challenging subjects.

As a college student, you cannot afford to be afraid of a challenging idea. Physical cowardice is bad enough, but mental cowardice is worse. No doubt you are well stocked with favorite ideas and beliefs. If you really think well of your favorites, you will be glad to back them against any hostile ideas. You will expect to win much of the time but not always. If you leave college with all your ideas unchanged, you may feel that yours was a dubious investment in higher education.

This book does not try to avoid controversial matters, such as communism, race prejudice, religion, the place of women, the meaning of freedom, the threat of science. You already have opinions on most of these subjects, and your point of view will doubtless be supported by some of the selections. Doubtless, too, some of your most cherished beliefs will be challenged by other selections. For example, you may be sensitive to the very word *Communism.* Many people are. You will not be afraid, however, to find out what communism is and to pit democratic ideas against the best it has to offer. Another touchy subject is religion. Again, you have reasons for believing as you do. If something you read runs counter to your beliefs, you will examine the new idea with the same fairness which you would wish extended to your ideas.

If you have something to say, you will find a way to say it. Even the mechanics of your writing—spelling, the placing of commas, the arrangement of your sentences—will be improved by the desire to say something. The selections in this book will give focus to things you already know. The questions at the end of the selections will serve as guides to a review of your reading. If you answer the questions, you will have plenty of raw material from which a paper may be fashioned. Then, at the end of each chapter, are numerous specific suggestions for writing. These will help you to hold your idea to a single channel. Choose and write!

Contents

1. The Desire to Know

2. Of Myself

3. Kinds of Delinquency

4. Focus on English

5. Jobs

6. Perfectionists

7. Two College Problems: Athletics and Fraternities

8. Advertising

9. War

10. Segregation and De-segregation

11. The Meaning of Freedom

Contents

12. Democracy Versus Communism

13. God and Man

14. Science and Man

15. Love and Marriage

16. Women and Men

17. About Education

18. Some Essentials of the Poetic Experience

19. Poems and Ideas

20. Fiction and Ideas

21. Writing About Books

～ *THE DESIRE TO KNOW*

AT THE BEGINNING OF A COLLEGE CAREER, it is no waste of time to weigh one's basic aptitude for doing college work. The desire to know—intellectual curiosity—is an essential without which a student is sure to feel a constant sense of frustration, of not belonging to a community of seekers. College provides the broadest opportunity for first stimulating and then providing the means for satisfying one's urge to know.

The first selection in this chapter, written about three hundred years ago, presents a shrewd analysis of four easily recognized types of students, as easily recognized today as they were in the seventeenth century. Your instructors, sooner or later, may be tempted to drop you into one of these categories. Which, do you think, it should be?

The other five selections are an invitation to you to assess the relative sharpness of your curiosity by measuring it against this quality as described by a sports writer, a scientist, an author, and a poet. By placing the selections on curiosity first in this book, I am deliberately suggesting that an intellectual curiosity is the first requirement for success in your English course—and, for that matter, in all your college work.

Paul Gallico examines his responses to the numerous sensations which are experienced by athletes. In his autobiographical essay, which he calls "The Feel," he justifies the curiosity—a specialized

1

sort of curiosity—which drove him to participate in almost every recognized sport. His object was to improve the quality and truth of his work as a sports writer.

"In the Laboratory with Agassiz" is a report on curiosity directed toward the sharpening of the power of observation. Again, as in "The Feel," observation was a means to an end, a scientific method, for "facts are stupid things . . . until brought into connection with some general law."

Walter Prichard Eaton suggests that the power of observation "comes by the grace of Heaven" and is not to be acquired. His curiosity, like that of Gallico and Scudder, has a practical application: the gaining of A's at Harvard and the making of a living as a professional writer.

The journalist, the scientist, and the author make it clear that good journalism, good science, and good writing are hardly possible without the stimulus of the desire to know. Finally, Tennyson, in two poems, examines curiosity as a driving force in the life of Ulysses, a Greek adventurer, and then shows in "The Lotos Eaters" how men, in the absence of energy, can argue for the pleasures of a vegetative existence. Ulysses, it will be noted, does not propose any usefulness to his quest, for he says that

> . . . all experience is an arch wherethro'
> Gleams that untravell'd world, whose margin fades
> Forever and forever when I move.

The victims of the lotos, facing the same world, ask:

> Death is the end of life; ah, why
> Should life all labour be?

The reader will note that curiosity, in its favorable sense, connotes the presence of energy. Indeed, an apathetic curiosity would be a contradiction in terms. Why? What, then, is meant by the phrase "idle curiosity"?

❧ *Four Types of Students*

Thomas Fuller

. . . Experienced schoolmasters may quickly make a grammar of boys' natures, and reduce them all, saving some few exceptions, to these general rules:

(a) Those that are ingenious and industrious. The conjunction of two such planets in a youth presage much good unto him. To such a lad a frown may be a whipping, and a whipping a death; yea, where their master whips them once, shame whips them all the week after. Such natures he useth with all gentleness.

(b) Those that are ingenious and idle. These think, with the hare in the fable, that, running with snails (so they count the rest of their schoolfellows), they shall come soon enough to the post, though sleeping a good while before their starting. Oh, a good rod would finely take them napping!

(c) Those that are dull and diligent. Wines, the stronger they be, the more lees they have when they are new. Many boys are muddy-headed till they be clarified with age, and such afterwards prove the best. Bristol diamonds are both bright, and squared and pointed by nature, and yet are soft and worthless; whereas orient ones in India are rough and rugged naturally. Hard, rugged, and dull natures of youth acquit themselves afterwards the jewels of the country, and therefore their dullness at first is to be borne with, if they be diligent. That schoolmaster deserves to be beaten himself, who beats nature in a boy for a fault. And I question whether all the whipping in the world can make their parts, which are naturally sluggish, rise one minute before the hour nature hath appointed.

(d) Those that are invincibly dull and negligent also. Correction may reform the latter, not amend the former. All the whetting in the world can never set a razor's edge on that which hath no steel in it. Such boys he consigneth over to other professions. Shipwrights and boatmakers will choose those crooked pieces of timber which other carpenters refuse. Those may make excellent merchants and mechanics who will not serve for scholars.

From "The Good Schoolmaster," *The Holy and the Profane State*, first published in 1642.

QUESTIONS ON CONTENT

1. In what sense does Fuller use the word *grammar?*
2. Define *ingenious; ingenuous.*
3. "The conjunction of . . . planets" refers to what "science"?
4. To what story does "the hare in the fable" refer?
5. What are *lees?*
6. What use does the author make of the figure of speech about Bristol and Indian diamonds?
7. In the last paragraph, what does *steel* represent?
8. What do "crooked pieces of timber" represent?
9. How many of the four types of student will benefit from whippings?

❧ *The Feel*

PAUL GALLICO

A child wandering through a department store with its mother is admonished over and over again not to touch things. Mother is convinced that the child only does it to annoy or because it is a child, and usually hasn't the vaguest inkling of the fact that Junior is "touching" because he is a little blotter soaking up information and knowledge, and "feel" is an important adjunct to seeing. Adults are exactly the same, in a measure, as you may ascertain when some new gadget or article is produced for inspection. The average person says: "Here, let me see that," and holds out his hand. He doesn't mean "see," because he is already seeing it. What he means is that he wants to get it into his hands and feel it so as to become better acquainted.

I do not insist that a curiosity and capacity for feeling sports is necessary to be a successful writer, but it is fairly obvious that a man who has been tapped on the chin with five fingers wrapped up in a leather boxing glove and propelled by the arm of an expert knows more about that particular sensation than one who has not, always provided he has the gift of expressing himself. I once inquired of a heavyweight prizefighter by the name of King Levinsky,

Reprinted from *Farewell to Sport* by Paul Gallico, by permission of Alfred A. Knopf, Inc. Copyright 1938 by Paul Gallico.

in a radio interview, what it felt like to be hit on the chin by Joe Louis, the King having just acquired that experience with rather disastrous results. Levinsky considered the matter for a moment and then reported: "It don't feel like nuttin'," but added that for a long while afterwards he felt as though he were "in a transom."

I was always a child who touched things and I have always had a tremendous curiosity with regard to sensation. If I knew what playing a game felt like, particularly against or in the company of experts, I was better equipped to write about the playing of it and the problems of the men and women who took part in it. And so, at one time or another, I have tried them all, football, baseball, boxing, riding, shooting, swimming, squash, handball, fencing, driving, flying, both land and sea planes, rowing, canoeing, skiing, riding a bicycle, ice-skating, roller-skating, tennis, golf, archery, basketball, running, both the hundred-yard dash and the mile, the high-jump and shot-put, badminton, angling, deep-sea, stream-, and surf-casting, billiards and bowling, motorboating and wrestling, besides riding as a passenger with the fastest men on land and water and in the air, to see what it felt like. Most of them I dabbled in as a youngster going through school and college, and others, like piloting a plane, squash, fencing, and skiing, I took up after I was old enough to know better, purely to get the feeling of what they were like.

None of these things can I do well, but I never cared about becoming an expert, and besides, there wasn't time. But there is only one way to find out accurately human sensations in a ship two or three thousand feet up when the motor quits, and that is actually to experience that gone feeling at the pit of the stomach and the sharp tingling of the skin from head to foot, followed by a sudden amazing sharpness of vision, clear-sightedness, and coolness that you never knew you possessed as you find the question of life or death completely in your own hands. It is not the "you" that you know, but somebody else, a stranger, who noses the ship down, circles, fastens upon the one best spot to sit down, pushes or pulls buttons to try to get her started again, and finally drops her in, safe and sound. And it is only by such experience that you learn likewise of the sudden weakness that hits you right at the back of the knees after you have climbed out and started to walk around her and that comes close to knocking you flat as for the first time since the engine quit its soothing drone you think of destruction and sudden death.

Often my courage has failed me and I have funked completely, such as the time I went up to the top of the thirty-foot Olympic diving-tower at Jones Beach, Long Island, during the competitions, to see what it was like to dive from that height, and wound up crawling away from the edge on hands and knees, dizzy, scared, and a little sick, but with a wholesome respect for the boys and girls who hurled themselves through the air and down through the tough skin of the water from that awful height. At other times sheer ignorance of what I was getting into has led me into tight spots such as the time I came down the Olympic ski run from the top of the Kreuzeck, six thousand feet above Garmisch-Partenkirchen, after having been on skis but once before in snow and for the rest had no more than a dozen lessons on an indoor artificial slide in a New York department store. At one point my legs, untrained, got so tired that I couldn't stem (brake) any more, and I lost control and went full tilt and all out, down a three-foot twisting path cut out of the side of the mountain, with a two-thousand-foot abyss on the left and the mountain itself on the right. That was probably the most scared I have ever been, and I scare fast and often. I remember giving myself up for lost and wondering how long it would take them to retrieve my body and whether I should be still alive. In the meantime the speed of the descent was increasing. Somehow I was keeping my feet and negotiating turns, how I will never know, until suddenly the narrow patch opened out into a wide, steep stretch of slope with a rise at the other end, and *that* part of the journey was over.

By some miracle I got to the bottom of the run uninjured, having made most of the trip down the icy, perpendicular slopes on the flat of my back. It was the thrill and scare of a lifetime, and to date no one has been able to persuade me to try a jump. I know when to stop. After all, I am entitled to rely upon my imagination for something. But when it was all over and I found myself still whole, it was also distinctly worth while to have learned what is required of a ski runner in the breakneck *Abfahrt* or downhill race, or the difficult *slalom*. Five days later, when I climbed laboriously (still on skis) halfway up that Alp and watched the Olympic downhill racers hurtling down the perilous, ice-covered, and nearly perpendicular *Steilhang*, I knew that I was looking at a great group of athletes who, for one thing, did not know the meaning of the word "fear." The slope was studded with small pine trees and rocks, but half of the field gained precious seconds by hitting that slope all out, with complete contempt for disaster rushing up at them at a speed better than sixty miles an hour. And when an unfortunate Czech skidded off the course at the bottom of the slope and into a pile of rope and got himself snarled up as helpless as a fly in a spider's web, it was a story that I could write from the heart. I had spent ten minutes getting myself untangled after a fall *without* any rope to add to the difficulties. It seems that I couldn't find where my left leg ended and one more ski than I had originally donned seemed to be involved somehow. Only a person who has been on those fiendish runners knows the sensation.

It all began back in 1922 when I was a cub sports-writer and consumed with more curiosity than was good for my health. I had seen my first professional prizefights and wondered at the curious behavior of men under the stress of blows, the sudden checking and the beginning of a little fall forward after a hard punch, the glazing of the eyes and the loss of locomotor control, the strange actions of men on the canvas after a knockdown as they struggled to regain their senses and arise on legs that seemed to have turned into rubber. I had never been in any bad fist fights as a youngster, though I had taken a little physical punishment in football, but it was not enough to complete the picture. Could one think under those conditions?

I had been assigned to my first training-camp coverage, Dempsey's at Saratoga Springs, where he was preparing for his famous fight with Luis Firpo. For days I watched him sag a spar boy with what seemed to be no more than a light cuff on the neck, or pat his face with what looked like no more than a caressing stroke of his arm, and the fellow would come all apart at the seams and collapse in a useless heap, grinning vacuously or twitching strangely. My burning curiosity got the better of prudence and a certain reluctance to expose myself to physical pain. I asked Dempsey to permit me to box a round with him. I had never boxed before, but I was in good physical shape, having just completed a four-years stretch as a galley slave in the Columbia eight-oared shell.

When it was over and I escaped through the ropes, shaking, bleeding a little from the mouth, with rosin dust on my pants and a vicious throbbing in my head, I knew all that there was to know about being hit in the prize ring. It seems that I had gone to an expert for tuition. I knew the sensation of being stalked and pursued by a relentless, truculent professional destroyer whose trade and business it was to injure men. I saw the quick flash of the brown forearm that precedes the stunning shock as a bony, leather-bound fist lands on cheek or mouth. I learned more (partly from photographs of the lesson, viewed afterwards, one of which shows me ducked under a vicious left hook, an act of which I never had the slightest recollection) about instinctive ducking and blocking than I could have in ten years of looking at prizefights, and I learned, too, that as the soldier never hears the bullet that kills him, so does the fighter rarely, if ever, see the punch that tumbles blackness over him like a mantle, with a tearing rip as though the roof of his skull were exploding, and robs him of his senses.

There was just that—a ripping in my head and then sudden blackness, and the next thing I knew, I was sitting on the canvas covering of the ring floor with my legs collapsed under me, grinning idiotically. How often since have I seen that same silly, goofy look on the faces of dropped fighters—and understood it. I held onto the floor with both hands, because the ring and the audience outside were making a complete clockwise revolution, came to a stop, and then went back again counter-clockwise. When I struggled to my feet, Jack Kearns, Dempsey's manager, was counting over me, but I neither saw nor heard him and was only conscious that I was in a ridiculous position and that the thing to do was to get up and try to fight back. The floor swayed and rocked beneath me like a fishing dory in an off-shore swell, and it was a welcome respite when Dempsey rushed into a clinch, held me up, and whispered into my ear: "Wrestle around a bit, son, until your head clears." And then it was that I learned what those little love-taps to the back of the neck and the short digs to the ribs can mean to the groggy pugilist more than half knocked out. It is a murderous game, and the fighter who can escape after having been felled by a lethal blow has my admiration. And there, too, I learned that there can be no sweeter sound than the bell that calls a halt to hostilities.

From that afternoon on, also, dated my antipathy for the spectator at prizefights who yells: "Come on, you bum, get up and fight! Oh, you big quitter! Yah yellow, yah yellow!" Yellow, eh? It is all a man can do to get up after being stunned by a blow, much less fight back. But they do it. And how a man is able to muster any further interest in a combat after being floored with a blow to the pit of the stomach will always remain to me a miracle of what the human animal is capable of under stress.

Further experiments were less painful, but equally illuminating. A couple of sets of tennis with Vinnie Richards taught me more about what is required of a top-flight tournament tennis-player

than I could have got out of a dozen books or years of reporting
tennis matches. It is one thing to sit in a press box and write caus-
tically that Brown played uninspired tennis, or Black's court
covering was faulty and that his frequent errors cost him the set.
It is quite another to stand across the net at the back of a service
court and try to get your racket on a service that is so fast that the
ear hardly detects the interval between the sound of the server's
bat hitting the ball and the ball striking the court. Tournament
tennis is a different game from week-end tennis. For one thing, in
average tennis, after the first hard service has gone into the net
or out, you breathe a sigh of relief, move up closer and wait for
the cripple to come floating over. In big-time tennis second service
is practically as hard as the first, with an additional twist on the
ball.

It is impossible to judge or know anything about the speed of
a fore-hand drive hit by a champion until you have had one fired
at you, or, rather away from you, and you have made an attempt to
return it. It is then that you first realize that tennis is played more
with the head than with the arms and the legs. The fastest player
in the world cannot get to a drive to return it if he hasn't thought
correctly, guessed its direction, and anticipated it by a fraction of a
second.

There was golf with Bob Jones and Gene Sarazen and Tommy
Armour, little Cruickshank and Johnny Farrell, and Diegel and other
professionals; and experiments at trying to keep up in the water with
Johnny Weismuller, Helen Madison, and Eleanor Holm, attempts
to catch football passes thrown by Benny Friedman. Nobody
actually plays golf until he has acquired the technical perfection to
be able to hit the ball accurately, high, low, hooked or faded and
placed. And nobody knows what real golf is like until he has played
around with a professional and seen him play, not the ball, but the
course, the roll of the land, the hazards, the wind, and the texture
of the greens and the fairways. It looks like showmanship when a
topflight golfer plucks a handful of grass and lets it flutter in the
air, or abandons his drive to march two hundred yards down to
the green and look over the situation. It isn't. It's golf. The average
player never knows or cares whether he is putting with or across
the grain of a green. The professional *always* knows. The same
average player standing on the tee is concentrated on getting the
ball somewhere on the fairway, two hundred yards out. The professional when preparing to drive is actually to all intents and purposes

playing his *second* shot. He means to place his drive so as to open up the green for his approach. But you don't find that out until you have played around with them when they are relaxed and not competing, and listen to them talk and plan attacks on holes.

Major-league baseball is one of the most difficult and precise of all games, but you would never know it unless you went down on the field and got close to it and tried it yourself. For instance, the distance between pitcher and catcher is a matter of twenty paces, but it doesn't seem like enough when you don a catcher's mitt and try to hold a pitcher with the speed of Dizzy Dean or Dazzy Vance. Not even the sponge that catchers wear in the palm of the hand when working with fast-ball pitchers, and the bulky mitt are sufficient to rob the ball of shock and sting that lames your hand unless you know how to ride with the throw and kill some of its speed. The pitcher, standing on his little elevated mound, looms up enormously over you at that short distance, and when he ties himself into a coiled spring preparatory to letting fly, it requires all your self-control not to break and run for safety. And as for the things they can do with a baseball, those major-league pitchers . . . ! One way of finding out is to wander down on the field an hour or so before game-time when there is no pressure on them, pull on the catcher's glove, and try to hold them.

I still remember my complete surprise the first time I tried catching for a real curve-ball pitcher. He was a slim, spidery left-hander of the New York Yankees, many years ago, by the name of Herb Pennock. He called that he was going to throw a fast breaking curve and warned me to expect the ball at least two feet outside the plate. Then he wound up and let it go, and that ball came whistling right down the groove for the center of the plate. A novice, I chose to believe what I saw and not what I heard, and prepared to catch it where it was headed for, a spot which of course it never reached, because just in front of the rubber it swerved sharply to the right and passed nearly a yard from my glove. I never had a chance to catch it. That way, you learn about the mysterious drop, the ball that sails down the alley chest high but which you must be prepared to catch around your ankles because of the sudden dip it takes at the end of its passage as though someone were pulling it down with a string. Also you find out about that queer fade-away, the slow curve, the fast in- and out-shoots that seem to be timed almost as delicately as shrapnel, to burst, or rather break, just when they will do the most harm—namely, at the moment when the batter is swinging.

Facing a big-league pitcher with a bat on your shoulder and trying to hit his delivery is another vital experience in gaining an understanding of the game about which you are trying to write vividly. It is one thing to sit in the stands and scream at a batsman: "Oh, you bum!" for striking out in a pinch, and another to stand twenty yards from that big pitcher and try to make up your mind in a hundredth of a second whether to hit at the offering or not, where to swing and when, not to mention worrying about protecting yourself from the consequences of being struck by the ball that seems to be heading straight for your skull at an appalling rate of speed. Because, if you are a big-league player, you cannot very well afford to be gun-shy and duck away in panic from a ball that swerves in the last moment and breaks perfectly over the plate, while the umpire calls: "Strike!" and the fans jeer. Nor can you afford to take a crack on the temple from the ball. Men have died from that. It calls for undreamed-of niceties of nerve and judgment, but you don't find that out until you have stepped to the plate cold a few times during batting practice or in training quarters, with nothing at stake but the acquisition of experience, and see what a fine case of the jumping jitters you get. Later on, when you are writing your story, your imagination, backed by the experience, will be able to supply a picture of what the batter is going through as he stands at the plate in the closing innings of an important game, with two or three men on base, two out, and his team behind in the scoring, and fifty thousand people screaming at him.

The catching and holding of a forward pass for a winning touchdown on a cold, wet day always makes a good yarn, but you might get an even better one out of it if you happen to know from experience about the elusive qualities of a hard, soggy, mud-slimed football rifled through the air, as well as something about the exquisite timing, speed, and courage it takes to catch it on a dead run, with two or three 190-pound men reaching for it at the same time or waiting to crash you as soon as your fingers touch it.

Any football coach during a light practice will let you go down the field and try to catch punts, the long, fifty-yard spirals and the tricky, tumbling end-over-enders. Unless you have had some previous experience, you won't hang on to one out of ten, besides knocking your fingers out of joint. But if you have any imagination,

SALEM COLLEGE LIBRARY
WINSTON - SALEM, N. C.

thereafter you will know that it calls for more than negligible nerve
to judge and hold that ball and even plan to run with it, when there
are two husky ends bearing down at full speed, preparing for a
head-on tackle.

In 1932 I covered my first set of National Air Races, in Cleveland,
and immediately decided that I had to learn how to fly to find
out what that felt like. Riding as a passenger isn't flying. Being up
there all alone at the controls of a ship is. And at the same time
began a series of investigations into the "feel" of the mechanized
sports to see what they were all about and the qualities of mentality,
nerve, and physique they called for from their participants. These
included a ride with Gar Wood in his latest and fastest speedboat,
Miss America X, in which for the first time he pulled the throttle
wide open on the Detroit River straightaway; a trip with the Indianapolis Speedway driver Cliff Bergere, around the famous brick
raceway; and a flip with Lieutenant Al Williams, one time U. S.
Schneider Cup race pilot.

I was scared with Wood, who drove me at 127 miles an hour,
jounced, shaken, vibrated, choked with fumes from the exhausts, behind which I sat hanging on desperately to the throttle bar, which
after while got too hot to hold. I was on a plank between Wood
and his mechanic, Johnson, and thought that my last moment had
come. I was still more scared when Cliff Bergere hit 126 on the
Indianapolis straightaway in the tiny racing car in which I was
hopelessly wedged, and after the first couple of rounds quite resigned to die and convinced that I should. But I think the most
scared I have ever been while moving fast was during a ride I took
in the cab of a locomotive on the straight, level stretch between
Fort Wayne, Indiana, and Chicago, where for a time we hit 90
miles per hour, which of course is no speed at all. But nobody
who rides in the comfortable Pullman coaches has any idea of the
didos cut up by a locomotive in a hurry, or the thrill of pelting
through a small town, all out and wide open, including the crossing
of some thirty or forty frogs and switches, all of which must be set
right. But that wasn't sport. That was just plain excitement.

I have never regretted these researches. Now that they are over,
there isn't enough money to make me do them again. But they paid
me dividends, I figured. During the Great Thompson Speed Trophy
race for land planes at Cleveland in 1935, Captain Roscoe Turner
was some eight or nine miles in the lead in his big golden, low-wing,

SALEM COLLEGE LIBRARY
WINSTON-SALEM, N. C.

speed monoplane. Suddenly, coming into the straightaway in front of the grandstands, buzzing along at 280 miles an hour like an angry hornet, a streamer of thick, black smoke burst from the engine cowling and trailed back behind the ship. Turner pulled up immediately, using his forward speed to gain all the altitude possible, turned and got back to the edge of the field, still pouring out that evil black smoke. Then he cut his switch, dipped her nose down, landed with a bounce and a bump, and rolled up to the line in a perfect stop. The crowd gave him a cheer of sympathy because he had lost the race after having been so far in the lead that had he continued he could not possibly have been overtaken.

There was that story, but there was a better one too. Only the pilots on the field, all of them white around the lips and wiping from their faces a sweat not due to the oppressive summer heat, knew that they were looking at a man who from that time on, to use their own expression, was living on borrowed time. It isn't often when a Thompson Trophy racer with a landing speed of around eighty to ninety miles an hour goes haywire in the air, that the pilot is able to climb out of the cockpit and walk away from his machine. From the time of that first burst of smoke until the wheels touched the ground and stayed there, he was a hundred-to-one shot to live. To the initiated, those dreadful moments were laden with suspense and horror. Inside that contraption was a human being who any moment might be burned to a horrible, twisted cinder, or smashed into the ground beyond all recognition, a human being who was cool, gallant, and fighting desperately. Every man and woman on the field who had ever been in trouble in the air was living those awful seconds with him in terror and suspense. I, too, was able to experience it. That is what makes getting the "feel" of things distinctly worth while.

QUESTIONS ON CONTENT

1. Why is this article called "The Feel"?
2. Who is called "a little blotter"? Why?
3. What is "a transom"? What did Levinsky mean to say?
4. From the list of sports in the third paragraph has Gallico omitted any activity which may be classed as a sport?
5. Why didn't the author care about being an expert at sports? What expertness did he want?

6. Was Gallico a fearless man?

7. What was the author's first attempt to gain the "feel" of a sport?

8. Did Gallico want to repeat his experience once he had "the feel"?

9. What type of student, according to the classification in "Four Types of Student" (see previous selection), would you say Gallico was?

10. Was there a focus to Gallico's curiosity or was it undirected?

❧ *In the Laboratory with Agassiz*

SAMUEL H. SCUDDER

It was more than fifteen years ago [from 1874] that I entered the laboratory of Professor Agassiz, and told him I had enrolled my name in the Scientific School as a student of natural history. He asked me a few questions about my object in coming, my antecedents generally, the mode in which I afterwards proposed to use the knowledge I might acquire, and, finally, whether I wished to study any special branch. To the latter I replied that, while I wished to be well grounded in all departments of zoology, I purposed to devote myself specially to insects.

"When do you wish to begin?" he asked.

"Now," I replied.

This seemed to please him, and with an energetic "Very well!" he reached from a shelf a huge jar of specimens in yellow alcohol.

"Take this fish," said he, "and look at it; we call it a haemulon; by and by I will ask what you have seen."

With that he left me, but in a moment returned with explicit instructions as to the care of the object entrusted to me.

"No man is fit to be a naturalist," said he, "who does not know how to take care of specimens."

I was to keep the fish before me in a tin tray, and occasionally moisten the surface with alcohol from the jar, always taking care to replace the stopper tightly. Those were not the days of ground-glass stoppers and elegantly shaped exhibition jars; all the old students will recall the huge neckless glass bottles with their leaky, wax-

From *Every Saturday*, XVI (April 4, 1874), 369–370.

besmeared corks, half eaten by insects, and begrimed with cellar dust. Entomology was a cleaner science than ichthyology, but the example of the Professor, who had unhesitatingly plunged to the bottom of the jar to produce the fish, was infectious; and though this alcohol had a "very ancient and fishlike smell," I really dared not show any aversion within these sacred precincts, and treated the alcohol as though it were pure water. Still I was conscious of a passing feeling of disappointment, for gazing at a fish did not commend itself to an ardent entomologist. My friends at home, too, were annoyed when they discovered that no amount of eau-de-Cologne would drown the perfume which haunted me like a shadow.

In ten minutes I had seen all that could be seen in that fish, and started in search of the Professor—who had, however, left the Museum; and when I returned, after lingering over some of the odd animals stored in the upper apartment, my specimen was dry all over. I dashed the fluid over the fish as if to resuscitate the beast from a fainting-fit, and looked with anxiety for a return of the normal sloppy appearance. This little excitement over, nothing was to be done but to return to a steadfast gaze at my mute companion. Half an hour passed—an hour—another hour; the fish began to look loathsome. I turned it over and around; looked it in the face— ghastly; from behind, beneath, above, sideways, at a three-quarters' view—just as ghastly. I was in despair; at an early hour I concluded that lunch was necessary; so, with infinite relief, the fish was carefully replaced in the jar, and for an hour I was free.

On my return, I learned that Professor Agassiz had been at the Museum, but had gone, and would not return for several hours. My fellow-students were too busy to be disturbed by continued conversation. Slowly I drew forth that hideous fish, and with a feeling of desperation again looked at it. I might not use a magnifying-glass; instruments of all kinds were interdicted. My two hands, my two eyes, and the fish: it seemed a most limited field. I pushed my finger down its throat to feel how sharp the teeth were. I began to count the scales in the different rows, until I was convinced that that was nonsense. At last a happy thought struck me—I would draw the fish; and now with surprise I began to discover new features in the creature. Just then the Professor returned.

"That is right," said he; "a pencil is one of the best of eyes. I am glad to notice, too, that you keep your specimen wet, and your bottle corked."

With these encouraging words, he added:

"Well, what is it like?"

He listened attentively to my brief rehearsal of the structure of parts whose names were still unknown to me: the fringed gill-arches and movable operculum; the pores of the head, fleshy lips and lidless eyes; the lateral line, the spinous fins and forked tail; the compressed and arched body. When I had finished, he waited as if expecting more, and then, with an air of disappointment:

"You have not looked very carefully; why," he continued more earnestly, "you haven't even seen one of the most conspicuous features of the animal, which is as plainly before your eyes as the fish itself; look again, look again!" and he left me to my misery.

I was piqued; I was mortified. Still more of that wretched fish! But now I set myself to my task with a will, and discovered one new thing after another, until I saw how just the Professor's criticism had been. The afternoon passed quickly; and when, toward its close, the Professor inquired:

"Do you see it yet?"

"No," I replied, "I am certain I do not, but I see how little I saw before."

"That is next best," said he, earnestly, "but I won't hear you now; put away your fish and go home; perhaps you will be ready with a better answer in the morning. I will examine you before you look at the fish."

This was disconcerting. Not only must I think of my fish all night, studying, without the object before me, what this unknown but most visible feature might be; but also, without reviewing my discoveries, I must give an exact account of them the next day. I had a bad memory; so I walked home by Charles River in a distracted state, with my two perplexities.

The cordial greeting from the Professor the next morning was reassuring; here was a man who seemed to be quite as anxious as I that I should see for myself what he saw.

"Do you perhaps mean," I asked, "that the fish has symmetrical sides with paired organs?"

His thoroughly pleased "Of course! of course!" repaid the wakeful hours of the previous night. After he had discoursed most happily and enthusiastically—as he always did—upon the importance of this point, I ventured to ask what I should do next.

"Oh, look at your fish!" he said, and left me again to my own devices. In a little more than an hour he returned, and heard my new catalogue.

"That is good, that is good!" he repeated; "but that is not all; go on"; and so for three long days he placed that fish before my eyes, forbidding me to look at anything else, or to use any artificial aid. "Look, look, look," was his repeated injunction.

This was the best entomological lesson I ever had—a lesson whose influence has extended to the details of every subsequent study; a legacy the Professor has left to me, as he has left it to many others, of inestimable value, which we could not buy, with which we cannot part.

A year afterward, some of us were amusing ourselves with chalking outlandish beasts on the Museum blackboard. We drew prancing starfishes; frogs in mortal combat; hydra-headed worms; stately crawfishes, standing on their tails, bearing aloft umbrellas; and grotesque fishes with gaping mouths and staring eyes. The Professor came in shortly after, and was as amused as any at our experiments. He looked at the fishes.

"Haemulons, every one of them," he said; "Mr. —— drew them."

True; and to this day, if I attempt a fish, I can draw nothing but haemulons.

The fourth day, a second fish of the same group was placed beside the first, and I was bidden to point out the resemblances and differences between the two; another and another followed, until the entire family lay before me, and a whole legion of jars covered the table and surrounding shelves; the odor had become a pleasant perfume; and even now, the sight of an old, six-inch, worm-eaten cork brings fragrant memories.

The whole group of haemulons was thus brought in review; and, whether engaged upon the dissection of the internal organs, the preparation and examination of the bony framework, or the description of the various parts, Agassiz's training in the method of observing facts and their orderly arrangement was ever accompanied by the urgent exhortation not to be content with them.

"Facts are stupid things," he would say, "until brought into connection with some general law."

At the end of eight months, it was almost with reluctance that I left these friends and turned to insects; but what I had gained by this outside experience has been of greater value than years of later investigation in my favorite groups.

QUESTIONS ON CONTENT

1. Darwin's *Origin of Species* was published in 1859. Could Scudder have read this before he entered "the Scientific School"?
2. What was Agassiz's first generalization about naturalists?
3. How long did Scudder on the first occasion spend looking at the fish? How long did he spend all told looking at the first fish?
4. Why didn't he use a microscope?
5. What helped "open" his eyes to new features of fish?
6. Was Agassiz chiefly concerned with amassing facts?
7. What process followed the examining of the first fish?
8. Have you ever been submitted to a discipline similar to the one described in this article?
9. Which type of student (see "Four Types of Students") would you say Scudder probably was?
10. What do Scudder and Gallico (see "The Feel") have in common?
11. Was Scudder's curiosity more sharply focused than Gallico's?

❧ *The Daily Theme Eye*

WALTER PRICHARD EATON

When I was an undergraduate at Harvard our instructors in English composition endeavored to cultivate in us a something they termed "The Daily Theme Eye." This peculiar variety of optic, I fear, always remained a mystery to a majority of the toilers after clearness, force, and elegance. Clearness, force, and even a certain degree of elegance, may be acquired; but the daily theme eye, like the eye for the sights of a rifle, may be discovered, developed, trained—but not acquired. It comes by the grace of Heaven, not of the Harvard or any other English department, and its possession is often one of the marks of the man whose destiny compels him to write. The Harvard English department has but given it a name; it has no local habitation. It is found in Henry James and the police reporter of the New York *Sun;* it illuminates the pages of *The Harvard Monthly* (sometimes) and of George Moore. It winks at you in Heine and peers solemnly in Mrs. Humphry Ward. And it flashes

From *The Atlantic Monthly*, XCIX (March 1907), 427–429. Reprinted by permission of *The Atlantic Monthly*.

and beams in a little lady I know who has written nothing save sprightly letters all the days of her life and never opened Hill's *Rhetoric* under the shade of the Washington Elm.

The fairy who stood over my cradle, though he forgot the gold spoon and much else besides, at least bestowed the gift of this wonderful optic. It brought me my college degree; for when other courses failed—which means when I failed in other courses—there was always English; it has brought me a living since; but more than all else it has brought me enjoyment, it has clothed the daily walk with interest, the teeming, noisy town with color and beauty, "the society of my contemporaries," to use Emerson's big phrase for my little purpose, with stimulating excitement. It has turned the panorama of existence into a play, or rather a thousand plays, and brought after sorrow or pain the great comfort of composition.

Daily themes in my day had to be short, not over a page of handwriting. They had to be deposited in a box at the professor's door not later than ten five in the morning. A classmate of mine, when an epigram was called for, once wrote, "An epigram is a lazy man's theme written at ten-three A.M." And because of this brevity, and the necessity of writing one every day whether the mood was on you or not, it was not always easy—to be quite modest—to make these themes literature, which, we were told by our instructors, is the transmission through the written word, from writer to reader, of a mood, an emotion, a picture, an idea. I hate to think how few, in fact, of all the thousands that were poured into that yawning box were literature, how seldom the poor instructors could dip their pens into their pots of red ink and write the magic "A" on the back. Their sarcastic comments were surely excusable. I have even forgiven the young man with hair like yellow corn-tassels, who scrawled on verses of mine, required to be written in imitation of some poet, "This may be O'Shaughnessy, it isn't poetry." Did he think thus to kill two song birds with one stone? Well, the effort of those of us who were sincere and comprehending in our pursuit of the elusive power to write was to make our themes literature as often as possible, and to do this the first essential was the choice of a subject. Not everything one sees or does or thinks can take shape on a page of paper and reproduce itself for the reader. Selection was the first requirement.

It became needful, then, to watch for and treasure incidents that were sharply dramatic or poignant, moods that were clear and definite, pictures that created a single clean impression. The tower of Memorial seen across the quiet marshes against the cool pink sky of evening; the sweep of a shell under the bridge and the rush of the spectators to the other rail to watch the needle-bow emerge, and the bent, brown backs of the crew; the chorus girls, still rubbing the paint from their cheeks with a tiny handkerchief wrapped over the forefinger, coming out of a stage entrance into the snow; the first sharp impression of a book just read or a play just seen,—these were the things we cherished, for these we could put on a page of paper with a beginning, a middle, and an end, and with some show of vividness. What we came to do, then, was to keep a note-book of our impressions, and when in June our themes were returned to us we had a precious record for the year. By training the daily theme eye, we watched for and found in the surroundings of our life, as it passed, a heightened picturesqueness, a constant wonder, an added significance. That hardened cynic, the professional writer, will smile and say, "You saw copy." Yes, we saw copy, but to see copy is to see the significant, to clarify what the ear and heart and eye receive, to add light and shadow to the monochrome of life.

My college roommate, a blessed boy full of good humor and serious purpose, was as incapable of acquiring the daily theme eye as a cat of obeying the eighth commandment. His idea of a daily theme was a task, not a pleasure. If there was no chance to write a political editorial, he supplied an anecdote of his summer vacation. Once he described a cliff he had seen in Newfoundland, and, determined to be pictorial, he added, "tumbling waterfalls" and "sighing pines." Unfortunately, the instructor who read it had also been in Newfoundland, and he pointed out that his investigations of the cliff in question had failed to disclose either "tumbling water-falls" or "sighing pines." My roommate treated the matter as a joke; he could not see that he had been guilty of any fault. And yet he is a much more moral man than I, with a far more troublesome conscience. Truth to his principles he would die for. But truth to the picture his mind retained and his hand tried to portray in the medium of literature, to him so trivial and unimportant, he could not grasp. What did it matter? So it would never occur to him to record in his themes the fleeting impressions of his daily life, to sit up half the night trying to pack into the clumsy frame of words the recollection of a strangely innocent face seen suddenly in the flash of an opened door down a dark, evil alley where the gusts of winter swirled. He went to bed and never knew a headache or a jumpy nerve. Yet I could not help thinking then that there was something in life he was missing besides the ultimate mark in our composition course. And I cannot help thinking that there is something in life he misses still.

But perhaps that is only my fancy. George Moore says that happiness is no more than a faculty for being surprised; and it is the sudden vista, the beauty of a city square seen through falling snow, a street-car drama, the face of a passing woman, the dialogue of friends, which make the surprises for the man with the eye for copy. George Moore himself has a daily theme eye of preternatural keenness, and he may be speaking only for a class. Happiness for my roommate lies, I suspect, rather in his faculty for not being surprised. A sudden accession of emotion at the sight of an unexpected view, for instance, would probably be immensely disconcerting. And if he should go into an art museum, as I did the other day, and see a little marble boy with a slightly parted mouth wet his lips with his tongue, I truly believe he would rush off to the doctor's at once, very unhappy, instead of rushing joyfully home to try to put the illusion into a sonnet! Well, every class has its Pharisaism, which in reality isn't a form of priggishness, at all, but merely a recognition of difference. He thinks I am unpractical, a bit odd, not quite a grown man. I think he is—a charming fellow. We are about quits on that!

QUESTIONS ON CONTENT

1. When does the author first define "the daily theme eye"?
2. Does he think this "optic" can be acquired?
3. What is meant by "seeing copy"?
4. What is the eighth commandment (King James' Version)?
5. Was the author's roommate a dishonest person?
6. "A faculty for being surprised" defines what?
7. What made the author think he had seen "a little marble boy . . . wet his lips"?
8. Are you akin to the author or to the author's roommate?
9. Do Eaton, Gallico ("The Feel"), and Scudder ("In the Laboratory with Agassiz") have anything in common? Explain. How do they differ?
10. Which type of student (see "Four Types of Students") would you say Eaton probably was?

❧ *Ulysses*

Alfred, Lord Tennyson

It little profits that an idle king,
By this still hearth, among these barren crags,
Match'd with an aged wife, I mete and dole
Unequal laws unto a savage race,
That hoard, and sleep, and feed, and know not me.   5
I cannot rest from travel: I will drink
Life to the lees: all times I have enjoy'd
Greatly, have suffer'd greatly, both with those
That loved me, and alone; on shore, and when
Thro' scudding drifts the rainy Hyades   10
Vext the dim sea: I am become a name;
For always roaming with a hungry heart
Much have I seen and known: cities of men,
And manners, climates, councils, governments,
Myself not least, but honour'd of them all;   15
And drunk delight of battle with my peers,
Far on the ringing plains of windy Troy.
I am a part of all that I have met;
Yet all experience is an arch wherethro'
Gleams that untravell'd world, whose margin fades   20
For ever and for ever when I move.
How dull it is to pause, to make an end,
To rust unburnish'd, not to shine in use!
As tho' to breathe were life. Life piled on life
Were all too little, and of one to me   25
Little remains: but every hour is saved
From that eternal silence, something more,
A bringer of new things; and vile it were
For some three suns to store and hoard myself,
And this gray spirit yearning in desire   30
To follow knowledge like a sinking star,
Beyond the utmost bound of human thought.
     This is my son, mine own Telemachus,

Poems, 1842.

To whom I leave the sceptre and the isle—
Well-loved of me, discerning to fulfil 35
This labour, by slow prudence to make mild
A rugged people, and thro' soft degrees
Subdue them to the useful and the good.
Most blameless is he, centred in the sphere
Of common duties, decent not to fail 40
In offices of tenderness, and pay
Meet adoration to my household gods,
When I am gone. He works his work, I mine.
   There lies the port; the vessel puffs her sail:
There gloom the dark broad seas. My mariners, 45
Souls that have toil'd, and wrought, and thought with me—
That ever with a frolic welcome took
The thunder and the sunshine, and opposed
Free hearts, free foreheads—you and I are old;
Old age hath yet his honour and his toil; 50
Death closes all: but something ere the end,
Some work of noble note, may yet be done,
Not unbecoming men that strove with Gods.
The lights begin to twinkle from the rocks:
The long day wanes: the slow moon climbs: the deep 55
Moans round with many voices. Come, my friends,
'Tis not too late to seek a newer world,
Push off, and sitting well in order smite
The sounding furrows; for my purpose hold
To sail beyond the sunset, and the bath: 60
Of all the western stars, until I d: Isles,
It may be that the gulfs will   we knew.
It may be we shall tou   es; and tho'
And see the great ; that which in old days 65
Tho' much is   heroic hearts, that which we are, we are;
We are ume and fate, but strong in will
M   seek, to find, and not to yield.

70

QUESTIONS ON CONTENT

1. To whom, if to anyone, is Ulysses talking?
2. Write a summary of what Ulysses says. What are the differences between your summary and the total effect of the poem?
3. Does Ulysses call on all men to follow in his ways? Discuss.
4. Contrast Ulysses and his son, Telemachus.
5. Would Ulysses have been happy in the laboratory with Agassiz? Why or why not?
6. Which lines in this poem do you regard as most memorable? Why?
7. In what way is "Ulysses" a definition through dramatic symbol of the abstraction, *curiosity?*

❧ *The Lotos-Eaters*

ALFRED, LORD TENNYSON

Choric Song

I

The
Than is sweet music here that softer falls
Or night from blown roses on the grass,
Of shadowy on still waters between walls
Music that gen in a gleaming pass;
Than tir'd eyelids the spirit lies,   5
Music that brings swee spirit lies,
Here are cool mosses deeyes;
And thro' the moss the ivies vn from the blissful skies.
And in the stream the long-leav
And from the craggy ledge the P

II   10

Why are we weigh'd upon with heaviness,
And utterly consumed with sharp distress,
While all things else have rest from weariness?

Poems, 1842.

All things have rest: why should we toil alone,   15
We only toil, who are the first of things,
And make perpetual moan,
Still from one sorrow to another thrown:
Nor ever fold our wings,
And cease from wanderings,   20
Nor steep our brows in slumber's holy balm;
Nor harken what the inner spirit sings,
'There is no joy but calm!'
Why should we only toil, the roof and crown of things?

III

Lo! in the middle of the wood,   25
The folded leaf is woo'd from out the bud
With winds upon the branch, and there
Grows green and broad, and takes no care,
Sun-steep'd at noon, and in the moon
Nightly dew-fed; and turning yellow   30
Falls, and floats adown the air.
Lo! sweeten'd with the summer light,
The full-juiced apple, waxing over-mellow,
Drops in a silent autumn night.
All its allotted length of days,   35
The flower ripens in its place,
Ripens and fades, and falls, and hath no toil,
Fast-rooted in the fruitful soil.

IV

Hateful is the dark-blue sky,
Vaulted o'er the dark-blue sea.   40
Death is the end of life; ah, why
Should life all labour be?
Let us alone. Time driveth onward fast,
And in a little while our lips are dumb.
Let us alone. What is it that will last?   45
All things are taken from us, and become
Portions and parcels of the dreadful Past.
Let us alone. What pleasure can we have
To war with evil? Is there any peace
In ever climbing up the climbing wave?   50

All things have rest, and ripen toward the grave
In silence; ripen, fall, and cease:
Give us long rest or death, dark death, or dreamful ease.

V

How sweet it were, hearing the downward stream,
With half-shut eyes ever to seem   55
Falling asleep in a half-dream!
To dream and dream, like yonder amber light,
Which will not leave the myrrh-bush on the height;
To hear each other's whisper'd speech;
Eating the Lotos day by day,   60
To watch the crisping ripples on the beach,
And tender curving lines of creamy spray;
To lend our hearts and spirits wholly
To the influence of mild-minded melancholy;
To muse and brood and live again in memory,   65
With those old faces of our infancy
Heap'd over with a mound of grass,
Two handfuls of white dust, shut in an urn of brass!

VI

Dear is the memory of our wedded lives,
And dear the last embraces of our wives   70
And their warm tears: but all hath suffer'd change:
For surely now our household hearths are cold:
Our sons inherit us: our looks are strange:
And we should come like ghosts to trouble joy.
Or else the island princes over-bold   75
Have eat our substance, and the minstrel sings
Before them of the ten years' war in Troy
And our great deeds, as half-forgotten things.
Is there confusion in the little isle?
Let what is broken so remain.   80
The Gods are hard to reconcile:
'Tis hard to settle order once again.
There *is* confusion worse than death,
Troubles on trouble, pain on pain,
Long labour unto aged breath,   85

Sore task to hearts worn out by many wars
And eyes grown dim with gazing on the pilot-stars.

VII

But, propt on beds of amaranth and moly,
How sweet (while warm airs lull us, blowing lowly)
With half-dropt eyelid still,   90
Beneath a heaven dark and holy,
To watch the long bright river drawing slowly
His waters from the purple hill—
To hear the dewy echoes calling
From cave to cave thro' the thick-twined vine—   95
To watch the emerald-colour'd water falling
Thro' many a wov'n acanthus-wreath divine!
Only to hear and see the far-off sparkling brine,
Only to hear were sweet, stretch'd out beneath the pine.

VIII

The Lotos blooms below the barren peak: 100
The Lotos blows by every winding creek:
All day the wind breathes low with mellower tone:
Thro' every hollow cave and alley lone
Round and round the spicy downs the yellow Lotos—dust is blown.
We have had enough of action, and of motion we,   105
Roll'd to starboard, roll'd to larboard, when the surge was seething
    free,
Where the wallowing monster spouted his foam-fountains in the
    sea.
Let us swear an oath, and keep it with an equal mind,
In the hollow Lotos-land to live and lie reclined
On the hills like Gods together, careless of mankind.   110
For they lie beside their nectar, and the bolts are hurl'd
Far below them in the valleys, and the clouds are lightly curl'd
Round their golden houses, girdled with the gleaming world:
Where they smile in secret, looking over wasted lands,
Blight and famine, plague and earthquake, roaring deeps and fiery
    sands,   115
Clanging fights, and flaming towns, and sinking ships, and praying
    hands.
But they smile, they find a music centred in a doleful song

Steaming up, a lamentation and an ancient tale of wrong,
Like a tale of little meaning tho' the words are strong;
Chanted from an ill-used race of men that cleave the soil,   120
Sow the seed, and reap the harvest with enduring toil,
Storing yearly little dues of wheat, and wine and oil;
Till they perish and they suffer—some, 'tis whisper'd—down in hell
Suffer endless anguish, others in Elysian valleys dwell,
Resting weary limbs at last on beds of asphodel.   125
Surely, surely, slumber is more sweet than toil, the shore
Than labour in the deep mid-ocean, wind and wave and oar;
Oh rest ye, brother mariners, we will not wander more.

QUESTIONS ON CONTENT

1. Ulysses was the leader of the men who have partaken of the
   lotos. What kind of action would you expect him to take to counteract the apathy? (Compare the preceding poem.)
2. Who is speaking in this poem? To whom?
3. Write a summary of the arguments in favor of the non-strenuous
   life. Would you call the arguments good illustrations of rationalization? Explain.

SUGGESTIONS FOR PAPERS

You have been asked, perhaps many times, "What do you want
to be?" You may never have been asked, "How strong is your *desire
to know?*" This second question is what you are now being asked.
Your first paper will be an answer to that question. Some suggestions on how to get at your answer are offered herewith. Whatever
suggestion you may decide to follow, you should be able to make
effective and specific reference to the various selections in this
chapter.

1. What are the present limits of your curiosity? You may have
a sharply defined curiosity. What first made you aware of the particular direction of your desire to know? How far have you gone
toward satisfying this desire? How will you go on? To what eventual goal?

2. Your desire to know may be without focus at the present. Do
you ignite easily? Do you take to a succession of new enthusiasms
which die out quickly? Tell your reader about the rise and fall of
your desire to know.

3. Newspapers attempt to satisfy almost every sort of interest. How much of a newspaper do you read? Can you measure your curiosity by what you read? Do you read, for example, all the comics? The sports page? Advice to the lovelorn? The foreign news? The local news? The financial page? The weather map? Do you regularly "keep up with" any specific feature of the newspaper? Why?

4. A university or college has been accurately described as "a bookish place." You may already have your textbooks for your courses. Can you tell how you *feel* toward these books? Pick up one of these books. Read the title. Look at the table of contents. So far as your paper is concerned, it does not matter whether you feel eager to study the book or not. What does matter is an honest telling of *how* you do feel.

5. Fit yourself into one of Fuller's categories in "Four Types of Students." What modifications are necessary to make the fit more exact? Is the estimate you have of yourself the same, so far as you know, as your high-school teachers had of you? Discuss reasons for any differences.

6. Scudder sat for hours examining a haemulon. You can write a valuable and entertaining paper if you will report the results of applying Agassiz's method of observation to almost any conceivable object: a blotter, a pencil, a flower, a fly. Try it on the book you are now reading. What is the color of the book? What is the size? How much does it weigh? How is it put together? What are the parts of the book? What is the purpose of each part? Report the processes of your mind while you are observing the facts.

7. Would you say that Paul Gallico put himself through a self-imposed, postgraduate course in sports journalism? Can you compare what he did with what Scudder did in the laboratory? How are the methods alike? How do they differ? Which procedure appeals to *you* more? Why?

8. Compare and contrast Eaton and Scudder. Did Eaton examine minutely or painstakingly or did he depend upon quick impressions? Do you think that he would have submitted himself to Agassiz's discipline? On the other hand, do you suppose that Scudder had a "daily theme eye"? After you have drawn up a series of comparisons and contrasts, take sides—that is, give reasons why you feel sympathetic with Eaton's or Scudder's kind of curiosity.

9. Ulysses of Tennyson's poem was motivated by what practical considerations, if any? Is he more like Scudder, Gallico, or Eaton

in his zest for life? How does he differ from all three? Was he a specialist? Did he think he had a chance to reach his goal? Did reaching a goal matter? Attack or defend his attitude towards life.

10. Compare and contrast Ulysses and Telemachus and say a word about Ulysses' "aged wife."

11. After writing out prose summaries of "Ulysses" and "The Lotos-Eaters" compare and contrast the ways of life represented in the two poems. Show where your own sympathies lie.

SOME TITLES FOR PAPERS

1. Types of Students I Have Known
2. Fuller's Figures of Speech Analyzed
3. Definitions of Curiosity
4. Things I Don't Want to Know
5. The Scope of My Curiosity
6. My Curiosity: A History
7. Will College Satisfy My Desire to Know?
8. Curiosity Killed a Cat
9. How to Develop Curiosity
10. The Questioning Spirit
11. Love of Knowledge Rules the World
12. "All Experience Is an Arch"
13. "The Feel": My Version
14. I Tried Agassiz's Method
15. Don't Ask Embarrassing Questions
16. Importance of the Question Mark
17. My Roommate's Curiosity
18. A Weekly Theme Eye
19. Ignorance Is Bliss
20. 'Tis Folly to Be Wise
21. Every Man a Ulysses?
22. Attractions of Lotos Land
23. Genuine Curiosity Demands Energy

❧ *OF MYSELF*

ONE FORM OF CURIOSITY is directed within ourselves. "Know thyself" is as much a ceaseless quest as "Know thy environment." One's chief task is to combine these two admonitions. "Know thyself in relation to environment." Environment may be defined as the sum of all the forces which affect you. It is a valuable exercise to write out an experience that will help you to explain "you."

Complete honesty in self-analysis is not easy to attain. Rousseau tells of this difficulty in part of the preface to his very frank autobiography. He also announces his intention to expose ruthlessly everything he knows about himself. His work, therefore, became a public confession, as intimate as that which one might, were he a Roman Catholic, whisper to a priest.

While most people shy away from such public exposure of "odious" faults, all of us have some inclination toward autobiography. Our trouble arises from not knowing *how* to talk about ourselves. The selections in this chapter represent several different, though related, ways of communicating personal experiences to others.

Cornelia Otis Skinner, in recalling one of her most miserable childhood days, touches the subject with humor. Similarly, Mark Twain succeeds in gaining the reader's sympathy through inviting him to laugh at a boy's discomfiture, to laugh at what doubtless was no laughing matter when it happened.

Wordsworth, Floyd Dell, and Keats approach their self-revelations with serious and humorless intent. Wordsworth offers his experience as evidence of Nature's essential good-will towards sensitive boys. Floyd Dell, skilfully avoiding sentimentality, tells his story as matter-of-factly as possible and refuses to point a moral. Keats muses on his ambitions, on Love and Fame, and finds them dwindle to nothingness, overpowered by the thoughts of death.

The three "confessions" demonstrate the cleverness of the writers and reveal how difficult it is to acknowledge any truly disgraceful conduct.

Peter De Vries in "Through a Glass Darkly" pokes exaggerated fun at a personal weakness of his.

The worst fault in the telling of personal experiences is telling too much. The one thing constant in all the selections in this chapter is *economy*. Each author has a single controlling idea; every detail contributes to the development of that one idea; all other details, no matter how tempting, are rejected. While studying this chapter, take note of the target each author was shooting at and then score each sentence a hit or a miss in accordance with its accuracy in hitting the target. Score your own sentences in like manner!

❧ *The Principle of Autobiography*

Jean Jacques Rousseau

No one can write a man's life but himself. The character of his inner being, his real life, is known only to himself; but, in writing it, he disguises it; under the name of his life, he makes an apology; he shows himself as he wishes to be seen, but not at all as he is. The sincerest persons are truthful at most in what they say, but they lie by their reticences, and that of which they say nothing so changes that which they pretend to confess, that in uttering only a part of the truth they say nothing. I put Montaigne at the head of these falsely-sincere persons who wish to deceive in telling the truth. He shows himself with his faults, but he gives himself none but amiable ones; there is no man who has not odious ones. Montaigne paints his likeness, but it is a profile. Who knows whether some scar on the cheek,

From a rough draft of the introduction to Rousseau's *Confessions*, as quoted by Sainte-Beuve in his essay "Rousseau," first published in 1851.

or an eye put out, on the side which he conceals from us, would not have totally changed the physiognomy? . . .

If I wish to produce a work written with care, like the others, I shall not paint, I shall rouge myself. It is with my portrait that I am here concerned, and not with a book. I am going to work, so to speak, in the darkroom; there is no other art necessary than to follow exactly the traits which I see marked. I form my resolution then about the style as about the things. I shall not try at all to render it uniform; I shall write always that which comes to me, I shall change it, without scruple, according to my humour; I shall speak of everything as I feel it, as I see it, without care, without constraint, without being embarrassed by the medley. In yielding myself at once to the memory of the impression received and to the present sentiment, I shall doubly paint the state of my soul, namely, at the moment when the event happened to me and the moment when I describe it; my style, unequal and natural, sometimes rapid and sometimes diffuse, sometimes wise and sometimes foolish, sometimes grave and sometimes gay, will itself make a part of my history. Finally, whatever may be the way in which this book may be written, it will be always, by its object, a book precious for philosophers; it is, I repeat, an illustrative piece for the study of the human heart, and it is the only one that exists.

QUESTIONS ON CONTENT

1. Why does Rousseau call Montaigne a "falsely-sincere" person?
2. What does Rousseau mean to convey by the words, "rouge myself"?
3. Interpret: "I shall doubly paint the state of my soul."
4. Rousseau thought his *Confessions* would always be valuable to philosophers. Why?

❧ *One Day*

CORNELIA OTIS SKINNER

One day, which still remains in my memory as "the calico-dress and express-wagon day," was the most miserable of that none too carefree year. Mother had made me a dress which, as I recall it, must have been one of unusual charm and imagination. She had come across the material in the country store near Conshohocken, an ancient, dingy emporium whose shelves were laden with bolts of fascinating dress goods, of almost ante-bellum vintage. For this particular garment, she chose a pretty calico, darkish blue, with an enchanting pattern of tiny stars and crescent moons. For model, she copied a frock from a Kate Greenaway illustration, with puffed sleeves and an Empire-like high waist. It was trimmed at the bottom with two rows of white rickrack. In taste and originality it probably put to shame Elise's modish sailor suits made, as she told everybody, by her mother's Chestnut Street tailor. Mother took great pains with it, I thought it was just lovely, and the first time I put it on, the admiring Crawfords said I was a "picture." Pleased and happy, I went off to school. The picture the Crawfords had in mind may have been one of pristine charm and quaintness, but the one I presented to my Comanche schoolmates was something, apparently, to be equaled in humor only by something out of the funny papers. They nudged one another, they pointed at me, they tittered and Elise passed an ultimate verdict on my frock by calling it "poor-folksy!" The morning passed for me in complete misery and I counted the minutes until Johnnie the coachman would call for me in the runabout and take me away from the hateful place. Eventually the final bell sounded, and I was called for, not by Johnnie in the runabout, but by Alan in the express wagon. The express wagon was a battered vehicle used for transporting pigeon crates to and from the station, and Alan was a farmhand equally battered. Today he looked worse than usual, his ragged blue jeans were spotted with birdlime, and his chin was furry with a three days' growth of beard. Ordinarily I welcomed a chance to ride in the express wagon. One

From *Family Circle*, by Cornelia Otis Skinner; published by Houghton Mifflin Company, 1948, and reprinted by their permission.

could sit beside Alan on the driver's seat and feel vastly important or one could sit back amid the pigeon crates, on one's own seat, and feel vastly uncomfortable but adventuresome. Alan was a taciturn son of the soil, a generous coating of which he bore on his person, and he smelled to high heaven, but I thought him rather wonderful. I had not heard of class consciousness and Alan and the express wagon seemed to me as felicitous a means of transportation as any. But today, as I looked out of the window, drawn up beside my rustic equipage was Elise's glistening dogcart with its smart little cob and the groom impressive in the Murphy livery, and my heart, which was already pretty low, sank to new depths of wretchedness. I hoped with my soul that I might be able to slink away without being seen, but, quick as a ferret, Elise spotted the wagon and guessed—from my expression—that it was there for me.

"Look!" she squealed with delight, "Cinderella's coach has called for her! See what Chameleon's family sent her to school in!" Then her black, malicious eye fell upon Alan and with mock politeness she said: "Is that your father driving it?"

If I hadn't been the small fool of the world, I would have fought back and even now the memory fills me with a desire to take a train to the town where Elise now leads a reformed and exemplary life and amaze her with a long-delayed uppercut to the jaw. However, all I did at the time was to grab my corduroy school bag (Elise's was of the finest leather) and run out of the building, blinded with tears of fury and hurt.

With a child's instinctive shyness at sharing private grievances with parents, I told Mother nothing of what had happened. But she knew something was tearing at my confused emotions when, at supper, I burst into uncontrollable tears. Wisely she let me cry it all out—then gently asked me what the trouble was. All I told her was that I never again wanted to wear that "poor child's dress." From observations I had made she figured out the situation and, after reassuring me, quietly put away the little frock over which she had taken such tender pains.

QUESTIONS ON CONTENT

1. What does *ante-bellum* mean? *vintage?* Is *vintage* normally used to apply to dress goods? Justify the use here.
2. Does this episode illustrate "class consciousness"? How?
3. Why didn't the author fight back?

4. What kind of person does the mother in this episode appear to be? Be specific.

❧ *A Cub Pilot's Experience*

MARK TWAIN

. . . The *Paul Jones* was now bound for St. Louis. I planned a siege against my pilot, and at the end of three hard days he surrendered. He agreed to teach me the Mississippi River from New Orleans to St. Louis for five hundred dollars, payable out of the first wages I should receive after graduating. I entered upon the small enterprise of "learning" twelve or thirteen hundred miles of the great Mississippi River with the easy confidence of my time of life. If I had really known what I was about to require of my faculties, I should not have had the courage to begin. I supposed that all a pilot had to do was to keep his boat in the river, and I did not consider that that could be much of a trick, since it was so wide.

The boat backed out from New Orleans at four in the afternoon, and it was "our watch" until eight. Mr. Bixby, my chief, "straightened her up," ploughed her along past the sterns of the other boats that lay at the Levee, and then said, "Here, take her; shave those steamships as close as you'd peel an apple." I took the wheel, and my heart-beat fluttered up into the hundreds; for it seemed to me that we were about to scrape the side off every ship in the line, we were so close. I held my breath and began to claw the boat away from the danger; and I had my own opinion of the pilot who had known no better than to get us into such peril, but I was too wise to express it. In half a minute I had a wide margin of safety intervening between the *Paul Jones* and the ships; and within ten seconds more I was set aside in disgrace, and Mr. Bixby was going into danger again and flaying me alive with abuse of my cowardice. I was stung, but I was obliged to admire the easy confidence with which my chief loafed from side to side of his wheel, and trimmed the ships so closely that disaster seemed ceaselessly imminent. When he had cooled a little he told me that the easy water was close ashore and the current outside, and therefore we must hug the bank, up-stream, to get the benefit of the former, and stay well out,

From *Life on the Mississippi,* Harper & Brothers (1883).

down-stream, to take advantage of the latter. In my own mind I resolved to be a down-stream pilot and leave the up-streaming to people dead to prudence.

Now and then Mr. Bixby called my attention to certain things. Said he, "This is Six-Mile Point." I assented. It was pleasant enough information, but I could not see the bearing of it. I was not conscious that it was a matter of any interest to me. Another time he said, "This is Nine-Mile Point." Later he said, "This is Twelve-Mile Point." They were all about level with the water's edge; they all looked about alike to me; they were monotonously unpicturesque. I hoped Mr. Bixby would change the subject. But no; he would crowd up around a point, hugging the shore with affection, and then say: "The slack water ends here, abreast this bunch of China-trees; now we cross over." So he crossed over. He gave me the wheel once or twice, but I had no luck. I either came near chipping off the edge of a sugar plantation, or I yawed too far from shore, and so dropped back into disgrace again and got abused.

The watch was ended at last, and we took supper and went to bed. At midnight the glare of a lantern shone in my eyes, and the night watchman said: "Come, turn out!"

And then he left. I could not understand this extraordinary procedure; so I presently gave up trying to, and dozed off to sleep. Pretty soon the watchman was back again, and this time he was gruff. I was annoyed. I said:

"What do you want to come bothering around here in the middle of the night for? Now, as like as not, I'll not get to sleep again to-night."

The watchman said:

"Well, if this ain't good, I'm blessed."

The "off-watch" was just turning in, and I heard some brutal laughter from them, and such remarks as "Hello, watchman! ain't the new cub turned out yet? He's delicate, likely. Give him some sugar in a rag, and send for the chambermaid to sing 'Rock-a-by Baby,' to him."

About this time Mr. Bixby appeared on the scene. Something like a minute later I was climbing the pilothouse steps with some of my clothes on and the rest in my arms. Mr. Bixby was close behind, commenting. Here was something fresh—this thing of getting up in the middle of the night to go to work. It was a detail in piloting that had never occurred to me at all. I knew that boats ran all night, but somehow I had never happened to reflect that somebody had to get up out of a warm bed to run them. I began to fear that piloting was not quite so romantic as I had imagined it was; there was something very real and worklike about this new phase of it.

It was a rather dingy night, although a fair number of stars were out. The big mate was at the wheel, and he had the old tub pointed at a star and was holding her straight up the middle of the river. The shores on either hand were not much more than half a mile apart, but they seemed wonderfully far away and ever so vague and indistinct. The mate said:

"We've got to land at Jones's plantation, sir."

The vengeful spirit in me exulted. I said to myself, "I wish you joy of your job, Mr. Bixby; you'll have a good time finding Mr. Jones's plantation such a night as this; and I hope you never *will* find it as long as you live."

Mr. Bixby said to the mate:

"Upper end of the plantation, or the lower?"

"Upper."

"I can't do it. The stumps there are out of the water at this stage. It's no great distance to the lower, and you'll have to get along with that."

"All right, sir. If Jones don't like it, he'll have to lump it, I reckon."

And then the mate left. My exultation began to cool and my wonder to come up. Here was a man who not only proposed to find this plantation on such a night, but to find either end of it you preferred. I dreadfully wanted to ask a question, but I was carrying about as many short answers as my cargo-room would admit of, so I held my peace. All I desired to ask Mr. Bixby was the simple question whether he was ass enough to really imagine he was going to find that plantation on a night when all plantations were exactly alike and all of the same color. But I held in. I used to have fine inspirations of prudence in those days.

Mr. Bixby made for the shore and soon was scraping it, just the same as if it had been daylight. And not only that, but singing: "Father in heaven, the day is declining," etc. It seemed to me that I had put my life in the keeping of a peculiarly reckless outcast. Presently he turned on me and said:

"What's the name of the first point above New Orleans?"

I was gratified to be able to answer promptly, and I did. I said I didn't know.

"Don't *know?*"

This manner jolted me. I was down at the foot again, in a moment. But I had to say just what I had said before.

"Well, you're a smart one!" said Mr. Bixby. "What's the name of the *next* point?"

Once more I didn't know.

"Well, this beats anything. Tell me the name of *any* point or place I told you."

I studied a while and decided that I couldn't.

"Look here! What do you start out from, above Twelve-Mile Point, to cross over?"

"I—I—don't know."

"You—you—don't know?" mimicking my drawling manner of speech. "What *do* you know?"

"I—I—nothing, for certain."

"By the great Caesar's ghost, I believe you! You're the stupidest dunderhead I ever saw or ever heard of, so help me Moses! The idea of *you* being a pilot—*you!* Why, you don't know enough to pilot a cow down a lane."

Oh, but his wrath was up! He was a nervous man, and he shuffled from one side of his wheel to the other as if the floor was hot. He would boil a while to himself, and then overflow and scald me again.

"Look here! What do you suppose I told you the names of those points for?"

I tremblingly considered a moment, and then the devil of temptation provoked me to say:

"Well—to—to—be entertaining, I thought."

This was a red rag to the bull. He raged and stormed so (he was crossing the river at the time) that I judged it made him blind, because he ran over the steering-oar of a trading-scow. Of course the traders sent up a volley of red-hot profanity. Never was a man so grateful as Mr. Bixby was; because he was brimful, and here were subjects who could *talk back*. He threw open a window, thrust his head out, and such an irruption followed as I never had heard before. The fainter and farther away the scowmen's curses drifted, the higher Mr. Bixby lifted his voice and the weightier his adjectives grew. When he closed the window he was empty. You could have drawn a seine through his system and not caught curses enough to disturb your mother with. Presently he said to me in the gentlest way:

"My boy, you must get a little memorandum-book; and every

time I tell you a thing, put it down right away. There's only one way to be a pilot, and that is to get this entire river by heart. You have to know it just like A B C."

That was a dismal revelation to me; for my memory was never loaded with anything but blank cartridges. However, I did not feel discouraged long. I judged that it was best to make some allowances, for doubtless Mr. Bixby was "stretching." Presently he pulled a rope and struck a few strokes on the big bell. The stars were all gone now, and the night was as black as ink. I could hear the wheels churn along the bank, but I was not entirely certain that I could see the shore. The voice of the invisible watchman called up from the hurricane-deck:

"What's this, sir?"

"Jones's plantation."

I said to myself, "I wish I might venture to offer a small bet that it isn't." But I did not chirp. I only waited to see. Mr. Bixby handled the engine-bells, and in due time the boat's nose came to the land, a torch glowed from the forecastle, a man skipped ashore, a darky's voice on the bank said, "Gimme de k'yarpetbag, Mass' Jones," and the next moment we were standing up the river again, all serene. I reflected deeply a while and then said—but not aloud—"Well, the finding of that plantation was the luckiest accident that ever happened; but it couldn't happen again in a hundred years." And I fully believed it *was* an accident, too.

By the time we had gone seven or eight hundred miles up the river, I had learned to be a tolerably plucky upstream steersman, in daylight, and before we reached St. Louis I had made a trifle of progress in night-work, but only a trifle. I had a note-book that fairly bristled with the names of towns, "points," bars, islands, bends, reaches, etc.; but the information was to be found only in the note-book—none of it was in my head. It made my heart ache to think I had only got half the river set down; for as our watch was four hours off and four hours on, day and night, there was a long four-hour gap in my book for every time I had slept since the voyage began.

My chief was presently hired to go on a big New Orleans boat, and I packed my satchel and went with him. She was a grand affair. When I stood in her pilot-house I was so far above the water that I seemed perched on a mountain; and her decks stretched so far away, fore and aft, below me, that I wondered how I could ever have considered the little *Paul Jones* a large craft. There were other differences, too. The *Paul Jones's* pilot-house was a cheap, dingy, battered rattletrap, cramped for room; but here was a sumptuous glass temple; room enough to have a dance in; showy red and gold window curtains; an imposing sofa; leather cushions and a back to the high bench where visiting pilots sit, to spin yarns and "look at the river"; bright, fanciful "cuspadores," instead of a broad wooden box filled with sawdust; nice new oilcloth on the floor; a hospitable big stove for winter; a wheel as high as my head, costly with inlaid work; a wire tiller-rope; bright brass knobs for the bells; and a tidy, white-aproned black "texas-tender," to bring up tarts and ices and coffee during mid-watch, day and night. Now this was "something like"; and so I began to take heart once more to believe that piloting was a romantic sort of occupation after all. The moment we were under way I began to prowl about the great steamer and fill myself with joy. She was as clean and as dainty as a drawing-room; when I looked down her long, gilded saloon, it was like gazing through a splendid tunnel; she had an oil-picture, by some gifted sign-painter, on every stateroom door; she glittered with no end of prism-fringed chandeliers; the clerk's office was elegant, the bar was marvellous, and the barkeeper had been barbered and upholstered at incredible cost. The boiler-deck (*i.e.*, the second story of the boat, so to speak) was as spacious as a church, it seemed to me; so with the forecastle; and there was no pitiful handful of deck-hands, firemen, and roustabouts down there, but a whole battalion of men. The fires were fiercely glaring from a long row of furnaces, and over them were eight huge boilers! This was un-utterable pomp. The mighty engines—but enough of this. I had never felt so fine before. And when I found that the regiment of natty servants respectfully "sir'd" me, my satisfaction was complete.

QUESTIONS ON CONTENT

1. What was Mr. Bixby's first order to his pupil?
2. Why did the cub pilot hope "Mr. Bixby would change the sub-ject"?
3. "Mr. Bixby was close behind, commenting." How do you know that this is an understatement?
4. What incident turned Mr. Bixby's wrath away from Mark Twain?
5. Comment on: "My memory was never loaded with anything but blank cartridges." Prove that this is an exaggeration.

❧ *"Fair Seed-time Had My Soul"*

WILLIAM WORDSWORTH

Fair seed-time had my soul, and I grew up
Fostered alike by beauty and by fear:
Much favoured in my birth-place, and no less
In that beloved Vale to which erelong
We were transplanted; there were we let loose   5
For sports of wider range. Ere I had told
Ten birth-days, when among the mountain slopes
Frost, and the breath of frosty wind, had snapped
The last autumnal crocus, 't was my joy
With store of springes o'er my shoulder hung   10
To range the open heights where woodcocks run
Along the smooth green turf. Through half the night,
Scudding away from snare to snare, I plied
That anxious visitation;—moon and stars
Were shining o'er my head. I was alone,   15
And seemed to be a trouble to the peace
That dwelt among them. Sometimes it befell
In these night wanderings, that a strong desire
O'erpowered my better reason, and the bird
Which was the captive of another's toil   20
Became my prey; and when the deed was done
I heard among the solitary hills
Low breathings coming after me, and sounds
Of undistinguishable motion, steps
Almost as silent as the turf they trod.   25

Nor less, when spring had warmed the cultured Vale,
Moved we as plunderers where the mother-bird
Had in high places built her lodge; though mean
Our object and inglorious, yet the end
Was not ignoble. Oh! when I have hung   30
Above the raven's nest, by knots of grass

Written between 1799 and 1805; published posthumously in *The Prelude*,
I:301–356 (1850).

And half-inch fissures in the slippery rock
But ill sustained, and almost (so it seemed)
Suspended by the blast that blew amain,
Shouldering the naked crag, oh, at that time   35
While on the perilous ridge I hung alone,
With what strange utterance did the loud dry wind
Blow through my ear! the sky seemed not a sky
Of earth—and with what motion moved the clouds!

Dust as we are, the immortal spirit grows   40
Like harmony in music; there is a dark
Inscrutable workmanship that reconciles
Discordant elements, makes them cling together
In one society. How strange, that all
The terrors, pains, and early miseries,   45
Regrets, vexations, lassitudes interfused
Within my mind, should e'er have borne a part,
And that a needful part, in making up
The calm existence that is mine when I
Am worthy of myself! Praise to the end!   50
Thanks to the means which Nature deigned to employ;
Whether her fearless visitings, or those
That came with soft alarm, like hurtless light
Opening the peaceful clouds; or she would use
Severer interventions, ministry   55
More palpable, as best might suit her aim.

QUESTIONS ON CONTENT

1. How old was the poet when he began trapping woodcocks?
2. What actions disturbed the boy's conscience? How did Nature participate in arousing his sense of guilt?
3. Explain: ". . . the end/Was not ignoble" (lines 29–30).
4. What credit does the poet give to Nature for his mature "calm existence"?
5. What does the word *fearless* (line 52) mean? *hurtless* (line 53)?
6. Does Wordsworth look at his childhood in a way that Rousseau ("Principles of Autobiography") would approve? Explain.

❧ *When I Have Fears That I May Cease To Be*

JOHN KEATS

When I have fears that I may cease to be
Before my pen has gleaned my teeming brain,
Before high pilèd books, in charact'ry,
Hold like rich garners the full-ripened grain;

When I behold, upon the night's starred face,   5
Huge cloudy symbols of a high romance,
And think that I may never live to trace
Their shadows, with the magic hand of chance;

And when I feel, fair creature of the hour!
That I shall never look upon thee more,   10
Never have relish in the faery power
Of unreflecting love!—then on the shore
Of the wide world I stand alone, and think
Till Love and Fame to nothingness do sink.

QUESTIONS ON CONTENT

1. Why does Keats use the phrase "fair creature *of the hour*"?
2. What is an "abstraction"? What are the abstractions in this poem?

Composed in 1821, published 1848.

❧ *Christmas*

FLOYD DELL

Memories of childhood are strange things. The obscurity of the
past opens a little lighted space—a scene, unconnected with anything else. One must figure out when it happened. There may be

From *Homecoming: An Autobiography*, by Floyd Dell, copyright 1933, by
Floyd Dell. Reprinted by permission of Rinehart and Company, Inc., Publishers.

anomalies in the scene, which need explanation. Sometimes the scenes are tiny fragments only. Again they are long dramas. Having once been remembered, they can be lived through again in every moment, with a detailed experiencing of movement and sensation and thought. One can start the scene in one's mind and see it all through again. Exactly so it was—clearer in memory than something that happened yesterday, though it was forty years ago. And, oddly enough, if there is some detail skipped over, lost out of the memory picture, no repetition of the remembering process will supply it—the gap is always there.

That fall, before it was discovered that the soles of both my shoes were worn clear through, I still went to Sunday school. And one time the Sunday-school superintendent made a speech to all the classes. He said that these were hard times, and that many poor children weren't getting enough to eat. It was the first time that I had heard about it. He asked everybody to bring some food for the poor children next Sunday. I felt very sorry for the poor children.

Also little envelopes were distributed to all the classes. Each little boy and girl was to bring money for the poor, next Sunday. The pretty Sunday-school teacher explained that we were to write our names, or to have our parents write them, up in the left-hand corner of the little envelopes. . . . I told my mother all about it when I came home. And my mother gave me, the next Sunday, a small bag of potatoes to carry to Sunday school. I supposed the poor children's mothers would make potato soup out of them. . . . Potato soup was good. My father, who was quite a joker, would always say, as if he were surprised, "Ah! I see we have some nourishing soup today!" It was so good that we had it every day. My father was at home all day long and every day, now; and I liked that, even if he was grumpy as he sat reading Grant's *Memoirs*. I had my parents all to myself, too; the others were away. My oldest brother was in Quincy, and memory does not reveal where the others were: perhaps with relatives in the country.

Taking my small bag of potatoes to Sunday school, I looked around for the poor children; I was disappointed not to see them. I had heard about poor children in stories. But I was told just to put my contribution with the others on the big table in the side room.

I had brought with me the little yellow envelope, with some money in it and sealed it up. My mother wouldn't tell me how much money she had put in it, but it felt like several dimes. Only she wouldn't let me write my name on the envelope. I had learned to write my name, and I was proud of being able to do it. But my mother said firmly, *no*, I must *not* write my name on the envelope; she didn't tell my why. On the way to Sunday school I had pressed the envelope against the coins until I could tell what they were; they weren't dimes but pennies.

When I handed in my envelope, my Sunday-school teacher noticed that my name wasn't on it, and she gave me a pencil; I could write my own name, she said. So I did. But I was confused because my mother had said not to; and when I came home, I confessed what I had done. She looked distressed. "I told you not to!" she said. But she didn't explain why. . . .

I didn't go back to school that fall. My mother said it was because I was sick. I did have a cold the week that school opened; I had been playing in the gutters and had got my feet wet, because there were holes in my shoes. My father cut insoles out of cardboard, and I wore those in my shoes. As long as I had to stay in the house anyway, they were all right.

I stayed cooped up in the house, without any companionship. We didn't take a Sunday paper any more, but the *Barry Adage* came every week in the mails; and though I did not read small print, I could see the Santa Clauses and holly wreaths in the advertisements.

There was a calendar in the kitchen. The red days were Sundays and holidays; and that red 25 was Christmas. (It was on a Monday, and the two red figures would come right together in 1893; but this represents research in the *World Almanac*, not memory.) I knew when Sunday was, because I could look out of the window and see the neighbor's children, all dressed up, going to Sunday school. I knew just when Christmas was going to be.

But there was something queer! My father and mother didn't say a word about Christmas. And once, when I spoke of it, there was a strange silence; so I didn't say anything more about it. But I wondered, and was troubled. Why didn't they say anything about it? Was what I had said I wanted (memory refuses to supply that detail) too expensive?

I wasn't arrogant and talkative now. I was silent and frightened. What was the matter? Why didn't my father and mother say anything about Christmas? As the day approached, my chest grew tighter with anxiety.

Now it was the day before Christmas. I couldn't be mistaken.

But not a word about it from my father and mother. I waited in painful bewilderment all day. I had supper with them, and was allowed to sit up for an hour. I was waiting for them to say something. "It's time for you to go to bed," my mother said gently. I *had* to say something.

"This is Christmas Eve, isn't it?" I asked, as if I didn't know. My father and mother looked at one another. Then my mother looked away. Her face was pale and stony. My father cleared his throat, and his face took on a joking look. He pretended he hadn't known it was Christmas Eve, because he hadn't been reading the papers. He said he would go downtown and find out.

My mother got up and walked out of the room. I didn't want my father to have to keep on being funny about it, so I got up and went to bed. I went by myself without having a light. I undressed in the dark and crawled into bed.

I was numb. As if I had been hit by something. It was hard to breathe. I ached all through. I was stunned—with finding out the truth.

My body knew before my mind quite did. In a minute, when I could think, my mind would know. And as the pain in my body ebbed, the pain in my mind began. I *knew*. I couldn't put it into words yet. But I knew why I had taken only a little bag of potatoes to Sunday school that fall. I knew why there had been only pennies in my little yellow envelope. I knew why I hadn't gone to school that fall—why I hadn't any new shoes—why we had been living on potato soup all winter. All these things, and others, many others, fitted themselves together in my mind, and meant something.

Then the words came into my mind and I whispered them into the darkness:

"*We're poor!*"

That was it. I was one of those poor children I had been sorry for, when I heard about them in Sunday school. My mother hadn't told me. My father was out of work, and we hadn't any money. That was why there wasn't going to be any Christmas at our house.

Then I remembered something that made me squirm with shame —a boast. (Memory will not yield this up. Had I said to some nice little boy, "I'm going to be President of the United States"? Or to a nice little girl: "I'll marry you when I grow up"? It was some boast as horribly shameful to remember.)

"*We're poor.*" There in bed in the dark, I whispered it over and over to myself. I was making myself get used to it. (Or—just torturing myself, as one pressed the tongue against a sore tooth? No, memory says not like that—but to keep myself from ever being such a fool again: suffering now, to keep this awful thing from ever happening again. Memory is clear on that; it was more like pulling the tooth, to get it over with—never mind the pain, this will be the end!)

It wasn't so bad, now that I knew. I *just hadn't known!* I had thought all sorts of foolish things; that I was going to Ann Arbor— going to be a lawyer—going to make speeches in the Square, going to be President! Now I knew better.

I had wanted (something) for Christmas. I didn't want it now. I didn't want anything.

I lay there in the dark, feeling the cold emotion of renunciation. (The tendrils of desire unfold their clasp on the outer world of objects, withdraw, shrivel up. Wishes shrivel up, turn black, die. It is like that.)

It hurt. But nothing would ever hurt again. I would never let myself want anything again.

I lay there stretched out straight and stiff in the dark, my fists clenched hard upon Nothing. . . .

In the morning it had been like a nightmare that is not clearly remembered—that one wishes to forget. Though I hadn't hung up any stocking, there was one hanging at the foot of my bed. A bag of popcorn, and a lead pencil, for me. They had done the best they could, now they realized that I knew about Christmas. But they needn't have thought they had to. I didn't want anything.

QUESTIONS ON CONTENT

1. What is the purpose of the first paragraph? Many years lie between the occurrences recorded here and the setting them down on paper. In what way does this lapse of time make the author's job a difficult one?
2. Is this something more than a Christmas story? If so, what?
3. Examine each detail for its contribution to the central effect. Could anything have been left out without damaging the impact of the story?
4. If you consider this writing effective, try to tell how the effectiveness is achieved. Are there any figures of speech? Is the language simple or ornate? Is sincerity evident? Explain.

❧ The Most Disgraceful Thing I Ever Did

1. The Scandal of the Anthology

ALDOUS HUXLEY

"I should like to show you," she said, and hesitated, blushing; embarrassed, she looked more ravishing than ever. "I should like to show you the little poem I wrote yesterday. I believe it's the best thing I've ever done."

I was only too delighted, of course. A man and a *bourgeois*— how could I fail to be delighted? This dazzling young aristocrat, so assured, so complete, so gloriously careless about everything and everyone except herself and her own fun, had actually, in our grandmother's phrase, "set her cap at me." She had taken the trouble to be charming. With what a delicious naïve sincerity and an obvious ignorance of all my works, she had flattered me. How much she had enjoyed all those books of mine, which she hadn't read! I basked in her radiance.

"Here it is." She pulled out of her bosom a folded paper. "Don't be too severe with it," she added, almost anxiously.

I adjusted my *pince-nez* and unfolded the document. "O Love," I began to read.

> O Love is sweet when April showers fall,
> And Love is lush when roses bloom in June,
> And Love beneath the swelt'ring harvest moon
> Is seldom pure; for love. . . .

I read it over twice slowly, wondering what on earth I should say. Why couldn't she be content with just living? And why, if she must *do* something, did she choose verse? There was the piano, there was the water-color sketching! . . . I looked up at her, and found myself confronted by her dark, intent eyes. She looked like Cleopatra, and twenty, and her body—oh, serpent of old Nile!— was sheathed in a skin of cloth-of-silver.

"What do you think of it?" she asked.

From *Vanity Fair* (October 1923); copyright The Condé Nast Publications Inc. Reprinted by permission of the author and the publisher.

SALEM COLLEGE LIBRARY
WINSTON-SALEM, N. C.

"I think it quite wonderful," I said with enthusiasm.

Her smile of pleasure was the loveliest thing in the world.

"I'm so glad," she said, with an air of detachment, "that you are compiling an anthology of the best modern verse."

A gloom suddenly descended on my spirit. I nodded. I couldn't deny it; everybody knew my anthology. It was going to be the very best of its kind—rigorously, austerely select.

"I thought," she said, and smiled at me again, "I thought that, perhaps, as you liked my little poem so much, you might. . . ."

QUESTIONS ON CONTENT

1. What does the author's *bourgeois* have to do with this episode?
2. Why did a "gloom suddenly descend" on Huxley's spirit?
3. Would Rousseau consider Huxley's act disgraceful?

2. *The Invasion of the Sanctuary*

F. Scott Fitzgerald

It was Christmas eve. In a fashionable church were gathered the great ones of the city in a pious swoon. For the hour bankers had put out of their weary minds the number of farmers on whom they must foreclose next day in order to make their twenty per cent. Real estate men had ceased worrying what gaudy lies should embellish their prospectuses on the following Monday. Even fatigued flappers had returned to religion and were wondering if the man two pews ahead really looked like Valentino, or whether it was just the way his hair was cut in the back.

And at that moment, I, who had been suppering heavily in a house not two doors from the church, felt religion descending upon me also. A warm current seemed to run through my body. My sins were washed away and I felt, as my host strained a drop or so from the ultimate bottle, that my life was beginning all over again.

"Yes," I said softly to myself, drawing on my overshoes, "I will go to church. I will find some friend, and sitting next to him, we will sing the Christmas hymns."

The church was silent. The rector had mounted to the pulpit and was standing there motionless, conscious of the approving gaze of Mrs. T. T. Conquadine, the wife of the flour king, sitting in the front row.

SALEM COLLEGE LIBRARY
WINSTON-SALEM, N. C.

I entered quietly and walked up the aisle toward him, searching the silent ranks of the faithful for some one whom I could call my friend. But no one hailed me. In all the church there was no sound but the metallic rasp of the buckles on my overshoes as I plodded toward the rector. At the very foot of the pulpit a kindly thought struck me—perhaps inspired by the faint odor of sanctity which exuded from the saintly man. I spoke.

"Don't mind me," I said, "go on with the sermon."

Then, perhaps unsteadied a bit by my emotion, I passed down the other aisle, followed by a sort of amazed awe, and so out into the street. The papers had the extra out before midnight.

QUESTIONS ON CONTENT

1. What is a *flapper?* How does this word serve to date this episode? Does the name *Valentino* make dating even more certain?
2. Does the last sentence help or harm the effect?
3. What is the significance of "the ultimate bottle"?

3. *The Episode of the Bean-Shooter*

HEYWOOD BROUN

The boy who lived across the street (his name was Valentine) boasted that his mother was horribly ailing. He said she had nervous prostration. My brother and I were interested, but sceptical. We could see her reading by the window of the library, and her nervous prostration did not show at all.

Possibly the experiment with the bean-shooter and the buck-shot was in the interest of science. My brother bought the weapons and then we took up a position on the little balcony outside our room. First we put out the lights, and then opened fire. The house of Valentine's mother was a shining mark. She herself was plainly visible as she rocked to and fro.

At the first crash of the shot against the window pane, she leaped high out of her chair. And it was the same with the next. Valentine seemed more truthful than we had imagined, for it was quite evident that his mother was a nervous woman. My brother and I took turns at shooting, and after each drive we ducked down behind the wall so that we were completely hidden in the darkness of the balcony.

Detection must have come merely from the direction of the attack, for we found ourselves the center of a family council the next morning. Valentine's mother had sent in a note of complaint. After rebukes and reproaches came the sentence. We must go and apologize. My brother, as the elder, apologized first. He said, "I want to apologize." Then I said, "I'll never do it again."

No horrible example at a temperance meeting, or murderer confessing to full court, ever had a greater thrill of pride. For the first time in my life I stood forth admittedly a sinner. The fact that my career was cut short by this pledge of reform lessened my enjoyment not at all. After all, I had lived.

And now, for the first time, I am ready to confess the shamelessness of it all. The dramatic possibilities of the situation tempted me beyond my strength. The truth of the matter is that I had not hit the window; no, not once. I had *tried* to hit it, but effort toward evil is not enough. But my aim and my manipulation of the bean-shooter were inferior. From my hands the lead missiles fell harmlessly to the street below, or sailed over the roof of the stricken woman's house. No crash of shaken glass rested on my conscience, but eagerly and passionately I accepted guilt and clung to it. So much did I long for an evil reputation that I was even willing to lie for it.

It has marked me. To this day, if any lady were ever kind enough to say to me, "I suppose you're a gay dog," I know I should smile a weak protest, blush a little, drop my head, and try to make her believe that the charge had hit home.

QUESTIONS ON CONTENT

1. Why does the author say that "Possibly the experiment with the bean-shooter and the buckshot was in the interest of science"?
2. Explain: "Effort towards evil is not enough." Is this notion morally correct?
3. Compare Broun's confession with Huxley's; with Fitzgerald's. Which of the acts confessed to do you consider genuinely disgraceful?
4. How would Rousseau regard these "confessions"?

🙌 *Through a Glass Darkly*

PETER DE VRIES

I have a mackintosh that is the apple of my eye, two topcoats, and a smoked melton, yet when a plugger in a clothing store recently detained me with a quick-change skit in which he whipped off a raglan, turned it inside out, and whipped it on again, with a hanky-panky on its behalf as a garment suitable for wet days, I bought it. Why? Because I am unable to rescue myself from demonstrators. Once my attention has been speared by a pitchman paring a potato with a trick knife, I stand mesmerized by the lengthening peel, powerless to move on till the operation is over and I have plunked down my quarter. I have thought of hiring an analyst to clean my coils, but the matter isn't really complicated enough for that. I'll give a few more examples of my trouble and then say what I think is at the bottom of it.

Not long ago, I was sauntering up Seventh Avenue in the Forties when a rap on the window of a store I was passing brought my head around in a reflex. Behind the glass, a man in a barber's tunic buttered his palms with a pomade called Lustrine and ground it into the noodle of a Latin youth seated before him on a three-legged stool. The stooge had dark, liquid eyes, which sought mine with a look of mute patience, as though for me alone was he taking this drubbing. When it was over and his locks were being combed into glossy undulations, I stepped inside for my trial size.

Later that week, a man in a tan duster banged a wand imperiously on a store pane in the East Thirties, alerting me and a middle-aged couple. He directed our attention to the skeleton of a human foot and then pointed to a printed sign alleging that the bones had been mangled by unscientific shoes. The couple moseyed along, but I was inside in a trice. A man in quasi-surgical garb shucked off my brogans and led me in stocking feet to a fluoroscope, which laid bare the dismal secrets of my own metatarsals. Ten minutes later I hobbled out scientifically shod, carrying my former footgear under my arm.

Reprinted by permission of the author. Copyright 1949 The New Yorker Magazine, Inc.

It was a few months later that another unguarded moment—one in the basement of a downtown emporium—brought me suddenly face to face with a bull-necked man on a dais who, having taken a spraddled stance, pulled the legs of a pair of denim pants in opposite directions till I thought he would pop, then gave up with a good-natured laugh, thus acknowledging himself hopelessly bested by the workmanship in the crotch. Some other shoppers who had paused went on, leaving me stranded. The man strained at the dungarees a second time and a third, his eyes reproaching me for my apparent immunity to reasonable proof. Something had to give, and it was me—four ninety-eight.

So it goes. I have the feeling these birds can spot me, or can spot the gelatinous type. I once read that suckers have their affliction written clearly in their features, so I decided to try the experiment of concealing as much of mine as possible one recent Saturday afternoon. I donned the reversible raglan, turning the collar up around my ears, drew on a soft hat, pulling it well down over one eye, and swaddled myself up to and including the chin in a heavy woollen muffler, leaving little visible of my face but my nose and a single eye. Even my gait was altered, for my scientifically constructed shoes had substantially deranged one foot.

Thus dressed, I strolled up Sixth Avenue clenching an unlighted cigar and humming an air from "Die Fledermaus." Just short of Central Park, I heard the familiar clatter of a stick on glass. It was in a drug store window on my immediate right. I stopped but didn't turn. Deliberately, I struck a match on my thumbnail, set fire to the cigar, and puffed till I stood in a dense cloud of smoke. The rap came again, this time more insistently. I inhaled a deep lungful and let it out leisurely, snapping the match into the gutter. A third summons sounded, prolonged and peremptory. I swung to.

A man in a laboratory jacket stood in the window. He drew my attention crisply to a chart down which digestive organs meandered in color. Having, by deftly flipping the pages of a folio on an easel, enumerated the ills that lay in wait for me if they had not already begun secretly to waste me, he picked up a bottle filled with purple liquid and shook it to a bright froth, holding up three fingers to indicate that I was to take this three times a day. I nodded and went inside.

These instances will suffice to illustrate the compulsion. As for elucidating it, I will have to relate an incident in my past in which it is most likely rooted. This involves an interval when I was myself, very briefly, a demonstrating salesman. I graduated from college in 1931, the year that marked the depth of the depression. You took anything you could get, those days. I took a job selling pressure cookers, which were then being promoted on a wide scale for the first time. The company I worked for emphasized group demonstrations. You cooked a meal in the kitchen of a woman who had called in her friends or neighbors for the occasion, they ate it, and you signed up as many of the women as you could. I was given a short course in operating the pressure cooker and sent into the field. This was in Chicago in the summer.

My first prospect was a widow named Mrs. Tannenbaum, whom I knew slightly. She agreed to gather a group of housewives for a bridge supper, which I was to fix. I arrived about four-thirty on the day of the demonstration, lugging the pressure cooker, in its leather case, and a pot roast under one arm. We were to have potatoes with the pot roast, of course, and I had told Mrs. Tannenbaum I thought carrots would be nice. We had used carrots in class. Mrs. Tannenbaum supplied the vegetables.

The ladies clustered in the kitchen while I ran through the fine points of the cooker for them, got the roast on, and set the valve. Then I shooed them to their bridge tables and peeled my potatoes and scraped my carrots. Mrs. Tannenbaum shut the kitchen door, leaving me alone. I got my vegetables on, and strayed out to the back porch and sat down on a glider with a magazine, to wait for the meal to be done. A little later, as I was thumbing through the magazine, an acrid odor reached my nostrils. I hurried in to the stove. I have since been at pains to forget the incident to the point of no longer clearly knowing what a pressure cooker looks like, but as I recall it, instead of closing the valve I had left it open, thus dissipating the steam, boiling all the water away, and burning everything, including the roast, to a crisp.

I stood, stricken, in the middle of the kitchen, debating what to do. A shred of laughter floated in above the hubbub at the front of the house. I lifted the smoking pot off the stove, tiptoed out the back door, down the stairs, along the walk beside the garage, to the alley, and dropped the whole works, cooker and all, into the garbage can. I set the lid back on the can and stole up the alley to the street, where I broke into a trot.

The recollection of that occurrence has haunted me ever since. I never showed up at the pressure-cooker office again and I never saw Mrs. Tannenbaum again—except that I still see her in my mind's eye, standing flabbergasted in the empty kitchen, her hungry and baffled guests around her. I don't know whether that or the vision of myself creeping away behind the garages is the more oppressive. Like Lord Jim, I carry down the years the adhesive memory of cowardice, but mine, unlike his, is cowardice without scope.

Thus, at the bottom of my constant purchases of paring knives and trial sizes is a quest for absolution. I have an expiatory urge that makes me secretly *want* situations in which I become a customer, an at times almost voluptuous desire for the buyer-seller relation, so that I can punish myself by being symbolically identified with my victims of that afternoon, especially Mrs. Tannenbaum. In fact, I try to *outdo* Mrs. Tannenbaum as a victim, because she didn't actually buy, while I do, in a sacrificial gesture that must be repeated, over and over again.

QUESTIONS ON CONTENT

1. Explain the following words and phrases: *hanky-panky; pitchman; clean my coils; noodle; stooge; moseyed along.*
2. What does the title mean?
3. At what point is the theme of this selection announced?
4. Would you classify the author's trouble as "an amiable weakness"?
5. The organization of this selection is simple and effective: I What my trouble is; II Examples of my trouble; III How my trouble started. What are the subheads for II and III?

SUGGESTIONS FOR PAPERS

Your paper is to be about yourself or about the selections in this chapter. If it is about yourself, it will take the form of either a straight narrative without a moral or a narrative with a moral. You may not have had an experience so venturous as Mark Twain's, but certainly you have had dozens of experiences as commonplace as those described by Wordsworth or Miss Skinner. You may have some peculiar weakness (a strength would do as well) which may be illustrated by a series or related occurrences. (See "Through a Glass Darkly.") Whatever you choose to write about, resolve to be specific. Do not simply glance at the episode; *look* at it; *stare* at it until the essential details are fixed in your mind. (If you feel a restraint in writing *I*, use the third person. Write about yourself as though you were someone else. This impersonal approach may enable you to see the episode or episodes more clearly.)

1. Have you had a romantic notion about something that you wanted to do? Have you tried learning to do it, only to find much of the romance turn to hard work? Select your subject; then devote the first part of your paper to your dream of what the job would be like and the second part to a specific statement of what it was really like. (Some possible subjects: Cowpunching; Sodajerking; a Newspaper Route; Gardening; In a Grocery Store; Delivery Boy; Hostess; Team Manager.)

2. Have you been told that you were a sensitive child? If so, how did you get this reputation? Tell in intimate detail one or two episodes that would justify describing you as sensitive. (You may feel that you gained something from acting a part; if so, add details to point this out.)

3. Do people think that you are tough fibered, perhaps a little heartless? If so, do you know upon what this impression is based? Tell in intimate detail one or two episodes which would justify you as insensitive. (If you have been misjudged, explain how.)

4. Rousseau says that everyone is guilty at one time or another of "odious" conduct. Wordsworth confesses to two petty crimes and then recalls his terror and sense of guilt. Can you recall a childhood "crime" and how *you* felt about it? If so, make your reader follow your mental processes before and after the deed.

5. Reread the little story told by Miss Skinner, "One Day." Put yourself in the position of the little snob, Elise, and retell the story from *her* point of view. Could she justify her conduct? What experience in your own life makes you confident that you understand Elise?

6. Wordsworth gives credit to Nature for gently preparing him for a later life. He says: "Thanks to the means which Nature deigned to employ." Reread his poem; then write your paper on the "means" which the poet had in mind. Finally, and most important, test your relations with Nature. Do you feel that Nature has taught you anything?

7. From whence came Peter De Vries's title, "Through a Glass Darkly"? After you have looked up the title (see *Bartlett's Familiar Quotations*), go to the original work and read the quotation in con-

text. Now, write a paper on how applicable the title is to De Vries's article.

8. It is possible that everyone has some special weakness, some peculiar susceptibility. What is yours? If you have such a weakness, describe it carefully; then give a series of specific examples to show what you mean.

9. What is your chief strength—that is, what can you always resist doing or saying? If you have some resolve to which you stick no matter what, tell about it and of the times you have been tempted to violate your rule. (Examples: "I never gossip"; "I never listen to gossip"; "I am never late"; "I am never profane"; "I am never cowardly"; "I am never unpleasant." You will not, of course, take these topics too seriously!)

10. Analyze any one of the selections in this chapter for method. How does the author gain the sympathy of the reader? How might he have lost that sympathy? Rewrite a part of the selection to show how conceit might have alienated the reader.

11. Which selection in this chapter is most appealing? Write a paper in which you make a series of comparisons to justify your choice of a particular selection as best.

12. Normally, it is thought, men and women shy away from revealing any of their truly wicked actions. Yet just as normal is the desire to confess. Criminals, after years of freedom, give themselves up, confess all, and say they feel better. Catholics confess regularly. Protestants enjoy testimonial meetings. Literary men, poets in particular, like to reveal their shortcomings. Could you write an essay on "The Joys of Being Found Out"? You should be able to cite many incidental examples but should concentrate on one major illustration.

SOME TITLES FOR PAPERS

1. A Disillusioning Experience
2. It Looked Wonderful, But . . .
3. Confessions of a Bully
4. Miserable Thin Skin
5. A Childhood Crime
6. My First Feeling of Guilt
7. Honest Confession Is Good
8. "I shall Rouge Myself"
9. I Can't Say No
10. My Most Vulnerable Point
11. My Most Disgraceful Act
12. Tripped By a Coincidence
13. Can Anyone Tell the Truth?
14. Now It Can Be Told
15. "When I Have Fears . . ."
16. A Revealing Christmas

(See also 1 and 9 under Suggestions for Papers.)

CHAPTER 3

❧ *KINDS OF DELINQUENCY*

WHERE DOES MISCHIEF STOP and delinquency begin? When do pranks become misdemeanors? At what point do adults decide to abandon —always reluctantly—the soothing formula of "boys will be boys" and conclude that boys may be social menaces?

The first two selections tell of the diverting activities of two contrasting mischief-makers. O. Henry's young hellion, Red Chief, is a model, properly exaggerated, of mischievous small boys. His extraordinary physical energy overflows and inundates some unsuspecting—and lovable—evil-doers. Mr. Rovere's Wallace is an intellectual counterpart of Red Chief. His excess mental energy is released against a boy's natural enemies, school teachers. Do Red Chief and Wallace qualify as juvenile delinquents?

If they do not, how do their activities differ from those of Sunshine, whose case history is reported by Agnes Meyer in "Schoolboy Racketeers"? Why do we laugh at Red Chief and Wallace but smile not at all at Sunshine? And if we do not smile at Sunshine, what is our response to his anti-social conduct? Do O. Henry and Rovere say anything about environment? Does Agnes Meyer stress environment?

❧ *The Ransom of Red Chief*

O. Henry

It looked like a good thing: but wait till I tell you. We were down South, in Alabama—Bill Driscoll and myself—when this kidnapping idea struck us. It was, as Bill afterward expressed it, "during a moment of temporary mental apparition"; but we didn't find that out till later.

There was a town down there, as flat as a flannel-cake, and called Summit, of course. It contained inhabitants of as undeleterious and self-satisfied a class of peasantry as ever clustered around a Maypole.

Bill and me had a joint capital of about six hundred dollars, and we needed just two thousand dollars more to pull off a fraudulent townlot scheme in Western Illinois with. We talked it over on the front steps of the hotel. Philoprogenitiveness, says we, is strong in semi-rural communities; therefore, and for other reasons, a kidnapping project ought to do better there than in the radius of newspapers that send reporters out in plain clothes to stir up talk about such things. We knew that Summit couldn't get after us with anything stronger than constables and, maybe, some lackadaisical bloodhounds and a diatribe or two in the *Weekly Farmers' Budget*. So, it looked good.

We selected for our victim the only child of a prominent citizen named Ebenezer Dorset. The father was respectable and tight, a mortgage fancier and a stern, upright collection-plate passer and forecloser. The kid was a boy of ten, with bas-relief freckles, and hair the color of the cover of the magazine you buy at the newsstand when you want to catch a train. Bill and me figured that Ebenezer would melt down for a ransom of two thousand dollars to a cent. But wait till I tell you.

About two miles from Summit was a little mountain, covered with a dense cedar brake. On the rear elevation of this mountain was a cave. There we stored provisions.

One evening after sundown, we drove in a buggy past old Dorset's house. The kid was in the street, throwing rocks at a kitten on the opposite fence.

From *Whirligigs* by O. Henry. Copyright 1907 by Doubleday & Company, Inc.

"Hey, little boy!" says Bill, "would you like to have a bag of candy and a nice ride?"

The boy catches Bill neatly in the eye with a piece of brick.

"That will cost the old man an extra five hundred dollars," says Bill, climbing over the wheel.

That boy put up a fight like a welter-weight cinnamon bear; but, at last, we got him down in the bottom of the buggy and drove away. We took him up to the cave, and I hitched the horse in the cedar brake. After dark I drove the buggy to the little village, three miles away, where we had hired it, and walked back to the mountain.

Bill was pasting court-plaster over the scratches and bruises on his features. There was a fire burning behind the big rock at the entrance of the cave, and the boy was watching a pot of boiling coffee, with two buzzard tail-feathers stuck in his red hair. He points a stick at me when I come up, and says:

"Ha! cursed paleface, do you dare to enter the camp of Red Chief, the terror of the plains?"

"He's all right now," says Bill, rolling up his trousers and examining some bruises on his shins. "We're playing Indian. We're making Buffalo Bill's show look like magic-lantern views of Palestine in the town hall. I'm Old Hank, the Trapper, Red Chief's captive, and I'm to be scalped at daybreak. By Geronimo! that kid can kick hard."

Yes sir, that boy seemed to be having the time of his life. The fun of camping out in a cave had made him forget that he was a captive himself. He immediately christened me Snake-eye, the Spy, and announced that, when his braves returned from the warpath, I was to be broiled at the stake at the rising of the sun.

Then we had supper; and he filled his mouth full of bacon and bread and gravy, and began to talk. He made a during-dinner speech something like this:

"I like this fine, I never camped out before; but I had a pet-'possum once, and I was nine last birthday. I hate to go to school. Rats ate up sixteen of Jimmy Talbot's aunt's speckled hen's eggs. Are there any real Indians in these woods? I want some more gravy. Does the trees moving make the wind blow? We had five puppies. What makes your nose so red, Hank? My father has lots of money. Are the stars hot? I whipped Ed Walker twice, Saturday. I don't like girls. You dassent catch toads unless with a string. Do oxen make any noise? Why are oranges round? Have you got beds to sleep on in this cave? Amos Murray has got six toes. A parrot can talk, but a monkey or a fish can't. How many does it take to make twelve?"

Every few minutes he would remember that he was a pesky redskin, and pick up his stick rifle and tiptoe to the mouth of the cave to rubber for the scouts of the hated paleface. Now and then he would let out a war-whoop that made Old Hank the Trapper shiver. That boy had Bill terrorized from the start.

"Red Chief," says I to the kid, "would you like to go home?"

"Aw, what for?" says he. "I don't have any fun at home. I hate to go to school. I like to camp out. You won't take me back home again, Snake-eye, will you?"

"Not right away," says I. "We'll stay here in the cave awhile."

"All right!" says he. "That'll be fine. I never had such fun in all my life."

We went to bed about eleven o'clock. We spread down some wide blankets and quilts and put Red Chief between us. We weren't afraid he'd run away. He kept us awake for three hours, jumping up and reaching for his rifle and screeching: "Hist! pard," in mine and Bill's ears, as the fancied crackle of a twig or the rustle of a leaf revealed to his young imagination the stealthy approach of the outlaw band. At last, I fell into a troubled sleep, and dreamed that I had been kidnapped and chained to a tree by a ferocious pirate with red hair.

Just at daybreak, I was awakened by a series of awful screams from Bill. They weren't yells, or howls, or shouts, or whoops, or yawps, such as you'd expect from a manly set of vocal organs— they were simply indecent, terrifying, humiliating screams, such as women emit when they see ghosts or caterpillars. It's an awful thing to hear a strong, desperate, fat man scream incontinently in a cave at daybreak.

I jumped up to see what the matter was. Red Chief was sitting on Bill's chest, with one hand twined in Bill's hair. In the other he had the sharp caseknife we used for slicing bacon; and he was industriously and realistically trying to take Bill's scalp, according to the sentence that had been pronounced upon him the evening before.

I got the knife away from the kid and made him lie down again But, from that moment, Bill's spirit was broken. He laid down on his side of the bed, but he never closed an eye again in sleep as long as that boy was with us. I dozed off for a while, but along toward sun-up I remembered that Red had said I was to be burned at the stake at the rising of the sun. I wasn't nervous or afraid; but I sat up and lit my pipe and leaned against a rock.

"What you getting up so soon for, Sam?" asked Bill.

"Me?" says I. "Oh, I got a kind of pain in my shoulder. I thought sitting up would rest it."

"You're a liar!" says Bill. "You're afraid. You was to be burned at sunrise, and you was afraid he'd do it. And he would, too, if he could find a match. Ain't it awful, Sam? Do you think anybody will pay out money to get a little imp like that back home?"

"Sure," said I. "A rowdy kid like that is just the kind that parents dote on. Now, you and the Chief get up and cook breakfast, while I go up on the top of the mountain and reconnoitre."

I went up on the peak of the little mountain and ran my eye over the contiguous vicinity. Over towards Summit I expected to see the sturdy yeomanry of the village armed with scythes and pitchforks beating the countryside for the dastardly kidnappers. But what I saw was a peaceful landscape dotted with one man ploughing with a dun mule. Nobody was dragging the creek; no couriers dashed hither and yon, bringing tidings of no news to the distracted parents. There was a sylvan attitude of somnolent sleepiness pervading that section of the external outward surface of Alabama that lay exposed to my view. "Perhaps," says I to myself, "it has not yet been discovered that the wolves have borne away the tender lambkin from the fold. Heaven help the wolves!" says I, and I went down the mountain to breakfast.

When I got to the cave I found Bill backed up against the side of it, breathing hard, and the boy threatening to smash him with a rock half as big as a cocoanut.

"He put a red-hot boiled potato down my back," explained Bill, "and then mashed it with his foot; and I boxed his ears. Have you got a gun about you, Sam?"

I took the rock away from the boy and kind of patched up the argument. "I'll fix you," says the kid to Bill. "No man ever yet struck the Red Chief but he got paid for it. You better beware!"

After breakfast the kid takes a piece of leather with strings wrapped around it out of his pocket and goes outside the cave unwinding it.

"What's he up to now?" says Bill, anxiously. "You don't think he'll run away, do you, Sam?"

"No fear of it," says I. "He don't seem to be much of a home body. But we've got to fix up some plan about the ransom. There don't seem to be much excitement around Summit on account of his disappearance; but maybe they haven't realized yet that he's gone. His folks may think he's spending the night with Aunt Jane or one of the neighbors. Anyhow, he'll be missed to-day. To-night we must get a message to his father demanding the two thousand dollars for his return."

Just then we heard a kind of war-whoop, such as David might have emitted when he knocked out the champion Goliath. It was a sling that Red Chief had pulled out of his pocket, and he was whirling it around his head.

I dodged, and heard a heavy thud and a kind of a sigh from Bill, like a horse gives out when you take his saddle off. A nigger-head rock the size of an egg had caught Bill just behind his left ear. He loosened himself all over and fell in the fire across the frying pan of hot water for washing the dishes. I dragged him out and poured cold water on his head for half an hour.

By and by, Bill sits up and feels behind his ear and says: "Sam, do you know who my favorite Biblical character is?"

"Take it easy," says I. "You'll come to your senses presently."

"King Herod," says he. "You won't go away and leave me here alone, will you, Sam?"

I went out and caught that boy and shook him until his freckles rattled.

"If you don't behave," says I, "I'll take you straight home. Now, are you going to be good, or not?"

"I was only funning," says he, sullenly. "I didn't mean to hurt Old Hank. But what did he hit me for? I'll behave, Snake-eye, if you won't send me home, and if you'll let me play the Black Scout to-day."

"I don't know the game," says I. "That's for you and Mr. Bill to decide. He's your playmate for the day. I'm going away for a while on business. Now, you come in and make friends with him and say you are sorry for hurting him, or home you go, at once."

I made him and Bill shake hands, and then I took Bill aside and told him I was going to Poplar Grove, a little village three miles from the cave, and find out what I could about how the kidnapping had been regarded in Summit. Also, I thought it best to send a peremptory letter to old man Dorset that day, demanding the ransom and dictating how it should be paid.

"You know, Sam," says Bill, "I've stood by you without batting an

eye in earthquakes, fire and flood—in poker games, dynamite outrages, police raids, train robberies, and cyclones. I never lost my
nerve yet till we kidnapped that two-legged skyrocket of a kid.
He's got me going. You won't leave me long with him, will you,
Sam?"

"I'll be back some time this afternoon," says I. "You must keep
the boy amused and quiet till I return. And now we'll write the
letter to old Dorset."

Bill and I got paper and pencil and worked on the letter while Red
Chief, with a blanket wrapped around him, strutted up and down,
guarding the mouth of the cave. Bill begged me tearfully to make
the ransom fifteen hundred dollars instead of two thousand. "I
ain't attempting," says he, "to decry the celebrated moral aspect of
parental affection, but we're dealing with humans, and it ain't human
for anybody to give up two thousand dollars for that forty-pound
chunk of freckled wildcat. I'm willing to take a chance at fifteen
hundred dollars. You can charge the difference up to me."

So, to relieve Bill, I acceded, and we collaborated a letter that
ran this way:

EBENEZER DORSET, ESQ.:

We have your boy concealed in a place far from Summit. It is
useless for you or the most skillful detectives to attempt to find him.
Absolutely, the only terms on which you can have him restored to
you are these: We demand fifteen hundred dollars in large bills for
his return; the money to be left at midnight to-night at the same
spot and in the same box as your reply—as hereinafter described.
If you agree to these terms, send your answer in writing by a solitary messenger to-night at half-past eight o'clock. After crossing
Owl Creek on the road to Poplar Grove, there are three large trees
about a hundred yards apart, close to the fence of the wheat field
on the right-hand side. At the bottom of the fence-post, opposite
the third tree, will be found a small pasteboard box.

The messenger will place the answer in this box and return immediately to Summit.

If you attempt any treachery or fail to comply with our demand
as stated, you will never see your boy again.

If you pay the money as demanded, he will be returned to you
safe and well within three hours. These terms are final, and if you
do not accede to them no further communication will be attempted.

TWO DESPERATE MEN.

I addressed this letter to Dorset, and put it in my pocket. As I was about to start, the kid comes up to me and says:

"Aw, Snake-eye, you said I could play the Black Scout while you was gone."

"Play it, of course," says I. "Mr. Bill will play with you. What kind of a game is it?"

"I'm the Black Scout," says Red Chief, "and I have to ride to the stockade to warn the settlers that the Indians are coming. I'm tired of playing Indian myself. I want to be the Black Scout."

"All right," says I. "It sounds harmless to me. I guess Mr. Bill will help you foil the pesky savages."

"What am I to do?" asks Bill, looking at the kid suspiciously.

"You are the hoss," says Black Scout. "Get down on your hands and knees. How can I ride to the stockade without a hoss?"

"You'd better keep him interested," said I, "till we get the scheme going. Loosen up."

Bill gets down on his all fours, and a look comes in his eye like a rabbit's when you catch it in a trap.

"How far is it to the stockade, kid?" he asks, in a husky manner of voice.

"Ninety miles," says the Black Scout. "And you have to hump yourself to get there on time. Whoa, now!"

The Black Scout jumps on Bill's back and digs his heels in his sides.

"For Heaven's sake," says Bill, "hurry back, Sam, as soon as you can. I wish we hadn't made the ransom more than a thousand. Say, you quit kicking me or I'll get up and warm you good."

I walked over to Poplar Grove and sat around the post-office and store, talking with the chaw-bacons that come in to trade. One whiskerando says that he hears Summit is all upset on account of Elder Ebenezer Dorset's boy having been lost or stolen. That was all I wanted to know. I bought some smoking tobacco, referred casually to the price of black-eyed peas, posted my letter surreptitiously, and came away. The postmaster said the mail-carrier would come by in an hour to take the mail to Summit.

When I got back to the cave Bill and the boy were not to be found. I explored the vicinity of the cave, and risked a yodel or two, but there was no response.

So I lighted my pipe and sat down on a mossy bank to await developments.

In about half an hour I heard the bushes rustle, and Bill wabbled out into the little glade in front of the cave. Behind him was the kid, stepping softly like a scout, with a broad grin on his face. Bill stopped, took off his hat, and wiped his face with a red handkerchief. The kid stopped about eight feet behind him.

"Sam," says Bill, "I suppose you'll think I'm a renegade, but I couldn't help it. I'm a grown person with masculine proclivities and habits of self-defense, but there is a time when all systems of egotism and predominance fail. The boy is gone. I sent him home. All is off. There was martyrs in old times," goes on Bill, "that suffered death rather than give up the particular graft they enjoyed. None of 'em ever was subjugated to such supernatural tortures as I have been. I tried to be faithful to our articles of depredation; but there came a limit."

"What's the trouble, Bill?" I asked him.

"I was rode," says Bill, "the ninety miles to the stockade, not barring an inch. Then, when the settlers was rescued, I was given oats. Sand ain't a palatable substitute. And then, for an hour I had to try to explain to him why there was nothin' in holes, how a road can run both ways, and what makes the grass green. I tell you, Sam, a human can only stand so much. I takes him by the neck of his clothes and drags him down the mountain. On the way he kicks my legs black and blue from the knees down; and I've got to have two or three bites on my thumb and hand cauterized.

"But he's gone"—continues Bill—"gone home. I showed him the road to Summit and kicked him about eight feet nearer there at one kick. I'm sorry we lose the ransom; but it was either that or Bill Driscoll to the madhouse."

Bill is puffing and blowing, but there is a look of ineffable peace and growing content on his rose-pink features.

"Bill," says I, "there isn't any heart disease in your family, is there?"

"No," says Bill, "nothing chronic except malaria and accidents. Why?"

"Then you might turn around," says I, "and have a look behind you."

Bill turns and sees the boy, and loses his complexion and sits down plump on the ground and begins to pluck aimlessly at grass and little sticks. For an hour I was afraid of his mind. And then I told him that my scheme was to put the whole job through immediately and that we would get the ransom and be off with it by midnight if old Dorset fell in with our proposition. So Bill braced up enough to give the kid a weak sort of a smile and a promise to play the Russian in a Japanese war with him as soon as he felt a little better.

I had a scheme for collecting that ransom without danger of being caught by counterplots that ought to commend itself to professional kidnappers. The tree under which the answer was to be left—and the money later on—was close to the road fence with big, bare fields on all sides. If a gang of constables should be watching for any one to come for the note, they could see him a long way off crossing the fields or in the road. But no, sirree! At half-past eight I was up in that tree as well hidden as a tree toad, waiting for the messenger to arrive.

Exactly on time, a half-grown boy rides up the road on a bicycle, locates the pasteboard box at the foot of the fence-post, slips a folded piece of paper into it, and pedals away again back toward Summit.

I waited an hour and then concluded the thing was square. I slid down the tree, got the note, slipped along the fence till I struck the woods, and was back at the cave in another half an hour. I opened the note, got near the lantern, and read it to Bill. It was written with a pen in a crabbed hand, and the sum and substance of it was this:

TWO DESPERATE MEN.

Gentlemen: I received your letter to-day by post, in regard to the ransom you ask for the return of my son. I think you are a little high in your demands, and I hereby make you a counter-proposition, which I am inclined to believe you will accept. You bring Johnny home and pay me two hundred and fifty dollars in cash, and I agree to take him off your hands. You had better come at night, for the neighbors believe he is lost, and I couldn't be responsible for what they would do to anybody they saw bringing him back. Very respectfully,

EBENEZER DORSET.

"Great pirates of Penzance," says I; "of all the impudent—"

But I glanced at Bill, and hesitated. He had the most appealing look in his eyes I ever saw on the face of a dumb or a talking brute.

"Sam," says he, "what's two hundred and fifty dollars, after all? We've got the money. One more night of this kid will send me to a bed in Bedlam. Besides being a thorough gentleman, I think Mr. Dorset is a spendthrift for making us such a liberal offer. You ain't going to let the chance go, are you?"

"Tell you the truth, Bill," says I, "this little he ewe lamb has somewhat got on my nerves too. We'll take him home, pay the ransom, and make our getaway."

We took him home that night. We got him to go by telling him that his father had bought a silver-mounted rifle and a pair of moccasins for him, and we were to hunt bears the next day.

It was just twelve o'clock when we knocked at Ebenezer's front door. Just at the moment when I should have been abstracting the fifteen hundred dollars from the box under the tree, according to the original proposition, Bill was counting out two hundred and fifty dollars into Dorset's hand.

When the kid found out we were going to leave him at home he started up a howl like a calliope and fastened himself as tight as a leech to Bill's leg. His father peeled him away gradually, like a porous plaster.

"How long can you hold him?" asks Bill.

"I'm not as strong as I used to be," says old Dorset, "but I think I can promise you ten minutes."

"Enough," says Bill. "In ten minutes I shall cross the Central, Southern, and Middle Western States, and be legging it trippingly for the Canadian border."

And, as dark as it was, and as fat as Bill was, and as good a runner as I am, he was a good mile and a half out of Summit before I could catch up with him.

QUESTIONS ON CONTENT

1. What did Bill mean by "temporary mental apparition"? How does this set the tone of the story?
2. Why was King Herod Bill's favorite Biblical character?
3. For what purpose did the kidnapers want $2,000?
4. What does *philoprogenitiveness* mean? What effect is gained by the use of this learned word?
5. Were you prepared for Ebenezer Dorset's reply to the Two Desperate Men?
6. How does the author manage to elicit the reader's sympathy for each of the characters?

7. Which of the kidnapers is the better educated? Does this difference in education give the author an advantage in telling his
   story? How?

❧ *Wallace*

RICHARD H. ROVERE

As a schoolboy, my relations with teachers were almost always
tense and hostile. I disliked my studies and did very badly in them.
There are, I have heard, inept students who bring out the best in
teachers, who challenge their skill and move them to sympathy and
affection. I seemed to bring out the worst in them. I think my personality had more to do with this than my poor classroom work.
Anyway, something about me was deeply offensive to the pedagogic
temperament.

Often, it took a teacher no more than a few minutes to conceive
a raging dislike for me. I recall an instructor in elementary French
who shied a textbook at my head the very first day I attended his
class. We had never laid eyes on each other until fifteen or twenty
minutes before he assaulted me. I no longer remember what, if anything, provoked him to violence. It is possible that I said something
that was either insolent or intolerably stupid. I guess I often did.
It is also possible that I said nothing at all. Even my silence, my
humility, my acquiescence, could annoy my teachers. The very
sight of me, the mere awareness of my existence on earth, could
be unendurably irritating to them.

This was the case with my fourth-grade teacher, Miss Purdy. In
order to make the acquaintance of her new students on the opening
day of school, she had each one rise and give his name and address
as she called the roll. Her voice was soft and gentle, her manner
sympathetic, until she came to me. Indeed, up to then I had been
dreamily entertaining the hope that I was at last about to enjoy a
happy association with a teacher. When Miss Purdy's eye fell on
me, however, her face suddenly twisted and darkened with revulsion. She hesitated for a few moments while she looked me up and
down and thought of a suitable comment on what she saw. "Aha!"

Reprinted by permission of the author. Copyright 1950 The New Yorker
Magazine, Inc.

she finally said, addressing not me but my new classmates, in a voice that was now coarse and cruel. "I don't have to ask *his* name. There, boys and girls, is Mr. J. Pierpont Morgan, lounging back in his mahogany-lined office." She held each syllable of the financier's name on her lips as long as she was able to, so that my fellow-students could savor the full irony of it. I imagine my posture was a bit relaxed for the occasion, but I know well that she would not have resented anyone else's sprawl as much as she did mine. I can even hear her making some friendly, schoolmarmish quip about too much summer vacation to any other pupil. Friendly quips were never for me. In some unfortunate and mysterious fashion, my entire being rubbed Miss Purdy and all her breed the wrong way. Throughout the fourth grade, she persisted in tormenting me with her idiotic Morgan joke. "And perhaps Mr. J. P. Revere can tell us all about Vasco da Gama this morning," she would say, throwing in a little added insult by mispronouncing my surname.

The aversion I inspired in teachers might under certain circumstances have been turned to good account. It might have stimulated me to industry; it might have made me get high marks, just so I could prove to the world that my persecutors were motivated by prejudice and perhaps by a touch of envy; or it might have bred a monumental rebelliousness in me, a contempt for all authority, that could have become the foundation of a career as the leader of some great movement against all tyranny and oppression.

It did none of these things. Instead, I became, so far as my school life was concerned, a thoroughly browbeaten boy, and I accepted the hostility of my teachers as an inescapable condition of life. In fact, I took the absolutely disastrous view that my teachers were unquestionably right in their estimate of me as a dense and altogether noxious creature who deserved, if anything, worse than he got. These teachers were, after all, men and women who had mastered the parts of speech, the multiplication tables, and a simply staggering number of countries. They could add up columns of figures the very sight of which made me dizzy and sick to the stomach. They could read "As You Like It" with pleasure—so they said, anyway, and I believed everything they said. I felt that if such knowledgeable people told me that I was stupid, they certainly must know what they were talking about. In consequence, my grades sank lower and lower, my face became more noticeably blank, my manner more mulish, and my presence in the classroom more aggravating to whoever presided over it. To be sure, I hated my teachers for their hatred of me, and I missed no chance to abuse them behind their backs, but fundamentally I shared with them the view that I was a worthless and despicable boy, as undeserving of an education as I was incapable of absorbing one. Often, on school days, I wished that I were dead.

This was my attitude, at least, until my second year in preparatory school, when, at fourteen, I fell under the exhilarating, regenerative influence of my friend Wallace Duckworth. Wallace changed my whole outlook on life. It was he who freed me from my terrible awe of teachers; it was he who showed me that they could be brought to book and made fools of as easily as I could be; it was he who showed me that the gap between their knowledge and mine was not unbridgeable. Sometimes I think that I should like to become a famous man, a United States senator or something of that sort, just to be able to repay my debt to Wallace. I should like to be so important that people would inquire into the early influences on my life and I would be able to tell them about Wallace.

I was freshly reminded of my debt to Wallace not long ago when my mother happened to come across a packet of letters I had written to her and my father during my first two years in a boarding school on Long Island. In one of these, I reported that "There's a new kid in school who's supposed to be a scientifical genius." Wallace was this genius. In a series of intelligence and aptitude tests we all took in the opening week, he achieved some incredible score, a mark that, according to the people who made up the tests, certified him as a genius and absolutely guaranteed that in later life he would join the company of Einstein, Steinmetz, and Edison. Naturally, his teachers were thrilled—but not for long.

Within a matter of weeks, it became clear that although Wallace was unquestionably a genius, or at least an exceptionally bright boy, he was disposed to use his considerable gifts not to equip himself for a career in the service of mankind but for purely anti-social undertakings. Far from making the distinguished scholastic record everyone expected of him, he made an altogether deplorable one. He never did a lick of schoolwork. He had picked up his scientific knowledge somewhere but evidently not from teachers. I am not sure about this, but I think Wallace's record, as long as he was in school, was even worse than mine. In my mind's eye there is a picture of the sheet of monthly averages thumbtacked to the bulletin board across the hall from the school post office; my name is one from the bottom, the bottom name being Wallace's.

As a matter of fact, one look at Wallace should have been enough to tell the teachers what sort of genius he was. At fourteen, he was somewhat shorter than he should have been and a good deal stouter. His face was round, owlish, and dirty. He had big, dark eyes, and his black hair, which hardly ever got cut, was arranged on his head as the four winds wanted it. He had been outfitted with attractive and fairly expensive clothes, but he changed from one suit to another only when his parents came to call on him and ordered him to get out of what he had on.

The two most expressive things about him were his mouth and the pockets of his jacket. By looking at his mouth, one could tell whether he was plotting evil or had recently accomplished it. If he was bent upon malevolence, his lips were all puckered up, like those of a billiard player about to make a difficult shot. After the deed was done, the pucker was replaced by a delicate, unearthly smile. How a teacher who knew anything about boys could miss the fact that both expressions were masks of Satan I'm sure I don't know. Wallace's pockets were less interesting than his mouth, perhaps, but more spectacular in a way. The side pockets of his jacket bulged out over his pudgy haunches like burro hampers. They were filled with tools—screwdrivers, pliers, files, wrenches, wire cutters, nail sets, and I don't know what else. In addition to all this, one pocket always contained a rolled-up copy of *Popular Mechanics*, while from the top of the other protruded *Scientific American* or some other such magazine. His breast pocket contained, besides a large collection of fountain pens and mechanical pencils, a picket fence of drill bits, gimlets, kitchen knives, and other pointed instruments. When he walked, he clinked and jangled and pealed.

Wallace lived just down the hall from me, and I got to know him one afternoon, a week or so after school started, when I was wrestling with an algebra lesson. I was really trying to get good marks at the time, for my father had threatened me with unpleasant reprisals if my grades did not show early improvement. I could make no sense of the algebra, though, and I thought that the scientific genius, who had not as yet been unmasked, might be generous enough to lend me a hand.

It was study period, but I found Wallace stretched out on the floor working away at something he was learning to make from *Popular Mechanics*. He received me with courtesy, but after hearing my request he went immediately back to his tinkering. "I could do that algebra, all right," he said, "but I can't be bothered with it.

Got to get this dingbat going this afternoon. Anyway, I don't care about algebra. It's too twitchy. Real engineers never do any of that stuff. It's too twitchy for them." I soon learned that "twitch" was an all-purpose word of Wallace's. It turned up, in one form or another, in about every third sentence he spoke. It did duty as a noun, an adjective, a verb, and an adverb.

I was disappointed by his refusal of help but fascinated by what he was doing. I stayed on and watched him as he deftly cut and spliced wires, removed and replaced screws, referring, every so often, to his magazine for further instruction. He worked silently, lips fiendishly puckered, for some time, then looked up at me and said, "Say, you know anything about that organ in the chapel?"

"What about it?" I asked.

"I mean do you know anything about how it works?"

"No," I said. "I don't know anything about that."

"Too bad," Wallace said, reaching for a pair of pliers. "I had a really twitchy idea." He worked at his wires and screws for quite a while. After perhaps ten minutes, he looked up again. "Well, anyhow," he said, "maybe you know how to get in the chapel and have a look at the organ?"

"Sure, that's easy," I said. "Just walk in. The chapel's always open. They keep it open so you can go in and pray if you want to, and things like that."

"Oh" was Wallace's only comment.

I didn't at all grasp what he had in mind until church time the following Sunday. At about six o'clock that morning, several hours before the service, he tiptoed into my room and shook me from sleep. "Hey, get dressed," he said. "Let's you and I twitch over to the chapel and have a look at the organ."

Game for any form of amusement, I got up and went along. In the bright, not quite frosty October morning, we scurried over the lawns to the handsome Georgian chapel. It was an hour before the rising bell.

Wallace had brought along a flashlight as well as his usual collection of hardware. We went to the rear of the chancel, where the organ was, and he poked the light underneath the thing and inside it for a few minutes. Then he got out his pliers and screwdrivers and performed some operations that I could neither see nor understand. We were in the chapel for only a few minutes. "There," Wallace said as he came up from under the keyboard. "I guess I got her twitched up just about right. Let's go." Back in my room, we talked

softly until the rest of the school began to stir. I asked Wallace
what, precisely, he had done to the organ. "You'll see," he said with
the faint, faraway smile where the pucker had been. Using my
commonplace imagination, I guessed that he had fixed the organ
so it would give out peculiar noises or something like that. I didn't
realize then that Wallace's tricks were seldom commonplace.

Church began as usual that Sunday morning. The headmaster
delivered the invocation and then announced the number and title
of the first hymn. He held up his hymnal and gave the genteel,
throat-clearing cough that was his customary signal to the organist
to get going. The organist came down on the keys but not a peep
sounded from the pipes. He tried again. Nothing but a click.

When the headmaster realized that the organ wasn't working,
he walked quickly to the rear and consulted in whispers with the
organist. Together they made a hurried inspection of the instrument, peering inside it, snapping the electric switch back and forth,
and reaching to the base plug to make certain the juice was on.
Everything seemed all right, yet the organ wouldn't sound a note.

"Something appears to be wrong with our organ," the headmaster
said when he returned to the lectern. "I regret to say that for this
morning's service we shall have to—"

At the first word of the announcement, Wallace, who was next
to me in one of the rear pews, slid out of his seat and bustled noisily
down the middle aisle. It was highly unusual conduct, and every eye
was on him. His gaudy magazines flapped from his pockets, his
portable workshop clattered and clanked as he strode importantly
to the chancel and rose on tiptoe to reach the ear of the astonished
headmaster. He spoke in a stage whisper that could be heard everywhere in the chapel. "Worked around organs quite a bit, sir," he
said. "Think I can get this one going in a jiffy."

Given the chance, the headmaster would undoubtedly have declined Wallace's kind offer. Wallace didn't give him the chance.
He scooted for the organ. For perhaps a minute, he worked on it,
hands flying, tools tinkling.

Then, stuffing the tools back into his pockets, he returned to the
headmaster. "There you are, sir," he said, smiling up at him. "Think
she'll go all right now." The headmaster, with great doubt in his
heart, I am sure, nodded to the organist to try again. Wallace stood
by, looking rather like the inventor of a new kind of airplane waiting to see his brain child take flight. He faked a look of deep
anxiety, which, when a fine, clear swell came from the pipes, was

replaced by a faint smile of relief, also faked. On the second or third chord, he bustled back down the aisle, looking very solemn and businesslike and ready for serious worship.

It was a fine performance, particularly brilliant in its timing. If Wallace had had to stay at the organ even a few seconds longer— that is, if he had done a slightly more elaborate job of twitching it in the first place—he would have been ordered back to his pew before he had got done with the repairs. Moreover, someone would probably have guessed that it was he who had put it on the fritz in the first place. But no one did guess it. Not then, anyway. For weeks after that, Wallace's prestige in the school was enormous. Everyone had had from the beginning a sense of honor and pride at having a genius around, but no one up to then had realized how useful a genius could be. Wallace let on after church that Sunday that he was well up on the workings not merely of organs but also of heating and plumbing systems, automobiles, radios, washing machines, and just about everything else. He said he would be pleased to help out in any emergency. Everyone thought he was wonderful.

"That was a real good twitch, wasn't it?" he said to me when we were by ourselves. I said that it certainly was.

From that time on, I was proud and happy to be Wallace's cup-bearer. I find it hard now to explain exactly what his victory with the organ, and all his later victories over authority, meant to me, but I do know that they meant a very great deal. Partly, I guess, it was just the knowledge that he enjoyed my company. I was an authentic, certified dunce and he was an acknowledged genius, yet he like being with me. Better yet was my discovery that this super-brain disliked schoolwork every bit as much as I did. He was bored silly, as I was, by "Il Penseroso" and completely unable to stir up any enthusiasm for "Silas Marner" and all the foolish goings on over Eppie. Finally, and this perhaps was what made me love him most, he had it in his power to humiliate and bring low the very people who had so often humiliated me and brought me low. . . .

I no longer remember all of Wallace's inventions in detail. Once, I recall, he made, in the chemistry laboratory, some kind of invisible paint—a sort of shellac, I suppose—and covered every blackboard in the school with it. The next day, chalk skidded along the slate and left about as much impression as it would have made on a cake of ice. The dormitory he and I lived in was an old one of frame construction, and when we had fire drills, we had to climb down outside fire escapes. One night, Wallace tied a piece of flypaper securely around each rung of each ladder in the building, then rang the fire alarm. Still another time, he went back to his first love, the organ, and put several pounds of flour in the pipes, so that when the organist turned on the pumps, a cloud of flour filled the chapel. One of his favorite tricks was to take the dust jacket from a novel and wrap it around a textbook. In a Latin class, then, he would appear to be reading "Black April" when he should have been reading about the campaigns in Gaul. After several of his teachers had discovered that he had the right book in the wrong cover (he piously explained that he put the covers on to keep his books clean), he felt free to remove the textbook and really read a novel in class.

Wallace was expelled shortly before the Easter vacation. As the winter had drawn on, life had become duller and duller for him, and to brighten things up he had resorted to pranks of larger conception and of an increasingly anti-social character. He poured five pounds of sugar into the gasoline tank of the basketball coach's car just before the coach was to start out, with two or three of the team's best players in his car, for a game with a school about twenty-five miles away. The engine functioned adequately until the car hit an isolated spot on the highway, miles from any service place. Then it gummed up completely. The coach and the players riding with him came close to frostbite, and the game had to be called off. The adventure cost Wallace's parents a couple of hundred dollars for automobile repairs. Accused of the prank, which clearly bore his trademark, Wallace had freely admitted his guilt. It was explained to his parents that he would be given one more chance in school; another trick of any sort and he would be packed off on the first train.

Later, trying to justify himself to me, he said, "You don't like that coach either, do you? He's the twerpiest twitch here. All teachers are twitchy, but coaches are the worst ones of all."

I don't recall what I said. Wallace had not consulted me about several of his recent escapades, and although I was still loyal to him, I was beginning to have misgivings about some of them.

As I recall it, the affair that led directly to his expulsion was a relatively trifling one, something to do with blown fuses or short circuits. At any rate, Wallace's parents had to come and fetch him home. It was a sad occasion for me, for Wallace had built in me the foundations for a sense of security. My marks were improving, my father was happier, and I no longer cringed at the sight of a teacher. I feared, though, that without Wallace standing behind me and giving me courage, I might slip back into the old ways. I was very near to tears as I helped him pack up his turbines, his tools, and his stacks of magazines. He, however, was quite cheerful. "I suppose my Pop will put me in another one of these places, and I'll have to twitch my way out of it all over again," he said.

"Just remember how dumb all those teachers are," he said to me a few moments before he got into his parents' car. "They're so twitchy dumb they can't even tell if anyone else is dumb." It was rather a sweeping generalization, I later learned, but it served me well for a number of years. Whenever I was belabored by a teacher, I remembered my grimy genius friend and his reassurances. I got through school somehow or other. I still cower a bit when I find that someone I've met is a schoolteacher, but things aren't too bad and I am on reasonably civil terms with a number of teachers, and even a few professors.

QUESTIONS ON CONTENT

1. Why does the author go into so much detail about his experiences with schoolteachers? Why did he not simply tell the story of Wallace?
2. Does the author ever adequately explain the attitude of teachers toward him?
3. What type of student was the author? Wallace? (See Fuller's "Four Types of Students.")
4. How are Wallace and Red Chief ("Ransom of Red Chief") alike? How do they differ?
5. What were the "two most expressive things" about Wallace?
6. The author says that Wallace "had picked up his scientific knowledge somewhere." Can you name the probable source of the knowledge?
7. What specific pieces of literature are mentioned in this story? What was Wallace and the author's attitude toward literature?
8. How does the author explain Wallace's good influence on him?
9. Why does the author fail to mention any other schoolmates?
10. Keep Wallace in mind as you read about Sunshine in the next selection.

❧ Schoolboy Racketeers

AGNES E. MEYER

When a spectacular case of juvenile delinquency breaks upon an American community, the reaction often is one of anxiety approaching hysteria. Yet these incidents would reveal to us what is wrong with our methods of dealing with youth if we would take the time to use them as case studies.

Consider, for example, what happened at Paul Junior High School in Washington, D.C. A fourteen-year-old boy, whose nickname is "Sunshine," was arrested on November 11 and charged with fourteen counts of robbing other Paul Junior students of sums varying from 5 cents to a dollar between September 22 and November 10. The principal, Thomas F. Ferry, had received an anonymous letter in the school suggestion box, early in October, telling him of the shakedowns and naming the culprit. The principal called Sunshine into his office and gave him a warning, but could do no more, as he had no proof upon which to take more drastic action.

A month passed during which a few more hints of the shakedowns reached the principal. On Wednesday, November 11, one of the pupils, Mike Hantman, went to the principal and asked him for a dollar, as he had been told by Sunshine to produce a dollar by 3 P.M. or take a beating.

The police gave Mike a marked dollar which he surrendered to Sunshine, who was thereupon arrested. Word got around the school that Mike Hantman had caused the arrest. Thursday night and Friday after the arrest, young Hantman and his mother received anonymous telephone calls telling them that Mike was going to get it for "ratting." By Friday afternoon, it was all over the school that Mike was in for a beating.

That night on the way home from a fraternity dance, Mike, with two friends, David Fram and Melvin Mackler, and the girls they were taking home, noticed that they were being followed by three automobiles, one of which tried to sideswipe their car. In front of Fram's home Mike saw a boy known to him jump out of the lead

Atlantic Monthly, March, 1954. Reprinted by permission of the author and the *Atlantic Monthly*.

car and heard him say, "All right, this is it." The boy pulled Fram out of the front seat and hit him. As Mike got out of the rear door, he was beaten and kicked into insensibility. Fram's parents, who were returning from a movie, arrived to find the girls screaming and Mike and their son knocked unconscious. The third boy, Mackler, had been hit only once before the attackers fled.

What are the facts behind the facts? Sunshine had been holding up boys for money—the teachers know of about thirty cases, the school children say sixty or seventy—ever since the beginning of school. He began with the little boys and worked up to the big ones, who had more pocket money.

Some of the Paul Junior youngsters told me that they are still afraid of Sunshine's friends who remain at the school, as they were not mixed up in the beating episode. The mothers of the beaten boys are bewildered and one of them plans to send her child to a private school.

It is commonly known at Paul that not only Sunshine but several of his friends have police records. Together they had been terrorizing the whole school, unbeknown to their teachers, from the onset of the autumn term. Can the principal and the teachers be criticized for this? By no means. They are not given the police records of the boys who are dumped on their hands, either at Paul Junior High or at any other school, although the grapevine among the youngsters usually disseminates the information to every pupil.

Even the police cannot keep track of the boys who have passed through their hands and have been referred to Juvenile Court, because they are never informed what happens to the boys subsequently. The secrecy that surrounds Juvenile Court decisions prevents it. As a consequence, most public school teachers, like those of Paul Junior High, in their crowded classes of forty or more children, are expected to cope with maladjusted children ranging from the slow learner to the subnormal, from those who are neurotics or suffer from other serious emotional disturbances to those who have already committed serious offenses.

It is high time that we make up our minds what the public schools can and cannot do. For at present the average teacher is expected to be a policeman, a psychiatrist, a public health expert, a doctor, a clergyman, a night club entertainer, and a parent. All this we demand from one underpaid public servant because the nation lacks the wisdom and the will power to face its social problems with honest, effective, and comprehensive insight.

2

Sunshine, the juvenile holdup man, is typical of the problem children to be found in our public schools. He comes from a broken home. The parents were divorced when the boy was three or four years old, according to his own recollection. Yet he remembers having been beaten by his father, who has now landed in a mental hospital. Sunshine still hates him.

His mother has done her best. She has worked for the support of her four children. Sunshine is the only one who has given her trouble. The backbone of the family is a grandmother who has Sunshine's only real devotion.

Sunshine's teachers believe in him with the innocence of people who do not understand his type. His home-room teacher, Mrs. Berch, is sure that he "would have been all right if he hadn't gotten into bad company." There is such a chasm between the ethical tradition of the teachers and the standards of the children that the former are often taken in by the rough and confused youngsters who, through experience with the police and the courts, develop a clever technique of manipulating both young people and adults. When Sunshine was confronted by the five pupils who preferred charges against him, he turned to them unctuously and said, "We can still be pals, can't we?" He also knew just what to say to his teachers in order to give them the illusion that they can reform him. This slick type of youngster anticipates exactly how adults will react to him and plays on their sensibilities with great skill.

But as Mrs. Berch said of him, "He also breaks down and gets real mean." On one occasion when he did some good work, his teacher felt she had him started on the straight and narrow path. He told her firmly he could not continue to do well, as he had his reputation to protect. "I have a reputation as a bad boy, and this is as important to me as your reputation for being good is to you."

This reputation was also the reason why he had a large following in the school. All adolescents feel admiration for the child who flouts authority and is willing to expose himself to danger. You can't get the hero worship of this age group by excelling at lessons. The good children at Paul admired Sunshine as much as the others but were saved from his influence by constructive interests. The potential bullies followed him slavishly because he was braver than they in his misdemeanors.

He was able to intimidate the whole school and extract money at will from the good children because they feared not only his superior strength and the long knife he carried, but the overwhelming power of his sycophantic adherents, who were not an organized gang but a loosely knit group of hero worshipers. Thus can one desperate character corrupt the atmosphere of a whole school.

Well, Sunshine is now awaiting trial at the Receiving Home. He is resentful because his pals who did the beating are out on parole in custody of their parents. "I'll have to take the rap for the whole lot of them," he told me resentfully, "even though I was in the clink and had nothing to do with the fight."

The demoralization we create in our children through this kind of legal confusion is unbelievable. Different social workers will make totally different decisions as to two children involved in the same case. This naturally creates resentment in the child who gets the more severe sentence.

Small wonder that Sunshine was confused about the difference between his treatment and that of the boys who did the beating. For surely the vicious maltreatment of smaller youngsters out of pure revenge is a serious business. Furthermore, Sunshine could never have been so successful in extracting money from his victims if the other ruffians had not increased his power with their support. If the boys who actually carried out the beating are not held responsible, it will undermine permanently the morale not only of the Paul school but of the other Washington schools as well.

Young Sunshine early became a truant, and truancy is often the first step toward delinquency. His truancy is traceable to his reading difficulties, which began when he was still in parochial school and continued undiscovered in various public schools until he went to Paul, where he was recently given his first individual lessons in remedial reading. His inability to keep up with his classmates became the source of his rebellion against school and authority in general. It is now known that a reading difficulty may be one of the reasons why children become delinquents.

Yet Sunshine was promoted from year to year with his age group, regardless of achievement. Each year he was less able to cope with the class assignments. He himself told me that he paid no attention to homework because he could not read the words or understand them when he could read them. He sat in class with a constantly deepening inferiority complex and a growing sense of isolation.

For this he compensated himself by skill in dancing, very important among the young today, and by becoming ever more aggressive toward a society which, from his point of view, lacked all possibility of genuine satisfaction. The isolation of such children is appalling when we consider that they move from families which give them no sense of belonging into schoolrooms so overcrowded that they feel like identical grains of sand.

The highly developed gang life which is now a characteristic of every large city is nothing but a defense mechanism against the feeling of solitude that affects adults as well as youth in our large-scale industrial society. Even Sunshine's coterie of admirers informed me that he was a "lone wolf."

The false ideals which the young develop under such conditions are inevitable. Even the normal boys are afraid of being called cowards, a fear which impelled Mike Hantman to go to the dance practically taking his life in his hands. I asked the boys implicated in the beating of Hantman why they took revenge on an "outsider." (Usually these gangs reserve revenge for an "insider" who betrays his pals.) I was informed that "ratting" is bad no matter what the circumstances and has to be punished— a code obviously identical with that portrayed in the gangster movies and the innumerable television programs of murderous revenge.

These misguided youngsters actually had the conviction that in beating Hantman they were carrying out a code of honor and a deed of virtue. When it became known that a fight was going to take place, several boys who knew neither Hantman nor his pursuers joined in the chase. The mere excitement which the threat of trouble created was a relief from the tedium of the empty existence of these fifteen-, sixteen-, and seventeen-year-olds.

This lack of interest-motivation in their lives, characteristic of many young folks, arises from the fact that we have unduly prolonged adolescence without providing an adequate program of education for boys who are not book-learners. Vocational training is largely a makeshift in an industrial society where most factory work can be learned quickly on the job. The best answer is a work and study program, used by some high schools, whereby the pupils spend half the day on the job and half in the classroom. At present the average school is not meaningful for this type of boy because the curriculum is not suitable and cannot hold his attention.

As far as the serious delinquents are concerned, no matter how well the principal knows that these maladjusted boys should not be in school, he has no authority to send them away without lengthy consultation with the Board of Education. Even though they learn nothing and are an obvious menace to the other students, the compulsory school law forces the principal to keep them. Needed are separate schools for serious offenders and another for those who can be easily rehabilitated. For delinquency is as contagious as measles and ten times more dangerous to the health of the student body. The code that prevails in the large schools is not that of the good boys but that of the desperadoes.

The leisure time of these big boys is equally empty. The usual recreation outlets that most cities afford exist in the Paul Junior High School area. But they are too namby-pamby for these vigorous young toughs of whom our country produces an abundance. They do not need Boy Scouting and other forms of recreation suitable for "nice children," but youth organizations devoted to boxing, wrestling, swimming, and other vigorous action programs that will furnish a real outlet for their pent-up energies.

To be sure, Sunshine and the crowd which participated in the beating must be punished. I am not advocating a "boys will be boys" attitude toward their misdemeanors. But let us keep in mind that these are bruised kids who have no plan for life except on a false basis because they have been exposed to more bad influences than good ones.

What can we expect of these boys when they are subjected daily to descriptions in newspapers and magazines, on radio and TV, of adult crimes more horrible than any our country has hitherto known? Getting rid of problem children by shipping them off to the Industrial Home School or, worse still, the National Training School is no answer. That is the path to moral and mental degradation for youngsters who can still be set on the right road if given the right kind of supervision.

3

The problem is, what to do with them? With that question we come to the tangled confusion, the inadequacy, and the outmoded nature of our whole system of handling juvenile offenders. What all these young boys need is guidance and correction, so that they will see their situation in all its moral implications, rather than incarceration and severity. Yet the District of Columbia and most other communities lack such corrective institutions. The best are private agencies like the Children's Village in New York, which are costly and so overloaded that they may not even have room for these boys.

Let's begin by looking at the various law enforcement agencies which are involved in the fate of juvenile offenders from Paul Junior High School. The Juvenile Squad of the police is headed by Captain Ryan and Sergeant Rasmussen, able men who have given their whole squad as much training as possible. But the police are interested in facts as facts and cannot take into account the deeper social and psychological aspects of juvenile crime. Moreover the Juvenile Squad, like all the other departments concerned with juvenile offenders, is understaffed. It has a staff of 33, of whom 9 are probationary detectives.

Not a day passes without parents coming in to say they cannot control their children. The Squad could do more adequate preventive work to keep children out of Juvenile Court if it had a better-trained and larger staff and eight cars instead of three. What complicates its duties is that the Juvenile Court does not inform the police whether the children received sentence, what the sentence was, and when the child may be expected back in his home. This creates more work for the police.

The staff of the Juvenile Court is equally over-worked. The 31 probation officers each carry a case load of 80, whereas 40 is the maximum if the probation officer is to do a good job. Furthermore, Judge Cockrill says that she is often forced to put on probation children who are not a good probation risk because the alternative is to send them to institutions where they cannot get proper care. Thus our lack of facilities leads to more delinquency.

Most people agree that the laws of the Juvenile Court should be revised. With an overworked staff, the careful preparation of each child's case is well-nigh impossible, and the heavy court calendar makes it necessary for children who have been sent to the Receiving Home by police to wait an average of thirty days until they come before the court. The capacity of the Receiving Home is 43, but the average daily population during the past few months has been 82, rising sometimes to 103. What would we think if adults were arbitrarily put in jail for that length of time without a court hearing? These children are deprived of their constitutional rights because they cannot afford a lawyer. Many of them are dismissed as innocent when their case is finally considered, yet they have spent thirty days in custody, exposed to evil influences, under the stress of removal from home and a frightening uncertainty as to their future.

Moreover, while the children are detained, they have almost nothing to do for lack of staff and facilities. Most of the children are in the fifteen-, sixteen-, and seventeen-year age group and the only activity possible for them is one hour daily of fresh air and exercise. The rest of the day they are locked up. This is sheer barbarism, unworthy of any humane civilization.

Here again we increase the number of delinquents and the seriousness of their offenses through the lack of proper administrative procedure, decent care, and adequate facilities. The Department of Public Welfare is not to blame. The staff is doing the best it can under impossible conditions.

What adds to the confusion is that no department—Police, Juvenile Court, or Welfare—knows what the others are doing. A centralized system of investigation and handling of juveniles is one of the first requisites. The Commission on Population Changes appointed by the District Commissioners outlined the need for coordinated services. But the public is indifferent because it does not know what sheer administrative inefficiency means in the way of broken lives, miscarriage of justice, and human misery. What, then, must be done?

1. Our communities must be reorganized and big urban centers broken down into neighborhood groups.

2. We must find sufficient boarding homes for our dependent children. We also lack the proper number of foster homes or boarding homes under the case-work department for children aged six or seven who could still be cured of their emotional difficulties. Many of our dependent children are in the well-managed Junior Village. But if they fail of adoption they graduate at twelve into the Industrial Home School. In other words, they become prisoners and are permanently stigmatized as such, although they have committed no offence.

3. We need homes that are a substitute for family care, where neglected children and mild offenders can lead a homelike life under trained personnel. (A model institution of this kind is the Milwaukee Children's Center.)

4. We need homes for serious behavior problems under the direction of psychiatrists.

5. The Industrial Home School should be of a cottage type with a well-rounded educational and vocational program. Fortunately, the white children in Washington moved into such a home in January. It took nearly thirty years to achieve this. Our Negro children are still in a horrible institution whose maximum population should be 190. It now has 500 in all, 75 per cent of whom are repeaters

largely because overcrowding leads to a too early dismissal. A new Industrial Home School for Negroes is promised for next year.

6. The secrecy surrounding the Juvenile Court must be modified so that better coordination may be developed between the court, the schools, the Welfare Department, and the Juvenile Police Squad.

4

Even more important than the correction and control of delinquency is its prevention. And the obvious focus for such a program is the public school, if only because it is the one public institution for the training of the young which exists in every American community.

Yet here is the area where our social imagination has failed us most conspicuously, largely because the American people, under the lure of materialism, forgot the importance of education. Had we valued it more, we would have foreseen well in advance that the education of all our people, together with a rapidly rising birth rate, called for more schoolrooms, more teachers, better-trained teachers, and more even quality of education throughout our country. We were not alert enough to the important role of the schools because we were and still are too little concerned about our postwar social problems. Above all, we failed to realize that the role of the school is very different in a society shattered by constant wars—whether hot or cold—constant migration, and broken homes.

We are bound to produce more and more unfortunate products like these Paul Junior culprits unless we can build an atmosphere in our public schools which will cushion the individual child against the influence of our mass civilization and its frightening depersonalization of the individual.

This effort must begin in our elementary schools, where the children are still young enough to be rescued from the evil effects of that no man's land between three and six, an age not often reached by the church, the school, or welfare groups. First of all, the American people must be willing to pay for more and better schools and more and better teachers, so that classes can be reduced to a maximum of twenty-five. All-day schools are essential in some areas where the majority of mothers work.

As long as the American people are willing to cheat their children out of a decent opportunity for self-development by herding them into school-pens like a lot of sheep, it is sheer hypocrisy to wring our hands in despair and wonder why we have so many moral, mental, and physical breakdowns. Only if the teacher can know her pupils as individuals and treat them as such can we counteract the trend toward anonymity which is the curse of our society.

With smaller classes, we could organize our schools in a more elastic manner and each child could receive careful study and be placed in a homogeneous group. The gap between the IQs in any class should not be so wide that it cannot be bridged even by the most expert teacher. Otherwise, both extremes suffer and we encourage delinquency in all of them. The bright students lose interest in school because their abilities are not challenged, and the slow learners acquire a spirit of defeatism, insecurity, and inferiority which manifests itself in various degrees of insubordination. Moreover, both groups hate each other, which makes for bad human relations and open friction.

Egalitarianism, a false interpretation of democracy, has led some educators to maintain that the maladjusted and the normal children, the slow learners and the bright pupils, must be kept together. As a result, the educational process is keyed to the lowest common denominator. When we penalize our best students in this way, we not only run the risk of destroying human character; we are depleting the greatest asset our nation possesses, a huge reservoir of human talents, capacities, and skills. If we do not give our strong children the opportunity to grow stronger, if we put all our emphasis on shielding the weak, the unstable, and the incompetent, we shall soon be not a welfare state but a hospital state, in which the productive citizens will have to spend most of their energies to support the vast number of the sick, the evildoers, and other unproductive types.

Since the home influences often leave much to be desired on any income level, our schools must develop closer ties with the family. That calls for an adequate staff of visiting teachers, familiar with class activities but also trained as psychologists. At Paul Junior High School there is one guidance teacher for 1530 pupils! Had there been constant contact with the homes of the pupils, the school never could have been terrorized by a small group of hoodlums, for Sunshine's racketeering would have been nipped in the bud.

Family counseling can be made readily accessible through visiting teachers in the local school who are already informed of the areas in which the child's family is weak. The visiting teachers can also constitute a referral bureau through which parents can be guided without loss of time to the numerous health and welfare facilities which exist in every city.

Obviously, such schools and the highly trained teachers they require will be beyond the reach of local tax resources in several of our less productive states. Therefore, Senator Hendrickson's Congressional committee which is investigating juvenile delinquency could not make a more practical approach to the cure of delinquency and crime than by requesting Federal aid for our public school system.

There is no doubt that it will be a costly business to counteract the rising tendency toward irresponsibility among boys and girls. But it will become more and more costly if we postpone action and allow our young people to degenerate through no fault of their own. It is high time to realize that the adults of our nation have been more delinquent in recognizing their responsibilities as citizens than have our neglected teen-agers.

QUESTIONS ON CONTENT

1. In what way does the author make full use of Sunshine's case history? Would her article be more, or less, effective if she had cited other cases of juvenile delinquency?
2. Where does the author think the blame for Sunshine's behavior should be placed? How does she excuse those who might have been able to control Sunshine?
3. Describe Sunshine's background. Do you think it inevitable that he should become a junior criminal? Explain.
4. Discuss the psychology of Sunshine's attitude.
5. Comment on the statement that youthful criminals are "bruised kids who . . . have been exposed to more bad influences than good ones."
6. Name the suggestions for correcting conditions which, the author says, lead to juvenile misconduct. Do you think these suggestions would be effective? Explain.
7. Compare Sunshine and Red Chief; Sunshine and Wallace.

SUGGESTIONS FOR PAPERS

Your paper this week may tell of mischief in which you or someone else was involved; or it may examine the essential differences between Red Chief and Wallace; or it may attempt to show the point at which mischief becomes juvenile delinquency.

1. Can you recall the time when you carefully planned to get the better of someone and then at the last moment had the tables turned on you? If so, select only the essential details for telling the episode as effectively as possible. Reject everything that does not bear directly on your story.

2. If you have turned the tables on someone who was trying to get the better of you, tell how you did it.

3. Do you know someone, perhaps yourself, who has gained a reputation as a mischievous boy or girl? If so, tell how he or she came to deserve—or not deserve—this reputation. Here you will be following the pattern in "Wallace" except that you should simply name, because of space limits, most of the mischievous actions and then tell in sufficient detail only one of the best examples.

4. What was the prime example of mischief committed during your four years in high school? Do you know the details well enough to give a reader the full flavor of the prank? What motivated it? How was it accomplished? What was the eventual result?

5. What were your grades in Deportment (if such grades were given at your school)? Explain the worst grade. Whether the grade was justified or not does not matter.

6. Draw up a series of likenesses and differences between Red Chief and Wallace: age, appearance, environment (time and place), parents, interests, attitudes toward their elders. Comb both stories for details to support your findings. Finally, can you decide which is the more effective character? Can you write an inductive definition of mischief?

7. Define "mischief" by setting it off against "juvenile delinquency." Use illustrations from the selections in this chapter to indicate the differences between these two terms.

8. Examine carefully Sunshine's case history. List the factors which the author thinks contributed to his delinquency. Are you convinced that this combination of circumstances made Sunshine's behavior inevitable? Explain. This sort of paper will be essentially a comment on the author's "bruised-kid" theory.

SOME TITLES FOR PAPERS

1. And the Class Roared
2. A Red Chief I Have Known
3. Mischief Requires Careful Planning
4. When Does Mischief Become Delinquency?
5. Adults Like Mischief Too!
6. The Tables Were Turned

7. My Attitude Towards Teachers
8. A Wallace I Have Known
9. Red Chief and Wallace: A Comparison
10. Which Is the Better Story, O. Henry's or Rovere's?
11. The Bruised-Kid Theory
12. The Causes of Juvenile Delinquency
13. A Sunshine I Have Known
14. A Remedy for the Delinquent

CHAPTER 4

❧ *FOCUS ON ENGLISH*

As YOU GO THROUGH course after course in college, you may sometimes wonder about the practical value of what you are learning. Are you, for example, among those who question the practical value of English? Do you say to yourself: "Since I am going to be an engineer, why should I study English?" or "I'm going to be a business man. What good is English to me?" One familiar answer to these questions is that a knowledge of how to write and speak effectively will make you a better citizen and will bring you a great deal of personal satisfaction. Another answer has been insistently ringing through the land of late. It is to this effect: learn to write well and to speak well or accept a crippling handicap in whatever you may choose as your life work.

Huge industries have become concerned over the enormous waste caused by bad communication. General Electric has issued a bulletin on "Why Study English?" It is reprinted here as representative of the attitude of all industry towards a serious problem. The attitude of business is well stated in a bulletin issued by The Amos Tuck School (Dartmouth): "Putting Words to Work." Both articles set forth persuasively the dollars-and-cents value of an ability to handle the English language effectively. (Further emphasis is given this point in Peter Drucker's article, "How To Be an Employee." See next chapter on Jobs.) These testimonials have been selected from literally dozens of similar articles which have appeared during the last few years.

Somerset Maugham in "Prose: Simple, Lucid, and Euphonious" tells of his efforts to improve as a writer and sprinkles in many observations about the great stylists of the past. His analysis of what makes for good contemporary writing contains useful suggestions on how to write.

W. H. Whyte points up the affectations of some modern writing, and E. B. White pokes fun at a system which tries to measure mathematically the quality of readability.

❧ *Why Study English?*

GENERAL ELECTRIC BULLETIN

If what Peter Drucker says is true, and we believe it is, you had better do something about your English.

Mr. Drucker wrote an article for the May, 1952, FORTUNE called "How to Be an Employee." [This article appears in Chapter 5, Jobs.] He said that the ability to express ideas in writing and in speaking heads the list of requirements for success.

"As soon as you move one step up from the bottom, your effectiveness depends on your ability to reach others through the spoken or written word. And the further away your job is from manual work, the larger the organization of which you are an employee, the more important it will be that you know how to convey your thoughts in writing or speaking. In the very large organizations, whether it is the government, the large business corporation, or the Army, this ability to express oneself is perhaps the most important of all the skills a man can possess."

It pleases us at General Electric to go on record as supporters of Mr. Drucker's statement. We know, of course, that there are many skills and personal qualifications leading to success. There is no doubt in our minds, for example, that you should have a genuine desire to exchange your best efforts in your employer's behalf for the chance to tackle increasingly more important, more challenging, and more rewarding assignments. We think that you should be able to look a fellow employee, including your boss, in the eye; that you should be reasonably neat and clean.

But right now we have much to say about English.

Issued in 1954. Reprinted by permission of General Electric Company.

The top engineer upstairs is on the telephone. He says to us: "Right before my eyes is a brief report made out by one of our young engineers. I have to guess what the fellow is driving at. I'm no English shark, but I find myself getting a little angry when I see four sentences tied together into one with commas. He has *principle* for *principal,* and he has also misspelled *accommodate* and *Cincinnati.* What if some of this fellow's bad sentences get into the hands of our customers?"

We sympathize, and we say somewhat lamely that it's up to him to suggest that the fellow hire a tutor.

The top engineer is wound up. "At the last meeting of our Association, representatives of all the major companies complained about the way their younger men were putting down their words—and futures—on paper. Can't someone tell us what to do?"

We reach for an answer.

"When boys and girls began avoiding mathematics like the plague," we remind him, "we began printing facts. It is now our duty and privilege to beat the drums for English! Our motives are partly selfish, because we want American business to succeed even more than it has in the past. But our motive is more than self-interest. We know because we rub shoulders with people, at work and in the community, that a solid background in English is prerequisite to happiness and well-being. Without a reasonably good command of English—as a means of communication—and without knowledge of what the best minds of all time have put into print, we are not educated for personal happiness, apart from the job, or for personal success in the exciting business of making a living."

"But I thought all boys and girls took English in high school and college?"

"Yes, they have put in their time. Their teachers have spread the feast, but some of them haven't been very hungry. Perhaps they will listen to us. Their teachers can tell them a thousand times that English is important, but they will say, 'Teacher means well, but she's trying to sell us on the importance of her subject.' Perhaps when a manufacturer of turbines, generators, jet engines, lamps, room air coolers, toasters, refrigerators, and 200,000 other electrical products says English is of tremendous importance, they will listen. After all, English is almost as important as math in our business, isn't it?"

The engineer's answer is deliberately emphatic: "Change the word *almost* to *just,* and, brother, you've said a mouthful! Tell them that English is important to them—and to us—because very soon their ability to read and to know and to remember what they have read, and to speak and to write well, will make all the difference, whether they and we or some other company of their career choice will succeed together."

At one time or another, all of us try our hand at writing.

A group of engineers applies the new principle to the development of a revolutionary type of gadget. The results of this effort are summed up in a typewritten report to the head of their department. The report is then mimeographed for the benefit of others in the organization.

The company prepares to put the new product on the market. Writers prepare literature describing its virtues, or explaining how to use it and keep it in working order.

This is indeed useful writing. No piece of company business can begin, progress, and achieve its purpose without the use of words. Writing, together with reading, is as much an integral part of the electrical manufacturing business (or any business) as your bones are part of your body.

Every day in your future you will be called upon to speak and write, and when you open your mouth, or write a letter or report, you will be advertising your progress and your potential worth.

Here is a verbatim extract from a laboratory notebook:

"Curt flew into the cloud, and I started the dispenser in operation. I dropped about three pounds (of dry ice) and then swung around and headed south.

"About this time I looked toward the rear and was thrilled to see long streamers of snow falling from the base of the cloud through which we had just passed. I shouted to Curt to swing around, and as we did so we passed through a mass of glistening snow crystals! We made another run though a dense portion of the unseeded cloud, during which time I dispensed about three more pounds of crushed dry ice . . . This was done by opening the the window and letting the suction of the passing air remove it. We then swung west of the cloud and observed draperies of snow which seemed to hang for 2–3000 feet below us and noted the cloud drying up rapidly, very similar to what we observe in the cold box in the laboratory . . . While still in the cloud as we saw the glinting crystals all over, I turned to Curt, and we shook hands as I said, 'We *did* it!' Needless to say, we were quite excited."

This extract is from the laboratory notebook of Vincent J. Schaefer. It is of historical significance because it describes the first artificial snow making outside the General Electric Research Laboratory. Without such record, other men could not have understood the purpose, procedure, and effect; would not have had a starting point from which to take off on their own investigations.

Since its beginning in 1900, the Research Laboratory has published nearly 2000 papers in technical journals, and these have recorded new facts, new basic discoveries, and new theories. Many are recognized the world over as classics, and are cited as authoritative references in their fields. Some opened up wholly new fields for exploration. Others cast new light on known phenomena. Some disclosed new tools for research.

But the recording of ideas and facts is not confined only to the engineering and scientific laboratories. Each year, thousands of General Electric mechanics, stenographers, accountants, and others write down their suggestions for improving the company products and procedures. To each whose suggestion is adopted is given a certain amount of money, but we suspect that real gain—for company and employee—is the focusing of attention upon those persons who can think of a better way and who can tell about it with words on paper.

We thought little of it at the time, but one night several of us were visiting over the back fence, and a college boy, home for the summer, joined us. He told us how he was enjoying his summer job as helper on a General Electric truck. We asked him who his boss was and how he liked him. He gave us the name and said, simply, "I like him very much. He is a well-spoken man." We think that you, too, if you will stop to think, prefer well-spoken men and women.

You will probably grant that General Electric knows a thing or two about its various specialties, but you may question whether our expertness extends to the English part of the education field. Let's get off the hook directly: your English teacher has probably forgotten more about the teaching of English than we will ever know. As a matter of fact, if someday your employer finds you wobbly in English, he will be critical of you, not some long-suffering teacher or parent.

One of our business colleagues, who would hate us if we gave away his name, has an interesting background. Early in his growing-up years, he dropped schooling so he could earn enough money to buy a Stutz roadster. Eight years later, after working in a shoe factory, another powerful desire took possession of him. He wanted a Harvard degree. For one year he studied all the specified high school subjects; he read everything he could lay his hands on. Then he took all the required high school examinations and passed them with an average of 95 per cent. At Harvard, he kept on reading everything he could squeeze into four years' time. To make a long story short, he's now doing better than all right.

Attitude makes all the difference!

If you are one of those "dese" and "dose" guys, and if it "don't make no sense" to you that your school and your employer "wants" you to become a literate person, all the teaching skill and the modern facilities can't win you over.

Did you ever hear of a mental block? It's a massive barrier in your mind, but like the Maginot Line, it can be penetrated.

That block may be mathematics or history or spelling or perhaps a feeling that no one likes you or something else. Do you remember how you learned to swim? You had flailed the water and sunk like a stone. But then a fortunate stroke propelled you forward, and now it doesn't occur to you when you dive off the board that you may not be able to swim to shore.

Too, your mind may be blocked because you imagine all well-read literate persons are precious, prissy characters who go around spouting Shakespeare. There may be a few of those people, but that is not Shakespeare's fault. We are just realistic enough to believe that some of the master poet's gracious writing style will rub off on you. We know that in a sense we become a part of what we read, and that what we call writing style is born from our unconscious attempt to imitate what we like.

We hope it has occurred to you that English extends beyond a single classroom; that your success or failure in your other classrooms is largely due to your ability to read, to understand, to speak, and to write. English is just as all-embracing in a business organization. Whether we are at drafting board, desk, machine, or calling on customers, we are involved more or less in communication.

We say that English—especially to American boys and girls—is an easy language to learn. Making English behave may be a little troublesome. You can play safe by writing dull little sentences, and they, of course, are less frustrating to the reader than involved wrong sentences. But since the sentence you write or speak is what the reader or listener uses as a criterion in judging you, it is good sense to learn how to become its master.

We know from our experience at General Electric that too many of our younger employees say to themselves before spreading their wings for a flight with words: "But if I write that report the way I *feel* it should be written, my boss will think that I am a child." If an engineer, for example, is testing an insulating material and it chars and smells like burned string beans, we can think of no reason why he should not say so.

Our business world needs young people whose minds are packed with facts, but with the boldness of imagination to release them in a form that is easy and pleasant to take.

We have on our desk copies of the GENERAL ELECTRIC RE-VIEW and the SCIENTIFIC AMERICAN—both written for thousands of top-flight engineers and scientists. The editors of both magazines know that factual reporting is necessary so that their readers, who are so brilliantly expert in many fields, will have confidence in the authority of their articles. But they know, too, that men and women, whatever their job or profession, are willing to begin and stay with an article only if it is well-written. Only you can guess how many books and articles you have thrown aside after tasting the first few paragraphs. Everyone who reads and listens is so very human.

Without interested readers, whether the magazine is SCHO-LASTIC or SCIENTIFIC AMERICAN, its survival depends upon the skill and labor-of-love that editors and authors lavish upon it. Your survival, too, as the adult you are aiming to be, depends upon your ability, desire, and courage to put your best foot forward in a world that will judge you by your words as well as your actions.

Who is the next most important man or woman in your life? We aren't thinking of the next prom date, but an understanding person who is sitting at a desk studying a filled-in application blank. Whether he's a college admissions or an employment officer, he hopes he is so right before saying *yes* or *no*.

Can you live up to your expressed desires? Will you fit in? Have you enough preparation, enough intellectual background? Can your brain direct your hands in performing skills? Can you stand the pace of competition? Can you accept responsibility? Will you worry a workaday problem, like a dog with a bone, till you have conquered it—and then brace yourself for a tougher assignment?

If what you have said on the application blank shows a glimmer of hope, you are brought in for a personal interview. This can be rough going if you haven't habituated yourself to accurate and well-organized expression.

The interviewer across the desk from you has been charged by his college or company to weigh your worth: he has accepted the responsibility of determining the future of the organization he represents—any good organization is but the lengthened shadow of qualified men.

Your job interests. Your participation in school activities. Your subject preferences. Your hobbies. Your ambitions. These and many other topics are brought forward for you to discuss.

The minutes speed by. You summon up the skills of presentation you have practiced in English and other classes. It strikes you, as you talk, that in neither writing nor speaking can you conceal your inadequacies.

As you move up the success ladder, what you write and what you say will determine in part your rate of climb. It is neither too early nor too late to become practiced in the art of communication; certainly not too late to accumulate background through reading experiences. . . .

We pause and listen to the unceasing whine of a motor across the yard. In the distance three green-gray columns of smoke are rushing upward from three yellow-brick chimneys. We see them as symbols of mechanical might controlled by the will, the wit, and the intelligence of earnest men. And these men, adventurers and pioneers of industry, can move ahead with their plans, because their own thought processes have been built upon such logical disciplines as history and math—and English.

QUESTIONS ON CONTENT

1. After examining the first five paragraphs of this article, jot down in your own words what each paragraph says and why the order of the paragraphs is effective (or ineffective). What is the purpose of the dialogue with the engineer? Of the eight paragraphs immediately following? Of the two paragraphs starting "Since its beginning in 1900 . . . "? What are other paragraph groupings in the article? Why are the paragraphs so short? Compare the paragraphs in Somerset Maugham's "Prose: Simple, Lucid, and Euphonious" (see below).

2. Show how the author of this article goes regularly from the

general to the specific. Cite examples. Are any generalizations
left unsupported by examples or illustrations? What is the effect
of this method?
3. List the reasons given here for regarding English as an important subject. Discuss.
4. What is said here about the study of literature? Of Shakespeare?
What do you deduce from what is said—that literature is useful
or useless?

~❧ *Putting Words to Work:*

What Business Has Learned About Writing

HERBERT C. MORTON

The businessman who complains that he is forced to read so
much poor writing often deserves sympathy; but not always. For
as a writer himself, he sometimes takes his own capacity to write
for granted—believing that only other people turn out wordy or
unnecessary memos, disorganized or obscure reports and inept or
unfriendly letters. Actually, as historian Jacques Barzun has phrased
it, clear and simple English "is no one's mother tongue; it has to be
worked for."

In many companies today, it is being worked for. More and more
executives realize that they cannot escape their dependence on
written communications, much as they might prefer the spoken
word. Thus instead of complaining about bad writing, they have
introduced programs to develop good writing—programs for themselves as well as for secretaries and correspondents. By doing so,
they have been able to reduce costs, to speed up the flow of letters
and reports and to improve the quality of written communications
within the firm and between the firm and its customers.

The techniques of the company writing counselors and consultants
are not new. They have been suggested by textbook writers, consultants and a few pioneering executives for 50 years. The novelty
is that they have been adopted by many firms and are within the

Reprinted by permission of The Amos Tuck School of Business Administration and *Dun's Review and Modern Industry*. First printed 1955.

reach of others that have not yet seriously attempted to put words to work more efficiently.

What are companies doing to encourage better writing, and what are the opportunities open to firms that are still inadvertently jamming their own communications?

Diagnosis Comes First

For years the language of business was bedeviled by a Gresham's law of its own: bad writing drove out the good. A *business-ese* was coined and perpetuated that made it easier for employees to write without thinking, to write without saying anything and to blunder ahead oblivious to the impact of what they wrote.

To replace this jerry-built lingo with a concise and more natural style is the major objective of any company writing program. But the training program is not the first step. Typically it follows an analysis of company writing (memos, reports and carbon copies of a cross section of correspondence) and conferences with top management and department heads on problems and objectives.

Why?

First, the consultant or company writing counselor wants to identify employees who are not qualified to write letters or reports or who need special help. The root of writing problems in some companies is the haphazard assignment of writing responsibilities. The mistaken belief persists that anyone can produce good letters and reports.

A second purpose of the survey is to determine typical writing problems so that workshop sessions, manuals and so on can be tailored to company and employee needs.

Third, the training director wants to identify recurring situations that may be handled more quickly and economically by form letters or guide letters. Form letters may be used to dispatch routine matters that do not require personal attention. Guide letters—or professionally written model letters that give the appearance of personally dictated replies—may save time and money, and minimize mistakes. A study published last January by the Hoover Task Force on Paperwork indicates how much may be saved by the use of guide letters and form letters. The following cost figures, which corroborate the finding of many companies and consultants, are based on 175-word letters:

Letters dictated to a stenographer	70 cents to $2.45 each
Letters dictated to a machine	60 cents to $2.25 each
Guide Letters	20 to 30 cents each
Form letters	8 to 15 cents each

A fourth purpose of the survey is to examine certain company policies. Are they clear and consistent? Are they understood by those who must intepret them or act on them in their writing? Consultants contend that management's claim that it knows what it wants is often contradicted by an analysis of written work or by interviews with employees. For example, one mail order firm called in a consultant to investigate the excessive number of complaint letters that led to costly back and forth correspondence. The company had a stated money-back guarantee policy, but many company correspondents were under the impression that they were supposed to dissuade unsatisfied customers from returning unwanted merchandise. Confronting management with the results of his investigation, the consultant asked: "Is the money-back guarantee unconditional or isn't it?" When he got hedging answers he pointed out bluntly that if the company wanted to cut down its complaints and improve its public relations it had to clarify its policy and stand by it. Management's decision to take back merchandise without questioning virtually eliminated the complaints.

In some companies the survey is broadened to include a review of writing systems or procedures. The consultant or company writing counselor may urge replacement of equipment. He may suggest the use of window envelopes for general correspondence in order to reduce duplicate typing. He may recommend streamlining the format of letters—eliminating indentions and standardizing side margins—in order to save secretarial time. (The publicized Simplified Letter, devised by the National Office Management Association, goes a step farther and eliminates the salutations and the complimentary close.) He may propose ways to standardize memos and reports.

He may also investigate obstacles to the flow of reports and letters. If incoming letters aren't answered fast enough, he may introduce a time control system that requires departments to report each month the number of letters that were answered in one day, two days, three days and so on. Time control reports not only provide a useful measure of productive efficiency, they may also disclose where the bottlenecks are that constrict the flow of letters. By installing a time control system, one firm was able to get 98 per cent of its incoming mail answered within three days. Another firm set a higher goal—to answer each letter the day it arrives. When it is unable to do so it sends out an acknowledgment form letter telling the policyholder that his letter is receiving attention.

An analysis of company writing, which may result in time control systems, equipment checks, revision of secretarial methods and preparation of training material, is an essential preliminary to the actual instruction of employees in better writing.

Telling Employees Why Writing Is Important

It is with an explanation of the importance of writing—to the individual and to the company—that a well-planned program begins. Writing is learned rather than taught. It improves more with practice than with instruction. An employee must want to write better if he is to benefit significantly from a training program. Without undervaluing the role of the consultant or teacher, it should be understood that in reality the employee must teach himself. The job of the instructor is primarily to motivate employees, to encourage them and to give them the right goals to aim at.

There are compelling reasons for learning to write better. To the employee seeking advancement, skill in language is a key requirement for success. In a leaflet entitled, *Why Study English*, the General Electric Company pointed out that "No piece of company business can begin, progress and achieve its purpose without the use of words. . . . Every day in your future you will be called upon to speak and write, and when you open your mouth or write a letter or report, you will be advertising your progress and your potential worth."

Anyone who can write clearly and persuasively possesses a skill that will be useful to him whatever job he holds or moves to. Writing is as essential to the accountant as to the salesman, to the secretary as to the supervisor. The subject matter, the length or style of the communication may change, but the principles of good English and good human relations do not.

Moreover, employees can be shown that if they are skilled at writing, they are more likely to enjoy it. It seems strange that people who are fastidious about their dress or proud of a par 4 on the 18th hole take so little pride in their ability to express themselves clearly, concisely and imaginatively in writing. There is satisfaction in any job well done, and employees should be helped to appreciate the satisfaction that comes from skill in self-expression.

The company also sets forth its reasons for introducing the program: the opportunities for cutting costs, the need for speeding up communication and clarifying them, the importance of public relations. For example, the importance of public relations is highlighted in the foreword to the *Effective Letters* portfolio issued by the New York Life Insurance Company:

"Anyone who writes a letter for New York Life holds a key position within the organization of the company, for he helps to determine, directly, by the kind of letters he writes, the nature of public feeling toward the Company, and toward the life insurance business as a whole."

In short, the arguments needed to persuade employees that writing is important are readily apparent. What is needed to launch an effective training program is the ingenuity and effort—the salesmanship—to put them across.

Telling Employees What Not To Do

A major objective of the writing program is to help employees get rid of bad habits. The recurring advice is: Eliminate clichés and jargon. Don't use more words than you need to convey your thought. Don't use big words and technical terms when everyday words will do. Don't antagonize your reader.

The clichés of business letter writing are time-worn, stock phrases that either have little meaning today or are roundabout ways of saying simple things that ought to be said more directly. L. E. "Cy" Frailey, consultant and author, has labeled them "whisker expressions." To a reader they are the tip-off that the writer is either dull, in a hurry or hopelessly behind the times. The catalog of "business-ese" includes *kindly advise, trusting to receive same, thanking you in advance, beg to call your attention*—a comprehensive list would fill a page. Since these tell-tale phrases are easy to identify, they are easy to eradicate.

More troublesome are the less obvious superfluous expressions that clutter business writing and rob it of its vigor. These words and phrases can, and should be scrapped. Last year The Pacific Telephone and Telegraph Company gave an example of what can be achieved by intelligent editing and rewriting. Reporting on its experience with a writing program set up by consultant Pauline Putnam, Pacific Telephone and Telegraph gave "before and after" samples of a company instruction sheet. The original was 465 words long. The revision, written by an employee who had taken the training course, covered the essentials in 197 words. The revision was not only shorter, it was also far easier to read and understand.

What should be scrapped? The clichés, of course, and also the doublets: *first and foremost, full and complete, appreciative and grateful.* Redundant phrases like *the situation as it actually exists* can be effectively shortened to the single word, *actually.* Judicious pruning can cut back the phrase *in the month of July* to read *in July.*

The fear of active verbs also adds to the clutter. Judging from typical letters and reports, businessmen who say "Hogan shot a 67" would write "a 67 was shot by Hogan"—if they were required to make the same statement in a report. Writing counselors, of course, do not ban the use of the passive voice; they merely warn against excessive use of it, since the passive is frequently longer and less effective. Business writers also weaken the impact of reports and letters by excessive use of the linking verb and noun. Instead of writing *compete,* they write *are in competition with;* instead of *show,* they write *are an indication of.*

Redundance and superfluous words waste the writer's time and the reader's time and add nothing to communication. They increase costs but not value. Rudolph Flesch once observed, after analyzing stacks of business correspondence and reports: "Roughly 50 per cent of the words are useless or even obstacles to communication."

In their effort to simplify and clarify business writing, consultants question the unnecessary use of big words and technical terms in ordinary correspondence. They deplore pompous expressions that are so often used in a misguided effort to appear scientific or scholarly, such as the following: "We must consider the future ramifications in addition to the inherent factors in existence at the time of the decision." Robert Gunning, consultant and author, has summed up the advice succinctly: "Write to express, not impress."

The list of don'ts includes warnings against ultimatums, preaching, hidden accusations such as *you forgot* or *I told you clearly in my last report,* and the curt *no* when a customer deserves a courteous, straightforward explanation.

But getting rid of bad habits is only a preparation for developing good ones.

What Business Writers Should Learn To Do

"Writing is essentially thinking," wrote Stephen Leacock, "or at least involves thinking as its first requisite." What does the reader want to know? What do you, as a writer, want to tell him? What do you want him to do? How do you want him to feel? What is the purpose of the message, the alternative ways of organizing and expressing it? These questions are worth thinking about before putting words on paper.

Actually the gobbledygook that writing counselors decry—the wordiness, pompousness and disregard of the "reader over your shoulder"—are merely symptoms. Often the cause of bad writing is the failure to think.

Ideally, of course, instruction in writing should include discipline in how to think straight, but the refinements of logic, essential as they are, typically are beyond the scope of the company training program. The writing consultant sets more modest goals. He tells employees what to think about rather than how to think.

Even elementary advice is useful because many simple ideas are ignored. For example, many employees profit from these two simple suggestions for planning their replies to incoming mail:

1. Underline the sentences and questions that need to be answered.

2. Jot down a few notes before dictating.

Advice on how to think about people is usually more detailed and more emphasized. It is summed up by the favorite admonition of consultants and counselors: "Adopt a YOU attitude." The point was put somewhat more explicitly for report writers many years ago in the Tuck School manual on research: "In your investigation, think of the subject. In your presentation, think of the reader."

It is in their discussion of the "you attitude" that writing counselors digress into a broader examination of human relations. For the "you attitude" is essentially the application of a knowledge of human relations and public relations to the task of writing. The "human touch" is often as important as the content of the message itself.

Employees are urged to write shorter sentences. And for a good reason. Short sentences are easier to understand and easier to write. A professional craftsman may write long sentences that are perfectly clear, but not the average writer in business. He is more likely to get hopelessly entangled in phrases and clauses. As a result the reader has to spend his time translating the message when he should be evaluating it.

Correctness for its own sake is not a major objective. The concern over split infinitives, the distinction between shall and will, the ban on prepositions at the end of a sentence—all of these rules that characterized instruction in business writing a generation ago—are frequently ignored. The critical questions today are: Is the message clear, complete, concise, accurate and persuasive? Does it win friends? Does it get action? Gross errors of grammar and usage get some attention, but the prevailing view seems to be that a knowledge of grammar is helpful only insofar as it helps a writer bring order out of the chaos of words in his mind. When devotion to usage forces him to sacrifice clear and forceful expression to achieve correctness, it becomes a barrier to communication. Furthermore perfect English is probably unattainable. The English language trips up its most professional practitioners. One expert who was deploring a certain violation of usage was himself caught in an infraction by E. B. White, the New Yorker magazine's perceptive and witty essayist. Whereupon Mr. White commented: "English usage is sometimes more than mere taste, judgment and education—sometimes it's sheer luck, like getting across the street." Luck can't be taught in a writing program.

The list of things that the typical company writing program covers also includes: word choice, particularly the superiority of concrete words over abstract words and simple words over complex; effective ways to begin and end letters; organization of long reports, including the usefulness of subheadings, charts, tables, and short introductory statements of conclusions and recommendations. (Programs even include detailed instruction on how to get along with stenographers: "Look at your secretary when you dictate . . . don't expect your words to ricochet off the window pane in her direction . . . Give specific instructions before you dictate . . . Dictate in phrases and clauses" and so on.) . . .

Techniques of Instruction

How are the do's and don'ts taught? What teaching devices are used?

The program usually gets underway with a series of workshops or clinical sessions on company time. Participation is either optional or compulsory. A skillfully-run program may get as good a turnout by voluntary participation as by required attendance, but wholly voluntary programs are not typical.

Classes are small, with 15 or fewer employees at each. There may be six to ten sessions lasting an hour or two. They are rarely lecture sessions. Usually they are informal group discussions that include analysis of good and bad company writing. Usually these sessions are supplemented by personal conferences between the program director and the employee.

The writing programs usually include the preparation of training manuals ranging from expensive volumes to simple mimeographed pamphlets. Manuals need not be elaborate to be effective and useful. It's the content that is important to management as well as to employees. Richard E. Morris, one of the most successful consultants, contends that until a manual is devised, management often doesn't know what its policies toward written communications are and employees do not understand what is expected of them. Preparing a manual helps management clarify its thinking and standardize its policies. To the employee, a manual is an up-to-date record of rules, procedures and objectives—a useful reference and reminder of what the company wants.

Short booklets that merely reiterate the need for good writing and the criteria of good writing are issued to remind employees who have already taken writing courses. Weekly or monthly bulletins are also used to advantage. Since they are issued periodically, they serve to remind employees of the importance of practice and of the company's continuing interest in good writing. Typically these bulletins are one-page mimeographed or printed sheets devoted to a single problem, such as how to begin a letter or a check list of trite phrases to avoid. During one two-year period the Mutual Benefit Life Insurance Company issued 43 of its "Good Letter Bulletins" covering a wide variety of topics.

Other devices to remind employees of the value of good writing include blotters, letter-appraisal charts, films, slides, and the readability guides, such as the plastic, jiffy "Reading-Ease Calculator" that has been used by General Motors Corporation and the simple "Writing Yardstick" folder prepared for the Prudential Insurance Company.

Readability formulas, which are both damned and praised, deserve a more extended comment because they have received so much attention in recent years. Unquestionably they have helped to dramatize the need for better writing and have stimulated popular interest in "readable writing." But readability formulas are primarily tests of written matter, not tools of writing. The tools of the writer are still information, ideas, words, an understanding of people and a disciplined mind. A mathematical formula or a calculator is no substitute for any of these and a dubious supplement. A writer cannot improve his product merely by keeping one hand on the calculator while the other is on the pen.

Moreover, there is reason to challenge the reliability of a formula as a measure of what has been written. Bad scores on a readability test may indicate conclusively that the written passage is difficult to read, but good scores do not prove excellence. A short sentence may pass a readability test without passing the subjective test of good communication. Sentences need not only to be short, they need to convey the intended meaning; and counting words, prefixes and so on does not yield a measurement of the more important qualities of content, organization and tone. The formulas have been blown up all out of proportion to their actual significance—not so much by those who have devised them and who recognize the limitations, as by those who seek to capitalize on them.

Any discussion of a single problem of business management runs the risk of exaggeration. There is a temptation to exalt potential benefits and to ignore the limitations of any proposed reform. Certainly business writing programs are no cure-all for sagging sales and poor public relations. If the company writing program has seemed overemphasized here, it is because the value of well-written reports and letters is still so frequently overlooked and because measures to improve them are so readily available. Actually what impresses an observer most is that so much can be achieved by a little first-aid. Despite the progress of recent years, one leading consultant confided that he is constantly amazed to find blue chip companies so desperately in need of a shake-up in their writing policies.

What business has learned about writing may be less than it needs to know, but it still is worth summing up:

1. Writing needs to be managed, just like production, marketing, industrial relations or finance. As a cost, it is too sizable to be neglected; as a tool, it is too useful to be left unsharpened or to be handled carelessly by unskilled workmen.

2. Techniques to reduce costs, to speed up the flow of letters and reports and to improve the quality of written communications are within reach. They include modernization of office procedures, train-

ing sessions, company manuals, bulletins and personal instruction.

3. Both consultant-directed and company-directed programs have proved successful.

4. To succeed, a writing improvement program needs the whole-hearted and continuing support of top management—a management that understands the problems of communications, that can set reasonable goals, that is receptive to proposed policy changes and that realizes the fundamental importance of changing the attitude of employees toward language and public relations.

QUESTIONS ON CONTENT

1. To whom is this article particularly addressed? What is the purpose of the first four paragraphs? Compare the first five paragraphs of "Why Study English?"
2. What is Gresham's Law?
3. How are the divisions of this article indicated? Discuss the logic of this arrangement.
4. Comment on the statement: "Writing is learned rather than taught."
5. What is the purpose of the first paragraph under "Telling Employees What Not To Do"?
6. What relationship is there between "Why Study English?" and this article? Between this article and E. B. White's "Calculating Machine" (see below)?
7. What are *clichés, passive verbs, redundancies?* Why should they be avoided?
8. Define, then discuss, the *you-attitude.*
9. Why is "correctness" considered "not a major objective"? Is correctness of no importance? Discuss.
10. Explain the term, *readability formula.* What attitude does the author take toward such a formula? Compare E. B. White's "Calculating Machine," below.
11. Is there a suggestion in this article that business writing should be sharply set aside from all other forms of writing, from, say, imaginative writing? Discuss.

❧ Prose: Lucid, Simple, and Euphonious

W. Somerset Maugham

I have never had more than two English lessons in my life, for though I wrote essays at school, I do not remember that I ever received any instruction on how to put sentences together. The two lessons I have had were given me so late in life that I am afraid I cannot hope greatly to profit by them. The first was only a few years ago. I was spending some weeks in London and had engaged as temporary secretary a young woman. She was shy, rather pretty, and absorbed in a love affair with a married man. I had written a book called *Cakes and Ale*, and, the typescript arriving one Saturday morning, I asked her if she would be good enough to take it home and correct it over the week-end. I meant her only to make a note of mistakes in spelling that the typist might have made and point out errors occasioned by a handwriting that is not always easy to decipher. But she was a conscientious young person and she took me more literally than I intended. When she brought back the typescript on Monday morning it was accompanied by four foolscap sheets of corrections. I must confess that at first glance I was a trifle vexed; but then I thought that it would be silly of me not to profit, if I could, by the trouble she had taken and so sat me down to examine them. I suppose the young woman had taken a course at a secretarial college and she had gone through my novel in the same methodical way as her masters had gone through her essays. The remarks that filled the four neat pages of foolscap were incisive and severe. I could not but surmise that the professor of English at the secretarial college did not mince matters. He took a marked line, there could be no doubt about that; and he did not allow that there might be two opinions about anything. His apt pupil would have nothing to do with a preposition at the end of a sentence. A mark of exclamation betokened her disapproval of a colloquial phrase. She had a feeling that you must not use the same word twice on a page and she was ready every time with a synonym to put in its

From *The Summing Up*, by W. Somerset Maugham. Copyright 1938 by W. Somerset Maugham, reprinted by permission of Doubleday & Company, Inc.

place. If I had indulged myself in the luxury of a sentence of ten lines, she wrote: 'Clarify this. Better break it up into two or more periods.' When I had availed myself of the pleasant pause that is indicated by a semicolon, she noted: 'A full stop'; and if I had ventured upon a colon she remarked stingingly: 'Obsolete.' But the harshest stroke of all was her comment on what I thought was rather a good joke: 'Are you sure of your facts?' Taking it all in all I am bound to confess that the professor at her college would not have given me very high marks.

The second lesson I had was given by a don, both intelligent and charming, who happened to be staying with me when I was myself correcting the typescript of another book. He was good enough to offer to read it. I hesitated, because I knew that he judged from a standpoint of excellence that is hard to attain; and though I was aware that he had a profound knowledge of Elizabethan literature, his inordinate admiration for *Esther Waters* made me doubtful of his discernment in the productions of our own day: no one could attach so great a value to that work who had an intimate knowledge of the French novel during the nineteenth century. But I was anxious to make my book as good as I could and I hoped to benefit by his criticisms. They were in point of fact lenient. They interested me peculiarly because I inferred that this was the way in which he dealt with the compositions of undergraduates. My don had, I think, a natural gift for language, which it has been his business to cultivate; his taste appeared to me faultless. I was much struck by his insistence on the force of individual words. He liked the stronger word rather than the euphonious. To give an example, I had written that a statue would be placed in a certain square and he suggested that I should write: the statue will stand. I had not done that because my ear was offended by the alliteration. I noticed also that he had a feeling that words should be used not only to balance a sentence but to balance an idea. This is sound, for an idea may lose its effect if it is delivered abruptly; but it is a matter of delicacy, since it may well lead to verbiage. Here a knowledge of stage dialogue should help. An actor will sometimes say to an author: 'Couldn't you give me a word or two more in this speech? It seems to take away all the point of my line if I have nothing else to say.' As I listened to my don's remarks I could not but think how much better I should write now if in my youth I had had the advantage of such sensible, broad-minded and kindly advice.

As it is, I have had to teach myself. I have looked at the stories I wrote when I was very young in order to discover what natural aptitude I had, my original stock-in-trade, before I developed it by taking thought. The manner had a superciliousness that perhaps my years excused and an irrascibility that was a defect of nature; but I am speaking now only of the way in which I expressed myself. It seems to me that I had a natural lucidity and a knack for writing easy dialogue.

When Henry Arthur Jones, then a well-known playwright, read my first novel, he told a friend that in due course I should be one of the most successful dramatists of the day. I suppose he saw in it directness and an effective way of presenting a scene that suggested a sense of the theatre. My language was commonplace, my vocabulary limited, my grammar shaky and my phrases hackneyed. But to write was an instinct that seemed as natural to me as to breathe, and I did not stop to consider whether I wrote well or badly. It was not until some years later that it dawned upon me that it was a delicate art that must be painfully acquired. The discovery was forced upon me by the difficulty I found in getting my meaning on paper. I wrote dialogue fluently, but when it came to a page of description I found myself entangled in all sorts of quandaries. I would struggle for a couple of hours over two or three sentences that I could in no way manage to straighten out. I made up my mind to teach myself to write. Unfortunately I had no one to help me. I made many mistakes. If I had had someone to guide me like the charming don of whom I spoke just now I might have saved much time. Such a one might have told me that such gifts as I had lay in one direction and that they must be cultivated in that direction; it was useless to try to do something for which I had no aptitude. But at that time a florid prose was admired. Richness of texture was sought by means of a jewelled phrase and sentences stiff with exotic epithets: the ideal was a brocade so heavy with gold that it stood up by itself. The intelligent young read Walter Pater with enthusiasm. My common sense suggested to me that it was anaemic stuff; behind those elaborate, gracious periods I was conscious of a tired, wan personality. I was young, lusty and energetic; I wanted fresh air, action, violence, and I found it hard to breathe that dead, heavily scented atmosphere and sit in those hushed rooms in which it was indecorous to speak above a whisper. But I would not listen to my common sense. I persuaded myself that this was

the height of culture and turned a scornful shoulder on the outside world where men shouted and swore, played the fool, wenched
and got drunk. I read *Intentions* and *The Picture of Dorian Gray*.
I was intoxicated by the colour and rareness of the fantastic words
that thickly stud the pages of *Salome*. Shocked by the poverty of
my own vocabulary, I went to the British Museum with pencil and
paper and noted down the names of curious jewels, the Byzantine
hues of old enamels, the sensual feel of textiles, and made elaborate
sentences to bring them in. Fortunately I could never find an opportunity to use them and they lie there yet in an old notebook ready
for anyone who has a mind to write nonsense. It was generally
thought then that the Authorized Version of the Bible was the
greatest piece of prose that the English language has produced. I
read it diligently, especially the Song of Solomon, jotting down for
future use turns of phrase that struck me and making lists of unusual
or beautiful words. I studied Jeremy Taylor's *Holy Dying*. In order
to assimilate his style I copied out passages and then tried to write
them down from memory.

The first fruit of this labour was a little book about Andalusia
called *The Land of the Blessed Virgin*. I had occasion to read parts
of it the other day. I know Andalusia a great deal better now than
I knew it then, and I have changed my mind about a good many
things of which I wrote. Since it has continued in America to have
a small sale it occurred to me that it might be worth while to revise
it. I soon saw that this was impossible. The book was written by
someone I have completely forgotten. It bored me to distraction. But
what I am concerned with is the prose, for it was as an exercise
in style that I wrote it. It is wistful, allusive and elaborate. It has
neither ease nor spontaneity. It smells of hot-house plants and
Sunday dinner like the air in the greenhouse that leads out of the
dining-room of a big house in Bayswater. There are a great many
melodious adjectives. The vocabulary is sentimental. It does not
remind one of an Italian brocade, with its rich pattern of gold,
but of a curtain material designed by Burne-Jones and reproduced
by Morris.

I do not know whether it was a subconscious feeling that this
sort of writing was contrary to my bent or a naturally methodical
cast of mind that led me then to turn my attention to the writers
of the Augustan Period. The prose of Swift enchanted me. I made
up my mind that this was the perfect way to write and I started to

work on him in the same way as I had done with Jeremy Taylor. I chose *The Tale of a Tub.* It is said that when the Dean re-read it in his old age he cried: 'What genius I had then!' To my mind his genius was better shown in other works. It is a tiresome allegory and the irony is facile. But the style is admirable. I cannot imagine that English can be better written. Here are no flowery periods, fantastic turns of phrase or high-flown images. It is a civilized prose, natural, discreet and pointed. There is no attempt to surprise by an extravagant vocabulary. It looks as though Swift made do with the first word that came to hand, but since he had an acute and logical brain it was always the right one, and he put it in the right place. The strength and balance of his sentences are due to an exquisite taste. As I had done before I copied passages and then tried to write them out again from memory. I tried altering words or the order in which they were set. I found that the only possible words were those Swift had used and that the order in which he had placed them was the only possible order. It is an impeccable prose.

But perfection has one grave defect: it is apt to be dull. Swift's prose is like a French canal, bordered with poplars, that runs through a gracious and undulating country. Its tranquil charm fills you with satisfaction, but it neither excites the emotions nor stimulates the imagination. You go on and on and presently you are a trifle bored. So, much as you may admire Swift's wonderful lucidity, his terseness, his naturalness, his lack of affectation, you find your attention wandering after a while unless his matter peculiarly interests you. I think if I had my time over again I would give to the prose of Dryden the close study I gave to that of Swift. I did not come across it till I had lost the inclination to take so much pains. The prose of Dryden is delicious. It has not the perfection of Swift nor the easy elegance of Addison, but it has a springtime gaiety, a conversational ease, a blithe spontaneousness that are enchanting. Dryden was a very good poet, but it is not the general opinion that he had a lyrical quality; it is strange that it is just this that sings in his softly sparkling prose. Prose had never been written in England like that before; it has seldom been written like that since. Dryden flourished at a happy moment. He had in his bones the sonorous periods and the baroque massiveness of Jacobean language and under the influence of the nimble and well-bred felicity that he learnt from the French he turned it into an instrument that was fit not only for solemn themes but also to express the light thought of the passing moment. He was the first of the rococo artists. If Swift reminds you of a French canal Dryden recalls an English river winding its cheerful way round hills, through quietly busy towns and by nestling villages, pausing now in a noble reach and then running powerfully through a woodland country. It is alive, varied, windswept; and it has the pleasant open-air smell of England.

The work I did was certainly very good for me. I began to write better; I did not write well. I wrote stiffly and self-consciously. I tried to get a pattern into my sentences, but did not see that the pattern was evident. I took care how I placed my words, but did not reflect that an order that was natural at the beginning of the eighteenth century was most unnatural at the beginning of ours. My attempt to write in the manner of Swift made it impossible for me to achieve the effect of inevitable rightness that was just what I so much admired in him. I then wrote a number of plays and ceased to occupy myself with anything but dialogue. It was not till five years had passed that I set out again to write a novel. By then I no longer had any ambition to be a stylist; I put aside all thought of fine writing. I wanted to write without any frills of language, in as bare and unaffected a manner as I could. I had so much to say that I could afford to waste no words. I wanted merely to set down the facts. I began with the impossible aim of using no adjectives at all. I thought that if you could find the exact term a qualifying epithet could be dispensed with. As I saw it in my mind's eye my book would have the appearance of an immensely long telegram in which for economy's sake you had left out every word that was not necessary to make the sense clear. I have not read it since I corrected the proofs and do not know how near I came to doing what I tried. My impression is that it is written at least more naturally than anything I had written before; but I am sure that it is often slipshod and I daresay there are in it a good many mistakes in grammar.

Since then I have written many other books; and though ceasing my methodical study of the old masters (for though the spirit is willing, the flesh is weak), I have continued with increasing assiduity to try to write better. I discovered my limitations and it seemed to me that the only sensible thing was to aim at what excellence I could within them. I knew that I had no lyrical quality. I had a small vocabulary and no efforts that I could make to enlarge it much availed me. I had little gift of metaphor; the original and striking simile seldom occurred to me. Poetic flights and the great imaginative sweep were beyond my powers. I could admire them in others as I could admire their far-fetched tropes and the unusual but suggestive language in which they clothed their thoughts, but my own invention never presented me with such embellishments; and I was tired of trying to do what did not come easily to me. On the other hand, I had an acute power of observation and it seemed to me that I could see a great many things that other people missed. I could put down in clear terms what I saw. I had a logical sense, and if no great feeling for the richness and strangeness of words, at all events a lively appreciation of their sound. I knew that I should never write as well as I could wish, but I thought with pains I could arrive at writing as well as my natural defects allowed. On taking thought it seemed to me that I must aim at lucidity, simplicity and euphony. I have put these three qualities in the order of the importance I assigned to them.

I have never had much patience with the writers who claim from the reader an effort to understand their meaning. You have only to go to the great philosophers to see that it is possible to express with lucidity the most subtle reflections. You may find it difficult to understand the thought of Hume, and if you have no philosophical training its implications will doubtless escape you; but no one with any education at all can fail to understand exactly what the meaning of each sentence is. Few people have written English with more grace than Berkeley. There are two sorts of obscurity that you find in writers. One is due to negligence and the other to wilfulness. People often write obscurely because they have never taken the trouble to learn to write clearly. This sort of obscurity you find too often in modern philosophers, in men of science, and even in literary critics. Here it is indeed strange. You would have thought that men who passed their lives in the study of the great masters of literature would be sufficiently sensitive to the beauty of language to write if not beautifully at least with perspicuity. Yet you will find in their works sentence after sentence that you must read twice to discover the sense. Often you can only guess at it, for the writers have evidently not said what they intended.

Another cause of obscurity is that the writer is himself not quite sure of his meaning. He has a vague impression of what he wants to say, but has not, either from lack of mental power or from laziness, exactly formulated it in his mind and it is natural enough that he should not find a precise expression for a confused idea. This is due largely to the fact that many writers think, not before, but as they write. The pen originates the thought. The disadvantage of this, and indeed it is a danger against which the author must be always on his guard, is that there is a sort of magic in the written word. The idea acquires substance by taking on a visible nature, and then stands in the way of its own clarification. But this sort of obscurity merges very easily into the wilful. Some writers who do not think clearly are inclined to suppose that their thoughts have a significance greater than at first sight appears. It is flattering to believe that they are too profound to be expressed so clearly that all who run may read, and very naturally it does not occur to such writers that the fault is with their own minds which have not the faculty of precise reflection. Here again the magic of the written word obtains. It is very easy to persuade oneself that a phrase that one does not quite understand may mean a great deal more than one realizes. From this there is only a little way to go to fall into the habit of setting down one's impressions in all their original vagueness. Fools can always be found to discover a hidden sense in them. There is another form of wilful obscurity that masquerades as aristocratic exclusiveness. The author wraps his meaning in mystery so that the vulgar shall not participate in it. His soul is a secret garden into which the elect may penetrate only after overcoming a number of perilous obstacles. But this kind of obscurity is not only pretentious; it is short-sighted. For time plays it an odd trick. If the sense is meagre time reduces it to meaningless verbiage that no one thinks of reading. This is the fate that has befallen the lucubrations of those French writers who were seduced by the example of Guillaume Apollinaire. But occasionally it throws a sharp cold light on what had seemed profound and thus discloses the fact that these contortions of language disguised very commonplace notions. There are few of Mallarmé's poems now that are not clear; one cannot fail to notice that his thought singularly lacked originality. Some of his phrases were beautiful; the materials of his verse were the poetic platitudes of his day.

Simplicity is not such an obvious merit as lucidity. I have aimed at it because I have no gift for richness. Within limits I admire richness in others, though I find it difficult to digest in quantity. I can read one page of Ruskin with delight, but twenty only with weariness. The rolling period, the stately epithet, the noun rich in poetic associations, the subordinate clauses that give the sentence weight and magnificence, the grandeur like that of wave following wave in the open sea; there is no doubt that in all this there is something inspiring. Words thus strung together fall on the ear like music. The appeal is sensuous rather than intellectual, and the beauty of the sound leads you easily to conclude that you need not bother about the meaning. But words are tyrannical things, they exist for their meanings, and if you will not pay attention to these, you cannot pay attention at all. Your mind wanders. This kind of writing demands a subject that will suit it. It is surely out of place to write in the grand style of inconsiderable things. No one wrote in this manner with greater success than Sir Thomas Browne, but even he did not always escape this pitfall. In the last chapter of *Hydriotaphia* the matter, which is the destiny of man, wonderfully fits the baroque splendour of the language, and here the Norwich doctor produced a piece of prose that has never been surpassed in our literature; but when he describes the finding of his urns in the same splendid manner the effect (at least to my taste) is less happy. When a modern writer is grandiloquent to tell you whether or no a little trollop shall hop into bed with a commonplace young man you are right to be disgusted.

But if richness need gifts with which everyone is not endowed, simplicity by no means comes by nature. To achieve it needs rigid discipline. So far as I know ours is the only language in which it has been found necessary to give a name to the piece of prose which is described as the purple patch; it would not have been necessary to do so unless it were characteristic. It was not always so. Nothing could be more racy, straightforward and alive than the prose of Shakespeare; but it must be remembered that this was dialogue written to be spoken. We do not know how he would have written if like Corneille he had composed prefaces to his plays. It may be that they would have been as euphuistic as the letters of Queen Elizabeth. But earlier prose, the prose of Sir Thomas More, for instance, is neither ponderous, flowery nor oratorical. It smacks of the English soil. To my mind King James's Bible has been a very harmful influence on English prose. I am not so stupid as to deny its great beauty. It is majestical. But the Bible is an oriental book. Its alien imagery has nothing to do with us. Those hyperboles, those luscious metaphors, are foreign to our genius. I cannot but think that not the least of the misfortunes that the Secession from Rome brought upon the spiritual life of our country is that this work for so long a period became the daily, and with many the only, reading of our people. Those rhythms, that powerful vocabulary, that grandiloquence, became part and parcel of the national sensibility. The plain, honest English speech was overwhelmed with ornament. Blunt Englishmen twisted their tongues to speak like Hebrew prophets. There was evidently something in the English temper to which this was congenial, perhaps a native lack of precision in thought, perhaps a naive delight in fine words for their own sake, an innate eccentricity and love of embroidery, I do not know; but the fact remains that ever since, English prose has had to struggle against the tendency to luxuriate. When from time to time the spirit of the language has reasserted itself, as it did with Dryden and the writers of Queen Anne, it was only to be submerged once more by the pomposities of Gibbon and Dr. Johnson. When English prose recovered simplicity with Hazlitt, the Shelley of the letters and Charles Lamb at his best, it lost it again with De Quincey, Carlyle, Meredith and Walter Pater. It is obvious that the grand style is more striking than the plain. Indeed many people think that a style that does not attract notice is not style. They will admire Walter Pater's, but will read an essay by Matthew Arnold without giving a moment's attention to the elegance, distinction and sobriety with which he set down what he had to say.

The dictum that the style is the man is well known. It is one of those aphorisms that say too much to mean a great deal. Where is the man in Goethe, in his birdlike lyrics or in his clumsy prose? And Hazlitt? But I suppose that if a man has a confused mind he will write in a confused way, if his temper is capricious his prose will be fantastical, and if he has a quick, darting intelligence that is reminded by the matter in hand of a hundred things he will, unless he has great self-control, load his pages with metaphor and simile. There is a great difference between the magniloquence of the Jacobean writers, who were intoxicated with the new wealth that had lately been brought into the language, and the turgidity of Gibbon and Dr. Johnson, who were the victims of bad theories. I can read every word that Dr. Johnson wrote with delight, for he had good sense, charm and wit. No one could have written better if he had not wilfully set himself to write in the grand style. He knew good English when he saw it. No critic has praised Dryden's prose more aptly. He said of him that he appeared to have no art other than that of expressing with clearness what he thought with vigour.

And one of his Lives he finished with the words: 'Whoever wishes to attain an English style, familiar but not coarse, and elegant but not ostentatious, must give his days and nights to the volumes of Addison.' But when he himself sat down to write it was with a very different aim. He mistook the orotund for the dignified. He had not the good breeding to see that simplicity and naturalness are the truest marks of distinction.

For to write good prose is an affair of good manners. It is, unlike verse, a civil art. Poetry is baroque. Baroque is tragic, massive and mystical. I cannot but feel that the prose writers of the baroque period, the authors of King James's Bible, Sir Thomas Browne, Glanville, were poets who had lost their way. Prose is a rococo art. It needs taste rather than power, decorum rather than inspiration and vigour rather than grandeur. Form for the poet is the bit and the bridle without which (unless you are an acrobat) you cannot ride your horse; but for the writer of prose it is the chassis without which your car does not exist. It is not an accident that the best prose was written when rococo with its elegance and moderation, at its birth attained its greatest excellence. For rococo was evolved when baroque had become declamatory and the world, tired of the stupendous, asked for restraint. It was the natural expression of persons who valued a civilized life. Humour, tolerance and horse sense made the great tragic issues that had preoccupied the first half of the seventeenth century seem excessive. The world was a more comfortable place to live in and perhaps for the first time in centuries the cultivated classes could sit back and enjoy their leisure. It has been said that good prose should resemble the conversation of a well-bred man. Conversation is only possible when men's minds are free from pressing anxieties. Their lives must be reasonably secure and they must have no grave concern about their souls. They must attach importance to the refinements of civilization. They must value courtesy, they must pay attention to their persons (and have we not also been told that good prose should be like the clothes of a well-dressed man, appropriate but unobtrusive?), they must fear to bore, they must be neither flippant nor solemn, but always apt; and they must look upon 'enthusiasm' with a critical glance. This is a soil very suitable for prose. It is not to be wondered at that it gave a fitting opportunity for the appearance of the best writer of prose that our modern world has seen, Voltaire. The writers of English, perhaps owing to the poetic nature of the language, have seldom reached the excellence that seems to have come so naturally to him. It is in so far as they have approached the ease, sobriety and precision of the great French masters that they are admirable.

Whether you ascribe importance to euphony, the last of the three characteristics that I mentioned, must depend on the sensitiveness of your ear. A great many readers, and many admirable writers, are devoid of this quality. Poets as we know have always made a great use of alliteration. They are persuaded that the repetition of a sound gives an effect of beauty. I do not think it does so in prose. It seems to me that in prose alliteration should be used only for a special reason; when used by accident it falls on the ear very disagreeably. But its accidental use is so common that one can only suppose that the sound of it is not universally offensive. Many writers without distress will put two rhyming words together, join a monstrous long adjective to a monstrous long noun, or between the end of one word and the beginning of another have a conjunction of consonants that almost breaks your jaw. These are trivial and obvious instances. I mention them only to prove that if careful writers can do such things it is only because they have no ear. Words have weight, sound and appearance; it is only by considering these that you can write a sentence that is good to look at and good to listen to.

I have read many books on English prose, but have found it hard to profit by them; for the most part they are vague, unduly theoretical, and often scolding. But you cannot say this of Fowler's Dictionary of Modern English Usage. It is a valuable work. I do not think anyone writes so well that he cannot learn much from it. It is lively reading. Fowler liked simplicity, straightforwardness and common sense. He had no patience with pretentiousness. He had a sound feeling that idiom was the backbone of a language and he was all for the racy phrase. He was no slavish admirer of logic and was willing enough to give usage right of way through the exact demesnes of grammar. English grammar is very difficult and few writers have avoided making mistakes in it. So heedful a writer as Henry James, for instance, on occasion wrote so ungrammatically that a schoolmaster, finding such errors in a schoolboy's essay, would be justly indignant. It is necessary to know grammar, and it is better to write grammatically than not, but it is well to remember that grammar is common speech formulated. Usage is the only test. I would prefer a phrase that was easy and unaffected to a phrase that was grammatical. One of the differences between French and English is that in French you can be grammatical with complete naturalness, but in English not invariably. It is a difficulty in writing English that the sound of the living voice dominates the look of the printed word. I have given the matter of style a great deal of thought and have taken great pains. I have written few pages that I feel I could not improve and far too many that I have left with dissatisfaction because, try as I would, I could do no better. I cannot say of myself what Johnson said of Pope: 'He never passed a fault unamended by indifference, nor quitted it by despair.' I do not write as I want to; I write as I can.

But Fowler had no ear. He did not see that simplicity may sometimes make concessions to euphony. I do not think a far-fetched, an archaic or even an affected word is out of place when it sounds better than the blunt, obvious one or when it gives a sentence a better balance. But, I hasten to add, though I think you may without misgiving make this concession to pleasant sound, I think you should make none to what may obscure your meaning. Anything is better than not to write clearly. There is nothing to be said against lucidity, and against simplicity only the possibility of dryness. This is a risk that is well worth taking when you reflect how much better it is to be bald than to wear a curly wig. But there is in euphony a danger that must be considered. It is very likely to be monotonous. When George Moore began to write, his style was poor; it gave you the impression that he wrote on wrapping paper with a blunt pencil. But he developed gradually a very musical English. He learnt to write sentences that fall away on the ear with a misty langour and it delighted him so much that he could never have enough of it. He did not escape monotony. It is like the sound of water lapping a shingly beach, so soothing that you presently cease to be sensible of it. It is so mellifluous that you hanker for some harshness, for an abrupt dissonance, that will interrupt the silky concord. I do not know how one can guard against this. I suppose the best chance is to have a more lively faculty of boredom than one's readers so that one is wearied before they are. One must always be on the watch for mannerisms and when certain cadences come too easily to the pen ask oneself whether they have not become mechanical. It is very hard to discover the exact point where the idiom one has formed to express oneself has lost its tang. As Dr. Johnson said: 'He that has once studiously formed a style, rarely writes afterwards with complete ease.' Admirably as I think

Matthew Arnold's style was suited to his particular purposes, I must admit that his mannerisms are often irritating. His style was an instrument that he had forged once for all; it was not like the human hand capable of performing a variety of actions.

If you could write lucidly, simply, euphoniously and yet with liveliness you would write perfectly: you would write like Voltaire. And yet we know how fatal the pursuit of liveliness may be: it may result in the tiresome acrobatics of Meredith. Macaulay and Carlyle were in their different ways arresting; but at the heavy cost of naturalness. Their flashy effects distract the mind. They destroy their persuasiveness; you would not believe a man was very intent on ploughing a furrow if he carried a hoop with him and jumped through it at every other step. A good style should show no sign of effort. What is written should seem a happy accident. I think no one in France now writes more admirably than Colette, and such is the ease of her expression that you cannot bring yourself to believe that she takes any trouble over it. I am told that there are pianists who have a natural technique so that they can play in a manner that most executants can achieve only as the result of unremitting toil, and I am willing to believe that there are writers who are equally fortunate. Among them I was much inclined to place Colette. I asked her. I was exceedingly surprised to hear that she wrote everything over and over again. She told me that she would often spend a whole morning working upon a single page. But it does not matter how one gets the effect of ease. For my part, if I get it at all, it is only by strenuous effort. Nature seldom provides me with the word, the turn of phrase, that is appropriate without being far-fetched or commonplace.

QUESTIONS ON CONTENT

1. What faults did the secretary find in Maugham's writing? Do you agree that they were faults? Why did the don's criticism seem more sensible?

2. What faults does Maugham ascribe to his early writing? What virtues? What means did he use to try to improve his style? Is writing, according to Maugham, learned or taught or both? Discuss.

3. List the books and authors mentioned as figuring in Maugham's search for a good prose style. What is said of Swift as compared with Dryden? What is said of Ruskin? Shakespeare? Arnold?

4. In the light of what you find in this essay, comment on the statement: "I had little gift for metaphor."
5. What attitude is taken towards obscurity in writing?
6. Examine carefully what is said about the King James Bible (page 119). Do you detect a possible contradiction? Discuss.
7. Distinguish between the terms *baroque* and *rococo,* both as used by Maugham and as defined in a dictionary.
8. Speculate on why Maugham's paragraphs are so much longer than those in the two preceding articles ("Why Study English?" and "Putting Words to Work").

❧ *You, Too, Can Write the Casual Style*

WILLIAM H. WHYTE, JR.

A revolution has taken place in American prose. No longer the short huffs and puffs, the unqualified word, the crude gusto of the declarative sentence. Today the fashion is to write casually.

The Casual Style is not exactly new. Originated in the early Twenties, it has been refined and improved and refined again by a relatively small band of writers, principally for the *New Yorker,* until now their mannerisms have become standards of sophistication. Everybody is trying to join the club. Newspaper columnists have forsaken the beloved metaphors of the sports page for the Casual Style, and one of the quickest ways for an ad man to snag an award from other ad men is to give his copy the low-key, casual pitch; the copy shouldn't sing these days—it should whisper. Even Dr. Rudolf Flesch, who has been doing so much to teach people how to write like other people, is counseling his followers to use the Casual Style. Everywhere the ideal seems the same: be casual.

But how? There is very little down-to-earth advice. We hear about the rapier like handling of the bromide, the keen eye for sham and pretension, the exquisite sense of nuance, the unerring ear for the vulgate. But not much about actual technique. The layman, as a consequence, is apt to look on the Casual Style as a mandarin dialect which he fears he could never master.

Nonsense. The Casual Style is within everyone's grasp. It has

Harper's Magazine, October, 1953. Reprinted by permission of the author.

now become so perfected by constant polishing that its devices may readily be identified, and they change so little that their use need be no more difficult for the novice than for the expert. (That's not quite all there is to it, of course. Some apparently casual writers, Thurber and E. B. White, among others, rarely use the devices.)

The subject matter, in the first place, is not to be ignored. Generally speaking, the more uneventful it is, or the more pallid the writer's reaction to it, the better do form and content marry. Take, for example, the cocktail party at which the writer can show how bored everyone is with everyone else, and how utterly fatuous they all are anyhow. Since a non-casual statement—*e.g.*, "The party was a bore"—would destroy the reason for writing about it at all, the Casual Style here is not only desirable but mandatory.

Whatever the subject, however, twelve devices are the rock on which all else is built. I will present them one by one, illustrating them with examples from such leading casual stylists as Wolcott Gibbs, John Crosby, John McCarten, and (on occasion) this magazine's "Mr. Harper." If the reader will digest what follows, he should be able to dash off a paragraph indistinguishable from the best casual writing being done today.

(1) Heightened Understatement. Where the old-style writer would say, "I don't like it," "It is not good," or something equally banal, the casual writer says it is *"something less than good."* He avoids direct statement and strong words—except, as we will note, where he is setting them up to have something to knock down. In any event, he qualifies. "Somewhat" and "rather," the bread-and-butter words of the casual writer, should become habitual with you; similarly with such phrases as "I suppose," "it seems to me," "I guess," or "I'm afraid." "Elusive" or "elude" are good, too, and if you see the word "charm" in a casual sentence you can be pretty sure that "eludes me," or "I find elusive," will not be far behind.

(2) The Multiple Hedge. Set up an ostensibly strong statement, and then, with your qualifiers, shoot a series of alternately negative and positive charges into the sentence until finally you neutralize the whole thing. Let's take, for example, the clause, "certain names have a guaranteed nostalgic magic." Challenge enough here; the names not only have magic, they have guaranteed magic. A double hedge reverses the charge. "Names which have, *I suppose* [hedge 1], a guaranteed nostalgic magic, *though there are times that I doubt it* [hedge 2]. . . ."

We didn't have to say they were guaranteed in the first place, of course, but without such straw phrases, we wouldn't have anything to construct a hedge on and, frequently, nothing to write at all. The virtue of the hedge is that by its very negating effect it makes any sentence infinitely expansible. Even if you have so torn down your original statement with one or two hedges that you seem to have come to the end of the line, you have only to slip in an anti-hedge, a strengthening word (*e.g.*, "definitely," "unqualified," etc.), and begin the process all over again. Witness the following quadruple hedge: "I found Mr. Home entertaining *from time to time* [hedge 1] on the ground, *I guess* [hedge 2], that the singular idiom and unearthly detachment of the British upper classes have *always* [anti-hedge] seemed *reasonably* [hedge 3] droll to me, *at least in moderation* [hedge 4]." The art of plain talk, as has been pointed out, does not entail undue brevity.

If you've pulled hedge on hedge and the effect still remains too vigorous, simply wipe the slate clean with a cancellation clause at the end. "It was all exactly as foolish as it sounds," says Wolcott Gibbs, winding up some 570 casual words on a subject, "and I wouldn't give it another thought."

(3) Narcissizing Your Prose. The casual style is nothing if not personal; indeed, you will usually find in it as many references to the writer as to what he's supposed to be talking about. For you do not talk about the subject; you talk about its impact on you. With the reader peering over your shoulder, you look into the mirror and observe your own responses as you run the entire range of the casual writer's emotions. You may reveal yourself as, in turn, listless ("the audience seemed not to share my boredom"); insouciant ("I was really quite happy with it"); irritated ("The whole thing left me tired and cross"); comparatively gracious ("Being in a comparatively gracious mood, I won't go into the details I didn't like"); or hesitant ("I wish I could say that I could accept his hypothesis").

(4) Preparation for the Witticism. When the casual writer hits upon a clever turn of phrase or a nice conceit, he uses this device to insure that his conceit will not pass unnoticed. Suppose, for example, you have thought of something to say that is pretty damn good if you say so yourself. The device, in effect, is to say so yourself. If you want to devastate a certain work as "a study of vulgarity in high places," don't say this flat out. Earlier in the sentence pre-

pare the reader for the drollery ahead with something like "what I am tempted to call" or "what could best be described as" or "If it had to be defined in a sentence, it might well be called. . . ."

Every writer his own claque.

(5) Deciphered Notes Device; or Cute-Things-I-Have-Said. In this one you are your own stooge as well. You feed yourself lines. By means of the slender fiction that you have written something on the back of an envelope or on the margin of a program, you catch yourself good-humoredly trying to decipher these shrewd, if cryptic, little jottings. *Viz.*: "Their diagnoses are not nearly as crisp as those I find in my notes"; ". . . sounds like an inadequate description, but it's all I have on my notes, and it may conceivably be a very high compliment."

(6) The Kicker. An echo effect. "My reactions [included] an irritable feeling that eleven o'clock was past Miss Keim's bedtime," —and now the Kicker—"*not to mention my own.*" This type of thing practically writes itself. "She returns home. She should never have left home in the first place, --- ------- ------ -." *

(7) Wit of Omission. By calling attention to the fact that you are not going to say it, you suggest that there is something very funny you could say if only you wanted to. "A thought occurred to me at this point," you may say, when otherwise stymied, "but I think we had better not go into that."

(8) The Planned Colloquialism. The casual writer savors colloquialisms. This is not ordinary colloquial talk—nobody is more quickly provoked than the casual writer by ordinary usage. It is, rather, a playful descent into the vulgate. Phrases like "darn," "awfully," "as all getout," "mighty," and other folksy idioms are ideal. The less you would be likely to use the word normally yourself the more pointed the effect. Contrast is what you are after, for it is the facetious interplay of language levels—a blending, as it were, of the East Fifties and the Sticks—that gives the Casual Style its off-hand charm.

(9) Feigned Forgetfulness. Conversation gropes; it is full of "what I really meant was" and "maybe I should have added," backings and fillings and second thoughts of one kind or another. Writing is different; theoretically, ironing out second thoughts beforehand is one of the things writers are paid to do. In the Casual Style, however, it is exactly this exposure of the writer composing in public that makes it so casual. For the professional touch, then, ramble,

---

* "And neither should I."

rebuke yourself in print ("what I really meant, I guess"), and if you have something you feel you should have said earlier, don't say it earlier, but say later that you guess you should have said it earlier.

(10) The Subject-Apologizer, or Pardon-Me-for-Living. The Casual Stylist must always allow for the possibility that his subject is just as boring to the reader as it is to him. He may forestall this by seeming to have stumbled on it by accident, or by using phrases like: "If this is as much news to you as it is to me," or "This, in case you've been living in a cave lately, is. . . ."

(11) The Omitted Word. This all began modestly enough the day a *New Yorker* writer dropped the articles "the" and "a" from the initial sentence of an anecdote (*e.g.*, "Man we know told us"; "Fellow name of Brown"). Now even such resolutely lowbrow writers as Robert Ruark affect it, and they are applying it to any part of speech anywhere in the sentence. You can drop a pronoun ("Says they're shaped like pyramids"); verb ("You been away from soap opera the last couple of weeks?"); or preposition ("Far as glamour goes . . .").

(12) The Right Word. In the lexicon of the casual writer there are a dozen or so adjectives which in any context have, to borrow a phrase, a guaranteed charm. Attrition is high—"brittle," "febrile," "confected," for example, are at the end of the run. Ten, however, defy obsolescence: *antic, arch, blurred, chaste, chill, crisp, churlish, disheveled, dim, disembodied.*

They are good singly, but they are even better when used in tandem: *c.f.*, "In an arch, antic sort of way"; "In an arch, blurred sort of way;" "In an arch, crisp sort of way." And so on.

Finally, the most multi-purpose word of them all: "altogether." Frequently it is the companion of "charming" and "delightful," and in this coupling is indispensable to any kind of drama criticism. It can also modify the writer himself (*e.g.*, "Altogether, I think . . ."). Used best, however, it just floats, unbeholden to any other part of the sentence.

Once you have mastered these twelve devices, you too should be able to write as casually as all getout. At least it seems to me, though I may be wrong, that they convey an elusive archness which the crisp literary craftsman, in his own dim sort of way, should altogether cultivate these days. Come to think of it, the charm of the Casual Style is something less than clear to me, but we needn't go into *that*. Fellow I know from another magazine says this point of view best described as churlish. Not, of course, that it matters.

QUESTIONS ON CONTENT

1. Examine the twelve criteria of a Casual Style. Are there any duplications or overlappings?
2. Why does the author call the style he is describing "casual" instead of, say, "sophisticated"?
3. What relation does the final paragraph of this satire bear to what has preceded?

❧ *Calculating Machine*

E. B. WHITE

A publisher in Chicago has sent us a pocket calculating machine by which we may test our writing to see whether it is intelligible. The calculator was developed by General Motors, who, not satisfied with giving the world a Cadillac, now dream of bringing perfect understanding to men. The machine (it is simply a celluloid card with a dial) is called the Reading-Ease Calculator and shows four grades of "reading ease"—Very Easy, Easy, Hard, and Very Hard. You count your words and syllables, set the dial, and an indicator lets you know whether anybody is going to understand what you have written. An instruction book came with it, and after mastering the simple rules we lost no time in running a test on the instruction book itself, to see how *that* writer was doing. The poor fellow! His leading essay, the one on the front cover, tested Very Hard.

Our next step was to study the first phrase on the face of the calculator: "How to test Reading-Ease of written matter." There is, of course, no such thing as reading ease of written matter. There is the ease with which matter can be read, but that is a condition of the reader, not of the matter. Thus the inventors and distributors of this calculator get off to a poor start, with a Very Hard instruction book and a slovenly phrase. Already they have one foot caught in the brier patch of English usage.

Not only did the author of the instruction book score badly on the front cover, but inside the book he used the word "personalize"

From *The Second Tree from the Corner*, by Harper and Brothers. Copyright, 1951, by E. B. White. Reprinted by permission of the author and publisher.

in an essay on how to improve one's writing. A man who likes the word "personalize" is entitled to his choice, but we wonder whether he should be in the business of giving advice to writers. "Whenever possible," he wrote, "personalize your writing by directing it to the reader." As for us, we would as lief Simonize our grandmother as personalize our writing.

In the same envelope with the calculator, we received another training aid for writers—a booklet called "How to Write Better," by Rudolf Flesch. This, too, we studied, and it quickly demonstrated the broncolike ability of the English language to throw whoever leaps cocksurely into the saddle. The language not only can toss a rider but knows a thousand tricks for tossing him, each more gay than the last. Dr. Flesch stayed in the saddle only a moment or two. Under the heading "Think Before You Write," he wrote, "The main thing to consider is your *purpose* in writing. Why are you sitting down to write?" And echo answered: Because, sir, it is more comfortable than standing up.

Communication by the written word is a subtler (and more beautiful) thing than Dr. Flesch and General Motors imagine. They contend that the "average reader" is capable of reading only what tests Easy, and that the writer should write at or below this level. This is a presumptuous and degrading idea. There is no average reader, and to reach down toward this mythical character is to deny that each of us is on the way up, is ascending. ("Ascending," by the way, is a word Dr. Flesch advises writers to stay away from. Too unusual.)

It is our belief that no writer can improve his work until he discards the dulcet notion that the reader is feeble-minded, for writing is an act of faith, not a trick of grammar. Ascent is at the heart of the matter. A country whose writers are following a calculating machine downstairs is not ascending—if you will pardon the expression—and a writer who questions the capacity of the person at the other end of the line is not a writer at all, merely a schemer. The movies long ago decided that a wider communication could be achieved by a deliberate descent to a lower level, and they walked proudly down until they reached the cellar. Now they are groping for the light switch, hoping to find the way out.

We have studied Dr. Flesch's instructions diligently, but we return for guidance in these matters to an earlier American, who wrote with more patience, more confidence. "I fear chiefly," he wrote, "lest my expression may not be *extra-vagant* enough, may not wander far enough beyond the narrow limits of my daily experience, so as to be adequate to the truth of which I have been convinced. . . . Why level downward to our dullest perception always, and praise that as common sense? The commonest sense is the sense of men asleep, which they express by snoring."

Run that through your calculator! It may come out Hard, it may come out Easy. But it will come out whole, and it will last forever.

QUESTIONS ON CONTENT

1. Although the author is having fun at the expense of the language calculators, he clearly has a serious point to make. What is it? Discuss.
2. Why does the author consider writing down to readers "a presumptuous and degrading idea"?
3. Compare what is said here about Rudolf Flesch with what is said about him in "Putting Words to Work" and in "You, Too, Can Write the Casual Style."

SUGGESTIONS FOR PAPERS

Not many, perhaps not even one, of the students who entered college with you will ever become a creative writer—a novelist, playwright, or poet. Almost all members of your class, however, will have to write professionally, that is, as a part of the jobs for which they expect to be paid. This week it is more important than usual that you should refer in your paper to the selections in this chapter, that you should know thoroughly the arguments presented, for it will not be very useful at a later date to say, "I wish someone had told me how important English is."

1. State in your own words the main points in "Why Study English?" Does the article consider only the practical value of English? What sort of example is given of a report on a technical subject? What may be deduced from this example? Could General Electric have an ulterior motive in publishing an article of this sort?

2. State in your own words the main points in "Putting Words to Work." Explain carefully each point; that is, under what to avoid in writing, define such words as *cliché, redundancy, passive verbs,* and show *why* they should be avoided. Under what to strive for in

writing, examine the *you-attitude*, the problem of correctness, and so on. If your paper is to be short, concentrate on either what not to do or on what to do.

3. Compare "Why Study English?" and "Putting Words to Work." List and discuss all points made by both articles; or list and discuss the points which are exclusive to each article.

4. Maugham says: "I had little gift for metaphor." Comb his essay for all figures of speech and then discuss the accuracy of this statement.

5. "Writing is learned rather than taught" ("Putting Words to Work"). Describe Maugham's experience, his search for a good style, and his own observations about learning to write. Use your own experiences with writing as a basis for commenting on Maugham's findings.

6. Read twenty-five pages of prose from any one of the writers mentioned by Maugham; then make tentative comments on all that Maugham has said about the author's style.

7. Select three of the twelve points made in the satire, "You, Too, Can Write the Casual Style," and fully explain them. Define terms.

8. Define *satire*. Show how "You, Too, Can Write the Casual Style" qualifies as satire. How does the final paragraph point up all that has gone before?

9. Compare E. B. White's "Calculating Machine" with what is said about reading formulas in "Putting Words to Work."

SOME TITLES FOR PAPERS

1. Industry's Concern with English
2. Business and English
3. Success Without English?
4. The Basic Value of English
5. English: Learned, not Taught
6. What to Avoid in Writing
7. What to Cultivate in Writing
8. Reading Helps Writing
9. Obscurity versus Clarity
10. I Like (Dislike) English
11. The Off-Hand Style
12. English: A Most Practical Subject
13. Why Write Down to People?
14. No Easy Road to Easy Writing
15. The Greatest Help to My Writing
16. No Substitute for Practice

❧ *JOBS*

You may know already exactly the job you want. You may not. The great variety of possibilities may seem overwhelming. How is one to reduce all jobs to some sort of order? Richard Cabot has attempted an answer to this question in "The Call of the Job." Through isolating seven qualities of all good jobs, he has provided a way to measure your job. Peter Drucker in "How To Be an Employee" tells how to reach a decision on what kind of an employee to be. His emphasis on the importance of skill in writing will remind you of the first two selections in Chapter 4. Drucker's article when considered in conjunction with Cabot's provides a ready means for determining the sort of place you should hope to find when you finish college. You will find it instructive to note the logical organization of these two articles.

Robert Frost's poem, "Two Tramps in Mud Time," emphasizes the philosophy of work, the object of which is to unite avocation and vocation, "love and need." You may feel that the poem, particularly in the last sixteen lines, is also an essay on "the call of the job."

❧ *The Call of the Job*

Richard Cabot

A camper starting into the woods on his annual vacation under-takes with enthusiasm the familiar task of carrying a Saranac boat upon a shoulder yoke. The pressure of the yoke on his shoulders feels as good as the grasp of an old friend's hand. The tautening of his muscles to the strain of carrying seems to gird up his loins and true up his whole frame. With the spring of the ground beneath him and the elastic rebound of the boat on its springy yoke, he seems to dance over the ground between two enlivening rhythms. It is pure fun.

In the course of half a mile or so, the carry begins to feel like work. The pleasant, snug fit of the yoke has become a very respecta-ble burden, cheerfully borne for the sake of the object in view, but not pleasant. The satisfaction of the carry is now something antici-pated, no longer grasped in the present. The job is well worth while, but it is no joke. It will feel good to reach the end and set the boat down.

Finally, if in about ten minutes more there is still no sight of the end, no blue sparkling glimmer of distant water low down among the trees, the work becomes drudgery. Will it ever end? Are we on the right trail at all? Is it worth while to go on?

Perhaps not, but to stop means painfully lowering the boat to the ground and later heaving it up again, which is the worst task of all —worse than going on as we are. So we hang to it, but now in scowling, stumbling, swearing misery, that edges always nearer to revolt.

In varying proportions every one's life mingles the experiences of that carry. At its best and for a few, work becomes play, at least for blessed jewel-like moments. By the larger number it is seen not a joy but as a tolerable burden, borne for the sake of the chil-dren's education, the butter on the daily bread, the hope of pro-motion. Finally, for the submerged fraction of humanity who are forced to labor without choice and almost from childhood, life seems

From *The Atlantic Monthly*, CXII (November 1913), 599–603. Reprinted by permission of *The Atlantic Monthly*.

drudgery, borne simply because they cannot stop without still greater misery. They are committed to it, as to a prison, and they cannot get out.

It is not often, I believe, that a whole life is possessed by any one of these elements,—play, work, or drudgery. Work usually makes up the larger part of life, with play and drudgery sprinkled in. Some of us at most seasons, all of us at some seasons, find work a galling yoke to which we have to submit blindly or angrily for a time, but with revolt in our hearts. Yet I have rarely seen drudgery so overwhelming as to crush out altogether the play of humor and good fellowship during the day's toil as well as after it.

In play you have what you want. In work you know what you want and believe that you are serving or approaching it. In drudgery no desired object is in sight; blind forces push you on.

In all work and all education the worker should be in touch with the distant sources of interest, else he is being trained to slavery, not to self-government and self-respect.

Present good, future good, no good,—these possibilities are mingled in the crude ore which we ordinarily call work. Out of that we must smelt, if we can, the pure metal of a vocation fit for the spirit of man. The crude mass of "work" as it exists to-day in mines, stores, railroads, schoolrooms, studies, and ships, contains elements that should be abolished, elements that are hard, but no harder than we need to call out the best of us, and here and there a nugget of pure delight.

Defined in this way, work is always, I suppose, an acquired taste. For its rewards are not immediate, but come in foretastes and aftertastes. It involves postponement and waiting. In the acquisition of wealth, economists rightly distinguish labor and waiting; but in another sense labor is always waiting. You work for your picture of your log-house because you want it, and because it cannot be had just for the asking. It awaits you in a future visible only to imagination. Into the further realization of that future you can penetrate only by work; meantime you must wait for your reward.

Further, this future is never perfectly certain. There is many a slip between the cup and the lip, and even when gross accidents are avoided, your goal,—your promotion, your home, the degree for which you have worked,—usually do not turn out to be what you have pictured them. This variation you learn to expect, to discount, perhaps to enjoy, beforehand, if you are a trained worker, just because you have been trained in faith. For work is always justified by faith. Faith, holding the substance (not the details) of things unseen, keeps us at our tasks. We have faith that our efforts will someday reach their goal, and that this goal will be something like we expected. But no literalism will serve us here. If we are willing to accept nothing but the very pattern of our first desires, we are forever disappointed in work and soon grow slack in it. In the more fortunate of us, the love of work includes a love of the unexpected, and finds a pleasant spice of adventure in the difference between what we work for and what we actually get.

Yet this working faith is not pure speculation. It includes a fore-taste of the satisfaction to come. We plunge into it as we jump into a cold bath, not because the present sensations are altogether sweet, but because they are mingled with a dawning awareness of the glow to follow. We do our work happily because the future is alive in the present,—not like a ghost but like a leader.

Where do we get this capacity to incarnate the future and to feel it swelling within us as a present inspiration? The power to go in pursuit of the future with seven-leagued boots or magic carpets can hardly be acquired or even longed for until we have had some actual experience of its rewards. We seem, then, to be caught in one of those circles which may turn out to be either vicious or virtuous. In the beginning something, or somebody, must magically entice us into doing a bit of work. Having done that bit, we can see the treasure of its results; these results will in turn spur us to redoubled efforts, and so once more to increased rewards. Given the initial miracle and we are soon established in the habit and in the enjoyment of work.

But there is a self-maintaining circularity in disease, idleness, and sloth, as well as in work, virtue, and health. Until we make the exertion (despite present pain and a barren outlook) we cannot taste the delightful result, or feel the spur to further effort. The wheel is at the dead point! Why should it ever move?

Probably some of us are moved at first by the leap of an elemental instinct in our muscles, which act before and beyond our conscious reason. Other people are tempted into labor by the irrational con-tagion of example. We want to be "in it" with the rest of our gang, or to win some one's approval. So we get past the dead point,—often a most alarming point to parents and teachers,—and once in motion, keep at it by the circular process just described.

Various auxiliary motives reinforce the ordinary energies of work. Here I will allude only to one—a queer pleasure in the mere stretch and strain of our muscles. If we are physically fresh and not worried, there is a grim exhilaration, a sort of frowning delight, in taking up a heavy load and feeling that our strength is adequate to it. It seems paradoxical to enjoy a discomfort, but the paradox is now getting familiar. For modern psychologists have satisfactorily bridged the chasm between pleasure and pain, so that we can now conceive what athletes and German poets have long felt, the delight in a complex of agreeable and disagreeable elements. In work we do not get as far as the "selige Schmerzen" so familiar in German lyrics, but we welcome difficulties, risks, and physical strains because (if we can easily conquer them) they add a spice to life,— a spice of play in the midst of labor.

Work gets itself started, then, by the contagion of somebody else's activity or by an explosion of animal energies within us. After a few turns of the work-rest cycle we begin to get a foretaste of rewards. A flavor of enjoyment appears in the midst of strain. Habit then takes hold and carries us along until the taste for work is definitely acquired.

In the crude job as we get it there is much rubbish. For work is a very human product. It is no better than we have made it, and even when it is redeemed from brutal drudgery it is apt to be scarred and warped by our stupidities and our ineptitudes. Out of the rough-hewn masses in which work comes to us it is our business—it is civilization's business—to shape a vocation fit for man. We shall have to remake it again and again; meantime, before we reject what we now have, it is worth while to see what we want.

What (besides better hours, better wages, healthier conditions) are the points of a good job? Imagine a sensible man looking for a satisfactory work, a vocational adviser guiding novices toward the best available occupation and a statesman trying to mold the industrial world somewhat nearer to the heart's desire,—what should they try for? Physical and financial standards determine what we get *out* of a job. But what shall we get *in* it? Much or little, I think, according to its fitness or unfitness for our personality,—a factor much neglected nowadays.

Among the points of a good job I shall name seven:—1. Difficulty and crudeness enough to call out our latent powers of mastery. 2. Variety and initiative balanced by monotony and supervision. 3. A boss. 4. A chance to achieve, to build something and to recognize what we have done. 5. A title and a place which is ours. 6. Connection with some institution, some firm, or some cause, which we can loyally serve. 7. Honorable and pleasant relations with our comrades in work.

Fulfil these conditions and work is one of the best things in life. Let me describe them more fully.

We want a chance to subdue. We want to encounter the raw and crude. Before the commercial age, war, hunting, and agriculture gave us this foil. We want it still, and for the lack of it often find our work too soft.

Of course, we can easily get an over-dose of crude resistance. A good job should offer us a fair chance of our winning. We have no desire to be crushed without a struggle. But we are all the better pleased if the fish makes a good fight before he yields.

Not only in the wilderness, but wherever we deal with raw material, our hands meet adventures. Every bit of wood and stone, every stream and every season has its own tantalizing but fascinating individuality, and as long as we have health and courage, these novelties strike not as a frustration but as a challenge.

Even in half-tamed products, like leather or steel, there are, experts tell me, incalculable variations which keep us on the alert if we are still close enough to the elemental to feel its fascinating materiality. When a clerk sells drygoods over the counter, I suppose he has to nourish his frontiersman's spirit chiefly in foiling the wily bargain-hunter or trapping the incautious countryman. But I doubt if the work is as interesting as a carpenter's or a plumber's. It reeks so strong of civilization and the "finished product" that it often sends us back to the woods to seek in a "vacation" that touch with the elemental which should properly form part of daily work.

We want both monotony and variety. The monotony of work is perhaps the quality of which we complain most, and often justifiably. Yet monotony is really demanded by almost everyone. Even children cry for it, though in doses smaller than those which suit their elders. Your secretary does not like her work, if you put more than her regular portion of variety into it. She does not want to be constantly undertaking new tasks, adapting herself to new situations. She wants some regularity in her traveling, some plain stretches in which she can get up speed and feel quantity of accomplishment,— that is, she wants a reasonable amount of monotony. Change and novelty in work are apt to demand fresh thought, and reduce our speed.

Naturally, there is a limit to this. We want some variety, some independence in our work. But we can easily get too much. I have heard as many complaints and felt in myself as many objections against variety as against monotony. I have seen and felt as much discontent with "uncharted freedom" as with irksome restraint. Bewilderment, a sense of incompetence and of rudderless drifting, are never far off from any one of us in our work. There is in all of us something that likes to trot along in harness,—not too tight or galling, to be sure,—but still in guidance and with support. That makes us show our best paces.

Nor is there anything slavish or humiliating in this. It is simply the admission that we are not ready at every moment to be original, inventive, creative. We have found out the immense strain and cost of fresh thinking. We are certain that we were not born to be at it perpetually. We want some rest in our work, some relief from high tension. Monotony supplies that relief. Moreover the rhythmic and habitual elements in us (ancient labor-saving devices) demand their representation. To do something again and again as the trees, the birds, and our own hearts do, is a fundamental need which demands and receives satisfaction in work as well as in play.

For the tragedies and abominations, the slaveries and degradations of manual labor we cannot put all the blame on the large element of monotony and repetition which such labor often contains. We should revolt and destroy any work that was not somewhat monotonous. But the point is that work should offer to each worker as much variety and independence as he has originality and genius, no more and no less. Give us either more or less than our share and we are miserable. We can be crushed and overdriven by too much responsibility, as well as by too little. Our initiative, as well as our docility, can be overworked.

We want a boss, especially in heavy or monotonous labor. Most monotonous work is of the sort that is cut out and supplied ready to hand. This implies that some one else plans and directs it. In so far as we want monotony, therefore, we want to be driven, though not overdriven, by a boss. If we are to do the pulling some one else should hold the reins. When I am digging my wife's garden beds I want her to specify where they shall go. We all want a master of some kind, and most of us want a master in human shape. The more manual our work is, the more we want him. Boatmen poling a scow through a creek need some one to steer and tell them which should push harder as they turn the bends of the stream. The steersman may be chosen by lot or each may steer in turn, but some boss we must have, for when we are poling we cannot well steer and we don't want the strain of trying fruitlessly to do both. This example is typical of the world's work. It demands to be bossed, and it is more efficient, even more original when it is bossed,—just enough!

Monotony, then, and bossing we need, but in our own quantity and also of our own kind. For there are different kinds (as well as different doses) and some are better than others. For example, to go to the same place of work every day is a monotony that simplifies life advantageously for most of us, but to teach the same subject over and over again is for most teachers an evil, though it may be just now a necessary evil.

We must try to distinguish. When we delight in thinking ourselves abused, or allow ourselves the luxury of grumbling, we often single out monotony as the target of our wrath. But we must not take all complaints (our own or other people's) at their face value. A coat is a misfit if it is too big or too small, or if it puckers in the wrong place. A job can be a misfit in twenty different ways and can be complained of in as many different tones. Let us be clear about this. If our discontent is as divine as it feels, it is not because all monotony is evil, but because our particular share and kind of monotony has proved to be a degrading waste of energy.

We want to see the product of our work. The bridge we planned, the house we built, the shoes we cobbled, help us to get before ourselves and so to realize more than a moment's worth of life and effort. The impermanence of each instant's thought, the transcience of every flush of effort tends to make our lives seem shadowy even to ourselves. Our memory is like a sieve through which most that we pick up runs back like sand. But in work we find refuge and stability, because in the accumulated product of many days' labor we can build up and present at last to our own sight the durable structure of what we meant to do. Then we can believe that our intentions, our hopes, our plans, our daily food and drink, have not passed through us for nothing, for we have funded their worth in some tangible achievement which outlasts them.

Further, such external proofs of our efficiency win us not only self-respect, but the recognition of others. We need something to show for ourselves, something to prove that our dreams are not impotent. Work gives us the means to prove it.

I want to acknowledge here my agreement in the charge often brought against modern factory labor,—namely that since no workman plans or finishes his product, no one can recognize his product, take pride in it or see its defects. Even when factory labor is well paid, its impersonal and wholesale merging of the man in the machine goes to make it unfit for men and women.

We want a handle to our name. Everyone has a right to the distinction which titles of nobility are meant to give, but it is from our work that we should get them. The grocer, the trapper, the night-watchman, the cook, is a person fit to be recognized, both by his own timid self and by the rest of the world. In time the title of our job comes to stand for us, to enlarge our personality and to give us permanence. Thus it supplements the standing which is given us by our product. To "hold down a job" gives us a place in the world, something approaching the home for which in some form or other everyone longs. "Have you any place for me?" we ask with eagerness, for until we find "a place" we are tramps,—men without a country.

A man with a job has, at least in embryo, the kind of recognition which we all crave. He has won membership in a club that he wants to belong to and especially hates to be left out of. To be in it as a member in full standing gives a taste of self-respect and self-confidence.

We want congeniality in our fellow workmen. One of the few non-physical "points" which people have already learned to look for in selecting work, is the temper and character of the "boss." Men, and especially women, care almost as much about this as about the hours and wages of the jobs. Young physicians will work in a laboratory at starvation wages for the sake of being near a great teacher, even though he rarely notices them. The congeniality of fellow workmen is almost as important as the temper of the boss. Two unfriendly stenographers in a single room will often give up their work and take lower wages elsewhere in order to escape each other.

All this is so obvious to those who look for jobs that I wonder why so few employers have noticed it. The housewives who keep their servants, the manufacturers who avoid strikes, are not always those who pay the best wages and offer the best conditions of work. The human facts—the personal relations of employer and employee —are often disregarded, but always at the employer's peril. The personal factor is as great as the economic in the industrial unrest of to-day. Are not even the "captains of industry" beginning to wake up to this fact?

Payment can be given a working man only for what some other man might have done,—because his pay is fixed by estimate of "what the work is worth," that is, what you can get other people to do it for. Hence you never pay anyone for what he individually does, but for what "a man like him," that fictitious being, that supposedly fair specimen of his type and trade, can be expected to do.

The man himself you cannot pay. Yet anyone who does his work well or gets satisfaction out of it, puts himself into it. Moreover he does things that he cannot be given credit for, finishes parts that no one else will notice. Even a mediocre amateur musician knows that the best parts of his playing, his personal tributes to the genius of the composer whom he plays, are heard by no one but himself and "the God of things as they are." There might be bitterness in the thought that in our work we get paid or praised only for what is not particularly ours, while the work that we put our hearts into is not recognized or rewarded. But in the struggle for spiritual existence we adapt ourselves to the unappreciative features of our environment and learn to look elsewhere for recognition. We do not expect people to pay us for our best. We look to the approval of conscience, to the light of our ideal seen more clearly when our work is good, or to the judgment of God. Our terms differ more than our tendencies. The essential point is that for appreciation of our best work we look to a Judge more just and keen-sighted than our paymaster. . . .

QUESTIONS ON CONTENT

1. Differentiate *play, work*, and *drudgery*.
2. "For work is always justified by faith." Explain.
3. Work produces pleasure; pleasure is a stimulant to more work; more work, more pleasure, and so on. How does the process get started?
4. The phrase *selige Schmerzen* means blissful melancholy or woe. What do athletes and German poets know about this odd combination?
5. Why are leather and steel called "half-tamed products"?
6. Is monotony the worst feature of a job? Or variety? Explain.
7. What connection is there between monotony and the need for a boss?
8. What is meant by the phrase "merging of the man in the machine"? Is there another name for this?
9. Which one of the seven characteristics of a job does the author fail to discuss?

10. "Payment may be given a working man only for what some
other man might have done." Explain. Is this still an acceptable
theory of wages?

❧ *Two Tramps in Mud Time*

ROBERT FROST

Out of the mud two strangers came
And caught me splitting wood in the yard.
And one of them put me off my aim
By hailing cheerily 'Hit them hard!'
I knew pretty well why he dropped behind   5
And let the other go on a way.
I knew pretty well what he had in mind:
He wanted to take my job for pay.

Good blocks of beech it was I split,
As large around as the chopping block;   10
And every piece I squarely hit
Fell splinterless as a cloven rock.
The blows that a life of self-control
Spares to strike for the common good
That day, giving a loose to my soul,   15
I spent on the unimportant wood.

The sun was warm but the wind was chill.
You know how it is with an April day
When the sun is out and the wind is still,
You're one month on in the middle of May.   20
But if you so much as dare to speak,
A cloud comes over the sunlit arch,
A wind comes off a frozen peak,
And you're two months back in the middle of March.

A bluebird comes tenderly up to alight   25
And turns to the wind to unruffle a plume

From *Complete Poems of Robert Frost* by Robert Frost. Copyright, 1916,
1923, 1949, by Henry Holt and Company, Inc. Copyright, 1936, 1942, 1943, by
Robert Frost.

His song so pitched as not to excite
A single flower as yet to bloom.
It is snowing a flake: and he half knew
Winter was only playing possum.   30
Except in color he isn't blue,
But he wouldn't advise a thing to blossom.

The water for which we may have to look
In summertime with a witching-wand,
In every wheelrut's now a brook,   35
In every print of a hoof a pond.
Be glad of water, but don't forget
The lurking frost in the earth beneath
That will steal forth after the sun is set
And show on the water its crystal teeth.   40

The time when most I loved my task
These two must make me love it more
By coming with what they came to ask.
You'd think I never had felt before
The weight of an ax-head poised aloft,   45
The grip on earth of outspread feet,
The life of muscles rocking soft
And smooth and moist in vernal heat.

Out of the woods two hulking tramps
(From sleeping God knows where last night,   50
But not long since in the lumber camps).
They thought all chopping was theirs of right.
Men of the woods and lumberjacks,
They judged me by their appropriate tool.
Except as a fellow handled an ax,   55
They had no way of knowing a fool.

Nothing on either side was said.
They knew they had but to stay their stay
And all their logic would fill my head:
As that I had no right to play   60
With what was another man's work for gain.
My right might be love but theirs was need.
And where the two exist in twain
Theirs was the better right—agreed.

But yield who will to their separation,   65
My object in living is to unite
My avocation and my vocation
As my two eyes make one in sight.
Only where love and need are one,
And the work is play for mortal stakes,   70
Is the deed ever really done
For Heaven and the future's sakes.

QUESTIONS ON CONTENT

1. Explain the puns in the title of this poem. What is the rime scheme? How many syllables in each line?
2. What motivation for the wood-chopping is implied by lines 13–16?
3. Explain line 24.
4. Paraphrase the lines about the bluebird.
5. Compare lines 44–48 with the statement in Cabot's "The Call of the Job" that man wants a chance to subdue, to get close to the elemental.
6. What is the "logic" in the two tramps' silence (see line 59)?
7. Explain "love and need" in relation to one's work. Can you relate this conception to any part of Cabot's "The Call of the Job"?
8. Did the tramps get the job? Explain.

❧ *How to Be an Employee*

PETER F. DRUCKER

Most of you graduating today will be employees all your working life, working for somebody else and for a pay check. And so will most, if not all, of the thousands of other young Americans graduating this year in all the other schools and colleges across the country.

Ours has become a society of employees. A hundred years or so ago only one out of every five Americans at work was employed, i.e., worked for somebody else. Today only one out of five is not employed but working for himself. And where fifty years ago "being

Reprinted from the May 1952 issue of *Fortune* Magazine by special permission of the Editors; copyright 1952 Time Inc.

employed" meant working as a factory laborer or as a farmhand, the employee of today is increasingly a middle-class person with a substantial formal education, holding a professional or management job requiring intellectual and technical skills. Indeed, two things have characterized American society during these last fifty years: the middle and upper classes have become employees; and middle-class and upper-class employees have been the fastest-growing groups in our working population—growing so fast that the industrial worker, that oldest child of the Industrial Revolution, has been losing in numerical importance despite the expansion of industrial production.

This is one of the most profound social changes any country has ever undergone. It is, however, a perhaps even greater change for the individual young man about to start. Whatever he does, in all likelihood he will do it as an employee; wherever he aims, he will have to try to reach it through being an employee.

Yet you will find little if anything written on what it is to be an employee. You can find a great deal of very dubious advice on how to get a job or how to get a promotion. You can also find a good deal on work in a chosen field, whether it be metallurgy or salesmanship, the machinist's trade or bookkeeping. Every one of these trades requires different skills, sets different standards, and requires a different preparation. Yet they all have employeeship in common. And increasingly, especially in the large business or in government, employeeship is more important to success than the special professional knowledge or skill. Certainly more people fail because they do not know the requirements of being an employee than because they do not adequately possess the skills of their trade; the higher you climb the ladder, the more you get into administrative or executive work, the greater the emphasis on ability to work within the organization rather than on technical competence or professional knowledge.

Being an employee is thus the one common characteristic of most careers today. The special profession or skill is visible and clearly defined; and a well-laid-out sequence of courses, degrees, and jobs leads to it. But being an employee is the foundation. And it is much more difficult to prepare for it. Yet there is no recorded information on the art of being an employee.

The Basic Skill

The first question we might ask is: what can you learn in college that will help you in being an employee? The schools teach a great many things of value to the future accountant, the future doctor, or the future electrician. Do they also teach anything of value to the future employee? The answer is: "Yes—they teach the one thing that it is perhaps most valuable for the future employee to know. But very few students bother to learn it."

This one basic skill is the ability to organize and express ideas in writing and speaking.

As an employee you work with and through people. This means that your success as an employee—and I am talking of much more here than getting promoted—will depend on your ability to communicate with people and to present your own thoughts and ideas to them so they will both understand what you are driving at and be persuaded. The letter, the report or memorandum, the ten-minute spoken "presentation" to a committee are basic tools of the employee.

If you work as a soda jerker you will, of course, not need much skill in expressing yourself to be effective. If you work on a machine your ability to express yourself will be of little importance. But as soon as you move one step up from the bottom, your effectiveness depends on your ability to reach others through the spoken or the written word. And the further away your job is from manual work, the larger the organization of which you are an employee, the more important it will be that you know how to convey your thoughts in writing or speaking. In the very large organization, whether it is the government, the large business corporation, or the Army, this ability to express oneself is perhaps the most important of all the skills a man can possess.

Of course, skill in expression is not enough by itself. You must have something to say in the first place. The popular picture of the engineer, for instance, is that of a man who works with a slide rule, T square, and compass. And engineering students reflect this picture in their attitude toward the written word as something quite irrelevant to their jobs. But the effectiveness of the engineer—and with it his usefulness—depends as much on his ability to make other people understand his work as it does on the quality of the work itself.

Expressing one's thoughts is one skill that the school can really teach, especially to people born without natural writing or speaking talent. Many other skills can be learned later—in this country there are literally thousands of places that offer training to adult people at work. But the foundations for skill in expression have to be laid early: an interest in and an ear for language; experience in organizing ideas and data, in brushing aside the irrelevant, in wedding outward form and inner content into one structure; and above all, the habit of verbal expression. If you do not lay these foundations during your school years, you may never have an opportunity again.

If you were to ask me what strictly vocational courses there are in the typical college curriculum, my answer—now that the good old habit of the "theme a day" has virtually disappeared—would be: the writing of poetry and the writing of short stories. Not that I expect many of you to become poets or short-story writers—far from it. But these two courses offer the easiest way to obtain some skill in expression. They force one to be economical with language. They force one to organize thought. They demand of one that he give meaning to every word. They train the ear for language, its meaning, its precision, its overtones—and its pitfalls. Above all they force one to write.

I know very well that the typical employer does not understand this as yet, and that he may look with suspicion on a young college graduate who has majored, let us say, in short-story writing. But the same employer will complain—and with good reason—that the young men whom he hires when they get out of college do not know how to write a simple report, do not know how to tell a simple story, and are in fact virtually illiterate. And he will conclude—rightly—that the young men are not really effective, and certainly not employees who are likely to go very far.

The next question to ask is: what kind of employee should you be? Pay no attention to what other people tell you. This is one question only you can answer. It involves a choice in four areas—a choice you alone can make, and one you cannot easily duck. But to make the choice you must first have tested yourself in the world of jobs for some time.

Here are the four decisions—first in brief outline, then in more detail:

1. Do you belong in a job calling primarily for faithfulness in the

performance of routine work and promising security? Or do you belong in a job that offers a challenge to imagination and ingenuity —with the attendant penalty for failure?

2. Do you belong in a large organization or in a small organization? Do you work better through channels or through direct contacts? Do you enjoy more being a small cog in a big and powerful machine or a big wheel in a small machine?

3. Should you start at the bottom and try to work your way up, or should you try to start near the top? On the lowest rung of the promotional ladder, with its solid and safe footing but also with a very long climb ahead? Or on the aerial trapeze of "a management trainee," or some other staff position close to management?

4. Finally, are you going to be more effective and happy as a specialist or as a "generalist," that is, in an administrative job?

Let me spell out what each of these four decisions involves:

1: *Is "Security" for You?*

The decision between secure routine work and insecure work challenging the imagination and ingenuity is the one decision most people find easiest to make. You know very soon what kind of person you are. Do you find real satisfaction in the precision, order, and system of a clearly laid-out job? Do you prefer the security not only of knowing what your work is today and what it is going to be tomorrow, but also security in your job, in your relationship to the people above, below, and next to you, and economic security? Or are you one of those people who tend to grow impatient with anything that looks like a "routine" job? These people are usually able to live in a confused situation in which their relations to the people around them are neither clear nor stable. And they tend to pay less attention to economic security, find it not too upsetting to change jobs, etc.

There is, of course, no such black-and-white distinction between people. The man who can do only painstaking detail work and has no imagination is not much good for anything. Neither is the self-styled "genius" who has nothing but grandiose ideas and no capacity for rigorous application to detail. But in practically everybody I have ever met there is a decided leaning one way or the other.

The difference is one of basic personality. It is not too much affected by a man's experiences; he is likely to be born with the one or the other. The need for economic security is often as not an outgrowth of a need for psychological security rather than a phenomenon of its own. But precisely because the difference is one of basic temperament, the analysis of what kind of temperament you possess is so vital. A man might be happy in work for which he has little *aptitude;* he might be quite successful in it. But he can be neither happy nor successful in a job for which he is *temperamentally* unfitted.

You hear a great many complaints today about the excessive security-consciousness of our young people. My complaint is the opposite: in the large organizations especially there are not enough job opportunities for those young people who need challenge and risk. Jobs in which there is greater emphasis on conscientious performance of well-organized duties rather than on imagination—especially for the beginner—are to be found, for instance, in the inside jobs in banking or insurance, which normally offer great job security but not rapid promotion or large pay. The same is true of most government work, of the railroad industry, particularly in the clerical and engineering branches, and of most public utilities. The book-keeping and accounting areas, especially in the larger companies, are generally of this type too—though a successful comptroller is an accountant with great management and business imagination.

At the other extreme are such areas as buying, selling, and advertising, in which the emphasis is on adaptability, on imagination, and on a desire to do new and different things. In those areas, by and large, there is little security, either personal or economic. The rewards, however, are high and come more rapidly. Major premium on imagination—though of a different kind and coupled with dogged persistence on details—prevails in most research and engineering work. Jobs in production, as supervisor or executive, also demand much adaptability and imagination.

Contrary to popular belief, very small business requires, above all, close attention to daily routine. Running a neighborhood drugstore or a small grocery store, or being a toy jobber, is largely attention to details. But in very small business there is also room for quite a few people of the other personality type—the innovator or imaginer. If successful, a man of this type soon ceases to be in a very small business. For the real innovator there is, still, no more promising opportunity in this country than that of building a large out of a very small business.

2: *Big Company or Small?*

Almost as important is the decision between working for a large and for a small organization. The difference is perhaps not so great as that between the secure, routine job and the insecure, imaginative job; but the wrong decision can be equally serious.

There are two basic differences between the large and the small enterprise. In the small enterprise you operate primarily through personal contacts. In the large enterprise you have established "policies," "channels" of organization, and fairly rigid procedures. In the small enterprise you have, moreover, immediate effectiveness in a very small area. You can see the effect of your work and of your decisions right away, once you are a little bit above the ground floor. In the large enterprise even the man at the top is only a cog in a big machine. To be sure, his actions affect a much greater area than the actions and decisions of the man in the small organization, but his effectiveness is remote, indirect, and elusive. In a small and even in a middle-sized business you are normally exposed to all kinds of experiences, and expected to do a great many things without too much help or guidance. In the large organization you are normally taught one thing thoroughly. In the small one the danger is of becoming a jack-of-all-trades and master of none. In the large one it is of becoming the man who knows more and more about less and less.

There is one other important thing to consider: do you derive a deep sense of satisfaction from being a member of a well-known organization—General Motors, the Bell Telephone System, the government? Or is it more important to you to be a well-known and important figure within your own small pond? There is a basic difference between the satisfaction that comes from being a member of a large, powerful, and generally known organization, and the one that comes from being a member of a family; between impersonal grandeur and personal—often much too personal—intimacy; between life in a small cubicle on the top floor of a skyscraper and life in a crossroads gas station.

3: *Start at the Bottom, or . . . ?*

You may well think it absurd to say that anyone has a choice between beginning at the bottom and beginning near the top. And indeed I do not mean that you have any choice between beginner's jobs and, let us say, a vice presidency at General Electric. But you do have a choice between a position at the bottom of the hierarchy and a staff position that is outside the hierarchy but in view of the top. It is an important choice.

In every organization even the smallest, there are positions that, while subordinate, modestly paid, and usually filled with young and beginning employees, nonetheless are not at the bottom. There are positions as assistant to one of the bosses; there are positions as private secretary; there are liaison positions for various departments; and there are positions in staff capacities, in industrial engineering, in cost accounting, in personnel, etc. Every one of these gives a view of the whole rather than of only one small area. Every one of them normally brings the holder into the deliberations and discussions of the people at the top, if only as a silent audience or perhaps only as an errand boy. Every one of these positions is a position "near the top," however humble and badly paid it may be.

On the other hand the great majority of beginner's jobs are at the bottom, where you begin in a department or in a line of work in the lowest-paid and simplest function, and where you are expected to work your way up as you acquire more skill and more judgment.

Different people belong in these two kinds of jobs. In the first place, the job "near the top" is insecure. You are exposed to public view. Your position is ambiguous; by yourself you are a nobody— but you reflect the boss's status; in a relatively short time you may even speak for the boss. You may have real power and influence. In today's business and government organization the hand that writes the memo rules the committee; and the young staff man usually writes the memos, or at least the first draft. But for that very reason everybody is jealous of you. You are a youngster who has been admitted to the company of his betters, and is therefore expected to show unusual ability and above all unusual discretion and judgment. Good performance in such a position is often the key to rapid advancement. But to fall down may mean the end of all hopes of ever getting anywhere within the organization.

At the bottom, on the other hand, there are very few opportunities for making serious mistakes. You are amply protected by the whole apparatus of authority. The job itself is normally simple, requiring little judgment, discretion, or initiative. Even excellent performance in such a job is unlikely to speed promotion. But one also has to fall down in a rather spectacular fashion for it to be noticed by anyone but one's immediate superior.

4: Specialist or "Generalist"?

There are a great many careers in which the increasing emphasis is on specialization. You find these careers in engineering and in accounting, in production, in statistical work, and in teaching. But there is an increasing demand for people who are able to take in a great area at a glance, people who perhaps do not know too much about any one field—though one should always have one area of real competence. There is, in other words, a demand for people who are capable of seeing the forest rather than the trees, of making over-all judgments. And these "generalists" are particularly needed for administrative positions where it is their job to see that other people do the work, where they have to plan for other people, to organize other people's work, to initiate it and appraise it.

The specialist understands one field; his concern is with technique, tools, media. He is a "trained" man; and his educational background is properly technical or professional. The generalist—and especially the administrator—deals with people; his concern is with leadership, with planning, with direction giving, and with co-ordination. He is an "educated" man; and the humanities are his strongest foundation. Very rarely is a specialist capable of being an administrator. And very rarely is a good generalist also a good specialist in a particular field. Any organization needs both kinds of people, though different organizations need them in different ratios. It is your job to find out, during your apprenticeship, into which of those two job categories you fit, and to plan your career accordingly.

Your first job may turn out to be the right job for you—but this is pure accident. Certainly you should not change jobs constantly or people will become suspicious—rightly—of your ability to hold any job. At the same time you must not look upon the first job as the final job; it is primarily a training job, an opportunity to analyze yourself and your fitness for being an employee.

The Importance of Being Fired

In fact there is a great deal to be said for being fired from the first job. One reason is that it is rarely an advantage to have started as an office boy in the organization; far too many people will still consider you a "green kid" after you have been there for twenty-five years. But the major reason is that getting fired from the first job is the least painful and the least damaging way to learn how to take a setback. And whom the Lord loveth he teacheth early how to take a setback.

Nobody has ever lived, I daresay, who has not gone through a period when everything seemed to have collapsed and when years of work and life seemed to have gone up in smoke. No one can be spared this experience; but one can be prepared for it. The man who has been through earlier setbacks has learned that the world has not come to an end because he lost his job—not even in a depression. He has learned that he will somehow survive. He has learned, above all, that the way to behave in such a setback is not to collapse himself. But the man who comes up against it for the first time when he is forty-five is quite likely to collapse for good. For the things that people are apt to do when they receive the the first nasty blow may destroy a mature man with a family, whereas a youth of twenty-five bounces right back.

Obviously you cannot contrive to get yourself fired. But you can always quit. And it is perhaps even more important to have quit once than to have been fired once. The man who walks out on his own volition acquires an inner independence that he will never quite lose.

When to Quit

To know when to quit is therefore one of the most important things—particularly for the beginner. For on the whole young people have a tendency to hang on to the first job long beyond the time when they should have quit for their own good.

One should quit when self-analysis shows that the job is the wrong job—that, say, it does not give the security and routine one requires, that it is a small-company rather than a big-organization job, that it is at bottom rather than near the top, a specialist's rather than a generalist's job, etc. One should quit if the job demands behavior one considers morally indefensible, or if the whole atmosphere of the place is morally corrupting—if, for instance, only yes men and flatterers are tolerated.

One should also quit if the job does not offer training one needs either in a specialty or in administration and the view of the whole. The beginner not only has a right to expect training from his first five or ten years in a job; he has an obligation to get as much training as possible. A job in which young people are not given real training—though, of course, the training need not be a formal "training program"—does not measure up to what they have a right and a duty to expect.

But the most common reason why one should quit is the absence of promotional opportunities in the organization. That is a compelling reason.

I do not believe that chance of promotion is the essence of a job. In fact there is no surer way to kill a job and one's own usefulness in it than to consider it as but one rung in the promotional ladder rather than as a job in itself that deserves serious effort and will return satisfaction, a sense of accomplishment, and pride. And one can be an important and respected member of an organization without ever having received a promotion; there are such people in practically every office. But the organization itself must offer fair promotional opportunities. Otherwise it stagnates, becomes corrupted, and in turn corrupts. The absence of promotional opportunities is demoralizing. And the sooner one gets out of a demoralizing situation, the better. There are three situations to watch out for:

The entire group may be so young that for years there will be no vacancies. That was a fairly common situation in business a few years back, as a result of the depression. Middle and lower management ranks in many companies were solidly filled with men in their forties and early fifties—men who were far too young to be retired but who had grown too old, during the bleak days of the Thirties, to be promotable themselves. As a result the people under them were bottled up; for it is a rare organization that will promote a young man around his older superior. If you find yourself caught in such a situation, get out fast. If you wait it will defeat you.

Another situation without promotional opportunities is one in which the group ahead of you is uniformly old—so old that it will have to be replaced long before you will be considered ready to move up. Stay away from organizations that have a uniform age structure throughout their executive group—old or young. The only organization that offers fair promotional opportunities is one in which there is a balance of ages.

And finally there is the situation in which all promotions go to members of a particular group—to which you do not belong. Some chemical companies, for instance, require a master's degree in chemistry for just about any job above sweeper. Some companies promote only engineering graduates, some government agencies only people who majored in economics, some railroads only male stenographers, some British insurance companies only members of the actuaries' association. Or all the good jobs may be reserved for members of the family. There may be adequate promotional opportunities in such an organization—but not for you.

Who Gets Promoted?

On the whole there are proportionately more opportunities in the big organization than in the small one. But there is very real danger of getting lost in the big organization—whereas you are always visible in the small one. A young man should therefore stay in a large organization only if it has a definite promotional program which insures that he will be considered and looked at. This may take several forms: it may be a formal appraisal and development program; it may be automatic promotion by seniority as in the prewar Army; it may be an organization structure that actually makes out of the one big enterprise a number of small organizations in which everybody is again clearly visible (the technical term for this is "decentralization").

But techniques do not concern us here. What matters is that there should be both adequate opportunities and fair assurance that you will be eligible for promotion. Let me repeat: to be promoted is not essential, either to happiness or to usefulness. To be considered for promotion is.

Your Life Off the Job

I have only one more thing to say: to be an employee it is not enough that the job be right and that you be right for the job. It is also necessary that you have a meaningful life outside the job.

I am talking of having a genuine interest in something in which you on your own, can be, if not a master, at least an amateur expert. This something may be botany, or the history of your country, or chamber music, cabinetmaking, Christmastree growing, or a thousand other things. But it is important in this "employee society" of ours to have a genuine interest outside of the job and to be serious about it.

I am not, as you might suspect, thinking of something that will keep you alive and interested during your retirement. I am speaking of keeping yourself alive, interested, and happy during your working life, and of a permanent source of self-respect and standing in the community outside and beyond your job. You will need such an interest when you hit the forties, that period in which most of us come to realize that we will never reach the goals we have set ourselves when younger—whether these are goals of achievement or of worldly success. You will need it because you should have one area in which you yourself impose standards of performance on your own work. Finally, you need it because you will find recognition and acceptance by other people working in the field, whether professional or amateur, as individuals rather than as members of an organization and as employees.

This is heretical philosophy these days when so many companies believe that the best employee is the man who lives, drinks, eats, and sleeps job and company. In actual experience those people who have no life outside their jobs are not the really successful people, not even from the viewpoint of the company. I have seen far too many of them shoot up like a rocket, because they had no interests except the job; but they also came down like the rocket's burned-out stick. The man who will make the greatest contribution to his company is the mature person—and you cannot have maturity if you have no life or interest outside the job. Our large companies are beginning to understand this. That so many of them encourage people to have "outside interests" or to develop "hobbies" as a preparation for retirement is the first sign of a change toward a more intelligent attitude. But quite apart from the self-interest of the employer, your own interest as an employee demands that you develop a major outside interest. It will make you happier, it will make you more effective, it will give you resistance against the setbacks and the blows that are the lot of everyone; and it will make you a more effective, a more successful, and a more mature employee.

You have no doubt realized that I have not really talked about how to be an employee. I have talked about what to know before becoming an employee—which is something quite different. Perhaps "how to be an employee" can be learned only by being one. But one thing can be said. Being an employee means working with people; it means living and working in a society. Intelligence, in the last analysis, is therefore not the most important quality. What is decisive is character and integrity. If you work on your own, intelligence and ability may be sufficient. If you work with people you are going to fail unless you also have basic integrity. And integrity—character—is the one thing most, if not all, employers consider first.

There are many skills you might learn to be an employee, many abilities that are required. But fundamentally the one quality demanded of you will not be skill, knowledge, or talent, but character.

QUESTIONS ON CONTENT

1. What is the purpose of the first five paragraphs? How do they emphasize the importance of what is to be said?
2. Defend or attack the notion that writing poetry or short stories is practical preparation for business writing.
3. Test yourself by answering the four sets of questions which the author poses. On the basis of your answers, what sort of job should you seek?
4. Does the author make a good case for being fired from a job? For quitting a job? Discuss.
5. How does this article supplement Cabot's "The Call of the Job"?

SUGGESTIONS FOR PAPERS

Since, in the broadest sense, a job is probably the central fact in everyone's life, a searching analysis of what a job should be is no waste of time. You have the opportunity to think this subject through, to relate it to yourself, and to set down on paper the results. Essentially, this sort of paper invites enumeration—that is, the listing of points with sufficient discussion to make each point clear.

1. Examine the seven "points of a good job" as discussed in "The Call of the Job." Measure any job that you have had by these requirements. The paper will be "self-organized," and its value must come from your ability to make clear the comparisons and contrasts.

2. How will the job which you hope to have after college measure up, so far as you can tell, to the seven points of a good job? If any of the seven points *may* be missing in your after-college job, will there be compensations? Discuss.

3. Professions are supposed to differ from jobs. Define *profession.* Name the vocations which are normally called professions. Select one for analysis of its "good points." Are its characteristics the same as those you associate with a job? What are the differences?

4. Young college women may write a particularly good paper by analysing the position known as "housewife" in the light of Cabot's seven essentials of a good job.

5. Ask your father about his job. Does he consider Cabot's seven points the essentials so far as his work is concerned? Would he add

other characteristics of a good job? Would he minimize or delete any of those in Cabot's list?

6. If one of the seven characteristics of a good job that Cabot discussed has seemed of particular importance to you, concentrate on this characteristic as the controlling idea of your paper.

(a) *We want a chance to subdue.* Reread Cabot's explanation of this statement. Then relate an experience in which you have subdued "the raw and the crude"—made something of beauty or usefulness from it.

(b) *We want both monotony and variety.* Cabot says that we want a balance between monotony and variety. Will this balance vary with the individual? Which do you prefer? Illustrate with an anecdote from your own experience.

(c) *We want a boss.* Do *you* want a boss? Why? Even if you say, "I want to be my own boss," are you sure that you also want to accept all the responsibility such a statement implies? Furthermore, the man who thinks that he is his own boss, may actually be serving many bosses. How? Discuss.

(d) *We want to see the product of our work.* This point suggests a besetting fault of our machine age: the assembly line. Can the average modern job fulfill this requirement? Are we now conditioned to be satisfied with seeing the product of teamwork—not of our work alone?

(e) *We want a handle to our name.* Again, you may call on personal experience to illustrate this point. What titles have been yours? To what title do you aspire?

(f) *We want congeniality in our fellow workmen.* Good personnel men consider this an essential. Why? How, exactly, does congeniality fit into the planned efficiency of an office, a factory, a playground, a team?

7. Relate "Two Tramps in Mud Time" to "The Call of the Job." The poem simply mentions "love and need" as the basic characteristics of a good job. It also mentions the merging of avocation and vocation. But you will find much in the poem suggesting other of Cabot's seven characteristics of the ideal job.

8. Organize a paper around your answers to the four sets of questions posed by Peter Drucker in "How To Be an Employee."

9. Consider the thesis of "Two Tramps in Mud Time" in relation to the section called "*Your Life Off the Job*" in "How To Be an Employee." In what way is Drucker's contention about vocation

and avocation different from Frost's? In what way is it like Frost's? Add your own comments.

SOME TITLES FOR PAPERS

1. An Analysis of the Perfect Job
2. Athletes and *Selige Schmerzen*
3. The Challenge of Manual Labor
4. I Want a Boss
5. I Do Not Want a Boss
6. Monotony on the Job
7. Too Much Responsibility
8. Jobs I Have Had
9. The Assembly Line (or, Man, the Machine)
10. House Work Is a Job Too!
11. My Father's (Mother's) Job: An Analysis
12. Love and Need in Relation to Work
13. Do I Want Security?
14. The Value of Being Fired
15. Starting Near the Top
16. Summary and Criticism of "How To Be an Employee"

❧ *PERFECTIONISTS*

SOMERSET MAUGHAM (Chapter 4) applied reason to his search for an improved style. He confesses that he is not a perfectionist, for, he thinks, perfection "is apt to be dull." Few persons care to give their lives, as they conceive life, to anything that is ultimate. They learn to settle for much less than perfection. What this means is that they become impatient with details, fretful at the demands that perfection, even human perfection, makes upon their time, energy, and attention. Yet, since all of us have some drops of the perfectionist's blood flowing in our veins, we bestow our homage on those who have the patience—and the talent—to strive for perfect things, and we understand and sympathize with those who have the patience—but not the talent—and go down to defeat.

Three types of perfectionists are presented in this chapter. First, there is Toscanini, one of the most famous names in music in our time. He has the vision, the talent, the energy, and the infinite patience of the successful perfectionist. Next, there is Mr. Gessler in Galsworthy's story "Quality." He makes boots. After you have read this story, you will decide whether or not Mr. Gessler has a spiritual kinship with Toscanini. Finally, there is "the artist with carpenter's hands." Perfection was out of his reach, but he refused to settle for anything less.

The fourth selection, "An Apology for Idlers," is really an argument for selective diligence, for recognizing that dreams have their value.

The fifth selection, "The Importance of Doing Things Badly," contends that many things worth doing are not worth doing well. One may conclude that an important condition of being a perfectionist is the willingness to do many things imperfectly.

 Toscanini

STEFAN ZWEIG

I love him who yearns for the impossible
Second part of Faust

Any attempt to detach the figure of Arturo Toscanini from the fugitive element of the music re-created under the magical spell of his baton, and to incorporate it in the more enduring substance of the written word, must, willy-nilly, become something more than the mere biography of a conductor. He who tries to describe Toscanini's services to the Spirit of Music and his wizard's influence over his audiences is describing, above all, an ethical deed. For Toscanini is one of the sincerest men of our time, devoting himself to the service of art with such fidelity, ardour, and humility as we are rarely privileged to admire in any other sphere of creative activity. He bows his head before the higher will of the master he interprets, so that he combines the mediating function of the priest with the fervour of the disciple, combines the strictness of the teacher with the unresting diligence and veneration of the pupil. This guardian of the hallowed and primal forms of music is always concerned with an integral effect rather than with detail, with faithful representation rather than with outward success. Since he invariably puts into his work his personal genius and the whole of his peculiar moral and spiritual energy, what he does sets an example, not in the realm of music alone, but for all artists in every domain. His individual triumphs transcend the boundaries of music to become the suprapersonal victory of creative will over the inertia of matter—a splendid proof that, even in a disintegrated and shattered age like ours, now and again it is possible for the gifted few to achieve the miracle of perfection.

From foreword by Stefan Zweig to *Toscanini* by Paul Stefan. Copyright 1936 by The Viking Press, Inc. Reprinted by permission of the Viking Press, Inc., New York.

For the fulfillment of his colossal task Toscanini has, year after year, steeled his soul with unparalleled inflexibility. Nothing but perfection will satisfy him. Thus he shoulders his burden, and manifests his moral grandeur. The fairly good, the nearly perfect, the approximate, he cannot endure. Toscanini detests compromise in all its forms, abominates an easy-going satisfaction. In vain will you remind him that the perfect, the absolute, are rarely attainable in this world; that, even to the sublimest will, no more is possible than an approach to perfection, since perfection is God's attribute, not man's. His glorious unwisdom makes it impossible for him to recognize this wise dispensation. For him the idea of the absolute is supreme in art; and like one of Balzac's heroes, he devotes his whole life to "la recherche de l'absolu." Now, the will of one who persistently endeavours to attain the unattainable has irresistible power both in art and in life.

When Toscanini wills, all must will; when he commands, all must obey. Every musician who has been guided by the movements of his wonder-working baton will testify that, within the range of the elemental energy that radiates from it, lassitude and inaccuracy are dispelled. By a mysterious induction some of his own electrical energy passes from him into every muscle and nerve, not only of the members of the orchestra, but also of all those who come to hear and to enjoy Toscanini's will; for as soon as he addresses himself to his tasks, each individual is inspired with the power of a divine terror, with a communicable strength which, after an initial phase of palsied alarm, induces in those affected by it a might which greatly transcends the ordinary. The discharge of his own tensions increases the capacity for musical appreciation of those who happen to be in his neighborhood, expanding the faculties of every musician and, one might even say, of the lifeless instruments as well. As out of every score he extracts its most deeply hidden mysteries, so, with his unceasing demands, does he extract from every performer in the orchestra the utmost of which each is capable, imposing a fanatical zeal, a tenseness of will and execution, which the individual, unstimulated by Toscanini, has never before known and may never again experience.

This forcible stimulation of the will is no easy or comfortable matter. Perfection must be fought for sternly, savagely, indefatigably. One of the most marvelous spectacles of our day, one of the most glorious revelations to every creative or interpretative artist, an hour never to be forgotten is the privilege of watching Toscanini when engaged in his struggle for perfection, in his contest for the maximum effect. The onlooker is enthralled, breathless, almost terrified, as he beholds. In general an artist's fight for supreme achievement takes place in privacy. The poet, the novelist, the painter, the composer, works alone.

From sketches and from much-corrected manuscripts one must guess the ardours of creation. But whoever witnesses a rehearsal conducted by Toscanini sees and hears Jacob wrestling with the angel—sights and sounds no less alarming and splendid than a thunderstorm.

In whatever medium an artist works, the study of Toscanini will help to keep him faithful to his ideals, that he may resemble the conductor who, with sublime patience and sublime impatience, constrains to fit into the scheme of a flawless vision so much that, but for him, would remain rough-hewn and indistinct. For—and this is Toscanini's most salient characteristic—his interpretation of a work does not come into being at rehearsal. A symphony he is to conduct will have been thoroughly worked over in his mind from the score, and the finest shades of its tonal reproduction will have been settled for him long before he takes his place at the desk. A rehearsal, for him, is no more than an instrumental adaptation to what he had already heard again and again with the mind's ear. His extraordinary frame needs only three or four hours' sleep in the twenty-four. Night after night he sits up, the composer's text close to his near-sighted eyes, scanning it bar by bar, note by note. He weighs every modulation, scrupulously ponders every tone, mentally rehearses the rhythmic combinations.

Since he is a man of unrivalled memory, the whole and the parts become incorporated into his being, and the written score is henceforward little more than waste paper. Just as in a Rembrandt etching the lightest line has made its peculiar, its personal contribution to the copper plate, so in Toscanini's most musical of brains has every phrase been indelibly registered before he begins to conduct the first rehearsal. All that remains for him to do is to impose on others the clarity of his own will; to transform his Platonic idea, his perfected vision, into orchestrated sound; to ensure the concerted outward reproduction of the music that exists in his mind; to make a multiplicity of instrumentalists obey the law which for him has already been formulated in imagined perfection.

This is an enterprise bordering on the impossible. An assemblage of persons having different temperaments and talents is to work as a unit, fulfilling and realizing, with photographic and phonographic accuracy, the inspired vision of one individual. A thousand times Toscanini has made a success of this undertaking, which is at once his torment and his delight. To have watched the process of unceasing assimilation whereby he transforms multiplicity into unity, energetically clarifying the vague, is a memorable lesson for anyone who reverences art in its highest form as symbolical of morality. It is thus that during rehearsal observer and auditor come to understand that Toscanini's work is ethical as well as artistic.

Public performance discloses to connoiseurs, to artists, to virtuosi, Toscanini as a leader of men, Toscanini celebrating one of his triumphs. This is the victorious march into the conquered realm of perfection. At rehearsal, on the other hand, we witness the struggle for perfection. There alone can be discerned the obscure but genuine and tragical image of the fighter; there alone are we enabled to understand the courage of Toscanini the warrior. Like battle-fields, his rehearsals are full of the tumult and the fever of fluctuating successes. In them, and only in them, are the depths of Toscanini's soul revealed.

Every time he begins a rehearsal, it is, in very truth, as if he were a general opening a campaign; his outward aspect changes as he enters the hall. At ordinary times, when one is alone with him, or with him among a circle of intimates, though his hearing is extraordinarily acute, one is inclined to fancy him rather deaf. Walking or sitting he has his eyes fixed on vacancy, in a brown study, his arms folded, his brows knitted, a man aloof from the world. Though the fact is shown by no outward signs, something is at work within him; he is listening to inner voices, is in a reverie, with all his senses directed inward. If you come close to him and speak to him, he starts; half a minute or more may elapse before his deep-set dark eyes light up to recognize even a familiar friend, so profoundly has he been shut away, spiritually deaf to everything but the inner music. A day-dreamer, in the isolation and concentration of the creative and interpretative artist—such is Toscanini when not "on the battle-field."

Yet the instant he raises his baton to undertake the mission he is to fulfill, his isolation is transformed into intimate communion with his fellows, his introspection is replaced by the alertness of the man of action. His figure stiffens and straightens; he squares his shoulders in martial fashion; he is now the commandant, the governor, the dictator. His eyes sparkle beneath their bushy brows; his mouth is firmly set; his movements are brisk, those of one ready for all emergencies, as he steps up to the conductor's desk and, with Napoleonic glance, faces his adversaries. For that is what the waiting crowd of instrumentalists has become to him at this supreme instant—adversaries to be subjugated, persons with conflicting wills, who have to be mastered, disciplined, and brought under the reign of law. Encouragingly he greets his fellow-musicians, lifts his baton, and therewith, like lightning into a lightningrod, the whole power of his will is concentrated into this slender staff.

A wave of the magic wand, and elemental forces are unchained; rhythmically the orchestra is guided by his clear-cut and virile movements. On, on, on; we feel, we breathe, in unison. Suddenly (the sudden cessation hurts, and one shrinks as from the thrust of a rapier), the performance, which to us, less sensitive than the conductor, has seemed to be going flawlessly, is stopped by a sharp tap on the desk. Silence fills the hall, till the startling stillness is startlingly broken by Toscanini's tired and irritable "Ma no! Ma no!" This abrupt negative, this pained exclamation, is like a sigh of reproach. Something has disturbed him. The sound of the instruments, plain to us all, has been discordant with the music of Toscanini's vision, audible to him alone.

Quietly, civilly, speaking very much to the point, the conductor now tries to make the orchestra understand how he feels the music ought to be rendered. He raises his baton once more, and the faulty phrase is repeated, less faultily indeed; but the orchestral reproduction is not yet in full harmony with the master's inward audition. Again he stops the performance with a tap. This time the explanation that ensues is less patient, more irritable. Eager to make his meaning perfectly plain, he uses all his powers of persuasion, and so great is his faculty for expression that in him the gesticulative talent proper to an Italian rises to the pitch of genius. Even the most unmusical of persons cannot fail to grasp, from his gestures, what he wants, what he demands, when he demonstrates the rhythm, when he imploringly throws his arms wide, and then fervently clasps them at his breast, to stress the need of a more lively interpretation; or when, setting his whole body plastically to work, he gives a visual image of the tone-sequences in his mind. More and more passionately does he employ the arts of persuasion, imploring, miming, counting, singing; becoming, so to say, each instrument in turn as he wishes to stimulate the performer who plays it; one sees him making the movements of a violinist, a flautist, kettledrummer. . . .

But if, despite this fiery incitation, despite this urgent exemplification, the orchestra still fails to grasp and to fulfill the conductor's wishes, Toscanini's suffering at their non-success and their mortal fallibility becomes intense. Distressed by the discordancy between the orchestral performance and the inward audition, he groans like a sorely wounded man, and seems beside himself because he cannot get on properly with his work. Forgetting the restraints of politeness, losing control, in his wrath against the stupidity of material obstacles, he rages, curses, and delivers volleys of abuse. It is easy to understand why none but his intimates are allowed to attend these rehearsals, at which he knows he will be overcome by his insatiable passion for perfection. More and more alarming grows the spectacle of the struggle, as Toscanini strives to wring from the instrumentalists the visioned masterpiece which has to be fashioned in the sphere of universally audible reality. His body quivers with excitement, his voice becomes hoarse, his brow is beaded with sweat; he looks exhausted and aged by these immeasurable hours of strenuous toil; but never will he stop an inch short of the perfection of his dream. With unceasingly renewed energy, he pushes onward and onward until the orchestra has at length been subjected to his will and can interpret the composer's music exactly as it has presented itself to the great conductor's mind.

Only he who has been privileged to witness this struggle for perfection hour after hour, day after day can grasp the heroism of a Toscanini; he alone can estimate the cost of the super-excellence which the public has come to expect as a matter of course. In truth the highest levels of art are never attained until what is enormously difficult seems to have been attained with consummate ease, until perfection appears self-evident. If you see Toscanini of an evening in a crowded concert-hall, the magician who holds sway over the dutiful instrumentalists, guiding them as if they were hypnotized by the movements of his baton, you might think his triumph won without effort—himself, the acme of security, the supreme expression of victory. In reality Toscanini never regards a task as definitely performed. What the public admires as completion has for him already become once more a problem. After fifty years' study of a composition, this man who is now verging upon seventy is never wholly satisfied with the results; he can in no case get beyond the stimulating uncertainty of the artist who is perpetually making new trials. Not for him a futile comfort; he never attains what Nietzsche calls the "brown happiness" of relaxation, of self-content. No other living man perhaps suffers so much as does this superlatively successful conductor from the imperfection of all the instrumental reproduction as compared with the music of his dreams.

Other inspired conductors are at least vouchsafed fleeting moments of rapture. Bruno Walter, for example, Toscanini's Apollonian brother in the realm of music, has them (one feels) from time to time. When he is playing or conducting Mozart, his face is now and again irradiated by the reflection of ecstasy. He is upborne on the waves of his own creation; he smiles unwittingly; he dreams as he is dandled in the arms of music.

But Toscanini, the insatiable, the captive of his longing for perfection, is never granted the grace of self-forgetfulness. He is consumed, as with undying fires, by the craving for ever-new forms of perfection. The man is absolutely sincere, incapable of pose. There is nothing studied about his behavior when, at the close of every concert, during the salvos of applause, he looks embarrassed and ashamed as he retires, coming back reluctantly and only through politeness when forced to respond to the acclamations of the audience. For him all achievement is mysterious, mournful. He knows that what he has so heroically wrested from fate is preëminently perishable; he feels, like Keats, that his name is "writ in water." The work of an interpretative artist cannot endure; it exists only for the moment, and leaves nothing that the senses of coming generations will be able to delight in. Thus his successes, magnificent though they are, can neither delude nor intoxicate him. He knows that in the sphere of orchestral reproduction there is nothing perdurable; that whatever is achieved must be re-achieved from performance to performance, from hour to hour. Who can be better aware than this man, to whom peace and full fruition are denied because he is insatiable, that art is unending warfare, not a conclusion but a perpetual recommencement?

Such moral strictness of conception and character is a signal phenomenon in art and in life. Let us not repine, however, that so pure and so disciplined a manifestation as Toscanini is a rarity, and that only on a few days each year can we enjoy the delight of having works so admirably presented to us by this master of his craft. Nothing can detract more from the dignity and the ethical value of art than the undue facility and triteness of its presentation thanks to the marvels of modern technique, whereby wireless and gramophone offer the sublime at any moment to the most indifferent; for thanks to this ease of presentation, most people forget the labour of creation, consuming the treasures of art as thoughtlessly and ir-reverently as if they were swilling beer or munching bread.

It is therefore, in such days as ours, a benefaction and a spiritual joy to behold one who so forcibly reminds us that art is sacramental labour, is apostolical devotion to the perpetually elusive and divine elements in our world; that it is not a chance gift of luck, but a hard-earned grace; is more than tepid pleasure, being likewise, and before all, creative need. In virtue of his genius and in virtue of his stead-fastness of character, Toscanini has wrought the miracle of compel-ling millions to accept our glorious patrimony of music as a con-stituent part of the living present. This interpretative wonder bears fruit far beyond its obvious frontiers; for what is achieved within the domain of any one art is an acquirement for art in general. Only an exceptional man imposes order upon others, and nothing arouses profounder veneration for this outstanding apostle of faith-fulness in work than his success in teaching a chaotic and incredu-lous epoch to feel fresh reverence for its most hallowed heritage.

QUESTIONS ON CONTENT

1. Explain the phrase "an ethical deed" at the end of the second sentence.
2. How does Toscanini's task differ from that of the poet, the novelist, the painter, and the composer?
3. Explain the reference to "Jacob wrestling with the angel." Is this an apt comparison?
4. Is there such a thing as "patient impatience"? Explain.
5. How much sleep does Toscanini need?
6. What is meant by "his Platonic idea"?
7. Why are only Toscanini's intimate friends allowed to attend his rehearsals?
8. Why are Toscanini's musicians called "adversaries"?
9. How and why is the phrase "writ in water" applied to Tosca-nini?
10. Can you summarize the "moral" of this description of a great artist?
11. "Art is sacramental labour." Explain.

❧ *Quality*

JOHN GALSWORTHY

I knew him from the days of my extreme youth, because he made my father's boots; inhabiting with his elder brother two little shops let into one, in a small by-street—now no more, but then most fashionably placed in the West End.

That tenement had a certain quiet distinction; there was no sign upon its face that he made for any of the Royal Family—merely his own German name of Gessler Brothers; and in the window a few pairs of boots. I remember that it always troubled me to account for those unvarying boots in the window, for he made only what was ordered, reaching nothing down, and it seemed so inconceivable that what he made could ever have failed to fit. Had he bought them to put there? That, too, seemed inconceivable. He would never have tolerated in his house leather on which he had not worked himself. Besides, they were too beautiful—the pair of pumps, so inexpressibly slim, the patent leathers with cloth tops, making water come into one's mouth, the tall brown riding-boots with marvellous sooty glow, as if, though new, they had been worn a hundred years. Those pairs could only have been made by one who saw before him the Soul of Boot—so truly were they prototypes incarnating the very spirit of all footgear. These thoughts, of course, came to me later, though even when I was promoted to him, at the age of perhaps fourteen, some inkling haunted me of the dignity of himself and brother. For to make boots—such boots as he made—seemed to me then, and still seems to me, mysterious and wonderful.

I remember well my shy remark, one day, while stretching out to him my youthful foot:

"Isn't it awfully hard to do, Mr. Gessler?"

And his answer, given with a sudden smile from out of the sardonic redness of his beard: "It is an Ardt!"

Himself, he was a little as if made from leather, with his yellow

Reprinted from *The Inn of Tranquillity* by John Galsworthy; copyright 1912 by Charles Scribner's Sons, 1940 by Ada Galsworthy; used by permission of the publishers.

crinkly face, and crinkly reddish hair and beard, and neat folds slanting down his cheeks to the corners of his mouth, and his guttural and one-toned voice; for leather is a sardonic substance, and stiff and slow of purpose. And that was the character of his face, save that his eyes, which were grey-blue had in them the simple gravity of one secretly possessed by the Ideal. His elder brother was so very like him—though watery, paler in every way, with a great industry—that sometimes in early days I was not quite sure of him until the interview was over. Then I knew that it was he, if the words, "I will ask my brudder," had not been spoken; and that, if they had, it was his elder brother.

When one grew old and wild and ran up bills, one somehow never ran them up with Gessler Brothers. It would not have seemed becoming to go in there and stretch out one's foot to that blue iron-spectacled glance, owing him for more than—say—two pairs, just the comfortable reassurance that one was still his client.

For it was not possible to go to him very often—his boots lasted terribly, having something beyond the temporary—some, as it were, essence of boot stitched into them.

One went in, not as into most shops, in the mood of: "Please serve me, and let me go!" but restfully, as one enters a church; and, sitting on the single wooden chair, waited—for there was never anybody there. Soon, over the top edge of that sort of well—rather dark, and smelling soothingly of leather—which formed the shop, there would be seen his face, or that of his elder brother, peering down. A guttural sound, and the tip-tap of bast slippers beating the narrow wooden stairs, and he would stand before one without coat, a little bent, in leather apron, with sleeves turned back, blinking—as if awakened from some dream of boots, or like an owl surprised in daylight and annoyed at this interruption.

And I would say: "How do you do, Mr. Gessler? Could you make me a pair of Russia leather boots?"

Without a word he would leave me, retiring whence he came, or into the other portion of the shop, and I would continue to rest in the wooden chair, inhaling the incense of his trade. Soon he would come back, holding in his thin, veined hand a piece of gold-brown leather. With eyes fixed on it, he would remark: "What a beaudiful biece!" When I, too, had admired it, he would speak again. "When do you wand dem?" and I would answer: "Oh! As soon as you conveniently can." And he would say: "To-morrow fordnighd?" Or if he were his elder brother: "I will ask my brudder!"

Then I would murmur: "Thank you! Good-morning, Mr. Gessler."
"Goot-morning!" he would reply, still looking at the leather in his
hand. And as I moved to the door, I would hear the tip-tap of his
bast slippers restoring him, up the stairs, to his dream of boots. But
if it were some new kind of footgear that he had not yet made me,
then indeed he would observe ceremony—divesting me of my boot
and holding it long in his hand, looking at it with eyes at once critical
and loving, as if recalling the glow with which he had created it,
and rebuking the way in which one had disorganised this masterpiece. Then, placing my foot on a piece of paper, he would two or
three times tickle the outer edges with a pencil and pass his nervous
fingers over my toes, feeling himself into the heart of my requirements.

I cannot forget that day on which I had occasion to say to him:
"Mr. Gessler, that last pair of town walking-boots creaked, you
know."

He looked at me for a time without replying, as if expecting me
to withdraw or qualify the statement, then said:

"Id shouldn'd 'ave greaked."

"It did, I'm afraid."

"You goddem wed before dey found demselves?"

"I don't think so."

At that he lowered his eyes, as if hunting for memory of those
boots, and I felt sorry I had mentioned this grave thing.

"Zend dem back!" he said; "I will look at dem."

A feeling of compassion for my creaking boots surged up in me,
so well could I imagine the sorrowful long curiosity of regard which
he would bend on them.

"Zome boods," he said slowly, "are bad from birdt. I can do noding
wid dem, I dake dem off your bill."

Once (once only) I went absentmindedly into his shop in a pair
of boots bought in an emergency at some large firm's. He took my
order without showing me any leather, and I could feel his eyes
penetrating the inferior integument of my foot. At last he said:

"Dose are nod my boods."

The tone was not one of anger, nor of sorrow, not even of contempt, but there was in it something quiet that froze the blood.
He put his hand down and pressed a finger on the place where the
left boot, endeavouring to be fashionable, was not quite comfortable.

"Id 'urds you dere," he said. "Dose big virms 'ave no self-respect.
Drash!" And then, as if something had given way within him, he

spoke long and bitterly. It was the only time I ever heard him discuss the conditions and hardships of his trade.

"Dey get id all," he said, "dey get id by adverdisement, nod by
work. Dey dake it away from us, who lofe our boods. Id gomes to
this—bresently I haf no work. Every year id gets less—you will
see." And looking at his lined face I saw things I had never noticed
before, bitter things and bitter struggle—and what a lot of grey
hairs there seemed suddenly in his red beard!

As best I could, I explained the circumstances of the purchase
of those ill-omened boots. But his face and voice made a so deep
impression that during the next few minutes I ordered many pairs.
Nemesis fell! They lasted more terribly than ever. And I was not
able conscientiously to go to him for nearly two years.

When at last I went I was surprised to find that outside one
of the two little windows of his shop another name was painted, also
that of a bootmaker—making, of course, for the Royal Family. The
old familiar boots, no longer in dignified isolation, were huddled in
the single window. Inside, the now contracted well of the one little
shop was more scented and darker than ever. And it was longer
than usual, too, before a face peered down, and the tip-tap of the
bast slippers began. At last he stood before me, and gazing through
those rusty iron spectacles, said:

"Mr. ——, isn'd it?"

"Ah! Mr. Gessler?" I stammered, "but your boots are really *too*
good, you know! See, these are quite decent still!" And I stretched
out to him my foot. He looked at it.

"Yes," he said, "beople do nod wand good boods, id seems."

To get away from his reproachful eyes and voice I hastily remarked: "What have you done to your shop?"

He answered quietly: "Id was too exbensif. Do you wand some
boods?"

I ordered three pairs, though I had only wanted two, and quickly
left. I had, I know not quite what feeling of being part, in his mind,
of a conspiracy against him; or not perhaps so much against him as
against his idea of boot. One does not, I suppose, care to feel like
that; for it was again many months before my next visit to his shop,
paid, I remember, with the feeling: "Oh, well, I can't leave the old
boy—so here goes! Perhaps it'll be his elder brother!"

For his elder brother, I knew, had not character enough to reproach me even dumbly.

And, to my relief, in the shop there did appear to be his elder brother, handling a piece of leather.

"Well, Mr. Gessler," I said, "how are you?"

He came close, and peered at me.

"I am breddy well," he said slowly; "but my older brudder is dead."

And I saw that it was indeed himself—but how aged and wan! And never before had I heard him mention his brother. Much shocked, I murmured: "Oh, I am sorry!"

"Yes," he answered, "he was a good man, he made a good bood; but he is dead." And he touched the top of his head, where the hair had suddenly gone as thin as it had been on that of his poor brother, to indicate, I suppose, the cause of death. "He could nod ged over losing de oder shop. Do you wand any boods?" And he held up the leather in his hand: "Id's a beaudiful biece."

I ordered several pairs. It was very long before they came—but they were better than ever. One simply could not wear them out. And soon after that I went abroad.

It was over a year before I was again in London. And the first shop I went to was my old friend's. I had left a man of sixty, I came back to one of seventy-five, pinched and worn and tremulous, who genuinely, this time, did not at first know me.

"Oh! Mr. Gessler," I said, sick at heart; "how splendid your boots are! See, I've been wearing this pair nearly all the time I've been abroad; and they're not half worn out, are they?"

He looked long at my boots—a pair of Russia leather, and his face seemed to regain steadiness. Putting his hand on my instep, he said:

"Do day vid you here? I 'ad drouble wid dat bair, I remember."

I assured him that they had fitted beautifully.

"Do you wand any boods?" he said. "I can make dem quickly; id is a slack dime."

I answered: "Please, please! I want boots all round—every kind!"

"I will make a vresh model. Your food must be bigger." And with utter slowness, he traced round my foot, and felt my toes, only once looking up to say:

"Did I dell you my brudder was dead?"

To watch him was painful, so feeble had he grown; I was glad to get away.

I had given those boots up, when one evening they came. Opening the parcel, I set the four pairs out in a row. Then one by one I tried them on. There was no doubt about it. In shape and fit, in finish and quality of leather, they were the best he had ever made me. And in the mouth of one of the town walking-boots I found his bill. The amount was the same as usual, but it gave me quite a shock. He had never before sent it in till quarter day. I flew downstairs and wrote a cheque, and posted it at once with my own hand.

A week later, passing the little street, I thought I would go in and tell him how splendidly the new boots fitted. But when I came to where his shop had been, his name was gone. Still there, in the window, were the slim pumps, the patent leathers with cloth tops, the sooty riding-boots.

I went in, very much disturbed. In the two little shops—again made into one—was a young man with an English face.

"Mr. Gessler in?" I said.

He gave me a strange, ingratiating look.

"No, sir," he said; "no. But we can attend to anything with pleasure. We've taken the shop over. You've seen our name, no doubt, next door. We make for some very good people."

"Yes, yes," I said; "but Mr. Gessler?"

"Oh!" he answered; "dead."

"Dead! But I only received these boots from him last Wednesday week."

"Ah!" he said; "a shockin' go. Poor old man starved 'imself."

"Good God!"

"Slow starvation, the doctor called it! You see he went to work in such a way! Would keep the shop on; wouldn't have a soul touch his boots except himself. When he got an order, it took him such a time. People won't wait. He lost everybody. And there he'd sit, goin' on and on—I will say that for him—not a man in London made a better boot! But look at the competition! He never advertised! Would 'ave the best leather, too, and do it all 'imself. Well, there it is. What could you expect with his ideas?"

"But starvation——!"

"That may be a bit flowery, as the sayin' is—but I know myself he was sittin' over his boots day and night, to the very last. You see, I used to watch him. Never gave 'imself time to eat; never had a penny in the house. All went in rent and leather. How he lived so long I don't know. He regular let his fire go out. He was a character. But he made good boots."

"Yes," I said, "he made good boots."

QUESTIONS ON CONTENT

1. What does "the Soul of Boot" mean? Compare the later statement that Mr. Gessler was "one secretly possessed of the Ideal." Can you relate these statements to Toscanini's "Platonic Idea"?
2. How did the narrator of this story tell the brothers Gessler apart?
3. Upon what does Mr. Gessler blame his plight?
4. Explain: "Nemesis fell."
5. Zweig found Toscanini's approach to art a lesson in ethics. What ethical lesson, if any, can you find in Mr. Gessler's approach to his "art"?

❧ *Artist with Carpenter's Hands*

ROBERT C. RUARK

Last week a lean, starved-looking young man with wild hair committed suicide here in New York. The papers called him a poet. First he jumped off a building in Greenwich Village and when that didn't kill him, he went home and strung himself up from a pipe.

His name was Jack Demoreland. The police knew little about him; the papers less. The art critic whom he visited just before he leaped off the roof knew him scarcely at all. He attracted attention only because his first attempt at suicide failed to kill him.

I knew Demoreland well. He was a friend of mine for many years, before the war. He wasn't a poet. He was an artist—a painter and a cartoonist. We had worked together on The Washington *Daily News*. I have several of his pictures.

The anatomy of suicide is a strange, complex thing; rarely the same in any man. I know why Demoreland killed himself. He killed himself because he saw the most beautiful pictures any man ever saw. They were right there, clamoring to come out of his head, but his hands weren't good enough to draw them forth.

Jack knew what he wanted to put on paper, knew it so well that it hurt him. But when he picked up the brush or pen it was

Published in the Scripps-Howard newspapers, September 13, 1948. Reprinted by permission of the author.

always a bad distortion of what he was trying to say. He was like a man whose head rings with wondrous music, but, when he opens his mouth to sing, only croaks emerge.

An alienist would say that the man was a definite psychopath, and so, I suppose, he was. He had tried to kill himself once before, long ago, in a fit of horrid depression. He had spent a short time in a mental hospital. It was the one true case of complete artistic frustration I ever knew.

Demoreland used to do little line sketches for me on sports stories, and later illustrated the top city-side feature of the day. During the first days of the war we set him to doing the daily military map. Those maps finally got him. Here was a guy who wanted to scream out loud with a paintbrush, and he was over in the corner with an inkwell, tracing the progress of the Germans against the Russians, the Japs against the Americans.

Most of the time Demoreland was a quiet, seemingly "normal" human being, who wore neckties, shaved, drank moderately, went out with a variety of women, and who rarely talked art. But occasionally the black desperation would stifle him, and he would forget to come home. He would forget to eat, to sleep, to wash.

It was then that a girl reporter used to take him in hand. She would throw a big slug of bourbon into him, feed him forcibly and plant him on the divan, where he'd sleep for 20 hours or so and snap back to his cartoons and his maps. I think the girl loved him very much, but there wasn't much future in it; his head was too full of pictures—pictures that couldn't be born.

You meet a lot of dilettante artists in big cities like New York. They live in Greenwich Village, mostly, and spend more time in the smoky little cheap-gin joints looking picturesque than they spend in front of an easel or at a typewriter.

Jack Demoreland was no dilettante. He was a worker. He would work 24, 36 hours at a crack, striving for a perfection he knew, actually, he'd never achieve. There was no bogus Bohemian in Jack —at least not through the years I knew him. He dressed like a young business executive, when he was off on one of his "tranquil" stretches, which sometimes ran for a year at a crack. He was a handsome youngster. He talked well. There was never anything "arty" about him.

Something, I guess, finally went really wrong in his head. New York, which he once told me seemed like the answer, obviously couldn't supply the necessary skill his hands lacked. He tried, and he tried again, and finally he got so tired it all seemed too tough to live with.

But a great artist lies in the morgue as I write this. It wasn't his fault that he was born with a carpenter's hands.

QUESTION ON CONTENT

1. "He saw the most beautiful pictures any man ever saw." Compare "the flawless vision" of Toscanini; the ideal of Mr. Gessler.

❧ *An Apology for Idlers*

ROBERT LOUIS STEVENSON

"Boswell: We grow weary when idle.
"Johnson: That is, sir, because others being busy, we want company; but if we were idle, there would be no growing weary; we should all entertain one another."

Just now, when every one is bound, under pain of a decree in absence convicting them of *lèse*-respectability, to enter on some lucrative profession, and labor therein with something not far short of enthusiasm, a cry from the opposite party who are content when they have enough, and like to look on and enjoy in the meanwhile, savors a little of bravado and gasconade. And yet this should not be. Idleness so called, which does not consist in doing nothing, but in doing a great deal not recognized in the dogmatic formularies of the ruling class, has as good a right to state its position as industry itself. It is admitted that the presence of people who refuse to enter in the great handicap race for sixpenny pieces, is at once an insult and a disenchantment for those who do. A fine fellow (as we see so many) takes his determination, votes for the sixpences, and in the emphatic Americanism, "goes for" them. And while such a one is ploughing distressfully up the road, it is not hard to understand his resentment, when he perceives cool persons in the meadows by the wayside, lying with a handkerchief over their ears and a glass at their elbow. Alexander is touched in a very delicate place by the disregard of Diogenes. Where was the glory of having taken Rome for these tumultuous Barbarians, who poured into the Senate

Published in 1877.

house, and found the Fathers sitting silent and unmoved by their success? It is a sore thing to have labored along and scaled the arduous hilltops, and when all is done, find humanity indifferent to your achievement. Hence physicists condemn the unphysical; financiers have only a superficial toleration for those who know little of stocks; literary persons despise the unlettered; and people of all pursuits combine to disparage those who have none.

But though this is one difficulty of the subject, it is not the greatest. You could not be put in prison for speaking against industry, but you can be sent to Coventry for speaking like a fool. The greatest difficulty with most subjects is to do them well; therefore, please to remember this is an apology. It is certain that much may be judiciously argued in favor of diligence; only there is something to be said against it, and that is what, on the present occasion, I have to say. To state one argument is not necessarily to be deaf to all others, and that a man has written a book of travels in Montenegro, is no reason why he should never have been to Richmond.

It is surely beyond a doubt that people should be a good deal idle in youth. For though here and there a Lord Macaulay may escape from school honors with all his wits about him, most boys pay so dear for their medals that they never afterward have a shot in their locker, and begin the world bankrupt. And the same holds true during all the time a lad is educating himself, or suffering others to educate him. It must have been a very foolish old gentleman who addressed Johnson at Oxford in these words: "Young man, ply your book diligently now, and acquire a stock of knowledge; for when years come upon you, you will find that poring upon books will be but an irksome task." The old gentleman seems to have been unaware that many other things besides reading grow irksome, and not a few become impossible, by the time a man has to use spectacles and cannot walk without a stick. Books are good enough in their own way, but they are a mighty bloodless substitute for life. It seems a pity to sit, like the Lady of Shalott, peering into a mirror, with your back turned on all the bustle and glamor of reality. And if a man reads very hard, as the old anecdote reminds us, he will have little time for thoughts.

If you look back on your own education, I am sure it will not be the full, vivid, instructive hours of truantry that you regret; you would rather cancel some lacklustre periods between sleep and waking in the class. For my own part, I have attended a good many lectures in my time. I still remember that the spinning of a top is a case of Kinetic Stability. I still remember that Emphyteusis is not a disease, nor Stillicide a crime. But though I would not willingly part with such scraps of science, I do not set the same store by them as by certain other odds and ends that I came by in the open street while I was playing truant. This is not the moment to dilate on that mighty place of education, which was the favorite school of Dickens and of Balzac, and turns out yearly many inglorious masters in the Science of the Aspects of Life. Suffice it to say this: if a lad does not learn in the streets, it is because he has not faculty of learning. Nor is the truant always in the streets, for if he prefers, he may go out by the gardened suburbs into the country. He may pitch on some tuft of lilac over a burn, and smoke innumerable pipes to the tune of the water on the stones. A bird will sing in the thicket. And there he may fall into a vein of kindly thought, and see things in a new perspective. Why, if this be not education, what is? We may conceive Mr. Worldly Wiseman accosting such a one, and the conversation that should thereupon ensue:—

"How, now, young fellow, what dost thou here?"

"Truly, sir, I take mine ease."

"Is this not the hour of the class? and should'st thou not be plying thy Book with diligence, to the end thou mayest obtain knowledge?"

"Nay, but thus also I follow after Learning, by your leave."

"Learning, quotha! After what fashion, I pray thee? Is it mathematics?"

"No, to be sure."

"Is it metaphysics?"

"Nor that."

"Is it some language?"

"Nay, it is no language."

"Is it a trade?"

"Nor a trade neither."

"Why, then, what is't?"

"Indeed, sir, as a time may soon come for me to go upon Pilgrimage, I am desirous to note what is commonly done by persons in my case, and where are the ugliest Sloughs and Thickets on the Road; as also, what manner of Staff is of the best service. Moreover, I lie here, by this water, to learn by root-of-heart a lesson which my master teaches me to call Peace, or Contentment."

Hereupon Mr. Worldly Wiseman was much commoved with passion, and shaking his cane with a very threatful countenance, broke forth upon this wise: "Learning, quotha!" said he: "I would have all such rogues scourged by the Hangman!"

And so he would go his way, ruffling out his cravat with a crackle of starch, like a turkey when it spreads its feathers.

Now this, of Mr. Wiseman's, is the common opinion. A fact is not called a fact, but a piece of gossip, if it does not fall into one of your scholastic categories. An inquiry must be in some acknowledged direction, with a name to go by; or else you are not inquiring at all, only lounging and the workhouse is too good for you. It is supposed that all knowledge is at the bottom of a well, or the far end of a telescope. Sainte-Beuve, as he grew older, came to regard all experience as a single great book, in which to study for a few years ere we go hence; and it seemed all one to him whether you should read in Chapter xx. which is the differential calculus, or in Chapter xxxix., which is hearing the band play in the gardens. As a matter of fact, an intelligent person, looking out of his eyes and hearkening in his ears, with a smile on his face all the time, will get more true education than many another in a life of heroic vigils. There is certainly some chill and arid knowledge to be found upon the summits of formal and laborious science; but it is all round about you, and for the trouble of looking, that you will acquire the warm and palpitating facts of life. While others are filling their memory with a lumber of words, one-half of which they will forget before the week be out, your truant may learn some really useful art: to play the fiddle, to know a good cigar, or to speak with ease and opportunity to all varieties of men. Many who have "plied their book diligently," and know all about some one branch or another of accepted lore, come out of the study with an ancient and owl-like demeanor, and prove dry, stockish, and dyspeptic in all the better and brighter parts of life. Many make a large fortune, who remain underbred and pathetically stupid to the last. And meantime there goes the idler, who began life along with them —by your leave, a different picture. He has had time to take care of his health and his spirits; he has been a great deal in the open air, which is the most salutary of all things for both body and mind; and if he has never read the great Book in very recondite places, he has dipped into it and skimmed it over to excellent purpose. Might not the student afford some Hebrew roots, and the business man some of his half-crowns, for a share of the idler's knowledge of life at large, and Art of Living? Nay, and the idler has another and more important quality than these. I mean his wisdom. He who has much looked on at the childish satisfaction of other people in their hobbies, will regard his own with only a very ironical indulgence. He will not be heard among the dogmatists. He will have a great and cool allowance for all sorts of people and opinions. If he finds no out-of-the-way truths, he will identify himself with no very burning falsehood. His way takes him along a by-road, not much frequented, but very even and pleasant, which is called Commonplace Lane, and leads to the Belvedere of Commonsense. Thence he shall command an agreeable, if no very noble prospect; and while others behold the East and West, the Devil and the Sunrise, he will be contentedly aware of a sort of morning hour upon all sublunary things, with an army of shadows running speedily and in many different directions into the great daylight of Eternity. The shadows and the generations, the shrill doctors and the plangent wars, go by into ultimate silence and emptiness; but underneath all this, a man may see, out of the Belvedere windows, much green and peaceful landscape; many firelit parlors; good people laughing, drinking, and making love as they did before the Flood or the French Revolution; and the old shepherd telling his tale under the hawthorn.

Extreme *busyness*, whether at school or college, kirk or market, is a symptom of deficient vitality; and a faculty for idleness implies a catholic appetite and a strong sense of personal identity. There is a sort of dead-alive, hackneyed people about, who are scarcely conscious of living except in the exercise of some conventional occupation. Bring these fellows into the country, or set them aboard ship, and you will see how they pine for their desk or their study. They have no curiosity; they cannot give themselves over to random provocations; they do not take pleasure in the exercise of their faculties for its own sake; and unless Necessity lays about them with a stick, they will even stand still. It is no good speaking to such folk; they *cannot* be idle, their nature is not generous enough; and they pass those hours in a sort of coma, which are not dedicated to furious moiling in the goldmill. When they do not require to go to the office, when they are not hungry and have no mind to drink, the whole breathing world is a blank to them. If they have to wait an hour or so for a train, they fall into a stupid trance with their eyes open. To see them, you would suppose there was nothing to look at and no one to speak with; you would imagine they were paralyzed or alienated; and yet very possibly they are hard workers in their own way, and have good eyesight for a flaw in a deed or a turn of the market. They have been to school and college, but all the time they had their eye on the medal; they have gone about in the world and mixed with clever people, but all the time they were thinking of their own affairs. As if a man's soul were not too small to begin with, they have dwarfed and narrowed theirs by a life of all work and no play; until here they are at forty, with a listless attention, a mind vacant of all material of amusement, and not one thought to rub against another while they wait for the train. Before he was breeched, he might have clambered on the boxes; when he was twenty, he would have stared at the girls; but now the pipe is smoked out, the snuffbox empty, and my gentleman sits bolt upright upon a bench, with lamentable eyes. This does not appeal to me as being Success in Life.

But it is not only the person himself who suffers from his busy habits, but his wife and children, his friends and relations, and down to the very people he sits with in a railway carriage or an omnibus. Perpetual devotion to what a man calls his business is only to be sustained by perpetual neglect of many other things. And it is not by any means certain that a man's business is the most important thing he has to do. To an impartial estimate it will seem clear that many of the wisest, most virtuous, and most beneficent parts that are to be played upon the Theatre of Life are filled by gratuitous performers, and pass, among the world at large, as phases of idleness. For in that Theatre, not only the walking gentlemen, singing chambermaids, and diligent fiddlers in the orchestra, but those who look on and clap their hands from the benches, do really play a part and fulfil important offices toward the general result. You are no doubt very dependent on the care of your lawyer and stockbroker, of the guards and signalmen who convey you rapidly from place to place, and the policemen who walk the streets for your protection; but is there not a thought of gratitude in your heart for certain other benefactors who set you smiling when they fall in your way, or season your dinner with good company? Colonel Newcome helped to lose his friend's money; Fred Bayham had an ugly trick of borrowing shirts; and yet they were better people to fall among than Mr. Barnes. And though Falstaff was neither sober nor very honest, I think I could name one or two long-faced Barabbases whom the world could better have done without. Hazlitt mentions that he was more sensible of obligation to Northcote, who had never done him anything he could call a service, than to his whole circle of ostentatious friends; for he thought a good companion emphatically the greatest benefactor. I know there are people in the world who cannot feel grateful unless the favor has been done them at the cost of pain and difficulty. But this is a churlish disposition. A man may send you six sheets of letter-paper covered with the most entertaining gossip, or you may pass half an hour pleasantly, perhaps profitably, over an article of his; do you think the service would be greater, if he had made the manuscript in his heart's blood, like a compact with the devil? Do you really fancy you should be more beholden to your correspondent, if he had been damning you all the while for your importunity? Pleasures are more beneficial than duties because, like the quality of mercy, they are not strained, and they are twice blest. There must always be two to a kiss, and there may be a score in a jest; but wherever there is an element of sacrifice, the favor is conferred with pain, and, among generous people, received with confusion. There is no duty we so much underrate as the duty of being happy. By being happy, we sow anonymous benefits upon the world, which remain unknown even to ourselves, or when they are disclosed, surprise nobody so much as the benefactor. The other day, a ragged, barefoot boy ran down the street after a marble, with so jolly an air that he set every one he passed into a good-humor; one of these persons, who had been delivered from more than usually black thoughts, stopped the little fellow and gave him some money with this remark: "You see what sometimes comes of looking pleased." If he had looked pleased before, he had now to look both pleased and mystified. For my part, I justify this encouragement of smiling rather than tearful children; I do not wish to pay for tears anywhere but upon the stage; but I am prepared to deal largely in the opposite commodity. A happy man or woman is a better thing to find than a five-pound note. He or she is a radiating focus of good-will; and their entrance into a room is as though another candle had been lighted. We need not care whether they could prove the forty-seventh proposition; they do a better thing than that, they practically demonstrate the great Theorem of the Livableness of Life. Consequently, if a person cannot be happy without remaining idle, idle he should remain. It is a revolutionary precept; but thanks to hunger and the workhouse, one not easily to be abused; and within practical limits, it is one of the most incontestable truths in the whole Body of Morality. Look at one of your industrious fellows for a moment, I beseech you. He sows hurry and reaps indigestion; he puts a vast deal of activity out to interest, and receives a large measure of nervous derangement in return. Either he absents himself entirely from all fellowship, and lives a recluse in the garret, with carpet slippers and a leaden inkpot; or he comes among people swiftly and bitterly, in a contraction of his whole nervous system, to discharge some temper before he returns to work. I do not care how much or how well he works, this fellow is an evil feature in other people's lives. They would be happier if he were dead. They could easier do without his services in the Circumlocution Office, than they can tolerate his fractious spirits. He poisons life at the well-head. It is better to be beggared out of hand by a scapegrace nephew, than daily hag-ridden by a peevish uncle.

And what, in God's name, is all this pother about? For what cause do they embitter their own and other people's lives? That a man should publish three or thirty articles a year, that he should finish or not finish his great allegorical picture, are questions of little interest to the world. The ranks of life are full; and although a thousand fall, there are always some to go into the breach. When they told Joan of Arc she should be at home minding women's work, she answered there were plenty to spin and wash. And so, even with your own rare gifts! When nature is "so careless of the single life," why should we coddle ourselves into the fancy that our own is of exceptional importance? Suppose Shakespeare had been knocked on the head some dark night in Sir Thomas Lucy's preserves, the world would have wagged on better or worse, the pitcher gone to the well, the scythe to the corn, and the student to his book; and no one been any the wiser of the loss. There are not many works extant, if you look the alternative all over, which are worth the price of a pound of tobacco to a man of limited means. This is a sobering reflection for the proudest of our earthly vanities. Even a tobacconist may, upon consideration, find no great cause for personal vainglory in the phrase; for although tobacco is an admirable sedative, the qualities necessary for retailing it are neither rare nor precious in themselves. Alas and alas! you may take it how you will, but the services of no single individual are indispensable. Atlas was just a gentleman with a protracted nightmare! And yet you see merchants who go and labor themselves into a great fortune and thence into the bankruptcy court; scribblers who keep scribbling at little articles until their temper is a cross to all who come about them, as though Pharaoh should set the Israelites to make a pin instead of a pyramid; and fine young men who work themselves into a decline, and are driven off in a hearse with white plumes upon it. Would you not suppose these persons had been whispered, by the Master of Ceremonies, the promise of some momentous destiny? and that this lukewarm bullet on which they play their farces was the bull's-eye and center-point of all the universe? And yet it is not so. The ends for which they give away their priceless youth, for all they know, may be chimerical or hurtful; the glory and riches they expect may never come, or may find them indifferent; and they and the world they inhabit are so inconsiderable that the mind freezes at the thought.

QUESTIONS ON CONTENT

1. Try to interpret the allusions in this essay by shrewd guessing. What, for example, do you think the following sentence must mean: "Alexander is touched in a very delicate way by the disregard of Diogenes"? How does the context (information surrounding the sentence) help to make the reference clear? If guessing fails, consult a biographical dictionary for information about Alexander and Diogenes.
2. Stevenson does not mention perfection nor perfectionists. What attitude of mind does he advocate, however, which would make even an approach to perfection impossible? Is diligence a characteristic of the perfectionist?

∾ *The Importance of Doing Things Badly*

I. A. WILLIAMS

Charles Lamb wrote a series of essays upon popular fallacies. I do not, at the moment, carry them very clearly in my memory; but, unless that treacherous servant misleads me more even than she usually does, he did not write of one piece of proverbial so-called wisdom that has always seemed to me to be peculiarly pernicious. And this saw, this scrap of specious advice, this untruth masquerading as logic, is one that I remember to have had hurled

From *The Outlook*, LI (London, April 21, 1923). By permission of the author.

at my head at frequent intervals from my earliest youth right up to my present advanced age. How many times have I not been told that "If a thing is worth doing at all, it is worth doing well"?

Never was there a more untruthful word spoken in earnest. For the world is full of things that are worth doing, but certainly not worth doing well. Was it not so great a sage as Herbert Spencer who said to the young man who had just beaten him at billiards, "Moderate skill, sir, is the sign of a good eye and a steady hand, but skill such as yours argues a youth misspent"? Is any game worth playing supremely well, at the price of constant practice and application?

Against the professional player I say nothing; he is a public entertainer, like any other, and by his skill in his particular sport he at least fulfills the first social duty of man—that of supporting himself and his family by his own legitimate exertions. But what is to be said of the crack amateur? To me he seems one of the most contemptible of mankind. He earns no money, but devotes himself, for the mere selfish pleasure of the thing, to some game, which he plays day in day out; he breaks down the salutary distinction between the amateur and the professional; eventually his skill deserts him, and he leaves behind him nothing that is of service to his fellow men—not a brick laid, not an acre ploughed, not a line written, not even a family supported and educated by his labor.

It is true that he has provided entertainment for a certain number of persons, but he has never had the pluck to submit himself to the test by which we demand that every entertainer should justify his choice of a calling—the demonstration of the fact that the public is willing to pay him for his entertainment. And, when his day is over, what is left, not even to the world, but to himself? Nothing but a name that is at once forgotten, or is remembered by stout gentlemen in clubs.

The playing of games, certainly, is a thing which is not worth doing well.

But that does not prove that it is not worth doing at all, as the proverb would, by implication, persuade us. There is nothing more agreeable and salutary than playing a game which one likes, and the circumstance of doing it badly interferes with the pleasure of no real devotee of any pastime. The man who minds whether or not he wins is no true sportsman—which observation is trite, but the rule it implies is seldom observed, and comparatively few people really play games for the sheer enjoyment of the *playing*. Is this not proved by the prevalence and popularity of handicaps? Why should we expect to be given points unless it be that we wish to win by means other than our own skill?

"Ah! but," my reader may say, "the weaker player wants to receive points in order that he may give the stronger one a better game." Really, I do not believe that that is so. Possibly, sometimes, a strong and vainglorious player may wish to *give* points, in order that his victory may be the more notable. But I do not think that even this is the true explanation. That, I suspect, was given to me the other day by the secretary of a lawn-tennis tournament, in which I played. "Why all this nonsense of handicaps? Why not let us be squarely beaten, and done with it?" I asked him. "Because," he replied, "if we did not give handicaps, none of the less good players would enter." Is that not a confession that the majority of us have not realized the true value of doing a trivial thing badly, for its own sake, and must needs have our minds buoyed and cheated into a false sense of excellence?

Moreover it is not only such intrinsically trivial things as games that are worth doing badly. This is a truth which, oddly enough, we accept freely of some things—but not of others—and as a thing which we are quite content to do ill let me instance acting. Acting, at its best, can be a great art, a thing worth doing supremely well, though its worth, like that of all interpretative arts, is lessened by its evanescence. For it works in the impermanent medium of human flesh and blood, and the thing that the actor creates—for what we call an interpretative artist is really a creative artist working in a perishable medium—is an impression upon, an emotion or a thought aroused in, the minds of an audience, and is incapable of record.

Acting, then, let me postulate,—though I have only sketched ever so briefly the proof of my belief,—can be a great art. But is anyone ever deterred from taking part in amateur theatricals by the consideration that he cannot act well? Not a bit of it! And quite rightly not, for acting is one of the things about which I am writing this essay—the things that are worth doing badly.

Another such thing is music; but here the proverbial fallacy again exerts its power, as it does not, for some obscure and unreasoning discrimination, in acting. Most people seem to think that if they cannot sing, or play the piano, fiddle, or sackbut, admirably well, they must not do any of these things at all. That they should not indiscriminately force their inferior performances upon the public, or even upon their acquaintance, I admit. But that there is no place "in the home" for inferior musical performances, is an untruth that I flatly deny.

How many sons and daughter have not, with a very small talent, given their parents—and even the less fondly prejudiced ears of their friends—great pleasure with the singing of simple songs? Then one day there comes to the singer the serpent of dissatisfaction; singing-lessons are taken, and—if the pupil is of moderate talent and modest disposition—limitations are discovered. And then, in nine cases out of ten, the singing is dropped, like a hot penny. How many fathers have not banished music from their homes by encouraging their daughters to take singing-lessons? Yet a home may be the fresher for singing that would deserve brickbats at a parish concert.

I may pause here to notice the curious exception that people who cannot on any account be persuaded to sing in the drawing-room, or even in the bath, will without hesitation uplift their tuneless voices at religious meetings or in church. There is a perfectly good and honorable explanation of this, I believe, but it belongs to the realm of metaphysics and is beyond my present scope.

This cursed belief, that if a thing is worth doing at all, it is worth doing well, is the cause of a great impoverishment in our private life, and also, to some extent, of the lowering of standards in our public life. For this tenet of proverbial faith has two effects on small talents: it leads modest persons not to exercise them at all, and immodest persons to attempt to do so too much and to force themselves upon the public. It leads to the decay of letter-writing and of the keeping of diaries, and, as surely, it leads to the publication of memoirs and diaries that should remain locked in the writers' desks.

It leads Mr. Blank not to write verses at all—which he might very well do, for the sake of his own happiness, and for the amusement of his friends—and it leads Miss Dash to pester the overworked editors of various journals with her unsuccessful imitations of Mr. de la Mare, Mr. Yeats, and Dr. Bridges. The result is that our national artistic life now suffers from two great needs: a wider amateur practice of the arts, and a higher, more exclusive, professional standard. Until these are achieved we shall not get the best out of our souls.

The truth is, I conceive, that there is for most of us only one thing—beyond, of course, our duties of citizenship and our personal duties as sons, or husbands, or fathers, daughters, or wives, or mothers—that is worth doing well—that is to say, with all our energy. That one thing may be writing, or it may be making steam-engines, or laying bricks. But after that there are hundreds of things that are worth doing badly, with only part of our energy, for the sake of the relaxation they bring us, and for the contacts which they give us with our minds. And the sooner England realizes this, as once she did, the happier, the more contented, the more gracious, will our land be.

There are even, I maintain, things that are in themselves *better* done badly than well. Consider fishing, where one's whole pleasure is often spoiled by having to kill a fish. Now, if one could contrive always to try to catch a fish, and never to do so, one might— But that is another story.

QUESTIONS ON CONTENT

1. What, according to the author, is "the first social duty of man"?
2. What is the significance of a "handicap"?
3. Define "an interpretative artist." Compare Toscanini.
4. The author recognizes two great needs of "our national artistic life." What are these? How would a willingness to do certain things badly serve these needs?
5. What one thing in each person's life is worth doing well?

SUGGESTIONS FOR PAPERS

You have perhaps not yet settled on the direction in which you will strive for perfection. Indeed, you may have already accepted compromise as the sensible way to live; a C attitude is less rewarding but more comfortable than an A attitude. Yet the chances are that you do want to be best at something. Your paper on the general idea of perfectionism may be mainly personal with incidental references to the selections in this chapter, or it may be mainly impersonal with incidental references to your beliefs or experiences. Comparison and contrast will be the obvious method of this paper.

1. Write a paper in which you isolate as narrowly as you can the one thing which you wish to do supremely well. In your first paragraph, define what this one thing is which you wish to do supremely well. In the remainder of your paper (two or three paragraphs) make clear what subordinate things you must learn to do well before

you can be sure of achieving your central ambition. Try to find ways to refer to passages from the selections in this chapter.

2. List those things which you do but do not do well. Do you consider them worth doing badly? Why? The answer will require perhaps an analysis of what constitutes a well-balanced life.

3. What is specialization? Can you name several reasons for the rise of specialization in the twentieth century? Does it have a connection with the idea of perfectionism? Or is it simply a necessity forced upon a highly complex society? (Does football provide a good example of detailed specialization?)

4. Zweig insists that Toscanini provides an ethical lesson for his generation. What kind of lesson could one learn from the experiences of Mr. Gessler? Of "the artist with carpenter's hands"? This analysis will call for (1) a listing of the requirements for successful specialization; (2) the application of the terms of this list to the three persons (Toscanini, Gessler, and the artist); (3) the reaching a conclusion on the basis of the analysis and the application.

5. Follow the suggestions under 4 above but use examples of your own. Draw your examples from people you know or from people you have read about.

6. Write a careful, detailed comparison of Toscanini and the artist with carpenter's hands. Compare "the vision," the patience, the energy, the talent, the personal satisfaction, and the result. What conclusion do you arrive at? That all men are created equal? That one man's dream is another man's nightmare? How does your conclusion apply to yourself?

7. Write a careful, detailed comparison of Mr. Gessler and the artist with carpenter's hands. Use the details of comparison suggested in 6 above. Note, however, the totally different causes for defeat in the two men. Arrive at some conclusion and apply the conclusion to yourself.

8. Write a careful, detailed comparison of Mr. Gessler and Toscanini. Use the details of comparison in 6 above. Add usefulness and personality to the list. What do you conclude? How does your conclusion apply to yourself?

9. All three of the perfectionists described in the selections of this chapter feel a more or less acute sense of frustration. Show of what this frustration consisted in each instance. What do you conclude about the dangers of perfectionism?

10. A poet has said that it is not what man *does* but what he *would do* that counts. This same poet has said that "all services

rank the same with God." Apply these conceptions to the three perfectionists described in this chapter. By the poet's reasoning, would the three end in a tie? Explain.

11. Write a paper explaining all the allusions in "An Apology for Idlers."

12. Compare "An Apology for Idlers" and "The Importance of Doing Things Badly." Is the central point of both essays similar? How do the essays differ? What is your criticism of what both authors have to say?

13. Attack or defend the chief contention in "The Importance of Doing Things Badly." Does the author mean that *all* things should be done badly? How does he distinguish between the amateur and the professional? Is he really anti-perfectionist?

SOME TITLES FOR PAPERS

1. The A Attitude
2. The C Attitude
3. The Perfection I Covet
4. The Ethics of Perfectionism
5. Penalties of Perfectionism
6. Quality in a Machine Age
7. The Price of Diligence
8. Perfectionism Gives Focus to Life
9. Perfection Is for Heaven
10. Idlers: Pro and Con
11. The Ethics of Doing Things Badly
12. Live and Let Live

❧ *TWO COLLEGE PROBLEMS: ATHLETICS AND FRATERNITIES*

THE PLACE OF ATHLETICS and fraternities in college life is perennially debated. There are those who regard both athletics and fraternities as side shows which have drawn most of the customers (students) away from the main tent: education. There are those who defend athletics and fraternities as essential contributors to the whole educative process.

So far as athletics are concerned the cycle seems clear. It started with the observation that "All study and no exercise make Joseph College a dull boy." That seemed logical and, educators thought, something should be done about it. "Much study and some exercise make Joseph less dull." That seemed better. "Less study and much exercise make Joseph still less dull." That began to be questionable doctrine. "No study and all exercise make Joe a dull boy." That's logical but bad. The original statement is now topsy-turvy. Joe—no longer Joseph—likes exercise, physical exercise; he does not care so much for mental exercise, and even if he did, he would have little time for it. His attitude would matter less if it were not for the amazing public interest in Joe's exercise. The public in this matter consists of most college presidents, some faculty members, almost all the students and alumni of all the colleges, and a vast body of sports-minded outsiders.

A recent analysis of college athletics in relation to higher education is provided by Harold W. Stoke in "College Athletics: Education or Show Business?" Mr. Stoke describes the golden knot which holds together the incompatibles of education and partly professionalized athletics. His cure? Cut the knot. But what of the young men who participate in athletics? Do they feel exploited? Apparently some do and some do not. Speaking for those who do is Allen Jackson, in an article with a self-explanatory title: "Too Much Football." Speaking for those who do not is Arnie Weinmeister, in an article with an equally self-explanatory title: "Why I Love Football." Both authors speak from experience. Which one argues more convincingly?

Even in an era of generous subsidy for college athletes, the chief recompense for stupendous effort is glory. How lasting, however, is this reward? Housman's poignant little poem, "To an Athlete Dying Young," answers for a village-hero runner, but the answer may stand for all athletes in their quest for glory. E. B. White, using reduction to absurdity as his method, surveys the whole sports scene in his satire, "The Decline of Sports (A Preposterous Fable)."

If athletics are more or less a headache to colleges, what about the fraternity system (sororities included)? The oversimplified question is this: are fraternities, in relation to what colleges profess to stand for, black, white, or gray? William S. Carlson calls the system black in his article: "Fraternities: Evil Force on the Campus." Robert T. McCracken thinks otherwise and says so in an address on "The Influence of the Fraternity."

In reading controversial materials, one should regard himself, first of all, as a judge of the debate, impartial and open-minded. With a firm grasp of the facts as presented, one should take the next step and render a verdict. One's own experiences when applicable may be used in determining the validity of the differing arguments. As college students you are in a good position to judge arguments involving either athletics or fraternities. By taking sides you do not have to lose your respect for what is sane and logical in the opposing point of view.

❧ *College Athletics: Education or Show Business?*

HAROLD W. STOKE

1

On the morning of December 7, 1951, in the General Sessions Court in New York City, fourteen tall young men stood before Judge Saul S. Streit. The scene was the climax of the notorious basketball scandals in which players had been convicted of receiving bribes from professional gamblers for throwing basketball games in Madison Square Garden. The judge was stern, but for the culprits he tempered justice. Jail sentences and fines were few and light. Judge Streit then looked over the heads of the defendants and hurled angry words at the colleges and universities they represented. He charged that these institutions had so far forgotten their educational mission and had so overemphasized athletics that they themselves had made this scene in his courtroom all but inevitable.

Addressing himself to the colleges, Judge Streit demanded immediate and drastic reforms. Among these were the restoration of athletic responsibilities to faculties and to the academic administrative authorities; the revitalization of the National Collegiate Athletic Association; the establishment of an amateur code and of a capable, well-financed policing authority.

While there was some dismay (if little surprise) in university circles at the basketball scandals, there was genuine puzzlement about the judge's suggestion for reform. The point that had escaped him was that all his proposals had been tried for years—uniformly without success. If Judge Streit and the countless educators who have tackled this problem had asked themselves why Bradley University, Kentucky, New York University, North Carolina State, or any other university should ever play basketball in Madison Square Garden, they would have started on a line of inquiry which

Atlantic Monthly, March, 1954. Reprinted by permission of the author and the *Atlantic Monthly.*

would have brought about a better understanding. Obviously it was no educational interest that brought the teams there, no huge concentration of alumni, no essential training program. It wasn't wholly a matter of money. They were there in response to a far more complex and subtle compulsion: to assist their schools as a part of the system of American higher education to carry out that system's latest and growing responsibility—namely, to provide public entertainment.

In our American society the need for entertainment is an inevitable consequence of the changing conditions of our lives—the lengthening life span, the shorter work week, speed and mobility, industrialization and prosperity. These changes create social vacuums, and for filling social vacuums the American system of education—and particularly higher education—is one of the most efficient devices invented. It is flexible, highly varied, and in touch with virtually the entire population; furthermore, it is characterized by a genuine spirit of service. It is manned by aggressive and accommodating people; it is suffused with a thoroughly practical philosophy. Hence, to its already great and growing array of services —its teaching, research, adult education, military training, and general public service—it has added another, public entertainment. This responsibility has been accepted in some instances eagerly, in some instances reluctantly, but nonetheless accepted. Drama, music, radio, and television widen the educational as well as the entertainment services of the universities; wherever these touch the public they possess more of the characteristics of entertainment than of education. Yet of all the instrumentalities which universities have for entertaining the public, the most effective is athletics.

What educational institutions thus far have not seen is that the responsibility for supplying public entertainment is a responsibility different in kind from those they have previously performed. The failure to understand this fact has led to endless strain in the management of athletics, to bewilderment among educators and the public, and even to outright scandal. Conceived as education, athletics is inexplicable, corrupting, and uncontrollable; as public entertainment, and even as public entertainment to be provided by educational institutions, athletics becomes comprehensible and manageable.

The most essential distinction between athletics and education lies in the institution's own interest in the athlete as distinguished from its interest in its other students. Universities attract students in order to teach them what they do not already know; they recruit athletes only when they are already proficient. Students are educated for something which will be useful to them and to society after graduation; athletes are required to spend their time on activities the usefulness of which disappears upon graduation or soon thereafter. Universities exist to do what they can for students; athletes are recruited for what they can do for the universities. This makes the operation of the athletic program in which recruited players are used basically different from any educational interest of colleges and universities.

The fundamental distinctions between athletics and education are somewhat obscured by several arguments frequently heard. The first is that athletics has "educational values." This is the familiar "character building," "team spirit," "sportsmanship" argument. Anyone who knows the actual operations of athletics will admit that such values could be realized far better if athletics were handled as recreation and physical education. The second argument is that many fine athletes make fine scholastic records—implying that there must not, after all, be any conflict between athletics and education. Again the answer can be short. Big-time athletics requires 20 to 28 hours per week of its devotees, aside from the time spent away from the campus; hence it is bound to detract from an athlete's education. But how can an impoverished athlete get a chance at a college education? I'll answer that question with another: Is he any more entitled to it than anyone else?

2

College athletics *is* public entertainment. Last year football audiences numbered 40 million, and now basketball is outstripping football in attendance. It is estimated that the public pays $100 million a year to the colleges for admission tickets, and television has added enormously to the number of spectators and to the revenue. Public interest as measured in publicity, newspaper coverage, and attention is far beyond that given to any educational activity. In no major school does the attention given to the appointment of a president compare with that given to the appointment of a coach, and the general public can name many more coaches than presidents.

The organization of this public entertainment is intricate. Most of the larger colleges and universities, private and public, are organized into athletic conferences managed by highly paid commissioners. Through them, complicated athletic schedules are worked out with all the finesse of the international bargaining table, and considerations of finance, publicity, the prospective careers of coaches and even presidents, are balanced in equations which would baffle electronic computers. Stadiums, field houses, and playing fields are constructed with the entertainment-seeking public primarily in mind. At the time the Yale Bowl was built it would have seated the entire adult population of New Haven, while Michigan could have put twice the population of Ann Arbor into its stadium. The University of Southern California and the University of California at Los Angeles are big schools, but even they would scarcely need the Memorial Stadium for their students and faculty. Obviously the real underwriters of bonds which build athletic plants are not students, but the public. Many an athletic director caught in a squeeze of high costs and inadequate gate receipts wishes to heaven he had all of the student tickets to sell to the people willing to pay more for them.

The same force lies back of the other features of athletics—the numerous and high-priced coaching specialists, the elaborate half-time shows, the colorful bands (supported almost as completely by scholarships as are the athletes and for the same purpose), the frolicsome majorettes, the carefully planned and executed spontaneous student rallies and demonstrations, the food, drink, and program concessions. None of these could possibly serve an educational purpose for which a college or university exists, but they are wonderful aids to public entertainment.

Perhaps most significant of all is the fact that the rules of the games themselves are now constructed and reconstructed with their entertainment value uppermost. Like dramatic coaches and directors bringing into being a Broadway production, the coaches and athletic directors gather each year to adjust the rules of football and basketball for the purpose of heightening the dramatic and entertainment value. The substitution rule, who may run with the ball, what may be allowed to happen within the ten-yard line or within the last four minutes, the nature of the penalties, and, currently, the one- or two-platoon system in football are matters which are governed by their effect upon the entertainment and upon the welfare of the enterprise. In basketball, the rules have been changed to encourage high scoring, constant running and action, alternate chances at scoring in order to provide the murderously exciting finishes which now characterize the game. Revisions are made each year only after the most elaborate study and consideration and with a wariness which would do credit to the fuse workers in a munitions factory.

Consider the Bowl games. They are important influences on athletic policies and at the same time irrefutable evidence that athletics, so far as the Bowls are concerned, have no educational significance whatsoever. So far as I know, no one seriously claims that they do.

All of the Bowls for obvious reasons are located in the South or in winter vacation areas. They are immensely successful business promotions; there is nothing about them remotely related to education. As one man put it: "Rose Bowl, Sugar Bowl, Orange Bowl—all are gravy bowls!" A half-million people saw the games in the eight major bowls last January 1, and it is estimated 70 million more heard them on radio or saw them on television. Receipts were almost $2.5 million. The distribution of the money follows a kind of formula in each conference—a large percentage to each school participating in the Bowl, a smaller percentage to each school in the conference and to the conference treasury itself. A more subtle formula to ensure support for Bowl games could hardly be devised. Participation in one of the Big Four Bowls—Rose, Sugar, Cotton, and Orange—may bring each participating school as much as $125,-000. Everyone profits—except the players, whose amateur status has thus far confined them to such grubby rewards as gifts of gold watches, blankets, free tickets which can be scalped, sometimes a little cash—the last usually secretly. Under pressure from the players and perhaps from a sense of institutional guilt at the indefensible exploitation, the rewards to players are improving, but they still are far below the A.S.C.A.P. and Equity pay scales for big-time entertainers.

3

How is all this to be made compatible with the nation's educational system? Most troubles arise from the failure of colleges to see that in supplying public entertainment they have embarked upon an operation which is different from their educational functions—and one that requires different management. Colleges have acted as if athletics were merely an extension of student recreation. Since athletes come from the same high schools as other students, are about the same age, and do get a kind of education, it has been assumed that the academic regulations applicable to the general run of students should also apply to athletes. We overlook completely the different reasons for which each is there. Hence schools have prescribed the same formal academic requirements for both the athlete and the nonathlete—a minimum number of hours must be taken, a certain number of courses must be passed, a systematic progress, however slow, must be made toward a degree, and a host of other regulations must be followed.

Yet athletics, like a corrosive acid, has eaten through every academic regulation—to the great frustration, bewilderment, and cynicism of the educational community. It has defeated faculties, forced the resignations of presidents, wrecked coaches, and undercut the support of institutions where the efforts to apply academic regulations have been insistent. Where such regulations have been successfully applied they have all but killed the athletic programs, or put them in abeyance, as at New York University, Fordham, or Pittsburgh, until a more "understanding" attitude permits revival. There are, of course, many schools—Oberlin, Swarthmore, Haverford, Bowdoin, to name a few—that attract little attention from the entertainment-seeking public because they make little attempt to supply public entertainment.

The truth is that the appetite of the public cannot be satisfied by the quality of entertainment which can be provided by athletics governed by academic regulations. Consequently, at institutions which are meeting the public's demands, academic regulations must be ignored, compromised, or eliminated. Admission requirements for athletes have become less formidable than they used to be, and usually an arrangement can be made for the boys to make up high school deficiencies. The requirements as to courses, progress toward degrees, and even grades can generally be met by either a flexible elective system or the "tailored curriculum" leading to a highly specialized "degree" in which many hours of handball, swimming, and coaching can be included. Where this does not suffice, every athletic department of any size provides at its own expense counseling and tutoring service for any of its men likely to get into trouble. Not all athletes need these negations of educational regulations, but the point is that when required the negations must be available. How compelling the necessity is can be estimated by the situations which come to light when these compromises are not sufficient—the wholesale cheating at West Point, the alteration of records at William and Mary, special examinations, and countless other devices involving various degrees of accommodation or even fraud and misdemeanor. No matter what the regulation, if it prevents athletics from supplying the public entertainment for which it exists, a way around must be found. This has been the fate which has uniformly attended the regulative efforts of faculties, administrators, code committees, accrediting associations, and even the N.C.A.A. itself.

Why should this conflict be so irreconcilable? There are many reasons, but perhaps the most compelling is that adequate entertainment can only be provided by winning teams. No amount of gushy sentiment about "playing the game" will conceal the fact that the public wants its teams to win. Victory is a part of the total titillation. If the public can't have it from one source it will transfer its loyalties and money to some other. Chick Meehan filled Yankee Stadium with football fans roaring for N.Y.U., but when de-emphasis came, N.Y.U. found that 6000 was a good crowd to watch it play Fordham, the archrival. "When Michigan loses, someone has to pay" may be a slogan at Ann Arbor, but it sums up the attitude of all schools with athletic entertainment programs. This means that to supply the entertainment, the schools must get the entertainers.

The recruitment of players is the key to most of the athletic anxieties of college presidents, the desperation of coaches, the pressure of alumni, and the activities of outside influences, business and otherwise. A chain reaction of undesirable consequences follows. The school must get the player, and the best one; the player knows this, and the bidding starts. Sometimes negotiations are carried on by a parent or other relative in order that the player may be technically free of all nonamateur bargains; otherwise he becomes a part of a corrupt bargain about which, if questions arise, he must lie or forever keep silent. Gradually the "board, room, and tuition" formula—plus a little extra, if necessary—has won acceptance. Sometimes the myth of employment persists as the justification for such payments, but it is now generally acknowledged to be a myth. The effort to limit the number of such scholarships is actually an effort to equalize competition between schools. The conferences often set a limit—but there are ways around it, the junior college "farm system" for one.

The bidding, of course, is highest for the best. In this field rumor is rife. There is the cartoon of the coach who angrily turns to one of his players and says: "Jones, you're through! Turn in your suit and your convertible." The deal may have a hundred variations, from a pledge to help the ambitious athlete on through medical school to assistance to various relatives. My own experience leads me to believe that the bizarre bargain is less frequent than educators and the public think, but is crucial nonetheless. One or two stars can transform a team into a winner and are worth what they cost. Schools bargain with all kinds of appeals—the prestige of the Ivy League may appeal to the boy from the Middle West; religious affiliation may take a boy to Notre Dame; the lavish dormitory facilities for athletes may tip the scales for Louisiana State or Texas. Most conferences have rules which prevent an athlete who has signed with one school from leaving it to join another, even though he later discovers the immense advantages of the second school. Conferences resent scouts from outside their territory, yet raiding is universal. By a dozen devices high school coaches are encouraged to become feeders for particular colleges and universities, sometimes by the flattering appointment to a coaching school staff, support for a bigger job, or even cash. Thus the web of recruitment is widespread, subtle, and effective.

The services of the American educational system in the field of public entertainment cannot be taken lightly—least of all by the educational institutions themselves. It may not be an ideal use of an educational institution to supply public entertainment, but the public interest exists; and for the institutions, either the necessity or the willingness to supply it also exists. The schools which would like to refuse will be compelled to supply it to keep up with their willing rivals. Their only choice is whether they will manage the entertainment in such a way as to prevent damage which the present methods certainly entail. These methods frequently create financial obligations which imperil educational development because they have contractual priority over educational budgets. Those who recruit players and the players who are recruited are too often corrupted not because of the bargains they strike, but because the bargains are in violation of pledges all have agreed to uphold. Influences outside universities are encouraged to seek control of educational operations—influences which are seldom willing to confine their interests to athletics. Athletics requires an atmosphere of academic accommodation to its necessities, to the great cynicism of faculties and students. It has bred a kind of humiliating schizophrenia in educational administrators who are compelled to defend with platitudes what they do not believe or to keep an uneasy silence. It has created a kind of amused tolerance toward institutions on the part of the very public which buys the entertainment—a tolerance which says that whatever the virtues and respectability of higher education on all other scores, it must be given the privilege of this secret sin.

4

At the risk of scornful disagreement let me outline how, it seems to me, the great strain in our educational institutions can be reduced. The first and most crucial step is purely intellectual: to make the admission, both inside and outside the universities, that our programs of intercollegiate athletics are operated primarily as public entertainment and not as educational responsibilities. This will lay a foundation for entirely new solutions to the problem.

With the acceptance of this concept most of the undesirable stresses and strains will begin to disappear. Athletics—that is, *winning* athletics—now becomes a legitimate university operation. Recruiting becomes not only legal but justifiable. To get the best athletes becomes not only understandable but commendable in exactly the same way that one seeks for excellence in any department of the university. One gives the athlete what the resources will allow—just as Illinois offers the graduate assistant in history or chemistry what it can to attract the best. No one thinks the less of Illinois because it can outbid Montana for graduate students. In short, athletic practices which are not at all appropriate to "educational" activities become acceptable and legitimate as parts of a program of public entertainment.

The same principle clarifies the position and character of the coaching staff. Let it be the best that can be obtained, as large and specialized as the situation requires. Let it be freed to meet its obligations without the moral strain imposed by the necessity to circumvent impossible requirements. The financial situations likewise becomes manageable. Since athletics is to be managed as entertainment, it need not in logic or in fact be a charge on the educational budget; and just as no educational institution expects to support itself from athletics, so athletics should not expect to be a charge on education. Self-support for athletics as public entertainment is at once a financial liberation and a restraint.

And why should there be concern about the academic record of a young man who comes to a university primarily to play on a team and whom the university has brought for exactly that purpose? I submit that nothing is lost by relieving all athletes of the obligation to meet academic requirements, if they cannot or do not wish to do so. Let us be courageous enough to admit that the university's interest in them is that they be good athletes, not that they be good students. It is the insistence that they be students which creates the problem both for the faculty and for the athletic managers, and to the detriment of both. Of course, if a boy wishes to be a student as well as an athlete, by all means encourage him, but in that case the fact that he is an athlete need not enter into his status as a student any more than his grades as a student should be made to affect his effectiveness as an athlete. The athlete will then for the first time be on a par with every other student who works his way through school. His academic progress will be exactly proportional to the time and interest he has beyond the demands of his employment.

What if the athlete has no interest whatsoever in his further education? A team entirely made up of professionals is not the solution for the colleges. The best solution is a prescription of academic work suited to the tastes and talents of the athlete but with the clear understanding by professors and athletes alike that the record as a student will be neither a hindrance nor a help to athletic success.

What! someone says. Have unbridled bidding for athletes? No eligibility rules? No discipline? By no means—but let these things arise, as they will, from athletic and not from academic sources and necessities. Let eligibility rules be drawn and enforced by those who are most concerned about them—the athletic managements— not by faculties. Who can be counted on to expose infractions of eligibility rules? Opponents! Every roster of players is exchanged between coaches—why should a faculty committee bother? Who is hurt if the ineligible player plays? The opposition! Who is the best insurance that he won't? The opposition! No, faculties and administrators have gratuitously assumed a lot of unnecessary burdens— and to what purpose or to what effect it is hard to see.

The relinquishment of formal academic—not institutional—control over athletics will have very substantial advantages both for athletics and for education. The first is the restoration of institutional and personal integrity. Gone will be the necessity to keep up the pretense that at the present time suffuses the discussion of athletics as a part of an educational program. The establishment of single-mindedness will be the greatest advantage, for educational institutions are basically devoted to intellectual honesty. Such honesty will free athletics as well as education from the schizophrenia from which they both now suffer.

A very valuable outcome will also be the dissipation of the sentimentality which currently surrounds college athletics in the mind of the public. This myth is carefully preserved not for its truth but for its utility. Listen to any major coach talk about his team and you will see how little such sentimentality is justified. He refers to his "material," not to boys; he discusses weakness at end and tackle and backfield, completely oblivious of the feelings of his men. There is not a player whom he will not instantly displace if he can get a better one. One of the most unhappy tasks that athletic managements must perform is to get rid of players to whom scholarships have been given—commitments made—but who can't quite make the grade on the field. Perhaps the public which sees the universities as operating departments of public entertainment and see athletes as assistants in the department will come to think of the whole matter a little differently—to the great relief of everyone concerned.

When doctors find that a given treatment results in no improvement, they re-examine their diagnosis; when scientists find that experiments produce no anticipated results, they revise their basic hypothesis. Educators now find that what was once the recreation of students in school has been transformed into a responsibility of the educational system to supply the public with entertainment. It is essential that educators carry through a fundamental revision of concepts of athletic management appropriate to this transformation.

QUESTIONS ON CONTENT

1. What were the basketball scandals referred to in the first paragraph? What does the author find wrong with Judge Streit's suggestions for reform?

2. With what other services of universities does the author classify athletics? In what essential ways does athletics differ from these other services? How does the author dispose of the arguments which tend to obscure the "fundamental distinctions between athletics and education"?

3. What is the purpose of section 2 of this article? Does it advance the argument or is it primarily descriptive of things as they are?
4. In what way does section 3 re-inforce section 2?
5. How do the first three sections prepare the way for section 4? How does the controlling idea of the entire article become evident in the final section? What is the controlling idea?
6. List all the elements in the author's solution to the problem of college athletics. Discuss each of these elements. Do you think the author's ideas make sense? Defend your point of view.

❧ Too Much Football

ALLEN JACKSON

Football is a complicated game, and the intense competition fostered by the business practices of big-time college football causes this complication to be increased. The result is that the players, if they wish to play the game at all, must spend more time on the gridiron than they bargained for. However, any spectator will tell you there are certain benefits connected with playing college football, such as being part of a school's tradition, learning fair play, having one's character built, traveling to different parts of the country, and being glorious. All of these compensate the athlete for the loss of school time. But after having played four years at guard for the University of Michigan, which possesses the largest college football stadium in the world, I can see that the supposed benefits of big-time football are either grossly exaggerated or completely imaginary, and it seems to me that most of the enormous amount of time I spent on the gridiron was wasted.

One of the most harmful aspects of the highly organized and regimented athleticism which is the result of a college sport having become "big time" is that the spontaneity has been taken out of the sport. In professional athletics the individual player expects to devote his whole person to his game because his livelihood depends upon consistent, "professional" performance. But the college athlete is primarily a student, not a professional, and when he is forced

From *The Atlantic Monthly,* October, 1951. Copyright 1951, by *The Atlantic Monthly.* Reprinted by permission.

into the overorganization and overperfection which the big-time game demands, he can no longer decide for himself whether he should study or play football on a particular day.

Probably few of the freshmen who try out for the team realize how much of their time will eventually be exacted by football. I remember discovering with dismay, as a freshman, that if I were to keep up with the rest of the men who were competing for positions on the varsity I would have to report for spring practice. Practicing football for six weeks during the warm and budding spring did not strike me as being either a glorious or a worthwhile occupation, but I needed to do it during both my freshman and sophomore years if I was to get in the lineup. I was engaged in actual practice on the field for about twenty hours a week during the spring semester, and during the fall my working week was boosted to about twenty-eight hours. Of course this includes only the time actually spent on the field, and does not include such things as evening movies of the next week's opponent, study time wasted because of fatigue, extra time demanded by game trips to other schools, and time spent in whirlpools and under heat lamps in the training room.

The four-year total actually spent on the field, counting three extra weeks of Rose Bowl practice, come to about 1350 hours. Although it was hard for me to realize it at the sophomoric height of my athletic zeal, my reason now tells me that football is only a single, minor, and unacademic part of a college education, and that it should not be more important than other single parts of college —such as, for example, the study of history. At Michigan I took six courses in history, each of them meeting three times a week for fifteen weeks, and each requiring an average of two hours of study for each hour in class. The total number of hours here is 810, about half of the time that I spent on the gridiron.

Of course many of the men on the Michigan team receive excellent grades despite their football playing. Last year the team average was higher than the school average, and the two players with the highest grades were an engineer and a premedical student. But these very men have agreed with me that high grades do not mean a satisfactory learning, and that football interferes with learning. Besides demanding that the student forego concerts, visiting lecturers, and outside reading during the football semester, big-time football also requires students with heavy loads to take part of their courses in summer school, and to skimp and cram their way through the fall semester as best they can.

A significant little adage which circulates in Michigan athletic circles says in effect that there are three aspects of college life at Michigan—intellectual, social, and athletic—but that the student has time for only two. This idea can circulate only where athletics have become, or are thought to have become, as important as the academic work of the University. The student who plays football is expected to sacrifice his studies for the sake of the game, and he is very darkly frowned upon if he misses practice for the sake of his studies. When after one Saturday game I limped off the field with a twisted ankle, I knew that I would be expected to spend a good deal of Sunday in the training room taking treatment for the injury. But since Sunday was the only time that I was able to study for a coming examination, I stayed away from the training room. As a result the ankle stiffened and on the practice field I was made to feel guilty for the rest of the week. The coaches are aware that in theory studies come first, but they are also aware that, in a big-time league, if studies actually come first, second-rate teams are likely to be the result.

One of my teammates, a philosophy student who at the time played fourth string, possessed a scholarship which would have enabled him to study in Europe. However, if he made use of this scholarship he would be unable to return in time to play football the following season. He asked the coaches' advice on this, hoping that they would tell him to go to Europe by all means, and come back and play for them when he was ready. But instead it was hinted that if he stayed he might well get to the "top" the next season, whereas if he took the scholarship it was quite possible that someone else would have his place when he got back. These suggestions were further implemented by numerous long-distance telephone calls from alumni who were amazed that anyone should consider taking a trip to Europe when there was a chance he might make the Michigan team. So he stayed, and the next season played third string.

Another teammate of mine decided during his junior year to use his GI Bill to cultivate a long-standing desire to study the piano. He had already earned a varsity letter as a sophomore center on Michigan's '48 National Championship team, and was looking forward to playing first string in his senior year, inasmuch as the man ahead of him was graduating. But during the following spring semester he became so engrossed in his piano playing that, although he still intended to play football in the autumn, he decided not to turn out for spring practice. Consequently, when he returned for practice in the fall of his senior year he was promptly and without explanation assigned to the fifth string. He was replaced by men who had practiced the previous spring and who because of this were evidently considered better gambles toward a winning combination.

The reasonable and sensible thing to do in such a situation would be to quit football because it was now obvious that he had fallen from favor and would never make the first team. But it is impossible to be sensible in the midst of people who are afflicted with football. Making what the fanatic football alumnus would call a courageous display of determination, he decided to try to win back his position, a decision which he now thinks foolish and wasteful. The result of his efforts was that by the end of the season he was still nothing more than a third-string center; and with the exception of two non-conference games and the waning, reserve-flooded minutes of the other games, he spent most of his time sitting on the bench.

2

While examining the nature of big-time football it will be necessary for me at times to criticize the position of the coaches. I wish to make the point here that it is not the individual but the position with which I find fault, and that this position must be criticized because it is one of the major means through which big-time football accomplished its distortion of the sporting spirit.

One of the ideas most thoroughly drummed into the heads of young Michigan football players is that it is a very valuable thing to be associated with Michigan football tradition. These men talk about Michigan's record, the fine men who have played for Michigan, in a manner almost liturgical, and the implication is that such things happen only at Michigan. Although much of this talk is sincere it is nevertheless misguided; it ignores the fact that Michigan tradition means basically that Michigan has always won more games than it has lost, and it means to keep on doing so.

At Michigan to win is of utmost importance; fair play and sportsmanship are fine, but to win is of utmost importance. Judging from the loud noises I have heard from chauvinistic, unathletic alumni from other big football schools, the Michigan people are not unique in proclaiming a "We're the best" athletic philosophy. But thanks to Fielding H. Yost and his point-a-minute teams of 1901 through 1905, the Michigan alumni have a better record to boast of than do the alumni of most other schools.

Yost was one of the first coaches to begin the custom of ensuring a winning record by encouraging large men to come to Michigan primarily to play football—a custom which is still zealously fostered. He was so successful in obtaining skillful players that between 1901 and 1905 his teams won 55 games in a row, and each year averaged 548 points to the opponents' 8 points. Most of the old-time Michigan alums will tell you that Fielding Yost was successful because he was ahead of his time as a coach, and this is certainly true. In pioneering player-recruitment and in consciously or unconsciously promoting a public acceptance of the idea that winning, and winning by a big score, is an end in itself, Yost acted in strict accordance with some of the most basic elements in modern football.

I do not quarrel with Yost's winning record as such, but I do quarrel with the tendency in modern football to *emphasize* winning as an end in itself, and the tendency toward a "kick him when he's down" attitude which such an emphasis fosters. Such an attitude, it seems to me, was more evident than the good sportsman's attitude when Yost's teams consistently ran up scores like 128 to 0, 88 to 0, and 139 to 0 against little schools without recruiting systems, such as Buffalo, West Virginia, and Ferris Institute. Such records, of course, are possible only when the public gives prestige to those who trample weak competition.

Whether big-time football distorts the values of the football-following public by its win emphasis or whether the public makes possible such emphasis by giving prestige to the teams which trample weak competition is a problem similar to the chicken and egg question. But whatever the cause, the result is that teams which feel the need of strengthening their reputation do so by keeping their reserves on the bench and running up the score on the first weak opponent encountered.

When the 1947 Michigan team went to the Rose Bowl there was a difference of opinion, among football experts, over whether Michigan or Notre Dame had the greatest team in the world. This controversy probably had much to do with the fact that most of the

Michigan first team was kept in the Rose Bowl game until the latter part of the fourth quarter, by which time it had run up a score of 49 to 0 on the weaker Southern California team. But even with this large accumulation of points there was almost a full team of Michigan reserve players who did not get into the game or who played for only a few seconds—the reason being, clearly, that if Southern Cal was prevented from scoring, the record would look much more impressive, and it would be obvious to the football experts that Michigan undoubtedly had the greatest team in the world.

3

The prestige which the college football business has succeeded in gaining for schools with winning records often produces an unsavory bigotry which goes beyond ordinary pride among both the players and students from a big football school. At Michigan one of those bigotry-fostering, tradition-conscious pre-game speeches which were impressive to sophomores but tiresome to seniors was to this effect: The men whom we were about to play would be battling *Michigan;* they would as a result be intimidated; and we should take advantage of this fine opportunity to dominate them. As a psychological device this idea was probably useful in giving confidence to sophomore players—but whether it worked or not, the point is that good sportsmen do not emphasize the use of their grandfathers' reputation to intimidate an opponent.

"When Michigan loses, someone has to pay." I heard the first of many repetitions of this illogical idea in 1949 when Michigan's 25-game winning streak was decisively broken by Army. Since then I have heard it repeated with dogged monotony by the coaches after each Michigan loss, including Michigan's loss to Michigan State last fall. During the practice week following this game I personally counted forty-three repetitions of the slogan. This one slogan symbolizes to me the perversion of the sporting spirit which has been produced by big-time football. The slogan not only implies that Michigan *shouldn't* have lost, but it also suggests that the loss was caused by something wrong somewhere—perhaps something shady on the part of the other team.

The point of view suggested by this slogan becomes positively unchristian in its implication that revenge will be sought at the expense of next week's opponent. This desire for revenge is doubly evil in that it cannot be directed at the people who seem to have inflicted the injury but must be spent upon the first innocent victim who happens along. But the brass-tack meaning of "When Michigan loses, someone has to pay" is simply that since Michigan prestige and Michigan gate receipts depend upon a spectacular winning record, a lost game must be counteracted, if possible, with a larger than usual winning score the following Saturday. And the slogan is successful in arousing these attitudes. Many of the players continue to deify the coaches long after they should have outgrown this, and to them everything said on the field is gospel. Those who do not care for much of what goes on are in the game too deep to get out, and if they wish to stay on the team they must close their minds to reason and allow themselves to be directed.

I do not wish to imply that the players are actually taught unfair tactics at Michigan: this is certainly not true. But the Michigan coaches find it necessary to emphasize winning to a much greater degree than is natural or reasonable, and in a game like football this sort of emphasis is bound to lead to unsportsmanlike conduct. Indeed, the feeling that it is terribly necessary to win is so strong, and the resultant feeling of relief after having won a game is so pronounced, that if any questionable tactics have been used by Michigan men during the game they are merely laughed off.

Virtually all of my teammates on last year's squad were very clean players, but the atmosphere of big football often turned team spirit into mob spirit when the group as a whole accepted actions which to the individual would seem unsportsmanlike. One of the key players on last year's team was noted for his feats in the boxing ring and for his quick temper. When on Monday afternoons the team would watch movies of the preceding Saturday's game, this player would occasionally be seen handing a seemingly accidental left-hook on an opposing player's chin. Of course the movies of any football game are likely to show up actions which appear to be underhanded; but the point here is that such actions—especially by the hotheaded boxer—would invariably strike the coaches as funny, and they would run the play over again in slow motion so that everyone could see and laugh.

The assembled players took their cues from the coaches and also laughed heartily to see such fun. Then, a few plays later on the screen, the coaches would solemnly draw our attention to the fact that the other team was "gang tackling," and that we would have to look for just "this sort of thing" from our next week's opponent because it was *that* kind of team. Michigan's maize and blue players are not encouraged to "gang tackle" of course; they are simply ordered to cover the opposing ball-carrier with "a blanket of blue."

4

Another bromide which the big-time football votaries like to administer to promising young athletes is that there is something wonderful about being part of the "team spirit" found in big-name teams. Human beings have long since proved themselves social animals, and it seems reasonable that they should enjoy team games. But big football has perverted the team spirit as well as the sporting spirit.

In the first place the competition for individual positions on big teams is altogether too stiff, and this does more to break down than to build up team spirit. The bigness of the game, the publicity and prestige which go along with a first-team position, and the large number of grim and intense young athletes who are drawn to the gridiron by these abnormalities cause a spirit of internecine conflict to be as much in evidence as *esprit de corps.*

Besides this, the increasing specialization demanded by big-time football does nothing toward engendering social cohesion on the team. The compulsion to win generated by the game's big-business aspect demands that the individual players become precise and accurate in their various specialties to a degree unnatural in college athletics. On the Michigan practice field the ends, backs, and linemen all spend much of their time in separate corners of the field, performing their various specialties with monotonous repetition. During the week there are only one or two hour-long scrimmages, on the average, and the rest of the time is devoted to various forms of dummy practice, running of signals, and practicing specialties. All of this is necessary to produce a winning team in a big-time league, but it is not much fun. Any sport which requires a week's practice of specialties for each sixty-minute game has become too mechanized to allow the spontaneous sort of team spirit which would seem to be the special value of college football.

Everyone has seen football teams gather in the center of the field just before the opening kickoff for a last-minute handshake, and this sight, plus the stock sport page photographs of men on the bench who are "trying just as hard as the men in the game," seems to indicate that team spirit is an actual and worthwhile reality in big-time football. I should like to state plainly and emphatically that much of the huddled handshaking and bench emotion is artificial. The players know that in order to win it is necessary to get "worked up" for the game, whether they feel like it or not. Also, the bigness and complexity of modern football produces a decrease in team homogeneity and a corresponding decrease in spontaneity. The players sense that they will be less effective without such homogeneity, and they attempt to regain this feeling on the practice field and in the big game by an artificial emphasis upon such devices as the pre-game handshake and the bench chatter.

My first experience with the automaton spirit which big-time coaches often find it necessary to enforce in order to make their teams efficient winning machines was when, as a freshman, I was used as a human dummy to test the proficiency of the '47 Rose Bowl varsity. Occasionally, when one of my freshman or reserve teammates would be laid out by the business-like efficiency of the varsity, in such a way that play could not be resumed until the field was cleared, the coaches would promote big-time football's party-line attitude toward such a situation by reciting this slogan: "Well, move the ball or move the body." The varsity players, tickled by such wit, would then move the ball to an uncluttered part of the field and resume play.

When I became a varsity player I began to notice other evidences that big-time football cannot afford to depend upon spontaneous team spirit. At the training table on the Friday night before a game the Michigan players were expected to show that they were in the process of "storing it up" for the next day's contest by eating their meal with a quiet intensity which precluded laughter or any evidence of high spirits. Probably there were a few players who actually felt a sort of judgment-day taciturnity, but for many of the players it was an artificially imposed atmosphere, and bad for the digestion. If, as often happened, some of the lighter hearts would forget for a moment that they were supposed to be grim on Friday evenings, there would be ominous and foreboding looks from the coaches' table—and if the unwholesome gaiety persisted, the coaches would silence it by uttering with gloomy irony, "We hope you'll all be this happy tomorrow night."

Another instance in which the Michigan players had an attitude externally imposed upon them will serve to exemplify the pernicious effect which big-time football has had upon the reputations of schools which sponsor big-name teams. A few days before we started on our Rose Bowl journey we were summoned for an orientation lecture, a surprising amount of which was devoted to our table manners and general deportment while in Pasadena. It seemed that many of the teams which had in the past gone to the Rose Bowl had been guilty of ungentlemanly conduct—one team, we were told, had been fond of throwing bread rolls the length of a table in the hotel dining room and flipping squares of butter against the ceiling, where they stuck. But Michigan, we were told, did not do that sort of thing. Although it was good to hear that Michigan did not do that sort of thing, neither I nor my teammates had ever been in the habit of throwing butter at the ceilings of plush hotels, and we wondered why we were being so energetically told to act in a normal manner.

The reason was that the big-time football system has unconsciously superimposed a mercernary stereotype upon the college football player, and people often *expect* a visiting football team to be rowdy; because of this, the coaches were at pains to impress us with lurid examples, of questionable authenticity, of how not to act. In Pasadena we conducted ourselves with a normal amount of gentility—neither better nor worse than the average of the teams which preceded us, a waitress told me. But the Michigan players heard themselves complimented profusely on their conduct.

The point of all this is that when an entire athletic group, like college football players, has such a reputation that players who conduct themselves with ordinary grace are looked upon as above average, there is something wrong with the system. Moreover, schools which sponsor big-name teams, and so associate themselves with this bad reputation, subtly lose prestige in the eyes of the general public. Big-time football has promoted a syllogism something like this: football players are something less than students; therefore, universities which sponsor big football teams, though famous, are something less than universities.

5

In order to exhibit one of big-time football's most unscrupulous practices, I shall have to explain the nature and function of the "red shirts," as they are called at Michigan. The generally used term is "cannon fodder." Because modern football is such a complicated game, the head coaches are able to attend to only the first two or three teams, called "blues" at Michigan. However, it is necessary to have at least two more teams, the red shirts, against whom the blues can scrimmage, or who can hold the dummies for the blues to block. The blues do not play amongst themselves because they are likely to hurt one another and be lost for the big game on Saturday. Also it is necessary for the varsity blues to feel their power and be able to march up and down the field through the weaker red shirts.

A few of the red shirts know that they will never rise in the varsity hierarchy, and they are still content to come out for practice season after season to be used by the blues. But there are not enough of these men. The rest of the red shirts are players who dream of making at least the third-string varsity one day, but who the coaches are reasonably sure will never make the grade. Instead of telling these men that their chances of making the varsity are extremely small, the coaches, because they need men on whom their varsity can sharpen its claws, encourage the red shirts to return each year to try again. Of course all this is a matter of subtle suggestion; it is impossible to prove actual misrepresentation of facts, but I have spoken to and played against a number of disenchanted red shirts who for four years held dummies and waited their turn to be mashed by the blues, only because it was hinted that they might make it one day.

To a young boy who is fresh out of high school—where he was a big man because of his football playing—the slightest hint by a big college coach that he might make the varsity is enough to set the home town buzzing and to increase the player's illusion of prestige. When he fails to make the varsity team, it seems one of life's most terrible tragedies.

Two years ago, such a player came to Michigan. As a great high school star and a holder of state records in track he was looked upon by his friends and home-town supporters as a potential All-American, and when the Michigan coaches watched him operate on the freshman team they seemed to agree. The following season—last fall—the player's picture was in every sporting magazine in the country, and since such publicity could occur only with the coaches' sanction, it was assumed that he would do great things. Then the football season began, and game after game the highly publicized player was left sitting on the bench. Although he dressed for all the games, and made all the trips, for some reason unknown to himself or to his teammates he was never allowed to play, except for a few seconds in one game, and by the end of the season it was apparent that he would not make a varsity letter. When Michigan prepared to make its second trip to the Rose Bowl, a trip on which ten more than the usual number of players were taken, so that even some of the red shirts went along, the coaches refused to take him, and in so doing as much as told him that he would never play for Michigan.

To a boy who had been heralded as a second Tom Harmon this was a crushing blow, especially since any reasonable person would assume that the football system, after publicizing the player with such vigor, would feel honor-bound to take him along on the Rose Bowl trip. What happened to this boy represents in concentrated form what happens to most of the students who play big-time football. They are first deluded into thinking that they are great and that football is great; then they are used by the system and finally discarded with at best nothing to show but a scrapbook full of redundant and inaccurate clippings.

Of course such build-up and subsequent disappointment occurs elsewhere in life, particularly in a professional sport like baseball. But this is all part of the professional scene, and it has no place in college athletics. College football should have all the benefits of a strictly amateur sport; but it is losing these and acquiring the undesirable aspects of a professional sport.

6

Any accusation that football leaves the player with nothing but a scrapbook full of clippings will move the defenders of the game immediately to demand that some mention be made of the "character building" upon which football seems to have a priority. Aside from the probability that the coaches who direct uncommercialized college sports, such as track, wrestling, and gymnastics, could present good arguments showing these sports to be just as effective builders of character as football, it seems to me that anyone who assumes that athletics are an extraordinary factor in the development of an individual's character is guilty of ignoring the many forces which contribute to such development.

But in the football world there is great emphasis placed upon character development; and if, in the coaches' not infallible judgment, an individual player's character does not seem to be developing in the manner prescribed by the big-time football system, his position on the team will be endangered. Because all big-time football players and coaches have grown up with the idea that it is necessary to give your all for the alma mater, anyone who does not seem willing to do this is looked upon as a coward.

The importance of winning in big-time football makes it absolutely necessary to field the best team possible on important Saturdays, regardless of injuries. When the modern compulsion to win is superimposed upon the old give-your-all idea, the pressure on an injured player to play despite his injury is immense. No matter how many times a player proves himself in battle, the first time he decides that an injury should keep him off the playing field he is given the raised eyebrow and accusing stare by the coaches, trainer, and even some of his teammates. This subtle accusation is caused by the team's collective dread of weakening the winning combination, and it is especially acute if the injury is not obvious and the coming game is expected to be close.

Near the end of my junior year, when I was a first-string, battle-scarred veteran of many games, I received what I considered to be a very serious knee injury a week before Michigan was to play Ohio State for the conference championship. The knee was badly swollen, and it was impossible for the doctor who looked at it to make a valid diagnosis until the swelling subsided. But, since I could not walk, and since it was necessary for me to spend two days in the hospital, I assumed that I would not be expected to play in the big game.

However, the man who substituted for me lacked both my weight and experience. So I found to my dismay that as soon as I could walk I was expected to "gut it out," as the Michigan training-room slogan would describe it, by reporting to the practice field, having my knee trussed up with tape, and preparing to give my all for Michigan. Although I could feel loose things inside my knee, I was so intimidated by this frightening preoccupation with guts that I hobbled dutifully out onto the practice field.

On the field I found that my obvious inability to play was looked upon with suspicion, and I began to hear remarks that I was allowing the knee to get the better of me. Instead of being ordered back to my hospital bed for a thorough examination, I was merely told that whether I played or not was entirely up to me. At this point it was clear that I was expected to play, and if I did not I would be dubbed a quitter. Like everyone else, I think there are certain things for which it is worth while to give my all, but I de-

cided then that the primitive alma-materism of an obsolete generation of college playboys was not one of them, and I did not play.

About a week later the knee became locked in a rigid position,
and it was necessary for me to return to the hospital. It was now
possible to see that a piece of cartilage had been torn in such a
way that there was little chance of its growing back together, and
an operation would be required. The operation did more than fix
my knee, because now the coaches knew that I had not been faking
and that I could once more be depended upon to give my all for
Michigan. But the point had been made: big-time football has no
respect for either the individual's word or his body.

7

A word must be said about the rabid football alumni and the
overzealous football fans. I find no fault with anyone who has a
normal interest in athletics, but the perverted bigness of football
produces people with a perverted interest in sport. Although the
number of the most adhesive of these hangers-on to the football
scene is not large, their presence is distressing because they are undoubtedly the articulate representatives of a much larger group
whose interest in and attitude toward big-time football allow the
unhealthy and prolonged hysteria which permeates the college
football scene each fall.

Except for a fawning and familiar interest in a few back-field
stars, many of the football alumni whom I met had no real interest
in the players as individuals; indeed their interest in the stars was
usually based only upon athletic reputation and seldom upon
character. Many of the football alumni who help destitute athletes
through school, from my observation, do this because of a selfish
interest in the perpetuation of the school's winning record, with
which they have identified themselves, and not because of a personal
interest in the welfare of the particular athlete. It is this sort of
person who exerts the pressure which fires coaches when the team
has not won enough games to satisfy the alumni's collective ego.
These are the men who are influential in promoting among young
boys a distorted idea of what it really means to play big football;
and these are the ones who think that other people's judgments
of men are as superficial as their own when they say that football
players will have no trouble finding jobs, because everyone is glad
to hire a football player.

Concerning the finding of jobs, it would be my guess that largely because of *very* widespread recruiting practices, the term football player has become synonymous with ape, and because of this it is often better for the job applicant to save mention of his gridiron record until after he has become acquainted with a prospective employer. Concerning the meaty subsidization question, I am glad to say that the University does none of it. A few of the players receive help from alumni, but a school with Michigan's prestige and record can usually get all the football material it needs without such aid.

During my four years at Michigan I played in games which took me from New York to California, but I was never given the opportunity to meet or speak to an opposing player. If there is any value in having an intercollegiate schedule, it would seem that such value would come from the opportunity which game trips afford to become acquainted with men from other schools and other parts of the country. But big football has no time for palaver. Indeed, on almost every trip we took, we were cautioned to keep to ourselves—because, and this is another slogan that I unfortunately know by heart, "We are here for only one purpose, and that is to win."

Often during a game I would develop a genuine fondness for some of the players with whom I was exchanging blows, and I would have valued a friendly glass of beer with them after the game. But the visiting team was always whisked off to its train with businesslike alacrity; about the only thing I learned from traveling to other schools was that in every college stadium the grass is more or less green.

Nor did I learn anything from making the Rose Bowl trip—I merely verified my suspicion that of all the farces connected with big-time football, the Rose Bowl was the biggest. The so-called honor and glory of playing in the Rose Bowl is transient and meaningless, as is any glory and honor which is nothing more than the product of a publicity man's imagination; the three-week extra practice is not justified by the benefits of the game; and the trip to the coast is crowded and regimented. But the visiting team does at least get a trip out of it, and this is more than the host team gets. Of course I had no opportunity to speak to any of the California players, but it is impossible for me to understand how they, as Rose Bowl participants, could think of themselves as anything but extremely unlucky. For them there is no send-off, no cross-country trip, and no guided tours—nothing but three more weeks of drudgery under a southern California sun.

So, after four years of seeing everything there is to see in big-time college football—victories, defeats, publicity, hospitals, championships, and bowls—of being known as a "football player" rather than a human being, of seeing myself and my teammates misrepresented and misquoted by sportswriters who seldom attempted to know the players personally, of playing in a 97,000-seat stadium in which my nonpaying student friends were forced to sit in the end zone, of having my natural desire for physical exercise corrupted and commercialized, of giving up pleasant afternoons in favor of kicking and rolling in the dust and muck of the practice field—I have decided that big-time football is a poor bargain for the boys who play the game.

QUESTIONS ON CONTENT

1. Compare the first and last paragraphs of this article. What do they have in common?
2. How relevant to each other are the author's estimates of the time he spent on football and the time he spent on six courses in history?
3. Comment on this statement: "The coaches are aware that in theory studies come first, but they also are aware that, in a big-time league, if studies actually come first, second-rate teams are likely to result." What if *all* colleges had second-rate teams?
4. What is the moral of the philosophy student's experience? Of the piano-playing student's experience?
5. Discuss the ethics of winning games by large scores. Can coaches do anything about this problem?
6. Comment on the Friday night intensity "which precluded laughter."
7. How true is the syllogism offered on p. 216?
8. Do you agree with the author's condemnation of the use of the "red shirts" as "cannon fodder"?
9. What point, if any, is made by telling the story of the much publicized player who did not make the team?
10. In what way does this article supplement "College Athletics: Education or Show Business?"
11. Does the author make the charge that Michigan players are subsidized?

❧ *Why I Love Football*

ARNIE WEINMEISTER

Football is, to my mind, the best sport of all. I'd rather watch it than any other game. Everything about it is exciting, the crisp crack of leather against leather, the crowded stadium, the thrill of watching a play in which every assignment is carried out perfectly, of seeing the fullback smacked down by a jarring tackle, or a halfback break loose for a long gain, or the defending line hold for downs within their five-yard line.

But, above all, I love to play it. And the greatest of football thrills for me is that of bodily contact. When I start a game I feel that I must hit my opponent first, and hardest. Of course, many times I get "waffled" on the first play, and I'll admit that I don't enjoy getting knocked on my back. But football is a fiercely competitive game, and it's this competitive aspect—the risk—that heightens the excitement. I've never known a really good football player who didn't like the contact involved in the sport.

Orban "Spec" Sanders loved physical contact as much as anyone I've known. We played together on the New York Yankees of 1948 and 1949. Spec used to sit in a whirlpool bath—sometimes for the better part of a week—to get rid of the Charley horses he'd suffered in the previous game. Whenever he had the choice of running out of bounds to avoid a tackler or running into him Spec would lower his head and ram the tackler for that extra yard or two.

It's this fierce competition and excitement of the game, plus a natural desire for rugged exercise, which makes football my first love in sports.

My earliest recollections of football go back to a time when the kids gathered in my back yard to tackle a dummy made of a burlap bag packed tightly full of autumn leaves. The bag was then tied to a stout branch of a tree, and we took turns trying to rip it apart. As I remember, my father liked this "practice" we held, because it served a twofold purpose. It kept us off the streets and, perhaps more important, it was the only way he could get me to rake the leaves. The harder we hit the dummy the more thrilled we

From *Holiday*, November, 1954. Reprinted by permission of the author.

were, and the boy who tore it down—rope, bag and all—was the hero of the moment.

In grammar school we played a game from which football, some maintain, originated—soccer. In our version of the game—being unable to afford a soccer ball—we substituted a horse chestnut, an abundance of which grew along the shaded streets of Portland, Oregon. You can imagine what shins and ankles looked like when ten or twelve boys aimed kicks at such a small object, missing it more than really necessary. This game probably helped develop a keen eye, good co-ordination, and more particularly—aggressiveness. Many years after I left Portland I ran into a friend who had played high-school football with me, and also the soccer game. He remembered me as the boy with the "Li'l Abner" boots—they had steel caps on the toes and made me the terror of the field.

From this game we progressed to sand-lot football. The biggest guy was the fullback and he always carried the ball. The little fellows not only couldn't tackle him; they couldn't argue with him. I was about twelve and my family thought I was to be the smallest of four boys, so I didn't carry the ball very often. I got a lot of practice tackling, which probably was fortunate, since most of my success in football was to be as a tackle. However, I grew to six feet four inches and two hundred and fifty pounds.

In high school I had my first taste of organized football. Here I learned that the big men around school were usually stars on the football field. I used to look up to the varsity players as supermen. I remember how excited I became when the coach would wander over to observe me in the long, hard practice sessions.

The first time I was sent into a game I was so nervous I didn't know where to line up. But once I was hit the nervousness vanished. It's something I've never got over; even now, as a professional player, I am emotionally tied up before a game and not until after the first play can I settle down.

After high school I went to the University of Washington and there my football career took a rather strange twist. I had played tackle in high school. Now I was told to play end. I was fast enough, but I lacked the deft hands so necessary to a pass receiver. At the end of a year I entered the service. I spent three years in the field artillery and returned to Washington aspiring to play fullback. During spring practice I was touted as a "cinch" All-American at this new position. In the fall we opened against St. Mary's and I had an excellent day for a debut, but we lost 24-20 to a team which featured Herman Wedemeyer. I dropped eleven pounds during the game, playing about fifty-seven minutes. The next week a tough team from U.C.L.A. beat us 33-9. During the third quarter I had my knee creased by a mountainous center and great line backer, Don Paul. After a couple of weeks of rest I was back in scrimmage. On one play I carried the ball around my left end and cut sharply to avoid a tackler. I heard a "crack" and the ball flew in one direction, I in another. My knee had buckled completely. I was helped from the field in tears; I uttered a weak "So long, fellows," certain I would never play football again.

Thanks to Dr. Rex B. Palmer, our team physician, I had a successful knee operation that fall and returned the following year to finish my collegiate football career. My coach, Ralph "Pest" Welch, felt that playing tackle would place less strain on my knee, so that's where I played.

Football is a more emotional game than is realized. I can recall players twenty-five to thirty years of age crying in the locker room. There was the time at the University of Washington when Jimmy Phelan gave such an inspirational talk that the team ran onto the field in a sort of trance. This was not unusual, except that someone forgot to open the door. The players plunged right through it. One of the tough line backers in the pro loop was Jerry Shipkey, a fullback from U.C.L.A. He would rather meet a runner coming through the line with his face than any other way. During practice sessions for the Pro Bowl, an all-star game in which Jerry and I played in Los Angeles, I would point to the fence and say, "O.K., Jerry, run through that fence." It wouldn't have surprised me to see him do it. It is fellows like Shipkey who have the spirit to make football what it is. It is a game that must be played without fear of bodily contact.

I didn't realize what the word "contact" meant until I became a professional. I'll never forget the day I reported to the New York Yankees' training camp in Cheshire, Connecticut. There were six of us returning from the college all-star game in Chicago, where the pro Cardinals had taught us quite a lesson during a 28-0 drubbing. That year, sports writers said we had the greatest array of collegiate talent ever assembled. There were John Lujack, Bobby Lane, Charles Conerly, Bob Chappius, George Connor, Paul Cleary and others of equal reputation. I gazed around and saw only men who looked like giants. One, in particular, was in a pair of shorts.

He was deeply tanned, with a brawny, hairy chest, and he was hitting a practice blocking sled with his bare shoulder. I remember remarking to my buddy, Paul Cleary, All-American end from U.S.C., "This is no place for me."

While with the Yankees under Ray Flaherty we lost our first two games of the 1948 season. Next we were slated to play San Francisco in Kezar Stadium. We flew from New York and arrived at Sonoma *Mission Inn* late on a Wednesday night. At noon Thursday we had a lunch of hamburger steak and onions, and were on the field in pads at 2:30 P.M. The temperature was 63 degrees when we left New York. At Sonoma it was 94 degrees. That afternoon I encountered the most brutal physical beating I have ever taken. Flaherty ran us in the heat for three hours and twenty minutes. We formed in two lines, about ten men to each, at one end of the field. As a kicker punted the ball down field the lead man in each line raced toward the halfback catching the ball, then turned and tried to beat the receiver back to the starting point. The only rest a man got was waiting his turn to repeat the whole thing. But soon men began toppling over so fast that by the time a runner returned to the starting position he would be first in line again. Before long, players all over the field were on hands and knees, actively ill. Flaherty yelled, "Look at Cheatham—he's the only one in shape." But when he finished one more sprint, Lloyd Cheatham was as sick as everyone else.

I don't have to tell fans what happened in the following Sunday's game: we were beaten 41-0 as the San Francisco 49ers scored two touchdowns within two minutes. We were as listless as one would expect, but we never stopped trying. After we returned East and Baltimore took us for our fourth consecutive loss, Red Strader was named coach during a meeting which endeared Dan Topping to me as an owner. Here we were a team badly beaten physically, with its morale almost gone, and Dan Topping told us to take four days off and rest. It worked, because we came back to win six of the next eight games for a season's record of 6-6. Topping's attitude impressed upon me the necessity of morale on a professional football team. All professional teams are about equal in weight and ability. The team with the best morale is usually the winning team.

A player cannot expect to get himself mentally ready to play on the day of the game. This preparation must start early in the week. I can think of many instances when players as well as coaches were worried because the practice attitude was not just right.

Steve Owen, famous coach for the New York Giants, claims he can walk into a dressing room an hour before game time and tell whether a team is set to go. Usually, if a team is ready, there is a minimum of locker-room banter.

I might add that Stout Steve has had plenty of football satisfaction when he felt that his clubs were ready. I remember back a few years ago when those wonderful teams of Paul Brown's at Cleveland, with Otto Graham throwing strikes to many fine receivers, were winning everything in sight. The Giants went out to play in that big Cleveland stadium determined to stop the Browns' streak with what, that year, the newspapers called Owen's "umbrella defense" against Graham's uncanny passes. The so-called "umbrella" was simply a method of covering potential receivers wherever they popped up on the field, in the flat zone or in the deep areas. But just covering receivers won't beat Cleveland. Not when Paul Brown had those great ball carriers booming up the middle and whanging the tackles with trap plays. And the Giant line knew it. We were ready to put the "umbrella" over the air routes to our goal line, but this particular Sunday there was a fine, unspoken determination to bottle up the Cleveland running game too. Nobody announced it. Not with words. But on the first Cleveland offensive play of the game, Graham in the T-quarterback slot, started that nice fakery of his with the ball, began his fade to pass, and vanished! That Giant line rolled into the Brown backfield like a tidal wave and that one collective charge set the pattern for the afternoon. Otto got his pants dirty. Al De-Rogatis, right tackle, and Jon Baker, guard, were really putting the pressure on Otto, making him throw the ball that fraction of a second early which leads to interceptions. We won. Not by much. Nobody was beating that Cleveland team by much. But then nobody expected the Giants to be that hot that day. The team was ready. The score was 6-0—the only game in which Cleveland was ever blanked.

One of the great, if seldom expressed, thrills of football lies in that sudden, sure conviction that you are a member of a team that is playing as one man.

On days like that most of the things that happen are good. The breaks go your way simply because you are more alert, higher keyed, faster than you have a right to be. I remember a game in Washington against George Marshall's Redskins, another Sunday with that usual good Washington crowd tearing its throat out above the big, brassy music of the Redskin band, and the turf just right and the day bright and all the guys full of beans . . . and maybe me a bit too beany. We had the ball and, as I recall, the play was a straight off-tackle smash with young Eddie Price, the Tulane flash, carrying the ball. My assignment was to brush-block the guy in front of me and then to remove the strong-side line backer. I missed the man in front of me, got the wrong angle on the line backer and missed him too. But it was one of those days. I kept driving. The play was being squeezed toward the sidelines and the Washington safety man, maybe Bullet Bill Dudley, was coming up fast to smack Eddie out of bounds. I rolled into him with what proved to be the key block and Price went almost all the way. I think they got him down around the three-yard line . . . Of course, nobody noticed that I'd missed two blocks except the whole team and Bill Dudley. As we were getting up, he looked at me sadly and said, "Why the hell can't you stay up there in the line and let us play this game right?"

As a pro I used to think I was calm before each contest, but my wife, Shirley, tells me that I am like a lion in a cage the morning of a game. She says she is careful not to discuss anything controversial because I'll "bite her head off." Most players develop a sort of pre-game ritual. I have one that goes something like this: I awaken at 9:00 A.M. (*if* I have been able to sleep that late). At 10:00 A.M. I have my battle breakfast, which consists of orange juice, steak, baked potato, toast and coffee. Then, I go to the stadium at 11:30 to begin dressing for the 2:00 P.M. game. Players have idiosyncrasies about dressing, such as putting stockings on inside out, taping on sponges or pads in some special way, and other foibles that sound crazy but relieve tensions.

These locker-room sessions, before and after any game, are part of the memories and the affinities all players own. I can remember backs with their ankles and shins taped to the point that they looked like ballet dancers up on their toes, and all those goofball conversations which attend the weird sights of grown men mincing about in pads and bandages.

"Hey, butter-butt, what do you do on that new A-Play?" "What do I do? Why I lay down fast and roll to the right so's I don't get hit none. Ain't that the play where you stand up and count the gate?"

"Hey, boy, that big guy from the Coast says that today's the day you get yours. He says he's ripe to cream you." "I cream nice but I don't mash so good."

"Let's get this one over fast today, fellows. I got a date." "Where you goin' to take her?" "He ain't goin' to take her. After this one, they're gonna sit in the lobby whilst she counts his loose teeth." "Gum her one for me, pal."

This is the comradeship, the nonsense, the bubbles, the family at home and working up to be glad of it. Nobody ever forgets it.

Football gets into your blood so deeply that it is difficult to tear yourself away from the game. I have talked to many ex-professional players who have told me that the first year out of football is tough. They say you get like a race horse. When the season rolls around you have that urge to start running to pile into somebody. There must be something catching about it, because the display of this aggressiveness draws around 15,000,000 fans each year to the stadia throughout the country. Why do these thousands turn out on Saturday and Sunday afternoons to watch football? Some of them come for the spectacle of the stadium itself: the colorful banners, the music of the bands, the jostling, cheering crowds. But more of them come for the vicarious thrill they get each time a halfback scampers for a long gain, intercepts a pass, or smacks someone down. Too, there is always the imminent likelihood of the entire complexion of the game changing quick as lightning. Anything can happen.

I remember one of the few games in which I played fullback in college. We were facing a highly touted St. Mary's eleven— mentioned earlier—featuring that superb halfback, Herman Wedemeyer. As the game got under way we see-sawed back and forth, neither team gaining decisively. I was held to a minimum of yardage in line plunging, which was supposed to be my specialty, but I had made some progress around the ends. Our quarterback decided to call an off-tackle slant. The situation was third down and two yards to go for a first down on our own forty-three-yard line. The ball was given to me, the off-tackle hole opened and I went through it. I cut toward the safety man in the middle of the field, then veered to avoid him and there was the goal line—fifty-seven yards away. I turned on full speed and I thought this was it. I could hear the safety in pursuit—could I make it? As I crossed the five-yard line I felt the clutches of a tackler and hit the turf—on the one-yard line. I was disappointed not to have gone all the way. But two plays later I scored on a line plunge. I'll be a long time forgetting this thrill, for in the very next scrimmage session I injured my knee and never again played fullback.

In 1948 I was invited to play with the Collegiate All-Stars in the annual game against the professional champions. When I arrived at training camp I knew who would play the tackles. Frank Leahy was head coach and he had his two great tackles on hand, George Connor and "Ziggy" Zcarobski. I felt deflated. At each practice session I tried my best, and midway through the two-week period Frank Leahy called me aside and asked if I would mind playing offensive guard. He added, "You see, Arnie, you've impressed us as a football player." These words have inspired me all through my football career.

This big charity game is played on a mid-August night at Soldier Field in Chicago before a crowd of more than 100,000. Just before the kick-off all the lights are turned out and the players are introduced. As each player is announced, he runs onto the field with a single spotlight following him. Running onto the field under that spotlight is one of the most dramatic moments of my football memories.

The average pay of a professional player is about $5000 or $6000 for a season which, including training camp, lasts about five and a half months. The minimum I know of is $3600 for a lineman and the maximum is $25,000 for a star quarterback. Many times we wonder whether all the lumps and bruises are worth it.

But maybe when all's said and done, the highlights and the incidents aren't quite enough to sum up this vastly technical game of man-to-man and team skills. Maybe the real answer to the lure of this sport goes deeper. Maybe it's man's eternal memories, the gladiator, soldier, warrior symbols in modern dress of a time when all the racers were young, strong and very willing to match blows for blood or fun. And in the autumn of the year when the air is crisp and the days are blue with the iron of frost, when the urge to move is compelling— . . . what a time to play football!

QUESTIONS ON CONTENT

1. Do all the details of this article contribute to the central idea: why I love football?
2. How does Weinmeister differ from Jackson ("Too Much Football") on the following points: injuries, emotions, do-or-die, coaches, team morale, "locker-room banter"?
3. Does the author mention his scholastic work at the University

of Washington? Considering the central purpose of the article, would such references have been appropriate? Discuss.
4. In "The Importance of Doing Things Badly" (Chapter 5), the author draws a clear line between amateurs and professionals. Does this distinction possibly account for the difference in Jackson's and Weinmeister's attitudes towards football? Discuss.
5. Does the final paragraph of this article offer perhaps the basic reason behind the appeal of football? Why, or why not?

❧ *The Decline of Sport*

(A Preposterous Parable)

E. B. WHITE

In the third decade of the supersonic age, sport gripped the nation in an ever-tightening grip. The horse tracks, ballparks, the rings, the gridirons, all drew crowds in steadily increasing numbers. Every time a game was played, an attendance record was broken. Usually some other sort of record was broken, too—such as the record for the number of consecutive doubles hit by left-handed batters in a Series game, or some such thing as that. Records fell like ripe apples on a windy day. Customs and manners changed, and the five-day business week was reduced to four days, then to three, to give everyone a better chance to memorize the scores.

Not only did sport proliferate but the demands it made on the spectator became greater. Nobody was content to take in one event at a time, and thanks to the magic of radio and television nobody had to. A Yale alumnus, class of 1962, returning to the Bowl with 197,000 others to see the Yale-Cornell football game would take along his pocket radio and pick up the Yankee Stadium, so that while his eye might be following a fumble on the Cornell twenty-two-yard line, his ear would be following a man going down to second in the top of the fifth, seventy miles away. High in the blue sky above the Bowl, skywriters would be at work writing the scores of other major and minor sporting contests, weaving an interminable

From *The Second Tree from the Corner,* by Harper and Brothers. Copyright, 1948, by E. B. White. Reprinted by permission of the author and publisher.

record of victory and defeat, and using the new high-visibility pink news-smoke perfected by Pepsi-Cola engineers. And in the frames of the giant video sets, just behind the goal-posts, this same alumnus could watch Dejected win the Futurity before a record-breaking crowd of 249,872 at Belmont, each of whom was tuned to the Yale Bowl and following the World Series game in the video and searching the sky for further news of events either under way or just completed. The effect of this vast cyclorama of sport was to divide the spectator's attention, oversubtilize his appreciation, and deaden his passion. As the fourth supersonic decade was ushered in, the picture changed and sport began to wane.

A good many factors contributed to the decline of sport. Substitutions in football had increased to such an extent that there were very few fans in the United States capable of holding the players in mind during play. Each play that was called saw two entirely new elevens lined up, and the players whose names and faces you had familiarized yourself with in the first period were seldom seen or heard of again. The spectacle became as diffuse as the main concourse in Grand Central at the commuting hour.

Express motor highways leading to the parks and stadia had become so wide, so unobstructed, so devoid of all life except automobiles and trees that sport fans had got into the habit of traveling enormous distances to attend events. The normal driving speed had been stepped up to ninety-five miles an hour, and the distance between cars had been decreased to fifteen feet. This put an extraordinary strain on the sport lover's nervous system, and he arrived home from a Saturday game, after a road trip of three hundred and fifty miles, glassy-eyed, dazed, and spent. He hadn't really had any relaxation and he had failed to see Czlika (who had gone in for Trusky) take the pass from Bkeeo (who had gone in for Bjallo) in the third period, because at that moment a youngster named Lavagetto had been put in to pinch-hit for Art Gurlack in the bottom of the ninth with the tying run on second, and the skywriter who was attempting to write "Princeton 0-Lafayette 43" had banked the wrong way, muffed the "3," and distracted everyone's attention from the fact that Lavagetto had been whiffed.

Cheering, of course, lost its stimulating effect on players, because cheers were no longer associated necessarily with the immediate scene but might as easily apply to something that was happening somewhere else. This was enough to infuriate even the steadiest performer. A football star, hearing the stands break into a roar before the ball was snapped, would realize that their minds were not on him, and would become dispirited and grumpy. Two or three of the big coaches worried so about this that they considered equipping all players with tiny ear sets, so that they, too, could keep abreast of other sporting events while playing, but the idea was abandoned as impractical, and the coaches put it aside in tickler files, to bring up again later.

I think the event that marked the turning point in sport and started it downhill was the Midwest's classic Dust Bowl game of 1975, when Eastern Reserve's great right end, Ed Pistachio, was shot by a spectator. This man, the one who did the shooting, was seated well down in the stands near the forty-yard line on a bleak October afternoon and was so saturated with sport and with the disappointments of sport that he had clearly become deranged. With a minute and fifteen seconds to play and the score tied, the Eastern Reserve quarterback had whipped a long pass over Army's heads into Pistachio's waiting arms. There was no other player anywhere near him, and all Pistachio had to do was catch the ball and run it across the line. He dropped it. At exactly this moment, the spectator—a man named Homer T. Parkinson, of 35 Edgemere Drive, Toledo, O.—suffered at least three other major disappointments in the realm of sport. His horse, Hiccough, on which he had a five-hundred-dollar bet, fell while getting away from the starting gate at Pimlico and broke its leg (clearly visible in the video); his favorite shortstop, Lucky Frimstitch, struck out and let three men die on base in the final game of the Series (to which Parkinson was tuned); and the Governor Dummer soccer team, on which Parkinson's youngest son played goalie, lost to Kent, 4-3, as recorded in the sky overhead. Before anyone could stop him, he drew a gun and drilled Pistachio, before 954,000 persons, the largest crowd that had ever attended a football game and the *second*-largest crowd that had ever assembled for any sporting event in any month except July.

This tragedy, by itself, wouldn't have caused sport to decline, I suppose, but it set in motion a chain of other tragedies, the cumulative effect of which was terrific. Almost as soon as the shot was fired, the news flash was picked up by one of the skywriters directly above the field. He glanced down to see whether he could spot the trouble below, and in doing so failed to see another skywriter approaching. The two planes collided and fell, wings locked, leaving a confusing trail of smoke, which some observers tried to interpret as a late sports score. The planes struck in the middle of the nearby eastbound coast-to-coast Sunlight Parkway, and a motorist driving a convertible coupé stopped so short, to avoid hitting them, that he was bumped from behind. The pileup of cars that ensued involved 1,482 vehicles, a record for eastbound parkways. A total of more than three thousands lost their lives in the highway accident, including the two pilots, and when panic broke out in the stadium, it cost another 872 in dead and injured. News of the disaster spread quickly to other sports arenas, and started other panics among the crowds trying to get to the exits, where they could buy a paper and study a list of the dead. All in all, the afternoon of sport cost 20,003 lives, a record. And nobody had much to show for it except one small Midwestern boy who hung around the smoking wrecks of the planes, captured some aero newssmoke in a milk bottle, and took it home as a souvenir.

From that day on, sport waned. Through long, noncompetitive Saturday afternoons, the stadia slumbered. Even the parkways fell into disuse as motorists rediscovered the charms of old, twisty roads that led through main streets and past barnyards, with their mild congestions and pleasant smells.

QUESTIONS ON CONTENT

1. What specific features of modern sports is the author satirizing? List them.
2. What is a *parable?* Does "The Decline of Sport" fit the definition?

❧ *To an Athlete Dying Young*

A. E. HOUSMAN

The time you won your town the race
We chaired you through the market-place;
Man and boy stood cheering by,
And home we brought you shoulder-high.

From *A Shropshire Lad* by A. E. Housman. Reprinted by permission of Henry Holt and Company, Inc.

To-day, the road all runners come, 5
Shoulder-high we bring you home,
And set you at your threshold down,
Townsman of a stiller town.

Smart lad, to slip betimes away
From fields where glory does not stay 10
And early though the laurel grows
It withers quicker than the rose.

Eyes the shady night has shut
Cannot see the record cut,
And silence sounds no worse than cheers 15
After earth has stopped the ears:

Now you will not swell the rout
Of lads that wore their honours out,
Runners whom renown outran
And the name died before the man. 20

So set, before its echoes fade,
The fleet foot on the sill of shade,
And hold to the low lintel up
The still-defended challenge-cup.

And round that early-laurelled head 25
Will flock to gaze the strengthless dead,
And find unwithered on its curls
The garland briefer than a girl's.

QUESTIONS ON CONTENT

1. What is the contrast between stanzas 1 and 2?
2. Why is the champion runner called "Smart lad"? Do stanzas 4 and 5 justify the phrase?
3. What does *laurel* signify? Does it actually wither "quicker than the rose"? Discuss.
4. To what *record* does the poet refer in stanza 4?
5. What is the *low lintel?*
6. How would you express the theme of this poem?

❦ *Fraternities: Evil Force on the Campus*

WILLIAM S. CARLSON

The letter was one of dozens stacked on my desk.

"Have you no regard," read its bold, angry scrawl, "for the ideals of all American co-eds? You are destroying all they have tried to build up through the years. I demand you reconsider in regards to liquidating sororities in the State of New York."

I tried the next letter: "Only under a dictatorship would such an action be authorized."

After the third ("Only in a Communistic or other such dominated form of government could such action take place") I gave up any thought of replying personally to my correspondents. All were young college students, members of various sororities and fraternities in many states.

The letters—ungrammatical, illegible, abusive, and based upon false information and faulty reasoning—obviously were inspired by the professional executives who run this nation's seventy-odd college social fraternities and sororities. I was called a dictator, a Communist, undemocratic, prejudiced, "not of the right type" for a fraternity; and accused of unwholesome acts, grave mistakes, unfairness, injustice, perpetrating "what would take place in Russia," and "dealing the educational system a telling blow." My associates and I were sued in Federal court, and had to go all the way to the United States Supreme Court in defending ourselves.

What aroused the storm? Merely this: Disturbed by the irresponsible actions of many of the fraternity national officers in the fall of 1953, I recommended to the Trustees of the State University of New York that we require all the national-affiliated fraternities and sororities within the State University of New York to go on a "local" basis. Giving them up to five years to work out their new status and prevent hardships in transfer of chapter houses, etc., we nevertheless urged them to discontinue their national affiliation without delay.

In a parallel action at the same time, we warned *all* our fraternal

The Saturday Review, September 10, 1955. Reprinted by permission of the author.

units—national and local alike—to eliminate absolutely any racial-religious discrimination in their membership practices. This is scarcely a new regulation in itself, for several other colleges—Amherst, Dartmouth, Columbia, the University of Connecticut, for instance—already forbid the race clause in fraternities' constitutions. And our own State of New York, by law, prohibits such artificial criteria in employment or admissions practices generally. In a sense, then, New York's State University was only insuring that its students act in accord with the law. Am I, then, a dictator or a subversive, as accused in those unlovely fraternity letters? Why were we forced into the Federal courts to defend our regulations of student groups? What aroused the fraternities' hatred—and fear?

The answer is simple. Many of the fraternities do not fear the college that tells them to break up discriminatory practices because they're confident that they are bigger than the law. National headquarters of these fraternities tells them, in effect: "We'll show an acceptable constitution—but you go ahead and blackball any Negro, or Jew, or Catholic, or anyone else that you want to keep out, and who'll ever know the reason? It's a secret vote, isn't it? And you active members aren't going to let the subversive element run our fraternity . . . are you?"

In their earliest origins, roughly a century ago, college fraternities were small clubs organized on a single campus. They grew up in a manner very similar to the neighborhood gang that the same boys had organized when only a few years younger. The early secret ritual was a logical upshot of what happens when youngsters form a club.

This format of the fraternity is described by the National Interfraternity Conference itself in a booklet published to explain and defend the fraternity system. The National Interfraternity Conference points out that in the early days poor communication virtually isolated the colleges and their fraternities, and adds: "The government, therefore, of fraternities was of boys, for boys, and by boys." But all that has been ended, happily in the National Interfraternity Conference view: Occasional conventions of affiliated fraternities became "in theory, at least," the governing bodies of the emerging national fraternities. But this "did not do away with the need of a central force to govern *ad interim.*"

"In general," the National Interfraternity Conference explains innocently, "the council was a small body, usually alumni, elected by the convention and clothed with executive, judicial and administrative authority over the whole fraternity during the recesses be-tween conventions. These councils functioned like the board of di-rectors of a corporation." The NIC then adds that the business of running national fraternities became "so complicated in detail as to require a fixed and complete organization with a corps of officers and employes to attend to them."

"Paid officers were placed in charge of the central administrative office who devoted most, if not all, of their time to the work of administration. Thus, there grew to be permanent executive secre-taries, though variously called, presiding over the central office in which the business affairs of their particular fraternity go steadily on. These men become expert in their work, *and their influence is widely asserted*" (italics mine).

The principles of old remain today, in the National Interfraternity Conference view: "Cultivation of the mind, refinement of conduct and manners, enrichment of the human soul," etc. Apart from the extent to which fraternities serve such principles in practice, these elements hardly are promoted more effectively by a national rather than an individual approach.

Obviously the national officers recognize their vulnerability. Little wonder, then, that they fear the move of State University of New York in breaking their power. Natural enough, too, for the National Interfraternity Conference to sue, seeking to restrain State Uni-versity of New York on "constitutional" grounds. The suit was dis-missed in the United States district court by a special panel, with the late Judge Augustus Hand writing the opinion. Later the Supreme Court upheld this opinion. It was logical, too, for the national officers to inspire the letter-writing campaign. I dis-miss the possibility that college boys the country over spontane-ously initiated a mass letter-writing effort. The professionals thought it up, hoping to intimidate me or the State University's trustees. They never had a chance.

In the same broadside which I've cited above the National Fra-ternity Conference interpolates glibly: "The college law is the law of the fraternity as the latter is an integral part of the college itself."

Nonsense. In the first place, the fraternity is a social adjunct tolerated (although, in rare cases, encouraged) by the college. I know of only a few instances in which a realistic president or trus-tee views the fraternity as an indispensable part of the educational apparatus. More important, the NIC's professed submission to the "college law" is not supported by the facts. I reject it entirely and so, I believe, will any candid president who has ever dealt with a national fraternity's organization. The National Fraternity Conference's true attitude toward the "college law" is demonstrated vividly by its suit against the State University of New York for having established a law to govern fraternal relations within the university.

First, a bit of background: the State University of New York is composed of twenty-seven geographically separated colleges, most of which antedate the university's own founding in 1948.

On the campuses of many of these colleges national fraternities were organized before 1948. The number of different national fraternities and sororities involved was approximately twenty-five. Among the State University campuses with national organizations is the State University Teachers College in Cortland. In 1952 membership of one sorority there erupted in a mass resignation of some thirty-seven girls who protested discriminatory practices enforced on the local chapter by the national organization. An inquiry sustained the girls' complaints and brought the sorority's national representative on a hurry-up emergency visit to reiterate that national policy forbade the girls' pledging a Negro girl, as they wished to do.

The national handed down these ultimatums: The girls at Cortland were "distinctly local-minded and didn't realize what it meant to be national"; they were slack in some things that "national" required of them; they must sign a loyalty statement in order to "remain national." All these were euphemisms for taking the national's policies, including discrimination—or else.

Undoubtedly, constraint was upon the girls to preclude their pledging Negro girls. Yet, to my subsequent queries, the sorority's national officers repeatedly declared that the sorority had "no discriminatory restrictions whatsoever . . . because of race, color, creed, or national origin. . . ."

True enough, the sorority's constitution contained no such restrictions. But word-of-mouth policy—as inflexible as any constitution—prohibits pledging of Negro girls. And not merely were we confronted with a "silent" constitution; the responsible officers deliberately concealed the real facts. We wanted assurance that the sorority was non-discriminatory, not only in specific mandates of the constitution, but in those tacit, unwritten practices and understandings. In direct contrast to the evidence unearthed in the Cortland ultimatum and resignations, the national officers did assure me that the sorority had "no agreements or tacit unwritten practices and understandings" contrary to the constitution. Obviously this conflicting evidence destroyed my faith in the national officers of that particular sorority. We suspended the sorority's chapter at Cortland and another at the State University College for Teachers in Buffalo. They remain under suspension today.

We went through the same frustrating procedure with a second sorority in Cortland in which the students themselves rebelled against pressure from the national organization. The national officers simultaneously were denying the girls permission to pledge a Negro and assuring me that their constitution and unwritten practices lacked discriminatory clauses. This sorority also was suspended.

In a third instance of unquestioned discrimination at a State University college suspension proved unnecessary because the members simply broke up the chapter. All sixty-two were in a fraternity at the State University College for Teachers in Albany, and they resigned from their national to form their own locally-governed group. National headquarters refused to let them pledge five Jewish students after the Albany chapter led—successfully, it thought—a fight to eliminate a "white gentile" clause in the national's constitution. The national officers had simply started one of those "gentleman's agreements" and shifted the offending clause to the ritual, making it unacceptable to anyone other than gentiles.

These three shockingly cynical evasions by fraternities and sororities which profess great admiration for the "college law" coincided with our study to learn if fraternity and sorority constitutions flout State law. We uncovered just one offending constitution among twenty-five—and that one did not involve any of these three groups where discriminatory practices were proved.

Clearly, here was a pattern of misrepresentation. The national fraternities and sororities misinformed and misled me—and their own young members—whenever it best served their purpose. I concluded that I had no way of determining the actual practice of national fraternities at any time the officers decided to withhold facts.

A proposal made to me by one of the nation's leading proponents of fraternities, a man whose leadership probably is second to none in those circles, bolstered this belief. In a letter assuring me of his powerful organization's "support" in eliminating discriminatory practices, he suggested a novel deal: Remove the selective clause from fraternity and sorority documents—but "continue their ancient custom of permitting the majority of chapters to pass judgment on any pledge before he or she could be initiated." In other words, continue the status quo so that discrimination might be perpetuated by subterfuge. Needless to say, I rejected the proposal that I and the State University of New York become parties to fraternity under-the-table dealing. But I was discouraged to find the topmost fraternity authorities specifically backing up the doubletalk and deceit that individual fraternities were revealing.

Discrimination is just one aspect—though the most glaring—of conduct and misconduct in fraternity affairs. Read any handbook for the fraternity advocate, or the proceedings of any serious fraternity meeting, and you will encounter many more examples of what the fraternities themselves recognize as their weak spots. Time after time you'll find troubled references to sub-par scholarship among the members; social conduct ranging from drinking to systematic evasion of chaperones; hazing and the infamous "Hell Week"; unpaid bills (including many large ones to the national organizations); and numerous others.

Customarily, though, the fraternities try to put any outside critic on the defensive by casting aspersions at his motives. In one recent national fraternity handbook a chapter on "Criticism of the Fraternity System" was devoted largely to such remarks as these: "What opposition still obtains is largely founded upon personal pique and disappointment, and the general criticism of certain other organizations hostile by the very nature of their group"; "that the fraternity may be discriminatory in their selections (of members) is no basis for criticism"; and "the origin and source of opposition to fraternities have often been attributed to personal pique or bias and prejudice naturally arising from the disappointment some individual feels because he or she failed to be invited to join a fraternity or sorority." An advertisement for a fraternity booklet titled "Discrimination? No, It's Only Selection" says that this "fine, clear, concise analysis" will "effectively answer all the hullabaloo over fraternity discrimination whipped up into a frenzy by, well, you know whom!"

The allusion, of course, is to such troublemakers as Communists— or just the kids who got blackballed or didn't have the money to join. To the allegations that the critics are either jealous social outcasts or dangerous radicals, I offer some thoughts in rebuttal. The most ardent anti-fraternity men, I find, are *ex*-fraternity men who have learned the truth on the inside—and there's not a radical in a carload. I, myself, was a brother until I resigned.

All the many eternal "problems" with which the fraternities shadow-box should be under the control of the college or university. No item in the social life of any college-recognized group should be hidden from the dean of students or other authority. Similarly, no fraternity or fraternity-member should be accountable to an off-campus hierarchy for standards of conduct. For too long America's colleges have paid a heavy price for the benefits which the fraternities and sororities claim for themselves. The only answer to re-aligning dog and tail in proper wagging sequence is for college administrators and trustees to seize the initiative as the State University of New York has done.

My experience with national fraternities offers proof that they do exercise, as they say, "widely asserted influence" over the immature college boy and girl. They do, indeed, wield their self-advertised "executive, judicial, and administrative authority" whenever and however they wish. The teen-ager who yields to the national fraternity's blandishments during Rush Week is tying himself up in many unsuspected ways. I, for instance, could not resign from my fraternity by writing to anyone at the University of Michigan, where I joined. I had to address national headquarters, and some professional brother there replied that my resignation in itself wasn't enough. The fraternity's "supreme council" had to pass on it. If the council didn't like my reason for resigning I presumably would be tied to my fraternity for life. I would, in effect, be bound unwillingly to whatsoever policy its national officers wished to promulgate.

Permitting off-campus organizations to boss the college's students is dangerous, in a discriminatory membership policy or wherever else the interests of "the national" and the college may not harmonize. Any competent college administrator can supervise the young people in his charge, if he has no outside interference. He has no real hope of doing his job if the student owes an allegiance elsewhere—an allegiance that may very well involve more secrets than even the rituals provide. Can any college president justify his abdicating the direction of his young charges? Parents send their children to college expecting not only proper curricular direction, but adequate supervision in social affairs. No president or dean can afford to be unable to govern his students' activities while they are in his charge.

This is, however, precisely the position of the national fraternities. They arrogate to themselves the power to control social standards of America's young college people. Neither the students themselves, nor the faculty, can challenge the higher, subtle, yet mandatory authority of the fraternity.

Not every sorority and fraternity, of course, is as deception-ridden as those I've cited here. Some that came to my attention during our study demonstrated their integrity without question. But the stakes are high, and today's friendly "national" may well prove tomorrow's Svengali. One national sorority president, for example, finally came out against us with all claws bared: "There are definite limitations of the power and authority of government and public educational institutions over the rights of individuals and private organizations engaged in lawful activities." This, from a group permitted to come on our campuses on good behavior. The behavior hasn't been good enough, I say.

Through refusal of colleges and universities to recognize national social fraternities and sororities the power of the fraternity professionals can be broken. Each fraternity should be a locally-owned and operated club, instead of just one more unit of a chain-store syndicate whose powerful and often cynical national office runs the show. Then, I am confident, the young men and women who as college students accept the dictation of non-collegiate authorities with "executive, judicial, and administrative" powers will be able to reassert dominion over their own affairs. No one will lose— except the professional fraternity jobholders and some of their less enlightened supporters. Everyone will gain—chiefly the young people and the colleges who then can act independently to end the "problems" with which the national fraternities struggle endlessly and, by and large, fruitlessly.

The fraternities' power is vast—for good or for evil. Properly channeled by *college* authorities their broad social activities can at last be diverted to the welfare of the educational program. By the violence of their reaction to the localizing decree of the State University of New York the nationals reveal that they realize it's now a fight for their lives.

QUESTIONS ON CONTENT

1. What is the purpose of the first five paragraphs? Of the sixth paragraph? To what does the author refer as "irresponsible actions"?
2. What is the central charge brought against the fraternities? Is the author opposed to any sort of fraternal organization?
3. Why does the author quote so extensively from the booklet issued by the National Fraternity Council?
4. What method is used to establish "a pattern of misrepresentation"?
5. Comment on the fraternity "weak spots" mentioned on p. 241. Do these seem more significant than the central charge brought against the fraternities? Discuss.
6. Why did the author resign from his fraternity? Does he say?
7. All points considered, justify or condemn the action taken by the State University of New York.

❧ *The Influence of the Fraternity*

ROBERT T. McCRACKEN

I think it may well be maintained that the most formative years in the life of a man who has gone through college are the years that he spent there. If he is fortunate in the choice of his college, and of his associations there, they may also be among his happiest years. But whether or not this latter be the case, the former is almost invariably true. It is during that period that he grows up, comes out of the shell of adolescence, and becomes a man. For the first time he is associating with young men, and if he finds himself in a co-educational institution, with young women. Some of the upper-classmen are of voting age. They are about to take their place in the body politic. They are thinking, at least occasionally, about what is ahead. All of that has a profound influence, not only on themselves, but upon those in the classes below them. The first faint stirrings of a thing called responsibility, never before really encountered, begin to manifest themselves. And with that comes a

The keynote address at the 46th Annual Meeting of the National Interfraternity Conference, 1954. Reprinted by permission of the author.

sense of freedom—slightly limited freedom of action, unlimited freedom of thought.

The influences brought to bear on such a young man are of enormous importance in his future development. He is passing through a stage of great sensitivity. He is discovering things in a region hitherto unknown. He is, consciously or unconsciously, testing them. His instincts are at work, approving some of them, rejecting others. He is unsure of himself, and hence a little shy. He is desperately eager to achieve and retain the respect and good will of his fellow students—even of some of the faculty. But he can't do it alone. He has to have help. And that help must come from those closest to him, those new friends to whom he is attracted and who are attracted to him. Just here is where the magic of the fraternity becomes the pricesless ingredient in his career.

When a man has been out of college for fifty years and looks back over that vista, the warmest spot on which his memory lingers is his fraternity. Certainly that is true with this graduate. The fraternity, the chapter, were to me a complete, cosy, homelike world within a world. My brothers in the chapter had been chosen, as I had, by men whom I considered extremely wise. I say this without any false modesty, but so greatly did I revere those who were conducting the chapter's affairs, that I often wondered why they chose me. As to the other men in the chapter, I had no doubt that every one had been elected after careful investigation, and for good and sufficient reasons. The thought that any one of them had been mistakenly elected never entered my mind. We have a song in my fraternity in which the words, "the chosen few," appear. Those words, and the thought that they conveyed, had a magic touch for me. For the first time in my seventeen years, I had been selected as one of a "chosen few." And selected by men whom I looked up to with profound respect. What a compliment that was—what a lift to one's self confidence—to one's self esteem! Armed with it, I began to feel that I could conquer almost anything. However small and negligible I might appear to be, and indeed was, the warm, intimate, cheering thought was always near—"At least I am a Psi U." I would come back to the chapter house from all sorts of rebuffs and disappointments, such as that when the family physician insisted that I give up trying to run the 440 because the training was endangering my health, and I knew that I should never win the varsity letter I returned to the chapter house to find there a haven of refuge and cheer which would soon make a new man of me. Like

Anteus, who acquired redoubled strength every time he touched the ground, I became refreshed and reinspired for new ventures by a few days in the atmosphere of the chapter house.

This blind devotion, this absolute certainty of the high quality of my brothers in the fraternity soon extended beyond the bounds of my own chapter. In the spring of my freshman year, the Pennsylvania chapter was the host to the annual convention. The delegates came from all parts of the country—men from Yale, Amherst, Dartmouth, other New England colleges; men from Cornell, from Michigan, from Chicago, and other smaller colleges. To my untutored, but deeply biased eye, they were all alike. They seemed to bear a stamp, some kind of impress from an ancient die, fashioned by the founders. A secret and very firm bond was established with the clasping of hands in the grip. Something seemed to flow through one from that grip—an affinity, a comradeship that was unique— set-apart, almost sacred. It was inherent in the brotherhood of the fraternity. It did not exist anywhere else.

I dare say that many of you went through this same thrilling experience. To my mind it is of incalculable import in the life of a college student. It has a very direct bearing on his development. He learns to believe in other men, to respect them, to look only for their good qualities—never for their faults. Soon enough, when he gets out into the world, he will encounter the spirit of criticism. Soon enough he will find that it is fashionable to look for the clay in the feet of the idol. But here is a period, all too short perhaps, but long enough to leave its impress on him, a period when he can, in the great words of Stevenson, retain a few friends, but those without capitulation. Some of them will be life-long friends. Some may drift away through marriage, removal to a distance, or for other reasons. But the memory of those golden days will still be there. Those brothers constituted a group apart, unlike any other group. We have with them an undefinable, but, nonetheless, tightly woven bond which is perceptible whenever and wherever we meet.

Now all of this is bound to have its influence on the college as well as on the student. Whatever may be said against the fraternity —and we all know that much has been said—that it is exclusive, that it is undemocratic, that it breaks up the unity of class association, that it is hard on the men who never make one—all of this is, in my judgment, heavily counter-balanced by the contribution it makes.

To begin with, it is a natural association. Birds of a feather flock together. They always have; they always will. What is more natural, therefore, than that they should establish a center where the flocking is good? No fraternity aspires to be the only one on the campus. If other groups establish chapters, that is so much the better. If there are not enough chapters to go around and include the entire student body, other methods of association may be found by those who are outside the ranks. Or students may found their own societies, and perhaps apply to a national fraternity for a charter. There is nothing to stop them. The best things in life are free—and friendship is one of them.

But such an association would be of far less value if it were not organized. Your college freshman embarks on what is to him an uncharted course. He doesn't really know where he is going or how to get there. He badly needs advice; he requires direction; he wants encouragement, he may even be the better for a little prodding. Much of his value to the college arises from the impetus given to him in his chapter.

The fraternity chapter, moreover, if it is well managed, recognizes that it is only an adjunct to the larger world of the college or university. I well remember that it was dinned into us from the beginning by the older men: "Remember that you are a Pennsylvania man first and a Psi U afterward." We were also constantly reminded that we wouldn't be of any use to either the fraternity or the university if we flunked out. Considerable emphasis was placed, in my day, on the passing of examinations. No college faculty could complain of that.

The problem of homesickness, very serious sometimes, is best taken care of in the chapter house. Any wise college administrator will recognize this. Here, into a strange and distant community, comes a boy who, perhaps, has never been away from home before. He may even be subject, at first, to a bit of hazing. Unless he has been to a boarding school—and a very great number have not—he is totally unprepared for what is happening to him. He is lonely; of course, he is lonely. He will be lonely at times even in his fraternity house, but much less lonely. He will come much more quickly to love the college if his loneliness is early dispelled.

Moreover, pride in the position of the fraternity on the campus ofttimes impels men to undertake college activities to which they might not have otherwise aspired. Every fraternity wants to be represented on the athletic teams, on the class offices and committees, on the publications and other student organizations. Accordingly, encouragement is afforded to chapter members to go out and try to make the team, or the editorial board, or the class presidency. Many a man who might have drifted through college doing nothing except keep up with his work and enjoy himself has acquired lively interests in important college functions through the urging of his fraternity, and has maintained these interests in the years following his graduation. No university administration could complain of that.

It has been asked by some, why the national fraternity? Why wouldn't it be just as well if the local chapter were a club with no intercollegiate connections? I submit that this view is deplorably provincial. This is a great country. Colleges and universities flourish in every section of it. Their alumni scatter to all parts of the land, to live and carry on their several vocations. We are a gregarious people. We like association with our fellow men—hence the Masonic lodges—and other fraternal organizations. They carry with them a bond, rendering this desired fellowship more readily obtainable and at the same time more permanent. Such association is a primitive urge, one strongly developed in the American character. Membership in a college fraternity, with its national scope, fits precisely into this scheme of living. It is naturally most apparent during undergraduate years when students visit colleges other than their own to view or take part in athletic contests and so on, and find themselves welcomed in the local chapter house of their fraternity. But it also is carried on through later years. The grip means something even to men who have been out of college for half a century. I can testify to that.

More important than this is the matter of standards and ideals. Established many years ago by the founders, they have been preserved and honored by all the chapters until they have become as much a part of the fraternity as the Greek letters by which it is known. The very fact that the principles and purposes set forth in the constitution of the fraternity are observed throughout the United States, and often throughout the Dominion of Canada, adds tremendous force to their influence upon every chapter. It is a splendid thing to have a group of college students realize, and never forget, that they are part of a powerful organization, with lofty standards and fine traditions, and that they are bound to that organization with unbreakable ties.

There have been some attempts recently by college or university administrations to dissolve the union between the chapter and the parent fraternity. No one can complain if the college authorities establish and enforce certain rules of conduct for the local chapters, such as forbidding the keeping of liquor or the entertainment of young women in the chapter house, or even the time and extent of the rushing period. That is proper campus discipline. But no set of officials who insist, as they all do, on academic freedom untrammeled should interfere with a student group's choice of its associates—its social and personal freedom, at least so long as these associates are proper associates. And what difference can it make if some of them are students in sister colleges? I can see no excuse for an iron curtain in college or university life.

But it is with the beauty, the stimulation, and the glorious comfort of fraternity life that we are concerned today. Every man in this room knows what it means. All of us have experienced the warm glow of the chapter house, the sheltering safety which it threw around us, the inspiration to fresh effort which we gained from it. No spot on the campus could take its place. At no other place did we feel that complete freedom from competition or rivalry, that unfettered companionship, that unbounded support and encouragement. There was the center of our college life. From there we went out into the larger sphere of the college and took our appropriate part in its activities, backed by the fraternity whenever backing was required. But we always came back, with or without our trophies, to the welcome and cheer of the chapter house. There we were at home. There we recovered from the blows that fell upon us, from the anxieties and disappointments which we all experienced, and which are as much a part of college life as of life itself. There we wove the brightest picture in the tapestry of our college careers. Let us hope, let us endeavor to see to it, that those who come after us, when they come into this priceless heritage, possess and enjoy it in the same measure.

QUESTIONS ON CONTENT

1. What is the purpose of the first two paragraphs?
2. Comment on the statement: "But he can't do it alone." What does "it" represent? Why can't the college student do "it" alone?
3. What argument in favor of fraternities is advanced in the third paragraph? Discuss.
4. What kind of influences (list the points) does the author think fraternities have on the colleges? Could any other force besides the fraternity produce the same influence?
5. Pages 246–248 take up the central point of President Carlson's

article, "Fraternities: An Evil Influence on the Campus." Does Mr. McCracken successfully refute President Carlson's arguments? Discuss. Does he attempt to meet the charge of "irresponsible actions" on the part of the national fraternity offices?

SUGGESTIONS FOR PAPERS

A. Athletics

Is athleticism a problem at your college or university? If all is well in this respect, then you may choose to write an analysis of this fortunate situation. If all is less than well, you have the opportunity now of sizing up the trouble—with assistance from the selections in this chapter—and suggesting a remedy.

1. If you participate in any form of athletics, you may write a paper on the extent to which your sport is professionalized. (Structure: I The extent of my participation; II How professionalized my sport was in high school; III How professionalized in college; IV Conclusion.)

2. If you do not participate in athletics, you may write a paper on the professional status of your favorite spectator sport. (Structure: I What is done for [and to] athletes; II The status of the coaching staff; III The relation of the sport to the rest of the college.)

3. Make a careful study of Stoke's "College Athletics: Education or Show Business?" Summarize each of the four sections. Show how the first three sections prepare the way for the fourth section.

4. Defend or attack the solution to the problem of college athletics as advanced in the fourth section of "College Athletics: Education or Show Business?" Some parts of the argument may seem valid, others less so. Point up these differences and then come to a conclusion of your own.

5. List the points made in "Too Much Football." Are they all of equal weight? If not, separate the major from the minor charges. Deal with the minor charges in a single paragraph by the process of enumeration ("The author brings a number of minor charges against big-time football, such as. . . ."). Next, discuss more fully, at least one paragraph each, two or three major points. End your paper with an estimate of the reasonableness of this attack on football.

6. List the points made in "Why I Love Football"; then answer the questions and follow the procedure suggested in 5, above.

7. Show how "Too Much Football" may be used to supplement and illustrate "College Athletics: Education or Show Business?" What is Stoke's central point? What is Jackson's? Are they similar? How do they differ? What is Stoke's solution? What is Jackson's, if any?

8. Show how "Too Much Football" and "Why I Love Football" differ. List the differences. Offer an explanation which may partly account for these differences.

9. Tell why you love football, or why you dislike it, or why you are indifferent. Use the method of organization of either "Too Much Football" or of "Why I Love Football."

10. Housman's "To an Athlete Dying Young" concentrates on the brevity of athletic fame. Write your own version of the impermanency of an athlete's laurels. (Test of team fame: can you name the football teams which played last year's bowl games? Or the top ten teams in last year's national standing? Test of individual fame: name a half-dozen All-Americans for any year along with their year and the positions they played.)

11. If you wish to defend athletes from the charge of impermanent fame, you could compare their impact on the public with that made by winners of scholastic honors. You probably do not know the names of *any* brilliant students at other colleges. Do you know the best students in your own college? Do you know the difference between Phi Beta Kappa and Phi Kappa Phi? Is either of these organizations on your campus? What are the requirements for membership? (Note: if you choose this subject, do not ask others for the answers to these questions. The interest and value of the paper will come from an honest appraisal of what you do or do not know about scholars and the rewards of scholarship.)

12. Examine the possibilities of a thorough-going professionalizing of college athletics. (I The absurdities of the present system; II The easy steps to full professionalizing; III Advantages to the athletes, to the college, to the public.)

B. Fraternities

Fraternities have been attacked and defended since their beginnings on American campuses. Members and non-members have equally good reasons for examining critically the claims which fraternities make: members see the workings from within and can detect whatever differences there may be between promises and performance; non-members may take an objective view of the theory and practice of fraternities. Both will read attentively what an opponent and a proponent of the system have to say.

13. If you are a member of a fraternity, set forth the advantages and disadvantages of membership. What does the fraternity propose to offer? What does it actually offer? What are its ideal attitude and its real attitude towards good scholarship (grades), towards racial or religious discrimination in selecting members, towards extra-curricular activities, towards other features of college life? (If you are not a member of a fraternity, you may wish to examine these points as an outsider.)

14. Summarize "Fraternities: An Evil Influence on the Campus." Support or attack the action taken by the State University of New York. (I What the action was; II Why it was taken; III Why it was the right action [or the wrong action]).

15. Summarize "The Influence of the Fraternities." Support or attack the points made in favor of the fraternity system. Determine whether this is a realistic or a sentimental appraisal of fraternities.

16. Discuss the issue of local versus national fraternities. Draw your points from the two articles on fraternities. Add your own conclusion on this argument.

SOME TITLES FOR PAPERS

A. Athletics

1. Athletics: More Work than Play
2. The Latest Code for Amateurs
3. Every Athlete Is a Needy Athlete
4. Far-flung Recruiting (consult a football program)
5. Athletes Should Be Paid
6. What a Good Team Does for a College (or to a College)
7. A Football Player's Weekly Schedule
8. The Cross Purpose of Athletics and Higher Education
9. The Public's Right to College Football Spectacles
10. Ten-cent Football
11. Bachelor of Athletics
12. Amateurs *vs.* Professionals
13. Horse Racing on a Collegiate Footing
14. High-paid Coaches

B. Fraternities

15. Values in Fraternities
16. The Ideal and the Actual in Fraternities
17. I'm Glad I Joined
18. I'm Glad I Didn't Join
19. Birds of a Feather
20. Local *vs.* National Fraternities
21. Hell Week or Help Week?
22. Study Conditions in Fraternity Houses
23. Fraternities Are (Are Not) Democratic
24. Selection, Not Discrimination
25. The Ideal Fraternity Man (Sorority Girl)

❧ *ADVERTISING*

NOTHING IN AMERICA so insistently demands our attention as advertising. Quite literally it is everywhere, at the breakfast table, on every means of public transportation, on billboards and handbills, in the air, newspapers, magazines, and mailboxes. It is inescapable.

The advertising man would be the first to say that advertising has produced the American way of life. It stimulates the demand for goods; a stimulated demand for goods increases production; increased production makes prosperity; prosperity provides money for all the people; money for all the people makes it possible for the advertising man to redouble his efforts to stimulate the demand for goods. It is a perfect circle and self-perpetuating.

Nevertheless, advertising irritates many people for many reasons, and the selections in this chapter set forth some of the reasons for public irritation. The speaker in "Talks on Advertising" brings two general charges against advertising men, one moral, the other esthetic. The sort of person this speaker perhaps has in mind is described in "Self-hypnotist," a report of an interview with a spectacularly successful ad-man. In "Where Are the Ads of Yesteryear?" the author, Robert L. Heilbroner, laments the passing of ads with a punch and cites, among others, some of the copy produced by the "self-hypnotist." This sort of article provides background material for examining critically current practices in advertising.

The arguments justifying advertising are advanced by Bruce Barton in "Advertising: Its Contribution to the American Way of Life." Mr. Barton finds in the publicizing of products and services

254

not only the key to successful capitalism but also a strong element of philanthropic good through service to the people—the service of helpful information. His stand contrasts sharply with that of Herman Wouk in "Talks on Advertising."

❧ *Talks on Advertising*

An After-dinner Oration by the Artist

HERMAN WOUK

Marquis, while you were talking I looked around this table and saw that (nearly) everyone here wins subsistence through the activity called advertising. Now, I realize that you invited me in the absence, enforced by your sedentary ways, of stuffed tiger heads or other trophies on your walls, a live artist being the equivalent of a dead beast as a social ornament. I will not question your motive because it has given me a chance to do a beautiful and good thing. I should like to entreat all these gentlemen to redeem the strange, bittersweet miracle of their lives, while there is yet time, by giving up the advertising business at once.

Has it ever occurred to any of you gentlemen to examine the peculiar fact that you find bread in your mouths daily? How does this happen? Who is it that you have persuaded to feed you? The obvious answer is that you buy your food, but this just states the question in another, less clear way, because money is nothing but an exchange token. Drop the confusing element of money from the whole process, and the question I've posed must confront you bleakly. What is it that you do, that entitles you to eat?

A shoemaker gives shoes for his bread. Well. A singer sings for her supper. Well. A capitalist leads a large enterprise. Well. A pilot flies, a coal-miner digs, a sailor moves things, a minister preaches, an author tells stories, a laundryman washes, an auto worker makes cars, a painter makes pictures, a street car conductor moves people, a stenographer writes down words, a lumberjack saws, and a tailor sews. The people with the victuals appreciate these services and cheerfully feed the performers. But what does an advertising man do?

From *Aurora Dawn*, copyright, 1947, by Herman Wouk. Reprinted by permission of Simon and Schuster, Publishers.

He induces human beings to want things they don't want.

Now, I will be deeply obliged if you will tell me by what links of logic anybody can be convinced that your activity—the creation of want where want does not exist—is a useful one and should be rewarded with food. Doesn't it seem, rather, the worst sort of mischief, deserving to be starved into extinction?

None of you, however, is anything but well fed; yet I am sure that until this moment it has never occurred to you on what a dubious basis your feeding is accomplished. I shall tell you exactly how you eat. You induce people to use more things than they naturally desire—the more useless and undesirable the article, the greater the advertising effort needed to dispose of it—and in all the profit from that unnatural purchasing, you share. You are fed by the makers of undesired things, who exchange these things for food by means of your arts and give you your share of the haul.

Lest you think I oversimplify, I give you an obvious illustration. People naturally crave meat; so the advertising of meat is on a negligible scale. However, nobody is born craving tobacco, and even its slaves instinctively loathe it. So the advertising of tobacco is the largest item of expense in its distribution. It follows, of course, that advertising men thrive most richly in the service of utterly useless commodities like tobacco or under-arm pastes, or in a field where there is a hopeless plethora of goods, such as soap or whisky.

But the great evil of advertising is not that it is unproductive and wasteful; were it so, it would be no worse than idleness. No. Advertising blasts everything that is good and beautiful in this land with a horrid spreading mildew. It has tarnished Creation. What is sweet to any of you in this world? Love? Nature? Art? Language? Youth? Behold them all, yoked by advertising in the harness of commerce!

Aurora Dawn! Has any of you enough of an ear for English to realize what a crime against the language is in that (trade) name? Aurora *is* the dawn! The redundancy should assail your ears like the shriek of a bad hinge. But you are so numbed by habit that it conveys no offense. So it is with all your barbarities. Shakespeare used the rhyming of "double" and "bubble" to create two immortal lines in *Macbeth*. You use it to help sell your Dubl-Bubl Shampoo, and you have no slightest sense of doing anything wrong. Should someone tell you that language is the Promethean fire that lifts man above the animals and that you are smothering the flame in mud, you would stare. You are staring. Let me tell you without images, then, that you are cheapening speech until it is ceasing to be an honest method of exchange, and that the people, not knowing that the English in a radio commercial is meant to be a lie and the English in the President's speech which follows, a truth, will in the end fall into a paralyzing skepticism in which all utterance will be disbelieved.

God made a great green wonderland when he spread out the span of the United States. Where is the square mile inhabited by men wherein advertising has not drowned out the land's meek hymn with the blare of billboards? By what right do you turn Nature into a painted hag crying "Come buy"?

A few heavenly talents brighten the world in each generation. Artistic inspiration is entrusted to weak human beings who can be tempted with gold. Has advertising scrupled to buy up the holiest of these gifts and set them to work peddling?

And the traffic in lovely youth! By the Lord, gentlemen, I would close every advertising agency in the country tomorrow, if only to head off the droves of silly girls, sufficiently cursed with beauty, who troop into the cities each month, most of them to be stained and scarred, a few to find ashy success in the hardening life of a model! When will a strong voice call a halt to this dismal pilgrimage, this Children's Crusade to the Unholy Land? When will someone denounce the snaring allurements of the picture magazines? When will someone tell these babies that for each girl who grins on a magazine cover a hundred weep in back rooms, and that even the grin is a bought and forced thing that fades with the flash of the photographer's bulb, leaving a face grim with scheming or heartbreak?

To what end is all this lying, vandalism, and misuse? You are trying to Sell; never mind what, never mind how, never mind to whom—just Sell, Sell, Sell! Small wonder that in good old American slang "sell" means "fraud"! Come now! Do you hesitate to promise requited love to miserable girls, triumph to failures, virility to weaklings, even prowess to little children, for the price of a mouth wash or a breakfast food? Does it ever occur to you to be ashamed to live by preying on the myriad little tragedies of unfulfillment which make your methods pay so well?

I trust that I am offending everybody very deeply. An artist has the privileges of the court fool, you know. I paint because I see with a seeing eye, an eye that familiarity never glazes. Advertising strikes me as it would a man from Mars and as it undoubtedly appears to the angels: an occupation the aim of which is subtle prevarication for gain, and the effect of which is the blighting of everything fair and pleasant in our time with the garish fungus of greed. If I have made all of you, or just one of you, repent of this career and determine to seek decent work, I will not have breathed in vain today.

QUESTIONS ON CONTENT

1. How does the artist-orator define the function of an advertising man?
2. "The more useless and undesirable the article, the greater the advertising effort needed to dispose of it." Comment.
3. What does *plethora* mean? If you don't know, guess the meaning from the context.
4. What is *Promethean fire?*
5. Could you find the specific newspaper or magazine advertisements referred to on page 256?
6. Name the two complaints against advertising voiced in this speech.

❧ *Self-hypnotist*

THE EDITORS OF *The New Yorker*

After seeing "The Hucksters," the film about advertising men and their woes, we decided to have a talk with an advertising man we have long heard about, Mr. John Caples, a vice-president of Batten, Barton, Durstine & Osborn, a distinguished member of the pushcart set for over twenty years, and a man who did as much as Calvin Coolidge to contribute to the merriment of the middle twenties. Mr. Caples was quick to tell us that the clients he has dealt with have been nothing like the spitting soap king who dominates "The Hucksters." "I haven't been interfered with," he said, "and, in fact, I have never laid eyes on many of the men I've written ads for." Mr. Caples' ads are among the most famous ever penned. Who does not remember his immortal "They Laughed When I Sat Down at the Piano—But When I Started to Play!" or his "They Grinned When the Waiter Spoke to Me in French—But Their Laughter Changed to Amazement at My Reply!" Mr. Caples put these together when he was only twenty-five and could barely make his way

From Talk of the Town, August 23, 1947. Reprinted by permission. Copyright 1947 The New Yorker Magazine, Inc.

through either "Chopsticks" or a French menu. We asked him how his inspiration came to him, and found him as inarticulate as a poet on that score. "I was just a young copy writer at Ruthrauff & Ryan and got hold of a couple of mailorder accounts," he said. "I was sitting around thinking about them one day and out popped that business about the piano. The waiter and the French followed naturally." Mr. Caples was interrupted at this point by the telephone. When he'd hung up, he courteously informed us about the call. "That was a friend of mine," he said. "Wanted to know who could handle copy on a method of teaching piano by lights. Don't do any of that stuff any more, but it certainly was good basic training."

Mr. Caples asked us if we'd like to see his scrapbook and, when we said we would, broke out a formidable volume, on the first page of which were the arresting and familiar headline "Fat Men!" and, beneath it, a sketch of a portly gentleman whose midriff had been shaded to emphasize starkly his proper proportions. "Damn thing still pulls," remarked Mr. Caples contentedly, turning to a page that screamed, "Dandruff? I'll End It in 48 Hours or No Cost!" We browsed through similar copy until we came upon the line "I Can Make You Magnetic—Irresistible! Give Me Five Days to Prove It—Free," strung over the photograph of a gray-haired, imposing figure. "Who's that?" we inquired. "That's a model," Mr. Caples told us. "The fellow selling the personality was too weak-looking for the ad." Quite a few of the ads in Mr. Caples' collection included triumphant personal stories by men called James Perkins, James Blackford, and James C. Crawford, all of whom turned out to be Mr. Caples. "Those were wild days," he said. "A few pseudonyms gave testimonials authenticity. Everybody did it." While we were trying to digest that thought, he related one of his difficulties with the They-Laughed-When ads. "I wrote an ad saying that the thing the fellow played after he sat down was Beethoven's 'Moonlight Sonata,'" Mr. Caples said, "but a lot of teachers jumped on it and said that after years of practice *they* couldn't play the 'Sonata' easily. I substituted 'Liebestraum,' and everybody seemed to be satisfied."

Mr. Caples closed his scrapbook with a faraway look in his eye. "Those *were* the days!" he said. "How about these days?" we inquired. Mr. Caples looked solemn. "I am in charge of a committee on the Continuing Study of Newspaper Reading of the American Association of Advertising Agencies," he said. "It's designed to learn what captures the interest of people reading newspapers and to apply the findings to advertising." He went to the wall and pulled down a large photostat of the first page of a newspaper. "You see this item on Truman's budget report?" he asked. "Well, it got twenty-three per cent of the women. But this item on three boys putting a splint on the leg of a dog that had been struck by an automobile got forty-four per cent of the men and forty-five per cent of the women." "Gosh!" we said. "Before you go," said Mr. Caples, "let me give you a copy of my 'Tested Advertising Methods.'" Back at the office, we opened the volume and came upon the passage "Use a process of self-hypnotism. Say to yourself that Smith's Liver Pills are the best pills in the world—that no other pills are like them—that they can produce any conceivable result, turn weaklings into giants, oldsters into youngsters, rejuvenate the human race in twenty-four hours."

QUESTIONS ON CONTENT

1. Advertising men are called hucksters. Why? What would a "member of the pushcart set" be?
2. For one of the "most famous" ads referred to in paragraph 1, see p. 262.
3. Does this interview point up the fundamental unreliability of all advertising or only of some advertising?
4. Must the advertising man believe what he says? Can he so believe? (See the title of this interview.)

❧ *Where Are the Ads of Yesteryear?*

ROBERT L. HEILBRONER

Let me begin by stating that I am a devotee of advertising. Its social significance, or its cultural insignificance, doesn't faze me a bit. I am not one of those who deplore the Human Wastage of the profession, nor do I view with alarm its gentle prevarications. The caricature of admen as hucksters amuses me, but doesn't raise my blood pressure a single notch. I just get a tremendous kick out of watching the advertising brain knock itself out in a bid for my patronage.

Harper's Magazine, June, 1953. Reprinted by permission of the author and *Harper's Magazine*.

Nevertheless, I have a bone to pick with the trade. I don't think advertising packs the wallop it used to. Maybe the trouble is in me: maybe I'm older and more jaded and no longer the susceptible quarry I undoubtedly once was. But I think there's more to it than that. I have a feeling that advertising doesn't come at you the way it once did—that it doesn't take you by the lapels, back you into a corner, and leave you stupefied, glazed, and as pantingly acquisitive as it did in the good old days.

There was a time, I am convinced, when a copywriter who couldn't sell an icebox to an Eskimo wouldn't have been worth his $17.50 a week.

That was back in the days when people still thought cultured pearls were only worn by uncultured people. So some hero composed this masterpiece for the Técla Pearl firm, and in exactly thirty-five words and five figures wrote what I consider to be an absolute rockcrusher of an ad:

A $10,000 Mistake

CLIENT for whom we had copied a necklace of Oriental Pearls, seeing both necklaces before her, said: *Well, the resemblance is remarkable, but this is mine!*

Then she picked up ours!

T E C L A

398 Fifth Avenue, New York
10 Rue de la Paix, Paris

The man who wrote that could have signed up Carrie Nation as a Woman of Distinction.

Or take this one. It sold the most dreary and intangible of goods: learning piano by mail. It did it in a closely-packed page of print from which not one cliché of the English language was omitted. But the effect? Well, read it and judge for yourself:

"Can he really play?" a girl whispered. "Heavens no!" Arthur exclaimed. "He never played a note in his life."

They Laughed When I Sat Down At the Piano But When I Started to Play!—

Arthur had just played "The Rosary."

The room rang with applause. I decided that this would be a dramatic moment for me to make my debut. To the amazement of all my friends, I strode confidently over to the piano and sat down.

"Jack is up to his old tricks," somebody chuckled. The crowd laughed. They were certain that I couldn't play a note.

"Can he really play?" I heard a girl whisper to Arthur.

"Heavens, no," Arthur exclaimed. "He never played a note in all his life. . . ."

I decided to make the most of the situation. With mock dignity I drew out a silk handkerchief and lightly dusted off the piano keys. Then I rose and gave the revolving piano stool a quarter of a turn as I had seen an imitator of Paderewski do in a vaudeville sketch.

"What do you think of his execution?" called a voice from the rear.

"We're in favor of it!" came back the answer and the crowd rocked with laughter.

Then I started to play.

Instantly a tense silence fell on the guests. The laughter died on their lips as if by magic. I played through the first few bars of Beethoven's immortal "Moonlight Sonata." I heard gasps of amazement. My friends sat breathless—spellbound.

I played on, and as I played, I forgot the people around me. I forgot the hour, the place, the breathless listeners. The little world I lived in seemed to fade—seemed to grow dim—unreal. Only the music was real. Only the music and visions it brought me. Visions as beautiful and as changing as the wind blown clouds and drifting moonlight that long ago inspired the master composer.

That, to me, is advertising. I *am* the guy at whom they laughed, and the prospect of Arthur slinking out of the room (I'll bet he never played "The Rosary" again) is my personal triumph. The starry-eyed girls, the breathlessly hushed guests—why, it's *me* they're clapping!

Yes, those were the days when an advertising man was a poet. A commercial poet, of course, for it was sheer larceny what his verses did to you.

You picked up a magazine, you saw the picture of a tender young woman, her fingers raised to her parted lips, you noted her tear-touched happiness, and then you read with her this unbeatable note:

To Peggy - for marrying me in the first place...

for bringing up our children—while I mostly sat back and gave advice.

for the 2,008 pairs of socks you've darned.

for finding my umbrella and my rubbers Heaven knows how often!

for tying innumerable dress ties.

for being the family chauffeur, years on end.

for never getting sore at my always getting sore at your bridge playing.

for planning a thousand meals a year — and having them taken for granted.

for a constant tenderness I rarely notice but am sure I couldn't live without.

for wanting a *good* watch ever so long . . . and letting your slow-moving husband think he'd hit on it all by himself.

for just being you . . . *Darling, here's your Hamilton with all my love!* Jim

I'll give you a moment while you blow your nose. Please note that Hamilton is mentioned but once, at the very end. But who could stop reading sooner? Some sixty-odd people wrote to the company just thanking them for running the ad at all.

Do you want to know what all these ads had? One thing. A love for prose—pure, rich, beaded prose. They didn't sell cigarettes in those days with the purchasable hauteur of a society matron; they sold 'em with "Not a Cough in a Carload"—at least until the Federal Trade Commission made them stop. They didn't sell cars with dyna, hydra, torque, and flyte; they sold them with a picture of Walter P. Chrysler leaning purposefully on a fender and saying to you, "Look at All Three!" (The Plymouth dealers were mobbed.) When they sold handkerchiefs they didn't give you this stuff about Father's Day; Weber and Heilbroner ran an ad which simply said, "We traveled 2,000 miles to save you 65 cents." When B. Altman's wanted to get rid of some corsages they did it with this superlative full-page spread:

We believe there are at least 500 men in New York who love their wives—and want to give them flowers for Easter. So we've provided 500 old-fashioned bouquets. . . . ready now and packed in beautiful boxes. They're just inside the Fifth Avenue entrance . . . all at one price, and that one price very easy to afford.

Who could resist?

They sold a memory course with the unforgettable picture of one middle-aged man advancing to meet another and saying, "I remember you. You're Addison Sims of Seattle." They sold an etiquette book with a picture of a bewildered girl, ill at ease in a swanky restaurant amid the shiny napery and the French menus: "Again She Orders—'A Chicken Salad, Please!'" And they punched that one home with this subhead: *"Are you conscious of your crudities?* . . . Would you use your fork for your fruit salad or a spoon? Would you cut your roll with a knife or break it with your fingers? Would you take olives with a fork?" (Two million people were sufficiently conscious of their crudities to buy the book.)

Social taboos? They mowed them down with ads like this one for Odorono:

> ### Within the Curve of a Woman's Arm
>
> A frank discussion of a subject too often avoided
>
> A woman's arm! Poets have sung of its grace; artists have painted its beauty.
>
> It should be the daintiest, sweetest thing in the world.
>
> And yet, unfortunately, it isn't always.

And a hundred others—slogans hammered from the gold. Ask The Man Who Owns One; B. O.; The Skin You Love to Touch; You Press the Button—We Do the Rest; Even Her Best Friend Wouldn't Tell Her. They did their Trojan bit for Packard, Lifebuoy, Woodbury, Kodak, and Listerine respectively.

That for me was advertising at its peak. It beguiled, it tickled, it intrigued, it *sold*. That was the prose that made America sit up and take nourishment from Campbell's Soup, that made its sinks sparkle with Sapolio, that launched a thousand million ships of Ivory Soap, that stacked Dr. Eliot's shelf from here to the moon, that awakened America first with a whisper and then with a shout, that made it reach for Luckies instead of sweets.

Are those days gone forever? Sometimes I fear so. I emerge from the Christmas issue of a magazine which had weighed on my lap like a telephone book and I feel bothered and bewildered, but definitely not bewitched. I read the insides of match-book covers and the outsides of delivery trucks, the one-inch ads that furtively hawk the Secrets of Life, the two-inchers that tell you how to build your own kennel, the six inchers that extol cantilevering devices for all the parts of the human body that need cantilevering, and when I'm all done, damned if I can remember who's selling what.

Worse than that, I feel I am being positively unsold by ads which seize on the macabre and the bizarre in an effort to arrest my roving eye. I resent being sold a necktie by the scabrous device of peeking under a man's beard to see one. My thirst for bitters is not whetted by sadistic little cartoons of what happens to people who don't use them. My liking for shirts is offset by a deep-seated distrust for a Cyclops.

And then so much advertising is such a bore. I am tired unto the death of beautiful girls drinking beer. I am weary beyond belief of cars, all two city blocks long, and all souped up to travel at dangerous speeds. I am immune—utterly immune—to the meaningless superlative and unconvinced by the inconclusive comparative (They're Milder . . .). Isn't anyone ever going to *sell* me a cigarette again, instead of telling me that it's less irritating (which implies that it's still somewhat irritating)? How long must I listen to business men telling business men to believe in the business system? Down how many alimentary canals must I wander with Dr. Schnurrbart of the Wiener Schnitzel Institute?

Is the end product of the advertising imagination no more inspiring than the gimmick? Are my children to believe that the alphabet runs ABCLSMFT?

I'm not quite reduced to a state of despair. Good prose has been pretty near clubbed to death, but it's still breathing. There was a Lever Brothers ad comparing margarine to you-know-what that was so persuasive it actually got me to trot around to the store and try their product. There are the jaunty penguins smoking Kools and the mouth-watering Guinness ads; the clever ones for *Holiday;* the brocade of Gimbels' prose ("Big, bargain-y Gimbels' sprawls right out at the hub of the universe"); the wanderlust-creating travel-to-England ads; the brilliant brevity of Modess (Because . . .); the Bache & Company financial ads ("Don't be a two percenter"); the continuing good humor of the Burma-Shave jingles.

Good advertising is getting scarce, but it's still around. So stand back, you copywriters, and give prose a little air. Give us back those wonderful meat-axe ads. Away with the precious, the pallid, and the paltry. As a parting shot, to remind you of the incomparable power of the properly chosen word, let me recommend to you this, perhaps the greatest of all advertisements. It appeared in a little box in the London *Times* of 1900. A few lines of type, no pictures, no women, no coupons, no gimmicks, no rhymes, no tinsel. It pulled answers from all over England:

> Men wanted for Hazardous Journey. Small wages, bitter cold, long months of complete darkness, constant danger, safe return doubtful. Honor and recognition in case of success.—*Sir Ernest Shackleton.*

QUESTIONS ON CONTENT

1. Is there an element common to all the striking ads the author remembers? Are the ads more brazen or more subtle than most ads today?
2. Try to determine what the ad-man had in mind as the chief sales-point of his copy. Consider each ad separately.
3. Does the author's own style fit the subject he is discussing? Explain.

❧ ADVERTISING: Its Contribution to the American Way of Life

BRUCE BARTON

One day when I was young in advertising, I slipped a piece of paper into my typewriter and wrote an advertisement for a life insurance company. It was addressed to young husbands and fathers. One of the coupons received in reply came from a traveler in Rio de Janeiro, whose home was in New Jersey. He was 38 years old, married, and the father of three children. He wanted information on a policy that, in case of his death, would guarantee his family an income of $3000 a year.

On the man's return to New Jersey, the policy was written and the first payment made. A few days later he went to his dentist to have a wisdom tooth extracted. Somehow the cavity became infected, the infection spread and he died.

That incident made a deep impression on me. Many times in the intervening years I have been reminded that somewhere in New Jersey there are a mother and three children, now grown up, who, without the slightest suspicion of my existence, have had their whole lives changed by the fact that one day I put together some words that were printed in a magazine, and read in a faraway country by their husband and father, who was influenced to do what I suggested.

It is a terrific power we wield, we men and women in advertising; it needs to be handled carefully, truthfully, sometimes even prayer-

Reader's Digest, April, 1955. Reprinted by permission.

fully. It is one of the most potent of all the forces that, for better or worse, can influence and change human lives.

Roy Durstine once made this sage comment: "Advertising came into the world when man became too impatient to wait for Mrs. Jones to tell Mrs. Smith that Brown's pickles were good." That's an interesting way of pointing out that advertising, as a technique, is simply mass selling. But in its wide influence on our American way of life, advertising is much more than that. It is a creative force that has generated new jobs, new ideas, has expanded our economy and helped to give us the highest standard of living in the world.

Take jobs. In 1900 almost nobody was building automobiles. Now we have a ten-billion-dollar, 772,000-worker industry which depends on additional thousands of workers in steel, rubber, glass, petroleum and allied fields.

Advertising did not invent the products or services which called forth those jobs, nor inspire the pioneering courage that built factories and machinery to produce them. What advertising did was to stimulate ambition and desire—the craving to possess, which is the strongest incentive to produce. To satisfy this craving the little factory was impelled to turn itself into a growing factory; and then, by the pressure of mass demand, into many factories. Mass production made possible mass economies, reflected in declining prices, until the product that began as the luxury of the rich became the possession of every family that was willing to work.

This happy result, if it could have been achieved at all without advertising, would have taken many years longer. The patent on the sewing machine was granted to young Elias Howe in 1846, but most of his mature years were passed in disappointment and poverty because no one bought his machine—advertising was too limited to spread the good news of its arrival. A whole generation of housewives, whose work could have been made lighter and pleasanter, died without ever having heard that such a wonderful homehelper had been born.

There is no such waste of time and life in the present-day world. The mechanical refrigerator, dishwasher, home freezer and dozens of other utilities and comforts were made known almost instantly to America's millions of women and became a welcome part of their lives—at prices that dropped lower and lower—as more factories were built and equipped.

With the coming of the washing machine, the vacuum cleaner and other household utilities, I prepared an advertising campaign for the women's magazines. The illustration of each advertisement was different—a tired woman bending over a wash-tub, scrubbing the floor, or performing some other distasteful duty. The copy was brief and unchanged throughout the series; it read:

Any woman who is doing any household task that a little electric motor can do is working for three cents an hour. Human life is too precious to be sold at a price of three cents an hour.

This and similar campaigns were widely effective. The wholesale emancipation of women from the drudgery of kitchen, laundry and cellar is one of the dramatic phenomena of our times, carrying with it vast enrichment of the intellectual, social, religious and political life of the nation. Advertising didn't inaugurate it, but it speeded it up.

Writing in *The Reader's Digest* 32 years ago, Earnest Elmo Calkins, one of the leaders to whom advertising owes a great debt, pointed out that "few have noticed the remarkable effects of advertising upon those who use it. It lays the advertiser under the necessity of living up to his advertising."

One of my early experiences was inaugurating a campaign of institutional advertising in which my advertisements set forth the public-service ideals of the corporation's management. One day a disgruntled dealer stormed into the president's office, threw down on the desk a magazine containing one of the ads, and exclaimed: "I see that you claim to be a very high-minded organization. I just want to tell you from my experience that you are nothing of the kind!"

The president sent for me, and said: "Bruce, maybe we are pitching our campaign a little too high!"

I protested violently. "It's my business to walk out in front with a big banner," I argued. "It's your business not to call me back, but to bring the business up to me." He agreed, and bit by bit the big business shaped up according to the picture we had painted for it.

The important part played by advertising in standardizing prices is rarely remembered now. "Fifty years ago," Mr. Calkins pointed out, "the prices in stores were not marked intelligibly to the customer. The selling price was whatever the salesman could get. The higher the price, the better the salesman. The secret price was an injustice to most customers. Only good bargainers could beat the salesman at his own game.

"Along came advertising. Some merchant, feeling around for a message, a story that would give him the individuality at which all advertising aims, abolished the secret price and announced: 'All goods plainly marked.' A new era in selling had begun which was to continue until goods could be returned if unsatisfactory, money cheerfully refunded; until the customer's continued satisfaction was placed higher than the profits on any sale. It is only within the memory of men now living that it has been believed that both parties to a bargain could be satisfied."

Without advertising, our newspapers would be four- or six-page flyers printed on cheap paper, with poor, if any, illustrations. Our popular magazines and trade and professional publications would be nonexistent. The publishers of *The Saturday Evening Post*, now selling at 15 cents a copy, estimate that, without advertising, the price would have to be 60 cents.

In my long and cheerful years of marriage my wife superintended the remodeling and redecorating of five houses and one apartment. In every case she sat down in advance with the architect, and brought to the conference a huge bundle of clippings which she had garnered from the magazines devoted to home building and decoration. The so-called women's magazines were her inspiration for our better living, better eating, better health and better parenthood. No money estimate can ever measure the contribution of their influence on the American way of life. As for the trade and professional publications, which are the postgraduate universities of the doctor, the lawyer, as well as the engineer, the executive and the plumber, there are 2187 of them. And 1169 publications that cultivate the vineyards of religion.

Advertising is of the very essence of democracy. An election goes on every minute of the business day across the counters of hundreds of thousands of stores and shops where the customers state their preferences and determine which manufacturer and which product shall be the leader today, and which shall lead tomorrow. In this fair but fierce competition for public preference every manufacturer must strive through continuous research to improve his product. Incidentally, what little advertising there is under totalitarianism is rigidly controlled, and understandably so. It is dangerous to let a captive people choose freely their food, their clothing, their tools or their homes; such freedom can too easily expand to the ultimate goal of choosing their leaders and their way of life.

Advertising has its follies, and its faults. To quote Mr. Calkins again: "Advertising was once looked upon with justifiable suspicion.

Patent-medicine people and out-and-out swindlers owed their existence to it. Publishers began to see that they were fouling their own nests in accepting business that destroyed the confidence that is the lifeblood of business. Edward Bok, editor of the *Ladies' Home Journal*, launched a crusade that stirred the patent-medicine world to its depth. The magazines cleaned house. They were followed by the newspapers."

Too many printed advertisements still make exaggerated claims. Too many still insult the sensitive intelligence and offend good taste. Too many radio and TV commercials are too long and too loud. But the business is young, less than 100 years old. It turns out some 30 million publication advertisements every year, something like 155 million radio and TV commercials. Under the pressure of such mass production there is bound to be a percentage of error and poor taste.

But during an examination of more than a million advertisements of all types, the Federal Trade Commission labeled less than three percent as possibly misleading. If advertising sometimes encourages men and women to live beyond their means, so sometimes does matrimony. If advertising is too often tedious, garrulous and redundant, so is the United States Senate.

The American people like advertising, want it, depend on it for information and, if it were abolished, the demand for its return would be overwhelming. For 11 days in the fall of 1953, most of the newspapers of New York City were out of business because of a strike. The effect on the business and social life of the city was cataclysmic. Department stores sales dropped as much as 25 percent. Job applications fell; the sale of used cars sagged. Even funeral attendance dropped because no death notices could be run. On the day the strike ended, a survey organization asked people: "What did you miss most in not having your paper?" Forty-two percent answered, "The advertisements."

Clients know too that advertising brings a bonus in better morale of employees who take pride in working for a well-known and widely respected company and do a better job because of it. Today's national advertiser asks the agency not, "How little can you get along with?" but, "How much can we profitably spend?"

Another impressive development has been the widespread recognition of the need for better "public relations." There is today no major industry that is not constantly urging its advertising agency to make fresh studies of the public's likes or dislikes. Every big industry is publicly owned, and knows that in a democracy it is the people who will finally decide who shall be in business, and under what conditions.

Every three seconds of the business day a baby is born in America; each month we add to the consuming public a city the size of Omaha. And pacing this population growth is an ever-higher standard of living throughout the country. Our economy is based on huge production, financed by tremendous consumer purchases, propelled by more advertising than is done by all the rest of the world together. It sustains a system that has made us the leaders of the free world: The American Way of Life.

QUESTIONS ON CONTENTS

1. What is the purpose of the first two paragraphs? Of the last paragraph?
2. The author calls advertising a "creative force"? Why?
3. What moral does the author draw from the experience of Elias Howe and his sewing machine?
4. List and discuss all the virtues of advertising as set forth in this article.
5. Do you think the author tends to minimize the sins of modern advertising? See p. 271.
6. Comment on this statement: "Advertising is the very essence of democracy." How does the author make a case for this point of view? And, if this is so, what should one say of the growth of consumers' organizations with their goal of exposing the fallacies in advertising? Are such organizations anti-democratic, or simply another element in the "essence of democracy"?

SUGGESTIONS FOR PAPERS

It would be difficult to find anyone in America completely indifferent to advertising. Most of us express ourselves volubly about the excess of this "art." You will find material for your paper at hand in a thousand forms. Selection of definite points of attack—or defense, if you wish—will be your chief problem.

1. The selection, "Talks on Advertising," accuses the writers of advertisements of a woeful lack of taste. Write your paper on this point. Choose advertisements from newspapers, magazines, or radio

which, you feel, offend good taste because they are too childish, too sentimental, too crude, too suggestive, or too ugly. Match these examples with others illustrating opposite qualities.

2. Another charge against advertising is its fundamental dishonesty. Since blatant dishonesty in advertising is illegal, you will have to show the ways advertisers evade the law by suggestion rather than outright claims. Study ten magazine advertisements, and judge the truth of what they say. (This is an inductive study—that is, you will be reasoning from particulars to a generalization.) What do you conclude about the honesty of advertising?

3. "Self-hypnotism" brings no direct charges against ad-men. Carefully study this selection and, on the basis of what this ad-man admits, draw up a set of conclusions about the ethics of advertising. Refer to "Talks on Advertising" for appropriate quotations.

4. Listen to four radio commercials advertising cigarettes. To what sort of audience are the commercials directed? What is the central point of their appeal? Does any one of them appeal to an adult level of intelligence? Rate the four commercials in the order of their dignity and good taste.

5. "The more useless and undesirable the article the greater the advertising effort needed to dispose of it." Test this statement and write about the results. Here are two suggested approaches: (1) Select a magazine which carries many advertisements. Make up lists to show which articles are given double pages, which are given a single page, which a half page, which a quarter page. Those products given the most space should be less useful and desirable than those given less space. Does it work out this way? (2) The most desirable and the most costly radio hours are evening hours from seven to ten, Sunday through Friday. What articles have purchased this radio time? According to the statement quoted above, what can you conclude about these products?

6. It is said that radio and television belong to the people. Both are supported by advertisers. To whom, then, do they belong? Discuss the advantages and disadvantages of this sort of ownership, with perhaps references to the current campaign for subscription TV.

7. Analyze "Where Are the Ads of Yesteryear?" What is the appeal sought for in each of the ads cited? Is the approach subtle or blatant, in good taste or not, essentially truthful or deliberately misleading, intentionally humorous or, perhaps, unintentionally so?

8. As the author of "Advertising: Its Contribution to the American Way of Life" indicates, ad-men take their function seriously. Should

they? List all the good points as given by Mr. Barton. Show how he strives to prove these points. Now list the sins of advertising. How are these treated? What do you conclude?

9. Consumers' organizations attempt to find out the truth behind advertisements. They do this through the testing of competing products and report findings to their subscribers. Investigate one of these reports (*Consumers' Union* or *Consumers' Research*), and estimate the advantages and disadvantages of this approach to buying.

SOME TITLES FOR PAPERS

1. Ethics of the Ad-man
2. What Billboard Advertising Does to a City (or to Country Roads)
3. Advantages to the Consumer of Advertising
4. Examples of Dignified Advertisements
5. Advertising Everywhere
6. Advertisers Cannot Please Everybody
7. The Worst Radio Advertising
8. The Best Radio Advertising
9. The Amazing Perfumes!
10. Least Wanted, Most Advertised
11. Fifty Magazine Advertisements: An Analysis
12. Health Advertisements: What Claims!
13. Advertisers Who Support Culture
14. Radio and Television Are for the People
15. Mass Media and Aristocratic Culture
16. The Lowest Common Denominator
17. Should Radio and Television Be Responsible for Culture?
18. Radio and Television Are Exclusively for the People's Amusement

❧ *WAR*

MAN, THOROUGHLY PERPLEXED by his apparent inability to avoid war, cannot be charged with thoughtlessness on the subject. Library shelves are overflowing with the results of the best thinking that the best brains can give to the subject. Every road, every bypath that might lead nations into conflict has been minutely surveyed and drawn to a scale for the world to see. Perhaps not enough people read these charts. Perhaps those who read them do not translate their meaning into a working, active faith that war can be avoided. It is certain that few subjects in our time are of more compelling significance or worth more hard, clear thinking.

William James in "The Moral Equivalent of War" does some hard, clear thinking, but so far his proposed solution to the problem has caused much comment but not action. War, he says, serves a positive need; one will find no cure for war if he blinks this fact. Suppose, he goes on, one can isolate and positively identify what this need is. The next step would be to find an adequate substitute which would be just as satisfactory to man but less harmful.

This approach is logically sound, but Will Durant in "Why Men Fight" calls James's proposal a "nostrum" which fails to take into account all the causes of war. In spite of his conviction that war is inevitable (he was writing this article on the verge of World War II), he concludes that we must "wage peace" as whole-heartedly as we always wage war.

Neither William James nor Will Durant could foresee the factor of atomic weapons which might make war unthinkable. Harold C. Urey, as spokesman for most physicists who have had a part in creating the awesome weapons, concludes in "How Does It All Add Up?" that if war comes again man will go. The question is this: if war has always been "inevitable" for the reasons given by William James, Will Durant, and a host of others, will this new danger negate those reasons? What do you think?

ᴖ *The Moral Equivalent of War*

WILLIAM JAMES

The war against war is going to be no holiday excursion or camping party. The military feelings are too deeply grounded to abdicate their place among our ideals until better substitutes are offered than the glory and shame that come to nations as well as to individuals from the ups and down of politics and the vicissitudes of trade. There is something highly paradoxical in the modern man's relation to war. Ask all our millions, north and south, whether they would vote now (were such a thing possible) to have our war for the Union expunged from history, and the record of a peaceful transition to the present time substituted for that of its marches and battles, and probably hardly a handful of eccentrics would say yes. Those ancestors, those efforts, those memories and legends, are the most ideal part of what we now own together, a sacred spiritual possession worth more than all the blood poured out. Yet ask those same people whether they would be willing in cold blood to start another civil war now to gain another similar possession, and not one man or woman would vote for the proposition. In modern eyes, precious though wars may be, they must not be waged solely for the sake of the ideal harvest. Only when forced upon one, only when an enemy's injustice leaves us no alternative, is a war now thought permissible.

It was not thus in ancient times. The earlier men were hunting men, and to hunt a neighboring tribe, kill the males, loot the village and possess the females, was the most profitable, as well as the most exciting, way of living. Thus were the more martial tribes selected,

From William James, *Memories and Studies* (1911), Longmans, Green and Company, Inc. Appeared first in *International Conciliation* (1910), No. 27.

and in chiefs and peoples a pure pugnacity and love of glory came to mingle with the more fundamental appetite for plunder.

Modern war is so expensive that we feel trade to be a better avenue to plunder; but modern man inherits all the innate pugnacity and all the love of glory of his ancestors. Showing war's irrationality and horror is of no effect upon him. The horrors make the fascination. War is the *strong* life; it is life *in extremis;* war taxes are the only ones men never hesitate to pay, as the budgets of all nations show us.

History is a bath of blood. The *Iliad* is one long recital of how Diomedes and Ajax, Sarpedon and Hector, *killed.* No detail of the wounds they made is spared us, and the Greek mind fed upon the story. Greek history is a panorama of jingoism and imperialism— war for war's sake, all the citizens being warriors. It is horrible reading, because of the irrationality of it all—save for the purpose of making "history"—and the history is that of the utter ruin of a civilization in intellectual respects perhaps the highest the earth has ever seen.

Those wars were purely piratical. Pride, gold, women, slaves, excitement, were their only motives. In the Peloponnesian War, for example, the Athenians asked the inhabitants of Melos (the island where the "Venus of Milo" was found), hitherto neutral, to own their lordship. The envoys meet, and hold a debate which Thucydides gives in full, and which, for sweet reasonableness of form, would have satisfied Matthew Arnold. "The powerful exact what they can," said the Athenians, "and the weak grant what they must." When the Meleans say that sooner than be slaves they will appeal to the gods, the Athenians reply: "Of the gods we believe and of men we know that, by a law of their nature, wherever they can rule they will. This law was not made by us, and we are not the first to have acted upon it; we did but inherit it, and we know that you and all mankind, if you were strong as we are, would do as we do. So much for the gods; we have told you why we expect to stand as high in their good opinion as you." Well, the Meleans still refused, and their town was taken. "The Athenians," Thucydides quietly says, "thereupon put to death all who were of military age and made slaves of the women and children. They then colonized the island, sending thither five hundred settlers of their own."

Alexander's career was piracy pure and simple, nothing but an orgy of power and plunder, made romantic by the character of the hero. There was no rational principle in it, and the moment he died his generals and governors attacked one another. The cruelty of those times is incredible. When Rome finally conquered Greece, Paulus Aemilius was told by the Roman Senate to reward his soldiers for their toil by "giving" them the old kingdom of Epirus. They sacked seventy cities and carried off a hundred and fifty thousand inhabitants as slaves. How many they killed I know not; but in Etolia they killed all the senators, five hundred and fifty in number. Brutus was "the noblest Roman of them all," but to reanimate his soldiers on the eve of Philippi he similarly promises to give them the cities of Sparta and Thessalonica to ravage, if they win the fight.

Such was the gory nurse that trained societies to cohesiveness. We inherit the warlike type; and for most of the capacities of heroism that the human race is full of we have to thank this cruel history. Dead men tell no tales, and if there were any tribes of other type than this they have left no survivors. Our ancestors have bred pugnacity into our bone and marrow, and thousands of years of peace won't breed it out of us. The popular imagination fairly fattens on the thought of wars. Let public opinion once reach a certain fighting pitch, and no ruler can withstand it. In the Boer War both governments began with bluff, but couldn't stay there; the military tension was too much for them. In 1898 our people had read the word WAR in letters three inches high for three months in every newspaper. The pliant politician McKinley was swept away by their eagerness, and our squalid war with Spain became a necessity.

At the present day, civilized opinion is a curious mental mixture. The military instincts and ideals are as strong as ever, but are confronted by reflective criticisms which sorely curb their ancient freedom. Innumerable writers are showing up the bestial side of military service. Pure loot and mastery seem no longer morally avowable motives, and pretexts must be found for attributing them solely to the enemy. England and we, our army and navy authorities repeat without ceasing, arm solely for "peace"; Germany and Japan it is who are bent on loot and glory. "Peace" in military mouths today is a synonym for "war expected." The word has become a pure provocative, and no government wishing peace sincerely should allow it ever to be printed in a newspaper. Every up-to-date dictionary should say that "peace" and "war" mean the same thing, now *in posse*, now *in actu*. It may even reasonably be said that the intensely sharp competitive *preparation* for war by the nations *is the real war*, permanent, unceasing; and that the battles are only a sort of public verification of the mastery gained during the "peace" interval.

It is plain that on this subject civilized man has developed a sort of double personality. If we take European nations, no legitimate interest of any one of them would seem to justify the tremendous destructions which a war to compass it would necessarily entail. It would seem as though common sense and reason ought to find a way to reach agreement in every conflict of honest interests. I myself think it our bounden duty to believe in such international rationality as possible. But, as things stand, I see how desperately hard it is to bring the peace party and the war party together, and I believe that the difficulty is due to certain deficiencies in the program of pacificism which set the militarist imagination strongly, and to a certain extent justifiably, against it. In the whole discussion both sides are on imaginative and sentimental ground. It is but one utopia against another, and everything one says must be abstract and hypothetical. Subject to this criticism and caution, I will try to characterize in abstract strokes the opposite imaginative forces, and point out what to my own very fallible mind seems the best utopian hypothesis, the most promising line of conciliation.

In my remarks, pacifist though I am, I will refuse to speak of the bestial side of the war regime (already done justice to by many writers) and consider only the higher aspects of militaristic sentiment. Patriotism no one thinks discreditable; nor does anyone deny that war is the romance of history. But inordinate ambitions are the soul of every patriotism, and the possibility of violent death the soul of all romance. The militarily patriotic and romantic-minded everywhere, and especially the professional military class, refuse to admit for a moment that war may be a transitory phenomenon in social evolution. The notion of a sheep's paradise like that revolts, they say, our higher imagination. Where then would be the steeps of life? If war had ever stopped, we should have to reinvent it, on this view, to redeem life from flat degeneration.

Reflective apologists for war at the present day all take it religiously. It is a sort of sacrament. Its profits are to the vanquished as well as to the victor; and quite apart from any question of profit, it is an absolute good, we are told, for it is human nature at its highest dynamic. Its "horrors" are a cheap price to pay for rescue from the only alternative supposed of a world of clerks and teachers, of co-education and zoophily, of "consumer's leagues" and "associated charities," of industrialism unlimited and feminism unabashed. No scorn, no hardness, no valor any more! Fie upon such a cattleyard of a planet!

So far as the central essence of this feeling goes, no healthy-minded person, it seems to me, can help to some degree partaking of it. Militarism is the great preserver of our ideals of hardihood, and human life with no use for hardihood would be contemptible. Without risks or prizes for the darer, history would be insipid indeed; and there is a type of military character which everyone feels that the race should never cease to breed, for everyone is sensitive to its superiority. The duty is incumbent on mankind, of keeping military characters in stock—of keeping them, if not for use, then as ends in themselves and as pure pieces of perfection—so that [Theodore] Roosevelt's weaklings and mollycoddles may not end by making everything else disappear from the face of nature.

This natural sort of feeling forms, I think, the innermost soul of army writings. Without any exception known to me, militarist authors take a highly mystical view of their subject, and regard war as a biological or sociological necessity, uncontrolled by ordinary psychological checks and motives. When the time of development is ripe the war must come, reason or no reason, for the justifications pleaded are invariably fictitious. War is, in short, a permanent human *obligation*. General Homer Lea, in his recent book, *The Valor of Ignorance*, plants himself squarely on this ground. Readiness for war is for him the essence of nationality, and ability in it the supreme measure of the health of nations.

Nations, General Lea says, are never stationary—they must necessarily expand or shrink, according to their vitality or decrepitude. Japan now is culminating; and by the fatal law in question it is impossible that her statesmen should not long since have entered, with extraordinary foresight, upon a vast policy of conquest—the game in which the first moves were her wars with China and Russia and her treaty with England, and of which the final objective is the capture of the Philippines, the Hawaiian Islands, Alaska, and the whole of our coast west of the Sierra Passes. This will give Japan what her ineluctable vocation as a state absolutely forces her to claim, the possession of the entire Pacific Ocean; and to oppose these deep designs we Americans have, according to our author, nothing but our conceit, our ignorance, our commercialism, our corruption, and our feminism. General Lea makes a minute technical comparison of the military strength which we at present could oppose to the strength of Japan, and concludes that the islands, Alaska, Oregon, and Southern California, would fall almost without resistance, that San Francisco must surrender in a fort-night to a Japanese investment, that in three or four months the war would be over, and our Republic, unable to regain what it had heedlessly neglected to protect sufficiently, would then "disintegrate," until perhaps some Caesar should arise to weld us again into a nation.

A dismal forecast indeed! Yet not unplausible, if the mentality of Japan's statesmen be of the Caesarian type of which history shows so many examples, and which is all that General Lea seems able to imagine. But there is no reason to think that women can no longer be the mothers of Napoleonic or Alexandrian characters; and if these come in Japan and find their opportunity, just such surprises as *The Valor of Ignorance* paints may lurk in ambush for us. Ignorant as we still are of the innermost recesses of Japanese mentality, we may be foolhardy to disregard such possibilities.

Other militarists are more complex and more moral in their considerations. The *Philosophie des Krieges,* by S. R. Steinmetz, is a good example. War, according to this author, is an ordeal instituted by God, who weighs the nations in its balance. It is the essential form of the state, and the only function in which peoples can employ all their powers at once and convergently. No victory is possible save as the resultant of a totality of virtues, no defeat for which some vice or weakness is not responsible. Fidelity, cohesiveness, tenacity, heroism, conscience, education, inventiveness, economy, wealth, physical health and vigor—there isn't a moral or intellectual point of superiority that doesn't tell, when God holds his assizes and hurls the people upon one another. *Die Weltgeschichte ist das Weltgericht* ["The history of the world is the judgment of the world."]; and Dr. Steinmetz does not believe that in the long run chance and luck play any part in apportioning the issues.

The virtues that prevail, it must be noted, are virtues anyhow, superiorities that count in peaceful as well as in military competition; but the strain on them, being infinitely intenser in the latter case, makes war infinitely more searching as a trial. No ordeal is comparable to its winnowings. Its dread hammer is the welder of men into cohesive states, and nowhere but in such states can human nature adequately develop its capacity. The only alternative is "degeneration."

Dr. Steinmetz is a conscientious thinker, and his book, short as it is, takes much into account. Its upshot can, it seems to me, be summed up in Simon Patten's word, that mankind was nursed in pain and fear, and that the transition to a "pleasure economy" may be fatal to a being wielding no powers of defense against its disintegrative influences. If we speak of the *fear of emancipation from the fear regime,* we put the whole situation into a single phrase; fear regarding ourselves now taking the place of the ancient fear of the enemy.

Turn the fear over as I will in my mind, it all seems to lead back to two unwillingnesses of the imagination, one esthetic, and the other moral: unwillingness, first to envisage a future in which army life, with its many elements of charm, shall be forever impossible, and in which the destinies of peoples shall nevermore be decided quickly, thrillingly, and tragically, by force, but only gradually and insipidly by "evolution"; and, secondly, unwillingness to see the supreme theater of human strenuousness closed, and the splendid military aptitudes of men doomed to keep always in a state of latency and never show themselves in action. These insistent unwillingnesses, no less than other esthetic and ethical insistencies, have, it seems to me, to be listened to and respected. One cannot meet them effectively by mere counter-insistency on war's expensiveness and horror. The horror makes the thrill; and when the question is of getting the extremest and supremest out of human nature, talk of expense sounds ignominious. The weakness of so much merely negative criticism is evident—pacifism makes no converts from the military party. The military party denies neither the bestiality nor the horror, nor the expense; it only says that these things tell but half the story. It only says that war is *worth* them; that, taking human nature as a whole, its wars are its best protection against its weaker and more cowardly self, and that mankind can not *afford* to adopt a peace economy.

Pacifists ought to enter more deeply into the esthetical and ethical point of view of their opponents. Do that first in any controversy, says J. J. Chapman; *then move the point,* and your opponent will follow. So long as anti-militarists propose no substitute for war's disciplinary function, no *moral equivalent* of war, analogous, as one might say, to the mechanical equivalent of heat, so long they fail to realize the full inwardness of the situation. And as a rule they do fail. The duties, penalties, and sanctions pictured in the utopias they paint are all too weak and tame to touch the military-minded. Tolstoi's pacifism is the only exception to this rule, for it is profoundly pessimistic as regards all this world's values, and makes the fear of the Lord furnish the moral spur provided elsewhere by the fear of the enemy. But our socialistic peace advocates all believe absolutely in this world's values; and instead of the fear of the Lord and the fear of the enemy, the only fear they reckon with is the fear of poverty if one be lazy. This weakness pervades all the socialistic literature with which I am acquainted. Even in Lowes Dickinson's exquisite dialogue [*Justice and Liberty,* New York, 1909], high wages and short hours are the only forces invoked for overcoming man's distaste for repulsive kinds of labor. Meanwhile men at large still live as they always have lived, under a pain-and-fear economy —for those of us who live in an ease economy are but an island in the stormy ocean—and the whole atmosphere of present-day utopian literature tastes mawkish and dishwatery to people who still keep a sense for life's more bitter flavors. It suggests, in truth, ubiquitous inferiority.

Inferiority is always with us, and merciless scorn of it is the keynote of the military temper. "Dogs, would you live forever?" shouted Frederick the Great. "Yes," say our utopians, "let us live forever, and raise our level gradually." The best thing about our "inferiors" today is that they are as tough as nails, and physically and morally almost as insensitive. Utopianism would see them soft and squeamish, while militarism would keep their callousness, but transfigure it into a meritorious characteristic, needed by "the service," and redeemed by that from the suspicion of inferiority. All the qualities of a man acquire dignity when he knows that the service of the collectivity that owns him needs them. If proud of the collectivity, his own pride rises in proportion. No collectivity is like an army for nourishing such pride; but it has to be confessed that the only sentiment which the image of pacific cosmopolitan industrialism is capable of arousing in countless worthy breasts is shame at the idea of belonging to *such* a collectivity. It is obvious that the United States of America as they exist today impress a mind like General Lea's as so much human blubber. Where is the sharpness and precipitousness, the contempt for life, whether one's own or another's? Where is the savage "yes" and "no," the unconditional duty? Where is the conscription? Where is the blood tax? Where is anything that one feels honored by belonging to?

Having said thus much in preparation, I will now confess my own utopia. I devoutly believe in the reign of peace and in the gradual advent of some sort of socialistic equilibrium. The fatalistic view of the war function is to me nonsense, for I know that war-making is due to definite motives and subject to prudential checks and reasonable criticisms, just like any other form of enterprise. And when whole nations are the armies, and the science of destruction vies in intellectual refinement with the sciences of production, I see that war becomes absurd and impossible from its own monstrosity. Extravagant ambitions will have to be replaced by reasonable claims, and nations must make common cause against them. I see no reason why all this should not apply to yellow as well as to white countries, and I look forward to a future when acts of war shall be formally outlawed as between civilized peoples.

All these beliefs of mine put me squarely into the anti-militarist party. But I do not believe that peace either ought to be or will be permanent on this globe, unless the states pacifically organized preserve some of the old elements of army discipline. A permanently successful peace economy cannot be a simple pleasure economy. In the more or less socialistic future toward which mankind seems drifting we must still subject ourselves collectively to these severities which answer to our real position upon this only partly hospitable globe. We must make new energies and hardihoods continue the manliness to which the military mind so faithfully clings. Martial virtues must be the enduring cement; intrepidity, contempt of softness, surrender of private interest, obedience to command, must still remain the rock upon which states are built—unless, indeed, we wish for dangerous reactions against commonwealth fit only for contempt, and liable to invite attack whenever a center of crystallization for military-minded enterprise gets formed anywhere in their neighborhood.

The war party is assuredly right in affirming and reaffirming that the martial virtues, although originally gained by the race through war, are absolute and permanent human goods. Patriotic pride and ambition in their military form are, after all, only specifications of a more general competitive passion. They are its first form, but that is no reason for supposing them to be its last form. Men now are proud of belonging to a conquering nation, and without a murmur they lay down their persons and their wealth, if by so doing they may fend off subjection. But who can be sure that *other aspects of one's country* may not, with time and education and suggestion enough, come to be regarded with similarly effective feelings of pride and shame? Why should men not some day feel that it is worth a blood tax to belong to a collectivity superior in *any* ideal respect? Why should they not blush with indignant shame if the community that owns them is vile in any way whatsoever? Individuals, daily more numerous, now feel this civic passion. It is only a question of blowing on the spark till the whole population gets incandescent, and on the ruins of the old morals of military honor, a stable system of morals of civic honor builds itself up. What the whole community comes to believe in grasps the individual as in a vise. The war function has grasped us so far; but constructive interests may some day seem no less imperative, and impose on the individual a hardly lighter burden.

Let me illustrate my idea more concretely. There is nothing to make one indignant in the mere fact that life is hard, that men should toil and suffer pain. The planetary conditions once for all are such, and we can stand it. But that so many men, by mere accidents of birth and opportunity, should have a life of *nothing else* but toil and pain and hardness and inferiority imposed upon them, should have *no* vacation, while others natively no more deserving never get any taste of this campaigning life at all—*this* is capable of arousing indignation in reflective minds. It may end by seeming shameful to all of us that some of us have nothing but campaigning, and others nothing but unmanly ease. If now—and this is my idea— there were, instead of military conscription, a conscription of the whole youthful population to form for a certain number of years a part of the army enlisted against *Nature*, the injustice would tend to be evened out, and numerous other goods to the commonwealth would follow. The military ideals of hardihood and discipline would be wrought into the growing fiber of the people; no one would remain blind as the luxurious classes now are blind, to man's real relations to the globe he lives on, and to the permanently sour and hard foundations of his higher life. To coal and iron mines, to freight trains, to fishing fleets in December, to dish-washing, clothes-washing, and window-washing, to road-building and tunnel-making, to foundries and stoke-holes, and to the frames of skyscrapers, would our gilded youths be drafted off, according to their choice, to get the childishness knocked out of them, and to come back into society with healthier sympathies and soberer ideas. They would have paid their blood tax, done their own part in the immemorial human warfare against nature, they would tread the earth more proudly, the women would value them more highly, they would be better fathers and teachers of the following generation.

Such a conscription, with the state of public opinion that would have required it, and the many moral fruits it would bear, would preserve in the midst of a pacific civilization the manly virtues which the military party is so afraid of seeing disappear in peace. We should get toughness without callousness, authority with as little criminal cruelty as possible, and painful work done cheerily because the duty is temporary, and threatens not, as now, to degrade the whole remainder of one's life. I spoke of the "moral equivalent" of war. So far, war has been the only force that can discipline a whole community, and until an equivalent discipline is organized, I believe that war must have its way. But I have no serious doubt that the ordinary prides and shames of social man, once developed to a certain intensity, are capable of organizing such a moral equivalent as I have sketched, or some other just as effective for preserving manliness of type. It is but a question of time, of skillful propagandism, and of opinion-making men seizing historic opportunities.

The martial type of character can be bred without war. Strenuous honor and disinterestedness abound elsewhere. Priests and medical men are in a fashion educated to it, and we should all feel some degree of it imperative if we were conscious of our work as an obligatory service to the state. We should be *owned,* as soldiers are by the army, and our pride would rise accordingly. We could be poor, then, without humiliation, as army officers now are. The only thing needed henceforth is to inflame the civic temper as past history has inflamed the military temper. H. G. Wells, as usual, sees the center of the situation. "In many ways," he says, "military organization is the most peaceful of activities. When the contemporary man steps from the street, of clamorous insincere advertisement, push, adulteration, underselling and intermittent employment, into the barrack yard, he steps on to a higher social plane, into an atmosphere of service and co-operation and of infinitely more honorable emulations. Here at least men are not flung out of employment to degenerate because there is no immediate work for them to do. They are fed and drilled and trained for better services. Here at least a man is supposed to win promotion by self-forgetfulness and not by self-seeking." . . . [*First and Last Things,* 1908, p. 215.]

Wells adds that he thinks that the conceptions of order and discipline, the tradition of service and devotion, of physical fitness, unstinted exertion, and universal responsibility, which universal military duty is now teaching European nations, will remain a permanent acquisition, when the last ammunition has been used in the fireworks that celebrate the final peace. I believe as he does. It would be simply preposterous if the only force that could work ideals of honor and standards of efficiency into English or American natures should be the fear of being killed by the Germans or the Japanese. Great indeed is Fear; but it is not, as our military enthusiasts believe and try to make us believe, the only stimulus known for awakening the higher ranges of men's spiritual energy. The amount of alteration in public opinion which my utopia postulates is vastly less than the difference between the mentality of those black warriors who pursued Stanley's party on the Congo with their cannibal war cry of "Meat! Meat!" and that of the General Staff of any civilized nation. History has seen the latter interval bridged over: the former one can be bridged over much more easily.

QUESTIONS ON CONTENT

1. How would you vote on the author's questions about the Civil War? Does something besides "ideal harvest" influence your answer?
2. Do you agree that "appetite for plunder" is more fundamental than "pugnacity and love of glory"?
3. Does man pay "war taxes" because "War is the *strong* life"?
4. What does *jingoism* mean and how did it originate?
5. Do you think that James's theory of pugnacity is tenable?
6. Do the people *push* their rulers into war?
7. Explain the author's saying that *peace* and *war* mean the same thing.
8. At what point does the author begin his review of the militarist's attitude toward war? How sympathetic is he toward this attitude?
9. How nearly correct was General Homer Lea in his predictions about Japan?
10. What argument does Steinmetz offer to prove that war is good in itself?
11. Explain: *"fear of emancipation from the fear regime."*
12. What two "unwillingnesses" of man make him reluctant to turn pacifist?
13. Why does James spend so much time on the esthetics and the ethics of war? Does this emphasis serve his own purposes? Explain.
14. Comment on the phrase "pleasure economy."
15. Is it James's main point that martial virtue may be retained without war?
16. What one sentence contains the essence of James's idea for pushing war out of men's minds? How does he herald the sentence? How does he support it?

❧ *Why Men Fight*

WILL DURANT

I. Perspective

In the year 1830 a French customs official unearthed, in the valley of the Somme, strange implements of flint now recognized by the learned as the weapons with which the men of the Old Stone Age made war. These stones are called *coups de poing,* or "blows of the fist," for one end was rounded to be grasped in the hand, while the other end was pointed for persuasion. With these modest tools of death, it seems, Neanderthal men from what is now Germany, and Cro-Magnon men from what is now France, fought fifty thousand years ago for the mastery of the continent, and, after a day of lusty battle, left perhaps a score of dead on the field. Twenty years ago, modern Germans and modern Frenchmen fought again, in that same valley, for that same prize, with magnificent tools of death that killed ten thousand men in a day. One art alone has made indisputable progress in history, and that is the art of war.

For five hundred centuries, two thousand generations have struggled for the terrain in a calendar of wars whose beginning is as distant as its end. Our own children rest there, some of them, lured by fear or nobility into that ancient strife. Even the sophisticated mind, accustomed to magnitude and marvels, is appalled by the panorama of historic war, from the occasional brawls and raids of normally peaceful "savages," through the sanguinary annals of Sumer, Babylonia and Assyria, the endless fratricide of the Greek city states, the merciful conquests of Alexander and Caesar, the brutal triumphs of Imperial Rome, the holy carnage of expanding Islam, the glorious slaughters of Genghis Khan, Tamerlane's pyramid of skulls, the destruction of Vijayanagar, the Hundred Years' War, the War of the Spanish Succession, the Seven Years' War, the English, American, French and Russian Revolutions, the Civil Wars of England and America, the Napoleonic Wars, the War of 1812, the Crimean War, the Franco-Prussian War, the Spanish-American

From *The Saturday Evening Post,* July 10, 1937. Reprinted by permission of the author.

War, the Boer War, the Russo-Japanese War, the First World War, the suicide of Spain, the Sino-Japanese War. . . . This, in our pessimistic moments, seems to be the main and bloody current of history, beside which all the achievements of civilization, all the illumination of letters and the arts, all the tenderness of women and the courtesies of men, are but graceful incidents on the bank, helpless to change the course or character of the stream.

Such a chronicle of conflict exaggerates, without doubt, the rôle of war in the records of our race. Strife is dramatic, and, to most of our historians, peaceful generations appear to have no history. So our chroniclers leap from battle to battle, and unwittingly deform the past into a shambles. In our saner moments we know that it is not so; that lucid intervals of peace far outweigh, in any nation's story, the mad seizures of war and revolution; that the history of civilization—of science and invention, law and morals, religion and philosophy, literature and art—runs like hidden gold in the river bed of time. Even war cannot quite blacken the picture of man's development.

Nevertheless, war has always been. Will it always be? What are its causes in the nature of men and in the structure of societies? What are its effects, for good or evil, upon the soul, the species, and the state? Can it be prevented, or diminished in frequency, or in any measure controlled? Let us consider these questions as objectively as may be permitted to men and women standing on the brink of what may be the most brutal war that history has ever known.

II. Causes

The causes of war are psychological, biological, economic, and political—that is, they lie in the impulses of men, the competition of groups, the material needs of societies, and fluctuations of national power.

The basic causes are in ourselves, for the state is an enlarged picture of the soul. The five major instincts of mankind—food-getting, mating, parental love, fighting, and association—are the ultimate sources of war. Our inveterate habit of eating is the oldest and deepest cause of war. For thousands, perhaps millions, of years, men were uncertain of their food supply. Not knowing yet the bounty of the soil, they trusted to the fortunes of the hunt. Having captured prey, they tore or cut it to pieces, often on the spot, and gorged themselves to their cubic capacity with the raw flesh and the hot gore; how could they tell when they might eat again? Greed is eating, or hoarding, for the future; wealth is originally a hedge against starvation; war is at first a raid for food. All vices were only virtues, indispensable in the struggle for existence; they became vices only in the degree to which social order and increasing security rendered them unnecessary for survival. Once men had to chase, to kill, to grasp, to overeat, to hoard; a hundred millenniums of insecurity bred into the race those acquisitive and possessive impulses which no laws or ideals, but only centuries of security, can mitigate or destroy.

The desire for mates and the love of children write half of the private history of mankind, but they have only rarely been the direct causes of war. The fighting instinct enters more obviously into the analysis, even if it operates most freely in persons about the military age. Nature develops it vigorously as an aid in getting or keeping food or mates; it arms every animal with organs of offense and defense, and lends to the physically weaker species the advantages of cunning and association. Since, by and large, those individuals and groups survived that excelled in food-getting, mate-getting, caring for children, and fighting, these instincts have been selected and intensified with every generation, and have budded into a hundred secondary forms of acquisition, venery, kindliness, and contention.

As the quest for food has grown into the amassing of great fortunes, so the fighting instinct has swelled into the lust for power and the waging of war. The lust for power is in most men a wholesome stimulus to ambition and creation, but in exceptional men, dressed in great and lasting authority, it becomes a dangerous disease, an elephantiasis of the soul, which goads them on to fight a thousand battles by proxy. Nietzsche, nervous and sickly and disqualified for military service, thrilled at the sight and sound of cavalry galloping along a Frankfort street, and at once composed a paean in honor of war and "the will to power." Mussolini and Hitler have read Nietzsche, and may, by replacing parliaments with supermen, and the religion of peace with the religion of war, justify the gentle maniac's prediction that the future would divide history into B. N. and A. N. —Before Nietzsche and After Nietzsche. Nothing is so improbable as the future.

The instinct of flight is hardly a source of war, though war gives it an extensive field of operations. The instinct of action enters into the picture as a love of adventure, an escape from relative and routine. A richer source is the instinct of association. Men fear solitude and naturally seek the protection of numbers. Slowly a society develops within whose guarded frontiers men are free to live peaceably, to accumulate knowledge and goods, and to worship their gods. Since our self-love overflows into love of our parents and children, our homes and possessions, our habits and institutions, our wonted environment and transmitted faith, we form in time an emotional attachment for the nation and the civilization of which these are constituent parts; and when any of them is threatened, our instinct of pugnacity is aroused to the limit determined by the natural cowardice of mankind. Such patriotism is reasonable and necessary, for without it the group could not survive, and the individual could not survive without the group. Prejudice is fatal to philosophy, but indispensable to a people.

Put all these passions together, gather into one force the acquisitiveness, pugnacity, egoism, egotism, affection, and lust for power of a hundred million souls, and you have the psychological sources of war. It may be that these sources are not completely instinctive, not inevitably rooted in the blood; contemporary psychology is chary of instincts, and suspects that many of them are but habits formed in early years through the imitation of corrupt adults. We need not spend ourselves on the dispute, for in any case the practical problem would remain—we should still have to change the parents before we could change the children.

The experience of Russia indicates that the business of pursuing food and mates, of fighting and gathering together, of loving children and money and power, is more deeply ingrained in human character than fashionable theory believes. Or was it that the lenience of the Ogpu allowed too many adults to survive? It is hard to build tomorrow's society with the day-after-tomorrow's men. *Historia non facit saltum:* History, like nature, makes no leaps.

These psychological impulses, taken in their social mass, become the biological sources of war. The group, too, as well as the individual, can be hungry or angry, ambitious or proud; the group, too, must struggle for existence and be eliminated or survive. The protective fertility of organisms soon multiplies mouths beyond the local food supply; the hunger of the parts, as in the body, becomes the hunger of the whole, and species wars against species, group against group, for lands or waters that may give more support to abounding life. Euripides, twenty-three hundred years ago, attributed the Trojan War to the rapid multiplication of the Greeks. "States that have a surplus population," said the ancient Stoic philosopher Chrysippus, "send great numbers out to colonies, and stir up wars against their neighbors." If that was the case when infanticide and Greek friendship were tolerated as means of controlling population, consider the results where statesmen encourage fertility. For then the birth rate must be raised to provide soldiers for war; war must be waged to conquer land for an expanding population; and population expands because the birth rate is so high. It is a very pinwheel of logic, bright and frail, a form of reasoning puzzlingly whimsical until we add its concealed premise—the will to power.

Group hunger begets group pugnacity, and pugnacity develops in the group, as in the individual, organs of protection and attack. In the group these are called armament; and when they are powerful, they may themselves, like the boy's biceptual consciousness, become a secondary source of war. On either scale some armament is necessary, for struggle is inevitable, and competition is the trade of life. The tragedy of our ideals is that we hitch them to the falling stars of equality and peace, while nature blithely bases her inescapable machinery of development upon difference and inequality of endowment and ability, upon competition and war; what chance have our ideals, nurtured in the mutual aid of the family, against that supremest court of all? Even mutual aid becomes an organ of struggle. We cooperate as individuals that we may the better compete as groups; morality and order have been developed because they strengthened the group in the inexorable competition of the world. Only when another star attacks us will the earth know internal peace; only a war of the planets can produce, for a moment, the brotherhood of man.

The psychological and biological forces are the ultimate origins of human conflict. From them flow the national rivalries that generate the proximate causes of war—those economic and political causes with which superficial analysis so readily contents itself.

The basic economic cause is rivalry for land: land to receive a designedly expanding population, land to provide material resources, land to open up new subjects to conscription and taxation. So the ancient Greeks fought their way through the Aegean isles to the coasts of Asia Minor and the Black Sea, and through the Mediterranean to Africa, Sicily, Italy, France, and Spain; so the English spread through the world in the last two centuries. There is, in history, a law of colonial expansion almost as explosive as any law of expansion in physics; whenever a population fails to exploit the resources of its soil, it will sooner or later be conquered by a people able to exploit those resources and to pour them into the commerce and uses of mankind.

These ancient provocations to conquest have been sharpened and magnified by the Industrial Revolution. To make war successfully a modern nation must be wealthy; to be wealthy it must develop industry; to maintain industry it must, in most cases, import food, fuel, and raw materials; to pay for these it must export manufactured goods; to sell these it must find foreign markets; to win these it must undersell its competitors or wage successful war. As likely as not, it will make war for any of the goods it must import, or for control of the routes by which it imports them.

Even in antiquity, semi-industrial Athens waged war for the control of the Aegean, the Hellespont, and the Black Sea, because it was dependent upon Russian grain; Rome had to conquer Egypt because it needed corn and Asia Minor because it needed markets for its handicrafts and fortunes for its politicians. Egyptian wheat, Near Eastern oil, and Indian cotton explain many a battle in British history; Spanish silver explains the wars of Rome with Carthage; Spanish copper, not Fascist theory, explains in our time the German help to insurgent forces in Spain. Our sinless selves had a taste for sugar in 1898.

The business cycle adds it own contributions to the causes of modern war. Since men are by nature unequal—some strong and some weak, some able and some (as they tell us) virtuous—it follows that in any society a majority of abilities will be possessed by a minority of men; from which it follows that, sooner or later, in any society, a majority of goods will be possessed by a minority of men. But this natural concentration of wealth impeded the wide spread of purchasing power among the people; production, perpetually accelerated by invention, leaps ahead of consumption; surpluses rise and generate either depression or war. For either production must stop to let consumption catch up, or foreign markets must be found to take the surplus unbought at home. Foreign markets can be secured by underselling competitors or defeating them in war. To undersell our competitors is impracticable; our standard of living is too high for that; to lower it to the level of Japan's would bring revolution; apparently the choice is between depression and war. But another major depression, possibly made worse through the increased displacement of costly labor by economical machines, might also bring revolution. What is left but war—or an unprecedented change in the behavior of men?

Add a few political causes, and our recipe for war will be complete. The first law of governments is self-preservation; their appetite grows by what they feed on, and they are seldom content. But further, the distribution of power among nations is always changing —through the discovery or development of new natural resources, through the rise or decline of population, through the weakening of religion, morals, and character, or through some other material, or biological, or psychological circumstance; and the nation that has become strong soon asserts itself over the nation that has become weak. Hence the impossibility of writing a peace pact that will perpetuate a *status quo;* hence the absurdity of Article X of the League of Nations Covenant; hence the failure of sanctions and the breakdown of the Treaty of Versailles. Excellent indeed is the peace treaty that does not generate a war.

These, then, are the causes of war. How natural it seems now, in the perspective of science and history; how ancient its sources and how inscrutable its destiny!

Is it any wonder that peace is so often but invisible war, in which the nations rest only to fight again?

III.   Effects

Consider briefly the effects of war. We think of these too often, too seldom of the causes. A reminding summary will suffice.

There are psychological effects. A certain exaltation of spirit may come to a country embarked upon what it believes to be a just war; the mind and heart of the people are unified, hyphens drop out, and the diverse elements of the population are more closely fused into a homogeneous nation. The citizens acquire habits of order and discipline, or courage and tenacity; if they are not destroyed, they are made stronger. Against these gains there is the silent gloom of parents and children bereaved, the disorders of demobilization, the demoralization of men new-trained to habits of violence, promiscuity, and deceit.

For a time there is a revulsion against war: pacifism flourishes so long as the evils of war are fresh in the memory; generous men like the Abbé of St. Pierre and Immanuel Kant and Woodrow Wilson offer plans for perpetual peace, and many humane resolutions are made. But as a fresh generation grows up, pacifism subsides; aged reminiscence idealizes the past, and the young are ready to believe that war is 99 percent glory, and only 1 percent diarrhea. War loses some of its terrors; to give one's life for one's country is again sweet and beautiful; and to die in bed becomes a shameful fate reserved for noncombatants and generals.

Biologically, war reduces the pressure of population upon the means of subsistence—which is an academic way of saying that some millions of people have been killed. Probably as a result of this, the birth rate has, before our Malthusian days, risen after war; and for some unknown reason, the ratio of male to female births has increased. Dysgenic and eugenic processes go on side by side. The strong and brave go to meet their deaths; the weak remain, and the timid return to multiply their kind. Pugnacity and brutality are diminished by the superior death rate of the pugnacious and the brutal, both in war and in peace. But usually the finer, more cultured and artistic societies are crushed out, or dominated, by the cruder, and more warlike groups; Athens by Sparta, Greece by Macedonia and Rome, T'ang China by the Tartars, Sung China by Mongols, Gupta India by the Huns, Rome by the barbarians, Renaissance Italy by France, France by Germany. History is a war between war and art, as life is a war between life and death; life and art are always defeated, and always reborn.

To most participating nations, a modern war brings complex economic results. Science and industry are occasionally advanced by researchers derived from the stimulus and energy of war. Life and property are destroyed; vast sums are consumed in armament; impossible debts accumulate. Repudiation in some form becomes inevitable; currencies are depreciated or annulled, inflation relieves debtor governments and individuals, savings and investments are wiped out, and men patiently begin to save and lend again. Overexpansion in war is followed by a major depression in peace. International trade is disrupted by intensified nationalism, exalted tariffs, and the desire to develop at home all industries requisite in war. The vanquished are enslaved—physically, as in antiquity, financially and by due process of law today. The victorious masses gain little except in self-conceit; the ruling minority among the victors may gain much in conquered lands, markets, spheres of influence, supplies, and taxable population. This is the little point that Sir Norman Angell forgot.

Politically, war may bring, to the conquered, revolution; to the victors, a strengthened government, the domination of the exchequer by returning soldiers, and the transformation of good generals into bad statesmen.

The methods and institutions that won the war tend to spread abroad and to replace the methods and institutions that lost. The pride of triumph and the appetite for spoils encourage further war, until men and materials are thrown recklessly into the lap of Mars, and the victor, like Assyria and Rome, destroys itself with its victories.

IV.   Nostrums

If the foregoing analysis is substantially correct, we shall be spared from any detailed examination of the usual plans for ending war; it is clear that most of these plans have ignored the multiple and tenacious roots of war in the nature of man.

William James, in his kindly way, hoped that the enrollment of the nation's youth, for a year or two, in a wideflung "war against Nature" would give creative expression to the impulses of action, adventure, and association, and so provide a "moral equivalent for war." It is evident that such a procedure would not offer an outlet for the other and major causes of international strife.

The League of Nations, except under Briand and Stresemann, was a conspiracy of the victors to preserve the gains they had made; it had to fail as soon as the fertility and industry of the defeated had altered the balance of national power left by the Treaty of Versailles. An organization of peace designed to perpetuate the spoils of war defeats itself by definition. The life of nations cannot be strait-jacketed into immutability.

Pacifism would be a cure for war, and doubtless for sovereignty, if it could survive the call to arms or the visible peril of attack. Pacifism in England, in our time, was strong enough to endanger the British Empire through unpreparedness and timidity; but a few Fascist twists of the Lion's tail restored the latent vigor of the beast and pacifists voted great sums for rearmament. A wise people will love peace and keep its powder dry.

Vague appeals to the conscience of mankind to put an end to war have had little effect in history, for there is no conscience of mankind. Morality is a habit of order generated by centuries of compulsion; international morality awaits international order; international order awaits international force. Conscience follows the policeman.

An effective approach to the problem of war will proceed, not by large and generous emotions but by the specific study and patient adjustment of specific causes and disputes. Peace must be planned and organized as realistically as war—with provision for every factor, and provision for every detail. This cannot be done in an occasional moment stolen by statesmen from internal affairs; it requires the full-time attention of able minds. It should be a major function of the Department of State to wage peace vigorously and continuously on every front; to isolate the germs of war at their source and to sterilize them with understanding and negotiation. It is our good fortune that our Department of State is headed by Cordell Hull, a man who has a will, rather than merely a wish, for peace.

If now we look again at the causes of war, we shall recognize at once that, even with the best will and intelligence available, these causes can be at best mitigated, but not soon removed. We may slowly lessen the greed that breeds war, by reducing the economic insecurity of individuals and states. As the food supply becomes more secure, fear and pugnacity will decrease. As painful taxes melt back into the public mint the great fortunes generated by the contact of free ability with great natural resources, the stimulus to excessive acquisition will be reduced. Perhaps in time we shall distribute among a cabinet of first-class men appointed by and responsible to Congress, many of the burdens and powers now unbearably concentrated in the presidency; then the temptations and opportunities of the will to power will be diminished, though doubtless superior ability will still polarize power to its purposes. Possibly, the Civilian Conservation Corps can be developed as a "moral equivalent" for the impulses to action, wanderlust, adventure, and association. Conceivably, religion may achieve again the international unity and influence by which it reduced, in the Middle Ages, the frequency, extent and barbarity of war. The slow internationalization of culture through greater ease of communication and travel, and the restoration of trade in ideas as well as goods, may diminish the egotism in patriotism, as happened in the Hellenistic world, and may win more adherents to the International of the Mind. How could a people trained to love art and music go to war with Italy or Germany, or a people matured to relish great literature make war upon England, Russia, or France?

Since the chief biological source of war is the pressure of population upon the means of life, the falling birth rate in the democratic countries is a subtle stimulus to peace. The rise of the birth rate in

Germany and Russia is probably temporary; even dictators are helpless before the great tides of imitation that change the mores, or
customs, of mankind. It may be possible—after the next holocaust—
to organize international agreements pledging governments to refrain from artificial provocations to fertility. Such a move, however,
would demand as a prerequisite the reduction of the economic incentives to war.

Those incentives are so numerous and powerful that each of them
should be the major concern of an international commission specifically appointed for its consideration and adjustment. There are so
many specialists, economists, and diplomats, lying about—to use
this verb in a purely geographic sense—that we might well distribute them into commissions severally assigned to examine the
economic causes of war, to hear the disputing groups patiently, to
investigate possibilities of conciliation, to do their work without the
explosive excitement of publicity, and to make specific and practicable recommendations to their governments.

One such commission would study the problem of fertility, and
seek territorial outlets for congested populations; another would
consider the access of agriculturally limited peoples to foreign food
supplies; another, the access of industrial nations to foreign or colonial raw materials and fuels; another, the breaking down of barriers
to world trade; another, the opening of opportunities to investment
and enterprise. It might be economical to offer to Germany and Italy
access to coal and iron, copper and cotton and wheat, in return for
cooperation in the reduction of armaments, imperialistic sorties,
birth bonuses, and warlike orations. If the democratic nations prefer
the arbitrament of battle to such tentatives of peace, it will be hard
to absolve them from partial responsibility for the next world war.
It is true that nations so aided would be strengthened, but they
would be less dangerous in their prosperity than in their need.

Meanwhile, it is good to organize peace throughout the Western
Hemisphere, and to give an example of pacific policy at home. It is
good to support democracy wherever we can do it without war; for
democracies are less likely to make war than nations whose powers
are concentrated in a small number of irresponsible men. It may be
that the growing weight and terror of rival armaments will generate,
before this year passes, such secret willingness to peace as may make
another world conference a practicable and hopeful thing, instead
of a windy and mischievous futility. A gathering of this kind might
seek not solutions but a year's truce in arming and talking, while

commissions examine the causes of conflict, explore avenues of adjustment, and prepare their reports for a reconvened conference. The more briefly such conferences sit, and the more continuously such commissions labor, the better it will be for the peace of mankind. Perhaps oratory should be added to the major causes of war.

Other proposals swarm into the imagination, but we may be sure that they involve more difficulties than are dreamt of by amiable philosophers. Many are tempted toward the idea of a federation of the English-speaking peoples of the world; here, perhaps, would be a force able to forge an international order, conscience, and peace. But, presumably, such a federation would evoke an equal and opposite federation; it would make government too powerful for the good of our public liberties; and, even if secure from without, it would not end strife within—war would merely become "civil." We do not want a crushing conformity of minds and wills to however admirable a Titan of American virtue and British order; variety and freedom are worth the price we pay for them, even the price of war.

In the end we must steel our hearts against utopias and be content, like Aristotle, with a slightly better state. We must not expect the world to improve much faster than ourselves. Perhaps, if we can broaden our borders with intelligent study, modest travel, and honest thought, if we can become conscious of the natural hunger and needs of other peoples, and sensitive to the varied beauties of many cultures and diverse lands, we shall not so readily plunge into competitive homicide but shall find room in our hearts for a wider understanding and an almost universal sympathy. We, above all, who enjoy beyond our merits the grace of peace and unity conferred upon us by our encompassing seas, owe it as a debt to honor to see more generously the problems of nations divided by hostile frontiers, conflicting necessities, dissimilar languages, and unfamiliar ways. We shall find in all these people qualities and accomplishments from which we may learn and refresh ourselves, and by which we may enrich our inheritance and our posterity. Some day, let us hope, it will be permitted us to love our country without betraying mankind.

QUESTIONS ON CONTENT

1. What is the purpose of the section called "Perspective"?
2. Make a collection of quotable statements from this article.
3. Explain the figure of speech at the end of the second paragraph.

State the idea in your own words; then judge the extra power of the figure.

4. At what place in the article is the structure of the article indicated? Does the author answer in order the questions he poses? Check carefully to see.

5. Comment on these statements: "Virtues . . . became vices only in the degree to which social order and increasing security rendered them unnecessary"; "Prejudice is fatal to philosophy but indispensable to a people."

6. Why does the author regard "equality and peace" as "falling stars"?

7. Although the author takes a realistic, perhaps cynical, approach to ways of preventing wars, what are his ideas for reducing the tensions which lead to fighting? List them.

8. Has the United Nations devoted time to any of the ideas suggested on pp. 297–299?

❧ *How Does It All Add Up?*

HAROLD C. UREY

During the nineteenth century the elements and techniques of mass production were developed. They have been improved and exploited for peaceful purposes during this century and especially in this country, until today nearly everything we use is produced by mass methods. Without these methods the high standard of living in the United States would be impossible, and with them a high standard of living is possible in all the countries of the world that have reasonable resources. During the present century many scientific and engineering discoveries have been made that contribute to this high standard of living.

Also, unfortunately, mass-production methods and scientific discoveries have been used for purposes of war. In order to apply these methods and discoveries to a given purpose, we must have an opportunity to practice them. The First World War gave the first opportunity for adaptation of mass production to purposes of war.

Reprinted by permission from *One World or None,* edited by Dexter Masters and Katharine Way, copyright, 1946, by the McGraw-Hill Book Company Inc., N.Y.C.

But it was only an elementary course in the art of mass destruction. The Second World War gave the opportunity for the advanced course, and by the end of it the lessons were thoroughly learned. Today we have the scientific knowledge, the engineering talent and experience, and the industrial know-how to make war on a real mass-production basis. Another war would differ from this past one in the same degree as a modern automobile differs from the Model T Ford, or perhaps a horse and wagon. Another war would be so successful from the point of view of destruction that little of the physical and human bases of our civilization would be left. For our scientific and mass techniques now include the atomic bomb and probably other weapons not yet come to the attention of the general public.

The particular weapons that concern us here include the airplane, the pilotless flying bomb (V-1), the rocket bomb (V-2), and the atomic bomb. It is possible that other methods suitable for delivering the atomic bomb may be partially developed and as yet unknown to the public. Still other methods may be developed in the future. Only the B-29 bomber was used in this war for the delivery of the atomic bomb, but the combination of these two weapons made conditions intolerable to Japan. In the future these weapons, produced on a mass-production basis, will make war intolerable to all peoples of the world. This does not mean that war will not come. It does mean that the war will probably not be of long duration because of the vast destruction that will be quickly and decisively accomplished.

Let us review the facts in regard to the atomic bomb as we see them today and as the preceding chapters of this book have laid them before us.

The atomic bomb, because of its overwhelming increase in effectiveness, which makes all defenses known or foreseeable nearly useless and completely ineffective, is not best regarded as just another weapon. In the past many new weapons have been invented, and in many cases they have added greatly to the effectiveness of the attack as compared to the defense. But our present defenses against atomic bombs are about as effective as a Roman army armed with spears, javelins, and shields would be against a modern army equipped with machine guns. Within a few years the atomic bomb carried by a few airplanes has increased the advantage of attack by about as much as was accomplished in a thousand years in the past. These weapons can destroy all defenses that we can devise at the present time. . . .

Still, many people believe that there will always be a defense for every weapon. There will always be an exception to such glib rules. But is the statement true in any sense that is of interest to us? Is there a defense against bullets? Perhaps, but they killed many men in the past war. Is there a defense against submarines? Yes, definitely. But they destroyed a large fraction of the world's shipping during the past war. Is there a defense against airplanes? Certainly defenses are known, but only the United States among the major combatants of the Second World War escaped serious damage or nearly complete destruction of its cities. Similar answers to similar questions could be made with respect to tanks, naval vessels, and other weapons great and small.

Weapons disappear from war if they are superseded by more effective weapons, but so long as they are used in war they produce actual damage in spite of defenses and in a rather definite proportion to their ability to inflict damage. When more destructive weapons than atomic bombs are developed, atomic bombs will not be used; but so long as they are used, they will continue to destroy many square miles of cities for each bomb exploded. Perhaps a question points the argument. Can any of us imagine a defense so effective that, sometime in the future, a country such as the United States would decide not to manufacture atomic bombs because defenses again them made their manufacture inadvisable for purely military reasons? I think not. If atomic bombs are not made in the future, it will be for other reasons than the effectiveness of defense. No military defense exists, and none can be devised. Atomic bombs are able to destroy the cities of the world and they will do so, if used in another war.

This thesis assumes that atomic bombs can be made in sufficient numbers and at costs sufficiently low to be used effectively in another war. Unfortunately both assumptions are correct. Our mass-production methods, which give us our high standard of living, our automobiles, power plants, chemical products, electrical devices, etc., make possible the production of atomic bombs in large numbers and at low cost. In fact, war will be cheaper in the future so far as the production and use of weapons are concerned and far more expensive from the point of view of destruction accomplished. Even small countries can make these bombs in numbers if they are such utter fools as to engage in the lethal business. They will not, because they know that they would be completely destroyed if bombs were used. It is only powerful industrialized countries that may not realize that before this weapon all countries are small and weak.

Before the past war small countries realized that they must get along with their neighbors. The cheapness of the atomic weapon relative to its destructive power makes it necessary that *all* countries get along with each other.

The question is asked: Can other countries besides England and the United States produce these bombs? And the answer is: Of course they can. What weapon ever devised by man remained the sole possession of the country of origin? The production of atomic bombs was a tricky, intricate business, but so is the production of tanks, airplanes, and other major weapons of war. The United States is the greatest industrial power at the present time and could and did make these weapons faster than any other country. But it is nonsense for us to assume that other countries cannot learn all the details of their production and, in fact, improve on the methods. If the people of the United States or England believe otherwise, they engage in the most dangerous of delusions.

How long will it take other countries to devise these weapons? Estimates vary. Most scientific and technical men who helped to produce the bombs guess between five and ten years; a few think less and some think more. Drs. Seitz and Bethe give convincing reasons for their estimate of six years or less in Chapter 9. It is to be hoped that the time will be large rather than small, since that would give more time for a solution of the whole problem.

Some have suggested that the United States would be safe if it were to keep ahead of other countries in the development and production of atomic weapons. It is not certain that this country could succeed in this attempt over any great length of time and certainly not for all time, for others will surely come abreast of us— and perhaps in less time than we think. But let us look more closely at the suggestion. Supposing that the United States remains ahead of other countries in number or effectiveness of bombs, what good does it do us? Do we plan to attack other countries at a favorable moment? Following such an attack, it would be necessary to occupy the countries with our armies in order to prevent the manufacture of bombs in the future. Some 7 per cent of the world's population would have to keep its feet on the necks of the rest of the world's peoples. It does not seem likely that we would choose this role voluntarily, with a full understanding of its responsibility and hardships let alone other considerations.

Later, when other countries secure enough atomic bombs to destroy the cities and other appropriate targets of this country, we would be in a position to destroy their cities, and it would do us no good whatever to have bombs enough to destroy those targets more than once. Extra bombs would be useless once sufficient numbers were available to destroy all large military targets of any possible enemy. If our hypothetical enemy had sufficient bombs to destroy our military targets, in what way could we keep ahead of this enemy? Atomic bombs are different. Enough can be made to destroy completely all possible targets and kill the inhabitants of all major cities of any country. It is then impossible to destroy them twice or to kill people twice. Eventually, therefore, we cannot hope to keep ahead of other countries in an atomic war.

We turn to defensive measures again and specifically to the dispersal of cities and going underground. This appears to be the only effective defense that anyone has proposed as yet, and it is only a palliative, only a way of moderating the effects of the attack. The cost of such dispersal would be high, on the order of the cost of the Second World War to us, for the actual translocation of dwellings, industries, and transportation facilities. Dispersal would also impair the efficiency of our industrial system, since industries are usually placed where they are because of economic advantages, such as natural transportation facilities and availability of power or raw materials. In many manufacturing processes concentration is often of great advantage; for many industries it is necessary.

The psychological problems associated with the dispersal of cities would be great. Many of us, and perhaps most of us, for one reason or another like the places and conditions under which we live, though you and I may not understand why others do so. Dispersal would affect each of us in a very direct manner. Agreement to carry through such a program would never be unanimous, and possibly the decision in regard to it would rest on a mere majority, with a determined minority vigorously opposed to it. Proposals have been made that dispersal could and should be achieved in fifteen years; this seems too short a time, though in the face of the threat under which we all may live, we may decide to carry it through. It would probably require a dictatorship for its execution. And in the end it would not be a definite and decisive defense, for if somewhat larger bombs were secured a determined enemy could destroy our economy and our people just the same. The atomic bomb is a very effective and inexpensive weapon and will probably become more effective and less expensive with time.

Perhaps critical plants could be placed underground, but to what purpose? This would not prevent the destruction of the people above ground, and if military plants and installations cannot protect the citizens of a country, what are they for and why prevent *their* destruction? If the Navy, Army, Air Forces, and atomic bombs cannot protect the citizens of a country and their property, who cares whether or not the military forces can protect themselves?

This book is concerned primarily with the military threat of atomic energy rather than with its peacetime uses, but such possible uses have a bearing on the military applications. Radioactive materials for medical uses can be secured without large plants containing large amounts of fissionable materials, for example, U-235 or plutonium. However, atomic power plants must necessarily contain sufficient of these materials to make bombs. Undetected diversion of these materials for use in bombs might be comparatively easy, since all chemical plants lose some material and losses vary from plant to plant. Records could be falsified comparatively easily, if those operating the plants were determined on such falsification. A much more extensive inspection system would be needed to prevent diversion of material in operating plants than would be necessary to prevent the construction of these plants. The possibility of diversion would not be conducive to confidence on the part of the peoples of the world. And since confidence in the operation of world control of atomic bombs is so vitally important, everything should be done to promote it first. If proper controls could be secured and confidence established, the operation of power plants could *then* be considered.

Let us consider briefly what would be lost if no large-scale power plants were operated in any country until world control had been established on such a basis that reasonable confidence could be assured. Chapter IV reviews this situation in detail, and from that discussion we cannot truthfully contend that the immediate use of atomic power is of very great economic importance. In any case, atomic power would first and most logically be used in locations where there are no other sources of energy—for example, in northern Canada, the Amazon River Basin, and other such places where oil and coal are not found. Ships might use atomic power to avoid refueling and the storage of fuel, but this will probably not be economical for some time.

Naval vessels might be more likely consumers of atomic energy than other ships, since the economic factor is not important. However, if we plan to build and operate such naval vessels, we are deciding to prepare for further wars. To be logical we should then decide to make bigger and better atomic bombs, for others will use these bombs if we threaten to use naval vessels or other implements of war against them. If atomic power is developed for naval vessels, the world will inevitably slip back into the atomic-bomb armament race and the whole problem moves back to the use of, and defense against, these bombs. Control of atomic bombs must inevitably lead to the control of all weapons of war. It is foolish to think of controlling only atomic-bomb manufacture and then to let wars start and continue with other weapons until atomic-bomb plants can be put into operation in order to finish the wars. Nothing less than the total abolition of war will prevent their use. In particular the use of atomic power for naval vessels would complicate the control of the military use of atomic energy and, it is hardly necessary to add, almost certainly prevent that degree of confidence so necessary for control.

The postponement of the use of atomic energy for large power plants would make for easier control of the atomic bomb. It is a small price to pay for the accomplishment of this most desirable end. It would not be necessary to postpone the use of radioactive materials at the same time.

Freedom versus an Atomic Armament Race.

The citizens of the United States are justly proud of the personal freedom they enjoy. It has been celebrated in song and speech from the beginning of the republic. It is referred to in the first sentence of our Declaration of Independence. It has been continuously lauded in public addresses throughout the land on all public occasions. It has always been imperfect, with violations of its principles at some time in the lives of most individuals and, in some sections of the population, throughout their lives. But our personal freedom, considering the number of people in the country and the length of time over which it has existed, represents a very large fraction of all such freedom that has existed in the whole history of mankind.

There are many circumstances that have led to this condition. The traditions of the early pioneers who settled the country should be remembered. Politically freedom began with the English Magna Charta. But in this country people have attained freedom mostly sooner and to a greater extent than have their blood brothers of Europe. In very large degree this has been due to safety from external aggression provided by the broad expanse of the Atlantic Ocean, behind which we have been able to solve our internal problems without being crushed by a foreign power even during a long and disabling Civil War.

With improvements in transportation and particularly with the discovery and development of air transportation, isolation due to our water defense has disappeared. Today it no longer exists. Twice in this century this country has believed that it was forced to defend itself and its vital interests by sending its sons to fight in Europe and, in this past war, in Asia as well. The same has been true of other similarly situated countries, such as Canada, Australia, and New Zealand.

With the advent of modern airplanes, and now atomic bombs, all natural defenses of all countries of the world have disappeared. Rivers, mountains, and oceans are of no value as defenses now and never will be again. With the obliteration of these defenses, the freedom of this country will be seriously threatened, and, in fact, the threat has already begun. From our beginnings we have known the extent of our armed forces. Today we and our elected representatives do not know the extent of these forces. Atomic bombs are being manufactured in an amount unknown to us, and these bombs represent an armament equivalent to a Navy, a large Army, or a large Air Force. Even Congress does not know the extent of this power, which represents a threat to other countries and has an important effect on the relation of this country to other countries.

If an atomic armament race continues—it is already going on—the citizens of the country will know less and less in regard to vital questions of this kind and finally must accept decisions in regard to public affairs blindly and from a few men in power. Not knowing the size of its armament, the people of the country must trust men in Washington with important decisions previously made through their elected representatives. Men on horseback will rapidly appear on the public scene. Note the attempt to secure the passage of the May-Johnson Bill without proper hearings in Congress. Here was a bill originating in the War Department, which proposed to transfer all control over atomic energy to a few men who would be safeguarded in their acts from all scrutiny by the public through security provisions backed by the most drastic penalties. If that bill or any similar bill passes Congress and is signed by the President, the first abdication of the sovereign rights of the people of the United States will have occurred. The May-Johnson Bill was actually similar in intent and effect to the transfer of power from the German Reichstag to Hitler, though, of course, it would not have so completely destroyed representative government in one act. Many people did not realize the broad and tragic meaning of this bill. It was a definite beginning of the end of our representative government and of the Bill of Rights of our Constitution.

Why have these things occurred? The answer is fear. The atomic bomb is such a grave threat to all men in all countries that frantic and desperate means of handling the problem have been proposed. If the armament race continues, more and more such things will occur. We become afraid, and we destroy the freedom of science. We fear other countries and conceal the number of our atomic bombs. We fear that bombs will be smuggled into our cities and that we will have to introduce secret police to detect such bombs. We fear attacks on our cities and may disperse them regardless of the desires of the people of those cities and of the people of the countryside to which they are moved. We fear sudden attack from without and will transfer the right to declare war from Congress to a single man, and that man, whoever he may be, will be affected by that power. He will become a dictator. Absolute power corrupts absolutely.

The same trend will occur in all countries of the world, and the end will be deadly fear everywhere. But of all the countries of the world, the most industrialized countries will be the most vulnerable and the most likely to be attacked by atomic bombs. These weapons stopped the Second World War, and at the same time they ended the defenses of the United States. They also threaten our liberties.

But why shudder before these fears? Should we not vigorously grasp the situation and take the offensive? The United States might ally with itself as many countries of the world as possible and lead them to conquest of the remainder. In such an undertaking this country would have to supply most of the men and materials. It is a very great effort that would be required, with much sacrifice. Assuming the will to do it, and ultimate success, this nation would become the most hated country on earth, and the hatred would last for a century and perhaps more. Throughout all that time constant vigilance would be required to prevent rebellion in conquered lands. Our people would become brutalized, as the conquering always have. It is not a pleasant solution, and, our traditions being what they are, it would be impossible to secure the will and determination required of our people to carry the program through to the end. Though all proposals for the solution of the atomic bomb are difficult, I believe that this is the most impossible of all.

The advent of the atomic bomb has caused endless confusion in the thinking of men, and the confusion spreads to more people as they come to realize all the implications of this weapon. What do the facts add up to?

The people of the world have in their hands a weapon of transcending size and destructiveness. The knowledge of the existence of this weapon and the methods of its production can never be lost. It can never again be returned to the realm of the unknown. Bombs can be made in large numbers—and cheaply. There is no defense against them. They can destroy physically beyond our ability to comprehend. Fear of them will destroy our liberties. To take the offensive and attempt to dominate the world would wreck our whole lives and those of generations to come.

Civilizations have risen and fallen repeatedly in the history of the world. We all recall such examples as the Babylonia Empire, the ancient Egyptian civilization, the Roman Empire; and, on this hemisphere, the empires of the Incas and the Mayans. It is to be expected that the future will see rises and falls, too. Modern technological war as developed by the European civilization of which we are a part may cause its complete disintegration. A world war in which atomic weapons are used might very well weaken all of our countries and peoples to such an extent that they would not be able to survive in the future. And not only may our own culture be destroyed by these weapons of mass destruction, but all civilizations as they exist in the world may be retarded and weakened for centuries to come.

It all adds up to the most dangerous situation that humanity has ever faced in all history.

QUESTIONS ON CONTENT

1. What is the relation of mass production to war?
2. How does the author dispose of the notion that "there will always be a defense for every weapon"? Do you agree with this reasoning?
3. What is said of the expense of producing atomic weapons as compared with conventional weapons? Will it cost less to kill men in the future than it did in the past?
4. How does the author view the possibility of the United States using the atomic bomb to subdue the world? How do you view such a possibility?
5. How is our freedom related to security measures which surround

atomic fission? Comment on the quotation: "Absolute power corrupts absolutely."

6. Does the author propose a solution? What, then, *does* "it all add up to"?

7. Why is there no discussion here of the causes of war? Does the author assume that such causes as those cited by William James ("The Moral Equivalent of War") and by Will Durant ("Why Men Fight") are no longer applicable? Discuss.

8. Have there been any notable recent advances towards (a) controlling atomic weapons, or (b) preventing war?

SUGGESTIONS FOR PAPERS

There are two extreme attitudes toward war: that of the militarist and that of the pacifist. The absolute militarist and the absolute pacifist are comparatively rare, for most persons take a stand somewhere between these extremes. Every human being, and particularly the educated person, is duty bound to examine the question of war and to declare himself on the subject.

1. Define absolute pacifism. What is it? You may include what it is not—that is, it is not capable of compromise. Then, you should list, with brief discussion, the immediate and the long-run advantages and disadvantages of the pacifist idea. How far could you go in accepting this idea for yourself?

2. Define absolute militarism. This is not a definition of war. It is a definition of an attitude. William James's "Moral Equivalent of War" summarizes some basic thinking of the militarist. Examine this mode of thinking. How far do you go in accepting this thinking?

3. Is it possible strictly to distinguish a combatant from a noncombatant in modern warfare? Men and women in uniforms are combatants. Are the persons who supply the armed forces combatants? And what of the persons who supply the persons who supply the armed forces? What of women and children? Is it logic or sentiment which traditionally lists women and children as noncombatants? (Possible organization, by paragraphs, of this paper: I the problem; II obvious combatants; III questionable combatants; IV obvious noncombatants, if any.)

4. Some historians believe that leaders lead their people into war. Others (see William James) believe the people force their leaders

to lead them into war. Is there some truth in both points of view? State the two positions; then try to decide what the reciprocal action is which does produce war.

5. William James thinks that "war against Nature" would provide a "moral equivalent" for war in the traditional sense. Reread the closing paragraphs of James's essay, paraphrase his theory, then examine the logic of the idea. (James himself says that the horror of war is one of its fascinations; how would his "moral equivalent" satisfy man's craving for horror—if, indeed, he has such a craving?)

6. Will Durant names four reasons for war: psychological, biological, economic, and political. The psychological involves essentially man's pugnacity; the biological, his group's pugnacity; the economic, his group's acquisitiveness; the political, his group's statesmanship (making his state dominant). Which is the most important of these reasons? Without which of these causes would the remaining causes become inoperative?

7. Some writers list "the material needs of societies" as one of the causes of war. Can you reduce this "cause" to an absurdity?

8. William James speaks of the incredible cruelties of ancient wars. Is there any reason to believe that cruelty either in quality or quantity has been reduced in modern times? Is any discernible progress to be found in fact or in attitude?

9. How has the United Nations simplified on the one hand and complicated on the other hand the problem of war? State the theory, which is simple, of the U.N.'s way to control warfare. What are some of the factors which complicate the working of this theory?

10. Will Durant in "Why Men Fight" shows little faith that war will ever be outlawed. State the basic reasoning behind this view. Next, examine Urey's warnings ("How Does It All Add Up?") about an atomic war. Finally, decide whether or not you think the threat of destruction from atomic weapons will cancel out all the ancient and modern reasons for fighting.

11. Explain three striking statements in "Why Men Fight," such as: "All vices were only virtues, indispensable in the struggle for existence"; Prejudice is fatal to philosophy, but indispensable to a people"; "History, like nature, makes no leaps." Link these three quotations, or three others, to the question of war.

SOME TITLES FOR PAPERS

1. The Ideal Pacifist
2. The Ideal Militarist
3. War is Immoral: How Can There Be a Moral Equivalent?
4. No Noncombatants
5. The Philosophy of Passive Resistance
6. Force Is Force and Cannot Be Modified
7. War Is God's Test of Man
8. The Cost of Peace versus The Cost of War
9. Who Would Fight for More Land?
10. Cruelty, Then and Now
11. Wars to Prevent Wars
12. Our Economic Excuses for War
13. The Limits of Patriotism
14. Pulling the Eyeteeth of National Sovereignty
15. People Always (Sometimes, Never) Want War
16. The United Nations Are Disunited

❧ *SEGREGATION AND DE-SEGREGATION*

MUCH HAS BEEN DONE RECENTLY to advance the cause of racial tolerance and by that very advance to arouse regional tensions. That the problem of prejudice, whether regional, national, or international, has not yet been solved is made clear by the selections in this chapter.

"Segregation and the Church," by Aubrey Burns, is an honest, straightforward indictment of the churches, Northern as well as Southern, which profess to believe in the equal value of human souls, yet directly or indirectly enforce segregation of the races. The ballad, "The Touchin' Case of Mr. and Mrs. Massa," deftly punctures the myth that Southerners are peculiarly intuitive in their understanding of the Negro.

Roi Ottley, a Negro journalist, reports in "Top Hats and Tom-toms" his first elation at being treated as an equal by Europeans and his later disillusionment. He concludes that "history offers no parallel to the dramatic ascent of Negroes in the U.S.—slaves a mere eighty years ago."

Although the problem of prejudice is not confined to a region, the problem of segregation in America is fairly well restricted to the South. The unanimous decision of the Supreme Court outlawing segregation in the public schools is having its greatest effect in the states which at one time formed the Confederacy. The final two articles ("A Southerner Looks at the Supreme Court" and "School Kids Are Color Blind") debate the meaning of the Court's order against segregation.

❧ *Segregation and the Church*

Aubrey Burns

In a world which, like a hornet's nest, is eternally swarming with problems, we do not choose which problems we will face and deal with. Willy-nilly our attention centers upon the problem with the deepest, most immediate, and most persistent sting.

Domestically, the critical Gordian knot of our generation is the relationship between our Caucasian majority and our Negro minority. We hardly need sociologists, historians, statesmen, and prophets to tell us this obvious truth.

Some Americans are trying desperately to pull the knot safely tight again; some are struggling to loosen it; while others cry for the stroke of an Alexander's sword. But whatever the solution, this is one problem American can no longer ignore.

It is a strange sort of problem, in that the solution is apparent and simple. What makes it a problem at all is Caucasian unwillingness to accept that solution—our emotional fear that the cure will prove worse than the disease.

So, like items and subtotals falsified to support the falsified balance of an embezzler, the items of race discrimination are "justified" in a futile effort to shore up the central Master Race myth. For without discrimination in the areas of religion, education, economics, and politics, how could the sensitive crux of the whole matter—social segregation—be maintained? Therefore, even though it be at the price of hypocrisy, loss of self-respect, and humiliation before the world, Caucasian America cannot "turn loose of this wildcat" for fear of fear.

It is news to very few that these patterns are nationwide, and in no wise peculiar to the South. The Federal government itself main-

From *Southwest Review,* Vol. XXXIV, No. 2 (Spring 1949). Published by permission of the author and the *Southwest Review.*

tains and perpetuates them. If any doubt of this fact existed, it was dispelled completely by the Report of the President's Committee on Civil Rights. Every American who cares for our country's honor and destiny should own and study this report, *To Secure These Rights,* which costs only one dollar. Southerners as well as Northerners will find evidence here that it is not simply the ex-Confederate ships of an otherwise seaworthy American fleet which are leaking and water-logged, but that we are all in the same boat, even though we are not all on the same deck.

Quite aside from the tensions which our Master Race theory creates between the Caucasian and Negro segments of our population—and these are by no means negligible—a whole series of tensions is created *within* the Caucasian majority group by the contradiction between principle and practice, between law and fact.

Gunnar Myrdal has called this contradiction "An American Dilemma." The President's Committee on Civil Rights says: "The pervasive gap between our aims and what we actually do is creating a kind of moral dry rot which eats away at the emotional and rational bases of democratic beliefs."

In recent years, despite our prejudices and our fears, we have been becoming aware with increasing swiftness that this disease is intolerable, and that it threatens to destroy the very roots of our national integrity. There is the sound of a going in the tops of the mulberry trees, and even the great branches are shaken.

Lynching has declined. Poll tax laws have been repealed. Negro suffrage is rapidly becoming a reality in many southern states. Justice is less often perverted. Negroes are serving in Congress and in state legislatures. Negro policemen are no longer rare. Court decisions are rejecting discriminatory legislation and interpretations.

The C.I.O. repudiates all racial discrimination in union membership, and A.F. of L. unions are accepting increasing numbers of Negro members. Employers are opening to Negroes occupations formerly reserved for Caucasians. Negro motormen and conductors on San Francisco trolleys, and Negro bus operators, are accepted equally with Caucasian platform men. New York state has administered its recent civil rights statutes with excellent effect. Other states and cities have instituted fair employment practice laws. Negro baseball players have been introduced into both major leagues.

Oklahoma, Texas, and Arkansas are struggling to break the bonds of educational segregation. Intercultural education projects growing out of the Springfield Plan have multiplied throughout the country. Segregation has been abolished in the school systems of Gary and Trenton. More than sixty Negro teachers are faculty members in twenty-five non-Negro colleges. The very concept of "separate but equal" education is under heavy fire as a self-contradiction.

Nonsegregated residence is increasing as restrictive covenants fail. Marin City, across the Golden Gate Bridge from San Francisco, is but one of a number of nonsegregated housing developments which have proved over a period of several years that Negroes and Caucasians can live side by side harmoniously with mutual respect, and can become friends and neighbors in a perfectly normal way.

Segregation and discrimination in military service are beginning to break down. Several experiments during the last war proved that men can fight and die together as equals without impairing military efficiency. New Jersey recently made the Department of Defense accept its reformed National Guard, nonsegregation and all.

President Truman was elected last November, perhaps in spite of, but perhaps because of, his willingness to stake his political future on the program recommended by his Committee on Civil Rights. Should the Committee's report be translated fully into national policy and legislation, the pattern of Caucasian-Negro relationships in this country would be revolutionized. For this would amount to our taking "the American dilemma" firmly by the horns.

Today, then, we can look, not with complacency but with hope, upon evidences of race-relations progress in political, economic, educational, and social directions.

But what about religion? Is the Church true to her genius and dedication, marching ahead of all the other institutions of our society? Is religion blazing the trail for government, for business and industry, for education, and for personal and group social relationships?

In doctrine, in principle, in precept, the answer is Yes. Today the Church is unceasingly pointing out to the State, to business, to the schools, and to individuals the truth that God is our father and that all men are brothers. The combined weight of the Law, the Prophets, the Gospel, and the doctrines of the Church is being used to establish society's obligation to give all men equal justice, equal freedom, and equal opportunity. Official pronouncements more and more explicit have been issued more and more frequently by more and more denominations and ecclesiastical councils.

But in all this there is the suggestion of "Don't do as I do—do as I say do." In point of actual internal practice, we who love the Church cannot be proud when we look at the growing trend away from the prevailing patterns of discrimination. Scores of nationwide and local secular organizations and agencies are working earnestly for better race relations, and are joining Caucasian and Negro in common action toward socially constructive ends. But last in the procession, behold the Church, the spotless Bride of Christ, reluctantly dragging her heels.

The Church is White. The Church is Caucasian. The Church is Segregated. The Church, I am afraid we must admit, is of all our institutions the most race-conscious. And it is in the Protestant churches of America that the Master Race pattern prevails most inexorably. Here is the stronghold, the bastion, the sanction of the whole sordid business. Here the weight of Christ and the Cross, the authority and blessing of God, are placed, *not in principle* but *de facto,* upon the American pattern of discrimination, of segregation and prejudice.

The case is clearly stated by Dr. Howard Thurman in a recent lecture:

> It is in this connection that American Christianity has betrayed the religion of Jesus almost beyond redemption. . . . The result is that in the one place in which normal free contacts might be most naturally established and in which the relations of the individual to his God should take priority over conditions of class, race, power, status, wealth or the like,—this place is one of the chief instruments for guaranteeing barriers. . . . The situation is so tragic that men of good will in all the specious classifications within our society find more cause for hope in the secular relations of life than in those of religion.

Support for Dr. Thurman's position is found in the report of the World Council of Churches, which adjourned last September in Amsterdam. Section I of the report includes this sentence: "Even where there are no differences of theology, language, or liturgy, there exist churches segregated by race and color, a scandal within the Body of Christ."

And Section III proves that the Church is, for all its shortcomings, capable of the severest kind of self-criticism:

> If the Church can overcome the national and social barriers which now divide it, it can help society to overcome those barriers. This is especially clear in the case of racial distinction. It is here that

the Church has failed most lamentably, where it has reflected and then by its example sanctified the racial prejudice that is rampant in the world. . . . It knows that it must call society away from prejudice based on race or color, and from the practices of discrimination and segregation, as denials of justice and human dignity; but it cannot say a convincing word to society until it takes steps to eliminate these from the Christian community, because they contradict all that it believes about God's love for all his children.

Frank Loescher's recently published study, *The Protestant Church and the Negro,* spells out this indictment with documentation and statistics. Here are some of his findings:

There are approximately 8,000,000 Protestant Negroes. About 7,-500,000 are in separate Negro denominations. . . . The remaining 500,000 Negro Protestants—about 6 per cent—are in predominantly white denominations, and of these . . . at least 99 per cent . . . are in segregated congregations. . . . The number of white and Negro persons who ever gather together for worship under the auspices of Protestant Christianity is almost microscopic.

Nonsegregated worship, then, exists for one per cent of six per cent—or six one-hundredths of one per cent—of American Negro Protestants. *Just how microscopic can Christian fellowship get?*

As a Methodist, I am embarrassed by the Central Jurisdiction. The reunited Methodist Church is divided for administrative purposes into six Jurisdictions. Five of these are geographic, and the sixth—the Central Jurisdiction—has a deceivingly geographic name. But it is not geographic. It is an overlapping Jurisdiction, in a different dimension—the racial dimension. *It is the Jim Crow car of the Methodist train.* It was set up ostensibly as a sop to the M.E. Church, South, when race and segregation threatened to stand as barriers to the plan of union. But it is significant that all American Methodism, except in New England and the far western states, has taken advantage of its segregation function. It is symbolic that on the jurisdictional boundary map of the United States in *The Methodist Discipline,* the dark shading of the Central Jurisdiction lies over the white Jurisdictions like a great blot.

Methodism is not unconscious of this stain. There is strong agitation to abolish the Central Jurisdiction entirely and absorb its constituent Negro Conferences into five geographic Jurisdictions. Even now plans for this step are being drawn up.

But this will not change the basic pattern of segregation. Probably it will mean only that besides meeting with the Caucasian brethren once in four years at the General Conference session, Negro Methodist leaders will also meet with the Caucasian brethren once in four years at the Jurisdictional Conferences. The Caucasian Annual Conferences still will have to be integrated with the Negro Annual Conferences. And even after that, integration will have to be achieved at the local church level. Cut off thus by inches, as it will be if it is ever cut off at all, Methodist segregation is a tail that seems destined to wag the dog in the matter of race fellowship for a long time to come.

Even while Methodism *talks* sackcloth and ashes over this Central Jurisdiction blot, and *studies* plans for its eventual eradication, the blot is actually spreading, rather than shrinking. Between 1944 and 1948 the area of its domain has been extended by four states. This brings the total of states affected up to thirty-four. Of these, twenty-one are "Yankee" states. Only thirteen are "Dixie" states.

There are 8,500,000 members of the Methodist Church, of whom only about 400 are Negroes worshiping in unsegregated congregations. But more than 330,000 of them are Negroes worshiping in segregated Negro congregations. More than a million and a half Negroes are members of separate Negro Methodist denominations.

As a Methodist, I have no wish to make my own church out to be an only or even a chief offender. But the Methodist Church is the largest American Protestant denomination and this makes it a valid example. Further, in the confessional it is more seemly to particularize one's own sins than those of one's neighbor.

Will W. Alexander explains the better record of the Roman Catholic Church in America by pointing out that for Catholics the church fulfils an almost exclusively *worship* function. Protestants, on the other hand, give great importance to the *social* function of their churches. It is not because of *religious* discrimination, we infer, that Protestant segregation of Negroes prevails, but because of *social* discrimination. Catholic churches can be inclusive in their worship without the danger of being confronted by inter-racial social fellowship. But this danger would become a reality to Protestant churches the moment they abandoned segregation in worship.

Nevertheless the Catholics do not stand as a shining example for Protestants. Gunnar Myrdal says that in general the Roman Catholic Church encourages Negroes to attend all-Negro churches, and discourages them from attending white churches. And statistics from several sources indicate that there are only about 300,000 Negro

Catholics in the United States, of whom almost two-thirds are in separate Negro churches.

It is not only in church organization and worship that Protestantism discriminates against the Negro. Restrictive covenants are the chief means, outside the South, for the enforcement and perpetuation of residential segregation, which automatically acts to keep Caucasians in "white" churches and Negroes in Negro churches. Until very recently all Protestant denominations had been silent on this subject. One reason is the fact that some of them own property bound by such covenants.

In urban transition areas, where Negroes are moving into the territory served by a "white" church, Dr. Loescher's observation is that "the customary pattern in Protestantism is to resist the Negro invasion and then, when transition has occurred, to sell the property to a Negro group. . . . This survey . . . has failed to discover a single 'white' church with an 'open' or mixed membership *in an area undergoing transition.*"

Denominations employ large numbers of persons. But there is no evidence that in their role as employers they have taken occasion to provide an example to commercial employers by eliminating race as a factor in choosing their own employees.

Protestant denominations control a large segment of America's facilities for higher education. Here the record is no better. Leaving out of account the southern states where educational segregation is required by law, Loescher's researchers showed that nearly all northern Negroes who attend college enroll in either southern Negro colleges, northern state universities, or northern private universities, while only "an insignificant number" attend church-controlled colleges. And a majority of such colleges are without any Negro students whatever. Church-controlled colleges, universities, secondary schools, and theological seminaries, almost without exception, have no Negroes on either their faculties or their boards of trustees.

Many Protestant leaders who recognize the shameful irony of current ecclesiastical practice rationalize the sense of guilt thus: "We're coming along as fast as we can, but you can't move great masses of average people too rapidly. You can't get too far ahead of the membership or you will lose contact."

It is true that many top-level Protestants have aching consciences on this subject, and that encouragingly large numbers of them are saying and doing everything possible to correct the inconsistency. But these are chiefly among the clergy and the youth, the social service commissions, the missionary and religious education boards and staffs, some of the editors of religious publications, and inter-denominational agencies.

Three years ago the Federal Council of Churches of Christ in America officially renounced the pattern of segregation in race relations as "unnecessary and undesirable and a violation of the Gospel of love and human brotherhood," and *requested* its constituent denominations to do likewise. The resolution concluded: "As proof of their sincerity in this renunciation they will work for a non-segregated Church and a non-segregated society."

At least four denominations have adopted the statement as their own, three others have recommended that their churches welcome Negroes, and a few others have made kindred pronouncements.

Late in 1948 the Federal Council reaffirmed this position. But the communions participating in the Federal Council are entirely sovereign and autonomous, and are not subject to the authority of the Council. It must be borne in mind that it is the more enlightened and liberal leaders who usually represent their denominations in the Council. And even when a denomination has adopted a forthright statement, the pronouncement may be no nearer to realization in practice than some of the pronouncements of the Declaration of Independence and of our national Constitution. Or than some of the courageous stands in many a forgotten party platform.

It would be unfair not to give full credit to the leavening elements that do exist. But they are still merely voices crying in the wilderness, with few disciples. It is at the local church level that segregation touches the individual Negro worshiper, and only when non-segregation has reached the local church level *in practice* will it ever have any real meaning for the membership in general.

Unfortunately only a small minority of the pastors in the field are sensitive to the problem. And in most of the denominations their power to speak or act in this area is limited by "the realities of the situation."

In the congregationally governed denominations, and indirectly in the others as well, it is not good for a minister's tenure in his present pastorate, or for his advancement in his career, if he is too outspoken or too active in directions which arouse the disapproval of the majority of his lay membership, or even of a key handful possessed of money and influence. In recent years ministers have recognized that to be under suspicion of interracial leanings is to be on dangerous ground. It is more dangerous in some denominations than in others, and safer in some localities than in others. But the danger is there, and the pastors know it. Few pastors are eager to martyr themselves.

Catholic hierarchical authoritarianism creates grave difficulties for the freedom of individual thought, but let us admit that Protestant democracy creates a majority-rule authoritarianism which holds a long whip over individual conviction, especially in the ministry, and makes stability of principle difficult.

We Protestants believe that the Church belongs to the communicants, just as we believe that the State belongs to its citizens. But one unavoidable result is that ministers, like politicians, are pressed sorely to become weathervanes rather than compasses. For their courage Bishop William Scarlett of the Protestant Episcopal Church has these words: "There is . . . a tendency to overestimate the repercussions which will follow decisive Christian action. Repercussions there will be. The important thing, however, is not whether our churches are larger or smaller. The essential point is that those within that Church be committed to the Christian Cause."

But there are many who do not swing with the wind, and I have no doubt that there are hundreds of ministers who would answer Yes! to the following questions:

Would not the power of integrity prove more effective than the influence of size and prosperity?

If having a social function prevents Protestant churches from fulfilling their more important moral and religious function, then would it not be better for them to sacrifice the former in order to fulfil the latter?

Is it not probable that by fulfilling their moral and religious function, Protestant churches might soon find themselves able to resume their social function without excluding "God's stepchildren" from that fellowship?

Let the Protestant churches of America take to heart and ponder solemnly certain questions far more penetrating:

Ye are the salt of the earth: but if the salt have lost his savor, wherewith shall it be salted? . . . For what is a man profited, if he shall gain the whole world, and lose his own soul? . . . And why beholdest thou the mote that is in thy brother's eye, but perceivest not the beam that is in thine own eye? . . . Can the blind lead the blind? shall they not both fall into the ditch?

The Report of the President's Committee on Civil Rights makes mention of "the establishment of interracial churches in many communities." This development would reflect credit upon American Protestantism were it not for the fact that it has been *outside* the framework of the standard Protestant communions that most of these interracial churches have sprung up. They have struggled into existence against odds, usually as the expression of the dreams of single individuals or of small groups.

Nevertheless it appears that it is in these "volunteer" sprouts that the chief hope of redemption and regeneration for Protestantism lies, insofar as the critical race issue is concerned. For here there is no dead hand of tradition lying heavy with inhibiting rigidity. Here there is no moral inertia to be overcome. Here there is no momentum of habit to be broken. Here there is no structure of self-deceiving rationalization to be torn down. And here there are no vested interests in the status quo to be defended.

I do not mean to suggest that these struggling interracial churches are meeting with opposition from the established faiths. On the contrary, many liberal minds, some of them powerful leaders within the great denominations, are frankly looking to these experiments as to a star in the night, and are lending them every aid and encouragement, in the hope that this glimmer of light will prove a beacon to the standard religious communions. I know of at least one interracial church which survived its crucial first years by means of direct grants of money from one of the major Protestant bodies.

This interracial church, which I submit as an outstanding example, is San Francisco's Church for the Fellowship of All Peoples, founded five years ago by Dr. Alfred Fisk, professor of philosophy at San Francisco State College, who is also a Presbyterian minister.

A grant of $3,600 a year, a meeting place, counsel, and encouragement—all these were provided at the beginning by the Board of National Missions and Church Extension of the Presbyterian Church, U.S.A. Today, however, the congregation is organizationally and doctrinally autonomous, and financially self-supporting.

A characteristic feature of the plan of "Fellowship Church" is the copastorship of two ministers, one Negro and the other Caucasian. But the interracial basis of the church is not merely Negro-Caucasian. It is universally inclusive. A Nisei minister and a Mexican-American minister are frequent participants in the worship leadership. In the congregation, Japanese, Chinese, Filipino, Indonesian, Mexican, and other non-Anglo-Saxon faces are scattered among those more numerous of black, white, and intermediate shades.

No artificial control has been exercised to maintain these proportions, which prevail quite spontaneously. One reason for this is the deliberate location of the church sanctuary in a nonsegregated section of the city. Another reason is the careful avoidance of the "neighborhood church" or community settlement-house character.

For Fellowship Church does not exist to work on the problem of race relations. Like any normal church, it exists as a center of religion, personal and social. Its peculiar genius is that it frees the experience and practice of religion from the *exclusive* character which vitiates true Christian fellowship and mocks true Christian doctrine.

Yet this is no watered-down lowest-common-denominator love feast seeking to be all things to all men. Its worship is solemn and profound. Its intellectual life, in the sermons and in its well-attended study groups, demands the most strenuous grappling of which tough minds are capable. Mentally, Fellowship Church digs steadily into bedrock.

And to smooth the path for those who will follow after, this interracial church has exploded the bugaboo that haunts segregated Christendom, by enjoying a church life as thoroughly *social* as that practiced by Protestants anywhere in America. An after-service coffee hour, membership teas, neighborhood home parties, potluck church suppers, ethnic restaurant adventures, hayrides, and picnics —these are the delight of these heterogeneous people who actually love one another. Young people's groups, women's societies, men's groups, Church school gatherings of children, work projects for intercultural organizations—all are popular elements of the Fellowship Church program. In the relaxed, vigorous life of this congregation, whether in the sanctuary or out of it, one feels the living reality of the words of St. Paul:

> God . . . hath made of one blood all nations of men for to dwell on all the face of the earth . . . For ye are all the children of God. . . . There is neither Jew nor Greek, there is neither bond nor free, there is neither male nor female: for ye are all one in Christ Jesus.

Already the conventional church life of San Francisco and the entire Bay Area is coming to look upon Fellowship Church as religion's "child of promise" in this region. But not for this region alone. There are influences reaching out from this center which may leaven the whole lump of American Protestantism.

One promise of this is to be found in the internship character of the Caucasian copastorship. Texas-born Robert Meyners, a Congregational minister, is the first of a projected series of carefully selected divinity school graduates destined for the ministry in the various major Protestant communions, who will serve a two-year "internship" of pastoral service with this "melting-pot" congregation.

A second promise centers in the permanent Negro copastor, Dr. Howard Thurman, a Baptist minister who was formerly professor and dean of the chapel at Howard University. Since 1944 his has been the guiding spirit of Fellowship Church. The integrity of its direction and the wisdom of its social strategy are chiefly his contribution.

In the judgment of many who know preachers and preaching, Dr. Thurman has few peers in the American pulpit. The 1947 Ingersoll Lecture at Harvard University was but one of the numerous lectures he gives annually in colleges and universities throughout the nation. His San Francisco congregation encourages such engagements, in the conviction that through these lectures, and through the many guest sermons he delivers in "Caucasian" pulpits each year, he is sowing seeds of the inclusive fellowship idea which will take root in hundreds of minds in dozens of strategic centers.

It was for this reason that Fellowship Church concurred heartily in Dr. Thurman's decision to accept the invitation of the University of Iowa to join the faculty of its School of Religion temporarily for the spring semester, 1948, as professor of philosophy of religion. For through the selection of Catholic, Protestant, and Jewish professors of varying race and national origin, this seminary is undertaking, on the level of ministerial education, a venture in intercultural religion which is closely akin to the experiment which Fellowship Church is working out on the local church level.

But the third conclusive promise lies in the membership, which is not only inclusively interracial, but also intercreedal. Adherents of all faiths are welcomed as affiliate members. Members, affiliate and primary, are scattered throughout the United States and in several other parts of the world. Many loyal friends, who for various reasons do not enroll themselves as members, are regular participants in worship, in church activities, and in financial support. Besides Protestants of all denominations, a check of an average Sunday morning congregation will reveal also Catholics, Jews, humanists, and agnostics. Serious-minded people who love their fellow man, many of them disillusioned with organized religion on idealistic grounds, are enticed by enthusiastic friends to visit one service. They go away with their misgivings shaken, and come back again to see if it is really true.

And it is true. There is a creative spirit of life in this fellowship. It is like being at the tip of a silent, groping root. For this is the growing edge. This sanctuary is not a room bounded, enclosing something, excluding someone. It is an open door between two dimensions, where humanity meets divinity. For here man finds God *in his brother man*—man unmodified by label or classification. Religion here is not "separate but equal" (or more honestly "separate and partial") but rather *undivided,* and therefore whole.

QUESTIONS ON CONTENT

1. What three attitudes of mind toward the race question are represented in paragraph 3?
2. Name a few race discriminations in each of these areas: religion, education, economics, politics.
3. Is race discrimination a practice peculiar to the South? Discuss.
4. What is the purpose of showing progress in race relations?
5. Explain the Central Jurisdiction within the Methodist Church.
6. Explain the difference in Protestant and Catholic problems in relation to segregation.
7. "Ministers . . . are pressed sorely to become weathervanes rather than compasses." Discuss.
8. What is an "ethnic restaurant adventure"?
9. In Fellowship Church what promise does the author find for the future of segregation within churches?

❧ *The Touchin' Case of Mr. and Mrs. Massa*

St. Clair McKelway

> Oh, let's fix us a julep and kick us a houn'
> (Sing "Yassah! Yassah! Yassah!")
> And let's dig a place in de col', col' groun'
> For Mr. and Mrs. Massa!

[Boogie-Woogie]

Oh, this Mr. and Mrs. Massa have always lived in old Virginia and old North Carolina and old South Carolina and old Alabama and old Kentucky and old So Forth and old So On and nobody has ever understood the colored people the way they do because down in

Reprinted by permission of the author. Copyright 1943 The New Yorker Magazine, Inc.

old So Forth and old So On is where the white folks understand the colored folks like no other white folks on earth understand colored folks. Yassah, Massa! Yassah!

[Boogie-Woogie]

Oh, before the war and for some time afterward Mr. and Mrs. Massa understood the colored folks so well that they had a washerwoman they paid $1.50 a week and a cook they paid $1.75 a week and a butler they paid $2.25 a week and it was mighty lucky for these colored folks that the washerwoman was the cook's mother and the butler was the cook's husband because this enabled the three of them to live cozily in the fifth one-room shack from the left on the other side of the railroad tracks and thus pay $0.85 less a week for rent than the total of their combined salaries.

[Boogie-Woogie]

Oh, and over and above the total of their combined salaries Mrs. Massa every other week gave the cook a ham bone outright and Mr. Massa every other month gave the butler a whole quarter of a dollar extra right out of a clear sky. It was manna, Mammy! Manna!

[Boogie-Woogie]

Oh, but after the war had been going along for a while the butler, whose name was Charles F. Parker, came to Mr. Massa and told him he was going to quit because he had been offered a job as a counterman in the cafeteria of a defense plant at a salary of $15 a week plus three meals a day and Mr. Massa understood the colored folks so well he told Charles F. Parker that up to then he (Mr. Massa) had been able through influence to persuade the local draft board not to draft him (Charles F. Parker) but that if he (Charles F. Parker) quit his job as butler he (Mr. Massa) would have to persuade the draft board to go ahead and draft him (Charles F. Parker). Swing low, sweet Lincoln!

[Boogie-Woogie]

Oh, but then Charles F. Parker told Mr. Massa that as he (Charles F. Parker) understood the situation after conversations with the draft board he (Charles F. Parker) had already been classed as 4-F owing to a number of physical disabilities, including chronic hoecake poisoning, and that therefore he thought he would take the job at the defense-plant cafeteria but with all due respect to Mr. Massa, etc. and etc. Hit that hoecake, boys! Hit it!

[Boogie-Woogie]

Oh, so Mr. and Mrs. Massa saw the straws in the wind, saw which way the wind was blowing, and also recognized the trend of the time, so they took another tack, changed face, turned over new leaves, and each gave Charles F. Parker fifteen cents as a bonus and wished him success in his new job and raised the washerwoman (Esther G. Henderson) from $1.50 a week to $1.75 a week and raised the cook (Mrs. Charles F. Parker) from $1.75 a week to $1.85 a week with the understanding that Mrs. Esther G. Henderson would help out Mrs. Charles F. Parker in the kitchen and that Mrs. Charles F. Parker would wait on the table. Pass the hominy grits, boys! Pass it!

[Boogie-Woogie]

Oh, but at the end of the first week under the new arrangement Mrs. Charles F. Parker came to Mrs. Massa and said she was going to quit because she had been offered a job as cook at the defense-plant cafeteria at a salary of $22.50 per week plus three meals a day and Mrs. Massa jus' had to cry. Weep some mo', my lady, oh, weep some mo'!

[Boogie-Woogie]

Oh, and then the washerwoman (Esther G. Henderson) came to Mrs. Massa and said she was going to quit because she was eighty-two years old and her back ached and her daughter and son-in-law were going to support her for nothing, and Mrs. Massa jus' had to cry some mo'!

[Boogie-Woogie]

Oh, and then one day a week after that Mr. and Mrs. Massa were walking back home after a dinner at the Old Southern Greek Chop-house and they saw Charles F. Parker and Mrs. Charles F. Parker and Esther G. Henderson coming out of the colored section of a movie house after having seen a Technicolored feature featuring Jack Benny and Mr. and Mrs. Massa noticed that Charles F. Parker had on a new suit and looked happy and that Mrs. Charles F. Parker had on a new dress and looked happy and that Esther G. Henderson had on a new shawl and looked happy and moreover was still laughing at the jokes Jack Benny had made inside the movie house and Mr. and Mrs. Massa saw the three of them go into a three-room stucco bungalow where Esther G. Henderson had a room all to herself and Mr. and Mrs. Charles F. Parker had a room all to themselves and then Mr. and Mrs. Massa looked at each other understandingly and tears came into the eyes of Mrs. Massa and Mr. Massa put his hand on her shoulder and said to her softly, "Nevah you mind, there'll be a reckonin' one of these days!"

[Boogie-Woogie]

Oh, and so Mr. and Mrs. Massa finally closed up the house in old So Forth and old So On and came to New York and leased a suite at the Savoy-Plaza and the Savoy-Netherlands and the Savoy-So Forth and the Savoy-So On and any time you want to listen day or night as well as any time you don't want to listen day or night they will tell you for hours without stopping how they understand the colored people like no other white folks on earth understand colored folks and how the war and high wages are jus' ruinin' everything down in old So Forth and old So On and how never you mind there's goin' to be a reckonin' one of these days. Reckon twice and hit it again, boys! Hit it!

[Boogie-Woogie]

Oh, and the bones of Mr. and Mrs. Massa are not growing cold and their heads are not bending low and no angel voices are calling to them and if nobody will carry them back to old So Forth and old So On, oh, then . . .

[Boogie-Woogie]

Let's fix us a julep and kick us a houn'
(Sing "Yassah! Yassah! Yassah!")
And let's dig a place in de col', col' groun'
For Mr. and Mrs. Massa!

QUESTIONS ON CONTENT

1. What is "manna"? "hoecake"?
2. Is the matter of segregation mentioned? If so, is it satirized?
3. What is the central satire leveled at?
4. Is it probable, or not, that Southerners do understand Negroes better than Northerners do? Discuss.

❧ Top Hats and Tom-Toms

Roi Ottley

I felt the lift and magnitude of being an American abroad—Negro though I am! I shared abundantly the esteem, admiration and affection often lavished upon white men of America. These

From *No Green Pastures* by Roi Ottley; copyright 1951 by Roi Ottley. Reprinted by permission of the publishers, Charles Scribner's Sons.

were offered in a thousand ways, subtle and outlandish, even some-times exquisite. To be sure, this was exhilarating, but it had to be accepted initially with a grain of salt. Maybe, I thought, I was traveling under fraudulent colors, for when you live on the outskirts of American democracy, you are inclined to look a gift horse in the mouth, especially if one has Mississippi memories. But with the suddenness of a thunderclap, I realized that to be born an American citizen today is to be part of a real good thing—like being born into a rich and powerful family. America is the greatest success story in human history. I soon came to recognize that abroad I was a sort of walking neon sign advertising the nation's unique achievements. For my colored countrymen and I enjoy a share of material things which most white people do not enjoy elsewhere in the world today.

But beyond the thrilling implications of being American, Europe has much to offer which is distinctly satisfying to a Negro born and reared in the U.S. For one thing, he is given a unique sort of racial experience, often involving intangibles of the spirit, which enables him to realize himself as a whole being. He steps into the main-stream of Europe's community—a step from a feudal to a modern society, racially speaking. There is no need to accommodate himself to racial prejudice in the numerous subtle ways characteristic of the U.S.

The Negro while abroad need not observe any of the racial amenities that are carefully followed back in the U.S.—such as al-lowing a white man to precede him through the door. No white woman hastens her step anxiously at his approach on a dark street. He rarely has to debate with himself or his fellows where to eat, rent a hotel room, have his hair cut or where to find amusement and companionship. Doors to concert halls, museums, libraries and smart cafés are open to him. He is not compelled to obscure himself in dark corners of public places, nor to avoid a casual flirtation with a white woman he happens to meet. Briefly: in the absence of Amer-ica's elaborate racial etiquette, he enjoys a self-respect, dignity and personal worth unknown to Negroes in the U.S.

Listen to a widely traveled Negro journalist: "Trained to resist race prejudice or submit to it," says J. A. Rogers, "the Negro finds himself [abroad] without an enemy to attack or a fetish to bow to. Timidly he watches, fearing, and almost hoping, for some sign of dis-crimination—something that will make him feel at home. But as the days go by he meets, so far as his color is concerned, such respect, such courtesy, such appreciation as he would not receive from his

fellow Negroes in America. He begins to realize that he may go anywhere he wishes. Months pass and the days are like Paradise. When,
at last, he takes ship to return he feels like an escaped convict going
back to his jailers."

And yet I always doubted the genuine ardor of the European's
racial tolerance. I sometimes felt he was only playing a part to ag-
gravate skin-proud Americans—and in the process, making me the
fall guy. I soon found ample justification for this early racial cynicism. Actually, I discovered, there is a deep strain of racial prejudice
toward Negroes running through the cultural fabric of the Continent (and England), often so subtle that it is not always seen by
the naked eye. Consequently, even many sophisticated Negroes are
taken in by the shiny appearance of things—spectacular, to be sure,
when compared with the racial situation for Negroes in sections of
the U.S. But though relations between the races in Europe may be
less cruelly degrading than in the U.S., actually racial prejudice is
no less real.

Comparison with America is always implicit in a Negro's observations of places abroad. So, even Negroes who have shared abundantly in the good things of the United States become greatly impressed by the racial patterns abroad and applaud them beyond
their actual worth. They do so, I suppose, because American accomplishments win them acclaim in Europe, which is manifested in
social privileges and cultural associations not allowed Negroes in
the U.S. For example, upon arrival in England as one of the first
Negro war correspondents, Ollie Stewart began his first dispatch to
the Baltimore *Afro-American* newspaper with, "I am most happy to
report that London has not shown me even a hint of color prejudice."
Richard Wright, who wrote the blazing *Native Son* and is today perhaps the most feted American in Paris, bluntly declares: "There is
more freedom in one square block of Paris than in all of the United
States." Paul Robeson, lionized by Europeans, stumps in identical
vein. He says racial liberty is characteristic of Europe, especially of
those sections dominated by the Soviet Union.

Today, in parts of Europe where white men have few rights,
Negroes belatedly enjoy equal rights. Dr. Robert C. Weaver, Negro
director of the American Council on Race Relations, went abroad in
1946 as a member of a U.N.R.R.A. mission to study the economic
rehabilitation of the Ukraine. He appraised race relations there with
a professional eye and reported upon his return: "The Soviet Union,
which was rife with anti-Semitism and national hatreds before the

revolution, is today relatively free from inter-group tensions. Conflicts between these groups are unknown, and the man-in-the-street in Russia cannot understand how the United States can claim to be a democratic nation and still persecute its darker citizens. To the Soviet citizen, it seems much more logical and fair to liquidate an enemy of the State than to deny a black man equal rights because of the color of his skin.

"The Soviet Union," Dr. Weaver added, "has solved its minority problems by legislation, economic and educative action. Expressions of nationality or racial chauvinism are punishable by law, and I was told of the application of that law. A Negro newspaperman in Moscow,* told me that once when he was riding on a train from Moscow to Stalingrad, several Americans, who were assigned space in his compartment, objected loudly to his presence. Despite the fact that these Americans were engineers, and vital to the industrial development of the Soviet Union, they were promptly removed from the train and arrested."

Reports like these make exciting reading. Consequently, rank-and-file Negroes frequently are ill-prepared for the racial realities—indeed, such Negroes are very often innocents abroad and are dumfounded by the discovery of racialism, Continental style. This seems to have been the case during World War II, when Negro soldiers were stationed in Holland. A little town in the southern Netherlands, so the story goes, decided to celebrate *Sinterklaas* in full-blown fashion. According to Dutch tradition, Santa Claus hails from Southern Spain and always arrives accompanied by a Negro servant, called *Zwarte Piet* or Black Peter. The Dutch inhabitants, streamlining this version, borrowed a jeep from the Americans to convey Santa and his black servant about the town to distribute gifts. But to the shock and humiliation of the Negroes, they discovered Peter being impersonated offensively by a Dutch woman who had blackened her face with burnt cork.

To be sure, tolerance of different races and colors in Europe is no myth. But the Continent (and England) is no racial Utopia—indeed, the case for liberalism abroad has been greatly romanticized. The fact is, beyond earshot, Negro Americans are labeled with such terms as "exotic," "musical," "backward," and "oppressed," and even described as a "brutish people." But the chief reason why most Negro Americans escape the more nauseating aspects of Europe's

* Chatwood Hall, Associated Negro Press.

racial prejudice rests squarely upon the fact that they enjoy a unique status while abroad. They are glamorous novelties. Moreover, they are infinitesimal in number and therefore never in competition with white men socially or economically. Above all, Negro tourists (and transient soldiers, singers, dancers, musicians and boxers who often are lionized) are dollar-carrying Americans who benefit by the tradition that the customer is always right.

The story is quite a different one for the continent's home-grown Negroes, who are born, reared, and must make their living in Europe. For white men abroad react to the same racial illusions that feed the vanity of white men in the U.S. The bulk hold tenaciously to a belief in the superiority of the white race and inferiority of the Negro race—though manifestations of this belief rarely are crude, blustering or heavy-handed. But they do indulge themselves in blanket racial stereotypes no less degrading to the Negro in Europe than racial segregation is to the Negro in parts of America. For instance, with the exception of an ebony élite, Negroes are described as "primitive" and "savage," and held ill-equipped mentally to do white men's work. Even without the elaborate machinery of Jim Crow, they are relegated to the galleries of cabarets and dance halls —dancing, singing or tooting a horn in the way of employment, a fact which has driven many Negroes into crime. The bulk of blacks in Europe is abysmally poor.

Except for a handful of educated black Africans, most of the Negroes seen in Europe and the British Isles are backward and illiterate, often belonging to the Moslem faith, and unused to Western ways. This falsely documents the African's inferiority in the eyes of Europeans, a fact which affects Negro Americans indirectly. But this yardstick rarely is applied directly to Negro Americans (and West Indian Negroes); they are received with an indulgence not extended the colonial blacks.

Negro Americans never upset the social, economic or religious equilibrium. For as Christians and Americans they are products of Western civilization—and, as such, different from Europeans only in the color of their skins. And because they are essentially a racially mixed people of brown complexions mostly, Europeans are not inclined to place them in the same racial group as black Africans.* Many are surprised by the color (and cultural) contrast between

---

* According to the anthropologists, nearly eighty-two percent of the Negro population in the U.S. is of mixed ancestry.

Negro Americans and Negro Africans; even Negro Americans themselves often are amazed by the sheer ebony blackness of the pure-
blooded African.

To grasp the racial realities abroad, one must understand that feeling against Negroes increases the further up one goes in the social
and economic scale—whereas the reverse is the case in the U.S. But
the races do not live on different sides of the railroad tracks—essentially, differences are based on caste, not color exclusively, as in
America. The racial equation is one of top hats over tom-toms. But
any Negro—by solid achievement, family or wealth—may belong
to the upper classes and enjoy their privileges. Crown princes of
African tribes and nations are given lavish respect. But this implied
racial liberalism is wholly false, for the white man in Europe cannot survive the final and acid test of racial equality, which of course
consists of marriage between the races. The European will vigorously oppose his daughter's marriage to a black man, and call into
support all the hoary legends, stereotypes and folklore insinuating
the racial inferiority of the Negro.

Negro is clearly something negative in the minds of most Europeans, even cultivated ones. Count Hermann Keyserling, in attempting to illustrate the offensive characteristics of white Americans, used the Negro as a standard. He once remarked: "The
American presents a curious picture: a European with the manners
of a negro and the soul of an Indian." He declared that the "lively
temperament of the average American, which shows itself not only
at baseball games, but more particularly in an astonishing passion
for verbosity . . . resembles the 'chattering' of the negro village [in
Africa]." Jung, who believed that Negroes had exerted a profound
psychological influence upon American personality, said that the
inimitable Rooseveltian laughter was found in its primal form among
the American Negroes, and those swaying, loose-limbed hips, "observed so frequently among American women," were of Negro
origin. "The expressions of the religious emotions, the revival meetings, the Holy Rollers and other abnormalities," he declared, "are
strongly influenced by the negro—and the famous naïveté of the
Americans, in its charming as well as in its more unpleasant forms,
can be easily compared with the childlikeness of the negro."

The key to Europe's paradoxical racial mentality is found simply
in the fact that white men abroad possess Negro colonies, which
form the cornerstone of their economic wellbeing. I quickly noticed
that those countries which had never had Negro possessions were

the most liberal in their attitudes toward races and colors. The simple and inescapable conclusion is this: if a country has a Negro population, automatically that country is more or less prejudiced toward a dark skin. This is the logic of colony ownership. A nation with a Christian tradition is compelled to concoct something approaching a rational reason to justify subjugating black people. To use Lord Oliver's words, they have to invent the "sordid anthropological heresy" that Negroes are really not human. The manhandling of the colonial Negroes in Africa forms one of the worst aspects of European history, involving sheer cruelty, denial of schooling, forced labor, and even decimation of whole populations.

No blanket charge can be leveled against Europe, for each nation has a distinct attitude toward Negroes, as does each state in the United States. Loosely, the principal nations with Negro possessions might be described thus: The French are sentimental—a sentimentality inspired by the heroics of black colonials who form the backbone of French armies. The Germans, who owned Negro colonies for only thirty years, are more liberal than the French—but a liberalism underscored by a racial cynicism which makes them unpredictable. The Belgians are calculatingly brutal, but no one would guess this by the wholly civilized treatment accorded Negroes visiting Belgium. The Dutch have a shrewd racial realism—a realism which inclines them toward tolerance as a means of imperialistic survival. The Italians, neophytes in modern colonialism, are indifferent, with few preconceived racial notions. The English, who regard themselves as above the turbulence of racialism, actually are the most cruelly prejudiced people abroad—a profound fact because of the many black millions who come under the British flag. These nations inspire little hope in the hearts of black Africans, for losses in the Far East cause Europe to hold all the more tenaciously to Africa and to deal all the more arbitrarily and repressively with the aspirations of blacks.

The rank and file in Europe have no elbow contact with the racial problems of faraway black Africa. That permits them the righteous luxury of loudly criticizing the treatment of Negroes in the U.S. Nearly a half million Negroes were in Europe and Africa during World War II, as soldiers, sailors and merchant seamen. They represented every stratum of the Negro community in the U.S. The introduction of these Negroes gave people abroad intimately detailed knowledge of racial realities in America. They quickly came to believe that "for anyone with one iota of Negro blood there is no social mercy," and concluded that "the color problem [in the U.S.] is an abyss into which we can look only with terror." A detailed survey of the Negro problem in Europe's press, made recently by James W. Ivy, editor of *The Crisis* magazine, revealed the magnitude of concern today.

Even so, there is an appalling ignorance current about American racial folkways. Ironically, I was compelled to explain in and out of season, often defend, American institutions and racial morality, and deny accusations which white America did not deserve—though I, before going abroad, had criticized the failures of American democracy. I frequently felt helpless, as so many Negroes do, attempting to explain the "race problem" to people without any concept of conditions in America. If all Americans were violently anti-Negro, and nothing was being done to improve the condition of Negroes, the racial situation would be infinitely simpler to explain than it is.

But how, for example, could I answer questions with these tacit implications: "Why, since you've never done your white countryman any injury, does he hate the Negroes?" . . . "Why are Negroes not allowed to walk on the sidewalks alongside whites?" . . . "Why do Negroes all live in ghettos?" . . . "Did you ever see a Negro married to a white woman in the U.S.?" Believe me, this was like asking a man when did he stop beating his wife. The implications and subtleties of race relations in the U.S. are much too unique, nor is there an overall racial pattern for the nation at large. If Negroes were a primitive people, living beyond the borders of the country, and the color question had a colonial-imperialist basis, perhaps the equation would make sense to Europeans. But since the Negro is a full-fledged citizen, his separation from the white community bewilders the average person abroad, astonishes the sophisticated and delights the anti-American elements.

What principally makes people abroad, especially colored people, uneasy about racialism in the U.S., is the subjective feeling that it bears heavily upon their own status in the eyes of white Americans. No wonder intellectuals like Harold Laski could declare that American racialism contains a Fascist character. Consequently, as we more and more lecture people about their democratic failures, criticism of American democracy will daily increase in vigor and volume. Even the British would more loudly attack us, if Britain did not urgently need American dollars, diplomatic and military cooperation in maintaining her empire. But as the European flatterers, eager for loans and food, become disillusioned by U.S. inability to share the wealth, they will join the packs howling at our Achilles heel.

No dollar consideration silences the Russians. Propaganda assaults on the "American way" in treating Negroes are becoming more and more shrill, with echoes wherever the Soviet Union has influence, particularly today in Asia. But the Russians are not concerned with racial morality as such, which indeed explains the many curious blandishments directed at Negroes everywhere, especially Negro Americans: with racial equality as the watchword, they decorated Negro fliers for bravery during World War II, offered Negro scientists and skilled mechanics flattering salaries and privileges to work in Russian industries, invited influential Negroes to diplomatic functions at their embassies, officially declared the great Russian novelist Alexander Pushkin a Negro and more than once pressed in the United Nations for investigation of the Negro problem in the U.S. Object: obviously the Russians hope to show by calculated demonstration that Communism believes in the equality and dignity of all races, and thus to win Negroes to the Communist banner.

But back in 1942, when Mrs. Ivy Litvinoff accompanied her ambassador husband to the U.S., she held a press conference with representatives of the Negro newspapers at which she declared: "I have visited Washington's slums where many of your people live. Witnessing almost daily the practices of segregation still causes us wonderment and confusion. I asked our colored maid to go to a certain large department store and make some purchases for me. This she definitely refused to do saying, 'the place refused to serve her people.'" Madame Litvinoff recalled all the many Americans who visited the Soviet Embassy in Washington on her husband's arrival and remarked that not one Negro was among them, adding: "We felt most neglected as we had always numbered your people as our true friends."

Sheer hypocrisy in Europe frequently underscores criticism of racialism in the U.S. Nearly one hundred million Negroes come under the flags of white men abroad—principally Belgium, France, Holland and Great Britain. Yet, ironically, these supposedly liberal nations which belabor U.S. treatment of Negroes have produced few Negroes comparable to Marian Anderson, Paul Robeson, Dorothy Maynor, William Grant Still and Duke Ellington in music; Ethel Waters, Lena Horne and Katherine Dunham in the theater; George Washington Carver, Percy Julian, Louis T. Wright and Charles Drew in science and medicine; W. E. B. Du Bois, William Stanley

Braithwaite and Charles S. Johnson in scholarship; Mordecai Johnson and Mary MacLeod Bethune in education; A. Philip Randolph and Willard S. Townsend in labor; Gwendolyn Brooks (1950 Pulitzer Prize Winner in poetry), Willard Motley, Langston Hughes and Richard Wright in literature; Joe Louis and Jackie Robinson in sports; Edith Sampson and Ralph J. Bunche (Nobel Peace Prize winner) in diplomacy.

The existence of such Negroes as these, of distinguished schools of learning for Negroes, could not possibly be deduced from the many articles published abroad about Negroes and America. In the eyes of Europe, the Negro is only an eternal reproach to white America. Yet history offers no parallel to the dramatic ascent of Negroes in the U.S.—slaves a mere eighty-odd years ago. Even the white serfs of feudal Europe, though belonging to the ruling racial group, took hundreds of years to unload the shackles of inferiority and reach their present-day level. That literally thousands of American Negroes of comfortable means are able to go abroad yearly should be a fact not lost upon a continent where few people have the means to travel even from city to city. But if this unusual point is unnoticed by white Europeans, Negroes abroad find the fact mighty impressive. Today the fifteen million Negroes in America form a sort of aristocracy within the world's black community, because of their incomparable achievements and material possessions. They are envied and admired tremendously; indeed, black America provides Negroes abroad with racial heroes.

No country abroad has so dazzled Negroes. This fact has been reflected in mass migration of Negroes to the U.S. Nearly a half million have entered the country in the past fifty years; today their numbers are restricted only by the immigration regulations. They were neither visionaries nor Utopians. But they came, hopeful and empirical. Their expectations were simple and concrete. They expected a better life than had been open to them back in their native homelands—more food, more comfort, a job, a farm, perhaps a career in law, medicine, dentistry or teaching; citizenship, a stake in American society, reasonable opportunity for development according to their capacities, a chance to better themselves, a chance to give their children a still better chance. The overwhelming vote is "yea" that on the whole black immigrants got a measure of what they sought.

America still is the fabulous land of rags to riches, even for Negroes—at least in the eyes of Negroes abroad. One, John Carter, a

British subject formerly secretary of England's aggressive League of Coloured Peoples, toured the U.S. early in 1950 and got an eyeful. He afterwards made an astute appraisal of the Negro's progress in the U.S. and placed the whole situation in a neat nutshell. "I must say that my short visit to America," he wrote to an American friend, "has caused me to be very pro-American. Whatever might be the prejudice, whatever the outrages past and present against our people, where else in the world does the Negro get such splendid opportunity? Where else in the world will a Negro woman drive a Cadillac? Or will Negroes get the opportunity for education that they have in the U.S.?

Where indeed! Consequently, we can say to Europe with absolute justice, "Behold the mote in thine own eye."

QUESTIONS ON CONTENT

1. Why does the author call this chapter from his book "Top Hats and Tom-toms"?
2. What are the things Negroes appreciate most about the way Europeans treat them? Does legislation have anything to do with the attitude Europeans assume towards Negroes? Before answering, review what has been said about the Russians.
3. Who is Paul Robeson? Does he rightfully speak for American Negroes?
4. Does it seem to you "much more logical and fair to liquidate an enemy of the State than to deny a black man equal rights"? Discuss.
5. Do you feel that Negroes are being supersensitive when they object to black-face impersonations? What would you think of white-face impersonations? Would you be offended?
6. What two reasons does the author give for the popularity of American Negroes abroad?
7. What is the "acid test of racial equality"? Discuss.
8. How does the author interpret the effect of nations' owning Negro colonies? How sound is this observation?
9. Would department stores in your community refuse to serve colored people?
10. What is the purpose of naming Negro leaders in various fields?
11. Discuss the over-all impression of what is said here about the current status of American Negroes.

❦ *A Southerner Looks*
at the Supreme Court

CLIFFORD DOWDEY

The first reaction in the South to the Supreme Court's decision on segregation was one of studied calm. Though vestigial demagogues responded as their constitutents expected them to, their intemperate blasts bore no more relation to the problems to be solved than the pious hosannas uttered by Northern politicians in the name of democracy.

The educated Southerner is well aware of the considerations of world politics which were involved in this decision; he strongly suspects that these considerations much influenced the unanimity of the Court, and he declines the role of obstacle to "the march of human freedom." At the same time, he is equally aware that "the historic decision" related to America's world position as an abstraction and to himself in the complex details of a very old reality.

Outside of the South irresponsible pharisees ("thank God, I'm not as other men") could display their own humanity by applauding this step toward "equality," but the Southerner has seldom been able to afford this luxury of self-approbation. Since his is a section where the white and black races co-exist in a single society, only the Southerner is forced to consider the practical application of a dictum which involves the minutiae of two parallel communities under one roof. For the practical application of the Court's decision only superficially concerned schools.

In the humane words of Chief Justice Warren, the decision said, "Today education is perhaps the most important function of state and local governments. . . . Today it is a principal instrument in awakening the child to cultural values . . . and *in helping him to adjust to a normal environment.*" (Not Warren's italics.)

Now, in the South the normal environment of the white child is white and the normal environment of the colored child is colored. A

The Saturday Review, October 9, 1954. Reprinted by permission of *The Saturday Review.*

mixed school would not help the student of either race to adjust to his normal environment, since no mixed environment exists. If the Court's ukase were executed the effect would be to create a new mixed environment. Such a black-and-white environment would destroy the two parallel societies that have painfully evolved over the past century in the South, and produce an environment that is unique in America.

I think it is safe to say that, confronted by no matter what mandate, the Southerner will attempt to continue the two parallel societies. He will look at the North, where segregation is illegal, and simulate what the North has done whenever confronted by a similar density of colored population. He will evade the law much in the manner that the Eighteenth Amendment was evaded, where the evasions were determined by individual conditions. For there is no single Southern attitude toward the Negro any more than there was a single American attitude toward Prohibition.

The only single Southern attitude—in which he can find no difference from the rest of the country—is that he wants to live in a white society. It is not this desire that differentiates him from his fellow-Americans, but the peculiar circumstances of his total society, and the hereditary conditioning of his historical circumstance. Other sections have never faced the problem of a mixed society. Whenever a community has accumulated a density of colored population the problem has been tacitly evaded by the creation of "black belts," as in New York and Chicago. Where individual Negroes formed any sizable percentage of a school, even in the excellent public-school system of New York, families who could afford to immediately moved their children to private schools or moved themselves to suburbs. Church congregations have manifested the greatest reluctance to amalgamation, and many old-line places of worship have remained steadfast islands of whites in mixed communities; often churches have been abandoned entirely to Negroes. In living terms, the low percentage of Negro population in the majority of Northern communities has made it possible for the white to preen himself on his abstract humanity and lack of discriminatory laws, while practising *de facto* segregation.

Now that "de-segregation" has been made national policy, the Southerner will have to achieve the same *de facto* segregation within his society without the balm of moral unction. But he has developed a high degree of tolerance to living under the lash of moral superiority and, as with problems thrust upon him for the past hundred years, he will struggle with pragmatic solutions from day to day, in a continuing flux of shift and change in the total structure.

Despite all the worn cliches, to the average Southerner the problem has never been the individual Negro. Without publicity, individual Negroes now attend Southern educational institutions such as the Medical College in Richmond and the Virginia Episcopal Seminary, and Southerners going North to college or to live readily adjust to customs involving individual Negroes. On the other hand, Northern families moving South develop quick antipathies for the Negro in mass and—after experiences with colored house-servants— damn the Negro character in the bitterest denunciations. The point is that *de facto* segregation in the South presents problems that are different in kind from other sections and different in degree within the South.

It is commonplace for people to say, "Of course Mississippi is different," with a 45 per cent Negro population; but there is no norm, no average of colored population. In Virginia colored-school enrolment varies from less than 5 per cent in western counties to as high as 80 per cent in eastern counties; Richmond stands between with a 40 per cent colored-school population in a total population in which every third person is a Negro.

Neither the school with one colored student in twenty nor with one white student to four Negroes would prepare children for a normal Southern environment. The one Negro in twenty students would be more typical of Northern environments, while the one white child in five would be typical of no environment ever known in modern America. More typical of the average, statistical Southern environment would be the two colored children to three whites. This would represent truly "a mixed class" (as opposed to a white class which included several Negroes), and would be more representative of the new, mixed environment for which these children would be prepared in the South—though such an environment would exist nowhere else.

The fact of these varying densities of mixed population within the South immediately reduces the Court decision from the nobility of an abstraction to chaos in detail. The Southern white relates to the Negro differently according to the density, according to the history of density, and according to individual circumstances. The educated Southerner who has always related to the Negro as a servant in his home, for instance, is totally unlike the ignorant poor man who relates in economic rivalry; and neighboring farmers maintain still a third relationship. For the Negro and the white are not static forces in an unchanging society.

Since the destruction of its original society in 1865 the South has undergone a continuous struggle of adaptation to an order which was not only foreign to its nature but contrary to its conscious design. This struggle to adapt was made in terms of primal survival, against the bitterest poverty and against outside exploitation and discrimination. The three generations which bore the brunt of the struggle suffered constant upheavals in their social order and structural dislocations totally unrelated to the Negro. The Negro was caught up along with the white and the compassionate white might say, as did Lincoln, "You suffer because of us and we suffer because of you."

Yet, from the outside the South seems viewed as an abstraction, an exotic deviation in the past and a backward appendage in the present, steadfast in a bigotry which opposes the national crusade for human liberty. This view attributes a sustained moral purpose and rational progression to the events during which the South was acted upon by the abolitionists, the Civil War, and this last battle in the Supreme Court. This noble concept is somewhat remote from the facts.

The whole distortion began with the legal existence of the slave-trade, for which New Englanders imported Negroes from Africa and sold them as chattels in the Southern states. From the beginning New Englanders made the profits from slavery and the South got the Negro. Chattel slavery provided a form of mass-labor as a practical method for the large-scale production of one money-crop (usually cotton or tobacco) by which plantations made agriculture a Big Business, and planters rivaled industrial tycoons in power and privilege. But the great planters were less than 1 per cent of the Southern population, and less than 10 per cent of the Southern population (including Negro slaveholders) owned any slaves at all. Many of these manumitted their own slaves at a personal sacrifice, creating by the early nineteenth century a class of freed Negroes. Nonslaveholders, in opposition to the "peculiar institution," migrated steadily out of the region, and Southern slaveholders and non-slaveholders (not Northern abolitionists) created the first emancipationist movements.

The difference between the native emancipationist and the Northern abolitionist symbolized the historic difference over the Negro between the sections. To the abolitionist it was enough to say, "Let my people go." He assumed no responsibility for the freed Negro or his adjustment in a white society. The native had to ask, "Go where?" Not only was there no place for a freed slave in an agricultural society, but the Southerner from the first was forced to consider an American society of mixed races. Even Lincoln believed deportation to Africa was the solution for emancipated slaves. Contrary to the idealists who advocated a march toward equality of the races. Take his own words: ". . . and I will say in addition to this that there is a physical difference between the white and black races which I believe will forever forbid the races living together on terms of social and political equality."

He was not elected on a platform to free the slaves, but to contain slavery within the South. On abolition he said, "I think no wise man has yet perceived how it (slavery) could be at once eradicated without producing even a greater evil to the cause of human liberty itself." Then, stating that he believed he had no right to interfere with slavery where it existed, Lincoln wrote the Emancipation Proclamation as a war measure with full knowledge of the dislocations he was bringing on the South. He made it abundantly clear (as in his letter to Greeley) that his Proclamation against the rebellious states was an expedient for preserving the Union. He wrote that if he could preserve the Union without this measure *against* the Rebels (not *for* the Negro) he would do it.

Thus, the violent abolition of the slave in 1862 was not an organic extension of the abolitionist movement and was connected in no way with any crusade toward equality. As slavery was still permitted in loyal sections (even in the South), emancipation was obviously a war measure, and Lincoln undoubtedly expected to remedy, when the war was over, the inevitable dislocations it caused. But after his death the bars of the zoo were let down in Washington. The spoilsmen and cranks who took over, in cynical exploitation and forthright vindictiveness, in effect set the Negro against the defeated and impoverished white during the twelve years of military occupation called "Reconstruction." Behind the bayonets of the occupying army the desolated region was invaded by financial and political adventurers who came to batten off the defeated people, and by "missionaries" who came to elevate the Negro, not to equality of citizenship, but to positions of supremacy. The first acts of outsiders regarding the Negroes in the South overlooked the actual condition of the Negroes (then recently-freed slaves) and experimented with their advancement at the calculated expense of the white society. For instance, the missionaries founded the first free and unmixed schools, definitely segregated and limited to the Negro. Under these circumstances the Negro began his life of freedom in a bitter struggle for survival between the races, in a time of strife and disorder, in the wreckage of a society. Emotions were raw and violence close to the surface; white and colored alike picked through the physical ruins for sustenance, and no waking hours were free of distrust, fomented antagonisms, and smoldering hatreds. Yet, during this period of turmoil the rulers defined no ultimate purpose or future goal for the freed Negro in a white society.

In the Civil Rights Act, which was written in 1867 into the Constitution as the now-famous Fourteenth Amendment, the Iowan who sponsored the bill specifically disassociated the measure from mixed schools. In defining the terms Mr. Wilson said, "Do they mean that in all things civil, social, political, all citizens, without distinction of race or color, shall be equal? By no means can they be so construed . . . nor do they mean that . . . their children shall attend the same schools. These are not civil rights or immunities." When the Civil Rights Act was incorporated into the Fourteenth Amendment during Reconstruction adoption of the amendment was mandatory in the Southern states before their Representatives could be seated in Washington. Even though the majority of Representatives who wanted to be seated were Negroes, out-of-staters, and Unionist natives, not one state adopted any measures to establish amalgamated schools. Anti-Confederate legislators ruled that "white and colored persons shall not be taught in the same schools, but in separate schools." Manifestly, the enemies of the traditional South who wrote these measures into the state constitutions did not believe in social equality, and this was true of the majority of states in the Union. Thus, the expressed will of non-Southern white people, on winning the Civil War, was not to establish equality for the Negro but to establish two parallel societies. The two parallel societies within the South were begun by outside legislation, while the South was under outside domination and financial exploitation, and both races were left to adjust themselves as best they might.

The present South is not an extension of the South that ended at Appomattox. That old South was created by itself, on its own ideals. The South that arose from the debris of invading armies and the longest military occupation in modern history was created partly from without, partly in reaction to the outside, largely in reaction to the conditions forced upon it, and always in a succession of make-shifts, of short-range measures for immediate self-preservation. Dis-possessed farmers fended off hunger by offering themselves as pools of cheap labor for Northern industry which took the profits out of the South; former planters and former slaves combined in despera-tion to evolve the tenant-farmer system, with its attendant evils. Dispossessed Bourbons of the former ruling class fought for polit-ical power with the new farmers; and the Negro, after he was aban-doned by the exploiters and the do-gooders, became the political issue which created "white supremacy" as an expedient and the "demagogue" as a result.

While the two parallel societies grew out of this amalgam of forces, it would be hypocritical to deny that the white man came first —as he did nationally during the Depression. In the long Depression which was Southern history from 1865 to World War II certainly the "Negro Problem" was less pressing to the Southern whites than it was to their distant detractors. The Negro was merely one of his multiple and at times insoluble problems, though the Negro ex-acerbated all else. During the period from 1865 to World War II great changes occurred which, not visible from year to year, or even decade to decade, are tremendous when viewed across the entire span. While vestiges of plantation-agriculture remained along with the acute poverty of the small dirt farm, modern agricultural meth-ods had been introduced; local businesses and even industries spread money through the region and, while much of the industry was still predominantly owned by Northern capital, higher wages raised the total Southern standard of living. Politically men emerged who could lead without appeal to regional passions and prejudice, and voters brought themselves to trust the party which, founded originally on an anti-Southern platform, had legislated their disfranchisement and directed their post-bellum debasement. Individual Southerners were accepted among the liberals and gave evidence that enlightenment had not died in the South with Jefferson. With the recession of poverty, ignorance also receded. As the older generations died off and the terrible memories grew dim, younger people grew in com-passion and understanding for the Negro within their midst. Ad-vances in humanity toward the Negro in some sections of the South have been such as to make the present conditions incomprehensible to aged grandparents. There is a most encouraging development among Negro leaders themselves—in education, law, medicine, busi-ness—and in certain areas they participated in local government.

But, unregenerately committed to a white society, the most ideal-istic Southerners know no more what to do than did their native emancipationist ancestors 100 years ago. Even the most forward-looking can see no clear, shining goals in realistic terms, and—God knows—no purpose has been clarified for them by today's distant and vocal humanitarians. In this present complex society, from the most humane to the most bigoted, the reaction to the Court's decision was unanimous in that it was regarded as another problem forced on the region from the outside. The average Southerner did not even bother to discuss the validity of the Court's opinion that "segrega-tion is a denial of equal protection of the law." The Court did not stultify itself by claiming that its ruling fulfilled any logical, legal progression toward racial equality. Its decision made very clear that the Court was changing the existing laws to meet today's standards, and negating the Constitutional Amendment of 1867 on the grounds that the American Constitution is subject to reinterpretation by the Supreme Court.

With this repudiation of the document supposed to guarantee their protection, white Southerners accepted this legislation by the judici-ary as something else dumped in their laps, as was the freed Negro, for them to deal with in their own way. The fact that their own way constitutes evasion of a national law marks a most significant change for the South. When the Southern states seceded in 1861 it was be-cause they believed their interests would be discriminated against by the Administration coming into power. They believed the Con-stitution had ceased to afford them protection. Believing the same thing again, since secession was proven to be impractical, the peo-ple are as equally determined to see to their own protection now as they were in 1861. Only today, having lived in closer proximity to other Americans, they have become more guileful.

Even so, things did not remain quiet in the South after the initial reaction to the decision. Citizens erupted into unprecedented letter-writing to newspapers, though the expected vehemence was un-expectedly matched by reasonable attitudes of pros and cons. In private conversations, which were dominated by the subject, there were surprisingly few expressions of bigotry; and an understanding, compassionate attitude toward the Negro's position revealed a deep change in the educated Southerner. Many expressed gratification that, legally, "second-class citizenship" was removed from the Negro and that he would receive an affirmation in his long struggle for mortal dignity.

However, the burden of all conversations concerned the machinery of evading a law which the people felt was passed without consideration for the living details. Not since the last occupation troops left the South in 1877 has sectional consciousness been so aroused. When the Southern Governors met their opinions ranged as widely as those of private citizens, but there was the same unanimity on the basic course to pursue, regardless of the methods of detail.

This October [1954], when the Court hears the proposals of methods of effectuating its decision, the Southerners—whether or not they state it explicitly—will be talking of means of sustaining the parallel societies which are threatened by the decision applying specifically to schools. As of now the plans of evasion are as diverse as were the means of evading the Eighteenth Amendment—conditioned by financial circumstances, neighborhoods, and other practical considerations remote from the arena of the decision. Families in "protected" suburbs or with children in private schools are as unconcerned as were teetotalers. Families in borderline areas have besieged realtors for new houses elsewhere, and the few private dayschools have been forced to take their phones off the hook. These evasions concern people of more or less relative privilege.

For less privileged people in borderline areas there will be a gradual moving out and those areas will become, as in the North, black belts. Negroes now in borderline areas (without any actual polling) seem to prefer the eventuality of a totally colored section. The Negroes in these totally black sections will continue to attend all-colored schools since, as neighborhood schools, they will draw only colored children. For areas which cannot resolve themselves readily into white and black gerrymandering will be done in school districts.

But, with whatever measures, there will be many small communities of only two schools where none of these expedients will apply. This situation will apply also to high schools which draw on an entire city. In all of these cases the first actual detail to resolve is with the teachers. In the South, in the two-school system, Negroes teach Negroes, with the result that the state of Virginia alone has more colored teachers than all the non-segregated states together. Who is to teach the mixed school? Is a Negro teacher fitted to prepare a white student for his "normal environment," or a white teacher fitted to prepare a Negro for his? As of today the Negro, through no fault of his own, is less well prepared at home for the advantages of school education. Is the Southern white child, then, to be retarded in his own school education by the inclusion of less well-prepared students?

Finally, if teachers can agree to prepare students for an amalgamated society, the effect would be to create a hybrid environment which would belong neither to the colored nor to the white in the whole country. Neither the Court nor the praisers of its decision have stated that this is the objective—the purpose of the abolition of segregation in schools.

When a mixed race is the expressed goal of America, when the other sections show their eagerness to form such a society, then the Southerner will stand convicted of thwarting the will of the majority. In the present circumstance only the Southerner is affected locally by the Federal judicial ruling, and he does not believe that the majority has any sincere interest in his living problems.

Because of this ingrained Southern belief in the irresponsibility of outside legislation, there have been the extreme stands which, at least, threaten to abolish compulsory education. Legal-minded Southerners point out that, regardless of the abrogation of their state constitutions, no Federal law can force a state to spend money in any specific way.

There is an illustrative situation just outside of Richmond. In a fashionable new suburb of highly privileged people there is a small community of colored people who subsist largely as houseservants for the neighborhood. There is no possibility that the county school of this district, preparing students for Princeton and Vassar, will open its doors to mixed classes.

It is the gradation, the variation of necessary adjustments, which makes the execution of the Court's decision in the South anything except an abstraction on the road to equality. The human conditioning of environments being what it is, and individual circumstances varying as they do, it would look at this moment as if the historic decision might create historic chaos—unless, in October, when the Court listens to representatives of the locally affected scenes it truly considers the real problems of the Southern society in which the Negro lives. Otherwise there will be a definite roadblock in the Negro's sorrowful journey toward his mortal dignity and full citizenship.

QUESTIONS ON CONTENT

1. What are the "considerations of world politics" mentioned in paragraph 2?
2. Explain: "For the practical application of the Court's decision only superficially concerned schools."
3. What is "the only single Southern attitude," and how does it differ, if at all, from the attitude in other parts of the United States?
4. Why does the author offer so much history? What is he trying to prove?
5. Does the author write coolly and without passion? Are there any passages which warm up a bit? If so, cite them.
6. What is the central idea? Is it logically sustained?
7. Why did "the average Southerner . . . not even bother to discuss the validity of the Court's opinion that 'segregation is a denial of equal protection of the law' "?

❧ *School Kids Are Color Blind*

FRED RODELL

In the cold war of conflicting ideas, there is sometimes an area so sacrosanct, an intellectual territory so pregnant with emotion, a level of disagreement so deep, that it cannot ever become an open battlefield of give-and-take debate. You do not argue with a devout adherent of a demanding religion about the divinity of Buddha, Mohammed, Jesus Christ. You do not argue with a Communist about the fundamental rightness-or-wrongness of Marx or of Lenin. And you do not argue with a traditional Southerner about his ingrained attitude toward Negroes, founded as it is on a quite inarticulate major premise that underlies whatever words he speaks.

In the last issue of this magazine [*SR* Oct. 9] Clifford Dowdey defended the rumblingly rebellious reaction of the South—or, to be a bit more exact than he is, the reaction of many adult white people in many parts of the South—to the recent decision of the Supreme Court of the United States which forbids the segregation of white

The Saturday Review, October 16, 1954. Reprinted by permission of *The Saturday Review.*

and colored children in separate public schools. Mr. Dowdey's defense is eloquent, learned, largely temperate—and a little frightening. It is also more than a little irrelevant. For Mr. Dowdey, by presuming on the superior factual knowledge that Southerners so often assume on this subject, manages to make of his subterranean and sectional prejudices and predilections a matter of course rather than a proper matter for debate. Yet it is precisely these prejudices and predilections—these taken-for-granted tenets—that lie, unquietly, at the heart of the whole howdydo.

What Mr. Dowdey has to say is briefly this: The South will simply *not obey* the Supreme Court's orders. Not by open defiance but by the use of whatever "legal" devices it can dream up—from the technical turning over of public schools into private hands to the gerrymandering of school districts—the South will see to it that colored and white children do not go to school together. Just as millions of Americans evaded Prohibition until the Eighteenth Amendment was repealed (Mr. Dowdey seems to forget that there was little pretense of "legality" in the frequenting of bootleggers and speakeasies), so will the South effectively evade mixed education. And quite properly, says Mr. Dowdey.

For the South has "painfully evolved" over the years "two parallel societies"; "the normal environment of the white child is white and the normal environment of the colored child is colored." Hence, any effort to destroy or even dent this allegedly "normal" duality—by having kids with different skins sit in the same classroom—might lead to "chaos." And all this is something that no Northerner can ever understand because the proportion of Negroes in the North is so much smaller that there is no real Negro problem; moreover, Northerners hypocritically embrace more subtle forms of segregation—Harlem, the Black Belt of Chicago, and New Yorkers who send their children to private schools or move to the suburbs.

Indeed, Mr. Dowdey's dissertation in defense of the South is so redolent of a not-always-muted antagonism to the North that it is often strangely reminiscent of a somewhat similar screed penned by another Southerner not quite a hundred years ago. Mr. Dowdey notes the proclivity of the Northerner to "preen himself on his abstract humanity"; he says he envies "this luxury of self-approbation"; he refers to "the pious hosannas uttered by Northern politicians in the name of democracy." He also indulges in paragraph after paragraph of embittered and mostly ancient history in which he blames the Negro's unhappy plight almost wholly on the North—from the

days of the New England slavetraders, on through absentee aboli-
tionism and war-bred emancipation and ruthless reconstruction,
right up to the white-supremacy politics Mr. Dowdey claims is the
North's fault too. He does not use the word "damyankee," but he
might as well have used it. As might that other Southerner of a century past, whose name was, of course, Roger Brooke Taney, and
whose Dred Scott opinion reveled as gleefully in derogation of the
North as it roared in defense of slavery.

This is not to say that Mr. Dowdey is wrong in the factual details
of his historical survey or even in his jaundiced eying of the motives
of most Northern reformers-of-the-South, from Abraham Lincoln to
Chief Justice Warren. There is no doubt that the Emancipation Proclamation was more a military than a humanitarian measure; nor that
post-Civil-War "reconstruction"—civil rights laws, Fourteenth
Amendment, and all—really meant political and commercial sub-
jugation of the South; nor that millions of non-Southerners cluckingly
deplore the South's public policy of segregation while practising it
privately themselves. There is no doubt that world politics, as reflected in the wish to take a telling talking-point away from Russia,
played a major part, just as Mr. Dowdey says it did, in the Supreme
Court's decision outlawing "separate but equal" public schools; nor
is there any doubt that this reversal of the Court's own error of almost fifty years before (as Mr. Dowdey conspicuously does not say)
required but little courage on the part of the Justices—who were
merely doing, rather late, what both the Republican and Democratic
Parties outside the South were officially on record as wanting done.

But Mr. Dowdey's history, though not technically inaccurate, is so
self-defensively, or South-defensively, selective—as in its complete
omission of the South's own financial exploitation and social degradation of the Negro for over a century and a half—that it verges
on historical fantasy. To read it you might suppose, if otherwise un-
informed, that Southern whites had never treated their colored
compatriots any less than handsomely—or at least as handsomely as
those colored folk deserve. And here, of course, is the clear center
of the gigantic blind-spot, the inarticulate major premise, the area of
undebate, that makes inevitably superficial whatever else a traditional Southerner may say about the Negro. Bluntly and simply, the
traditional Southerner does not and will not consider any man of
African ancestry a full-fledged human being.

Listen to Mr. Dowdey as, for all his even-tempered talk, the slip
of his patronizing contempt keeps showing. "The educated South-

erner . . . has always related to the Negro as a servant in his home . . ." During depression "the Negro was merely one of his [the Southern white's] multiple and at times insoluble problems . . ." (not a person; "merely" a problem). "There is a most encouraging development among Negro leaders themselves—in education, law, medicine, business . . ." (note the subtle semantics by which only Negro "leaders" achieve anything—and guess whether Mr. Dowdey would similarly have specified "white leaders"). Finally: "In a fashionable new [Richmond] suburb of highly-privileged people there is a small community of colored people who subsist largely as houseservants for the neighborhood. There is no possibility that the county school of this district, preparing students for Princeton and Vassar, will open its doors to mixed classes." And a pity that it will not—for these "highly-privileged" boys and girls, kept clean of contamination up to college, may be rudely surprised to find themselves sitting in mixed classes at Princeton or Vassar, or at Yale or Harvard or Smith or Wellesley or Siwash.

Mr. Dowdey does not go so far as did some of his sectional antecedents who, in parts of the South before the Civil War, made it a crime to teach a Negro to read and write. But his notions about Negro education, some tacit, some openly expressed, tend uncomfortably in the same direction. He is shocked at the notion of Negro teachers for white students (or even *vice versa*); he is baffled by the problem, posed almost rhetorically as if there were no acceptable answer: "Who is to teach the mixed school?" And he ties it all up with the tender comment that "the Negro, through no fault of his own, is less well prepared at home for the advantages of school education."

Why is he less well prepared, Mr. Dowdey, and whose "fault" might it be? And will the next generation of Negro children be any better "prepared at home" if *their* parents, going to school *now*, are relegated, as you would have them, to what you deem to be a comparatively second-rate education in separate schools in which no foot is set by white teachers or white fellow students—both of these groups already blessed with superior home or formal training on account of their skins, not their innate mental capacities? It is a pretty little circle of white supremacy in education that you describe and that you would have go on presumably forever: colored children denied mixed schools because they are less well readied at home, because their parents have been past victims of identical segregation —as will be, by similar logic, their children and grandchildren and great-grandchildren. "Is the Southern white child, then," you ask, "to be retarded in his own school education by the inclusion of less well-prepared students?" And echo answers in a Southern accent: "Nevah, unto the *n*th generation."

Mr. Dowdey may, with some warrant, twit the North about its holier-than-thou attitude toward the South so far as some aspects of segregation, such as housing, are concerned; but few if any Northerners would defend as he does a deliberate policy of perpetual discrimination in the matter of schooling, especially public schooling, coldly and callously aimed against colored children. Almost everywhere in the North Negro and white school kids sit at adjoining desks, and laugh and play together at recess, oblivious of their shades of pigmentation. And they learn enough too, despite Mr. Dowdey's alleged intellectual drag of the Negroes on the whites, to get into college with a somewhat greater degree of success than do their white contemporaries from the segregated schools of the South.

Nor can Mr. Dowdey retort that mixed schools work in the North only because there is but one colored student to five or ten or twenty white ones. In New Haven, as in many Northern communities, there are public schools where the colored enrolment equals or exceeds the white enrolment—and where children of Yale faculty members study beside children of Yale janitors, colored and white, and come out better educated, and better citizens, for it. If Mr. Dowdey has read the papers recently, he must realize, to his probable discomfiture, that newly mixed schools are beginning to work here and there in the South too, from Washington, D. C., to Corpus Christi, Texas. Indeed, the rising rebelliousness against de-segregation in most of the South—from the plans to change laws or constitutions and the silly we-won't-play boycott of further Supreme Court hearings, threatened by several Southern states, to the sporadic Ku-Klux-like local incidents—all comes, not from the schoolchildren who are going to do the mixing but from that majority of white Southern adults, be they professional politicians or less publicized protestants, who are, unfortunately, more grown up as grown-upness is reckoned in years than measured by maturity of heart and mind.

The crux of the matter is the stark fact that it is the Southern adults, the supposedly wiser oldsters, who keep the un-Christian cross of discrimination ablaze—from segregated schools to occasional open violence. Children are born colorblind, so far as prejudice is concerned; a dark skin means no more to a white child than does dark hair to a blond child. South or North, only the insidious insistence of their elders that the difference is more than skin deep ever implants in the minds of the young the seeds of an assumed superiority. And even then the seeds sprout slowly, and take tenuous root.

There is not on record one single Southern community where white children have rebelled at, or so much as mildly resisted, going to school with their Negro neighbors—except at adult instigation. When the Supreme Court, in an earlier and narrower decision a couple of years back, ordered Negroes admitted to some Southern universities the Cassandras of everything from social ostracism to racial conflict were confounded by the white students' easy acceptance, indeed their warm welcoming, of the Negroes newly in their midst. And Southern boys who fought in World War II or in Korea developed a healthy respect for the essential equality of their colored and unsegregated comrades-in-arms on every level from intelligence to courage.

Even though it be today "normal," as Mr. Dowdey says it is, for white people and colored people to live apart—thanks to the hammering into children's heads, down the generations, of the nonsense that Negroes are, by nature, different and inferior beings—nevertheless, only by a naked *non sequitur* does it follow, as Mr. Dowdey says it follows, that because their families live apart colored and white children should learn apart. By learning together they might, as in many parts of the North, come in time to live together—in the same sections, the same blocks, the same apartment- or rooming-houses. But this indiscriminate intermingling is, of course, what Mr. Dowdey and his kind fear most.

And "fear" is the proper word. Although discrimination against the Negro in the South originally began as a by-product of financial greed—as a way of getting and keeping dirt-cheap labor to support Southern gentlemen and ladies among their mansions and magnolias—and although the cheap-labor incentive is, on a slightly different legal level, still rampant today—the emphasis of discrimination has shifted from money to emotions. You do not argue with a traditional Southerner about the Negro simply because his feeling of superiority to the colored man is unhappily essential to his own sense of self-respect. The fear is not of the Negroes rising *en masse* or raping at random white womanhood. It is the more gnawing type of fear that stems from self-doubt and inner insecurity, and so must seek a scapegoat, a someone-not-so-good-as-I-am, in order to create, by contrast, a synthetic approval of and pride in oneself. Emotionally mature Southern whites—and they are on the steady increase—do not need to bolster their egos at the expense of the Negro and do not favor segregation in public schools.

Eventually, for all the fear-bred resentment and rebellion, the separate schools of the South will go. The Supreme Court's long-belated decision—even though, after the initial ringing declaration, it will doubtless be supplemented and put into practical effect by the Justices gradually and gingerly—will still stand as a major step toward setting the Negro really free. Meanwhile, the kind of education most sorely needed in the South will remain, not the education of colored children in a civilized fashion, but the education of white adults in the brand of inner strength that breeds humility and true humanity—unsegregated.

QUESTIONS ON CONTENT

1. Does the second turn in a debate have its advantages? How possibly might Mr. Dowdey ("A Southerner Looks at the Supreme Court") have used an opportunity for rebuttal?
2. What is the purpose of paragraph 1?
3. Does the author offer a fair and complete summary of "A Southerner Looks at the Supreme Court"?
4. Which author, Mr. Dowdey or Mr. Rodell, writes with the greater animus? Or is it a draw in this respect? Cite passages to prove your contention.
5. Comment on this statement: "Bluntly and simply, the traditional Southerner does not and will not consider any man of African ancestry a full-fledged human being." What is the "flavor" of the word "traditional" in this sentence? Is there also a "traditional Northerner"? If so, how would you describe him?
6. What is the central idea? Is it logically sustained?

SUGGESTIONS FOR PAPERS

It is not difficult to face the theoretical problem of race prejudice. It is not easy, however, to face or clearly to understand the practical, personal problem. Nevertheless, every person is responsible for his own thinking and feeling on this subject. You can contribute to your own mental and moral growth by setting down on paper the reasons you have for thinking, feeling, and acting as you do toward Negroes.

1. If you belong to a church, write your paper on your church and its attitude toward Negroes. What is the *theory* of your church about Negroes? What is its *practice?* If theory and practice are not in harmony, what is the excuse for the practice? What would *you* have the practice be?

2. What is the attitude of your college toward Negroes? Is your college's policy set by state law? Or by church law? Or by registration procedures? Would you welcome Negroes as fellow students with all the social, athletic, and fraternal rights appertaining thereto?

3. What limits are placed upon Negroes in your community? Is there any sort of segregation, by Jim Crowism or by less obvious means? List all the forms of segregation of which you are aware. How many of these forms, if any, would you have abolished?

4. Do you believe that race prejudice is a national, not a purely Southern problem? If so, show how prejudice differs in the North and the South. Take into consideration the different forms of segregation, opportunity for education, jobs, social equality and the like.

5. What do you consider to be the most encouraging signs of progress in reducing race prejudice? The Supreme Court decisions which will require equal, unsegregated education for whites and Negroes? The breakdown of the barriers in athletics? Legislation which forbids discrimination in employment? Choose the evidence of progress which seems most far-reaching and significant to you and build your paper toward this as a climax. For example, you will briefly discuss this point, and then this one and this one—all signs of progress—but *this one* is most heartening of all.

6. Write your paper on athletics and race prejudice. Is the degree of prejudice dependent somewhat upon whether or not contact or noncontact sports are involved? Consider track. But what about tennis and golf? Consider football. But what about boxing? And baseball? Is baseball a "semicontact" sport? Is the problem solved in all organized baseball?

7. Define the word *prejudice*. Now, examine closely your personal thoughts and feelings toward Negroes. Are you prejudiced? You may want to check through the following questions: Do you think Negroes should vote? Hold public office? Be members of your church? Live next door? Work as a fellow employee? Be equal members in your fraternity or sorority? Marry into your family?

8. Does your prejudice, if any, extend to other groups of people besides Negroes? Using the list of questions at the end of suggestion

7, jot down an explanation of your reactions to some of the following races or nationals: British, Russians, Jews, Japanese, Germans, Mexicans, Italians, Chinese, Koreans, Poles, French. Choose for discussion only those groups which produce a strong response in you.

9. Prejudice shows up in many forms. Can you isolate a set of your prejudices? Can you "explain" how you acquired each prejudice? A reasonable dislike is not prejudice. Is your response to the items in the following list reasonable or otherwise? (1) southern cooking; (2) Koreans; (3) fellow travelers; (4) Richard Nixon; (5) Roman Catholic; (6) K.K.K.; (7) states' rights; (8) hillbilly music; (9) Shakespeare; (10) Dixiecrats; (11) Fair Deal; (12) Protestant; (13) whisky; (14) dancing; (15) sanity code (athletics); (16) Jews; (17) the Pope; (18) United Nations; (19) poetry; (20) atom bomb.

10. Analyze any one of the articles (or the ballad) in this chapter. (I Central point of the article and how it is sustained; II Arguments for or against or for and against this central point; III My point of view and why.)

11. Act as debate judge in the argument between Mr. Dowdey ("A Southerner Looks at the Supreme Court") and Mr. Rodell ("School Kids Are Color Blind"). (I Points made by Mr. Dowdey; II Appraisal of these points; III Points made by Mr. Rodell; IV Appraisal of these points; V The winner of the debate and why.)

SOME TITLES FOR PAPERS

1. Am I Prejudiced?
2. My Church and Segregation
3. My College and the Negro
4. The Negro in My Community
5. I Know Mr. and Mrs. Massa
6. Racial Tolerance Has Taken Great Strides
7. The Negro Athlete: How He Fares
8. Race Prejudice in the North
9. Race Prejudice in the South
10. The Problem of Intermarriage
11. White Supremacy as a Political Issue
12. Negroes Aren't the Only Victims of Prejudice
13. The Absurdity of Jim Crow Laws
14. I Search out My Prejudices
15. Anti-prejudice Can Be as Bad as Prejudice
16. Minority Tyranny

❧ *THE MEANING OF FREEDOM*

BECAUSE FREEDOM IS ONE of Man's noblest conceptions, it is not difficult to find noble utterances on the subject. Because freedom is never completely won but always in process of being won, it is a valuable discipline to think through for oneself the essential applied meaning of the word. Aid to this sort of thinking is provided in the selections of this chapter.

Throughout history freedom has had its isolated champions. One of the first of these was Socrates. Under threat of death, he refused to violate his intellectual honor. All the pressures of official Athens, of frightened little men who feared the keen assaults of Socrates on their secure little beliefs, could not force a change in the heroically stubborn old man. He accepted death but would not accept mental slavery.

For two thousand years after Socrates, freedom had its isolated voices which became a slowly augmented chorus as the centuries wore on. In mid-seventeenth century, Milton applied his great mind to the problem of a free press and, since all freedoms are interlaced, enunciated the classic requirement for freedom: freedom of choice. When choice is lacking, freedom is lacking.

Practical tests are needed for the ideas of Socrates and Milton.

One test involves the limit of freedom for teachers. Two clear and astute articles, both models of argument, present the case against communist teachers in college (Professor Sidney Hook) and the case for allowing such teachers in college (Dr. Alexander Meiklejohn). H. L. Mencken's "In Tennessee" is a right-wing attack on the pretensions of teachers who argue for academic freedom in the face of community opposition.

The final article, "The Mummification of Opinion" by Senator Fulbright, highlights a danger which confronts not only teachers but all citizens: the freezing of opinion when it becomes dangerous to speak or act as an individual.

❧ *"The Unexamined Life Is Not Worth Living"*

SOCRATES

[Socrates, charged with disbelief in the gods and with corrupting the youth of Athens, is on trial for his life. In the following passage he explains his code of intellectual integrity.]

Some one will say: And are you not ashamed, Socrates, of a course of life which is likely to bring you to an untimely end? To him I may fairly answer: There you are mistaken: a man who is good for anything ought not to calculate the chance of living or dying; he ought only to consider whether in doing anything he is doing right or wrong—acting the part of a good man or of a bad. . . . For wherever a man's place is, whether the place which he has chosen or that in which he has been placed by a commander, there he ought to remain in the hour of danger; he should not think of death or of anything but of disgrace. And this, O men of Athens, is a true saying.

Strange, indeed, would be my conduct, O men of Athens, if I who, when I was ordered by the generals whom you chose to command me at Potidaea and Amphipolis and Delium, remained where they placed me, like any other man, facing death—if now, when, as I conceive and imagine, God orders me to fulfil the philosopher's mission of searching into myself and other men, I were to desert my post

Taken from the *Apology* in *Dialogues of Plato* translated into English by Benjamin Jowett, Oxford University Press.

through fear of death, or any other fear; that would indeed be strange, and I might justly be arraigned in court for denying the existence of the gods, if I disobeyed the oracle because I was afraid of death, fancying that I was wise when I was not wise. For the fear of death is indeed the pretense of wisdom, and not real wisdom, being a pretense of knowing the unknown; and no one knows whether death, which men in their fear apprehend to be the greatest evil, may not be the greatest good. Is not this ignorance of a disgraceful sort, the ignorance which is the conceit that a man knows what he does not know? And in this respect only I believe myself to differ from men in general, and may perhaps claim to be wiser than they are:—that whereas I know but little of the world below, I do not suppose that I know; but I do know that injustice and disobedience to a better, whether God or man, is evil and dishonorable, and I will never fear or avoid a possible good rather than a certain evil. And therefore if you let me go now, and are not convinced by Anytus, who said that since I had been prosecuted I must be put to death (or if not that I ought never to have been prosecuted at all); and that if I escape now, your sons will all be utterly ruined by listening to my words—if you say to me, Socrates, this time we will not mind Anytus, and you shall be let off, but upon one condition, that you are not to enquire and speculate in this way any more, and that if you are caught doing so again you shall die;—if this was the condition on which you let me go, I should reply: Men of Athens, I honor and love you; but I shall obey God rather than you, and while I have life and strength I shall never cease from the practice and teaching of philosophy, exhorting anyone whom I meet and saying to him after my manner: You, my friend,—a citizen of the great and mighty and wise city of Athens,—are you not ashamed of heaping up the greatest amount of money and honor and reputation, and caring so little about wisdom and truth and the greatest improvement of the soul, which you never regard or heed at all? And if the person with whom I am arguing, says: Yes, but I do care; then I do not leave him or let him go at once; but I proceed to interrogate and examine and cross-examine him, and if I think that he has no virtue in him, but only says that he has, I reproach him with undervaluing the greater, and over-valuing the less. And I shall repeat the same words to everyone whom I meet, young and old, citizen and alien, but especially to the citizens, inasmuch as they are my brethren. For know that this is the command of God; and I believe that no greater good has ever happened in the state than my service to the God. For

I do nothing but go about persuading you all, old and young alike, not to take thought for your persons or your properties, but first and chiefly to care about the greatest improvement of the soul. I tell you that virtue is not given by money, but that from virtue comes money and every other good of man, public as well as private. This is my teaching, and if this is the doctrine which corrupts the youth, I am a mischievous person. But if anyone says that this is not my teaching, he is speaking an untruth. Wherefore, O men of Athens, I say to you, do as Anytus bids or not as Anytus bids, and either acquit me or not; but whichever you do, understand that I shall never alter my ways, not even if I have to die many times.

Men of Athens, do not interrupt, but hear me; there was an understanding between us that you should hear me to the end: I have something more to say, at which you may be inclined to cry out; but I believe that to hear me will be good for you, and therefore I beg that you will not cry out. I would have you know, that if you kill such an one as I am, you will injure yourselves more than you will injure me. Nothing will injure me, not Meletus nor yet Anytus—they cannot, for a bad man is not permitted to injure a better than himself. I do not deny that Anytus may, perhaps, kill him, or drive him into exile, or deprive him of civil rights; and he may imagine, and others may imagine, that he is inflicting a great injury upon him: but there I do not agree. For the evil of doing as he is doing—the evil of unjustly taking away the life of another—is greatest far.

And now, Athenians, I am not going to argue for my own sake, as you may think, but for yours, that you may not sin against the God by condemning me, who am his gift to you. For if you kill me you will not easily find a successor to me, who, if I may use such a ludicrous figure of speech, am a sort of gadfly, given to the state by God; and the state is a great and noble steed who is tardy in his motions owing to his very size, and requires to be stirred into life. I am that gadfly which God has attached to the state, and all day long and in all places am always fastening upon you, arousing and persuading and reproaching you. You will not easily find another like me, and therefore I would advise you to spare me. I dare say that you may feel out of temper (like a person who is suddenly awakened from sleep), and you think that you might easily strike me dead as Anytus advises, and then you would sleep on for the remainder of your lives, unless God in his care of you sent you another gadfly. When I say that I am given to you by God, the proof of my mission is this:—if I had been like other men, I should have not neglected all my own concerns or patiently seen the neglect of them during all these years,

and have been doing yours, coming to you individually like a father
or elder brother, exhorting you to regard virtue: such conduct, I say,
would be unlike human nature. If I had gained anything, or if my
exhortations had been paid, there would have been some sense in my
doing so; but now, as you will perceive, not even the impudence of
my accusers dares to say that I have ever exacted or sought pay of
any one; of that they have no witness. And I have a sufficient witness to the truth of what I say—my poverty.

QUESTIONS ON CONTENT

1. How does the first paragraph make clear that *discipline* is part
   of Socrates's conception of freedom? What two kinds of discipline are implied in the words: "whether the place which he
   has chosen or that in which he has been placed by a commander"?
2. What is "the philosopher's mission"?
3. What is an *oracle?*
4. Why is fear of death "a pretense of wisdom"?
5. To what does Socrates refer as "the world below"?
6. Comment on Anytus's idea that since Socrates had been prosecuted, he should be put to death.
7. Is it clear why Socrates was unpopular with Athenian citizens?
   Explain.
8. At what points does this speech of Socrates seem to be almost a
   stenographic transcription of what he said?
9. "A bad man is not permitted to injure a better than himself."
   Explain.
10. What is Socrates's conception of his function in society? How
    does he make vivid this conception?
11. How does he prove that he is God-appointed to his function?

❧ *Freedom to Choose*

JOHN MILTON

Good and evil we know in the field of this world grow up together
almost inseparably; and the knowledge of good is so involved and
interwoven with the knowledge of evil, and in so many cunning

From *Areopagitica* (1644).

resemblances hardly to be discerned, that those confused seeds which were imposed upon Psyche as an incessant labor to cull out, and sort asunder, were not more intermixed. It was from out the rind of one apple tasted that the knowledge of good and evil, as two twins cleaving together, leaped forth into the world. And perhaps this is that doom which Adam fell into of knowing good and evil, that is to say, of knowing good by evil.

As, therefore, the state of man now is, what wisdom can there be to choose, what continence to forbear, without the knowledge of evil? He that can apprehend and consider vice with all her baits and seeming pleasures, and yet abstain, and yet distinguish, and yet prefer that which is truly better, he is the true wayfaring Christian. I cannot praise a fugitive and cloistered virtue, inexercised and unbreathed, that never sallies out and sees her adversary, but slinks out of the race, where that immortal garland is to be run for, not without dust and heat. Assuredly we bring not innocence into the world; we bring impurity much rather; that which purifies us is trial, and trial is by what is contrary. That virtue, therefore, which is but a youngling in the contemplation of evil, and knows not the utmost that vice promises to her followers, and rejects it, is but a blank virtue, not a pure; her whiteness is but an excremental [superficial] whiteness, which was the reason why our sage and serious poet Spenser, whom I dare be known to think a better teacher than Scotus or Aquinas, describing true temperance under the person of Guion, brings him in with his palmer through the cave of Mammon, and the bower of earthly bliss, that he might see and know, and yet abstain.

Since, therefore, the knowledge and survey of vice is in this world so necessary to the constituting of human virtue, and the scanning of error to the confirmation of truth, how can we more safely, and with less danger, scout into the regions of sin and falsity than by reading all manner of tractates and hearing all manner of reason? And this is the benefit which may be had of books promiscuously read.

QUESTIONS ON CONTENT

1. Your instructor may ask for individual reports on (1) Psyche and the confused seeds; (2) Scotus; (3) Aquinas; (4) Spenser; (5) Guion's adventure in the Cave of Mammon (*Faerie Queene*, 2:7); (6) Guion's adventure in the Bower of Bliss (*Faerie Queene*, 2:12).

2. To what apple does Milton refer in the second sentence?
3. Explain the phrase "knowing good *by* evil."
4. How does Milton define "the true wayfaring Christian"?
5. Summarize Milton's argument as it applies to prohibition of evil.
6. Milton was a strong Protestant largely on the grounds that he assumed the rights of men in choosing a way of life without intervention on the part of a ritualistic church. Do present-day Protestant churches hold to the Miltonic tradition? Do they advocate that their members abstain before tasting or after tasting? Are they in general advocates of prohibitions and censorships?
7. Discuss the matter of choice as the essence of freedom. Is freedom to think and act as everyone else does genuine freedom? What, for example, would a test of freedom in the realm of politics be in the states of Vermont and South Carolina? Cite other possible tests of freedom.
8. Is freedom to make a *wrong* decision or choice a basic tenet of true freedom? Explain.

Should Communists Be Permitted to Teach?

SIDNEY HOOK

The academic community throughout the United States is currently being disturbed by the perennial issue of the nature and limits of academic freedom. The specific event which has precipitated intense interest and discussion, not only in college classrooms but in all circles interested in education, is the expulsion of some professors from the University of Washington for being members of the Communist party. The arresting thing about this case is that for the first time in the history of education the grounds given for the expulsion of the professors is that *they* have been guilty of violating the principles of academic freedom, and therefore of "conduct unbecoming a teacher."

Here is certainly a startling reversal which reflects the emergence of new problems in culture and education not dreamed of when

Reprinted from *The New York Times Magazine,* February 27, 1949, by permission of *The New York Times* and Mr. Hook.

John Dewey and Arthur T. Lovejoy organized the American Association of University Professors to further the interests of their profession and defend academic freedom and tenure.

Because the decision may set an important precedent in higher education, it invites a reconsideration of first principles in the light of the facts.

If, as Cardinal Newman has observed, the function of a university is the discovery and publication of the truth in all branches of knowledge, then academic freedom is essential to its very life. For without the freedom to inquire, to challenge and to doubt, truth cannot be well-grounded or error refuted. Since not everything which has been accepted is true, nor everything which is newly proposed is false, the result of inquiry sometimes undermines the customary and supports the novel. When this takes place in non-controversial areas, it is recognized as the natural operation of the discipline of scientific inquiry; when it affects controversial issues, vested interests and emotions are often aroused and attempts are made to safeguard some special doctrine and conclusion from the consequences of critical scrutiny.

Anything may be regarded as a controversial subject, from the heliocentric hypothesis and the theory of evolution to the causes of World War II and the wisdom of the Marshall Plan. That is why universities from the time of their origin have been compelled to fight the battle for academic freedom over and over again. Although in the West, in matters of pure science, there are no longer powerful special interests that can be outraged by the progress of inquiry, in the social studies, arts and philosophy, convictions are not so clearly a function of evidence. Conclusions in these fields touch on issues of contemporary political or social concern in relation to which almost everyone believes he is something of an authority. One man's truth is often another man's propaganda.

None the less no distinction in principle can be drawn between non-controversial and controversial themes, especially if we recognize that all human judgments are fallible. The presumption is that university professors engaged in the search for truth are qualified by their professional competence. The judges of their competence can only be their intellectual peers or betters in their own fields. If this is denied, the university loses its *raison d'etre* as an institution, not only for free research but critical teaching.

In consequence, any doctrinal impositions, no matter what their source, which set up limits beyond which the professor cannot go, affect him both as a scholar and a teacher. As a scholar, he loses professional standing in the intellectual community if it is suspected that his findings must fit the predetermined conclusions and prejudices of those whose first loyalty is not to the objective methods of seeking the truth. As a teacher, he cannot engage in the honest presentation and reasoned investigation of all relevant *alternatives* to the theories and policies he is considering. He runs the risk of forfeiting the respect of his students, who look to him for candid evaluation and intellectual stimulus, if they believe that he is time-serving or prudent beyond the call of scientific evidence.

If in the honest exercise of his academic freedom an individual reaches views which bring down about his head charges of "Communist," "Fascist," or what not, the academic community is duty bound to protect him irrespective of the truth of the charges. And since these words are often epithets of disparagement rather than of precise description, there is all the more reason why the university must stand firm. It places its faith in the loyalty of its teachers to the ethics and logic of scientific inquiry. The heresies of yesterday are often the orthodoxies of today. In the interests of winning new truths, it is better to err on the side of toleration than of proscription.

This means that the professor occupies a position of trust not only in relation to the university and his students, but to the democratic community which places its faith and hope in the processes of education. ("If a nation expects to be ignorant and free, in a state of civilization," wrote Jefferson, "it expects what never was and what never will be.") Academic freedom therefore carries with it duties correlative with rights. No professor can violate them under the pretext that he is exercising his freedom. That is why the graduate faculty of the New School of Social Research explicitly declares that in the interests of academic freedom, "no member of the faculty can be a member of any political party or group which asserts the right to dictate in matters of science or scientific opinion."

So far the analysis of principles can take us. There remains the important question of fact. Is a member of the Communist party, so long as he remains a member, free to exercise his rights and fulfill his duties as an objective scholar and teacher? To answer this question we must look at what the Communist party itself teaches, its conditions of membership, and what has come to light about the actual behavior of known members of the Communist party. We are not dealing now with the right to hold Communist *beliefs* but with what is entailed by the *act* of membership in the Community party as it affects educational practice.

First of all, it is important to recognize that there are no "sleepers" or passive members of the Communist party. The statutes of membership define a party member as one who not only "accepts the party program, attends the regular meetings of the membership branch of his place of work" but "who is *active* in party work." Inactivity as well as disagreement with the decisions of any party organization or committee are grounds for expulsion. The concluding sentence of the pledge which the member inducted into the Communist party takes since 1935 reads: "I pledge myself to remain at all times a vigilant and firm defender of the Leninist line of the party, the only line that insures the triumph of Soviet power in the United States." (*Daily Worker*, April 2, 1936.)

The "place of work" of the Communist party teacher is the school or university. How is a Communist party member active in party work at the university? Here are some directives from the official organ of the Communist party (*The Communist*, May, 1937):

"Party and Y. C. L. fractions set up within classes and departments must supplement and combat by means of discussions, brochures, etc., bourgeois omissions and distortions in the regular curriculum. *Marxist-Leninist analysis must be injected into every class.*

"Communist teachers must take advantage of their positions, without exposing themselves, to give their students to the best of their ability working-class education.

"To enable the teachers in the party to do the latter, the party must take careful steps to see that all teacher comrades are given thorough education in the teaching of Marxism-Leninism. Only when teachers have really mastered Marxism-Leninism will they be able skillfully to inject it into their teaching at the least risk of exposure and at the same time conduct struggles around the schools in a truly Bolshevik manner."

Two things are significant here. The first is the injunction to cooperate with Communist party fractions among students in order—I am still quoting from official sources—"*to guide and direct that spirit of rebelliousness which already exists.*" The practice, many years ago, was to organize Communist students and teachers in the same cells, but since this led to exposure when students dropped out, teachers and students are now separately organized and meet only through carefully selected committees.

The second noteworthy thing is that the Communist party teachers are fearful of exposure and quite aware that their practices violate accepted notions of academic freedom and responsibility. That is why when literature appears under their imprint it is anonymous. Since no one takes personal responsibility, what is said about things and persons, including non-Communist colleagues, is not likely to be scrupulous or accurate. Sometimes it is downright scurrilous.

How is it possible for the Communist party to control the thinking of its members who teach in so many different fields? What have literature, philosophy, science and mathematics got to do with its political program? The answer is to be found in the fact that according to the Communist party itself politics is bound up, through the class struggle, with every field of knowledge. On the basis of its philosophy of dialectical materialism, a party line is laid down for every area of thought from art to zoology. No person who is known to hold a view incompatible with the party line is accepted as a member. For example, if he is a historian he cannot become a member if he teaches that the economic factor is not the most decisive factor in history or, if a political scientist, that the state is not the executive committee of the ruling class or that the Soviet Union is not a democracy. Individuals have been denied membership in the Communist party because they did not believe in "dialectics" in nature.

If a philosopher, to cite cases from my own field, accepts the theories of Mach or Carnap or Husserl or Alexander or Dewey or T. H. Green or G. E. Moore, upon joining the Communist party he will criticize the doctrines he had espoused previously. He cannot ever criticize dialectical materialism or the theories of Lenin and Stalin whom he now regards as great philosophers. If a physicist or mathematician becomes a member of the Communist party he is required, wherever it is possible for him to do so, to relate his subject to the growth of technology, its impact upon social divisions, the class uses to which discovery is put, and the liberating role it can play in a Communist economy. The general theme is: science under capitalism makes for death and poverty; under communism, science makes for life and abundance.

The party line, however, is not constant in all fields. It changes with political exigencies. The life of a Communist party teacher, therefore, is not a happy one, since he may have to prove the opposite of what he once so fervently taught. His difficulties are mitigated by the fact that in different terms he faces different students whose memories are apt to be short in any event. But English teachers who have been members of the Communist party during the last few years have had to reverse their judgments about the same novelists, and sometimes even about the same books, e. g. Malraux's "Man's Fate," Dos Passos' "U.S.A.," Wright's "Native Son," because of changes in the party line toward these authors.

In the social sciences Communist party teachers taught in 1934 that Roosevelt was a Fascist; in 1936, during the Popular Front, a progressive; in 1940, during the Nazi-Stalin Pact, a warmonger and imperialist; in 1941, after Hitler invaded the Soviet Union, a leader of the oppressed peoples of the world.

Whether with respect to specific issues Communist teachers have been right or wrong in these kaleidoscopic changes is not the relevant question. What is relevant is that their conclusions are not reached by a free inquiry into the evidence. To stay in the Communist party, they must believe and teach what the party line decrees. If anyone doubts this we have the objective evidence provided by Granville Hicks in his public letter of resignation from the Communist party. Hicks resigned because he was refused even the right to *suspend judgment* on the Nazi-Stalin pact. "If the party," he writes, "had left any room for doubt, I could go along with it. . . . But they made it clear that if I eventually found it impossible to defend the pact, and defend it in their terms, there was nothing for me to do but resign." (*New Republic,* Oct. 4, 1939.)

It is argued by some civil libertarians, who are prepared to grant the foregoing, that this is still not sufficient evidence to impugn the integrity of teachers who are members of the Communist party. They must be judged by their individual actions in the classroom; they must, so to speak, be "caught in the act" of inculcating the party line in the minds of their students.

This has two fatal difficulties. It would require spying in every classroom to detect the party line, and disorganize or intimidate not only Communist party members but the entire faculty, since a member of the Communist party admits membership only when faced with a charge of perjury, and not always then. The academic community would wrathfully and rightfully repudiate any such practice.

Second, it would be very difficult to determine when a teacher was defending a conclusion because he honestly believed it followed from the evidence, and when he was carrying out his task as a good soldier in the party cause.

Those who contend that membership in the Communist party is *prima facie* evidence that a teacher does not believe in or practice academic freedom, insist that such membership is an *act*, not merely an expression of opinion. They deny that they are invoking the principle of guilt by association, for no one who joins and remains a member of the Communist party could be ignorant of what classroom practices are required of him. If he were ignorant, the Communist party itself would drop him for "inactivity."

It is interesting to note that this position is independent of the questions whether a teacher has a right to be a member of a legal party or whether the Communist party is or should be a legal organization. Paraphrasing Justice Holmes' famous remark about the Boston policeman, a man may have a constitutional right to be a member of the Communist party but he has no constitutional right to be a college professor unless he is free to accept the duties as well as rights of academic freedom. Anyone is free to join or leave the Communist party: but once he joins and remains a member, he is not a free mind.

Some administrative authorities have taken the position that they would not knowingly engage members of the Communist party, otherwise thought competent, but that they would not discharge them after they discovered the fact of their membership. This is obviously inconsistent. The reason which explains their reluctance to take on a member of the Communist party, if valid, still operates when he has already joined the faculty. If on educational grounds a Communist party member is objectionable *before* he has begun working for the party line, is he any less objectionable when he is actually in action? If anything, a person, known from the very outset as a member of the Communist party, may be assigned to a post where he can do far less damage than someone who has successfully concealed the fact of his membership.

There remains the question as to whether expulsion on grounds of membership in the Communist party does not set a dangerous precedent. Communists under fire in a sudden accession of concern for Catholics, express fear lest this threaten the tenure of teachers who are members of the Catholic Church.

As one who cannot be taxed with undue sympathy for Thomist doctrine, I should maintain there is no evidence whatsoever of the operation of Catholic cells in nonsectarian universities which impose a party line in all the arts and sciences that must be followed by all Catholic teachers on pain of excommunication. The comparison is a red herring. The danger to free inquiry in education from Catholic quarters comes not from teachers but from outside pressure groups.

If any other organization exists which operates like the Communist party, its members should be treated equitably with the members of the Communist party. Members of the Nazi party were under similar discipline. But in their case, before and after the Stalin-Hitler alliance, the Communists demanded their peremptory dismissal.

The problem of the *"fellow-traveler"* is even a more difficult and involved question. But its solution, paradoxical as it may appear, is simple. It must be left entirely to the enlightened good sense of the academic community, which can apply various sanctions short of dismissal. The term "fellow-traveler" is hopelessly vague. "Fellow-travelers" come and go. They are of all varieties. No one is wise enough to pick out the dumb, innocent sheep from the cunning and dishonest goats. So long as they are not under the discipline of the Communist party, they may still be sensitive to the results of honest inquiry. Whatever harm they do is incomparably less than the harm that would result from any attempt to purge them. Without the steel core of the Communist party fraction on the campus to magnetize them, they will fly off in all the directions their scattered wits take them.

Although the exclusion of Communist party teachers from the academic community seems justified in *principle,* this by itself does not determine whether it is a wise or prudent action in *all* circumstances. Sometimes the consequences of removing an unmitigated evil may be such as to make its sufferance preferable. If removal of Communist party members were to be used by other reactionary elements as a pretext to hurl irresponsible charges against professors whose views they disapprove, a case might be made for suspending action. On the other hand, failure to act in a situation where the academic process has been flagrantly suborned may lead to public suspicion and reprisals that injure innocent and guilty alike.

How to protect the innocent, as well as those who have genuinely broken with the Communist party, from dangers attending a policy justified in principle is too large a theme to explore here. But I am confident that *if the execution of the policy were left to university faculties themselves,* and not to administrators and trustees who are harried by pressure groups, there would be little ground for complaint. In the last analysis there is no safer repository of the integrity of teaching and scholarship than the dedicated men and women who constitute the faculties of our colleges and universities.

QUESTIONS ON CONTENT

1. What makes the expulsion of professors from the faculty of the University of Washington something new in the history of education?
2. What does Hook say about human fallibility?
3. According to the author, are there certain noncontroversial questions?
4. "The heresies of yesterday are often the orthodoxies of today." Explain and give examples.
5. Upon what essentially does Hook build his case against allowing communists to teach? Compare Meiklejohn's attitude on this point. Is there a true disagreement here?
6. Would a communist English teacher have more or less difficulty in following the party line than a communist teacher in some other field?
7. What two objections are there to judging the communist teacher by his actions and not simply by the fact that he is a communist?
8. Is there a legitimate analogy between communist teachers and Catholic teachers? Explain.
9. What is a "fellow-traveler"? What does the author think of such persons?
10. According to Hook, what group should have control of the policy toward communist teachers?

❧ Should Communists Be Allowed to Teach?

ALEXANDER MEIKLEJOHN

The president and regents of the University of Washington have dismissed three professors and have placed three others on probation. That statement fails to mention the most significant feature of

Reprinted from *The New York Times Magazine*, March 27, 1949, by permission of the author and the publisher.

what has been done. The entire faculty is now on probation. Every scholar, every teacher, is officially notified that if, in his search for the truth, he finds the policies of the American Communist party to be wise, and acts on that belief, he will be dismissed from the university.

In one of the dismissal cases, the evidence is not clear enough to enable an outsider to measure the validity of the decision. But the other five cases force an issue on which everyone who cares for the integrity and freedom of American scholarship and teaching must take his stand. Cool and careful consideration of that issue should be given by all of us, whether or not we agree with the teachers in question, but especially if we do not agree with them.

The general question in dispute is that of the meaning of academic freedom. But that question has three distinct phases. The first of these has to do with the organization of a university. It asks about the rights and duties of the faculty in relation to the rights and duties of the administration. And the principle at issue corresponds closely to that which, in the Government of the United States, is laid down by the First Amendment to the Constitution. Just as that Amendment declares that "Congress shall make no law abridging the freedom of speech," so, generally, our universities and colleges have adopted a principle which forbids the administration to abridge the intellectual freedom of scholars and teachers. And, at this point, the question is whether or not the president and regents at Washington have violated an agreement, made in good faith, and of vital importance to the work of the university.

The principle of academic freedom was clearly stated by Sidney Hook in THE NEW YORK TIMES Magazine of Feb. 27, 1949. After noting that "administrators and trustees" are "harried by pressure-groups," Mr. Hook concluded his argument by saying, "In the last analysis, there is no safer repository of the integrity of teaching and scholarship than the dedicated men and women who constitute the faculties of our colleges and universities." On the basis of that conviction, the Association of University Professors has advocated, and most of our universities, including Washington, have adopted, a "tenure system." That system recognizes that legal authority to appoint, promote, and dismiss teachers belongs to the president and regents. But so far as dismissals are concerned, the purpose of the tenure agreement is to set definite limits to the exercise of that authority.

This limitation of their power, governing boards throughout the nation have gladly recognized and accepted. To the Association of University Professors it has seemed so important that violations of it have been held to justify a "blacklisting" of a transgressor institution—a recommendation by the association that scholars and teachers refuse to serve in a university or college which has thus broken down the defenses of free inquiry and belief.

It is essential at this point to note the fact that the fear expressed by the tenure system is a fear of action by the president and regents. Since these officers control the status and the salaries of teachers, it is only through them or by them that effective external pressure can be used to limit faculty freedom. To say, then, as we must, that the explicit purpose of the tenure system is to protect freedom against the president and regents is not to say that these officials are more evil than others. It says only that they are more powerful than others. Theirs is the power by which, unless it is checked by a tenure system, evil may be done.

Under the excellent code adopted at the University of Washington, it is agreed that, after a trial period in which the university makes sure that a teacher is competent and worthy of confidence, he is given "permanence" of tenure. This means that he is secure from dismissal unless one or more of five carefully specified charges are proved against him. And the crucial feature of this defense of freedom is that the holding of any set of opinions, however unpopular or unconventional, is scrupulously excluded from the list of proper grounds for dismissal. The teacher who has tenure may, therefore, go fearlessly wherever his search for the truth may lead him. And no officer of the university has authority, openly or by indirection, to abridge that freedom.

When, under the Washington code, charges are made against a teacher, it is provided that prosecution and defense shall be heard by a tenure committee of the faculty, which shall judge whether or not the accusations have been established. In the five cases here under discussion, the only charge made was that of present or past membership in the American Communist party. Specific evidence of acts revealing unfitness or misconduct in university or other activities was deliberately excluded from the prosecution case. And, further, since the alleged fact of party membership was frankly admitted by the defense, the only question at issue was the abstract inquiry whether or not such membership is forbidden under the five provisions of the tenure code.

Upon that issue, the faculty committee decided unanimously that, in the cases of the ex-members of the Communist party, there were, under the code, no grounds for dismissal. And, by a vote of eight to three, the same conclusion was reached concerning the two men who were still members of the party. In the discussions of the committee, the suggestion was made that the code should be so amended that party membership would give ground for dismissal. But that action was not recommended. In its capacity as the interpreter of the code which now protects academic freedom, the committee, in all five cases, declared the charges to be not supported by the evidence presented.

In response to this judgment upon teachers by their intellectual peers, the regents, on recommendation of the president, dismissed the two party members. And, second, going beyond the recommendation of the president, they placed the three ex-members "on probation" for two years. These actions are clearly a violation of the agreement under which faculty members have accepted or continued service in the university. They deserve the condemnation of everyone who respects the integrity of a covenant, of everyone who values faculty freedom and faculty responsibility for the maintaining of freedom.

The second phase of the general question goes deeper than the forms of university organization. It challenges the wisdom of the tenure code as it now stands. It may be that, though the regents are wrong in procedure, they are right in principle. Here, then, we must ask whether President Allen is justified in saying that a teacher who is "sincere in his belief in communism" cannot "at the same time be a sincere seeker after truth which is the first obligation of the teacher." In a press interview, Mr. Allen is quoted as saying, "I insist that the Communist party exercises thought control over every one of its members. That's what I object to." Such teachers, he tells us, are "incompetent, intellectually dishonest, and derelict in their duty to find and teach the truth." Can those assertions be verified? If so, then the tenure code should be amended. If not, then the action of the university should be immediately and decisively reversed.

No one can deny that a member of the American Communist party accepts a "discipline." He follows a party "line." As the policies of the party shift, he shifts with them. That statement is in some measure true of all parties, whose members agree to work together by common tactics toward a common end. But the Communist discipline, it must be added, is unusually rigid and severe. Our question is, then, whether submission to that discipline unfits for university work men who, in grounds of scholarship and character, have been judged by their colleagues to be fitted for it.

For the judging of that issue we must examine the forces by means of which the discipline of the American Communist party is exercised. It is idle to speak of "thought control" except as we measure the compulsions by which that control is made effective. What, then, are the inducements, the dominations which by their impact upon the minds of these university teachers, rob them of the scholar's proper objectivity?

So far as inducements are concerned, good measuring of them requires that we place side by side the advantages offered to a scholar by the Communist party and those offered by the president and regents of a university. On the one hand, as seen in the present case, the administration can break a man's career at one stroke. It has power over every external thing he cares for. It can destroy his means of livelihood, can thwart his deepest inclinations and intentions. For example, in very many of our universities it is today taken for granted that a young scholar who is known to be a Communist has not the slightest chance of a faculty appointment. He is barred from academic work. And, as against this, what has the American Communist party to offer? Its "inducements" are the torments of suspicion, disrepute, insecurity, personal and family disaster.

Why, then, do men and women of scholarly training and taste choose party membership? Undoubtedly, some of them are, hysterically, attracted by disrepute and disaster. But, in general, the only explanation which fits the facts is that these scholars are moved by a passionate determination to follow the truth where it seems to lead no matter what may be the cost to themselves and their families. If anyone wishes to unearth the "inducements" which threaten the integrity of American scholarship he can find far more fruitful lines of inquiry than that taken by the administration of the University of Washington.

But Communist controls, we are told, go far deeper than "inducements." The members of the party, it is said, "take orders from Moscow"; they are subject to "thought control by a foreign power." Now, here again, the fact of rigid party discipline makes these assertions, in some ambiguous sense, true. But, in the sense in which President Allen and his regents interpret them, they are radically false.

Let us assume as valid the statement that, in the American Communist party "orders" do come from Moscow. But by what power are those orders enforced in the United States? In the Soviet Union, Mr. Stalin and his colleagues can, and do, enforce orders by police and military might. In that nation their control is violent and dictatorial. But by what form of "might" do they control an American teacher in an American university? What can they do to him? At its extreme limit, their only enforcing action is that of dismissal from the party. They can say to him, "You cannot be a member of this party unless you believe our doctrine, unless you conform to our policies." But, under that form of control, a man's acceptance of doctrines and policies is not "required." It is voluntary.

To say that beliefs are required as "conditions of membership" in a party is not to say that the beliefs are required by force, unless it is shown that membership in the party is enforced. If membership is free, then the beliefs are free.

Misled by the hatreds and fears of the cold war, President Allen and his regents are unconsciously tricked by the ambiguities of the words, "control," and "require," and "free," and "objective." The scholars whom they condemn are, so far as the evidence shows, free American citizens. For purposes of social action, they have chosen party affiliation with other men, here and abroad, whose beliefs are akin to their own. In a word, they do not accept Communist beliefs because they are members of the party. They are members of the party because they accept Communist beliefs.

Specific evidence to support the assertion just made was staring President Allen and his regents in the face at the very time when they were abstractly denying that such evidence could exist. Three of the five men whom they condemned as enslaved by party orders had already, by their own free and independent thinking, resigned from the party. How could they have done that if, as charged, they were incapable of free and independent thinking? Slaves do not resign.

At the committee hearings, these men explained, simply and directly, that under past conditions, they had found the party the most effective available weapon for attack upon evil social forces but that, with changing conditions, the use of that weapon seemed no longer advisable. Shall we say that the decision to be in the party gave evidence of a lack of objectivity while the decision to resign gave evidence of the possession of it? Such a statement would have no meaning except as indicating our own lack of objectivity.

In these three cases, as in the more famous case of Granville Hicks who, some years ago, resigned party membership with a brilliant account of his reasons for doing so, the charge made cannot be sustained. The accusation as it stands means nothing more than that the president and regents are advocating one set of ideas and are banning another. They are attributing to their victims their own intellectual sins. And the tragedy of their action is that it has immeasurably injured the cause which they seek to serve and, correspondingly, has advanced the cause which they are seeking to hold back.

The third phase of our question has to do with the wisdom, the effectiveness, of the educational policy under which teachers have been dismissed or put on probation. And, on this issue, the evidence against the president and regents is clear and decisive. However good their intention, they have made a fatal blunder in teaching method.

As that statement is made, it is taken for granted that the primary task of education in our colleges and universities is the teaching of the theory and practice of intellectual freedom, as the first principle of the democratic way of life. Whatever else our students may do or fail to do, they must learn what freedom is. They must learn to believe in it, to love it, and most important of all, to trust it.

What, then, is this faith in freedom, so far as the conflict of opinions is concerned? With respect to the world-wide controversy now raging between the advocates of the freedom of belief and the advocates of suppression of belief, what is our American doctrine? Simply stated, that doctrine expresses our confidence that whenever, in the field of ideas, the advocates of freedom and the advocates of suppression meet in fair and unabridged discussion, freedom will win. If that were not true, if the intellectual program of democracy could not hold its own in fair debate, then that program itself would require of us its own abandonment. That chance we believers in self-government have determined to take. We have put our faith in democracy.

But the president and regents have, at this point, taken the opposite course. They have gone over to the enemy. They are not willing to give a fair and equal hearing to those who disagree with us. They are convinced that suppression is more effective as an agency of freedom than is freedom itself.

But this procedure violates the one basic principle on which all teaching rests. It is impossible to teach what one does not believe. It is idle to preach what one does not practice. These men who advocate that we do to the Russians what the Russians, if they had the power, would do to us are declaring that the Russians are right and that we are wrong. They practice suppression because they have more faith in the methods of dictatorship than in those of a free self-governing society.

For many years the writer of these words has watched the disastrous educational effects upon student opinion and attitude when suppression has been used, openly or secretly, in our universities and colleges. The outcome is always the same. Dictatorship breeds rebellion and dissatisfaction. High-spirited youth will not stand the double-dealing which prates of academic freedom and muzzles its teachers by putting them "on probation."

If we suggest to these young people that they believe in democracy, then they will insist on knowing what can be said against it as well as what can be said for it. If we ask them to get ready to lay down their lives in conflict against an enemy, they want to know not only how strong or how weak are the military forces of that enemy, but also what he has to say for himself as against what we are saying for ourselves.

Many of the students in our colleges and universities are today driven into an irresponsible radicalism. But that drive does not come from the critics of our American political institutions. It comes chiefly from the irresponsible defenders of those institutions—the men who make a mockery of freedom by using in its service the forces of suppression.

Underlying and surrounding the Washington controversy is the same controversy as it runs through our national life. The most tragic mistake of the contemporary American mind is its failure to recognize the inherent strength and stability of free institutions when they are true to themselves. Democracy is not a weak and unstable thing which forever needs propping up by the devices of dictatorship. It is the only form of social life and of government which today has assurance of maintaining itself.

As contrasted with it, all governments of suppression are temporary and insecure. The regimes of Hitler and Mussolini flared into strength, and quickly died away. The power of the Soviet Union cannot endure unless that nation can find its way into the practices of political freedom. And all the other dictatorships are falling, and will fall, day by day. Free self-government alone gives promise of permanence and peace. The only real danger which threatens our democracy is that lack of faith which leads us into the devices and follies of suppression.

QUESTIONS ON CONTENT

1. Why should one "especially" consider the views of those with whom one disagrees?
2. Name the first phase of the dispute over academic freedom.
3. Do Professor Hook and Dr. Meiklejohn agree at any point? At what precise place in the argument do they part ways?
4. What is meant by "a tenure system"? How did the idea of tenure start? Discuss.
5. Try to find out if the "blacklisting" of an institution by the A.A.U.P. means exactly what Dr. Meiklejohn says it does.
6. Does the author name the five charges that are considered justification for dismissal?
7. What is "scrupulously excluded from the list of proper grounds for dismissal"? Why does the author emphasize this point?
8. How could the regents be "wrong in procedure" but "right in principle"?
9. Name the second phase of the dispute over academic freedom.
10. How does the author seek to dispose of the argument that "thought control" is practiced on American communists?
11. "Slaves do not resign." Explain.
12. Is the author willing to accept the word of a communist at its face value? Discuss.
13. Name the third phase of the dispute over academic freedom.
14. Is this phase the most important of all? Discuss.

❧ *In Tennessee*

H. L. MENCKEN

[Thomas Scopes, a schoolteacher, agreed to violate, as a test, the Tennessee law which forbade the teaching in public schools that man is a part of the evolutionary scheme. He was tried and convicted in July 1925. More than a hundred reporters attended the trial at Dayton, Tenn., and filed 165,000 words of coverage per day. Interest in academic freedom cannot claim full credit for all this excitement; the presence of Clarence Darrow, famous criminal

Reprinted from *The Nation*, CXXI (July 1, 1925), 21–22, by permission of *The Nation* and the author.

lawyer and atheist, as special defense attorney and William Jennings Bryan, great orator and fundamentalist, as special prosecuting attorney, accounted for much of the public's curiosity.]

Always in this great republic, controversies depart swiftly from their original terms and plunge into irrelevancies and false pretenses. The case of prohibition is salient. Who recalls the optimistic days before the Eighteenth Amendment, and the lofty prognostications of the dry mullahs, clerical and lay? Prohibition, we were told, would empty the jails, reduce the tax rate, abolish poverty, and put an end to political corruption. Today even the Prohibitionists know better, and so they begin to grow discreetly silent upon the matter. Instead, they come forward with an entirely new Holy Cause. What began as a campaign for a Babbitt's Utopia becomes transformed into a mystical campaign for Law Enforcement. Prohibition is a grotesque failure, but the fight must go on. A transcendental motive takes the place of a practical motive. One categorical imperative goes out and another comes in.

So, now, in Tennessee, where a rural pedagogue stands arraigned before his peers for violating the school law. At bottom, a quite simple business. The hinds of the State, desiring to prepare their young for life there, set up public schools. To man those schools they employ pedagogues. To guide those pedagogues they lay down rules prescribing what is to be taught and what is not to be taught. Why not, indeed? How could it be otherwise? Precisely the same custom prevails everywhere else in the world, wherever there are schools at all. Behind every school ever heard of there is a definite concept of its purpose—of the sort of equipment it is to give to its pupils. It cannot conceivably teach everything; it must confine itself by sheer necessity to teaching what will be of the greatest utility, cultural or practical, to the youth actually in hand. Well, what could be of greater utility to the son of a Tennessee mountaineer than an education making him a good Tennessean, content with his father, at peace with his neighbors, dutiful to the local religion, and docile under the local mores?

That is all the Tennessee anti-evolution law seeks to accomplish. It differs from other regulations of the same sort only to the extent that Tennessee differs from the rest of the world. The State, to a degree that should be gratifying, has escaped the national standardization. Its people show a character that is immensely different from the character of, say, New Yorkers or Californians. They retain, among other things, the anthropomorphic religion of an elder day.

They do not profess it; they actually believe in it. The Old Testament, to them, is not a mere sacerdotal whizz-bang, to be read for its pornography; it is an authoritative history, and the transactions recorded in it are as true as the story of Barbara Frietchie, or that of Washington and the cherry tree, or that of the late Woodrow's struggle to keep us out of the war. So crediting the sacred narrative, they desire that it be taught to their children, and any doctrine that makes game of it is immensely offensive to them. When such a doctrine, despite their protests, is actually taught, they proceed to put it down by force.

Is that procedure singular? I don't think it is. It is adopted everywhere, the instant the prevailing notions, whether real or false, are challenged. Suppose a school teacher in New York began entertaining his pupils with the case against the Jews, or against the Pope. Suppose a teacher in Vermont essayed to argue that the late Confederate States were right, as thousands of perfectly sane and intelligent persons believe—that Lee was a defender of the Constitution and Grant a traitor to it. Suppose a teacher in Kansas taught that prohibition was evil, or a teacher in New Jersey that it was virtuous. But I need not pile up suppositions. The evidence of what happens to such a contumacious teacher was spread before us copiously during the late uproar about Bolsheviks. And it was not in rural Tennessee but in the great cultural centers which now laugh at Tennessee that punishments came most swiftly, and we were most barbarous. It was not Dayton but New York City that cashiered teachers for protesting against the obvious lies of the State Department.

Yet now we are asked to believe that some mysterious and vastly important principle is at stake at Dayton—that the conviction of Professor Scopes will strike a deadly blow at enlightenment and bring down freedom to sorrow and shame. Tell it to the marines! No principle is at stake at Dayton save the principle that school teachers, like plumbers, should stick to the job that is set before them, and not go roving about the house, breaking windows, raiding the cellar, and demoralizing the children. The issue of free speech is quite irrelevant. When a pedagogue takes his oath of office, he renounces his right to free speech quite as certainly as a bishop does, or a colonel in the army, or an editorial writer on a newspaper. He becomes a paid propagandist of certain definite doctrines and attitudes, mainly determined specifically and in advance, and every time he departs from them deliberately he deliberately swindles his employers.

What ails Mr. Scopes, and many like him, is that they have been filled with subversive ideas by specialists in human liberty, of whom I have the honor to be one. Such specialists, confronted by the New York cases, saw a chance to make political capital out of them, and did so with great effect. I was certainly not backward in that enterprise. The liars of the State Department were fair game, and any stick is good enough to beat a dog with. Even a pedagogue, seized firmly by the legs, makes an effective shillelagh. (I have used, in my time, yet worse: a congressman, a psychiatrist, a birth controller to maul an archbishop.) Unluckily, some of the pedagogues mistook the purpose of the operation. They came out of it full of a delusion that they were apostles of liberty, of the search for knowledge, of enlightenment. They have been worrying and exasperating their employers ever since.

I believe it must be plain that they are wrong, and that their employers, by a necessary inference, are right. A pedagogue, properly so called—and a high-school teacher in a country town is properly so called—is surely not a searcher for knowledge. His job in the world is simply to pass on what has been chosen and approved by his superiors. In the whole history of the world no such pedagogue has ever actually increased the sum of human knowledge. His training unfits him for it; moreover, he would not be a pedagogue if he had either the taste or the capacity for it. He is a workingman, not a thinker. When he speaks, his employers speak. What he says has behind it all the authority of the community. If he would be true to his oath he must be very careful to say nothing that is in violation of the communal mores, the communal magic, the communal notion of the good, the beautiful, and the true.

Here, I repeat, I speak of the pedagogue, and use the word in its strict sense—that is, I speak of the fellow whose sole job is teaching. Men of great learning, men who genuinely know something, men who have augmented the store of human knowledge—such men, in their leisure, may also teach. The master may take an apprentice. But he does not seek apprentices in the hill towns of Tennessee, or even on the East Side of New York. He does not waste himself upon children whose fate it will be, when they grow up, to become Rotarians or Methodist deacons, bootleggers or moonshiners. He looks for his apprentices in the minority that has somehow escaped that fate—that has, by some act of God, survived the dreadful ministrations of schoolteachers. To this minority he may submit his doubts as well as his certainties. He may present what is dubious and of evil report along with what is official, and hence good. He may be wholly himself. Liberty of teaching begins where teaching ends.

QUESTIONS ON CONTENT

1. Why does the author open his article with a paragraph about prohibition?
2. Do you think the last sentence of paragraph 2 is a good definition of education?
3. Is the author making fun of Tennessee? What other states does he belabor and why?
4. How, according to the author, are teachers like plumbers?
5. When and in what way does a teacher swindle his employer?
6. Compare Mencken's conception of a teacher as a "paid propagandist" and Meiklejohn's ideal teacher who deserves full freedom. Which is the more realistic view?
7. Define *pedagogue*.
8. Is it valid to imply that "men of great learning" never come from "the hill towns of Tennessee" or "the East Side of New York"?

❧ *The Mummification of Opinion*

Senator J. William Fulbright

As far back as the 1830s *freedom* of discussion and the influence of the *majority opinion* thereon was a matter of real concern to thoughtful people. Alexis de Tocqueville put it well I think:

> I know of no country in which there is so little independence of mind and real freedom of discussion as in America. The will of man is not shattered, but softened, bent, and guided; men are seldom forced by it to act, but they are restrained from acting. The majority no longer says: "You shall think as I do or you shall die"; but it says: "You are free to think differently from me and to retain your life, your property, and all that you possess; but you are henceforth a stranger among your people. You may retain your civil rights, but they will be useless to you, for you will never be chosen by your fellow citizens if you solicit their votes; and

Address delivered January 25, 1955, and printed by *The Saturday Review*, February 12, 1955. Reprinted by permission of *The Saturday Review*.

they will affect to scorn you if you ask for their esteem. You will remain among men, but you will be deprived of the rights of mankind. Your fellow creatures will shun you like an impure being; and even those who believe in your innocence will abandon you, lest they should be shunned in their turn. Go in peace! I have given you your life, but it is an existence worse than death."

The sharp edge of that prophecy cuts deeply into us today, not alone because of the Senator from Wisconsin and not alone because of the driving pressure of his avowed followers. Restrictions on freedom of expression come from many sources, and in some cases for reasons unrelated to the ambitions of the Wisconsin revolutionary.

There is, for example, the narrowing effect inherent in the concentration of managerial control of the press, the radio, the movies—and, in the foreseeable future, television.

Within the last forty years, according to Morris Ernst, one-third of our daily newspapers have disappeared, and more than 3,000 weeklies have ceased publication. As of a recent date ten of our states did not have a single city with competing papers, and in the whole of America there are only a few more than 100 cities where one can find daily papers in competition. The pattern of concentration extends elsewhere. In radio one-fifth of the stations are interlocked with newspapers. Four networks dominate national radio, while less than two dozen advertisers account for 50 per cent of network income. And in the film industry five big companies exercise a dominant influence upon the industry.

Let me make one thing plain. I am not saying that what brought this to pass was in all cases the hand of monopoly grabbing for bigness as an end in itself. In some cases *cost*-account sheets *compelled* owners and managers to seek their survival by enlarging themselves through mergers. And it is to the credit of some of these that when they found themselves in a monopolistic position they tried to run the communications property as if it were a responsible public utility. But men of this outlook are, unfortunately, in the minority.

The general effect of what approaches monopoly control is that people hear, see, watch, read, and listen to only one side of public questions. And this in turn can adversely affect the public man to whom the guidance of public affairs is entrusted. He may know the truth and want to speak it. Yet he doubts whether his views, as transmitted to his constituents by those who control communication channels, will be fairly presented, or presented at all. So there often follows from this a chain reaction of cynicism leading to corruption.

This public man, to achieve anything at all, will not use the open road, but will crowd himself into the path of low intrigue. He will not boldly scout what lies ahead for the nation. He will bend his weight to the end of having everything stand still. He will voice no prophecies of what ought to be. He will speak only the sterile dogmas of the street, and only those bits of rumor which bear the general sanction of the lords of communication.

And what of the end result to all this? It can be a society shaped in imitation of an Egyptian mummy; a society where the embalmer holds the highest place of honor; a society of fixed, painted, and hard shells; a society feeding on its dry rot, until the fateful hour when a probing finger striking the shell from without makes it collapse on the empty center.

This vision of the future is not drawn from the thin air or from a fevered imagination. It came after reading the report on tax-exempt foundations issued recently by the Reece Committee of the House of Representatives. There, in one sentence, Chairman Reece put himself on the side of all the pharaohs from Rameses I to the gentleman whose solar ship was uncovered recently. "The trustees of the tax-exempt foundations" said the Reece report, "should . . . be very chary of promoting ideas, concepts, and opinion-forming material which run contrary to what the public currently *wishes, approves,* and *likes.*"

I said a moment ago that in addition to Senator McCarthy restrictions on freedom of expression have been imposed by the most respectable sources. Recently, for example, our military academies banned all student debate on the question of the recognition of Red China. The cadets at West Point and the midshipmen at Annapolis, who are destined to be our military chiefs, presumably could discuss how many angels can sit on the point of a needle, or any other celestially remote matter. But it was officially decreed that they should hold to the public posture of being blind, deaf, and dumb to the most tortured issue of the moment; an issue whose correct handling can determine whether the students themselves as well as the rest of us will live or will die.

I am indebted to the *Princeton Alumni Weekly* for another example in the same vein. The *Weekly*—scarcely a radical publication —took notice of undergraduate apathy toward political and social questions. And, in listing some of the underlying causes for a phenomenon common to other colleges, it included the pressures to conform exerted by our great industrial corporations on students. To illustrate, the *Weekly* then cited from a personnel pamphlet issued by the powerful Socony-Vacuum Oil Company, advising students how they should behave in college if they wished to be employed on graduation. The order of the day reads, and I quote from the pamphlet: "Personal views can cause a lot of trouble. The 'isms' are out. Business being what it is, it naturally looks with disfavor on the wild-eyed radical or even the moderate pink."

Consider the implications of this text. With one hand it gags the breath of student curiosity. With the other hand it dangles bread before his mouth as a reward for silence, unbroken even by a moderate gurgle. It says to the student, "You will be saved only if you consider yourself a beast of burden or a beast of prey." It says to him: "Production and not the producer is the object of life on earth." It says to him: "We ourselves are the judge and the jury of what a wild-eyed radical and a moderate pink is. And if you ask us what it is, in the act of asking you become the very thing we don't want." And it says to him: "If you must find some way to spend your energies as an undergraduate before we take complete charge of you there are football games, movies, and now television spectacles of magnificent dimensions which you may attend provided they have been screened for security and do not cause you to think."

How should those of us here bear ourselves in a climate where the pressures to conform are so remorseless?

To the politician who means to be faithful to his oath of office the answer is plain. It is to draw closer still to the letter and spirit of the Constitution. For in the degree to which he does this he can better follow the guide lines staked out by the Founders.

They were not prepared to lodge the rule of our society in the majority opinion. They knew it to be a quick and volatile thing; knew that it required a frame of law to steady it and bring it into creative focus. Neither did they say that the frame of law was itself limitless in what it could cover. They said the law itself should be limited to enumerated topics which are a proper concern of Caesar. All else—the dreams and speculations of artists, or any other manner of activity involving a connection between a man and his God—were not to be invaded by the law.

Beyond this, the Founders were under no illusions about the nature of power. "Give all power to the many," they said, "and they will oppress the few. Give all power to the few, they will oppress the many. Both, therefore, ought to have power that each may defend itself against the other." And with this in mind, the organ of government they framed was a balanced arrangement for unity and diversity, authority and liberty, security and freedom, continuity and new birth. Elsewhere other societies have divorced these coupled terms, saying that they were incompatible, and that one could survive only if the other was eliminated. And elsewhere, too, the effect of such a divorce has led directly to the dissolution of the society that was meant to prosper.

If the American politician draws close to the letter and spirit of the Constitution he will not only gain strength and direction from what the Founders first explored. He will be further reinforced when he grasps the keystone fact that the Constitution is superior to any majority or minority. In consequence of this, his oath of office does not require him to swing with every breeze. The oath requires of him that he should reflect the *deliberate* sense of the community. And this in turn means that he ought to consider himself a teacher, offering by precept and example a style and method of deliberation that can be imitated by the community at large as it seeks on its own to know, and then to do the good. It also means, as is often the case with teachers, that he must be prepared to accept banishment or destruction at the hands of the people because he has aroused their anger in the very act of serving them well.

And, finally, what of the writer? He has a unique responsibility to the political community of which he is a part. That responsibility arises from his talent, from his capacity to enlighten, to civilize those citizens to whose hands is entrusted the ultimate power in our society. The writer is the natural teacher of the people.

In this hurried mechanical age the artist and intellectual are among the few who have the serenity and sense of perspective which may help us to find a way out of the fevered confusion which presently afflicts us.

Through the writer the political community needs to be taught how and what to laugh at; how and what to scorn or to pity; needs to be taught continuously that honor is not the same as fame or notoriety; that physical bravery is not the only form of courage. It needs to be taught the proper objects of anger or of love. It needs to be taught the nature of justice. And, above all, through the writer the political community needs to be taught that the capacity of the human mind has yet to be explored, that there can be new possibilities for men themselves.

QUESTIONS ON CONTENT

1. How much truth do you find in Alexis de Tocqueville's observations on freedom of discussion in America? Cite examples to prove or disprove what he says.
2. Name the forces militating today against freedom of opinion.
3. What is the purpose of paragraph 4 on p. 386?
4. Who are the "lords of communication"? How complimentary is this term?
5. The author's title is emphasized on p. 387. How appropriate are the metaphors he uses?
6. What three examples does the author give of attempts to shut off possibly unorthodox opinions?
7. Should students anywhere be allowed to talk publicly about such issues as recognition of Red China?
8. Has the author accurately interpreted the advice to college students offered by a large oil company?
9. Why are conscientious American politicians compared to teachers?
10. What are the responsibilities of writers?

SUGGESTIONS FOR PAPERS

As the selections in this chapter have indicated, freedom is far from being a simple conception. Everybody must relinquish complete freedom in order to attain relative freedom. But how relative? At what point, in one direction, does freedom disappear, and at what point, in the other direction, does it become a license to encroach on the freedom of others? You are asked to discover for yourself, with all the assistance you can get from your reading, the basic reasonableness of relative freedom.

1. Socrates speaks of the state as a "noble steed" and of himself as "a gadfly" sent on a mission to keep the steed restless. Choose some contemporary public figure who apparently considers it his function to sting the nation (the state, the county, or the city) into restlessness. Such a figure is not likely to be popular. Do you think his actions worth defending even if you yourself do not agree with him?

2. Socrates did not think of freedom as absolute. A man, he thought, had duties to forces outside himself and to forces within

himself. Explain, with examples, this idea of freedom. (Reread paragraph 1 of "The Unexamined Life Is Not Worth Living.")

3. "Give me liberty, or give me death," said Patrick Henry. Show how this sort of choice—the ultimate freedom—is made reasonable by Socrates. Then explain why this conception is *not* the ideal of most men.

4. Would Milton consider a monastic life a good life in the moral sense? What would his attitude be toward censorship, prohibition, and any legislative restrictions on moral choices? Defend or attack his position.

5. Write a paper about freedom of the press. Is this a completely good thing? Suppose a city has a single newspaper or two newspapers owned by the same person or syndicate. Do advertisers affect newspaper policy? Do politics color the presentation of news stories? Is there any alternative to a free press?

6. What is "academic freedom"? Divide the term: What is "freedom"? What is the effect of "academic"? Does it broaden or narrow the word *freedom?* Does "academic freedom" represent a *need* or an *extra privilege?* Is it a benefit to the teacher alone? Does it consist solely of the right to state both sides of a question? For whom is this sort of freedom most necessary—for a communist teacher in Moscow, for a capitalistic teacher in Washington, or for a communist teacher in Washington and a capitalistic teacher in Moscow? Jot down answers to these questions; then organize a paper in which you state what academic freedom is *not* and then what it *is*. Quotations from your reading will strengthen your paper.

7. It has been said that "it is the purpose of higher education" to "unsettle the minds of young men, to widen their horizons, to inflame their intellects. It is not to reform them, to amuse them, or to make them expert technicians in any field. It is to teach them to think, to think straight, if possible; but to think for themselves." (Robert Maynard Hutchins.) Write your paper as a comment on this conception of education. (Suggested approach: I Hutchins' statement; II Meiklejohn's response; III Hook's response; IV Mencken's response; V My response.)

8. What constitutes a controversial question? Is it literally true that there are two sides to every question? If so, what becomes of the advice that professors can keep out of trouble by avoiding controversial questions? Or of the advice, actually given by a college president, that one, to avoid difficulties, needs only to teach the truth? Are

preferences different from *truths?* Can you relate *choice* as a basic element of freedom (see Milton, Chapter 14) to *controversy* which simply dramatizes choice?

9. Should a communist be allowed to teach in an American college? Before you answer this question, ask yourself this one: Would I exclude others besides communists? Would I exclude a Catholic? An atheist? An orthodox Jew? A fascist? An extreme conservative? A fundamentalist? (Assume for the sake of your argument that all these persons are adequately trained in the subject that they are to teach.) If you would exclude any of these others, would it be for the same reason each time? Does the communist differ essentially from the persons in these other categories?

10. Examine Meiklejohn's reasoning in his rebuttal to the charge that American communists are the victims of "thought control." Is the basic question this: Can there be an *American* communist? Does Dr. Meiklejohn assume that there can be? Does Professor Hook assume that there cannot ("Should Communists Be Permitted to Teach?")? Which reasoning and which facts appeal to you as more convincing?

11. Write out a close, point-by-point comparison of Dr. Meiklejohn's and Professor Hook's articles. Does Professor Hook offer some information about communism and communists which may justify his apparent disagreement with Dr. Meiklejohn? Be sure to add your own opinion to the discussion.

12. Compare Meiklejohn's and Hook's attitude toward teachers with Mencken's. Start by copying down exactly what each says about those who teach. You will discover some basic differences of opinion. After discussing these differences, place yourself as squarely as possible in one camp or the other.

13. In an article called "Teachers and Controversial Questions" (*Harper's Magazine,* June 1938, CLXXVII, 15–22), Dr. Meiklejohn advanced the thesis that teachers should be advocates of their personally held beliefs. Has Dr. Meiklejohn in any way modified this stand? Support or attack this idea. How, for example, would a propagandist differ from a teacher-advocate? Your answer should show what a teacher should not be and then what a teacher should be. What risks, if any, are involved in the practice of the theory of teacher-advocates? Are *you* willing to run such risks? Why, or why not?

14. Senator Fulbright in "The Mummification of Opinion" discusses the tyranny of the majority. Are there also dangers in a minor-

ity cutting too far into the rights of the majority? Examine both sides of this argument. (I Dangers from the majority, with illustrations; II Dangers from the minority, with illustrations; III The line to be drawn.)

SOME TITLES FOR PAPERS

1. Enforcing Social Customs
2. No Choice, No Freedom
3. Discipline and Freedom
4. Anytus Today (see the selection from Socrates)
5. You Can Kill a Man but Not an Idea
6. The Function of a Gadfly
7. Good and Evil: Intertwined
8. The True Wayfaring Christian
9. Books Promiscuously Read
10. The Legal Tyranny of the Majority
11. The Social Tyranny of the Majority
12. The Tyranny of the Minority
13. My Stake in Freedom of the Press
14. Give the People Light and They Will Find Their Way
15. All Mankind Minus One
16. The Value of Wrong Opinions
17. Temperate Controversy
18. How To Keep a Right Opinion Right
19. Should Demagogues Be Silenced?
20. The Ideal Controversialist: A Definition
21. Academic Freedom: A Need or a Privilege?
22. How To Avoid Controversial Subjects
23. One Man's Meat Is Another Man's Poison
24. Education Should Unsettle the Mind
25. The Teacher I Would Not Hire
26. Teachers Are Like Plumbers
27. Do I Know What My Teachers Believe?
28. Yesterday's Heresies Are Today's Orthodoxies
29. If I Were a Teacher
30. A Capitalist Teacher in Moscow: A Fantasy
31. Are Avowed Communist Teachers Dangerous?

CHAPTER 12

❧ *DEMOCRACY VERSUS COMMUNISM*

WHAT IS A DEMOCRATIC GOVERNMENT? The word *democratic* is used to describe the political systems of Russia, East Germany, and the United States. So used, the word loses its meaning. Obviously a more precise definition is needed.

Carl Becker in "The Ideal Democracy" presents the basic, historical definition of democracy and disentangles this definition from modern abuse of the term (1) as applied to nondemocratic governments and (2) as applied to the practical compromises in democratic politics which modify the ideal. The word *ideal* as used here means existing as the archetype or perfect original from which copies less perfect may be made. In other words, Becker describes the perfect pattern of democracy in which the source of political authority must be vested in the people, not in the ruler.

What is a communistic government? The word communistic is used to describe the political system in Russia and its satellites. It is significant that Russia uses and perverts the word *democratic*, but democratic states do not return the compliment by applying the word *communistic* to any part of their system. Ideal communism has been lost in actual practices, but shreds of it may be seen in the calm listing of "The Tenets of Communism" by Massimo Salvadori.

The appeal of revolutionary, equalitarian movements is supposed to be most attractive to the down-trodden. Edwin Markham's poem, "The Man with the Hoe," has historical significance through its description of a brutalized farm laborer, who, according to the poet, represented the world's oppressed. Carl Sandburg in "The People Will Live On" expresses his confidence in the ultimate destiny of the people. The man with the hoe will live on and become something better; as he improves, so will the effectiveness of the democratic process.

The slim chances of the people under nondemocratic regimes is made vivid by a former communist, Arthur Koestler, in his book *Darkness at Noon*, from which the excerpts, "The Arrest of Arlova and the End of Bogrov," are taken. In a powerful novel, *1984*, George Orwell has projected into the near future the bitter fate of man under communistic control. The excerpt from the book, "Memory Holes," shows the systematic degradation of the vast, exploited populace—the very men with hoes, the oppressed who were to be lifted up by the new system.

❧ *The Ideal Democracy*

CARL L. BECKER

I

Democracy, like liberty or science or progress, is a word with which we are all so familiar that we rarely take the trouble to ask what we mean by it. It is a term, as the devotees of semantics say, which has no "referent"—there is no precise or palpable thing or object which we all think of when the word is pronounced. On the contrary, it is a word which connotes different things to different people, a kind of conceptual Gladstone bag which, with a little manipulation, can be made to accommodate almost any collection of social facts we may wish to carry about in it. In it we can as easily pack a dictatorship as any other form of government. We have only to stretch the concept to include any form of government supported by a majority of the people, for whatever reasons and by

From Carl L. Becker's *Modern Democracy*, Yale University Press, 1941. Reprinted by permission of the publisher.

whatever means of expressing assent, and before we know it the empire of Napoleon, the Soviet regime of Stalin, and the Fascist systems of Mussolini and Hitler are all safely in the bag. But if this is what we mean by democracy, then virtually all forms of government are democratic, since virtually all governments, except in times of revolution, rest upon the explicit or implicit consent of the people. In order to discuss democracy intelligently it will be necessary, therefore, to define it, to attach to the word a sufficiently precise meaning to avoid the confusion which is not infrequently the chief result of such discussions.

All human institutions, we are told, have their ideal forms laid away in heaven, and we do not need to be told that the actual institutions conform but indifferently to these ideal counterparts. It would be possible then to define democracy either in terms of the ideal or in terms of the real form—to define it as government of the people, by the people, for the people; or to define it as government of the people, by the politicians, for whatever pressure groups can get their interests taken care of. But as a historian I am naturally disposed to be satisfied with the meaning which, in the history of politics, men have commonly attributed to the word—a meaning, needless to say, which derives partly from the experience and partly from the aspirations of mankind. So regarded, the term democracy refers primarily to a form of government, and it has always meant government by the many as opposed to government by the one— government by the people as opposed to government by a tyrant, a dictator, or an absolute monarch. This is the most general meaning of the word as men have commonly understood it.

In this antithesis there are certain implications, almost tacitly understood, which give a more precise meaning to the term. Peisistratus, for example, was supported by a majority of the people, but his government was never regarded as a democracy for all that. Caesar's power derived from a popular mandate, conveyed through established republican forms, but that did not make his government any less a dictatorship. Napoleon called his government a democratic empire, but no one, least of all Napoleon himself, doubted that he had destroyed the last vestiges of the democratic republic. Since the Greeks first used the term, the essential test of democratic government has always been this: the source of political authority must be and remain in the people and not in the ruler. A democratic government has always meant one in which the citizens, or a sufficient number of them to represent more or less effectively the common will, freely act from time to time, and according to established forms, to appoint or recall the magistrates and to enact or revoke the laws by which the community is governed. This I take to be the meaning which history has impressed upon the term democracy as a form of government. It is, therefore, the meaning which I attach to it in these lectures.

The most obvious political fact of our time is that democracy as thus defined has suffered an astounding decline in prestige. Fifty years ago it was not impossible to regard democratic government, and the liberties that went with it, as a permanent conquest of the human spirit. In 1886 Andrew Carnegie published a book entitled *Triumphant Democracy*. Written without fear and without research, the book was not an achievement of the highest intellectual distinction perhaps; but the title at least expressed well enough the prevailing conviction—the conviction that democracy had fought the good fight, had won the decisive battles, and would inevitably, through its inherent merits, presently banish from the world the most flagrant political and social evils which from time immemorial had afflicted mankind. This conviction could no doubt be most easily entertained in the United States, where even the tradition of other forms of government was too remote and alien to color our native optimism. But even in Europe the downright skeptics, such as Lecky, were thought to be perverse, and so hardheaded a historian as J. B. Bury could proclaim with confidence that the long struggle for freedom of thought had finally been won.

I do not need to tell you that within a brief twenty years the prevailing optimism of that time has been quite dispelled. One European country after another has, willingly enough it seems, abandoned whatever democratic institutions it formerly enjoyed for some form of dictatorship. The spokesmen of Fascism and Communism announce with confidence that democracy, a sentimental aberration which the world has outgrown, is done for; and even the friends of democracy support it with declining conviction. They tell us that democracy, so far from being triumphant, is "at the cross roads" or "in retreat," and that its future is by no means assured. What are we to think of this sudden reversal in fortune and prestige? How explain it? What to do about it?

II

One of the presuppositions of modern thought is that institutions, in order to be understood, must be seen in relation to the conditions of time and place in which they appear. It is a little difficult for us to look at democracy in this way. We are so immersed in its present fortunes that we commonly see it only as a "close-up," filling the screen to the exclusion of other things to which it is in fact related. In order to form an objective judgment of its nature and significance, we must therefore first of all get it in proper perspective. Let us then, in imagination, remove from the immediate present scene to some cool high place where we can survey at a glance five or six thousand years of history, and note the part which democracy has played in human civilization. The view, if we have been accustomed to take democratic institutions for granted, is a bit bleak and disheartening. For we see at once that in all this long time, over the habitable globe, the great majority of the human race has neither known nor apparently much cared for our favorite institutions.

Civilization was already old when democracy made its first notable appearance among the small city states of ancient Greece, where it flourished brilliantly for a brief century or two and then disappeared. At about the same time something that might be called democracy appeared in Rome and other Italian cities, but even in Rome it did not survive the conquest of the world by the Roman Republic, except as a form of local administration in the cities of the empire. In the twelfth and thirteenth centuries certain favorably placed medieval cities enjoyed a measure of self-government, but in most instances it was soon replaced by the dictatorship of military conquerors, the oligarchic control of a few families, or the encroaching power of autocratic kings. The oldest democracy of modern times is the Swiss Confederation, the next oldest is the Dutch republic. Parliamentary government in England does not antedate the late seventeenth century, the great American experiment is scarcely older. Not until the nineteenth century did democratic government make its way in any considerable part of the world—in the great states of continental Europe, in South America, in Canada and Australia, in South Africa and Japan.

From this brief survey it is obvious that, taking the experience of mankind as a test, democracy has as yet had but a limited and temporary success. There must be a reason for this significant fact. The reason is that democratic government is a species of social

luxury, at best a delicate and precarious adventure which depends
for success upon the validity of certain assumptions about the capacities and virtues of men, and upon the presence of certain material
and intellectual conditions favorable to the exercise of these capacities and virtues. Let us take the material conditions first.

It is a striking fact that until recently democracy never flourished
except in very small states—for the most part in cities. It is true that
in both the Persian and the Roman empires a measure of self-government was accorded to local communities, but only in respect to
purely local affairs; in no large state as a whole was democratic government found to be practicable. One essential reason is that until
recently the means of communication were too slow and uncertain to
create the necessary solidarity of interest and similarity of information over large areas. The principle of representation was well
enough known to the Greeks, but in practice it proved impracticable
except in limited areas and for special occasions. As late as the
eighteenth century it was still the common opinion that the republican form of government, although the best ideally, was unsuited to
large countries, even to a country no larger than France. This was
the view of Montesquieu, and even of Rousseau. The view persisted
into the nineteenth century, and English conservatives, who were opposed to the extension of the suffrage in England, consoled themselves with the notion that the American Civil War would confirm it
—would demonstrate that government by and for the people would
perish, if not from off the earth, at least from large countries. If their
hopes were confounded the reason is that the means of communication, figuratively speaking, were making large countries small. It is
not altogether fanciful to suppose that, but for the railroad and the
telegraph, the United States would today be divided into many small
republics maneuvering for advantage and employing war and diplomacy for maintaining an unstable balance of power.

If one of the conditions essential to the success of democratic government is mobility, ease of communication, another is a certain
measure of economic security. Democracy does not flourish in communities on the verge of destitution. In ancient and medieval times
democratic government appeared for the most part in cities, the
centers of prosperity. Farmers in the early Roman Republic and in
the Swiss Cantons were not wealthy to be sure, but equality of possessions and of opportunity gave them a certain economic security.
In medieval cities political privilege was confined to the prosperous
merchants and craftsmen, and in Athens and the later Roman Re-

public democratic government was found to be workable only on condition that the poor citizens were subsidized by the government or paid for attending the assemblies and the law courts.

In modern times democratic institutions have, generally speaking, been most successful in new countries, such as the United States, Canada, and Australia, where the conditions of life have been easy for the people; and in European countries more or less in proportion to their industrial prosperity. In European countries, indeed, there has been a close correlation between the development of the industrial revolution and the emergence of democratic institutions. Holland and England, the first countries to experience the industrial revolution, were the first also (apart from Switzerland, where certain peculiar conditions obtained) to adopt democratic institutions; and as the industrial revolution spread to France, Belgium, Germany, and Italy, these countries in turn adopted at least a measure of democratic government. Democracy is in some sense an economic luxury, and it may be said that in modern times it has been a function of the development of new and potentially rich countries, or of the industrial revolution which suddenly dowered Europe with unaccustomed wealth. Now that prosperity is disappearing round every next corner, democracy works less well than it did.

So much for the material conditions essential for the success of democratic government. Supposing these conditions to exist, democratic government implies in addition the presence of certain capacities and virtues in its citizens. These capacities and virtues are bound up with the assumptions on which democracy rests, and are available only in so far as the assumptions are valid. The primary assumption of democratic government is that its citizens are capable of managing their own affairs. But life in any community involves a conflict of individual and class interests, and a corresponding divergence of opinion as to the measures to be adopted for the common good. The divergent opinions must be somehow reconciled, the conflict of interests somehow compromised. It must then be an assumption of democratic government that its citizens are rational creatures, sufficiently so at least to understand the interests in conflict; and it must be an assumption that they are men of good will, sufficiently so toward each other at least to make those concessions of individual and class interest required for effecting workable compromises. The citizens of a democracy should be, as Pericles said the citizens of Athens were, if not all originators at least all sound judges of good policy.

These are what may be called the minimum assumptions and the necessary conditions of democratic government anywhere and at any time. They may be noted to best advantage, not in any state, but in small groups within the state—in clubs and similar private associations of congenial and like-minded people united for a specific purpose. In such associations the membership is limited and select. The members are, or may easily become, all acquainted with each other. Everyone knows, or may easily find out, what is being done and who is doing it. There will of course be differences of opinion, and there may be disintegrating squabbles and intrigues. But on the whole, ends and means being specific and well understood, the problems of government are few and superficial; there is plenty of time for discussion; and since intelligence and good will can generally be taken for granted there is the disposition to make reasonable concessions and compromises. The analogy must be taken for what it is worth. States may not be the mystical blind Molochs of German philosophy, but any state is far more complex and intangible than a private association, and there is little resemblance between such associations and the democracies of modern times. Other things equal, the resemblance is closest in very small states, and it is in connection with the small city of ancient Greece that the resemblance can best be noted.

The Greek states were limited in size, not as is often thought solely or even chiefly by the physiography of the country, but by some instinctive feeling of the Greek mind that a state is necessarily a natural association of people bound together by ties of kinship and a common tradition of rights and obligations. There must then, as Aristotle said, be a limit:

> For if the citizens of a state are to judge and distribute offices according to merit, they must know each other's characters; where they do not possess this knowledge, both the elections to offices and the decisions in the law courts will go wrong. Where the population is very large they are manifestly settled by haphazard, which clearly ought not to be. Besides, in overpopulous states foreigners and metics will readily acquire citizenship, for who will find them out?

It obviously did not occur to Aristotle that metics and foreigners should be free to acquire citizenship. It did not occur to him, or to any Greek of his time, or to the merchants of the self-governing medieval city, that a state should be composed of all the people inhabiting a given territory. A state was rather an incorporated body of people within, but distinct from, the population of the community.

Ancient and medieval democracies had thus something of the character of a private association. They were, so to speak, purely pragmatic phenomena, arising under very special conditions, and regarded as the most convenient way of managing the affairs of people bound together by community of interest and for the achievement of specific ends. There is no suggestion in Aristotle that democracy (polity) is intrinsically a superior form of government, no suggestion that it derives from a special ideology of its own. If it rests upon any superiority other than convenience, it is the superiority which it shares with any Greek state, that is to say, the superiority of Greek over barbarian civilization. In Aristotle's philosophy it is indeed difficult to find any clear-cut distinction between the democratic form of government and the state itself; the state, if it be worthy of the name, is always, whatever the form of government, "the government of freemen and equals," and in any state it is always necessary that "the freemen who compose the bulk of the people should have absolute power in some things." In Aristotle's philosophy the distinction between good and bad in politics is not between good and bad types of government, but between the good and bad form of each type. Any type of government—monarchy, aristocracy, polity—is good provided the rulers aim at the good of all rather than at the good of the class to which they belong. From Aristotle's point of view neither democracy nor dictatorship is good or bad in itself, but only in the measure that it achieves, or fails to achieve, the aim of every good state, which is that "the inhabitants of it should be happy." It did not occur to Aristotle that democracy (polity), being in some special sense in harmony with the nature of man, was everywhere applicable, and therefore destined by fate or the gods to carry throughout the world a superior form of civilization.

It is in this respect chiefly that modern democracy differs from earlier forms. It rests upon something more than the minimum assumptions. It is reinforced by a full-blown ideology which, by endowing the individual with natural and imprescriptible rights, sets the democratic form of government off from all others as the one which alone can achieve the good life. What then are the essential tenets of the modern democratic faith?

III

The liberal democratic faith, as expressed in the works of eighteenth- and early nineteenth-century writers, is one of the formulations of the modern doctrine of progress. It will be well, therefore, to note briefly the historical antecedents of that doctrine.

In the long history of man on earth there comes a time when he remembers something of what has been, anticipates something that will be, knows the country he has traversed, wonders what lies beyond—the moment when he becomes aware of himself as a lonely, differentiated item in the world. Sooner or later there emerges for him the most devastating of all facts, namely, that in an indifferent universe which alone endures, he alone aspires, endeavors to attain, and attains only to be defeated in the end. From that moment his immediate experience ceases to be adequate, and he endeavors to project himself beyond it by creating ideal worlds of semblance, Utopias of other time or place in which all has been, may be, or will be well.

In ancient times Utopia was most easily projected into the unknown past, pushed back to the beginning of things—to the time of P'an Ku and the celestial emperors, to the Garden of Eden, or the reign of King Chronos when men lived like gods free from toil and grief. From this happy state of first created things there had obviously been a decline and fall, occasioned by disobedience and human frailty, and decreed as punishment by fate or the angry gods. The mind of man was therefore afflicted with pessimism, a sense of guilt for having betrayed the divine purpose, a feeling of inadequacy for bringing the world back to its original state of innocence and purity. To men who felt insecure in a changing world, and helpless in a world always changing for the worse, the future had little to offer. It could be regarded for the most part only with resignation, mitigated by individual penance or well-doing, or the hope of some miraculous intervention by the gods, or the return of the god-like kings, to set things right again, yet with little hope that from this setting right there would not be another falling away.

This pervasive pessimism was gradually dispelled in the Western world, partly by the Christian religion, chiefly by the secular intellectual revolution occurring roughly between the fifteenth and the eighteenth centuries. The Christian religion gave assurance that the lost golden age of the past would be restored for the virtuous in the future, and by proclaiming the supreme worth of the individual in the eyes of God enabled men to look forward with hope to the good life after death in the Heavenly City. Meantime, the secular intellectual revolution, centering in the matter-of-fact study of history and science, gradually emancipated the minds of men from resignation to fate and the angry gods. Accumulated knowledge of history, filling in time past with a continuous succession of credible events, banished all lost golden ages to the realm of myth, and enabled men to live without distress in a changing world since it could be regarded as not necessarily changing for the worse. At the same time, a more competent observation and measurement of the action of material things disclosed an outer world of nature, indifferent to man indeed, yet behaving, not as the unpredictable sport of the gods, but in ways understandable to human reason and therefore ultimately subject to man's control.

Thus the conditions were fulfilled which made it possible for men to conceive of Utopia, neither as a lost golden age of the past nor as a Heavenly City after death prepared by the gods for the virtuous, but as a future state on earth of man's own devising. In a world of nature that could be regarded as amenable to man's control, and in a world of changing social relations that need not be regarded as an inevitable decline and fall from original perfection, it was possible to formulate the modern doctrine of progress: the idea that, by deliberate intention and rational direction, men can set the terms and indefinitely improve the conditions of their mundane existence.

The eighteenth century was the moment in history when men first fully realized the engaging implications of this resplendent idea, the moment when, not yet having been brought to the harsh appraisal of experience, it could be accepted with unclouded optimism. Never had the universe seemed less mysterious, more open and visible, more eager to yield its secrets to common-sense questions. Never had the nature of man seemed less perverse, or the mind of man more pliable to the pressure of rational persuasion. The essential reason for this confident optimism is that the marvels of scientific discovery disclosed to the men of that time a God who still functioned but was no longer angry. God the Father could be conceived as a beneficent First Cause who, having performed his essential task of creation, had withdrawn from the affairs of men, leaving them competently prepared and fully instructed for the task of achieving their own salvation. In one tremendous sentence Rousseau expressed the eighteenth-century world view of the universe and man's place in it. "Is it simple," he exclaimed, "is it natural that

God should have gone in search of Moses in order to speak to Jean Jacques Rousseau?"

God had indeed spoken to Rousseau, he had spoken to all men, but his revelation was contained, not in Holy Writ interpreted by Holy Church, but in the great Book of Nature which was open for all men to read. To this open book of nature men would go when they wanted to know what God had said to them. Here they would find recorded the laws of nature and of nature's God, disclosing a universe constructed according to a rational plan; and that men might read these laws aright they had been endowed with reason, a bit of the universal intelligence placed within the individual to make manifest to him the universal reason implicit in things and events. "Natural law," as Volney so clearly and confidently put it, "is the regular and constant order of facts by which God rules the universe; the order which his wisdom presents to the sense and reason of men, to serve them as an equal and common rule of conduct, and to guide them, without distinction of race or sect, toward perfection and happiness." Thus God had devised a planned economy, and had endowed men with the capacity for managing it: to bring his ideas, his conduct, and his institutions into harmony with the universal laws of nature was man's simple allotted task.

At all times political theory must accommodate itself in some fashion to the prevailing world view, and liberal-democratic political theory was no exception to this rule. From time immemorial authority and obedience had been the cardinal concepts both of the prevailing world view and of political and social theory. From time immemorial men had been regarded as subject to overruling authority—the authority of the gods, and the authority of kings who were themselves gods, or descended from gods, or endowed with divine authority to rule in place of gods; and from time immemorial obedience to such divine authority was thought to be the primary obligation of men. Even the Greeks, who were so little afraid of their gods that they could hobnob with them in the most friendly and engaging way, regarded mortals as subject to them; and when they lost faith in the gods they deified the state as the highest good and subordinated the individual to it. But the eighteenth-century world view, making man the measure of all things, mitigated if it did not destroy this sharp contrast between authority and obedience. God still reigned but he did not govern. He had, so to speak, granted his subjects a constitution and authorized them to interpret it as they would in the supreme court of reason. Men were still subject to an overruling authority, but the subjection could be regarded as voluntary because self-imposed, and self-imposed because obedience was exacted by nothing more oppressive than their own rational intelligence.

Liberal-democratic political theory readily accommodated itself to this change in the world view. The voice of the people was now identified with the voice of God, and all authority was derived from it. The individual instead of the state or the prince was now deified and endowed with imprescriptible rights; and since ignorance or neglect of the rights of man was the chief cause of social evils, the first task of political science was to define these rights, the second to devise a form of government suited to guarantee them. The imprescriptible rights of man were easily defined, since they were self-evident: "All men are created equal, [and] are endowed by their Creator with certain inalienable rights, among which are life, liberty, and the pursuit of happiness." From this it followed that all just governments would remove those artificial restraints which impaired these rights, thereby liberating those natural impulses with which God had endowed the individual as a guide to thought and conduct. In the intellectual realm, freedom of thought and the competition of diverse opinion would disclose the truth, which all men, being rational creatures, would progressively recognize and willingly follow. In the economic realm, freedom of enterprise would disclose the natural aptitudes of each individual, and the ensuing competition of interests would stimulate effort, and thereby result in the maximum of material advantage for all. Liberty of the individual from social constraint thus turned out to be not only an inherent natural right but also a preordained natural mechanism for bringing about the material and moral progress of mankind. Men had only to follow reason and self-interest: something not themselves, God and Nature, would do whatever else was necessary for righteousness.

Thus modern liberal-democracy is associated with an ideology which rests upon something more than the minimum assumption essential to any democratic government. It rests upon a philosophy of universally valid ends and means. Its fundamental assumption is the worth and dignity and creative capacity of the individual, so that the chief aim of government is the maximum of individual self-direction, the chief means to that end the minimum of compulsion by the state. Ideally considered, means and ends are conjoined in the concept of freedom: freedom of thought, so that the truth may prevail; freedom of occupation, so that careers may be open to talent; freedom of self-government, so that no one may be compelled against his will.

In the possibility of realizing this ideal the prophets and protagonists of democracy exhibited an unquestioned faith. If their faith seems to us somewhat naïve, the reason is that they placed a far greater reliance upon the immediate influence of good will and rational discussion in shaping the conduct of men than it is possible for us to do. This difference can be conveniently noted in a passage from the *Autobiography* of John Stuart Mill, in which he describes his father's extraordinary faith in two things—representative government and complete freedom of discussion:

> So complete was my father's reliance on the influence of reason over the minds of mankind, whenever it was allowed to reach them, that he felt as if all would be gained if the whole population were taught to read, if all sorts of opinions were allowed to be addressed to them by word and writing, and if by means of the suffrage they could nominate a legislature to give effect to the opinions they adopted. He thought that when the legislature no longer represented a class interest, it would aim at the general interest, honestly and with adequate wisdom; since the people would be sufficiently under the guidance of educated intelligence to make in general good choice of persons to represent them, and having done so to leave to those whom they had chosen a liberal discretion. Accordingly, aristocratic rule, the government of the few in any of its shapes, being in his eyes the only thing that stood between mankind and the administration of its affairs by the best wisdom to be found amongst them, was the object of his sternest disapprobation, and a democratic suffrage the principal articles of his political creed.

The beliefs of James Mill were shared by the little group of Philosophical Radicals who gathered about him. They were, indeed, the beliefs of all those who in the great crusading days placed their hopes in democratic government as a panacea for injustice and oppression. The actual working of democratic government, as these devoted enthusiasts foresaw it, the motives that would inspire men and the objects they would pursue in that ideal democracy which so many honest men have cherished and fought for, have never been better described than by James Bryce in his *Modern Democracies*. In this ideal democracy, says Bryce, the average citizen will give close and constant attention to public affairs, recognizing that this is his interest as well as his duty. He will try to comprehend the main issues of policy, bringing to them an independent and impartial mind, which thinks first not of its own but of the general interest. If, owing to inevitable differences of opinion as to what are the measures needed for the general welfare, parties become inevitable, he will join one, and attend its meetings, but will repress the impulses of party spirit. Never failing to come to the polls, he will vote for his party candidate only if satisfied by his capacity and honesty. He will be ready to . . . be put forward as a candidate for the legislature (if satisfied of his own competence), because public service is recognized as a duty. With such citizens as electors, the legislature will be composed of upright and capable men, single-minded in their wish to serve the nation. Bribery in constituencies, corruption among public servants, will have disappeared. Leaders may not always be single-minded, nor assemblies always wise, nor administrators efficient, but all will be at any rate honest and zealous, so that an atmosphere of confidence and good will will prevail. Most of the causes that make for strife will be absent, for there will be no privileges, no advantages to excite jealousy. Office will be sought only because it gives opportunity for useful public service. Power will be shared by all, and a career open to all alike. Even if the law does not— perhaps it cannot—prevent the accumulation of fortunes, these will be few and not inordinate, for public vigilance will close the illegitimate paths to wealth. All but the most depraved persons will obey and support the law, feeling it to be their own. There will be no excuse for violence, because the constitution will provide a remedy for every grievance. Equality will produce a sense of human solidarity, will refine manners, and increase brotherly kindness.

Such is the ideal form of modern democracy laid away in heaven. I do not need to tell you that its earthly counterpart resembles it but slightly.

QUESTIONS ON CONTENT

1. Define *semantics*.
2. What is the purpose of paragraph 1? Is a democracy "any form of government supported by a majority of the people"?
3. Discuss sentence 2 of paragraph 2.
4. To what does "this antithesis" refer in sentence 1 of paragraph 3?

5. Historically the essential test of a democratic government has been what?

6. What has happened to democracy during the twentieth century?

7. "Democracy has as yet had but a limited and temporary success." What reasons does the author advance for this fact?

8. What influence do the following factors have on democracy: means of communication, economic security?

9. What are the minimum assumptions concerning the people of a democracy?

10. How does Aristotle's idea of democracy differ from the modern idea?

11. What does the author call "the most devastating of all facts"?

12. Why did man first seek a Utopia in the past? What turned his eyes to the future?

13. How does the doctrine of progress promote democracy?

14. Examine James Bryce's description of ideal democracy. In what respects has this ideal particularly failed in its practical application?

∾ *The Tenets of Communism*

MASSIMO SALVADORI

For an understanding of the developments which are likely to take place within the communist movement, it is necessary to keep in mind the main aspirations of the "faithful" and their interpretation of the world in which they live. Similar aspirations and interpretations can be found in other movements: it is their combination in a well-integrated system that constitutes communism. This system can be summed up in the following points:

1. The primary stimulus to action for a communist is an emotional one: the consciousness and horror of economic suffering, both made possible by the freeing of human beings from various forms of political, economic, and intellectual bondage brought about by liberalism during the last two hundred years, either directly (where it triumphed) or indirectly (where it weakened and caused the col-

From *The Rise of Modern Communism,* 1952. Reprinted by permission of Henry Holt and Company.

lapse of traditional authoritarianism). How this is reconciled with the practice of ruthless cruelty is explained in Point 21.

2. On the practical level the communist desires to end the exploitation of man by man. *Exploitation* is understood exclusively in economic terms of a relationship between individuals within a certain social structure (see Point 10 below). Political and intellectual domination do not exist *per se;* if the employer is the impersonal representative of the collective will, there is no domination and no exploitation.

3. All individual and collective activities must be directed toward the goal of greater material welfare (more goods, more leisure, etc.). Communists here simply give greater emphasis to an aspiration which is also stressed by Western liberalism.

4. Points 2 and 3 can be achieved only through the establishment of a collectivistic society in which private ownership of the means of production has been abolished. This has been proved "scientifically" by Marx through the analysis—conducted dialectically—of human history.

5. Point 4 is so important that all means are legitimate which lead to the establishment of collectivism. Among these means *violence* is a most important one.

6. The triumph of collectivism requires the previous conquest of the state, which is nothing but organized violence.

7. Once the communists have conquered the state, no limit can be put to the exercise of their power. For the good of the toiling masses, there must be a dictatorship.

8. From this it follows that all power must be concentrated in the hands of the communists—that is, the state must be totalitarian. Communists reject categorically the fundamental liberal principle of the division of power. In a communist state there can be no separation between political power, economic power, and religious power, nor division within political power. Any autonomy that may exist is not a right of individuals or groups, but a concession made by the state for purely administrative reasons.

9. The universe is so ordained that collectivism is inevitable. The identification of their aspirations with a supposedly universal law has been of fundamental importance in strengthening the communists in the difficult stages of their political struggle. It is equivalent to the Crusaders' conviction that they were carrying out God's Will.

10. The reality of the universe is represented exclusively by Matter, which is inherently endowed with certain features and operates

on the basis of inherent laws. The communists deny emphatically any supernatural level of existence; God therefore does not exist.

11. The universe can be understood only through application of the dialectical principle corresponding to the process through which Matter changes and is transformed.

12. Reason is an attribute of Matter, like movement, energy, etc. The communists reject the identification of the universe with the spirit as emphatically as the concept of God.

13. Man is, of course, part of Matter. He is like clay, and as clay he is molded by the laws inherent in Matter itself. There is no such thing as an independent reason or an independent will; the individual's autonomy simply does not exist.

14. Man is molded by economic forces which act on the basis of laws inherent in the world of economic phenomena, and which are part of the laws of the universe.

15. As reason and will are merely attributes of Matter and expression of laws determining the universal material process, liberty does not exist. Man can only do what he is compelled to do by economic forces.

16. As morality, or evaluation of what is good and what is evil, and choice between them, implies liberty, and liberty is non-existent, so also morality is non-existent *per se*. What human beings call morality is an attribute of Matter and varies with the structure (economic organization) of the Matter.

17. The non-existence of morality *per se* leads the communists to deny the autonomous existence of the law as a system of moral principles, the observance of which is enforced by the state. The denial of law leads to the denial of the concept of the citizen, who is a physical individual endowed with rights and duties—that is, with moral elements.

18. Human reality is represented by categories (economic groups and social classes), and not by individual units included in the group; individual units have no more autonomy than the cells in the human body. Communism rejects categorically the "nominalism" which characterized Western thought from the eleventh to the twentieth centuries, and from which sprang humanism, Protestantism, and liberalism.

19. The liberal assumption of the self-sufficiency, autonomy, and responsibility of the individual is false. Communists are those who have been economically conditioned to discover the truth of human developments; the others are either too limited and cannot discover

the truth (and must therefore be led) or are economically determined not to accept the truth (and must therefore be destroyed).

20. The group, existing *per se*, has total control—political, economic, or religious—over the individual. The communist mind cannot conceive of majority and minority in a group; it is always "the proletariat," "the bourgeoisie," "the clergy," not "the proletarians," "the bourgeois," "the ministers," among whom some may follow one tendency and some another.

21. The individual who refuses to conform to the group to which he belongs is a cancer, a diseased element, and must therefore be destroyed. This postulate is important for an understanding of how communists can combine the concern for human suffering (Point 1) with the practice—and the theory [1]—of such disregard for human life as has rarely been witnessed in the history of mankind. In "nominalistic" terms, communist humanitarianism belongs to the level of abstractions (the collectivity) and is therefore compatible with cruel ruthlessness on the level of reality (the individual). What matters is the welfare of the proletariat, not of the proletarians. The mental approach here is similar to that of the nazis, who were indifferent to the sufferings of millions of Germans because what mattered to them was only the nation or race. Neither communists nor nazis can understand the Christian concepts of love and charity for individual man.

22. In broader terms, heresies and "deviations" are diseases in the social body and must therefore be extirpated. A healthy society requires that all its members conform completely to the type required by the society itself.

From these twenty-two points it is easy to see that communists are compelled by their own beliefs and by their understanding of the world in which we live to enforce political despotism and intellectual dogmatism. There is nothing in their attitude which has not been experimented with—at times fairly successfully (from their point of view)—by other movements; what is new is the possibility, supplied by technological progress, of exercising greater control over the individual than ever before.

The question is often asked whether communism can change its internal structure and go through a process of liberalization, or

[1] "In principle we have never renounced terror and cannot renounce it." Lenin, quoted in E. H. Carr, *The Bolshevik Revolution, 1917–1923* (New York: Macmillan, 1951), p. 156.

whether it is chained to authoritarianism to such an extent that all communist states must be police states. Both communist and non-communist Western intellectuals have often maintained that authoritarianism is only a passing phase, the result of capitalistic and imperialistic pressure; that, with the consolidation of communist regimes and the weakening of internal opposition and external aggression, an era of liberty will be introduced and the withering away of the state, foreseen by Marx, will become a reality. In theory most things are possible. On the basis of recent historical evidence, however, this optimistic view of the future of communism seems to be based on a number of misconceptions concerning certain fundamentals, particularly the nature of collectivism, the communist ideology, and the influence of political institutions brought into existence by communism.

Experience shows that discipline and authority are required for the proper functioning of economic enterprises. In a capitalistic society there are hundreds of thousands, or millions, of different enterprises. Because of their multiplicity, because of conflicting interests separating industry, agriculture, trade and credit, also separating employers and employees, management and labor—in other words, because of the division of power characteristic of democratic societies, the enforcement of authority and discipline is limited. In a collectivistic society there is one huge corporation embracing the whole of the economy; its very size requires a complicated and rigid authoritarian and disciplinarian structure; planning cannot be disrupted by autonomous decisions reached by this or that branch of the economy, by one or another group of producers; there is no division of power. It is difficult to see how, under such conditions, the economy can be run on a basis other than that of total authority and total discipline. And if the economy and the state are one, how can this one thing act in an authoritarian way in its economic activities and act freely in its political activities? If the collectivist state is politically free, it is always possible that the slowness, vacillations, dissent, and neutralization of conflicting forces, which often characterize democratic procedure, will bring the economy to a standstill; if the efficiency of the economy is to be maintained, democratic procedure must be abolished—as has been done in the Soviet Union, in China, and in the so-called "People's Democracies."

Since the beginning of civilization, there have been numerous collectivist societies. Not a single one has enjoyed free institutions. Apart from its political aspects, collectivism is not conducive to the expression of individual autonomy. Because of the absence of private wealth, whatever the individual wishes to achieve can be achieved only through state authorization. No magazine can be printed unless the state provides the newsprint; no organization can have its headquarters unless the state provides the building; no meeting can be held unless the state provides the place. Miracles can happen; but it is wiser to believe in miracles (especially economic and political miracles) after they have happened, and not before. Meanwhile, it is well to note that in the Soviet Union and in the People's Democracies despotism and collectivism have gone together, that communists are satisfied with what they have achieved politically in the states they control, that for them a police state is the same as liberty: "Repression at home has become superfluous, because with the suppression of exploitation and the disappearance of exploiters, there was no one left to repress." [2]

Freedom usually brings with it differentiation and division. In a free society there are conservatives and radicals, believers and unbelievers, those who work hard and those who do not. Democracy, through the recognition of the legitimacy of differences and of opposition, implies a procedure through which these varied groups can live more or less peacefully together. The communist mind does not conceive differentiation, nor does it conceive the legitimacy of opposition. For the communist, what is different is either error or evil, and cannot be put on the same level as the truth represented by the communist idea. If communists were to be tolerant, their tolerance would be like that of the Ottoman Turks who allowed the "infidels" to survive but considered them subhuman. Communists maintain that the problems of opposition and "deviation" cannot arise in a truly socialistic society, because all citizens, being economically equal, will be of one mind. They do not consider that incomes may be equal but that functions will be different, or that there is no evidence that all members of an economic group react in the same way (in free societies property owners are divided, farmers are divided, workers are divided).

Whatever may have been their original intentions, Lenin and his collaborators proceeded to organize Russia on the basis of a totalitarian dictatorship. Dictatorships (more of an oligarchic type than the Russian one) have been organized in the countries in which communists have seized power during the last few years. Once an

[2] Stalin, quoted in *Contemporary Political Science* (Paris: UNESCO, 1950), p. 404.

institution has been brought into existence, it is hard to kill it. Institutions often tend to develop according to a logic which has little or nothing to do with the concepts underlying them. There are very few instances of dictatorships ending of their own will. The end is usually the result of internal conflict or external attack; in the absence of either, dictatorships may last for centuries. If communist thinking included the autonomy of the individual, the control of the citizens over the government, the legitimacy of opposition, there would be a faint possibility of change. But these are the very ideas the communists have criticized most severely. It was their hatred for these ideas that induced them to cut themselves off from what had been until then the main stream of socialist thought.

It is possible to imagine that, having eliminated all opposition and dissent, communists might put an end to the use of the coercive powers of the state. It seems highly unlikely, however, that they will abandon the instruments required for the total enforcement of the communist will over the citizens. Were they to do so they would be no longer communists, but what they hate with the greatest passion: democratic socialists.

The "withering away" of the state is as out of the question as any minor "liberalization" in the organization of the movement, simply because any relaxation of political and intellectual pressure would bring into existence differences, deviations, and opposition, the legitimacy of which the communist mind cannot conceive. If communist societies continue to exist for some time, it is likely that they will evolve the institutions of self-perpetuating oligarchies (politburos or their equivalent) enforcing political tyranny, intellectual dogmatism, and economic monopoly.

After the seizure of political power, the main communist emphasis is on expansion of economic activities. Success will undoubtedly be achieved, thanks to the concentration of all available capital and of the direction of labor in the hands of a group with unlimited power. Results in the Soviet Union have been on the whole inferior to those achieved in capitalistic countries during the corresponding period of industrial expansion. The rate of economic expansion is not likely to increase, because the advantages of concentration and purposeful unified direction are offset by the repression of individual initiative and by bureaucracy. (In the United States the ratio of administrative workers to production workers is about 1 to 7; in the Soviet Union, 1 to 4; Soviet economic bureaucracy would fall into a morass of slowness, inefficiency, and waste unless held in line by exceptionally energetic individuals. But a bureaucratic society is not likely to produce many exceptionally energetic individuals.) For short periods the curve of economic expansion is likely to rise more in communist states than in countries with non-collectivistic economies. For longer periods (a decade or more), the opposite is likely to be true. The rate of economic expansion in communist states is important when we take into account their relations with non-communist states; it can however be considered relatively unimportant from the point of view of the internal strength of a communist state. Lacking the possibility of making comparisons, and unable to apply their critical faculties to the objective analysis of their conditions, citizens of communist states after a few years of dictatorship will believe whatever they are told by their leaders about the achievements of collectivism and its superiority over all other economic systems.

In the field of intellectual activities, the experience of communism is not likely to differ from that of other despotic societies. As long as there are minds formed in the pre-despotic period—where at least some liberty of thought was tolerated—a certain brilliancy may characterize mental developments. As generations go by, despotism gradually represses—sometimes to the point of suppression—the creativeness of the human mind, and intellectual stagnation and decadence follow. This process may be more rapid in a communist society than it has been in other authoritarian societies because (1) the communist conceptual framework (dialectical materialism) is a particularly narrow one, and because (2) means of thought control (particularly censorship and monopoly of education) are considerably more efficient in the twentieth century than they were in previous centuries. The curve indicating intellectual expression is likely to rise less and fall sooner than the curve of economic expansion.

Again on the basis of experiences made by other strongly authoritarian oligarchic states, it is legitimate to assume that, in spite of all efforts to enforce total conformity or orthodoxy, differences are likely to appear in the long run within the oligarchy, though not among the masses of citizens—or "subjects," as they should be called. Differences may arise on questions of principles or of policies, or simply on questions of personal interest. Often the greater the power, the more fierce is the struggle for power. To this must be added the economic incentive deriving from the fact that in a communist state political power is the best road to wealth, and that, as generations go by, the missionary spirit which at present is inspiring many communist leaders will be replaced more and more by materialistic considerations. In the European satellite states agreement is enforced by the all-powerful Politburo of the Soviet Union. But already in Yugoslavia the lack of control by the Soviet Politburo over the Yugoslav police has made it possible for Tito to "deviate." In China also the power is in the hands of a communist oligarchy autonomous vis-à-vis the Soviet one. A falling out of Chinese and Soviet communist leaders should not be expected in the near future, since the two groups are being held together by their common ideology and by strong common economic and political interests. But what is unlikely in the immediate future may not be an impossibility in the long run. In the Soviet Union itself there is no principle for the transfer of power; succession may be settled on the basis of an agreement among the members of the oligarchy. There will be occasions, however, when succession will have to be settled by force, and force may mean anything from a "palace revolution" to a civil war.

The present leaders of the communist states, from Mao to Rakosi, are mostly people endowed with strong personalities molded in a period of storm and stress. The younger leaders, as is already apparent in the Soviet Union, are as fanatic and bigoted as their elders, but their personalities are less impressive. They are the products of a highly bureaucratized society, and not of a hard struggle for survival in a competitive world. The qualities leading to communist success in a non-communist world are not the same as those leading to success within a communist society which demands servility, blind obedience, and absolute conformity. However dangerous it may be to prophesy, it is possible that, as time goes on, the quality of leadership of the communist societies will gradually deteriorate. Because in a totalitarian structure the impulse to action can only come from those who monopolize political power, their deterioration is likely to be reflected, in the long run, in the deterioration of communist institutions. Minds will stagnate, and so will all forms of individual and collective activities.

However vague and uncertain, a conclusion can be drawn from what has been stated in the last few paragraphs. Communism, as we have seen, is strong today. It may not be the strongest single movement existing in the world at the opening of the second half of the twentieth century, but it is certainly one of the strongest. Its strength derives mainly from a revulsion for conditions of suffering in which lived hundreds of millions of human beings in the Eastern

Hemisphere. Once communism is on its own, the strength it derives from the defects of non-communist societies disappears. Because of its totalitarian structure, a communist state cannot produce the energy required to maintain fresh life in its institutions. It is therefore bound, if not to decay, certainly to stagnate. It is impossible to say how much time will be needed for this process to take place. But if non-communist states can—and there is no reason why they should not, unless seized by panic—hold their own for a generation or so, they are likely to be faced at the end of that period by a communism that has lost most of its present dynamic energy, a communism whose institutions are becoming empty and brittle shells, and whose leaders and followers, instead of being crusaders, have become mere bureaucrats.

If by *error* we mean engaging in action which gives different results from those expected, the communist leaders have already made a number of serious errors. Others can be expected. Three major and two minor past errors deserve mention. (1) In 1918 Lenin and his friends were convinced that within a few years all Europe would have gone communist; for five years, therefore, they engaged in revolutionary tactics which strengthened anti-communist forces. (2) In 1928 Stalin and the Comintern decided that the shortest cut to the triumph of communism in Europe was to help the authoritarian Right to destroy the main enemy—liberalism. The result was the sudden appearance of nazism, which proved to be stronger than either liberalism or communism, and which would have destroyed the Soviet Union if the latter had not been helped by what remained of liberal states. (3) In 1945 the Soviet Politburo was certain that an economic crisis would engulf the United States, and decided therefore on a policy of aggressiveness. The result was the strengthening of an anti-communist feeling in the United States and a greater resistance to Societ expansion. Among the minor mistakes, (4) Tito was excommunicated on the assumption that the Yugoslav masses would revolt against him. (5) The Korean war was launched on the assumption that the United States would not fight. Through the concourse of favorable unforeseen happenings, none of the errors proved to be lethal to the communist movement. But what has been true for the past may not necessarily hold for the future.

Concerning its position in world affairs, we have seen that by the end of 1950 the communist movement exercised undisputed control over a large area of the Eastern Hemisphere, from the Bering Straits to Thuringia in central Germany, from the Arctic Ocean to the frontiers of Indochina, India, and the Near East. Over 750,000,000 people live in this area. If it is true, as contemporary events seem to bear out, that an efficient and dynamic dictatorship cannot be eliminated by the efforts of internal opposition, it is to be expected, in view of the lack of pressure from outside, that communism will remain the dominant political force in that area. Its weakening is likely to take place only after it has lost its dynamic energy—a process which, as we have seen, is not to be expected in the immediate future.

At the opposite extreme are the seven nations of the English-speaking world, where communism has achieved its least success. There we find conscious opposition to the monistic ideologies and to the totalitarian practices of communism, and a fairly clear vision of the fundamental differences between a free society and a servile one. In view of their high level of cultural, economic, and political developments, the English-speaking countries naturally play the main role in checking the advance of communism outside the areas where it has achieved success, thanks to chaotic conditions created by the two World Wars.

Communism is also still relatively weak where traditional oligarchies exercise political power over mainly passive masses of citizens, and where intellectuals are few and have relatively little influence. This is true, in varying degree, not only of most Latin American countries, but also of the Moslem world, of India, of parts of the southwestern Pacific area, and of Negro Africa. The weakening of these traditional oligarchies and the awakening of the masses of the people will lead to a crisis which will open the way to the development of new political forces. Communism there will certainly have the active support of the communist-controlled states. Democracy, in its individualistic-capitalistic form or in its limited socialistic-collectivistic form, should receive the support of the nations which operate within the framework of free institutions. Under present conditions it is difficult to foresee an overthrow of either the totalitarian form of government in the communist area, or of the democratic form of government in the English-speaking world. The influence of both communism and democracy in shaping the future of mankind is likely to depend to a great extent on their respective abilities to determine the changes which will occur among a majority of the population of the world in the second half of the twentieth century. If there are more than 750,000,000 inhabitants in the entire communist empire, there are only a little over 300,000,000 in the states in which free institutions are solidly entrenched: the English-speaking nations, France, the smaller European democracies, two or three Latin American states, etc. This leaves 1,200,-000,000 people in the rest of the world. There is little doubt that the communist organizations are bracing themselves for the conquest of nations where democracy is shaky, and those nations which are only now emerging from their Middle Ages, as in the case of most Moslem countries, or are for the first time entering the world of civilization, as is the case of Negro Africa.

Whatever the importance of the attempts made to influence developments in the non-Western world, the main field of conflict at the middle of the century between the free or pluralistic form of society and the servile, monistic one, was represented by Continental western Europe. Because of the high level of cultural and economic activities, that section of Europe—in spite of the exhaustion caused by a succession of wars, civil wars, economic crises, and violent ideological conflicts—still plays an important role in world affairs. Nearly 250 million people live there, belonging to nations which only a generation ago were leading mankind, intellectually as well as politically and economically. They produce half as many goods and services as are produced in the whole of the communist world. If the human and material resources of Continental western Europe were to be controlled by the communists, they would come much closer to their realization of total triumph.

In that area there is probably a higher percentage of convinced fanatical communists than anywhere else. They can count on the support—varying from state to state—of anything between less than one tenth and nearly one third of the population. The majority of the people in France, Italy, Western Germany, and in the smaller states are definitely opposed to communism. This majority, however, is divided, and the various sections are considerably less dynamic than the communists. They often have a better understanding of what they do not want than of what they do want. Deep chasms separate the main anti-communist tendencies existing at present: Christian democracy (or Christian socialism), democratic socialism and liberalism (represented in various countries by several conflicting parties).[3] In parts of southern and central Europe fascism

---

[3] At the middle of 1951 there were thirteen states in Continental Europe in which the citizens could express their political will freely. Of the elected representatives of the people 36 percent belonged to Christian Democratic or similar parties, 27 percent to Democratic Socialist parties, and 17 percent to Liberal parties. The balance was made up by communists and by groups of the authoritarian Right.

still appeals to large sections of the population. Wherever there are fascist or semi-fascist dictatorships, their non-communist opponents are often drawn within the orbit of communist influence.[4]

Without disparaging the courageous democratic opponents of communism who, since the end of World War II, have conducted a brilliant and on the whole successful fight against totalitarianism, we may assume that what will happen in Continental western Europe during the near future will be the result more of external pressures (American and Russian) than of the autonomous working of internal forces. National communist parties and underground communist military organizations enjoy the powerful backing of the Soviet Union which provides skilled organizers, trained leadership, clear-cut directives, asylum to those who need it, and probably financial means. Through the Marshall Plan and the North Atlantic Treaty Organization the United States has tried, in conjunction with other measures concerning individual European states, to strengthen anti-communist forces and to give them greater cohesion.

Begun as one of the many extreme tendencies unknown to the general public at the turn of the century, communism stands today as possibly the most powerful single political movement, if not in the world, certainly in most of the Eastern Hemisphere. Among the factors which have contributed to its success are:

1. the economic suffering of large sections of mankind;
2. the impression made by this suffering on Marxist intellectuals who form the solid core of the communist movement, and whose thinking is characterized by emotional postulates and extreme dogmatism;
3. the chaotic conditions in which many areas of Europe and Asia found themselves after the two World Wars, which enabled small minorities of well-organized and determined communists to seize political power;
4. the willingness to use brute force and to ignore every principle of ethics;
5. an uncompromising attitude which brooks no opposition and no deviation, and which gives to communism a cohesion and a homogeneity unknown to all other movements (except the

[4] From a democratic point of view, one of the unfavorable aspects of the situation in many parts of non-Soviet Continental Europe is that the movement for checking communism can easily slide in the direction of unsavory Rightist totalitarianism. It happened in Italy in 1922 and in Germany in 1933, with tragic results for Europe and for the rest of mankind. It has happened in the Iberian peninsula; it may happen again in many countries. It is only in Switzerland, in the Scandinavian and in the Benelux states that democracy is as solidly entrenched as it is in the English-speaking world.

fascist one); with this goes an internal structure which puts a maximum of power into the hands of a minimum of leaders;

6. the promise of the Millennium, coupled with a deep belief in the inevitability of socialism, and a remarkable spirit of sacrifice;
7. the ability of present communist leaders to adjust their action to ever-changing conditions; and
8. the power and prestige of the Soviet Union.

Communism today is less utopian than it was in its early revolutionary phase (1917–1923). It has a popular base which was lacking then; it enjoys the advantages of skilled and courageous leadership; it has become first and foremost a machine for the conquest of political power. There had been a beautiful dream, which is still the dream of many intellectuals who have little contact with reality. For those who believe in freedom, the reality of communism is a tragic one,[5] and it is no use deluding oneself that it will be transformed through an internal process of the communist movement.

Looking at the institutions of the communist state and of the communist parties, at what is and not at what should or might be, one cannot escape the conclusion that communism negates the noble attempt made during the last three hundred years in Western civilization to make liberty the basis of the social order, to evolve institutions through which continuous peaceful change can take place, to replace arbitrary rule with rule by law, and government by force with government by discussion. The attempt has produced but limited results so far; success can be achieved only through an effort which includes an uncompromising opposition to communism.

QUESTIONS ON CONTENT

1. What is the basic difference between the theory of democracy and the theory of communism? How do all the minor differences proceed from this basic difference?
2. How do communists reconcile their professed humanitarianism with their practice of ruthless cruelty?

[5] "Communism, in its stage of so-called Utopia . . . taught love and kindness. . . . Upon becoming political . . . it turned to immorality, from love to hatred, the most intensified expression of which is Leninism." A. Gordin, *Communism Unmasked* (New York: Hord, 1940), p. 308. "An idea which has inspired whole generations to matchless heroism has become identified with the methods of a regime based on corruption, extortion and betrayal." Such is the revised opinion of the first secretary of the Comintern, A. Balabanova, *My Life as a Rebel* (New York: Harper, 1938), p. 319.

3. How do communists interpret the word, *exploitation?* Can a communist subject be exploited?
4. What attention does communism give to material welfare? To spiritual? If material progress is a communist ideal, why have communist states made less progress in this direction than has been made by democratic states?
5. Explain the relationship of communism to dictatorship? Has single dictatorship in Russia been abandoned?
6. Discuss point 8 concerning the concentration of all power—political, economic, intellectual, spiritual—in the state.
7. What are the chances that totalitarianism will cease or markedly decrease in communistic states?
8. What prediction does the author make concerning the future of communism? Discuss his reasoning.
9. Name the major errors the communists have committed. Can you add others?
10. What are the major factors which have contributed to communist success?

❧ *The Man with the Hoe*

Edwin Markham

Written after seeing Millet's world-famous painting of a toiler in the abyss of labor.

God made man in his own image: in the image of God made He him.—Genesis.

Bowed by the weight of centuries he leans
Upon his hoe and gazes on the ground,
The emptiness of ages in his face,
And on his back the burden of the world.
Who made him dead to rapture and despair, 5
A thing that grieves not and that never hopes,
Stolid and stunned, a brother to the ox?
Who loosened and let down this brutal jaw?

Copyright 1899 and 1924, reprinted by permission of Virgil Markham.

Whose was the hand that slanted back this brow?
Whose breath blew out the light within this brain?   10

Is this the Thing the Lord God made and gave
To have dominion over sea and land;
To trace the stars and search the heavens for power;
To feel the passion of Eternity?
Is this the dream He dreamed who shaped the suns   15
And markt their ways upon the ancient deep?
Down all the caverns of Hell to their last gulf
There is no shape more terrible than this—
More tongued with cries against the world's blind greed—
More filled with signs and portents for the soul—   20
More packt with danger to the universe.

What gulfs between him and the seraphim!
Slave of the wheel of labor, what to him
Are Plato and the swing of Pleiades?
What the long reaches of the peaks of song,   25
The rift of dawn, the reddening of the rose?
Thru this dread shape the suffering ages look;
Time's tragedy is in that aching stoop;
Thru this dread shape humanity betrayed,
Plundered, profaned and disinherited,   30
Cries protest to the Powers that made the world,
A protest that is also prophecy.

O masters, lords and rulers in all lands,
Is this the handiwork you give to God,
This monstrous thing distorted and soul-quencht?   35
How will you ever straighten up this shape;
Touch it again with immortality;
Give back the upward looking and the light;
Rebuild in it the music and the dream;
Make right the immemorial infamies,   40
Perfidious wrongs, immedicable woes?

O masters, lords and rulers in all lands,
How will the future reckon with this Man?
How answer his brute question in that hour
When whirlwinds of rebellion shake all shores?   45

How will it be with kingdoms and with kings—
With those who shaped him to the thing he is—
When this dumb Terror shall rise to judge the world,
After the silence of the centuries?

QUESTIONS ON CONTENT

1. You may find in your library a print of Millet's painting. Compare the picture and the poem. Which is more expressive?
2. Is the quotation from Genesis intended as irony? Explain.
3. What does "the world's blind greed" (line 19) have to do with the plight of the man with the hoe?
4. Explain: "A protest that is also prophecy" (line 32).
5. Does the poet suggest what will make "this dumb terror" rise against his oppressors?
6. Are men with the hoes ripe for democracy or for what? Discuss.

❧ *The People Will Live On*

CARL SANDBURG

The people will live on.
The learning and blundering people will live on.
They will be tricked and sold and again sold
And go back to the nourishing earth for rootholds,
The people so peculiar in renewal and comeback,   5
You can't laugh off their capacity to take it.
The mammoth rests between his cyclonic dramas.
The people so often sleepy, weary, enigmatic,
is a vast huddle with many units saying:
"I earn my living.   10
I make enough to get by
and it takes all my time.
If I had more time
I could do more for myself
and maybe for others.   15
I could read and study

From *The People, Yes,* by Carl Sandburg, copyright, 1936, by Harcourt, Brace and Company, Inc.

and talk things over
and find out about things.
It takes time.
I wish I had the time." 20

The people is a tragic and comic two-face: hero and hoodlum:
phantom and gorilla twisting to moan with a gargoyle
mouth: "They buy me and sell me . . . it's a game . . . sometime I'll break loose . . ."

Once having marched 25
Over the margins of animal necessity,
Over the grim line of sheer subsistence
Then man came
To the deeper rituals of his bones,
To the lights lighter than any bones, 30
To the time for thinking things over,
To the dance, the song, the story,
Or the hours given over to dreaming,
Once having so marched.

Between the finite limitations of the five senses 35
and the endless yearnings of man for the beyond
the people hold to the humdrum bidding of work and food
while reaching out when it comes their way
for lights beyond the prison of the five senses,
for keepsakes lasting beyond any hunger or death. 40
This reaching is alive.
The panderers and liars have violated and smutted it.
Yet this reaching is alive yet
for lights and keepsakes.

The people know the salt of the sea 45
and the strength of the winds
lashing the corners of the earth.
The people take the earth
as a tomb of rest and a cradle of hope.
Who else speaks for the Family of Man? 50
They are in tune and step
with constellations of universal law.

The people is a polychrome,
a spectrum and a prism

held in a moving monolith, 55
a console organ of changing themes,
a clavilux of color poems
wherein the sea offers fog
and the fog moves off in rain
and the Labrador sunset shortens 60
to a nocturne of clear stars
serene over the shot spray
of northern lights.
The steel mill sky is alive.
The fire breaks white and zigzag 65
shot on a gun-metal gloaming.
Man is a long time coming.
Man will yet win.
Brother may yet line up with brother:

This old anvil laughs at many broken hammers. 70
There are men who can't be bought.
The fireborn are at home in fire.
The stars make no noise.
You can't hinder the wind from blowing.
Time is a great teacher. 75
Who can live without hope?

In the darkness with a great bundle of grief the people march.
In the night, and overhead a shovel of stars for keeps, the people
march:
Where to? what next?" 80

QUESTIONS ON CONTENT

1. Are "learning and blundering" people the hope of a democracy?
2. Does Sandburg imply the same distinction between the people
   and overlords which Markham states clearly in "The Man with
   the Hoe"? (See, for example, line 23.) Is there a threat in "The
   People Will Live On"?
3. Discuss lines 10–20. Have you heard this sort of talk?
4. Is the theme of this poem that man will never be satisfied with
   material things, that man cannot truly live by bread alone? Cite
   lines to indicate that this may be the theme.
5. What are the "lights" and the "keepsakes" (line 44)?

6. What is "this old anvil" of line 70?
7. Does line 76, "Who can live without hope?", explain the statements of the previous six lines?
8. What, do you think, is the answer to the last two questions of this poem?

❧ *Darkness at Noon*

ARTHUR KOESTLER

[The following episodes represent models of the Soviet technique for making effective the will of No. 1. The central character is N. S. Rubashov, who is, according to Koestler, "a synthesis of the lives of a number of men who were victims of the so-called Moscow Trials." Arlova, an ardent revolutionist herself, is Rubashov's mistress. The first episode describes the preliminaries to the arrest of Arlova. The second episode occurs in a cell block of a Moscow prison after Rubashov himself has been arrested. All the prisoners know and use "the quadratic alphabet" to tap out messages to each other through the cell walls.]

The Arrest of Arlova

It was the time of preparation for the second great trial of the opposition. The air in the Legation had become peculiarly thin. Photographs and portraits disappeared from walls overnight; they had hung there for years, nobody had looked at them, but now the light patches leaped to the eye. The staff restricted their conversation to service matters; they spoke to each other with a careful and reserved politeness. At meals in the Legation canteen, when conversation was unavoidable, they stuck to the stock phrases of official terminology, which, in the familiar atmosphere, appeared grotesque and rather uneasy; it was as though, between requests for salt-cellar and mustard-pot, they called out to each other the catch-words of the latest Congress manifesto. Often it happened that somebody protested against a supposed false interpretation of what he had just said, and called his neighbors to witness, with precipitate exclamations of "I did not say that," or "That is not what I meant." The whole thing gave Rubashov the impression of

From Arthur Koestler, *Darkness at Noon*. Copyright 1941 by The Macmillan Company and used with their permission.

a queer and ceremonious marionette-play with figures, moving on wires, each saying their set piece. Arlova alone, with her silent, sleepy manner, seemed to remain unchanged.

Not only the portraits on the walls, but also the shelves in the library were thinned out. The disappearance of certain books and brochures happened discreetly, usually the day after the arrival of a new message from above. Rubashov made his sarcastic commentaries on it while dictating to Arlova, who received them in silence. Most of the works on foreign trade and currency disappeared from the shelves—their author, the People's Commissar for Finance, had just been arrested; also nearly all old Party Congress reports treating the same subject; most books and reference-books on the history and antecedents of the Revolution; most works by living authors on jurisprudence and philosophy; all pamphlets dealing with the problems of birth control; the manuals on the structure of the People's Army; treatises on trade unionism and the right to strike in the People's state; practically every study of the problems of political constitution more than two years old, and, finally, even the volumes of the *Encyclopaedia* published by the Academy —a new revised edition being promised shortly.

New books arrived, too; the classics of social science appeared with new footnotes and commentaries, the old histories were replaced by new histories, the old memoirs of dead revolutionary leaders were replaced by new memoirs of the same defunct. Rubashov remarked jokingly to Arlova that the only thing left to be done was to publish a new and revised edition of the back numbers of all newspapers.

In the meantime, a few weeks ago, an order had come from "above," to appoint a librarian who would take the political responsibility for the contents of the Legation library. They had appointed Arlova to this post. At first Rubashov had mumbled something about a "kindergarten" and had held the whole thing for an imbecility, up to the evening when, at the weekly meeting of the Legation Party cell, Arlova had been sharply attacked from several sides. Three or four speakers, amongst whom was the First Secretary, rose and complained that some of the most important speeches of No. 1 were not to be found in the library, that on the other hand, it was still full of oppositional works, and that books by politicians who had since been unmasked as spies, traitors and agents of foreign Powers had until quite recently occupied prominent positions in the shelves; so that one could hardly avoid a suspicion of an intentional demonstration. The speakers were dispassionate and cuttingly business-like; they used carefully selected phrases. It seemed as though they were giving each other the cues for a pre-arranged text. All speeches ended with the conclusion that the Party's chief duty was to be watchful, to denounce abuses mercilessly, and that whoever did not fulfil this duty made himself an accomplice of the vile *saboteurs.* Arlova, summoned to make a statement, said with her usual equanimity, that she was far from having any evil intent; and that she had followed every instruction given her; but while she was speaking in her deep, slightly blurred voice, she let her glance rest a long time on Rubashov, which she otherwise never did in the presence of others. The meeting ended with the resolution to give Arlova a "serious warning."

Rubashov, who knew only too well the methods lately brought into use in the Party, became uneasy. He guessed that there was something in store for Arlova and felt helpless, because there was nothing tangible to fight against.

The air in the Legation became even thinner. Rubashov stopped making personal comments while dictating, and that gave him a singular feeling of guilt. There was apparently no change in his relations with Arlova, but this curious feeling of guilt, which was solely due to the fact that he no longer felt capable of making witty remarks while dictating, prevented him stopping behind her chair and putting his hands on her shoulders, as he used to do. After a week, Arlova stayed away from his room one evening, and did not come the following evenings either. It was three days before Rubashov could bring himself to ask her the reason. She answered something about a migraine in her sleepy voice and Rubashov did not press her any further. From then on she did not come again, with one exception.

This was three weeks after the cell meeting which had pronounced the "serious warning," and a fortnight after she had first stopped visiting him. Her behavior was almost as usual, but the whole evening Rubashov had the feeling that she was waiting for him to say something decisive. He only said, however, that he was glad she was back again, and that he was overworked and tired— which actually was the case. In the night he noticed repeatedly that she was awake and staring into the dark. He could not get rid of this tormenting sense of guilt; also his toothache had started again. That was her last visit to him.

Next day, before Arlova had appeared in his office, the Secretary told Rubashov, in a manner which was supposed to be confidential, but with each sentence carefully formulated, that Arlova's brother and sister-in-law had been arrested a week ago "over there." Arlova's brother had married a foreigner; they were both accused of having treasonable connections with her native country in the service of the opposition.

A few minutes later Arlova arrived for work. She sat, as always, on her chair in front of the desk, in her embroidered blouse, slightly bent forward. Rubashov walked up and down behind her, and all the time he had before his eyes her bent neck, with the skin slightly stretched over the neck-bones. He could not take his eyes off this piece of skin, and felt an uneasiness which amounted to physical discomfort. The thought would not leave him that "over there" the condemned were shot through the back of the neck.

At the next meeting of the Party cell Arlova was dismissed from her post as librarian because of political untrustworthiness, on the motion of the First Secretary. No comment was made and there was no discussion. Rubashov, who was suffering from almost intolerable toothache, had excused himself from attending the meeting. A few days afterwards Arlova and another member of the staff were recalled. Their names were never mentioned by their former colleagues; but, during the months he remained in the Legation before he was himself recalled, the sisterly scent of her large, lazy body clung to the walls of his room and never left them. . . .

The End of Bogrov

Rubashov had never witnessed an execution—except, nearly, his own; but that had been during the Civil War. He could not well picture to himself how the same thing looked in normal circumstances, as part of an orderly routine. He knew vaguely that the executions were carried out at night in the cellars, and that the delinquent was killed by a bullet in the neck; but the details of it he did not know. In the Party death was no mystery, it had no romantic aspect. It was a logical consequence, a factor with which one reckoned and which bore rather an abstract character. Also death was rarely spoken of, and the word "execution" was hardly ever used; the customary expression was "physical liquidation." The words "physical liquidation" again evoked only one concrete idea: The cessation of political activity. The act of dying itself was a technical detail, with no claim to interest; death as a factor in a logical equation had lost any intimate bodily feature.

Rubashov stared into the darkness through his pince-nez. Had the proceedings already started? Or was it still to come? He had taken off his shoes and socks; his bare feet at the other end of the blanket stuck up palely in the darkness. The silence became even more unnatural. It was not the usual comforting absence of noise; it was a silence which had swallowed all sound and smothered it, a silence vibrating like a taut drum-skin. Rubashov stared at his bare feet and slowly moved the toes. It looked grotesque and uncanny, as though the white feet led a life of their own. He was conscious of his own body with unusual intensity, felt the lukewarm touch of the blanket on his legs and the pressure of his hand under his neck. Where did the "physical liquidation" take place? He had the vague idea that it must take place below, under the stairs which led down, beyond the barber's room. He smelled the leather of Gletkin's revolver belt and heard the crackling of his uniform. What did he say to his victim? "Stand with your face to the wall"? Did he add "please"? Or did he say: "Don't be afraid. It won't hurt . . ."? Perhaps he shot without any warning, from behind, while they were walking along—but the victim would be constantly turning his head round. Perhaps he hid the revolver in his sleeve, as the dentist hides his forceps. Perhaps others were also present. How did they look? Did the man fall forward or backwards? Did he call out? Perhaps it was necessary to put a second bullet in him to finish him off.

Rubashov smoked and looked at his toes. It was so quiet that one heard the crackling of the burning cigarette paper. He took a deep pull on his cigarette. Nonsense, he said to himself. Penny novelette. In actual fact, he had never believed in the technical reality of "physical liquidation." Death was an abstraction, especially one's own. Probably it was now all over, and what is past has no reality. It was dark and quiet, and No. 402 had stopped tapping.

He wished that outside somebody might scream to tear this unnatural silence. He sniffed and noticed that for some time already he had the scent of Arlova in his nostrils. Even the cigarettes smelled of her; she had carried a leather case in her bag and every cigarette out of it had smelled of her powder. . . . The silence persisted. Only the bunk creaked slightly when he moved.

Rubashov was just thinking of getting up and lighting another cigarette when the ticking in the wall started again. THEY ARE COMING, said the ticking.

Rubashov listened. He heard his pulses hammering in his temples and nothing else. He waited. The silence thickened. He took off his pince-nez and tapped:

I HEAR NOTHING. . . .

For a whole while No. 402 did not answer. Suddenly he tapped, loudly and sharply:

NO. 380. PASS IT ON.

Rubashov sat up quickly. He understood: the news had been tapped on through eleven cells, by the neighbours of No. 380. The occupants of the cells between 380 and 402 formed an acoustic relay through darkness and silence. They were defenseless, locked within their four walls; this was their form of solidarity. Rubashov jumped from his bunk, pattered over bare-footed to the other wall, posted himself next to the bucket, and tapped to No. 406:

ATTENTION. NO. 380 IS TO BE SHOT NOW. PASS IT ON.

He listened. The bucket stank; its vapours had replaced the scent of Arlova. There was no answer. Rubashov pattered hastily back to the bunk. This time he tapped not with the pince-nez but with his knuckles:

WHO IS NO. 380?

There was again no answer. Rubashov guessed that, like himself, No. 402 was moving pendulum-like between the two walls of his cell. In the eleven cells beyond him, the inhabitants were hurrying noiselessly, with bare feet, backwards and forwards between the walls. Now No. 402 was back again at his wall; he announced:

THEY ARE READING THE SENTENCE TO HIM. PASS IT ON.

Rubashov repeated his previous question:

WHO IS HE?

But No. 402 had gone again. It was no use passing the message on to Rip Van Winkle, yet Rubashov pattered over to the bucket side of the cell and tapped it through; he was driven by an obscure sense of duty, the feeling that the chain must not be broken. The proximity of the bucket made him feel sick. He pattered back to the bed and waited. Still not the slightest sound was heard from outside. Only the wall went on ticking:

HE IS SHOUTING FOR HELP.

HE IS SHOUTING FOR HELP, Rubashov tapped to 406. He listened. One heard nothing. Rubashov was afraid that the next time he went near the bucket he would be sick.

THEY ARE BRINGING HIM. SCREAMING AND HITTING OUT. PASS IT ON, tapped No. 402.

WHAT IS HIS NAME? Rubashov tapped quickly, before 402 had quite finished his sentence. This time he got an answer:

BOGROV. OPPOSITIONAL. PASS IT ON.

Rubashov's legs suddenly became heavy. He leant against the wall and tapped through to No. 406:

MICHAEL BOGROV, FORMER SAILOR ON BATTLESHIP POTEMKIN. COMMANDER OF THE EASTERN FLEET, BEARER OF THE FIRST REVOLUTIONARY ORDER, LED TO EXECUTION.

He wiped the sweat from his forehead, was sick into the bucket, and ended the sentence:

PASS IT ON.

He could not call back to his memory the visual image of Bogrov, but he saw the outlines of his gigantic figure, his awkward, trailing arms, the freckles on his broad, flat face with the slightly turned-up nose. They had been room-mates in exile after 1905; Rubashov had taught him reading, writing and the fundamentals of historical thought; since then, wherever Rubashov might happen to be, he received twice a year a hand-written letter, ending invariably with the words: "Your comrade, faithful unto the grave, Bogrov."

THEY ARE COMING, tapped No. 402 hastily, and so loudly that Rubashov, who was still standing next to the bucket with his head leaning back against the wall, heard it across the cell! STAND AT THE SPY-HOLE. DRUM. PASS IT ON.

Rubashov stiffened. He tapped the message through to No. 406: STAND AT THE SPY-HOLE. DRUM. PASS IT ON. He pattered through the dark to the cell door and waited. All was silent as before.

In a few seconds there came again the ticking in the wall: NOW.

Along the corridor came the low, hollow sound of subdued drumming. It was not tapping nor hammering: the men in the cells 380 to 402 who formed the acoustic chain and stood behind their doors like a guard of honour in the dark, brought out with deceptive resemblance the muffled, solemn sound of a roll of drums, carried by the wind from the distance. Rubashov stood with his eyes pressed to the spy-hole, and joined the chorus by beating with both hands rhythmically against the concrete door. To his astonishment, the stifled wave was carried on to the right, through No. 406 and beyond; Rip Van Winkle must have understood after all; he too was drumming. At the same time Rubashov heard to his left, at some distance still from the limits of his range of vision, the grinding of iron doors back on their slidings. The drumming to his left became slightly louder; Rubashov knew that the iron door which separated the isolation cells from the ordinary ones, had been opened. A bunch of keys jangled, now the iron door was shut again; now he heard the approach of steps, accompanied by sliding and slipping noises on the tiles. The drumming to the left rose in a wave, a steady, muffled crescendo. Rubashov's field of vision, limited by cells No. 401 and 407, was still empty. The sliding and squealing sounds approached quickly, now he distinguished also a moaning and whimpering, like the whimpering of a child. The steps quickened, the drumming to the left faded slightly, to the right swelled.

Rubashov drummed. He gradually lost the sense of time and of space, he heard only the hollow beating as of jungle tom-toms; it might have been apes that stood behind the bars of their cages, beating their chests and drumming; he pressed his eye to the judas, rising and falling rhythmically on his toes as he drummed. As before, he saw only the stale, yellowish light of the electric bulb in the corridor; there was nothing to be seen save the iron doors of Nos. 401 and 407, but the roll of drums rose, and the creaking and whimpering approached. Suddenly shadowy figures entered his field of vision: they were there. Rubashov ceased to drum and stared. A second later they had passed.

What he had seen in these few seconds, remained branded on Rubashov's memory. Two dimly lit figures had walked past, both in uniform, big and indistinct, dragging between them a third, whom they held under the arms. The middle figure hung slack and yet with doll-like stiffness from their grasp, stretched out at length, face turned to the ground, belly arched downwards. The legs trailed after, the shoes skated along on the toes, producing the squealing sound which Rubashov had heard from the distance. Whitish strands of hair hung over the face turned towards the tiles, with the mouth wide open. Drops of sweat clung to it; out of the mouth spittle ran thinly down the chin. When they had dragged him out of Rubashov's field of vision, further to the right and down the corridor, the moaning and whimpering gradually faded away; it came to him only as a distant echo, consisting of three plaintive vowels: "u-a-o." But before they had turned the corner at the end of the corridor, by the barber's shop, Bogrov bellowed out loudly twice, and this time Rubashov heard not only the vowels, but the whole word; it was his own name, he heard it clearly: Ru-ba-shov.

Then, as if at a signal, silence fell. The electric lamps were burning as usual, the corridor was empty as usual. Only in the wall No. 406 was ticking:

ARI[S]E, YE WRETCHED OF THE EARTH.

Rubashov was lying on his bunk again, without knowing how he had got there. He still had the drumming in his ears, but the silence was now a true silence, empty and relaxed. No. 402 was presumably asleep. Bogrov, or what had remained of him, was presumably dead by now.

"Rubashov, Rubashov. . . ." That last cry was branded ineffaceably in his acoustic memory. The optic image was less sharp. It was still difficult for him to identify with Bogrov that doll-like figure with wet face and stiff, trailing legs, which had been dragged through his field of vision in those few seconds. Only now did the white hair occur to him. What had they done to Bogrov? What had they done to this sturdy sailor, to draw this childish whimpering from his throat? Had Arlova whimpered in the same way when she was dragged along the corridor?

Rubashov sat up and leant his forehead against the wall behind which No. 402 slept; he was afraid he was going to be sick again. Up until now, he had never imagined Arlova's death in such detail. It had always been for him an abstract occurrence; it had left him with a feeling of strong uneasiness, but he had never doubted the logical rightness of his behaviour. Now, in the nausea which turned his stomach and drove the wet perspiration from his forehead, his past mode of thought seemed lunacy. The whimpering of Bogrov unbalanced the logical equation. Up till now Arlova had been a factor in this equation, a small factor compared to what was at stake. But the equation no longer stood. The vision of Arlova's legs in their high-heeled shoes trailing along the corridor upset the mathematical equilibrium. The unimportant factor had grown to the immeasurable, the absolute; Bogrov's whining, the inhuman sound of the voice which had called out his name, the hollow beat of the drumming, filled his ears; they smothered the thin voice of reason, covered it as the surf covers the gurgling of the drowning.

Exhausted Rubashov fell asleep, sitting—his head leaning against the wall, the pince-nez before his shut eyes.

QUESTIONS ON CONTENT

1. Keep in mind the contents of paragraph 2 and 3 as a preparation for reading "Memory Holes," the final selection in this chapter. Note particularly the last sentence of paragraph 3.

2. Why did Arlova "let her glance rest a long time on Rubashov"?

3. Why was Arlova dismissed from her job as librarian?

4. What fascinated Rubashov about the back of Arlova's neck?

5. What impression do you have of Arlova?

6. "In the Party death was no mystery." Why?

7. What are "the fundamentals of historical thought" which Rubashov had taught Bogrov?

8. What was the purpose of the drumming as Bogrov passed?

9. The author describes Bogrov as Rubashov had known him. Why?

10. Is there any connection between the way Bogrov closed his letters to Rubashov and the shouting of Rubashov's name at the end of this episode? Explain.

11. Did Rubashov have anything to do with the death of Arlova? Explain. (See question 2, above.)

❧ *Memory Holes*

GEORGE ORWELL

Glossary of Words

[*telescreen:* a device by which pictures and sound were transmitted to a central government receiving station. Operators at the government station could see and address directly anyone within range of the device. Telescreens were placed everywhere so that all "citizens" were under government scrutiny at all times, day and night.

speakwrite: a device which would record speech directly into typed form.

newspeak: a new, very much curtailed vocabulary through which only ideas acceptable to the dictator could be transmitted. A Newspeak word was formed as follows: *good; ungood; doubleungood; doubleplusungood.*

Big Brother: the name for the dictator.

Oceania: the one third of the world over which Big Brother ruled.

From *1984* by George Orwell. Copyright, 1949, by Harcourt, Brace and Company, Inc.

Two Minutes Hate: a daily frenzy of synthetic hatred directed against the current enemy of Oceania and against the imagined counter-revolutionists within Oceania.

vaporized: executed (compare the phrase "physical liquidation" in "The End of Bogrov").

the Party: Oceania has three levels of society: the Inner Party; the Party; the proletariat, or proles, a vast mass of people who live in squalor and ignorance which make Karl Marx's proletariat seem bourgeoisie.

Ingsoc: apparently an abbreviation for English Socialism.

the Spies: children trained to spy on their parents and neighbors and report their findings to the Thought Police.

Junior Anti-Sex League: children of party members who were taught to despise sex because sex involved tenderness, love and loyalty for persons rather than for party and Big Brother.]

With the deep, unconscious sigh which not even the nearness of the telescreen could prevent him from uttering when his day's work started, Winston pulled the speakwrite toward him, blew the dust from its mouthpiece, and put on his spectacles. Then he unrolled and clipped together four small cylinders of paper which had already flopped out of the pneumatic tube on the right-hand side of his desk.

In the walls of the cubicle there were three orifices. To the right of the speakwrite, a small pneumatic tube for written messages; to the left, a larger one for newspapers; and in the side wall, within easy reach of Winston's arm, a large oblong slit protected by a wire grating. This last was for disposal of waste paper. Similar slits existed in thousands or tens of thousands throughout the building, not only in every room but at short intervals in every corridor. For some reason they were nicknamed memory holes. When one knew that any document was due for destruction, or even when one saw a scrap of waste paper lying about, it was an automatic action to lift the flap of the nearest memory hole and drop it in, whereupon it would be whirled away on a current of warm air to the enormous furnaces which were hidden somewhere in the recesses of the building.

Winston examined the four slips of paper which he had unrolled. Each contained a message of only one or two lines, in the abbreviated jargon—not actually Newspeak, but consisting largely of New-

speak words—which was used in the Ministry for internal purposes.
They ran:

> times 17.3.84 bb speech malreported africa rectify
> times 19.12.83 forcasts 3 yp 4th quarter 83 misprints verify current issue
> times 14.2.84 miniplenty malquoted chocolate rectify
> times 3.12.83 reporting bb dayorder doubleplusungood refs unpersons rewrite fullwise upsub antefiling.

With a faint feeling of satisfaction Winston laid the fourth
message aside. It was an intricate and responsible job and had better
be dealt with last. The other three were routine matters, though
the second one would probably mean some tedious wading through
lists of figures.

Winston dialed "back numbers" on the telescreen and called for
the appropriate issues of the *Times*, which slid out of the pneumatic tube after only a few minutes' delay. The messages he had
received referred to articles or news items which for one reason
or another it was thought necessary to alter, or, as the official phrase
had it, to rectify. For example, it appeared from the *Times* of the
seventeenth of March that Big Brother, in his speech of the previous day, had predicted that the South Indian front would remain
quiet but that a Eurasian offensive would shortly be launched in
North Africa. As it happened, the Eurasian Higher Command had
launched its offensive in South India and left North Africa alone.
It was therefore necessary to rewrite a paragraph of Big Brother's
speech in such a way as to make him predict the thing that had
actually happened. Or again, the *Times* of the nineteenth of December had published the official forecasts of the output of various
classes of consumption goods in the fourth quarter of 1983, which
was also the sixth quarter of the Ninth Three-Year Plan. Today's
issue contained a statement of the actual output, from which it
appeared that the forecasts were in every instance grossly wrong.
Winston's job was to rectify the original figures by making them
agree with the later ones. As for the third message, it referred to a
very simple error which could be set right in a couple of minutes. As
short a time ago as February, the Ministry of Plenty had issued a
promise (a "categorical pledge" were the official words) that there
would be no reduction of the chocolate ration during 1984. Actually,
as Winston was aware, the chocolate ration was to be reduced
from thirty grams to twenty at the end of the present week. All that

was needed was to substitute for the original promise a warning that it would probably be necessary to reduce the ration at some time in April.

As soon as Winston had dealt with each of the messages, he clipped his speakwritten corrections to the appropriate copy of the *Times* and pushed them into the pneumatic tube. Then, with a movement which was as nearly as possible unconscious, he crumpled up the original message and any notes that he himself had made, and dropped them into the memory hole to be devoured by the flames.

What happened in the unseen labyrinth to which the pneumatic tubes led, he did not know in detail, but he did know in general terms. As soon as all the corrections which happened to be necessary in any particular number of the *Times* had been assembled and collated, that number would be reprinted, the original copy destroyed, and the corrected copy placed on the files in its stead. This process of continuous alteration was applied not only to newspapers, but to books, periodicals, pamphlets, posters, leaflets, films, sound tracks, cartoons, photographs—to every kind of literature or documentation which might conceivably hold any political or ideological significance. Day by day and almost minute by minute the past was brought up to date. In this way every prediction made by the Party could be shown by documentary evidence to have been correct; nor was any item of news, or any expression of opinion, which conflicted with the needs of the moment, ever allowed to remain on record. All history was a palimpsest, scraped clean and reinscribed exactly as often as was necessary. In no case would it have been possible, once the deed was done, to prove that any falsification had taken place. The largest section of the Records Department, far larger than the one in which Winston worked, consisted simply of persons whose duty it was to track down and collect all copies of books, newspapers, and other documents which had been superseded and were due for destruction. A number of the *Times* which might, because of changes in political alignment, or mistaken prophecies uttered by Big Brother, have been rewritten a dozen times still stood on the files bearing its original date, and no other copy existed to contradict it. Books, also, were recalled and rewritten again and again, and were invariably reissued without any admission that any alteration had been made. Even the written instructions which Winston received, and which he invariably got rid of as soon as he had dealt with them, never stated or implied that an act of forgery was to be committed; always the reference was to slips, errors, misprints, or misquotations which it was necessary to put right in the interests of accuracy.

But actually, he thought as he readjusted the Ministry of Plenty's figures, it was not even forgery. It was merely the substitution of one piece of nonsense for another. Most of the material that you were dealing with had no connection with anything in the real world, not even the kind of connection that is contained in a direct lie. Statistics were just as much a fantasy in their original version as in their rectified version. A great deal of the time you were expected to make them up out of your head. For example, the Ministry of Plenty's forecast had estimated the output of boots for the quarter at a hundred and forty-five million pairs. The actual output was given as sixty-two millions. Winston, however, in rewriting the forecast, marked the figure down to fifty-seven millions, so as to allow for the usual claim that the quota had been overfulfilled. In any case, sixty-two millions was no nearer the truth than fifty-seven millions, or than a hundred and forty-five millions. Very likely no boots had been produced at all. Likelier still, nobody knew how many had been produced, much less cared. All one knew was that every quarter astronomical numbers of boots were produced on paper, while perhaps half the population of Oceania went barefoot. And so it was with every class of recorded fact, great or small. Everything faded away into a shadow-world in which, finally, even the date of the year had become uncertain.

Winston glanced across the hall. In the corresponding cubicle on the other side a small, precise-looking, dark-chinned man named Tillotson was working steadily away, with a folded newspaper on his knee and his mouth very close to the mouthpiece of the speakwrite. He had the air of trying to keep what he was saying a secret between himself and the telescreen. He looked up and his spectacles darted a hostile flash in Winston's direction.

Winston hardly knew Tillotson, and had no idea what work he was employed on. People in the Records Department did not readily talk about their jobs. In the long, windowless hall, with its double row of cubicles and its endless rustle of papers and hum of voices murmuring into speakwrites, there were quite a dozen people whom Winston did not even know by name, though he daily saw them hurying to and fro in the corridors or gesticulating in the Two Minutes Hate. He knew that in the cubicle next to him the little woman with sandy hair toiled day in, day out, simply at tracking down and deleting from the press the names of people who had been vaporized and were therefore considered never to have existed. There was a certain fitness in this, since her own husband had been vaporized a couple of years earlier. And a few cubicles away a mild, ineffectual, dreamy creature named Ampleforth, with very hairy ears and a surprising talent for juggling with rhymes and meters, was engaged in producing garbled versions—definitive texts, they were called—of poems which had become ideologically offensive but which for one reason or another were to be retained in the anthologies. And this hall, with its fifty workers or thereabouts, was only one sub-section, a single cell, as it were, in the huge complexity of the Records Department. Beyond, above, below, were other swarms of workers engaged in an unimaginable multitude of jobs. There were the huge printing shops with their sub-editors, their typography experts, and their elaborately equipped studios for the faking of photographs. There was the teleprograms section with its engineers, its producers, and its teams of actors specially chosen for their skill in imitating voices. There were the armies of reference clerks whose job was simply to draw up lists of books and periodicals which were due for recall. There were the vast repositories where the corrected documents were stored, and the hidden furnaces where the original copies were destroyed. And somewhere or other, quite anonymous, there were the directing brains who coordinated the whole effort and laid down the lines of policy which made it necessary that this fragment of the past should be preserved, that one falsified, and the other rubbed out of existence.

And the Records Department, after all, was itself only a single branch of the Ministry of Truth, whose primary job was not to reconstruct the past but to supply the citizens of Oceania with newspapers, films, textbooks, telescreen programs, plays, novels— with every conceivable kind of information, instruction, or entertainment, from a statue to a slogan, from a lyric poem to a biological treatise, and from a child's spelling book to a Newspeak dictionary. And the Ministry had not only to supply the multifarious needs of the Party, but also to repeat the whole operation at a lower level for the benefit of the proletariat. There was a whole chain of separate departments dealing with proletarian literature, music, drama, and entertainment generally. Here were produced rubbishy newspapers containing almost nothing except sport, crime, and astrology, sensational five-cent novelettes, films oozing with sex, and sentimental songs which were composed entirely by mechanical means on a special kind of kaleidoscope known as a versificator. There was even a whole sub-section—*Pornosec,* it was called in New-speak—engaged in producing the lowest kind of pornography, which was sent out in sealed packets and which no Party member, other than those who worked on it, was permitted to look at.

Three messages had slid out of the pneumatic tube while Winston was working; but they were simple matters, and he had disposed of them before the Two Minutes Hate interrupted him. When the Hate was over he returned to his cubicle, took the Newspeak dictionary from the shelf, pushed the speakwrite to one side, cleaned his spectacles, and settled down to his main job of the morning.

Winston's greatest pleasure in life was in his work. Most of it was a tedious routine, but included in it there were also jobs so difficult and intricate that you could lose yourself in them as in the depths of a mathematical problem—delicate pieces of forgery in which you had nothing to guide you except your knowledge of the principles of Ingsoc and your estimate of what the Party wanted you to say. Winston was good at this kind of thing. On occasion he had even been entrusted with the rectification of the *Times* leading articles, which were written entirely in Newspeak. He unrolled the message that he had set aside earlier. It ran:

> times 3.12.83 reporting bb dayorder doubleplusungood refs un-persons rewrite fullwise upsub antefiling.

In Oldspeak (or standard English) this might be rendered:

> The reporting of Big Brother's Order for the Day in the Times of December 3rd 1983 is extremely unsatisfactory and makes references to nonexistent persons. Rewrite it in full and submit your draft to higher authority before filing.

Winston read through the offending article. Big Brother's Order for the Day, it seemed, had been chiefly devoted to praising the work of an organization known as FFCC, which supplied cigarettes and other comforts to the sailors in the Floating Fortress. A certain Comrade Withers, a prominent member of the Inner Party, had been singled out for special mention and awarded a decoration, the Order of Conspicuous Merit, Second Class.

Three months later FFCC had suddenly been dissolved with no reasons given. One could assume that Withers and his associates were now in disgrace, but there had been no report of the matter in the press or on the telescreen. That was to be expected, since it was unusual for political offenders to be put on trial or even publicly denounced. The great purges involving thousands of people, with public trials of traitors and thought-criminals who made abject confession of their crimes and were afterwards executed, were special showpieces not occurring oftener than once in a couple of years. More commonly, people who had incurred the displeasure of the Party simply disappeared and were never heard of again. One never had the smallest clue as to what had happened to them. In some cases they might not even be dead. Perhaps thirty people personally known to Winston, not counting his parents, had disappeared at one time or another.

Winston stroked his nose gently with a paper clip. In the cubicle across the way Comrade Tillotson was still crouching secretively over his speakwrite. He raised his head for a moment: again the hostile spectacle-flash. Winston wondered whether Comrade Tillotson was engaged on the same job as himself. It was perfectly possible. So tricky a piece of work would never be entrusted to a single person; on the other hand, to turn it over to a committee would be to admit openly that an act of fabrication was taking place. Very likely as many as a dozen people were now working away on rival versions of what Big Brother had actually said. And presently some master brain in the Inner Party would select this version or that, would re-edit it and set in motion the complex processes of cross-referencing that would be required, and then the chosen lie would pass into the permanent records and become truth.

Winston did not know why Withers had been disgraced. Perhaps it was for corruption or incompetence. Perhaps Big Brother was merely getting rid of a too-popular subordinate. Perhaps Withers or someone close to him had been suspected of heretical tendencies. Or perhaps—what was likeliest of all—the thing had simply happened because purges and vaporizations were a necessary part of the mechanics of government. The only real clue lay in the words "refs unpersons," which indicated that Withers was already dead. You could not invariably assume this to be the case when people were arrested. Sometimes they were released and allowed to remain at liberty for as much as a year or two years before being executed. Very occasionally some person whom you had believed dead long since would make a ghostly reappearance at some public trial where he would implicate hundreds of others by his testimony before vanishing, this time forever. Withers, however, was already an *unperson*. He did not exist; he had never existed. Winston decided that it would not be enough simply to reverse the tendency of Big

Brother's speech. It was better to make it deal with something totally unconnected with its original subject.

He might turn the speech into the usual denunciation of traitors and thought-criminals, but that was a little too obvious, while to invent a victory at the front, or some triumph of overproduction in the Ninth Three-Year Plan, was a piece of pure fantasy. Suddenly there sprang into his mind, ready-made as it were, the image of a certain Comrade Ogilvy, who had recently died in battle, in heroic circumstances. There were occasions when Big Brother devoted his Order for the Day to commemorating some humble, rank-and-file Party member whose life and death he held up as an example worthy to be followed. Today he should commemorate Comrade Ogilvy. It was true that there was no such person as Comrade Ogilvy, but a few lines of print and a couple of faked photographs would soon bring him into existence.

Winston thought for a moment, then pulled the speakwrite toward him and began dictating in Big Brother's familiar style: a style at once military and pedantic, and, because of a trick of asking questions and then promptly answering them ("What lessons do we learn from this fact, comrades? The lessons—which is also one of the fundamental principles of Ingsoc—that," etc., etc.), easy to imitate.

At the age of three Comrade Ogilvy had refused all toys except a drum, a submachine gun, and a model helicopter. At six—a year early, by a special relaxation of the rules—he had joined the Spies; at nine he had been a troop leader. At eleven he had denounced his uncle to the Thought Police after overhearing a conversation which appeared to him to have criminal tendencies. At seventeen he had been a district organizer of the Junior Anti-Sex League. At nineteen he had designed a hand grenade which had been adopted by the Ministry of Peace and which, at its first trial, had killed thirty-one Eurasian prisoners in one burst. At twenty-three he had perished in action. Pursued by enemy jet planes while flying over the Indian Ocean with important despatches, he had weighted his body with his machine gun and leapt out of the helicopter into the deep water, despatches and all—an end, said Big Brother, which it was impossible to contemplate without feelings of envy. Big Brother added a few remarks on the purity and single-mindedness of Comrade Ogilvy's life. He was a total abstainer and a nonsmoker, had no recreations except a daily hour in the gymnasium, and had taken a vow of celibacy, believing marriage and the care of a family to be incompatible with a twenty-four-hour-a-day devotion to duty. He had no subjects of conversation except the principles of Ingsoc, and no aim in life except the defeat of the Eurasian enemy and the hunting-down of spies, saboteurs, thought-criminals, and traitors generally.

Winston debated with himself whether to award Comrade Ogilvy the Order of Conspicuous Merit; in the end he decided against it because of the unnecessary cross-referencing that it would entail.

Once again he glanced at his rival in the opposite cubicle. Something seemed to tell him with certainty that Tillotson was busy on the same job as himself. There was no way of knowing whose version would finally be adopted, but he felt a profound conviction that it would be his own. Comrade Ogilvy, unimagined an hour ago, was now a fact. It struck him as curious that you could create dead men but not living ones. Comrade Ogilvy, who had never existed in the present, now existed in the past, and when once the act of forgery was forgotten, he would exist just as authentically, and upon the same evidence, as Charlemagne or Julius Caesar.

QUESTIONS ON CONTENT

1. The shortened form for various ministries of government were, for example, Miniplenty (Minister of Plenty). What does the prefix *mini* suggest? Comment.
2. What was Winston's job?
3. Why did the fourth item on his list interest him?
4. Is there anything ironical about the phrase, "the sixth quarter of the Ninth Three-Year Plan"?
5. Compare the account of the destruction and alteration of records in "Memory Holes" with a similar account in Arlova's Arrest. What conclusion do you draw from this sequence?
6. What is a *palimpsest*?
7. How do the statistics on the manufacture of boots demonstrate that "rectifying" the records was all nonsense?
8. The primary job of the Ministry of Truth (Minitruth) was what? Compare this function with that undertaken by the present regime in the USSR.
9. How often did the great purges occur?
10. Why was Winston confident that his piece on Comrade Ogilvy would be accepted?

SUGGESTIONS FOR PAPERS

Knowledge of theory is basic to an understanding of practice, and any system is best tested by comparing or contrasting it with an opposing system. Democracy and communism are poles apart in theory and practice. You know something about the political system under which you live. You can know it better (1) by examining its ideals and (2) by comparing those ideals with the ideals of another system.

1. Would you say that the last paragraph of "The Ideal Democracy" is true? If you think it is true, specifically cite examples of political practices which are hardly ideally democratic. Your own city or state government should provide enough examples.

2. Why does democracy work imperfectly? Search through "The Ideal Democracy" for the reasons. See particularly the quotation from James Bryce.

3. If you feel that you have taken democracy for granted, you might write a "confession" in which you reveal what you do *not* know about the practical working of a democratic system. How, for example, are candidates chosen for state representative, for mayor of your city, for county tax assessor, etc.?

4. Define a program of education best suited, in your opinion, for preparing youth to be citizens in an *ideal* democracy.

5. You have doubtless noted the structural symmetry of "The Ideal Democracy." Outline the essay and show how the three main sections form an excellent example of extended definition.

6. Whenever in America a club or association of any sort is formed, a committee is appointed or elected to draw up a constitution and by-laws. Americans, in short, constantly think in a democratic way. Examine critically the constitution and by-laws of some club with which you are associated. Are essentially democratic principles observed? Do you note a certain amount of impatience with the democratic process? Explain.

7. "If all mankind minus one, were of one opinion, and only one person were of the contrary opinion, mankind would be no more justified in silencing that one person, than he, if he had the power, would be justified in silencing mankind." (John Stuart Mill, *On Liberty*.) Does this add a new element to the definition of democracy as formulated in "The Ideal Democracy"?

8. "You do not allow a palpable madman to leap over precipices;

. . . his true liberty were that a wiser man, that any and every wiser man, could, by brass collars, or in whatever milder or sharper way, lay hold of him when he was going wrong, and order and compel him to go a little righter." (Thomas Carlyle, *Past and Present.*) Is this recommendation contrary to democratic procedure? Interpret this passage as it may be related by contrast to "The Ideal Democracy."

9. "The Man with the Hoe" contains a threat: the men with hoes will some day rise and sweep away bad rulers. There is something of this same threat in "The People Will Live On." Has this threat of the people been carried out anywhere yet? If so, with what advantage or disadvantage to the people?

10. Becker in "The Ideal Democracy" says that in the people must be vested political authority. "The Man with the Hoe" presents a representative specimen of the people. "The People Will Live On" takes a more hopeful view of the people's capacities. What is the dilemma suggested by the people on the one hand and the demands of democracy on the other? Is a working democracy harder to achieve than a working authoritarianism?

11. List the qualities an average person should have in order to take his place effectively in a democracy. (See "The Ideal Democracy.") How far short of these qualities do the people symbolized by "The Man with the Hoe" fall? Do the people in "The People Will Live On" come nearer to qualifying?

12. Discuss the equalitarian phase of communistic doctrine. Are all men equal? Would it be desirable to legislate equality? Assuming that such a law of equalization could be passed and enforced, what would be the result? Who would benefit? Would the superior person be the only one to suffer? (Structure: I. Are all men equal?; II. Can laws bring about equality or only equality of opportunity?; III. What would become of society under equalization laws?)

13. What are some popular misconceptions of communism? Think of persons on the local or national scene who have been accused of being communists. In so far as you know the personal beliefs of these persons, would you class them as communists? Discuss.

14. Discuss the so-called Marxian law of the greater and greater concentration of wealth into fewer and fewer hands. What forces of law have limited this concentration? What other forces have operated to spread ownership of large industries? Why are capitalists eager to see the slogan "Every man a capitalist" come true?

15. Many small communal experiments have been tried, both before and after Marx. What, do you suppose, made them fail? "From each according to his ability; to each according to his need." Examine that communist statement closely. Are both *ability* and *need* difficult to define for even a single individual?

16. Why may totalitarianism grow out of any economic system? Why, however, is it most likely to grow out of a system in which the state owns everything? How may a balance of ownership be maintained so that dictatorship may be avoided? What should the state own? What should individuals own? Devote a single paragraph to each of the first questions, and a paragraph to the last three.

17. A line from the communist song, the *Internationale*, is this: "Arise, ye wretched of the earth!" How is this line used in "The End of Bogrov"? Consider, too, "The Man with the Hoe" which describes one of the wretched of the earth. What has communism done for this man? If there are no individuals in the communist conception, *can* communism do anything for anybody?

18. Write your paper on the idea of *power*. Begin with an analysis of what you know about your own urge to have your own way. How far does this urge go? Does it have limits? If so, what are they? If not, what would best express a limitless power? Finally, if you had power, would you voluntarily give it up?

19. Is *fear* the basic characteristic of a totalitarian regime? Does this fear dominate the government and the people governed? Refer to the selections in this chapter. Why was Arlova arrested? Why was she executed? Why was Rubashov arrested, and Bogrov? Why all the elaborate effort to falsify (rectify) every written record in "Memory Holes"? Is democracy beset by such benumbing fears?

20. A democracy prizes opposition. Why? What would happen without it? Use a simple example to illustrate, an athletic team, perhaps. Why does a good coach create a B team? A dictatorship crushes opposition. Why? What would happen with it?

21. There are two preliminary steps to action: thought and communication (speech and/or writing). Is this the reason for the Thought Police? Is the slogan of the dictator: "Nip the action in the thought"? Does this explain the arrest of Arlova? Of Rubashov? Is the ultimate solution of such a problem some such device as telescreens?

22. Discuss any one or more of the twenty-two tenets of communism as listed by Massimo Salvadori in "The Tenets of Communism."

SOME TITLES FOR PAPERS

1. Why I Prefer Democracy
2. How to Improve Democracy
3. My Understanding of Ideal Democracy
4. "The Ideal Democracy": A Study in Structure
5. Is the Majority Always Right?
6. The Logic of Democracy
7. Men Free and Equal?
8. Can the People Be Trusted?
9. The People: A Definition
10. Millet's Picture and Markham's Poem: A Comparison
11. Would Science Approve Markham's Thesis?
12. "The People Will Live On": An Analysis
13. The Basis of Communism
14. Why I Prefer Capitalism
15. Property Rights Are Human Rights Too
16. The Proletarian in Theory and in Fact
17. The Capitalist in Theory and in Fact
18. Nothing to Gain but Chains
19. The Right to Be Wrong
20. Man's Inhumanity to Man
21. Fear Motivates Dictators
22. Some Tenets of Communism Considered
23. Man Control: New Techniques
24. Why Dictators Fear the Printed Word

❧ *GOD AND MAN*

FROM YOUR EARLIEST YEARS you have been taught certain attitudes toward religion. You may have discussed with your companions many questions pertaining to God and religion. It is unlikely, therefore, that you come to the reading in this chapter unprepared to understand what is said. Yet, because the approaches may be fresh to you, especially in the first selection, you may feel that the material is difficult and some of it, perhaps, disturbing. The university man or woman learns to examine critically conflicting points of view and then to exercise a liberty of choice, that basic requirement of Milton's "wayfaring Christian."

The five selections in this chapter consider man's relation to God, or to the Force which is behind or in all things. "Man against Darkness" asserts that the universe is purposeless and that whatever man does, he does as a result of a chain of causes over which he has little control. The blame for this dark view is laid at the door of science, which has pronounced that "Nature is nothing but matter in motion," a motion governed entirely by "blind force and laws." Man is matter and nothing more, and, therefore, his motions are also blindly governed. The author calls the belief in spirit and a benevolent God "That Great Illusion." The reader will ask, perhaps, if the older phrase, "The Grand Perhaps," is not at least more scientific than "The Great Illusion."

The conclusions of the first selection represent a minority report.

In the next three, the majority speaks its belief in a world of purpose presided over by a benign Deity whose immediate intentions may not be demonstrable—or even clear—but whose ultimate concern is to complete satisfactorily the lives of those who believe in Him. Fulton J. Sheen in "Man's Quest for God" speaks for this majority conviction.

In "The Biography Cure" the thesis is that God works differently in the hearts of various men, but that ultimately these differences will be resolved. The function of religion is to provide man with access to God and to secure for him God's friendliness. "The Biography Cure" shows how three men went about fulfilling the function of religion.

Tennyson's confession of faith—or strong hope—is expressed in the "Prologue" to *In Memoriam.* The poet summarizes the reasons which led him to a clear trust in God's purposes. The final selection, "High Flight," describes an ecstatic experience which made God an immediate reality for the poet.

❧ *Man against Darkness*

W. T. STACE

1

The Catholic bishops of America recently issued a statement in which they said that the chaotic and bewildered state of the modern world is due to man's loss of faith, his abandonment of God and religion. For my part I believe in no religion at all. Yet I entirely agree with the bishops. It is no doubt an oversimplification to speak of *the* cause of so complex a state of affairs as the tortured condition of the world today. Its causes are doubtless multitudinous. Yet allowing for some element of oversimplification, I say that the bishops' assertion is substantially true.

M. Jean-Paul Sartre, the French existentialist philosopher, labels himself an atheist. Yet his views seem to me plainly to support the statement of the bishops. So long as there was believed to be a God in the sky, he says, men could regard him as the source of their

From *The Atlantic Monthly*, CLXXXII (September 1948), 53–58. Reprinted by permission of the author and *The Atlantic Monthly.*

moral ideals. The universe, created and governed by a fatherly God, was a friendly habitation for man. We could be sure that, however great the evil in the world, good in the end would triumph and the forces of evil would be routed. With the disappearance of God from the sky all this has changed. Since the world is not ruled by a spiritual being, but rather by blind forces, there cannot be any ideals, moral or otherwise, in the universe outside us. Our ideals, therefore, must proceed only from our own minds; they are our own inventions. Thus the world which surrounds us is nothing but an immense spiritual emptiness. It is a dead universe. We do not live in a universe which is on the side of our values. It is completely indifferent to them.

Years ago Mr. Bertrand Russell, in his essay *A Free Man's Worship,* said much the same thing.

> Such in outline, but even more purposeless, more void of meaning, is the world which Science presents for our belief. Amid such a world, if anywhere, our ideals henceforward must find a home. . . . Blind to good and evil, reckless of destruction, omnipotent matter rolls on its relentless way; for man, condemned today to lose his dearest, tomorrow himself to pass through the gate of darkness, it remains only to cherish, ere yet the blow falls, the lofty thoughts that ennoble his little day; . . . to sustain alone, a weary but unyielding Atlas, the world that his own ideals have fashioned despite the trampling march of unconscious power.

It is true that Mr. Russell's personal attitude to the disappearance of religion is quite different from either that of M. Sartre or of the bishops or myself. The bishops think it a calamity. So do I. M. Sartre finds it "very distressing." And he berates as shallow the attitude of those who think that without God the world can go on just the same as before, as if nothing had happened. This creates for mankind, he thinks, a terrible crisis. And this I agree with him. Mr. Russell, on the other hand, seems to believe that religion has done more harm than good in the world, and that its disappearance will be a blessing. But his picture of the world, and of the modern mind, is the same as that of M. Sartre. He stresses the *purposelessness* of the universe, the facts that man's ideals are his own creations, that the universe outside him in no way supports them, that man is alone and friendless in the world.

Mr. Russell notes that it is science which has produced this situation. There is no doubt that this is correct. But the way in which it has come about is not generally understood. There is a popular belief that some particular scientific discoveries or theories, such as the Darwinian theory of evolution, or the views of geologists about the age of the earth, or a series of such discoveries, have done the damage. It would be foolish to deny that these discoveries have had a great effect in undermining religious dogmas. But this account does not at all go to the root of the matter. Religion can probably outlive any scientific discoveries which could be made. It can accommodate itself to them. The root cause of the decay of faith has not been any particular discovery of science, but rather the general spirit of science and certain basic assumptions upon which modern science, from the seventeenth century onwards, has proceeded.

2

It was Galileo and Newton—notwithstanding that Newton himself was a deeply religious man—who destroyed the old comfortable picture of a friendly universe governed by spiritual values. And this was effected, not by Newton's discovery of the law of gravitation nor by any of Galileo's brilliant investigations, but by the general picture of the world which these men and others of their time made the basis of the science, not only of their own day, but of all succeeding generations down to the present. That is why the century immediately following Newton, the eighteenth century, was notoriously an age of religious skepticism. Skepticism did not have to wait for the discoveries of Darwin and the geologists in the nineteenth century. It flooded the world immediately after the age of the rise of science.

Neither the Copernican hypothesis nor any of Newton's or Galileo's particular discoveries were the real causes. Religious faith might well have accommodated itself to the new astronomy. The real turning point between the medieval age of faith and the modern age of unfaith came when the scientists of the seventeenth century turned their backs upon what used to be called "final causes." The final cause of a thing or event meant the purpose which it was supposed to serve in the universe, its cosmic purpose. What lay back of this was the presupposition that there is a cosmic order or plan and that everything which exists could in the last analysis be explained in terms of its place in this cosmic plan, that is, in terms of its purpose.

Plato and Aristotle believed this, and so did the whole medieval

Christian world. For instance, if it were true that the sun and the moon were created and exist for the purpose of giving light to man, then this fact would explain why the sun and the moon exist. We might not be able to discover the purpose of everything, but everything must have a purpose. Belief in final causes thus amounted to a belief that the world is governed by purposes, presumably the purposes of some overruling mind. This belief was not the invention of Christianity. It was basic to the whole of Western civilization, whether in the ancient pagan world or in Christendom, from the time of Socrates to the rise of science in the seventeenth century.

The founders of modern science—for instance, Galileo, Kepler, and Newton—were mostly pious men who did not doubt God's purposes. Nevertheless they took the revolutionary step of consciously and deliberately expelling the idea of purpose as controlling nature from their new science of nature. They did this on the ground that inquiry into purposes is useless for what science aims at: namely, the prediction and control of events. To predict an eclipse, what you have to know is not its purpose but its causes. Hence science from the seventeenth century onwards became exclusively an inquiry into causes. The conception of purpose in the world was ignored and frowned on. This, though silent and almost unnoticed, was the greatest revolution in human history, far outweighing in importance any of the political revolutions whose thunder has reverberated through the world.

For it came about in this way that for the past three hundred years there has been growing up in men's minds, dominated as they are by science, a new imaginative picture of the world. The world, according to this new picture, is purposeless, senseless, meaningless. Nature is nothing but matter in motion. The motions of matter are governed, not by any purpose, but by blind forces and laws. Nature on this view, says Whitehead—to whose writings I am indebted in this part of my paper—is "merely the hurrying of material, endlessly, meaninglessly." You can draw a sharp line across the history of Europe dividing it into two epochs of very unequal length. The line passes through the lifetime of Galileo. European man before Galileo—whether ancient pagan or more recent Christian—thought of the world as controlled by plan and purpose. After Galileo European man thinks of it as utterly purposeless. This is the great revolution of which I spoke.

It is this which has killed religion. Religion could survive the discoveries that the sun, not the earth, is the center; that men are descended from simian ancestors; that the earth is hundreds of millions of years old. These discoveries may render out of date some of the details of older theological dogmas, may force their restatement in new intellectual frameworks. But they do not touch the essence of the religious vision itself, which is the faith that there is plan and purpose in the world, that the world is a moral order, that in the end all things are for the best. This faith may express itself through many different intellectual dogmas, those of Christianity, of Hinduism, of Islam. All and any of these intellectual dogmas may be destroyed without destroying the essential religious spirit. But that spirit cannot survive destruction of belief in a plan and purpose of the world, for that is the very heart of it. Religion can get on with any sort of astronomy, geology, biology, physics. But it cannot get on with a purposeless and meaningless universe.

If the scheme of things is purposeless and meaningless, then the life of man is purposeless and meaningless too. Everything is futile, all effort is in the end worthless. A man may, of course, still pursue disconnected ends, money, fame, art, science, and may gain pleasure from them. But his life is hollow at the center. Hence the dissatisfied, disillusioned, restless spirit of modern man.

The picture of a meaningless world, and a meaningless human life, is, I think, the basic theme of much modern art and literature. Certainly it is the basic theme of modern philosophy. According to the most characteristic philosophies of the modern period from Hume in the eighteenth century to the so-called positivists of today, the world is just what it is, and that is the end of all inquiry. There is no reason for its being what it is. Everything might just as well have been quite different, and there would have been no reason for that either. When you have stated what things are, what things the world contains, there is nothing more which could be said, even by an omniscient being. To ask any question about *why* things are thus, or what purpose their being so serves, is to ask a senseless question, because they serve no purpose at all. For instance, there is for modern philosophy no such thing as the ancient problem of evil. For this once famous question presupposes that pain and misery, though they seem so inexplicable and irrational to us, must ultimately subserve some rational purpose, must have their places in the cosmic plan. But this is nonsense. There is no such overruling rationality in the universe. Belief in the ultimate irrationality of everything is the quintessence of what is called the modern mind.

It is true that, parallel with these philosophies which are typical of the modern mind, preaching the meaninglessness of the world, there has run a line of idealistic philosophies whose contention is that the world is after all spiritual in nature and that moral ideals and values are inherent in its structure. But most of these idealisms were simply philosophical expressions of romanticism, which was itself no more than an unsuccessful counterattack of the religious against the scientific view of things. They perished, along with romanticism in literature and art, about the beginning of the present century, though of course they still have a few adherents.

At the bottom of these idealistic systems of thought were rationalizations of man's wishful thinking. They were born of the refusal of men to admit the cosmic darkness. They were comforting illusions within the warm glow of which the more tender-minded intellectuals sought to shelter themselves from the icy winds of the universe. They lasted a little while. But they are shattered now, and we return once more to the vision of a purposeless world.

3

Along with the ruin of the religious vision there went the ruin of moral principles and indeed of all values. If there is a cosmic purpose, if there is in the nature of things a drive towards goodness, then our moral systems will derive their validity from this. But if our moral rules do not proceed from something outside us in the nature of the universe—whether we say it is God or simply the universe itself—then they must be our own inventions. Thus it came to be believed that moral rules must be merely an expression of our own likes and dislikes. But likes and dislikes are notoriously variable. What pleases one man, people, or culture displeases another. Therefore morals are wholly relative.

This obvious conclusion from the idea of a purposeless world made its appearance in Europe immediately after the rise of science, for instance in the philosophy of Hobbes. Hobbes saw at once that if there is no purpose in the world there are no values either. "Good and evil," he writes, "are names that signify our appetites and aversions; which in different tempers, customs, and doctrines of men are different. . . . Every man calleth that which pleaseth him, good; and that which displeaseth him, evil."

This doctrine of the relativity of morals, though it has recently received an impetus from the studies of anthropologists, was thus really implicit in the whole scientific mentality. It is disastrous for morals because it destroys their entire traditional foundation. That is why philosophers who see the danger signals, from the time at least of Kant, have been trying to give to morals a new foundation, that is, a secular or nonreligious foundation. This attempt may very well be intellectually successful. Such a foundation, independent of the religious view of the world, might well be found. But the question is whether it can ever be a *practical* success, that is, whether apart from its logical validity and its influence with intellectuals, it can ever replace among the masses of men the lost religious foundation. On that question hangs perhaps the future of civilization. But meanwhile disaster is overtaking us.

The widespread belief in "ethical relativity" among philosophers, psychologists, ethnologists, and sociologists is the theoretical counterpart of the repudiation of principle which we see all around us, especially in international affairs, the field in which morals have always had the weakest foothold. No one any longer effectively believes in moral principles except as the private prejudices either of individual men or of nations or cultures. This is the inevitable consequence of the doctrine of ethical relativity, which in turn is the inevitable consequence of believing in a purposeless world.

Another characteristic of our spiritual state is loss of belief in the freedom of the will. This also is a fruit of the scientific spirit, though not of any particular scientific discovery. Science has been built up on the basis of determinism, which is the belief that every event is completely determined by a chain of causes and is therefore theoretically predictable beforehand. It is true that recent physics seems to challenge this. But so far as its practical consequences are concerned, the damage has long ago been done. A man's actions, it was argued, are as much events in the natural world as is an eclipse of the sun. It follows that men's actions are as theoretically predictable as an eclipse. But if it is certain now that John Smith will murder Joseph Jones at 2:15 P.M. on January 1, 1963, what possible meaning can it have to say that when that time comes John Smith will be *free* to choose whether he will commit the murder or not? And if he is not free, how can he be held responsible?

It is true that the whole of this argument can be shown by a competent philosopher to be a tissue of fallacies—or at least I claim that it can. But the point is that the analysis required to show this is much too subtle to be understood by the average entirely unphilosophical man. Because of this, the argument against free will is generally swallowed whole by the unphilosophical. Hence the thought that man is not free, that he is the helpless plaything of forces over which he has no control, has deeply penetrated the modern mind. We hear of economic determinism, cultural determinism, historical determinism. We are not responsible for what we do because our glands control us, or because we are the products of environment or heredity. Not moral self-control, but the doctor, the psychiatrist, the educationist, must save us from doing evil. Pills and injections in the future are to do what Christ and the prophets have failed to do. Of course I do not mean to deny that doctors and educationists can and must help. And I do not mean in any way to belittle their efforts. But I do wish to draw attention to the weakening of moral controls, the greater or less repudiation of personal responsibility which, in the popular thinking of the day, result from these tendencies of thought.

4

What, then, is to be done? Where are we to look for salvation from the evils of our time? All the remedies I have seen suggested so far are, in my opinion, useless. Let us look at some of them.

Philosophers and intellectuals generally can, I believe, genuinely do something to help. But it is extremely little. What philosophers can do is to show that neither the relativity of morals nor the denial of free will really follows from the grounds which have been supposed to support them. They can also try to discover a genuine secular basis for morals to replace the religious basis which has disappeared. Some of us are trying to do these things. But in the first place philosophers unfortunately are not agreed about these matters, and their disputes are utterly confusing to the non-philosophers. And in the second place their influence is practically negligible because their analyses necessarily take place on a level on which the masses are totally unable to follow them.

The bishops, of course, propose as remedy a return to belief in God and in the doctrines of the Christian religion. Others think that a new religion is what is needed. Those who make these proposals fail to realize that the crisis in man's spiritual condition is something unique in history for which there is no sort of analogy in the past. They are thinking perhaps of the collapse of the ancient Greek and Roman religions. The vacuum then created was easily filled by Christianity, and it might have been filled by Mithraism if Christianity had not appeared. By analogy they think that Christianity might now be replaced by a new religion, or even that Christianity itself, if revivified, might bring back health to men's lives.

But I believe that there is no analogy at all between our present state and that of the European peoples at the time of the fall of paganism. Men had at that time lost their belief only in particular dogmas, particular embodiments of the religious view of the world. It had no doubt become incredible that Zeus and the other gods were living on the top of Mount Olympus. You could go to the top and find no trace of them. But the imaginative picture of a world governed by purpose, a world driving towards the good— which is the inner spirit of religion—had at that time received no serious shock. It had merely to re-embody itself in new dogmas, those of Christianity or some other religion. Religion itself was not dead in the world, only a particular form of it.

But now the situation is quite different. It is not merely that particular dogmas, like that of the virgin birth, are unacceptable to the modern mind. That is true, but it constitutes a very superficial diagnosis of the present situation of religion. Modern skepticism is of a wholly different order from that of the intellectuals of the ancient world. It had attacked and destroyed not merely the outward forms of the religious spirit, its particularized dogmas, but the very essence of that spirit itself, belief in a meaningful and purposeful world. For the founding of a new religion a new Jesus Christ or Buddha would have to appear, in itself a most unlikely event and one for which in any case we cannot afford to sit and wait. But even if a new prophet and a new religion did appear, we may predict that they would fail in the modern world. No one for long would believe in them, for modern men have lost the vision, basic to all religion, of an ordered plan and purpose of the world. They have before their minds the picture of a purposeless universe, and such a world-picture must be fatal to any religion at all, not merely to Christianity.

We must not be misled by occasional appearances of revival of the religious spirit. Men, we are told, in their disgust and disillusionment at the emptiness of their lives, are turning once more to religion, or are searching for a new message. It may be so. We must expect such wistful yearnings of the spirit. We must expect men to wish back again the light that is gone, and to try to bring it back. But however they may wish or try, the light will not shine again,—not at least in the civilization to which we belong.

Another remedy commonly proposed is that we should turn to

science itself, or the scientific spirit, for our salvation. Mr. Russell and Professor Dewey both make this proposal, though in somewhat different ways. Professor Dewey seems to believe that discoveries in sociology, the application of scientific method to social and political problems, will rescue us. This seems to me to be utterly naïve. It is not likely that science, which is basically the cause of our spiritual troubles, is likely also to produce the cure for them. Also it lies in the nature of science that, though it can teach us the best means for achieving our ends, it can never tell us what ends to pursue. It cannot give us any ideals. And our trouble is about ideals and ends, not about the means for reaching them.

5

No civilization can live without ideals, or to put it in another way, without a firm faith in moral ideas. Our ideals and moral ideas have in the past been rooted in religion. But the religious basis of our ideals has been undermined, and the superstructure of ideals is plainly tottering. None of the commonly suggested remedies on examination seems likely to succeed. It would therefore look as if the early death of our civilization were inevitable.

Of course we know that it is perfectly possible for individual men, very highly educated men, philosophers, scientists, intellectuals in general, to live moral lives without any religious convictions. But the question is whether a whole civilization, a whole family of peoples, composed almost entirely of relatively uneducated men and women, can do this.

It follows, of course, that if we could make the vast majority of men as highly educated as the very few are now, we might save the situation. And we are already moving slowly in that direction through the techniques of mass education. But the critical question seems to concern the time-lag. Perhaps in a few hundred years most of the population will, at the present rate, be sufficiently highly educated and civilized to combine high ideals with an absence of religion. But long before we reach any such stage, the collapse of our civilization may have come about. How are we to live through the intervening period?

I am sure that the first thing we have to do is to face the truth, however bleak it may be, and then next we have to learn to live with it. Let me say a word about each of these two points. What I am urging as regards the first is complete honesty. Those who wish to resurrect Christian dogmas are not, of course, consciously dishonest. But they have that kind of unconscious dishonesty which consists in lulling oneself with opiates and dreams. Those who talk of a new religion are merely hoping for a new opiate. Both alike refuse to face the truth that there is, in the universe outside man, no spirituality, no regard for values, no friend in the sky, no help or comfort for any man of any sort. To be perfectly honest in the admission of this fact, not to seek shelter in new or old illusions, not to indulge in wishful dreams about this matter, this is the first thing we shall have to do.

I do not urge this course out of any special regard for the sanctity of truth in the abstract. It is not self-evident to me that truth is the supreme value to which all else must be sacrificed. Might not the discoverer of a truth which would be fatal to mankind be justified in suppressing it, even in teaching men a falsehood? Is truth more valuable than goodness and beauty and happiness? To think so is to invent yet another absolute, another religious delusion in which Truth with a capital T is substituted for God. The reason why we must now boldly and honestly face the truth that the universe is non-spiritual and indifferent to goodness, beauty, happiness, or truth is not that it would be wicked to suppress it, but simply that it is too late to do so, so that in the end we cannot do anything else but face it. Yet we stand on the brink, dreading the icy plunge. We need courage. We need honesty.

Now about the other point, the necessity of learning to live with the truth. This means learning to live virtuously and happily, or at least contentedly, without illusions. And this is going to be extremely difficult because what we have now begun dimly to perceive is that human life in the past, or at least human happiness, has almost wholly depended upon illusions. It has been said that man lives by truth, and that the truth will make us free. Nearly the opposite seems to me to be the case. Mankind has managed to live only by means of lies, and the truth may very well destroy us. If one were a Bergsonian one might believe that nature deliberately puts illusions into our souls in order to induce us to go on living.

The illusions by which men have lived seem to be of two kinds. First, there is what one may perhaps call the Great Illusion—I mean the religious illusion that the universe is moral and good, that it follows a wise and noble plan, that it is gradually generating some supreme value, that goodness is bound to triumph in it. Secondly, there is a whole host of minor illusions on which human happiness nourishes itself. How much of human happiness notoriously comes from the illusions of the lover about his beloved? Then again we work and strive because of the illusions connected with fame, glory, power, or money. Banners of all kinds, flags, emblems, insignia, ceremonials, and rituals are invariably symbols of some illusion or other. The British Empire, the connection between mother country and dominions, is partly kept going by illusions surrounding the notion of kingship. Or think of the vast amount of human happiness which is derived from the illusion of supposing that if some non-sense syllable, such as "sir" or "count" or "lord," is pronounced in conjunction with our names, we belong to a superior order of people.

There is plenty of evidence that human happiness is almost wholly based upon illusions of one kind or another. But the scientific spirit, or the spirit of truth, is the enemy of illusions and therefore the enemy of human happiness. That is why it is going to be so difficult to live with the truth.

There is no reason why we should have to give up the host of minor illusions which render life supportable. There is no reason why the lover should be scientific about the loved one. Even the illusions of fame and glory may persist. But without the Great Illusion, the illusion of a good, kindly, and purposeful universe, we shall *have* to learn to live. And to ask this is really no more than to ask that we become genuinely civilized beings and not merely sham civilized beings.

I can best explain the difference by a reminiscence. I remember a fellow student in my college days, an ardent Christian, who told me that if he did not believe in a future life, in heaven and hell, he would rape, murder, steal, and be a drunkard. That is what I call being a sham civilized being. On the other hand, not only could a Huxley, a John Stuart Mill, a David Hume, live great and fine lives without any religion, but a great many others of us, quite obscure persons, can at least live decent lives without it.

To be genuinely civilized means to be able to walk straightly and to live honorably without the props and crutches of one or another of the childish dreams which have so far supported men. That such a life is likely to be ecstatically happy I will not claim. But that it can be lived in quiet content, accepting resignedly what cannot be helped, not expecting the impossible, and thankful for small mercies, this I would maintain. That it will be difficult for men in general to learn this lesson I do not deny. But that it will be impossible I would not admit since so many have learned it already.

Man has not yet grown up. He is not adult. Like a child he cries for the moon and lives in a world of fantasies. And the race as a whole has perhaps reached the great crisis of its life. Can it grow up as a race in the same sense as individual men grow up? Can man put away childish things and adolescent dreams? Can he grasp the real world as it actually is, stark and bleak, without its romantic or religious halo, and still retain his ideals, striving for great ends and noble achievements? If he can, all may yet be well. If he cannot, he will probably sink back into the savagery and brutality from which he came, taking a humble place once more among the lower animals.

QUESTIONS ON CONTENT

1. What four opinions about man and God does the author cite? The author, the bishops, and M. Sartre agree in what way? How does Bertrand Russell differ?
2. What has science had to do with the decline in religion?
3. How did a shift from concern with purpose to concern with cause bring about a flood of skepticism?
4. The "essence of the religious vision itself . . . is the faith that there is plan and purpose in the world, that the world is a moral order, that in the end all things are for the best." Compare the idea that religion is designed "to give man access to the powers which seem to control him" and "to induce those powers to be friendly to him."
5. What is the basic view of modern philosophy?
6. Relate purposelessness in the universe to relativity of morals.
7. If every event is determined by a chain of causes, do man's actions become as predictable as a sun's eclipse? What example does the author use to illustrate this point? Can you detect a fallacy here? Define *determinism*.
8. If the masses are unable to follow the thinking of philosophers in their cerebrations on free will and the relativity of morals, does it not follow that maybe the masses haven't yet followed the scientists and philosophers who discredit purpose in the world? Discuss. Can you see a parallel here of the Biblical story of the Tower of Babel?

9. Does the author believe that a new philosophy or a new religion might cure the world? Discuss.

10. What does the author set up as two preliminary conditions for continuing to live in this world?

11. "Mankind has managed to live only by means of lies, and the truth may very well destroy us." Since a fallible man, the author of this article, makes this statement, does it carry any more authority than "the truth will make you free"? In other words, the first statement is an attempt to represent truth, and by that fact it puts the capital T back into the word *Truth*.

◗ *Man's Quest for God*

FULTON J. SHEEN

The quest for God is essentially the search for the full account and meaning of life. If we but had the power to take our soul from our body, put it in a crucible, and distil out the meaning of that quest, what would we find it to be? If we could but make the inmost heart of all humanity speak out its inmost yearnings, what would we discover them to be? Would we not find that every heart and mind and soul in creation desires fundamentally three realities and only three realities—Life, Truth, and Love? In fact, so deep are these three realities, Being, Truth, and Love, that we can say the whole universe overflows with them. Of each thing in the universe it can be said that it is. Of each thing in the universe it can be said that it is true, for it is related to a mind, and of each thing in the universe it can be said that it is love, for it is related to a will and a desire.

The first deep-seated yearning, then, in the human heart is the yearning for Life. Of all our treasures it is that which we surrender last, and with the greatest reluctance. Titles, joys, and wealth, power, ambition, honor—all of these we will let go provided we can hold on to that precious, palpitating, vibrating thing called Life. The very instinct which impels a man to put out his hand when he walks in

From *The Divine Romance* by Fulton J. Sheen. Copyright, 1930, by The Century Company. Reprinted by permission of the publishers Appleton-Century-Crofts, Inc.

the dark, proves that he is willing to sacrifice a part of his body rather than to endanger that which he holds most precious—his Life. Not even the sad fact of suicide disproves the reality of this yearning, for in every suicide there is an illusion and a sentiment. The illusion is that suicide is total destruction. The sentiment is the desire for repose or the will to shake off the worries of life. Suicide is not so much the desire that one wants to be annihilated, but rather that one wants to be at ease, which is just another way of saying one wants to have a different life.

The second most fundamental craving is the desire for Truth. The very first question we asked when we came into this world was the question "Why?"; a question which betrays that we are all born incipient philosophers. As children, we tear apart our toys to find out what makes the wheels go round. As grown-ups, never having lost the desire to know the "Why" and "Wherefore" of things, we tear apart, by our mental analysis, the very toy of the universe to find out what makes its wheels go round. We turn our telescopes on the sun and ask it to divulge its secrets; we ask the stars to tell us the story of their twinkling; and the very ocean to surrender the mystery of its depth. We are incurably bent on knowing and discovering the truth of things—that is why we hate to have secrets kept from us.

But that is not all. The third fundamental inclination of human nature is the desire to love and to be loved. From the first day in the Garden of Eden, when God said: "It is not good for man to be alone," on even to the crack of doom, man has thirsted and will thirst for Love. Each child that is born into the world instinctively presses itself to its mother's breast in testimony of affection. Later on he goes to his mother to have his play-wounds bound, and to shed his tears down the cheek of his mother. Finally, when the child has grown to man's estate, he looks for a companion, young like unto himself, one to whom he can "unpack his heart with words"; one who will measure up to that beautiful definition of friendship, "one in whose presence we can keep silence"—it is only before strangers that we must speak. Then the love of spouse for spouse is sealed in the bonds of matrimony, and when monotony threatens its sanctity, then there comes a child which makes an earthly Trinity. Thus the love of parents for children becomes the love of grandparents for grandchildren, and so the quest goes on from the cradle to the grave.

We desire life and truth and love, but do we find them in their plenitude on this earth? Do we carry within ourselves the energy, the force, and the power to realize them to the highest degree? Are we such masters and captains of our fate that we may give to ourselves an overflowing measure of these most precious of all gifts? We possess a fraction of life, a fraction of truth, and a fraction of love, but do we possess them in their fullness?

Certainly Life is not completely under our control. Successes of life are soon exhausted. Reputations wane and are forgotten. Schemes have their hour and come to naught. The science of one age is superseded by that of another. The taste of one age is unintelligible to the next. Poets become silent. Each tick of the clock brings us closer to the tomb; "our hearts are but muffled drums beating a funeral march to the grave." "From hour to hour we ripe and ripe; from hour to hour we rot and rot." Life may be a great torrent outpoured from the inexhaustible chalice of eternity, but we are permitted but a few drops of it in the cup of our own life.

And although Truth is a condition of our nature, neither do we possess it in its fullness, for the more we study the less we know, or rather the less we think we know. Learning opens up a thousand new vistas of knowledge down which we might travel for a lifetime, if we had a thousand lives. What man is there who has devoted his life to study who will not honestly avow that he really knows less now than what he thought he knew the night he graduated from high school? How often, too, the search for truth corrects the prejudices of youth, and how often earnest seekers after truth have come to mock and remain to pray. Great minds like Newton have confessed that all their knowledge seemed to leave them standing on the seashore of truth before which stretched an ocean of infinite truth. Thomas Aquinas, the greatest mind the world has ever produced, declared at the end of his life that all that he wrote seemed to him as straw compared to a vision which Divine Truth had accorded him.

Finally, Love in its perfected state is not to be found in this world. Broken hearts, ruined homes, young widows, divorce courts, orphans —all are so many eloquent proofs that man has not found a true and lasting love. Unfortunately, with the passing of time it often loses its delicacy. How rare, for example, is the young man who can treasure for days and for weeks and for years the gift of a rose or the touch of a hand of a friend. Quaff as he will the magic of love's wine and drink deep as he may of her springs, a day must finally come when the last cake is crumbled at life's great feast, and the last embrace is passed from friend to friend. The noblest and best of human love ends, and nothing is perfect that ends.

Though we are the lord and master of the universe, though we possess these strong yearnings, which are the very mainsprings of our beings, yet we do not find these yearnings fulfilled on this earth. Life is mingled with death; Truth is mingled with error; and Love is mingled with hate. Our life, then, is not in creatures; our Truth, then, is not in the spoken word; our Love, then, is not in what we see. Life cannot exist with death; Truth cannot exist with error; and Love cannot exist with hate.

But where find the source of these three realities? Where find the author of Existence and Truth and Love that vibrates through all creation? Shall we say that they have no source? But, if they have no source, how can they be, and how can they affect our lives at this moment? They are things that are reasonable and, therefore, must have been intelligently produced. They cannot come from the dismal slime of primeval jungles, for then the mind would be confronted with the absurdity that the nobler comes from the less noble. Where, then, find their source?

Suppose I am in search of the source of the light which is in this room. Where shall I find it? The source of the light is not to be found under that distant chair, for there light is mingled with shadow. The source of the light is not to be found under the table, for there too light is mingled with darkness. Where find the source of light? I must go out to something which is nothing but pure light, namely, the sun. So, too, if I am to find the source of the Life and the Truth and the Love that is in this world, I must go out to a Life that is not mingled with the shadow, death; I must go out to a Truth which is not mingled with the shadow, error; and I must go out to a Love which is not mingled with the shadow, hate. I must go out beyond "the margent of this world," out past the "golden gateways of the stars," out past the clotted clay of all humanity, out even to the "hid battlements of eternity," out to Some One who is Pure Life, Pure Truth, and Pure Love.

> "There is a quest that calls me
>   In nights when I am alone,
>   The need to ride where the ways divide
>   The Known from the Unknown.
>
> "I mount what thought is near me
>   And soon I reach the place,
>   The tenuous rim where the Seen grows dim,
>   And the sightless hides its face.

"I have ridden the wind,
I have ridden the sea,
I have ridden the moon and stars,
I have set my feet in the stirrup seat
Of a comet coursing Mars.

"And everywhere
Thro' the earth and air
My thought speeds, lightning-shod,
It comes to a place where checking pace
It cries 'Beyond lies God.' "

Oh, would that I had the speech of angel tongues or the language which Adam spoke in Eden, or a tongue like Isaiah which had been touched with a coal from the very altar of God—then, perhaps, I could make you understand what God is. But our untempered speech which descends "grimy and rough-cast from Babel's brick-layers," strong it is to damn, strong it is to speak of cheek and lip and bosom; for these things it moves with light ease in the speech of the working day. But to speak of God, it moves with the clumsiness of the hieroglyphs. Poor as it is, language may tell its story that God is not some dim far-off abstraction, not some "spatio-temporal configuration"; not "an epochal occasion"; not an energy, but the fullness of Life and Truth and Love. God is that Life Which has throbbed throughout the agelessness of eternity, wherein each moment is eternity and eternity is as a moment; that Life whence has come all existing things from the stars, the "glimmering tapers lit about the day's dead sanctities," on even to the smiling face of a babe in a crib.

God is that Truth in Whom darkness and ignorance can find no place, before Whom all is spread out in its widest extent and smallest detail; that Truth the Greek academicians sought as they walked the streets of Athens, the Truth the scientist seeks as he uncovers fossils in the strata of the earth, the Truth the saint seeks as he leaves the lights and glamours of the world for the shades and shadows of the cross where the saints are made.

God is that Love Who ever wills and loves the Good because it is His nature, that Love whence has come the love of spouse for spouse, and that yet stranger love of a Stephen who loved and prayed for those who stoned him in hate; and the purer love of "passionless passion and mild tranquillities" wherein the heart confides in God alone.

If, then, God is the source of the Life, the Truth, and the Love in the universe, and if the very existence of these things depends more upon Him than the evening rays upon the setting sun, do we not owe Him something in return? If there are gifts, shall there not be gratitude for gifts? If a man invents a machine, does not the government give him patent rights entitling him to returns on his invention? If an author writes a book, is he not entitled to royalties on his writings, simply because they are the creation of his mind? Now, we are God's invention, or better still, God's creation. Is not God, therefore, entitled to a return on His creation? Is He not entitled to royalties on His works? And since He has given us three great gifts which contain all other gifts, should He not be entitled to triple returns on those gifts? Since He has given us Truth, are we not in duty bound to know Him? Since He gave us Love, should we not love in return? Since He gave us Life, should we not serve Him? If we admit that triple bond, then we admit religion, or commerce between God and man, and such is the first lesson of the penny catechism: "Why did God make us? God made us to know Him, to love Him, to serve Him in this world and to be happy with Him forever in heaven."

Thus I come back to my starting point: The quest for God is essentially the search for the full account and meaning of life. And life has a meaning because the essence of God is Love.

God is not a Being Who does not know how to love; not one of those tepid hearts that have no flames, and whose tiny sparks have not the power of enkindling others, but fly back only upon themselves; not a powerless God Who knows how to love but cannot realize His dreams; not a God Who burns with love but has only cold words to say. God's love is not like a stream which runs deep and mighty as long as it is held within narrow banks, but like the great Feast at which five thousand sat and all did have their fill.

If we would know what God is, then we need only look into our own hearts. Something God-like is mirrored there—for whatever is best in the treasured lives of heroic men and the serene unwritten lives of innocent women; whatever is best in the loyalty of human hearts and the unwearying sweetness of a mother's love; whatever is noble in the sacrificing care of a father and the devotion of an unselfish friend, is but the dim reflection, the far-off echo, the faint shadow of that which in God is perfect. We are but enjoying a two-billionth part of the light and heat which streams from the sun, and it may equally be that we are receiving even a smaller fraction of the Love and Life and Truth which is in God.

Do not think that any heart can speak with such rapturous language but that there is a deeper heart, a greater love, and a nobler affection. If your own mother seems to you to be the incarnation of all that is loving in life, do you think the God Who made mothers can be any less loving? If your own father seems to you to be the realization of all that kindness in life can mean, do you think the God Who made fathers is any less kind? If your own heart and mind revel in the size of the planets and the nature of the spheres, do you not think it should thrill at the knowledge of Him before Whom all the nations of the earth are poised as the grains in the balance? If there are times when the joy of living almost transports us into other realms; if there are times when the discovery of a human truth lifts us into heights of ecstatic repose; if there are times when the human heart in its noblest reaches and purest affections has the power to cast us into an ecstasy, to thrill and exalt us, then what must be the great Heart of Hearts! If a human heart can increase the joy of living, then what must be the great Heart of God! *If the Spark is so bright, oh, what must be the Flame!*

QUESTIONS ON CONTENT

1. What are the "only three realities"? How does the author construct his essay around these three terms?
2. Although self-preservation is a strong urge, does it always take priority over "Titles, joys, and wealth, power, ambition, honor"?
3. What is the purpose of the first eight paragraphs? What, particularly, is the purpose of the fourth paragraph? The eighth?
4. Why is it, or is it not, an absurdity to suppose that the nobler may come from the less noble? Discuss.
5. What figures of speech does the author use in describing man's debt to God? Are they appropriate? Explain.
6. Is there anything in common between this essay and "Man Against Darkness"? Compare the style and the content of the two essays. Speculate on how two men, products of similar environment and examining the same evidence, can come to such opposed conclusions.
7. What evidence do you find that this selection might have been delivered as a sermon?
8. Is there any indication that the author is a Roman Catholic?
9. What are the basic assumptions upon which the author rests his case?

❧ *The Biography Cure*

LON CALL

I wonder if you have ever heard of the "Biography Cure." It is the remedy one finds for his spiritual ills by going to the lives of great men for inspiration and for insight and for interpretation of abstract ideas. When Longfellow wrote the great words, "Lives of great men all remind us, We can make our lives sublime," he was talking about the Biography Cure. . . .

This is especially true in religion. So today I am presenting three ways of looking at life by looking at three great religious men. The three men are John Henry Newman, the Catholic, Charles Haddon Spurgeon, the Baptist preacher and evangelist, and James Martineau, Unitarian minister, writer and scholar.

No names stand higher in any sphere than the three I have named, and they have much in common although they were worlds apart in religious conviction. They lived at the same time. They were contemporary Londoners, but I doubt if they ever met although each would have been the richer had he known the others. In his own way each achieved about as much honor as his church could bestow. They died as the nineteenth century was dying, but their lives continue to shine as stars in our time with increasing brightness. They were devout and honest men and sincerely questful of the kindly light of religious faith. Roman Catholic culture is embodied in Newman who sought the seat of religious authority and found it in Rome. Evangelical Protestantism is embodied in Spurgeon who sought religious authority and found it in the Bible. Liberal religion has never had a greater prophet than Martineau who found the source of religion, not in a Church or Book, but in the instincts of a pure conscience and in the convictions of unclouded reason. Today when so many find their ideal in Newman, while others find theirs in Spurgeon and still others in Martineau, it seems to me that we can learn to understand and appreciate these vastly conflicting points of view by knowing something of these three men. . . .

At fifteen Newman joined the Anglican Church, firmly convinced

Delivered as a sermon in March 1949. Reprinted by permission of the author.

that he was elected to eternal glory. At sixteen he had a profound conviction that for him marriage was not to be, and he held to that idea throughout life with occasional misgivings, as is likely to happen to any healthy-minded young man.

There was a time when he was drawn to religious liberalism. He and his associates in college formed a discussion club where everything was called into question with no appeal to authority other than reason. He did not become a liberal, but the experience freed him from narrow views of religion, gave him a breadth of sympathy for the point of view of others, and also served to make him restless with the orthodoxy he had inherited. Knowing that it was impossible to continue in orthodoxy, he faced the future with liberalism on the one hand and Rome on the other. He chose Rome.

His reasons for denouncing liberalism are interesting to us liberals, and I should like to bring you some of them gleaned from statements he made, not in his youth but in his full maturity. Here are seven of them:

First, as to mystery. The liberal says no one can believe what he does not understand. Then, says Newman, it follows that there are no mysteries in religion. But there are, for religion begins and ends in mystery.

Second, as to belief. The liberal asserts that a theological doctrine is nothing more than an opinion which happens to be held by certain groups of men. Then, says Newman, no creed is necessary for salvation. But it is, since salvation is by belief.

Third, as to his own profession, the priesthood. The liberal asserts that Christianity is modified by the growth of civilization and the exigencies of time and place. Then, says Newman, the Catholic priesthood, necessary to the Middle Ages, may be superseded now.

Fourth, as to Christianity. The liberal says there is a religious point of view more simply true than Christianity as it has been taught. Then, says Newman, Christianity is like a grain of wheat that has died, and may or may not eventually bear fruit. But it is Christianity alone that must bear fruit.

Fifth, as to science. The liberal holds that no doctrine can reasonably stand in the way of scientific conclusions. Then, says Newman, the science of political economy may reverse our Lord's teachings about poverty and riches.

Sixth, as to the church. The liberal declares the right of private judgment and asserts that there is no existing authority competent to interfere with the liberty of individuals to reason for themselves. Then, says Newman, religious establishments that require assent to dogmas, such as the church, are outmoded.

Seventh, as to morality. The liberal maintains that virtue is the child of knowledge and vice the child of ignorance. Then, says Newman, a population can be made moral and happy by education, literature, travel, ventilation and drainage. And this, of course, is certainly not the case.

Today, in view of our widespread acceptance of these principles of religious liberalism, it is clear that we are in quite another world from that in which the mystic and saintly Newman moved a hundred years ago.

So he went to Rome on a visit, and his reasons for becoming Catholic are worthy of note. At first he was very dubious of Catholicism. Standing on an eminence overlooking the Vatican he cried, "What shall I call thee, light of the wide west, or heinous error's seat?" At one sanctuary he was so impressed that he exclaimed, "Oh, that thy creed were sound, thou Church of Rome!" On his return to England his boat was becalmed for an entire week during which he was much alone with his tortured soul. It was at that time that he composed the noble poem, "Lead, kindly light." To sing that hymn at a funeral is a mistake. It is a hymn-poem for a restless soul seeking serenity. Two years more and Newman resigned his Anglican pastorate to become a Roman Catholic, but during those two years it is generally conceded that his sermons were extremely brilliant. As we read them today it is evident that we have no pulpit prose now to compare with them. One man who heard him often declared that you could listen to his sermon and come away still not believing in his creed, but you would have to be harder than most men if you did not feel more than ever ashamed of all coarseness and selfishness. Beauty of dream, of thought and of utterance, yes and of life, was Newman's passion. Having believed always in the unreality of material phenomena, he lived and moved and had his being in the world of the spirit. Looking back now at his career, one is tempted to say that all through his long life he strove to make the Arabian fairy tales come true.

Critics now agree that he always did credit to his imagination at the expense of his reason. He was not at home in his world. He liked to think himself back into the eighteenth century, even the seventeenth. Some even place him in the Middle Ages. No one ever rated him modern. He resented theological reform and declared that modern thought should itself be reformed in the light of the Christian revelation. He was unmoved by the social reforms of his time and gave himself completely to the development of Catholic doctrine, its growth even in a rationalistic age and the classics in an age of science. One of his biographers declared that he was a skeptic determined to be a saint. Newman declared that going into Catholicism was like putting into port after a rough voyage. The Church was for him the seat of authority, the kindly light of religious faith.

Newman was celebrating his forty-fourth birthday when a boy named Charles Spurgeon, a self-taught youngster, just turned sixteen, started one morning from his Cambridge home with a companion to conduct a Baptist meeting in a cottage in an outlying community. Each thought the other was to be the preacher of the occasion until they were actually at the meeting. Someone had tricked them. Well, it was Spurgeon who preached. Two years later he was pastor of a church. At twenty he gathered a church in London, rented a hall and outgrew it. At twenty-two he was the most popular preacher in London. The reasons for his popularity were many. Partly it was oratory; partly, at first, his youth; always it was his humor and his tears, also his endless stories and illustrations, his voice and manner and, of course, his orthodoxy.

Spurgeon rooted his faith in the Bible. He feared and scorned the appeal to reason and preached against it. He resented the developments of Biblical criticism. Sometime, somewhere, he seems to have been drawn to religious liberalism but we are at a loss to know when or where. Once he stated that he had made "one tempestuous sailing over the ocean of free thought . . . but faith took the helm and steered me back and I cast my anchor on Calvary."

He was not only anti-liberal, but anti-Catholic. He and Newman may have been in the same city, but they were poles apart in religious conviction. Spurgeon wrote a very scathing book against the Catholics which he called "Anti-Christ and Her Brood, or Popery Unmasked." Spurgeon could find no grounds for believing in the human reason, for sin he said had robbed mankind of such possibility. Neither could he find grounds for authority in the See of a bishop or pope. Only in the Bible did he fix his faith declaring that even if conscience dictates anything to the contrary, it must be the work of the devil.

Spurgeon once declared that "a chasm is opening between men who believe their Bible and the men who are prepared for an advance upon scripture. Inspiration and speculation cannot long abide in peace. We cannot hold to the inspiration of the Word and yet reject it; we cannot believe in the atonement and deny it; we cannot hold to the doctrine of the fall of man from his state of perfection and yet to the idea of the evolution of spiritual life from human nature. . . . One way or the other we must go." And Spurgeon went to the Bible. It was his kindly light.

Spurgeon spoke the language of the throng. He addressed himself to their untutored minds. He made the most of every opportunity to get converts. He advised every minister to do likewise and never to be satisfied with less than conversions at every meeting. He said, don't be like the boy who went fishing and came back to report, "Well, I didn't catch a single fish but I drowned a lot of worms."

The world has seldom seen a more popular preacher than Spurgeon. On one occasion twenty thousand people were turned away from a meeting at which he was to preach. Enormous collections were taken but remained uncounted because Sunday was no day to work, even in counting so much of the Lord's money. Much of the money went to charity. Over twenty-two hundred separate sermons were printed and distributed throughout the world, and Spurgeon's books reached amazing sales. His church, the London Metropolitan Tabernacle, numbered six thousand members. One man who heard him often declared that "Spurgeon is the world's greatest living talker." He spoke of trees as if he had studied nothing else. He seemed as familiar with the stars as a schoolmaster with the alphabet. He discussed physiology with the knowledge of a trained physician. And always, with his appeal to Biblical authority, was the urgency of human goodness. He was the avowed and constant enemy of evil.

There are many people who, when they think of beauty, recall the life and preaching of Cardinal Newman. There are also many who, when they think of goodness, think of the life and preaching of Charles H. Spurgeon. And there are very many indeed who, when they think of truth, recall the life and influence of James Martineau.

James Martineau was older than Spurgeon but younger than Newman. When Newman was reaching for his cardinal's robes, and Spurgeon was turning thousands away from his revival meetings, Martineau ended a Unitarian pastorate of twenty-five years in Liverpool and took a church in London. It was the world of Thomas Carlyle, John Stuart Mill, Alfred Tennyson, Charles Darwin and the great Gladstone, who once declared that Martineau was the first among living English thinkers.

It was said of Newman that he lifted one out of coarseness. It was said of Spurgeon that he was the world's best talker. And Gladstone said of Martineau that he was England's greatest living thinker.

Born into a Unitarian home, James was an unusually thoughtful child. There is one story out of his childhood to the effect that set by his mother to the task of Bible reading one rainy Sunday afternoon, he announced an hour or so later that he had finished it. "But you couldn't have," she replied. "Well," he said, "I skipped the nonsense." Martineau had his head set upon a career as an engineer, but the death of a dear friend so impressed him that he turned to religious study. He examined and re-examined the claims of the Roman Catholic Church. He studied the historical significance of the Christian religion. He delved deeply into the origin and character of the Bible, its authority and the claims made for its infallibility. But he gave pre-eminence to neither church nor book. He once declared that for more than fifty years his one aim had been the substitution of religion at first hand, straight out of the interaction of the soul and God, for religion at second hand fetched by what had been copied out of the anonymous traditions of the eastern Mediterranean world eighteen centuries before. He came through honest and rigorous study to see Jesus, not as a Jewish Messiah, but as a prince of human saints who revealed the highest possibilities of the human soul. The seat of religious authority he found in man himself; in man's reason, his conscience and his affections. The sphere of judgment he transferred from authorities outside of a man to springs of action within. He once declared that he could more surely feel that reason was the gift of God than any book or church.

Martineau felt that we must trust implicitly our natural powers; our senses as reporters of the world about us; our understanding as interpreters of that world; our reason and conscience in ordering that world, and reason and conscience in finding and knowing God.

The ultimate appeal—let us here proclaim it to our age as Martineau proclaimed it to his—the seat of authority, the basis of religion, is in reason and conscience. Whoever tries to shake that authority, though he think himself a saint in doing so, is an infidel. Whoever thinks or declares that any religious authority can be above reason or conscience, no matter what may be the book or the church, is secretly pulling up all belief by the roots. Whoever tells me that any apostle or prophet, priest or preacher can set himself above my own reason and conscience fixes upon such a messenger of God the sign of impostor. Without this appeal to the rational nature in man duty loses its sacredness, the spiritual values their significance and man becomes a slave, earth a prison, and God a devil.

Such was, all too sketchily, the abiding service of this great man. Here was a clear, honest, profound religious synthesis which transferred the sphere of judgment from outward authorities to inward springs of action. Here was the access of the soul to divine things. Here was first-hand religion. Here was the true ground for the idea of the indwelling God. Here was human freedom defined and vindicated. Here was the court of appeal from all authorities, from church and ceremony, from book and creed. Here was the kindly light.

And because James Martineau followed that light, you and I are today set where otherwise our feet would not have climbed. Because he ran and was not weary, we walk and do not faint.

QUESTIONS ON CONTENT

1. Examine Newman's seven reasons for "denouncing liberalism." Does authority underlie each of Newman's "reasons"?
2. "Going into Catholicism was like putting into port after a rough voyage." Comment. What was the "rough voyage"? What does the "port" represent?
3. What is meant by "evangelical protestantism"?
4. In what way were Newman and Spurgeon in agreement? In disagreement?
5. Why did Spurgeon reject: (*a*) human reason; (*b*) an authoritarian church; (*c*) conscience?
6. In what way is the account of Martineau's rapid reading of the Bible a key to his life?
7. Does Martineau agree in any way with Newman or Spurgeon?
8. Comment on each sentence of the third paragraph from the end.
9. Can you name a modern counterpart of John Henry Newman? Of Charles Spurgeon? Of Martineau?
10. Which of the religions represented by the three men considered here has had the greatest growth in our century? Try to explain why.
11. With which, if any, of the approaches advocated by these three men do you agree?

❧ *In Memoriam A. H. H.*

Alfred, Lord Tennyson

Obiit MDCCCXXXIII

Strong Son of God, immortal Love,
   Whom we, that have not seen thy face,
   By faith, and faith alone, embrace,
Believing where we cannot prove;

Thine are these orbs of light and shade;   5
   Thou madest Life in man and brute;
   Thou madest Death; and lo, thy foot
Is on the skull which thou hast made.

Thou wilt not leave us in the dust:
   Thou madest man, he knows not why;   10
   He thinks he was not made to die;
And thou hast made him: thou art just.

Thou seemest human and divine,
   The highest, holiest manhood, thou:
   Our wills are ours, we know not how;   15
Our wills are ours, to make them thine.

Our little systems have their day;
   They have their day and cease to be:
   They are but broken lights of thee,
And thou, O Lord, art more than they.   20

We have but faith: we cannot know;
   For knowledge is of things we see;
   And yet we trust it comes from thee,
A beam in darkness: let it grow.

From *In Memoriam*, 1850. A. H. H. are the initials of Arthur Henry Hallam, Tennyson's friend, whose sudden death in 1833 caused the poet to write *In Memoriam*. This "Prologue," though placed first, was written last.

Let knowledge grow from more to more, 25
But more of reverence in us dwell;
That mind and soul, according well,
May make one music as before,

But vaster. We are fools and slight;
We mock thee when we do not fear: 30
But help thy foolish ones to bear;
Help thy vain worlds to bear thy light.

Forgive what seem'd my sin in me;
What seem'd my worth since I began;
For merit lives from man to man, 35
And not from man, O Lord, to thee.

Forgive my grief for one removed,
Thy creature, whom I found so fair.
I trust he lives in thee, and there
I find him worthier to be loved. 40

Forgive these wild and wandering cries,
Confusions of a wasted youth;
Forgive them where they fail in truth,
And in thy wisdom make me wise.

QUESTIONS ON CONTENT

1. What are the "orbs of light and shade"?
2. Are "Death" and "the skull" the same thing? If so, what is meant by "thy foot/ Is on the skull"? Define *die*, line 11.
3. Explain the reasoning in Stanza 3. Is line 12 made up of two hypotheses? What are "the little systems" of line 17?
4. The poet calls knowledge "A beam in darkness." Contrast this view with that set forth in "Man against Darkness."
5. "We mock thee when we do not fear." Comment.
6. Why does the poet ask forgiveness for grief (line 37)?
7. What is meant by the line, "Confusions of a wasted youth"?
8. Is the reasoning of Tennyson similar to Newman's, Spurgeon's, or Martineau's? (See "The Biography Case.")

❧ *High Flight*

JOHN GILLESPIE MAGEE, JR.

Oh! I have slipped the surly bonds of Earth
    And danced the skies on laughter-silvered wings;
Sunward I've climbed, and joined the tumbling mirth
    Of sun-split clouds,—and done a hundred things
You have not dreamed of—wheeled and soared and swung
    High in the sunlit silence. Hov'ring there,
I've chased the shouting wind along, and flung
    My eager craft through footless halls of air. . . .
Up, up the long delirious, burning blue
    I've topped the wind-swept heights with easy grace,
Where never lark, or even eagle flew—
    And, while with silent, lifting mind I've trod
    The high untrespassed sanctity of space,
Put out my hand and touched the face of God.

QUESTIONS ON CONTENT

1. What is the "argument" of this poem? Compare the "Prologue" to *In Memoriam.*
2. Is the experience described here a form of ecstasy? Discuss.
3. Examine all the adjectives, and tell why each one is, or is not, appropriate.

SUGGESTIONS FOR PAPERS

Your own experience with religion will doubtless serve as a guide to your response to the selections in this chapter. You will note a sharp clash between the thought in the first article and the ideas in the remaining four selections. Try to understand clearly what is said; then in your paper take your stand.

1. The author of "Man against Darkness" writes confidently of "the disappearance of religion" because science has forced men to

Reprinted by permission of Mrs. John G. Magee.

abandon the older idea that everything in the universe fits into a cosmic scheme presided over by an Overruling Mind. Has religion disappeared? Is everyone aware that he lives in a purposeless universe? Can science prove its contention of purposelessness? Devote a paragraph to each of these questions; add personal comment.

2. Are there any new reasons for disbelieving in man's control—at least partial control—of his own destiny? It is said that a chain of circumstances leads to every action and that the action itself then takes its place as a link in the chain. Can man break the chain or is he simply pulled along by it? How many actions are unavoidable? Consider laziness, heroism, cowardice, alcoholism. Do these terms become meaningless if one denies free will?

3. The thesis of "Man against Darkness" is that religion is no longer possible. Does the author provide an argument for the necessity of religion? Whence, for example, comes the author's feeling that loss of religion is a calamity? Has religion ever been scientifically provable? (A scientific faith is a contradiction in terms, is it not?) *Can* faith be scientifically discredited?

4. Compare "Man against Darkness" and "Man's Quest for God." Here are two points you might consider: the conceptions of a purposeless universe versus one which is essentially a reflection of God; the conceptions of a world which just happened and could well be regulated differently versus one which must be the product of something nobler than itself. How does the language of the two essays differ? Can *what* is said in each essay be separated from *how* it is said?

5. Analyze "Man's Quest for God." How does the author seek to prove the paramount importance of Life, Truth, Love? How, then, does he relate these abstractions to man's search for God? Is this approach reasonable or emotional or both? What consideration is given to Ignorance and Hate? How are these opposites of Truth and Love explained?

6. Which person—Newman, Spurgeon, or Martineau ("The Biography Cure")—represents most nearly your own thinking about religion? Give reasons for rejecting the religious approach of two of these men and then give reasons for agreeing with one of them. Or reject all three and add your own independent view of religion.

7. Write a paper on Martineau ("The Biography Cure") as a civilized man. Use the definition of a civilized man as set forth in "Man against Darkness." Was Martineau a victim of "the Great Illusion"? If so, does he qualify otherwise as a civilized person?

8. On the basis of Tennyson's "Prologue," how would you compare the poet's beliefs with those of Newman? Spurgeon? Martineau? (All from "The Biography Cure.") Does Tennyson in stanza 3 add a justification for faith not included in any other selection?

9. First explain, then attack or defend any one of the following statements:

(*a*) "The chaotic and bewildered state of the modern world is due to man's loss of faith, his abandonment of God and religion."

(*b*) "Our ideals . . . must proceed from our own minds; they are our own inventions."

(*c*) "Blind to good and evil, reckless of destruction, omnipotent matter rolls on its relentless way."

(*d*) "Inquiry into purposes is useless for what science aims at: namely, the prediction and control of events."

(*e*) "The world is just what it is, and that is the end of all inquiry. There is no reason for its being what it is. Everything might just as well have been different, and there would have been no reason for that either."

(*f*) "Every man calleth that which pleaseth him, good; and that which displeaseth him, evil."

(*g*) "God hath appointed a strait and narrow way, that leadeth to life." Contrast with (*f*).

(*h*) "Pills and injections in the future are to do what Christ and the prophets failed to do."

(*i*) "Inspiration and speculation cannot long abide in peace."

(*j*) "The ultimate appeal . . . the seat of authority, the basis of religion, is in reason and conscience."

(*k*) Thou wilt not leave us in the dust:

> Thou madest man, he knows not why,
>
> He thinks he was not made to die;
>
> And thou hast made him: thou art just.

SOME TITLES FOR PAPERS

1. The Best Religion
2. *Cause* and *Purpose* Defined
3. Science Cannot Touch Religion
4. In the Heart, Not in the Head
5. Direction in a "Purposeless" World
6. I Am Morally Responsible
7. Religion and Morals Are Separate Things
8. What Is the Purpose of Purposelessness?

❧ SCIENCE AND MAN

THE FINDINGS OF SCIENCE have never before claimed such awed attention from so many people. There are numerous reasons for this: a greatly expanded educational program which enables more people to understand, at least partly, what scientists are up to; a shorter cut than heretofore from scientific theory to practical application; spectacular demonstrations such as those at Hiroshima and, experimentally, at Bikini and elsewhere. Most important, perhaps, is the fact of world tension which has dramatized the laboratories and focused anxious eyes on men of science. You as a college student have all these reasons for being vitally concerned with what science has so far done. You will not, of course, learn science in your English class, but it is an appropriate place for oral and written discussion of the findings of science and what these findings mean.

Thomas Henry Huxley, the greatest expositor of the claims of science, lays down the rules for scientific investigation. He establishes the close relationship between everyday reasoning and scientific reasoning. His comparisons are so homely and simple as to be disarming. You will have the feeling while reading "The Scientific Method" that nothing evil could possibly result from a process at once so human and so reasonable. And "On a Piece of Chalk" will arouse no fears, for in it he simply shows how expertly reasonable science can be, how resourceful in extracting the meaning from a commonplace piece of chalk.

So long as scientific experiments have involved chalk, vegetables and lower animals man has looked on with undisturbed interest. Scientists, however, have always had man as their ultimate interest and have moved ever closer to direct experimentation with human beings. So far they have, for the most part, merely described and measured and classified. They have amassed mountains of statistics.

All through the ages the man who would rule has used force either to gain his power or to maintain it. Men of science have always, consciously or unwittingly, been at hand to provide the latest sorts of force, the weapons of war. They are more busily at this job now than ever before in history. There is nothing new in this. What may be new is the slow realization of those ambitious to be rulers that the application of direct force is a means of gaining only a temporary control over men. Force, for example, has not yet been able to stamp out the desire for freedom. Has science an answer? Can science eliminate the desire for freedom? Can "brainwashing" be developed into a dependable technique?

Suppose science can provide a way for man to learn *without conscious effort.* J. D. Ratcliff's article, "Learn While You Sleep," sets forth the steps so far taken to accomplish this result. What are the good and the evil possibilities of sleep-learning?

As usual the announced purpose of producing a technique of sleep teaching is benefit to mankind. Aldous Huxley, however, in a classic of science fiction, *Brave New World,* visualizes the perfection of the technique. His "Stable Society" shows what science may do to man.

"An Outline of Scientists" pokes fun at some of the pretensions of science and blows some fresh air over the current awe with which many people regard everything labeled scientific.

The final selection, "The Myth of Science Fiction," drew many angry protests from addicts of this sort of reading. Why? What man can imagine, man has some chance of doing. This article shows the trend in the imaginings of science-fiction writers.

❧ *The Scientific Method*

THOMAS HENRY HUXLEY

The method of scientific investigation is nothing but the expression of the necessary mode of working of the human mind. It is simply the mode by which all phenomena are reasoned about, rendered precise and exact. There is no more difference, but there is just the same kind of difference, between the mental operations of a man of science and those of an ordinary person, as there is between the operations and methods of a baker or of a butcher weighing out his goods in common scales, and the operations of a chemist in performing a difficult and complex analysis by means of his balance and finely graduated weights. It is not that the action of the scales in the one case, and the balance in the other, differ in the principles of their construction or manner of working; but the beam of one is set on an infinitely finer axis than the other, and of course turns by the addition of a much smaller weight.

You will understand this better, perhaps, if I give you some familiar example. You have all heard it repeated, I dare say, that men of science work by means of induction and deduction, and that by the help of these operations, they, in a sort of sense, wring from Nature certain other things, which are called natural laws, and causes, and that out of these, by some cunning skill of their own, they build up hypotheses and theories. And it is imagined by many, that the operations of the common mind can be by no means compared with these processes, and that they have to be acquired by a sort of special apprenticeship to the craft. To hear all these large words, you would think that the mind of a man of science must be constituted differently from that of his fellow men; but if you will not be frightened by terms, you will discover that you are quite wrong, and that all these terrible apparatus are being used by yourselves every day and every hour of your lives.

There is a well-known incident in one of Molière's plays, where the author makes the hero express unbounded delight on being told that he had been talking prose during the whole of his life. In the same way, I trust that you will take comfort, and be delighted with

From *Collected Essays* (1893).

yourselves, on the discovery that you have been acting on the principles of inductive and deductive philosophy during the same period. Probably there is not one here who has not in the course of the day had occasion to set in motion a complex train of reasoning, of the very same kind, though differing of course in degree, as that which a scientific man goes through in tracing the causes of natural phenomena.

A very trivial circumstance will serve to exemplify this. Suppose you go into a fruiterer's shop, wanting an apple—you take up one, and on biting it, you find it is sour; you look at it, and see that it is hard and green. You take up another one and that too is hard, green, and sour. The shopman offers you a third; but, before biting it, you examine it, and find that it is hard and green, and you immediately say that you will not have it, as it must be sour, like those that you have already tried.

Nothing can be more simple than that, you think; but if you will take the trouble to analyse and trace out into its logical elements what has been done by the mind, you will be greatly surprised. In the first place you have performed the operation of induction. You found that, in two experiences, hardness and greenness in apples went together with sourness. It was so in the first case, and it was confirmed by the second. True, it is a very small basis, but still it is enough to find sourness in apples where you get hardness and greenness. You found upon that a general law that all hard and green apples are sour; and that, so far as it goes, is a perfect induction. Well, having got your natural law in this way, when you are offered another apple which you find is hard and green, you say, "All hard and green apples are sour; this apple is hard and green, therefore this apple is sour." That train of reasoning is what logicians call a syllogism, and has all its various parts and terms—its major premiss, its minor premiss, and its conclusion. And, by the help of further reasoning, which, if drawn out, would have to be exhibited in two or three other syllogisms, you arrive at your final determination, "I will not have that apple." So that, you see, you have, in the first place, established a law by induction, and upon that you have founded a deduction, and reasoned out the special particular case. Well now, suppose, having got your conclusion of the law, that at some time afterwards you are discussing the qualities of apples with a friend: you will say to him, "It is a very curious thing, but I find that all hard and green apples are sour!" Your friend says to you, "But how do you know that?" You at once reply, "Oh, because I have tried them over and over again, and have always found them to be so." Well, if we were talking science instead of common sense, we should call that an experimental verification. And, if still opposed, you go further, and say, "I have heard from the people in Somersetshire and Devonshire, where a large number of apples are grown, that they have observed the same thing. It is also found to be the case in Normandy, and in North America. In short, I find it to be the universal experience of mankind wherever attention has been directed to the subject." Whereupon, your friend, unless he is a very unreasonable man, agrees with you, and is convinced that you are quite right in the conclusion you have drawn. He believes, although perhaps he does not know he believes it, that the more extensive verifications are—that the more frequently experiments have been made, and results of the same kind arrived at—that the more varied the conditions under which the same results are attained, the more certain is the ultimate conclusion, and he disputes the question no further. He sees that the experiment has been tried under all sorts of conditions, as to time, place, and people, with the same result; and he says with you, therefore, that the law you have laid down must be a good one, and he must believe it. In science we do the same thing—the philosopher exercises precisely the same faculties, though in a much more delicate manner. In scientific inquiry it becomes a matter of duty to expose a supposed law to every possible kind of verification, and to take care, moreover, that this is done intentionally, and not left to a mere accident, as in the case of the apples. And in science, as in common life, our confidence in a law is in exact proportion to the absence of variation in the result of our experimental verifications. For instance, if you let go your grasp of an article you may have in your hand, it will immediately fall to the ground. That is a very common verification of one of the best established laws of nature—that of gravitation. The method by which men of science establish the existence of that law is exactly the same as that by which we have established the trivial proposition about the sourness of hard and green apples. But we believe it in such an extensive, thorough, and unhesitating manner because the universal experience of mankind verifies it, and we can verify it ourselves at any time; and that is the strongest possible foundation on which any natural law can rest.

So much, then, by way of proof that the method of establishing laws in science is exactly the same as that pursued in common life. Let us now turn to another matter (though really it is but another phase of the same question), and that is, the method by which, from the relations of certain phenomena, we prove that some stand in the position of causes towards the others.

I want to put the case clearly before you, and I will therefore show you what I mean by another familiar example. I will suppose that one of you, on coming down in the morning to the parlor of your house, finds that a tea-pot and some spoons which had been left in the room on the previous evening are gone—the window is open, and you observe the mark of a dirty hand on the window-frame, and perhaps, in addition to that, you notice the impress of hob-nailed shoes on the gravel outside. All these phenomena have struck your attention instantly, and before two seconds have passed you say, "Oh, somebody has broken open the window, entered the room, and run off with the spoons and the tea-pot!" That speech is out of your mouth in a moment. And you will probably add, "I know there has; I am quite sure of it!" You mean to say exactly what you know; but in reality you are giving expression to what is, in all essential particulars, an hypothesis. You do not know it at all; it is nothing but an hypothesis rapidly framed in your own mind. And it is an hypothesis founded on a long train of inductions and deductions.

What are those inductions and deductions, and how have you got at this hypothesis? You have observed in the first place, that the window is open; but by a train of reasoning involving many inductions and deductions, you have probably arrived long before at the general law—and a very good one it is—that windows do not open of themselves; and you therefore conclude that something has opened the window. A second general law that you have arrived at in the same way is, that tea-pots and spoons do not go out of a window spontaneously, and you are satisfied that, as they are not now where you left them, they have been removed. In the third place, you look at the marks on the window-sill, and the shoe-marks outside, and you say that in all previous experience the former kind of mark has never been produced by anything else but the hand of a human being; and the same experience shows that no other animal but man at present wears shoes with hob-nails in them such as would produce the marks in the gravel. I do not know, even if we could discover any of those "missing links" that are talked about, that they would help us to any other conclusion! At any rate the law which states our present experience is strong enough for my present purpose. You next reach the conclusion that, as these kinds of marks have not been left by any other animal than man, or are liable to be formed in any other way than by a man's hand and shoe, the marks in question have been formed by a man in that way. You have, further, a general law, founded on observation and experience, and that, too, is, I am sorry to say, a very universal and unimpeachable one—that some men are thieves; and you assume at once from all these premisses—and that is what constitutes your hypothesis—that the man who made the marks outside and on the windowsill, opened the window, got into the room, and stole your tea-pot and spoons. You have now arrived at a vera causa—you have assumed a cause which, it is plain, is competent to produce all the phenomena you have observed. You can explain all these phenomena only by the hypothesis of a thief. But that is a hypothetical conclusion, of the justice of which you have no absolute proof at all; it is only rendered highly probable by a series of inductive and deductive reasonings.

I suppose your first action, assuming that you are a man of ordinary common sense, and that you have established this hypothesis to your own satisfaction, will very likely be to go off for the police, and set them on the track of the burglar, with the view to the recovery of your property. But just as you are starting with this object, some person comes in, and on learning what you are about, says, "My good friend, you are going on a great deal too fast. How do you know that the man who really made the marks took the spoons? It might have been a monkey that took them, and the man may have merely looked in afterwards." You would probably reply, "Well, that is all very well, but you see it is contrary to all experience of the way tea-pots and spoons are abstracted; so that, at any rate, your hypothesis is less probable than mine." While you are talking the thing over in this way, another friend arrives, one of the good kind of people that I was talking of a little while ago. And he might say, "Oh, my dear sir, you are certainly going on a great deal too fast. You are most presumptuous. You admit that all these occurrences took place when you were fast asleep, at a time when you could not possibly have known anything about what was taking place. How do you know that the laws of Nature are not suspended during the night? It may be that there has been some kind of supernatural interference in this case." In point of fact, he declares that your hypothesis is one of which you cannot at all demonstrate the truth and that you are by no means sure that the laws of Nature are the same when you are asleep as when you are awake.

Well, now, you cannot at the moment answer that kind of reasoning. You feel that your worthy friend has you somewhat at a disadvantage. You will feel perfectly convinced in your own mind, however, that you are quite right, and you say to him, "My good friend, I can only be guided by the natural probabilities of the case, and if you will be kind enough to stand aside and permit me to pass, I will go and fetch the police." Well, we will suppose that your journey is successful, and that by good luck you meet with a policeman; that eventually the burglar is found with your property on his person, and the marks correspond to his hand and to his boots. Probably any jury would consider those facts a very good experimental verification of your hypothesis, touching the cause of the abnormal phenomena observed in your parlor, and would act accordingly.

Now, in this suppositious case, I have taken phenomena of a very common kind, in order that you might see what are the different steps in an ordinary process of reasoning, if you will only take the trouble to analyse it carefully. All the operations I have described, you will see, are involved in the mind of any man of sense in leading him to a conclusion as to the course he should take in order to make good a robbery and punish the offender. I say that you are led, in that case, to your conclusion by exactly the same train of reasoning as that which a man of science pursues when he is endeavoring to discover the origin and laws of the most occult phenomena. The process is, and always must be, the same; and precisely the same mode of reasoning was employed by Newton and Laplace in their endeavors to discover and define the causes of the movements of the heavenly bodies, as you, with your own common sense, would employ to detect a burglar. The only difference is, that the nature of the inquiry being more abstruse, every step has to be most carefully watched, so that there may not be a single crack or flaw in your hypothesis. A flaw or crack in many of the hypotheses of daily life may be of little or no moment as affecting the general correctness of the conclusions at which we may arrive; but, in a scientific inquiry, a fallacy, great or small, is always of importance, and is sure to be in the long run constantly productive of mischievous if not fatal results.

Do not allow yourselves to be misled by the common notion that an hypothesis is untrustworthy simply because it is an hypothesis. It is often urged, in respect to some scientific conclusion, that, after all, it is only an hypothesis. But what more have we to guide us in nine-tenths of the most important affairs of daily life than hypotheses, and often very ill-based ones? So that in science, where the evidence of an hypothesis is subjected to the most rigid examination, we may rightly pursue the same course. You may have hypotheses, and hypotheses. A man may say, if he likes, that the moon is made of green cheese: that is an hypothesis. But another man, who has devoted a great deal of time and attention to the subject, and availed himself of the most powerful telescopes and the results of the observations of others, declares that in his opinion it is probably composed of materials very similar to those of which our own earth is made up: and that is also only an hypothesis. But I need not tell you that there is an enormous difference in the value of the two hypotheses. That one which is based on sound scientific knowledge is sure to have a corresponding value; and that which is a mere hasty random guess is likely to have but little value. Every great step in our progress in discovering causes has been made in exactly the same way as that which I have detailed to you. A person observing the occurrence of certain facts and phenomena asks, naturally enough, what process, what kind of operation known to occur in Nature, applied to the particular case, will unravel and explain the mystery? Hence you have the scientific hypothesis; and its value will be proportionate to the care and completeness with which its basis had been tested and verified. It is in these matters as in the commonest affairs of practical life; the guess of the fool will be folly, while the guess of the wise man will contain wisdom. In all cases, you see that the value of the result depends on the patience and faithfulness with which the investigator applies to his hypothesis every possible kind of verification.

QUESTIONS ON CONTENT

1. What does the author mean by "the necessary mode of working of the human mind"?
2. How does the comparison of the butcher and the chemist help to make clear Huxley's definition of scientific method?
3. How does the author make clear the inductive method?
4. What necessary relationship is there between induction and deduction?
5. What is likely to be the greatest weakness in the inductive process?
6. Define "experimental verification."
7. How does the scientist differ from the layman in his demand for proof?

8. What illustration does Huxley use to show the method of proving that certain phenomena stand in the position of *causes* of other phenomena?

9. To what does the author allude in his reference to "missing links"? (Hint: this lecture was part of a series on Darwin.) And why does he use a "monkey" in one of the counter-hypotheses? Explain, too, the attitude of "one of the good kind of people" who mentions the possible suspending of the laws of Nature and supernatural interference.

10. "In a scientific inquiry, a fallacy, great or small, is always of importance." Comment. Is any scientific inquiry ever brought to conclusion?

❧ *On a Piece of Chalk*

Thomas Henry Huxley

If a well were sunk at our feet in the midst of the city of Norwich, the diggers would very soon find themselves at work in that white substance almost too soft to be called rock, with which we are all familiar as "chalk."

Not only here, but over the whole country of Norfolk, the well-sinker might carry his shaft down many hundred feet without coming to the end of the chalk; and, on the sea-coast, where the waves have pared away the face of the land which breasts them, the scarped faces of the high cliffs are often wholly formed of the same material. Northward, the chalk may be followed as far as Yorkshire; on the south coast it appears abruptly in the picturesque western bays of Dorset, and breaks into the Needles of the Isle of Wight; while on the shores of Kent it supplies that long line of white cliffs to which England owes her name of Albion.

Were the thin soil which covers it all washed away, a curved band of white chalk, here broader, and there narrower, might be followed diagonally across England from Lulworth in Dorset, to Flamborough Head in Yorkshire—a distance of over 280 miles as the crow flies. From this band to the North Sea, on the east, and the Channel, on the south, the chalk is largely hidden by other deposits; but, ex-

First published in 1868.

cept in the Weald of Kent and Sussex, it enters into the very foundation of all the southeastern counties.

Attaining, as it does in some places, a thickness of more than a thousand feet, the English chalk must be admitted to be a mass of considerable magnitude. Nevertheless, it covers but an insignificant portion of the whole area occupied by the chalk formation of the globe, much of which has the same general characters as ours, and is found in detached patches, some less, and others more extensive, than the English. Chalk occurs in north-west Ireland; it stretches over a large part of France,—the chalk which underlies Paris being, in fact, a continuation of that of the London basin; it runs through Denmark and Central Europe, and extends southward to North Africa; while eastward, it appears in the Crimea and in Syria; and may be traced as far as the shores of the Sea of Aral, in Central Asia. If all the points at which true chalk occurs were circumscribed, they would lie within an irregular oval about 3,000 miles long in diameter—the area of which would be as great as that of Europe, and would many times exceed that of the largest existing inland sea—the Mediterranean.

Thus the chalk is no unimportant element in the masonry of the earth's crust, and it impresses a peculiar stamp, varying with the conditions to which it is exposed, on the scenery of the districts in which it occurs. The undulating downs and rounded coombs, covered with sweet-grassed turf, of our inland chalk country, have a peacefully domestic and mutton-suggesting prettiness, but can hardly be called either grand or beautiful. But on our southern coasts, the wall-sided cliffs, many hundred feet high, with vast needles and pinnacles standing out in the sea, sharp and solitary enough to serve as perches for the wary cormorant, confer a wonderful beauty and grandeur upon the chalk headlands. And, in the East, chalk has its share in the formation of some of the most venerable of mountain ranges, such as the Lebanon.

What is this wide-spread component of the surface of the earth? and whence did it come?

You may think this no very hopeful inquiry. You may not unnaturally suppose that the attempt to solve such problems as these can lead to no result, save that of entangling the inquirer in vague speculations, incapable of refutation and of verification. If such were really the case, I should have selected some other subject than a "piece of chalk" for my discourse. But, in truth, after much deliberation, I have been unable to think of any topic which would so well enable me to lead you to see how solid is the foundation upon which some of the most startling conclusions of physical science rest.

A great chapter of the history of the world is written in the chalk. Few passages in the history of man can be supported by such an overwhelming mass of direct and indirect evidence as that which testifies to the truth of the fragment of the history of the globe, which I hope to enable you to read, with your own eyes, to-night. Let me add, that few chapters of human history have a more profound significance for ourselves. I weigh my words well when I assert, that the man who should know the true history of the bit of chalk which every carpenter carries about in his breeches-pocket, though ignorant of all other history, is like, if he will think his knowledge out to its ultimate results, to have a truer, and therefore a better, conception of this wonderful universe, and of man's relation to it, than the most learned student who is deep-read in the record of humanity and ignorant of those of Nature.

The language of the chalk is not hard to learn, not nearly so hard as Latin, if you only want to get at the broad features of the story it has to tell; and I propose that we now set to work to spell that story out together.

We all know that if we "burn" chalk the result is quicklime. Chalk, in fact, is a compound of carbonic acid gas, and lime, and when you make it very hot the carbonic acid flies away and the lime is left. By this method of procedure we see the lime, but we do not see the carbonic acid. If, on the other hand, you were to powder a little chalk and drop it into a good deal of strong vinegar, there would be a great bubbling and fizzing, and, finally, a clear liquid, in which no sign of chalk would appear. Here you see the carbonic acid in the bubbles; the lime, dissolved in the vinegar, vanished from sight. There are a great many other ways of showing that chalk is essentially nothing but carbonic acid and quicklime. Chemists enunciate the result of all the experiments which prove this, by stating that chalk is almost wholly composed of "carbonate of lime."

It is desirable for us to start from the knowledge of this fact, though it may not seem to help us very far towards what we seek. For carbonate of lime is a widely-spread substance, and is met with under very various conditions. All sorts of limestones are composed of more or less pure carbonate of lime. The crust which is often deposited by waters which have drained through limestone rocks, in the form of what are called stalagmites and stalactites, is carbonate of lime. Or, to take a more familiar example, the fur on the inside of a tea-kettle is carbonate of lime; and, for anything chemistry tells us to the contrary, the chalk might be a kind of gigantic fur upon the bottom of the earth-kettle, which is kept pretty hot below.

Let us try another method of making the chalk tell us its own history. To the unassisted eye chalk looks simply like a very loose and open kind of stone. But it is possible to grind a slice of chalk down so thin that you can see through it—until it is thin enough, in fact, to be examined with any magnifying power that may be thought desirable. A thin slice of the fur of a kettle might be made in the same way. If it were examined microscopically, it would show itself to be a more or less distinctly laminated mineral substance, and nothing more.

But the slice of chalk presents a totally different appearance when placed under the microscope. The general mass of it is made up of very minute granules; but, imbedded in this matrix, are innumerable bodies, some smaller and some larger, but, on a rough average, not more than a hundredth of an inch in diameter, having a well-defined shape and structure. A cubic inch of some specimens of chalk may contain hundreds of thousands of these bodies, compacted together with incalculable millions of the granules.

The examination of a transparent slice gives a good notion of the manner in which the components of the chalk are arranged, and of their relative proportions. But, by rubbing up some chalk with a brush in water and then pouring off the milky fluid, so as to obtain sediments of different degrees of fineness, the granules and the minute rounded bodies may be pretty well separated from one another, and submitted to microscopic examination, either as opaque or as transparent objects. By combining the views obtained in these various methods, each of the rounded bodies may be proved to be a beautifully-constructed calcareous fabric, made up of a number of chambers, communicating freely with one another. The chambered bodies are of various forms. One of the commonest is something like a badly-grown raspberry, being formed of a number of nearly globular chambers of different sizes congregated together. It is called *Globigerina*, and some specimens of chalk consist of little else than *Globigerinae* and granules. Let us fix our attention upon the *Globigerina*. It is the spoor of the game we are tracking. If we can learn what it is and what are the conditions of its existence, we shall see our way to the origin and past history of the chalk.

A suggestion which may naturally enough present itself is, that these curious bodies are the result of some process of aggregation which has taken place in the carbonate of lime; that, just as in winter, the rime on our windows simulates the most delicate and elegantly arborescent foliage—proving that the mere mineral water may, under certain conditions, assume the outward form of organic bodies—so this mineral substance, carbonate of lime, hidden away in the bowels of the earth, has taken the shape of these chambered bodies. I am not raising a merely fanciful and unreal objection. Very learned men, in former days, have even entertained the notion that all the formed things found in rocks are of this nature; and if no such conception is at present held to be admissible, it is because long and varied experience has now shown that mineral matter never does assume the form and structure we find in fossils. If any one were to try to persuade you that an oyster-shell (which is also chiefly composed of carbonate of lime) had crystallized out of sea-water I suppose you would laugh at the absurdity. Your laughter would be justified by the fact that all experience tends to show that oyster-shells are formed by the agency of oysters, and in no other way. And if there were no better reasons, we should be justified, on like grounds, in believing that *Globigerina* is not the product of anything but vital activity.

Happily, however, better evidence in proof of the organic nature of the *Globigerinae* than that of analogy is forthcoming. It so happens that calcareous skeletons, exactly similar to the *Globigerinae* of the chalk, are being formed, at the present moment, by minute living creatures, which flourish in multitudes, literally more numerous than the sands of the sea-shore, over a large extent of that part of the earth's surface which is covered by the ocean.

The history of the discovery of these living *Globigerinae,* and of the part which they play in rock building, is singular enough. It is a discovery which, like others of no less scientific importance, has arisen, incidentally, out of work devoted to very different and exceedingly practical interests. When men first took to the sea, they speedily learned to look out for shoals and rocks; and the more the burthen of their ships increased, the more imperatively necessary it became for sailors to ascertain with precision the depth of the waters they traversed. Out of this necessity grew the use of the lead and sounding line; and, ultimately, marine-surveying, which is the recording of the form of coasts and of the depth of the sea, as ascertained by the sounding lead, upon charts.

At the same time, it became desirable to ascertain and to indicate the nature of the sea-bottom, since this circumstance greatly affects its goodness as holding ground for anchors. Some ingenious tar, whose name deserves a better fate than the oblivion into which it has fallen, attained this object by "arming" the bottom of the lead with a lump of grease, to which more or less of the sand or mud, or broken shells, as the case might be, adhered, and was brought to the surface. But, however well adapted such an apparatus might be for rough nautical purposes, scientific accuracy could not be expected from the armed lead, and to remedy its defects (especially when applied to sounding in great depths) Lieut. Brooke, of the American Navy, some years ago invented a most ingenious machine, by which a considerable portion of the superficial layer of the sea-bottom can be scooped out and brought up from any depth to which the lead descends. In 1853, Lieut. Brooke obtained mud from the bottom of the North Atlantic, between Newfoundland and the Azores, at a depth of more than 10,000 feet, or two miles, by the help of this sounding apparatus. The specimens were sent for examination to Ehrenberg of Berlin, and to Bailey of West Point, and those able microscopists found that this deep-sea mud was almost entirely composed of the skeletons of living organisms—the greater proportion of these being just like the *Globigerinae* already known to occur in the chalk.

Thus far, the work had been carried on simply in the interest of science, but Lieut. Brooke's method of sounding acquired a high commercial value, when the enterprise of laying down the telegraph-cable between this country and the United States was undertaken. For it became a matter of immense importance to know, not only the depth of the sea over the whole line along which the cable was to be laid, but the exact nature of the bottom, so as to guard against chances of cutting or fraying the strands of that costly rope. The Admiralty consequently ordered Captain Dayman, an old friend and shipmate of mine, to ascertain the depth over the whole line of the cable, and to bring back specimens of the bottom. In former days, such a command as this might have sounded very much like one of the impossible things which the young Prince in the Fairy Tales is ordered to do before he can obtain the hand of the Princess. However, in the months of June and July, 1857, my friend performed the task assigned to him with great expedition and precision, without, so far as I know, having met with any reward of that kind. The specimens of Atlantic mud which he procured were sent to me to be examined and reported upon.[1]

The result of all these operations is, that we know the contours and the nature of the surface-soil covered by the North Atlantic for a distance of 1,700 miles from east to west, as well as we know that of any part of the dry land. It is a prodigious plain—one of the widest and most even plains in the world. If the sea were drained off, you might drive a wagon all the way from Valentia, on the west coast of Ireland, to Trinity Bay, in Newfoundland. And, except upon one sharp incline about 200 miles from Valentia, I am not quite sure that it would even be necessary to put the skid on, so gentle are the ascents and descents upon that long route. From Valentia the road would lie down-hill for about 200 miles to the point at which the bottom is now covered by 1,700 fathoms of sea-water. Then would come the central plain, more than a thousand miles wide, the inequalities of the surface of which would be hardly perceptible, though the depth of water upon it now varies from 10,000 to 15,000 feet; and there are places in which Mont Blanc might be sunk without showing its peak above water. Beyond this, the ascent on the American side commences, and gradually leads, for about 300 miles, to the Newfoundland shore.

Almost the whole of the bottom of this central plain (which extends for many hundred miles in a north and south direction) is covered by a fine mud, which, when brought to the surface, dries into a greyish-white friable substance. You can write with this on a blackboard, if you are so inclined; and, to the eye, it is quite like very soft, greyish chalk. Examined chemically, it proves to be composed almost wholly of carbonate of lime; and if you make a section of it, in the same way as that of the piece of chalk was made, and view it with the microscope, it presents innumerable *Globigerinae* imbedded in a granular matrix. I say substantially because there are a good many minor differences; but as these have no bearing on the question immediately before us,—which is the nature of the *Globigerinae* of the chalk,—it is unnecessary to speak of them.

Globigerinae of every size, from the smallest to the largest, are associated together in the Atlantic mud, and the chambers of many are filled by a soft animal matter. This soft substance is, in fact, the

---

[1] See Appendix to Captain Dayman's *Deep-sea Soundings in the North Atlantic Ocean between Ireland and Newfoundland, made in H.M.S. "Cyclops."* Published by order of the Lords Commissioners of the Admiralty, 1858. They have since formed the subject of an elaborate Memoir by Messrs. Parker and Jones, published in the *Philosophical Transactions* for 1865.

remains of the creature to which the *Globigerina* shell, or rather skeleton, owes its existence—and which is an animal of the simplest imaginable description. It is, in fact, a mere particle of living jelly, without defined parts of any kind—without a mouth, nerves, muscles, or distinct organs, and only manifesting its vitality to ordinary observation by thrusting out and retracting from all parts of its surface, long filamentous processes, which serve for arms and legs. Yet this amorphous particle, devoid of everything which, in the higher animals, we call organs, is capable of feeding, growing, and multiplying; of separating from the ocean the small proportion of carbonate of lime which is dissolved in sea-water; and of building up that substance into a skeleton for itself, according to a pattern which can be imitated by no other known agency.

The notion that animals can live and flourish in the sea, at the vast depths from which apparently living *Globigerinae* have been brought up, does not agree very well with our usual conceptions respecting the conditions of animal life; and it is not so absolutely impossible as it might at first sight appear to be, that the *Globigerinae* of the Atlantic sea-bottom do not live and die where they are found.

As I have mentioned, the soundings from the great Atlantic plain are almost entirely made up of *Globigerinae*, with the granules which have been mentioned, and some few other calcareous shells; but a small percentage of the chalky mud—perhaps at most some five percent. of it—is of a different nature, and consists of shells and skeletons composed of silex, or pure flint. These silicious bodies belong partly to the lowly vegetable organisms which are called *Diatomaceae*, and partly to the minute, and extremely simple, animals, termed *Radiolaria*. It is quite certain that these creatures do not live at the bottom of the ocean, but at its surface—where they may be obtained in prodigious numbers by the use of a properly constructed net. Hence it follows that these silicious organisms, though they are not heavier than the lightest dust, must have fallen, in some cases, through fifteen thousand feet of water, before they reached their final resting-place on the ocean floor. And considering how large a surface these bodies expose in proportion to their weight, it is probable that they occupy a great length of time in making their burial journey from the surface of the Atlantic to the bottom.

But if the *Radiolaria* and *Diatoms* are thus rained upon the bottom of the sea, from the superficial layers of its waters in which they pass their lives, it is obviously possible that the *Globigerinae* may be similarly derived; and if they were so, it would be much more easy to understand how they obtain their supply of food than it is at present. Nevertheless, the positive and negative evidence all points the other way. The skeletons of the full-grown, deep-sea, *Globigerinae* are so remarkably solid and heavy in proportion to their surface as to seem little fitted for floating; and, as a matter of fact, they are not to be found along with the *Diatoms* and *Radiolaria* in the uppermost stratum of the open ocean. It has been observed, again, that the abundance of *Globigerinae*, in proportion to other organisms, of like kind, increases with the depth of the sea; and that deep-water *Globigerinae* are larger than those which live in shallower parts of the sea; and such facts negative the supposition that these organisms have been swept by currents from the shallows into the deeps of the Atlantic. It therefore seems to be hardly doubtful that these wonderful creatures live and die at the depths in which they are found.[2]

However the important points for us are, that the living *Globigerinae* are exclusively marine animals, the skeletons of which abound at the bottom of deep seas; and that there is not a shadow of reason for believing that the habits of the *Globigerinae* of the chalk differed from those of the existing species. But if this be true, there is no escaping the conclusion that the chalk itself is the dried mud of an ancient deep sea.

In working over the soundings collected by Captain Dayman, I was surprised to find that many of what I have called the "granules" of that mud were not, as one might have been tempted to think at first, the mere powder and waste of *Globigerinae*, but that they had a definite form and size. I termed these bodies "*coccoliths*," and doubted their organic nature. Dr. Wallich verified my observation, and added the interesting discovery that, not unfrequently, bodies similar to these "coccoliths" were aggregated together into spheroids, which he termed "*coccospheres*." So far as we knew, these bodies, the nature of which is extremely puzzling and problematical, were

---

[2] During the cruise of H.M.S. *Bulldog*, commanded by Sir Leopold M'Clintock, in 1860, living star-fish were brought up, clinging to the lowest part of the sounding-line, from a depth of 1,260 fathoms, midway between Cape Farewell, in Greenland, and the Rockall banks. Dr. Wallich ascertained that the sea-bottom at this point consisted of the ordinary *Globigerina* ooze, and that the stomachs of the star-fishes were full of *Globigerinae*. This discovery removes all objections to the existence of living *Globigerinae* at great depths, which are based upon the supposed difficulty of maintaining animal life under such conditions; and it throws the burden of proof upon those who object to the supposition that the *Globigerinae* live and die where they are found.

peculiar to the Atlantic soundings. But, a few years ago, Mr. Sorby, in making a careful examination of the chalk by means of thin sections and otherwise, observed, as Ehrenberg had done before him, that much of its granular basis possesses a definite form. Comparing these formed particles with those in the Atlantic soundings, he found the two to be identical; and thus proved that the chalk, like the soundings, contains these mysterious coccoliths and coccospheres. Here was a further and most interesting confirmation, from internal evidence, of the essential identity of the chalk with modern deep-sea mud. *Globigerinae*, coccoliths, and coccospheres are found as the chief constituents of both, and testify to the general similarity of the conditions under which both have been formed.[3]

The evidence furnished by the hewing, facing and superposition of the stones of the Pyramids, that these structures were built by men, has no greater weight than the evidence that the chalk was built by *Globigerinae* and the belief that those ancient pyramid-builders were terrestrial and air-breathing creatures like ourselves, is not better based than the conviction that the chalk-makers lived in the sea. But as our belief in the building of the Pyramids by men is not only grounded on the internal evidence afforded by these structures, but gathers strength from multitudinous collateral proofs and is clinched by the total absence of any reason for a contrary belief; so the evidence drawn from the *Globigerinae* that the chalk is an ancient sea-bottom is fortified by innumerable independent lines of evidence; and our belief in the truth of the conclusion to which all positive testimony tends, receives the like negative justification from the fact that no other hypothesis has a shadow of foundation.

It may be worth while briefly to consider a few of these collateral proofs that the chalk was deposited at the bottom of the sea. The great mass of the chalk is composed, as we have seen, of the skeletons of *Globigerinae,* and other simple organisms, imbedded in granular matter. Here and there, however, this hardened mud of the ancient sea reveals the remains of higher animals which have lived and died, and left their hard parts in the mud, just as the oysters die and leave their shells behind them, in the mud of the present seas.

[3] I have recently traced out the development of the "coccoliths," from a diameter of 1/7000th of an inch up to their largest size (which is about 1/1000th), and no longer doubt that they are produced by independent organisms, which, like the *Globigerinae,* live and die at the bottom of the sea.

There are, at the present day, certain groups of animals which are never found in fresh waters, being unable to live anywhere but in the sea. Such are the corals; those corallines which are called *Polyzoa;* those creatures which fabricate the lamp-shells, and are called *Brachiopoda;* and pearly *Nautilus,* and all animals allied to it; and all the forms of sea-urchins and star-fishes. Not only are all these creatures confined to salt water at the present day; but, so far as our records of the past go, the conditions of their existence have been the same; hence, their occurrence in any deposit is as strong evidence as can be obtained, that that deposit was formed in the sea. Now the remains of animals of all kinds which have been enumerated, occur in the chalk, in greater or less abundance; while not one of those forms of shell-fish which are characteristic of fresh water has yet been observed in it.

When we consider that the remains of more than three thousand distinct species of aquatic animals have been discovered among the fossils of the chalk, that the great majority of them are of such forms as are now met with only in the sea, and that there is no rea-son to believe that any one of them inhabited fresh water—the col-lateral evidence that the chalk represents an ancient sea-bottom acquires as great force as the proof derived from the nature of the chalk itself. I think you will now allow that I did not overstate my case when I asserted that we have as strong grounds for believing that all the vast area of dry land, at present occupied by the chalk, was once at the bottom of the sea, as we have for any matter of history whatever; while there is no justification for any other belief.

No less certain it is that the time during which the countries we now call south-east England, France, Germany, Poland, Russia, Egypt, Arabia, Syria, were more or less completely covered by a deep sea, was of considerable duration. We have already seen that the chalk is, in places, more than a thousand feet thick. I think you will agree with me, that it must have taken some time for the skele-tons of animalcules of a hundredth of an inch in diameter to heap up such a mass as that. I have said that throughout the thickness of the chalk the remains of other animals are scattered. These remains are often in the most exquisite state of preservation. The valves of the shell-fishes are commonly adherent; the long spines of some of the sea-urchins, which would be detached by the smallest jar, often remain in their places. In a word, it is certain that these animals have lived and died when the place which they now occupy was the surface of as much of the chalk as had then been deposited; and that each has been covered up by the layer of *Globigerina* mud, upon which the creatures imbedded a little higher up have, in like manner, lived and died. But some of these remains proved the existence of reptiles of vast size in the chalk sea. These lived their time, and had their ancestors and descendants, which assuredly implies time, reptiles being of slow growth.

There is more curious evidence, again, that the process of covering up, or, in other words, the deposit of *Globigerina* skeletons, did not go on very fast. It is demonstrable that an animal of the cretaceous sea might die, that its skeleton might lie uncovered upon the sea-bottom long enough to lose all its outward coverings and appendages by putrefaction; and that, after this had happened, another animal might attach itself to the dead and naked skeleton, might grow to maturity, and might itself die before the calcareous mud had buried the whole.

Cases of this kind are admirably described by Sir Charles Lyell. He speaks of the frequency with which geologists find in the chalk a fossilized sea-urchin, to which is attached the lower valve of a *Crania*. This is a kind of shell-fish, with a shell composed of two pieces, of which, as in the oyster, one is fixed and the other free.

"The upper valve is almost invariably wanting, though occasionally found in a perfect state of preservation in the white chalk at some distance. In this case, we see clearly that the sea-urchin first lived from youth to age, then died and lost its spines, which were carried away. Then the young *Crania* adhered to the bared shell, grew and perished in its turn; after which, the upper valve was separated from the lower, before the Echinus became enveloped in chalky mud." [4]

A specimen in the Museum of Practical Geology, in London, still further prolongs the period which must have elapsed between the death of the sea-urchin, and its burial by the *Globigerinae*. For the outward face of the valve of a *Crania,* which is attached to a sea-urchin (*Micraster*), is itself overrun by an incrusting coralline, which spreads thence over more or less of the surface of the sea-urchin. It follows that, after the upper valve of the *Crania* fell off, the surface of the attached valve must have remained exposed long enough to allow of the growth of the whole coralline, since corallines do not live imbedded in mud.

The progress of knowledge may, one day, enable us to deduce from such facts as these the maximum rate at which the chalk can

[4] *Elements of Geology,* by Sir Charles Lyell, Bart. F.R.S., p. 23.

have accumulated, and thus to arrive at the minimum duration of the chalk period. Suppose that the valve of the *Crania* upon which a coralline has fixed itself in the way just described, is so attached to the sea-urchin that no part of it is more than an inch above the face upon which the sea-urchin rests. Then, as the coralline could not have fixed itself, if the *Crania* had been covered up with chalk mud, and could not have lived had itself been so covered, it follows, that an inch of chalk mud could not have accumulated within the time between the death and decay of the soft parts of the sea-urchin and the growth of the coralline to the full size which it has attained. If the decay of the soft parts of the sea-urchin; the attachment, growth to maturity, and decay of the *Crania;* and the subsequent attachment and growth of the coralline, took a year (which is a low estimate enough), the accumulation of the inch of chalk must have taken more than a year: and the deposit of a thousand feet of chalk must, consequently, have taken more than twelve thousand years.

The foundation of all this calculation is, of course, a knowledge of the length of time the *Crania* and the coralline needed to attain their full size; and, on this head, precise knowledge is at present wanting. But there are circumstances which tend to show that nothing like an inch of chalk has accumulated during the life of a *Crania;* and, on any probable estimate of the length of that life, the chalk period must have had a much longer duration than that thus roughly assigned to it.

Thus, not only it is certain that the chalk is the mud of an ancient sea-bottom; but it is no less certain, that the chalk sea existed during an extremely long period, though we may not be prepared to give a precise estimate of the length of that period in years. The relative duration is clear, though the absolute duration may not be definable. The attempt to affix any precise date to the period at which the chalk sea began, or ended, its existence, is baffled by difficulties of the same kind. But the relative age of the cretaceous epoch may be determined with as great ease and certainty as the long duration of that epoch.

You will have heard of the interesting discoveries recently made, in various parts of Western Europe, of flint implements, obviously worked into shape by human hands, under circumstances which show conclusively that man is a very ancient denizen of these regions. It has been proved that the whole populations of Europe, whose existence has been revealed to us in this way, consisted of savages, such as the Esquimaux are now; that, in the country which is now France, they hunted the reindeer, and were familiar with the ways of the mammoth and the bison. The physical geography of France was in those days different from what it is now—the river Somme, for instance, having cut its bed a hundred feet deeper between that time and this; and, it is probable, that the climate was more like that of Canada or Siberia, than that of Western Europe.

The existence of these people is forgotten even in the traditions of the oldest historical nations. The name and fame of them had utterly vanished until a few years back; and the amount of physical change which has been effected since their day renders it more than probable that, venerable as are some of the historical nations, the workers of the chipped flints of Hoxne or of Amiens are to them, as they are to us, in point of antiquity. But, if we assign to these hoar relics of long-vanished generations of men the greatest age that can possibly be claimed for them, they are not older than the drift, or boulder clay, which, in comparison with the chalk, is but a very juvenile deposit. You need go no further than your own sea-board for evidence of this fact. At one of the most charming spots on the coast of Norfolk, Cromer, you will see the boulder clay forming a vast mass, which lies upon the chalk, and must consequently have come into existence after it. Huge boulders of chalk are, in fact, included in the clay, and have evidently been brought to the position they now occupy by the same agency as that which has planted blocks of syenite from Norway side by side with them.

The chalk, then, is certainly older than the boulder clay. If you ask how much, I will again take you no further than the same spot upon your own coasts for evidence. I have spoken of the boulder clay and drift as resting upon the chalk. That is not strictly true. Interposed between the chalk and the drift is a comparatively insignificant layer, containing vegetable matter. But that layer tells a wonderful history. It is full of stumps of trees standing as they grew. Fir-trees are there with their cones, and hazel-bushes with their nuts; there stand the stools of oak and yew trees, beeches and alders. Hence this stratum is appropriately called the "forest-bed."

It is obvious that the chalk must have been upheaved and converted into dry land, before the timber trees could grow upon it. As the bolls of some of these trees are from two to three feet in diameter, it is no less clear that the dry land thus formed remained in the same condition for long ages. And not only do the remains of stately oaks and well-grown firs testify to the duration of this condition of things, but additional evidence to the same effect is afforded by the abundant remains of elephants, rhinoceroses, hippopotamuses, and other great wild beasts, which it has yielded to the zealous search of such men as the Rev. Mr. Gunn. When you look at such a collection as he has formed, and bethink you that these elephantine bones did veritably carry their owners about, and these great grinders crunch, in the dark woods of which the forest-bed is now the only trace, it is impossible not to feel that they are as good evidence of the lapse of time as the annual rings of the tree stumps.

Thus there is a writing upon the wall of cliffs at Cromer, and whoso runs may read it. It tells us, with an authority which cannot be impeached, that the ancient sea-bed of the chalk sea was raised up, and remained dry land, until it was covered with forest, stocked with the great game the spoils of which have rejoiced your geologists. How long it remained in that condition cannot be said; but, "the whirligig of time brought its revenges" in those days as in these. That dry land, with the bones and teeth of generations of long-lived elephants, hidden away among the gnarled roots and dry leaves of its ancient trees, sank gradually to the bottom of the icy sea, which covered it with huge masses of drift and boulder clay. Sea-beasts, such as the walrus now restricted to the extreme north, paddled about where birds had twittered among the topmost twigs of the fir-trees. How long this state of things endured we know not, but at length it came to an end. The upheaved glacial mud hardened into the soil of modern Norfolk. Forests grew once more, the wolf and the beaver replaced the reindeer and the elephant; and at length what we call the history of England dawned.

Thus you have, within the limits of your own county, proof that the chalk can justly claim a very much greater antiquity than even the oldest physical traces of mankind. But we may go further and demonstrate, by evidence of the same authority as that which testifies to the existence of the father of men, that the chalk is vastly older than Adam himself. The Book of Genesis informs us that Adam, immediately upon his creation, and before the appearance of Eve, was placed in the Garden of Eden. The problem of the geographical position of Eden has greatly vexed the spirits of the learned in such matters, but there is one point respecting which, so far as I know, no commentator has ever raised a doubt. This is, that of the four rivers which are said to run out of it, Euphrates and Hiddekel are identical with the rivers now known by the names of Euphrates and Tigris. But the whole country in which these mighty rivers take their origin, and through which they run, is composed of rocks which are either of the same age as the chalk, or of later date. So that the chalk must not only have been formed, but, after its formation, the time required for the deposit of these later rocks, and for their upheaval into dry land, must have elapsed, before the smallest brook which feeds the swift stream of "the great river, the river of Babylon" began to flow.

Thus, evidence which cannot be rebutted, and which need not be strengthened, though if time permitted I might indefinitely increase its quantity, compels you to believe that the earth, from the time of the chalk to the present day, has been the theatre of a series of changes as vast in their amount, as they were slow in their progress. The area on which we stand has been first sea and then land, for at least four alternations; and has remained in each of these conditions for a period of great length.

Nor have these wonderful metamorphoses of sea into land, and of land into sea, been confined to one corner of England. During the chalk period, or "cretaceous epoch," not one of the present great physical features of the globe was in existence. Our great mountain ranges, Pyrenees, Alps, Himalayas, Andes, have all been upheaved since the chalk was deposited, and the cretaceous sea flowed over the sites of Sinai and Ararat. All this is certain, because rocks of cretaceous, or still later, date have shared in the elevatory movements which gave rise to these mountain chains; and may be found perched up, in some cases, many thousand feet high upon their flanks. And evidence of equal cogency demonstrates that, though, in Norfolk, the forest-bed rests directly upon the chalk, yet it does so, not because the period at which the forest grew immediately followed that at which the chalk was formed, but because an immense lapse of time, represented elsewhere by thousands of feet of rock, is not indicated at Cromer.

I must ask you to believe that there is no less conclusive proof that a still more prolonged succession of similar changes occurred, before the chalk was deposited. Nor have we any reason to think that the first term in the series of these changes is known. The oldest sea-beds preserved to us are sands, and mud, and pebbles, the wear and tear of rocks which were formed in still older oceans.

But, great as is the magnitude of these physical changes of the world, they have been accompanied by a no less striking series of modifications in its living inhabitants. All the great classes of animals, beasts of the field, fowls of the air, creeping things, and things which dwell in the waters, flourished upon the globe long ages before the chalk was deposited. Very few, however, if any, of these ancient forms of animal life were identical with those which now live. Certainly not one of the higher animals was of the same species as any of those now in existence. The beasts of the field, in the days before the chalk, were not our beasts of the field, nor the fowls of the air such as those which the eye of man has seen flying, unless his antiquity dates infinitely further back than we at present surmise. If we could be carried back into those times, we should be as one suddenly set down in Australia before it was colonized. We should see mammals, birds, reptiles, fishes, insects, snails, and the like, clearly recognizable as such, and yet not one of them would be just the same as those with which we are familiar, and many would be extremely different.

From that time to the present, the population of the world has undergone slow and gradual, but incessant, changes. There has been no grand catastrophe—no destroyer has swept away the forms of life of one period, and replaced them by a totally new creation: but one species has vanished and another has taken its place; creatures of one type of structure have diminished, those of another have increased, as time has passed on. And thus, while the differences between the living creatures of the time before the chalk and those of the present day appear startling, if placed side by side, we are led from one to the other by the most gradual progress, if we follow the course of Nature through the whole series of those relics of her operations which she has left behind. It is by the population of the chalk sea that the ancient and the modern inhabitants of the world are most completely connected. The groups which are dying out flourish, side by side, with the groups which are now the dominant forms of life. Thus the chalk contains remains of those strange flying and swimming reptiles, the pterodactyl, the icthyosaurus and the plesiosaurus, which are found in no later deposits, but abounded in preceding ages. The chambered shells called ammonites and belemnites, which are so characteristic of the period preceding the cretaceous, in like manner die with it.

But, amongst these fading remainders of a previous state of things, are some very modern forms of life, looking like Yankee pedlars among a tribe of Red Indians. Crocodiles of modern type appear; bony fishes, many of them very similar to existing species, almost supplant the forms of fish which predominate in more ancient seas; and many kinds of living shell-fish first become known to us in chalk. The vegetation acquires a modern aspect. A few living animals are not even distinguishable as species, from those which existed at that remote epoch. The *Globigerina* of the present day, for example, is not different specifically from that of the chalk; and the same may be said of many other *Foraminifera*. I think it probable that critical and unprejudiced examination will show that more than one species of much higher animals have had a similar longevity; but the only example which I can at present give confidently is the snake's-head lamp-shell (*Terebratulina caput serpentis*), which lives in our English seas and abounded (as *Terebratulina striata* of authors) in the chalk.

The longest line of human ancestry must hide its diminished head before the pedigree of this insignificant shell-fish. We Englishmen are proud to have an ancestor who was present at the Battle of Hastings. The ancestors of *Terebratulina caput serpentis* may have been present at a battle of *Ichthyosauria* in that part of the sea which, when the chalk was forming, flowed over the site of Hastings. When all around has changed, this *Terebratulina* has peacefully propagated its species from generation to generation, and stands to this day, as a living testimony to the continuity of the present with the past history of the globe.

Up to this moment I have stated, so far as I know, nothing but well-authenticated facts, and the immediate conclusions which they force upon the mind. But the mind is so constituted that it does not willingly rest in facts and immediate causes, but seeks always after a knowledge of the remoter links in the chain of causation.

Taking the many changes of any given spot of the earth's surface, from sea to land and from land to sea, as an established fact, we cannot refrain from asking ourselves how these changes have occurred. And when we have explained them—as they must be explained—by the alternate slow movements of elevation and depression which have affected the crust of the earth, we go still further back, and ask, Why these movements?

I am not certain that any one can give you a satisfactory answer to that question. Assuredly I cannot. All that can be said, for certain, is, that such movements are part of the ordinary course of nature, inasmuch as they are going on at the present time. Direct proof may be given, that some parts of the land of the northern hemisphere are at this moment insensibly rising and others insensibly sinking; and there is indirect, but perfectly satisfactory, proof, that an enormous area now covered by the Pacific has been deepened thousands of feet, since the present inhabitants of that sea came into existence. Thus there is not a shadow of a reason for believing that the physical changes of the globe, in past times, have been affected by other than natural causes. Is there any more reason for believing that the concomitant modifications in the forms of the living inhabitants of the globe have been brought about in other ways?

Before attempting to answer this question, let us try to form a distinct mental picture of what has happened in some special case. The crocodiles are animals which, as a group, have a very vast antiquity. They abounded ages before the chalk was deposited; they throng the rivers in warm climates, at the present day. There is a difference in the form of the joints of the back-bone, and in some minor particulars, between the crocodiles of the present epoch and those which lived before the chalk; but, in the cretaceous epoch, as I have already mentioned, the crocodiles had assumed the modern type of structure. Notwithstanding this, the crocodiles of the chalk are not identically the same as those which lived in the times called "older tertiary," which succeeded the cretaceous epoch; and the crocodiles of the older tertiaries are not identical with those of the newer tertiaries, nor are these identical with existing forms. I leave open the question whether particular species may have lived on from epoch to epoch. But each epoch has had its peculiar crocodiles; though all, since the chalk, have belonged to the modern type, and differ simply in their proportions, and in such structural particulars as are discernible only to trained eyes.

How is the existence of this long succession of different species of crocodiles to be accounted for? Only two suppositions seem to be open to us—Either each species of crocodile has been specially created, or it has arisen out of some pre-existing form by the operation of natural causes. Choose your hypothesis; I have chosen mine. I can find no warranty for believing in the distinct creation of a score of successive species of crocodiles in the course of countless ages of time. Science gives no countenance to such a wild fancy; nor can even the perverse ingenuity of a commentator pretend to discover this sense, in the simple words in which the writer of Genesis records the proceeding of the fifth and sixth days of the Creation.

On the other hand, I see no good reason for doubting the necessary alternative, that all these varied species have been evolved from pre-existing crocodilian forms, by the operation of causes as completely a part of the common order of nature as those which have affected the changes of the inorganic world. Few will venture to affirm that the reasoning which applies to crocodiles loses its force among other animals, or among plants. If one series of species has come into existence by the operation of natural causes, it seems folly to deny that all may have arisen in the same way.

A small beginning has led us to a great ending. If I were to put the bit of chalk with which we started into the hot but obscure flame of burning hydrogen, it would presently shine like the sun. It seems to me that this physical metamorphosis is no false image of what has been the result of our subjecting it to a jet of fervent, though nowise brilliant, thought to-night. It has become luminous, and its clear rays, penetrating the abyss of the remote past, have brought within our ken some stages of the evolution of the earth. And in the shifting "without haste, but without rest" of the land and sea, as in the endless variation of the forms assumed by living beings, we have observed nothing but the natural product of the forces originally possessed by the substance of the universe.

QUESTIONS ON CONTENT

1. What are the evidences from this essay of a scientific mind at work? Of a literary mind?
2. Agassiz observed that "Facts are stupid things until brought into contact with some general law." (See p. 17.) How does Huxley connect his facts with a general law?
3. Is the reasoning of this essay carried on inductively or deductively? Explain.
4. Does Huxley admit any negative evidence? Does he show an open mind which can be swayed by observed facts only? Show that this is or is not so.
5. What is meant by "collateral proofs"?
6. What point does Huxley make of the *"Terebratulina caput serpentis"*? Is he amused by the sound of this large term?
7. Explain the purpose and comment on the effect of the last paragraph.
8. Find the points in this lecture which show the author's support of the idea of evolution.
9. At what point is reference made to the comparative value of a scientific and a humane education? Do you think Huxley's contention is valid? Discuss.

❧ *Learn While You Sleep*

J. D. RATCLIFF

In his book, *Brave New World*, Aldous Huxley pictured the world 600 years from now. In his grimly efficient civilization, children learned lessons while they slept—by means of "hypnopaedia" or sleep teaching.

Present evidence indicates, however, that we won't have to wait six centuries for sleep teaching. A machine to do the job is already available. In a series of remarkable experiments at the University of North Carolina, it has been shown that a person's brain can absorb knowledge while he is sleeping. Over and over again, a phonograph repeated a meaningless list of words to a group of soundly sleeping students. On awakening, they were able to memorize the list almost 20 per cent faster than another group of comparable intelligence.

The experiments, and their results, create an exciting prospect. Up to now, human beings have had to spend a third of their lives blacked out in sleep. The way may now be open to use profitably at least part of this time in constructive study.

For a long time, psychologists have guessed that at least part of the brain stays awake while the rest of the body sleeps. We roll to the edge of the bed, but rarely roll out. Some portion of the brain warns of danger. When bedcovers slip on cold nights, we pull them up without awakening. Mothers sleep peacefully through the scream of train whistles and the blare of auto horns—but are instantly alert when a child emits the faintest whimper. Apparently, some "warning area" of the brain stays awake, alert to danger—and possibly alert to new ideas.

There have been a number of attempts to implant thoughts in this wakeful area of the brain. Until fairly recently, workers in this field faced a series of handicaps. First, there was no way to determine positively when a subject was actually in deep sleep. The electrical brain-wave machine, the electroencephalograph readings, when diagrammed, showed that the brain gives off three basic wave

Reprinted from *Look* (March 14, 1950), pp. 46–53, by permission of Cowles Magazine, Inc.

patterns. In thought, the waves are short, sharp, slightly irregular and with a notably high per-second frequency. In relaxation (or the waking condition midway between thought and sleep), they are tall, relatively uniform in size and shape, clean and evenly spaced. In sleep, the electrical pattern is rambling, rounded off and almost lazy-looking.

Although the electroencephalograph solved the problem of how to recognize a sleeping brain, it could do nothing about teaching it something it didn't already know. Automatic and highly unusual phonographs were needed to drum thoughts into these brains. The phonographs would have to operate very quietly in order not to awaken the student. Necessarily, they would be equipped with a clocking device that could set the instrument in operation often and at any time during the night. Until a short time ago, such machines were not available.

This particular difficulty was corrected by Max Sherover, a remarkable mite of a man who is president of Linguaphone Institute of New York. This concern makes records for teaching 29 languages, including several African tribal languages such as Efik and Hausa. Sherover, who is barely over five feet tall and weighs 130 lbs., was born in Cracow, Austria (now Poland). He came to the United States in 1903, when he was 14 years old, and started climbing the American ladder three rungs at a time. In the next 25 years, he made several fortunes: as publisher of a world-trade magazine in Japan; as an importer of bricks from Belgium; as a world textile trader; as a promoter of inventions. His good fortune took a nose dive in 1928 when he financed a $3,000,000 apartment-hotel in Brooklyn and was caught by sky-rocketing construction costs. In a spirit of hope rather than desperation, he took a boat to France to look for a new export-import business. While there, he came upon the British-owned Linguaphone technique for teaching languages with phonograph records. The idea appealed to him and he acquired the American rights.

The imaginative Sherover saw possibilities in Linguaphone never grasped by its British sponsors. If you could play records to people and teach them while they were awake, said Sherover, why couldn't you teach them when they were asleep? If you could funnel knowledge into a sleeping mind, you could cut years from the educational process. Businessmen, engineers and doctors could familiarize themselves with difficult problems during the waste hours of midnight to 8 A.M. Lawyers could get a head start on complicated briefs. Overnight, men could absorb the scores of symphonies and in a few days learn calculus.

Sherover's interest was both strong and genuine and he turned first to small-scale experimenting. When his son Charles had to learn poems in grade school, Sherover would read them at his bedside while the boy slept. The process *seemed* to work. But it was monotonous business sitting up half the night reading to a sleeping boy. Sherover set about building a phonograph to do the job. His first model was a crude luggage-type machine with a clock attachment. It could be pre-set to play at any time during the night. Although it was workable, it was not entirely satisfactory. Sherover went on improving it. By the mid 40's he had perfected a clock-controlled phonograph which would play any record, or any selection of records, at any time during the night. It could be set to play at, say, 2 A.M. and at 4 A.M. for any desired lengths of time. At this point, all that was needed was a test of the validity of the basic sleep-teaching-by-phonograph idea.

The opportunity for such a test was presented by Charles P. Elliott, at the time working for his doctor's degree at the University of North Carolina. Under rigidly controlled conditions, Elliott set out to learn whether the brain of a sleeping person could absorb information.

He drew the outlines of his experiment. Two groups of subjects would be used with 20 students in each group. They would be pretested to determine their learning ability and to make certain that the intelligence of the two groups matched.

After this preliminary work was completed, experiments got under way. The work took two years to complete. Volunteer students were told that tests were being made with the brain-wave machine. Sleep teaching was never mentioned. The students agreed to sleep in a laboratory cubicle, alongside another laboratory where all the machinery was installed. Tested one at a time, students had electrodes from the machine fastened to their skulls with collodion.

This procedure was used on 20 students: When the brain-wave machine said they were soundly asleep, the phonograph was turned on sending sound through a concealed pillow microphone. Over and over again, for a total of 30 times, a record repeated a list of fifteen three-letter words: boy, egg, say, art, run, not, sir, leg . . . If the brain-wave machine showed that the students were about to awaken, the phonograph was silenced. Another 20 students went through exactly the same process, but with one difference: the phonograph did not play the list of words to them during the night.

The critical part of the experiment came when students awakened in the morning. All were asked to memorize the list of words. If those who heard it during the night learned it significantly faster, there would be but one conclusion. The sleeping brain could absorb knowledge.

Careful stop-watch checks showed that those who had heard the record during the night were able to memorize the list almost 20 per cent faster than those who had not. Further, they made far fewer errors in the course of learning. It was as if they were recalling something temporarily forgotten.

The North Carolina work does not promise that tomorrow's university will be an innerspring mattress. But it does indicate that exposure to new knowledge can, in a single night's time, measurably hasten the learning process. What of repeated exposure night after night? As yet, there is no sure answer to that. But another piece of work suggests what the answer may be.

Dr. Lawrence Leshan of the College of William and Mary wished to see what could be accomplished by suggestion during sleep. For his experiment, he selected 20 boys in an upstate New York summer camp. All were fingernail biters. He wanted to see if by suggestion made during sleep he could break them of the habit.

Over and over again, while the boys slept, a record repeated one sentence: "My fingernails taste terribly bitter. My fingernails taste terribly bitter. My fingernails . . ." The sentence was repeated 600 times each night.

The experiment got underway on July 5. For weeks it looked like it was leading nowhere, no matter how much the phonograph droned its monotonous message. Then, on Aug. 7, one boy stopped biting his nails. On August 20, two more gave up the unpleasant habit. On August 29, five more stopped. By the time camp closed for the summer, eight out of 20 had given up a firmly rooted habit. Dr. Leshan, a true scientist, naturally suspected that the camp environment, and not the recordings, brought on the improvements. Checks with other nail-biting campers proved this untrue—they were chewing their nails as busily as ever.

Some of the most challenging data turned up by Sherover's machine (it sells for a below-cost price of $85) has come from individual researchers. For example, one well-known psychiatrist used it in treating a problem child. Conflicts in school had grown to a point

where this youngster could no longer attend classes. Further education seemed out of the question. The world had another unruly,
rebellious misfit. Then treatment got underway. The psychiatrist
drew up points he wished to implant in the boy's mind and recorded
them at a radio station.

Monotonously, over and over again, the record played while the
boy slept: "You will always like to study hard and work hard because
you know that all things worthwhile are gotten by hard study and
hard work. You always study hard, then it will be fun to take
examinations, because you will know that you can pass examinations
easily. You will be proving to yourself and others that you have
studied and worked hard . . . that you have a better mind than
most people. All the great men and women in the world became
great by hard, honest study and work. You, too, want to be great.
. . . Playing, going to shows, going on trips will always be great
fun because you will know you have earned your fun. . . ."

Under the influence of this suggestion, repeated night after night,
the boy began to straighten out. Unconsciously, he accepted the
ideas expressed and began to adopt them as his own. Sherover's idea
was entering the effectual stage. . . .

How sleep teaching works, no one knows. For that matter, no
one knows what sleep itself is. One old theory states that sleep
comes when toxic products accumulate in the blood. But no one
has been able to find these toxic products. Further, one member of
a pair of Siamese twins will often doze while the other is wide awake
—despite the fact that they share a common blood supply. Another
theory states that we sleep when the volume of blood flowing to
the brain decreases. But there is no good explanation as to what
makes the blood supply diminish in the first place.

We don't know *why* the brain goes to sleep. But the work cited
here demonstrates pretty conclusively that some portion of the brain
is awake and on the job all the time.

So far, research men have made no more than a halting start
toward understanding sleep teaching. This is surprising in the light
of the idea's tremendous allure.

Education in large part consists of learning isolated facts: names,
dates, equations, the verse of renowned poets. . . . If sleep teaching
can hasten such learning no more than 20 per cent, it will still cut
years from the educational process. It could open cultural pursuits
to older people, now denied them by lack of time. It is even possible

to imagine educational radio programs which would run the night through, assisting people to learn languages, music, mathematics.

QUESTIONS ON CONTENT

1. How do psychologists "guess" that part of the brain remains awake?
2. Of what elements is the word *electroencephalograph* formed? What is the purpose of this device?
3. Explain the phrase: "climbing the American ladder three rungs at a time."
4. "If you could funnel knowledge into a sleeping mind, you could cut years from the educational process." Comment.
5. Does the Elliott experiment at the University of North Carolina illustrate Huxley's definition of the scientific? (See "The Scientific Method.")
6. How do the purposes of the Elliott test and the Leshan test differ? Is it a fundamental difference? Compare also the test on the "problem child."
7. "Education in large part consists of learning isolated facts." Comment.

❧ *A Stable Society*

ALDOUS HUXLEY

["A Stable Society" is taken from Aldous Huxley's novel, *Brave New World*. The "brave new world" is a society in which science has, with a few negligible exceptions, triumphed over all man's problems. It has particularly answered his craving for stability. It controls exactly and literally all man's actions from before birth to death. How this method of control originated and was brought to perfection is partly explained in this chapter.

There are five, strictly regulated classes of society ranging from the highly intelligent Alphas to the less intelligent Betas, to the middle-class Gammas, to the subnormal Deltas, and ending with the moronic Epsilons. Each class is produced in numbers sufficient to care for the work to be done by that class. The state controls the

From *Brave New World* by Aldous Huxley. Copyright, 1932, by Aldous Huxley. Reprinted by permission of Harper and Brothers.

hatcheries in which the embryo babies are grown in bottles. Intelligence within a group is standardized by a process involving varying degrees of brain-stunting in the embryos. After removal from the bottle, the infant is ready for conditioning, a process described in this chapter. Conditioning is largely devoted to making the infant, then the child, and finally the adult satisfied with his status in life. Hypnopaedia, or sleep teaching, is an important instrument in the conditioning program.

Henry Ford is the god in this new society, a position which he earned through his discovery of the assembly-line technique. This technique carried out to perfection has in the brave new world stabilized society. Since Ford is the god, "Oh, Ford" is a form of profanity.]

Mr. Foster was left in the Decanting Room. The D. H. C. [Director of Hatcheries and Conditioning] and his students stepped into the nearest lift and were carried up to the fifth floor.

INFANT NURSERIES. NEO-PAVLOVIAN CONDITIONING ROOMS, announced the notice board.

The Director opened a door. They were in a large bare room, very bright and sunny; for the whole of the southern wall was a single window. Half a dozen nurses, trousered and jacketed in the regulation viscose-linen uniform, their hair aseptically hidden under white caps, were engaged in setting out bowls of roses in a long row across the floor. Big bowls, packed tight with blossom. Thousands of petals, ripe-blown and silkily smooth, like the cheeks of innumerable little cherubs, but of cherubs, in that bright light, not exclusively pink and Aryan, but also luminously Chinese, also Mexican, also apoplectic with too much blowing of celestial trumpets, also pale as death, pale with the posthumous whiteness of marble.

The nurses stiffened to attention as the D. H. C. came in.

"Set out the books," he said curtly.

In silence the nurses obeyed his command. Between the rose bowls the books were duly set out—a row of nursery quartos opened invitingly each at some gaily coloured image of beast or fish or bird.

"Now bring in the children."

They hurried out of the room and returned in a minute or two, each pushing a kind of tall dumbwaiter laden, on all its four wire-netted shelves, with eight-month-old babies, all exactly alike (a Bokanovsky Group, it was evident) and all (since their caste was Delta) dressed in khaki.

"Put them down on the floor."

The infants were unloaded.

"Now turn them so that they can see the flowers and books."

Turned, the babies at once fell silent, then began to crawl towards those clusters of sleek colors, those shapes so gay and brilliant on the white pages. As they approached, the sun came out of a momentary eclipse behind a cloud. The roses flamed up as though with a sudden passion from within; a new and profound significance seemed to suffuse the shining pages of the books. From the ranks of the crawling babies came little squeals of excitement, gurgles and twitterings of pleasure.

The Director rubbed his hands. "Excellent!" he said. "It might almost have been done on purpose."

The swiftest crawlers were already at their goal. Small hands reached out uncertainly, touched, grasped, unpetaling the transfigured roses, crumpling the illuminated pages of the books. The Director waited until all were happily busy. Then, "Watch carefully," he said. And, lifting his hand, he gave the signal.

The Head Nurse, who was standing by a switchboard at the other end of the room, pressed down a little lever.

There was a violent explosion. Shriller and ever shriller, a siren shrieked. Alarm bells maddeningly sounded.

The children started, screamed; their faces were distorted with terror.

"And now," the Director shouted (for the noise was deafening), "now we proceed to rub in the lesson with a mild electric shock."

He waved his hand again, and the Head Nurse pressed a second lever. The screaming of the babies suddenly changed its tone. There was something desperate, almost insane, about the sharp spasmodic yelps to which they now gave utterance. Their little bodies twitched and stiffened; their limbs moved jerkily as if to the tug of unseen wires.

"We can electrify that whole strip of floor," bawled the Director in explanation. "But that's enough," he signalled to the nurse.

The explosions ceased, the bells stopped ringing, the shriek of the siren died down from tone to tone into silence. The stiffly twitching bodies relaxed, and what had become the sob and yelp of infant maniacs broadened out once more into a normal howl of ordinary terror.

"Offer them the flowers and books again."

The nurses obeyed; but at the approach of the roses, at the mere sight of those gaily-coloured images of pussy and cock-a-doodle-doo and baa-baa black sheep, the infants shrank away in horror; the volume of their howling suddenly increased.

"Observe," said the Director triumphantly, "observe."

Books and loud noises, flowers and electric shocks—already in the infant mind these couples were compromisingly linked; and after two hundred repetitions of the same or a similar lesson would be wedded indissolubly. What man has joined, nature is powerless to put asunder.

"They'll grow up with what the psychologists used to call an 'instinctive' hatred of books and flowers. Reflexes unalterably conditioned. They'll be safe from books and botany all their lives." The Director turned to his nurses. "Take them away again."

Still yelling, the khaki babies were loaded on to their dumb-waiters and wheeled out, leaving behind them the smell of sour milk and a most welcome silence.

One of the students held up his hand; and though he could see quite well why you couldn't have lowercaste people wasting the Community's time over books, and that there was always the risk of their reading something which might undesirably decondition one of their reflexes, yet . . . well, he couldn't understand about the flowers. Why go to the trouble of making it psychologically impossible for Deltas to like flowers?

Patiently the D. H. C. explained. If the children were made to scream at the sight of a rose, that was on grounds of high economic policy. Not so very long ago (a century or thereabouts), Gammas, Deltas, even Epsilons, had been conditioned to like flowers—flowers in particular and wild nature in general. The idea was to make them want to be going out into the country at every available opportunity, and so compel them to consume transport.

"And didn't they consume transport?" asked the student.

"Quite a lot," the D. H. C. replied. "But nothing else."

Primroses and landscapes, he pointed out, have one grave defect: they are gratuitous. A love of nature keeps no factories busy. It was decided to abolish the love of nature, at any rate among the lower classes; to abolish the love of nature, but *not* the tendency to consume transport. For of course it was essential that they should keep on going to the country, even though they hated it. The problem was to find an economically sounder reason for consuming transport than a mere affection for primroses and landscapes. It was duly found.

"We condition the masses to hate the country," concluded the

Director. "But simultaneously we condition them to love all country sports. At the same time, we see to it that all country sports shall entail the use of elaborate apparatus. So that they consume manufactured articles as well as transport. Hence those electric shocks."

"I see," said the student, and was silent, lost in admiration.

There was a silence; then, clearing his throat, "Once upon a time," the Director began, "while our Ford was still on earth, there was a little boy called Reuben Rabinovitch. Reuben was the child of Polish-speaking parents." The Director interrupted himself. "You know what Polish is, I suppose?"

"A dead language."

"Like French and German," added another student, officiously showing off his learning.

"And 'parent'?" questioned the D. H. C.

There was an uneasy silence. Several of the boys blushed. They had not yet learned to draw the significant but often very fine distinction between smut and pure science. One, at last, had the courage to raise a hand.

"Human beings used to be . . ." he hesitated; the blood rushed to his cheeks. "Well, they used to be viviparous."

"Quite right." The Director nodded approvingly.

"And when the babies were decanted . . ."

"'Born,'" came the correction.

"Well, then they were the parents—I mean, not the babies, of course; the other ones." The poor boy was overwhelmed with confusion.

"In brief," the Director summed up, "the parents were the father and mother." The smut that was really science fell with a crash into the boys' eye-avoiding silence. "Mother," he repeated loudly rubbing in the science; and leaning back in his chair, "These," he said gravely, "are unpleasant facts; I know it. But then most historical facts *are* unpleasant."

He returned to Little Reuben—to Little Reuben, in whose room, one evening, by an oversight, his father and mother (crash, crash!) happened to leave the radio turned on.

("For you must remember that in those days of gross viviparous reproduction, children were always brought up by their parents and not in State Conditioning Centres.")

While the child was asleep, a broadcast program from London suddenly started to come through; and the next morning, to the astonishment of his crash and crash (the more daring of the boys ventured to grin at one another), Little Reuben woke up repeating word for word a long lecture by that curious old writer ("one of the very few whose works have been permitted to come down to us"), George Bernard Shaw, who was speaking, according to a well-authenticated tradition, about his own genius. To little Reuben's wink and snigger, this lecture was, of course, perfectly incomprehensible and, imagining that their child had suddenly gone mad, they sent for a doctor. He, fortunately, understood English, recognized the discourse as that which Shaw had broadcasted the previous evening, realized the significance of what had happened, and sent a letter to the medical press about it.

"The principle of sleep-teaching, or hypnopaedia, had been discovered." The D. H. C. made an impressive pause.

The principle had been discovered; but many, many years were to elapse before that principle was usefully applied.

"The case of Little Reuben occurred only twenty-three years after Our Ford's first T-Model was put on the market." (Here the Director made a sign of the T on his stomach and all the students reverently followed suit.) "And yet . . ."

Furiously the students scribbled "*Hypnopaedia, first used officially in A. F. 214. Why not before? Two reasons. (a)* . . ."

"These early experimenters," the D. H. C. was saying, "were on the wrong track. They thought that hypnopaedia could be made an instrument of intellectual education . . ."

(A small boy asleep on his right side, the right arm stuck out, the right hand hanging limp over the edge of the bed. Through a round grating in the side of a box a voice speaks softly.

"The Nile is the longest river in Africa and the second in length of all the rivers of the globe. Although falling short of the length of the Mississippi-Missouri, the Nile is at the head of all rivers as regards the length of its basin, which extends through 35 degrees of latitude . . ."

At breakfast the next morning, "Tommy," some one says, "do you know which is the longest river in Africa?" A shaking of the head. "But don't you remember something that begins: The Nile is the . . ."

"The Nile-is-the-longest-river-in-Africa-and-the-second-in-length-of-all-the-rivers-of-the-globe . . ." The words came rushing out. "Although-falling-short-of . . ."

"Well now, which is the longest river in Africa?"

The eyes are blank. "I don't know."

"But the Nile, Tommy."

"The-Nile-is-the-longest-river-in-Africa-and-second . . ."

"Then which river is the longest, Tommy?"

Tommy bursts into tears. "I don't know," he howls.)

That howl, the Director made it plain, discouraged the earliest investigators. The experiments were abandoned. No further attempt was made to teach children the length of the Nile in their sleep. Quite rightly. You can't learn a science unless you know what it's all about.

"Whereas, if they'd only started on *moral* education," said the Director, leading the way towards the door. The students followed him, desperately scribbling as they walked and all the way up in the lift. "Moral education, which ought never, in any circumstances, to be rational."

"Silence, silence," whispered a loud speaker as they stepped out at the fourteenth floor, and "Silence, silence," the trumpet mouths indefatigably repeated at intervals down every corridor. The students and even the Director himself rose automatically to the tips of their toes. They were Alphas, of course; but even Alphas have been well conditioned. "Silence, silence." All the air of the fourteenth floor was sibilant with the categorical imperative.

Fifty yards of tiptoeing brought them to a door which the Director cautiously opened. They stepped over the threshold into the twilight of a shuttered dormitory. Eighty cots stood in a row against the wall. There was a sound of light regular breathing and a continuous murmur, as of very faint voices remotely whispering.

A nurse rose as they entered and came to attention before the Director.

"What's the lesson this afternoon?" he asked.

"We had Elementary Sex for the first forty minutes," she answered. "But now it's switched over to Elementary Class Consciousness."

The Director walked slowly down the long line of cots. Rosy and relaxed with sleep, eighty little boys and girls lay softly breathing. There was a whisper under every pillow. The D. H. C. halted and, bending over one of the little beds, listened attentively.

"Elementary Class Consciousness, did you say? Let's have it repeated a little louder by the trumpet."

At the end of the room a loud speaker projected from the wall. The Director walked up to it and pressed a switch.

". . . all wear green," said a soft but very distinct voice, beginning in the middle of a sentence, "and Delta Children wear khaki. Oh no, I don't want to play with Delta children. And Epsilons are still worse. They're too stupid to be able to read or write. Besides they wear black, which is such a beastly color. I'm *so* glad I'm a Beta."

There was a pause; then the voice began again.

"Alpha children wear grey. They work much harder than we do, because they're so frightfully clever. I'm really awfully glad I'm a Beta, because I don't work so hard. And then we are much better than the Gammas and the Deltas. Gammas are stupid. They all wear green, and Delta children wear khaki. Oh no, I *don't* want to play with Delta children. And Epsilons are still worse. They're too stupid to be able . . ."

The Director pushed back the switch. The voice was silent. Only its thin ghost continued to mutter from beneath the eighty pillows.

"They'll have that repeated forty or fifty times more before they wake; then again on Thursday, and again on Saturday. A hundred and twenty times three times a week for thirty months. After which they go on to a more advanced lesson."

Roses and electric shocks, the khaki of Deltas and a whiff of asafœtida—wedded indissolubly before the child can speak. But wordless conditioning is crude and wholesale; cannot bring home the finer distinctions, cannot inculcate the more complex courses of behavior. For that there must be words, but words without reason. In brief, hypnopaedia.

"The greatest moralizing and socializing force of all time."

The students took it down in their little books. Straight from the horse's mouth.

Once more the Director touched the switch.

". . . so frightfully clever," the soft, insinuating, indefatigable voice was saying. "I'm really awfully glad I'm a Beta, because . . ."

Not so much like drops of water, though water, it is true, can wear holes in the hardest granite; rather, drops of liquid sealing-wax, drops that adhere, incrust, incorporate themselves with what they fall on, till finally the rock is all one scarlet blob.

"Till at last the child's mind *is* these suggestions, and the sum of the suggestions *is* the child's mind. And not the child's mind only. The adult's mind too—all his life long. The mind that judges and desires and decides—made up of these suggestions. But all these suggestions are *our* suggestions!" The Director almost shouted in his triumph. "Suggestions from the State." He banged the nearest table. "It therefore follows . . ."

A noise made him turn round.

"Oh, Ford!" he said in another tone, "I've gone and woken the children."

QUESTIONS ON CONTENT

1. What does the D. H. C. mean when he says, "It might almost have been done on purpose."

2. Explain: "What man has joined, nature is powerless to put asunder." Compare "Learn While You Sleep."

3. Why were Deltas conditioned to dislike flowers and books?

4. Explain the phrase "consume transport."

5. Why does Huxley put the words "(crash, crash!)" after "mother?"

6. Compare the story of Reuben Rabinovich and the accounts of sleep-teaching experiments in "Learn While You Sleep."

7. What is the significance of making a sign of the "T" on the stomach?

8. Is there any logical fallacy in Huxley's representing the D. H. C. as a lecturer and students furiously scribbling notes?

9. What is described as "the greatest moralizing and socializing force of all time"?

10. Does this selection make you feel that the *instability* of society may be a blessing?

❧ *An Outline of Scientists*

JAMES THURBER

Having been laid up by a bumblebee for a couple of weeks, I ran through the few old novels there were in the cottage I had rented in Bermuda and finally was reduced to reading "The Outline of Science, a Plain Story Simply Told," in four volumes. These books were published by Putnam's fifteen years ago and were edited by J. Arthur Thomson, Regius Professor of Natural History at the University of Aberdeen. The volumes contained hundreds of articles written by various scientists and over eight hundred illustrations,

From *Let Your Mind Alone*, by James Thurber (Harper & Brothers, 1937). Reprinted by permission. Copyright 1936, James Thurber. Originally published in *The New Yorker*.

forty of which, the editor bragged on the flyleaf, were in color. A plain story simply told with a lot of illustrations, many of them in color, seemed just about the right mental fare for a man who had been laid up with a bee. Human nature being what it is, I suppose the morbid reader is more interested in how I happened to be laid up by a bee than in what I found in my scientific research, so I will dismiss that unfortunate matter in a few words. The bee stung me in the foot and I got an infection (staphylococcus, for short). It was the first time in my life that anything smaller than a turtle had ever got the best of me, and naturally I don't like to dwell on it. I prefer to go on to my studies in "The Outline of Science," if everybody is satisfied.

I happened to pick up Volume IV first, and was presently in the midst of a plain and simple explanation of the Einstein theory, a theory about which in my time I have done as much talking as the next man, although I admit now that I never understood it very clearly. I understood it even less clearly after I had tackled a little problem about a man running a hundred-yard dash and an aviator in a plane above him. Everything, from the roundness of the earth to the immortality of the soul, has been demonstrated by the figures of men in action, but here was a new proposition. It seems that if the aviator were traveling as fast as light, the stop watch held by the track judge would not, from the aviator's viewpoint, move at all. (You've got to make believe that the aviator could see the watch, which is going to be just as hard for you as it was for me.) You might think that this phenomenon of the unmoving watch hand would enable the runner to make a hundred yards in nothing flat, but, if so, you are living in a fool's paradise. To an aviator going as fast as light, the hundred-yard track would shrink to nothing at all. If the aviator were going *twice* as fast as light, the report of the track judge's gun would wake up the track judge, who would still be in bed in his pajamas, not yet having got up to go to the track meet. This last is my own private extension of the general theory, but it seems to me as sound as the rest of it.

I finally gave up the stop watch and the airplane, and went deeper into the chapter till I came to the author's summary of a scientific romance called "Lumen," by the celebrated French astronomer, M. Flammarion (in my youth, the Hearst Sunday feature sections leaned heavily on M. Flammarion's discoveries). The great man's lurid little romance deals, it seems, with a man who died in 1864, and whose soul flew with the speed of thought to one of the stars in the constellation Capella. This star was so far from the earth that it took light rays seventy-two years to get there, hence the man's soul kept catching up with light rays from old historical events and passing them. Thus the man's soul was able to see the battle of Waterloo, fought backward. First the man's soul—oh, let's call him Mr. Lumen—first Mr. Lumen saw a lot of dead soldiers and then he saw them get up and start fighting. "Two hundred thousand corpses, come to life, marched off the field in perfect order," wrote M. Flammarion. Perfect order, I should think, only backward.

I kept going over and over this section of the chapter on the Einstein theory. I even tried reading it backward, twice as fast as light, to see if I could capture Napoleon at Waterloo while he was still home in bed. If you are interested in the profound mathematical theory of the distinguished German Scientist, you may care to glance at a diagram I drew for my own guidance as follows:

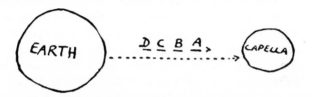

Now, A represents Napoleon entering the field at Waterloo and B represents his defeat there. The dotted line is, of course, Mr. Lumen, going hell-for-leather. C and D you need pay no particular attention to; the first represents the birth of Mr. George L. Snively, an obscure American engineer, in 1819, and the second the founding of the New England Glass Company, in 1826. I put them in to give the thing roundness and verisimilitude and to suggest that Mr. Lumen passed a lot of other events besides Waterloo.

In spite of my diagram and my careful reading and rereading of the chapter on the Einstein theory, I left it in the end with a feeling that my old grip on it, as weak as it may have been, was stronger than my new grip on it, and simpler, since it had not been mixed up with aviators, stop watches, Mr. Lumen, and Napoleon. The discouraging conviction crept over me that science was too much for me, that these brooding scientists, with their bewildering problems, many of which work backward, live on an intellectual level which I, who think of a hundred-yard dash as a hundred-yard dash, could never attain to. It was with relief that I drifted on to Chapter XXXVI, "The Story of Domesticated Animals." There wouldn't be anything in that going as fast as light or faster, and it was more the kind of thing that a man who has been put to bed by a bee should read for the alleviation of his humiliation. I picked out the section on dogs, and very shortly I came to this: "There are few dogs which do not inspire affection; many crave it. But there are some which seem to repel us, like the bloodhound. True, man has made him what he is. Terrible to look at and terrible to encounter, man has raised him up to hunt down his fellowman." Accompanying the article was a picture of a dignified and mournful-looking bloodhound, about as terrible to look at as Abraham Lincoln, about as terrible to encounter as Jimmy Durante.

Poor, frightened little scientist! I wondered who he was, this man whom Mr. J. Arthur Thomson, Regius Professor of Natural History at the University of Aberdeen, had selected to inform the world about dogs. Some of the chapters were signed, but this one wasn't, and neither was the one on the Einstein theory (you were given to understand that they had all been written by eminent scientists, however). I had the strange feeling that both of these articles had been written by the same man. I had the strange feeling that *all* scientists are the same man. Could it be possible that I had isolated here, as under a microscope, the true nature of the scientist? It pleased me to think so; it still pleases me to think so. I have never liked or trusted scientists very much, and I think now that I know why: they are afraid of bloodhounds. They must, therefore, be afraid of frogs, jack rabbits, and the larger pussycats. This must be the reason that most of them withdraw from the world and devote themselves to the study of the inanimate and the impalpable. Out of my analysis of those few sentences on the bloodhound, one of the gentlest of all breeds of dogs, I have arrived at what I call Thurber's Law, which is that scientists don't really know anything about anything. I doubt everything they have discovered. I don't think light has a speed of 7,000,000 miles per second at all (or whatever the legendary speed is). Scientists just think light is going that fast, because they are afraid of it. It's so terrible to look at. I have always suspected that light just plodded along, and now I am positive of it.

I can understand how that big baby dropped the subject of bloodhounds with those few shuddering sentences, but I propose to scare him and his fellow-scientists a little more about the huge and feral creatures. Bloodhounds are sometimes put on the trail of old lost ladies or little children who have wandered away from home. When a bloodhound finds an old lady or a little child, he instantly swallows the old lady or the little child whole, clothes and all. This is probably what happened to Charlie Ross, Judge Crater, Agnes Tufverson, and a man named Colonel Appel, who disappeared at the battle of Shiloh. God only knows how many thousands of people bloodhounds have swallowed, but it is probably twice as many as the Saint Bernards have swallowed. As everybody knows, the Saint Bernards, when they find travelers fainting in the snow, finish them off. Monks have notoriously little to eat and it stands to reason they couldn't feed a lot of big, full-grown Saint Bernards; hence they sick them on the lost travelers, who would never get anywhere, anyway. The brandy in the little kegs the dogs wear around their necks is used by the Saint Bernards in drunken orgies that follow the killings.

I guess that's all I have to say to the scientists now, except *boo!*

QUESTIONS ON CONTENT

1. Although this essay is written with the lightest touch, in what way does it set forth the problem of the scientist who writes for the layman and the layman who tries to understand the scientist?
2. "I had the strange feeling that *all* scientists are the same man." Do you have the same strange feeling about scientists?
3. What is Thurber's Law?
4. Can you deduce what the persons mentioned in the next to last paragraph had in common?

❧ *The Myth of Science Fiction*

SIEGFRIED MANDEL AND PETER FINGESTEN

Modern science fiction is a quest for a key to the universe. Inside the slick SF package is the desire to unlock the door of this world and escape into the beyond—where all is simple machines and clean space. To speed this wish SF has created a mythology which is a counterpart of the cults formed by primitive men who didn't know where the rain came from, or the wind, and who invented mysteries in order to dispel uncertainty. On the heels of mystery entered the elements also present in SF today: symbolism, ideology,

The Saturday Review, August 27, 1955. Reprinted by permission of *The Saturday Review* and the authors.

codes, priests, salvation, doctrinal terminology, tradition, and prophecy. The heart of the form is a moody discontent with things as
they are. It is magnified claustrophobia. Why are we earthbound,
isolated, and shut off from the infiniteness of the universe? As Groff
and Lucy Conklin have noted, science fiction "offers a welcome relief
from the confinement of our noisy, cluttered, and often dull and
wearisome everyday lives, and an escape from the restraints of
complex civilization."

Like Westerns, SF plots consist of a range of invention inside a
general form. Typical of the straightfaced narrative technique is
the story which opens in this fashion: "Ord sat in his swivel chair
and surveyed the solar system." Ord is a space-station sentinel
manning his post 2,000 miles above earth where he eventually con-
tracts "solitosis," an affliction which besets with hallucinations men
stranded in a deserted universe. "Realism" of this sort is but a trans-
ference of everyday objects and situations onto a cosmic plane.
Spacemen are, of course, afflicted only with psychological diseases,
as super-medicine has made obsolete the other kind.

In another story a select group jets its way into space and after
several galactic adventures reaches its destination in the far reaches
of astral infinity, but is refused an immigration permit after being
tagged as undesirable. The author has given himself here an opportunity to discuss liberal politics and theories of "group dynamics"
—all very modern. In this "rejection" story we also have an indication of the feeling of inferiority of SF man toward superior beings
in space, in contrast to his feeling of superiority toward fellow
earthmen who do not belong at all in the circle of the elect.

There is no limitation to the gimmicks that are engineered by SF
writers—from projections forward and backward in space-time to
interstellar wars and "end of the world" stories—especially since
they raid the encyclopedic sources of biology, anthropology, and
astronomy. Still, the best SF writers try not to let gimmicks dominate
their characters; they make an attempt to understand objectively how
the life of Future Man will have been affected by another 1,500 years
of engineering. What will Love be in 3500 A.D.? Loyalty? Ambition?
Patriotism?

Escape from confinement—from political, social, and personal
reality—always has occupied man's mind. This explains the dis-
interested attitude toward women in science fiction, and the absence
of pleasure-seeking *per se*. Discounting spurious space operettas
and fringe melodramas, legitimate SF does not assign women to

siren roles; there are no bosomy creatures to drive men to erotic distraction. They wait at home, like Penelope for Ulysses, and whatever they're doing there it's not heroic.

Three things account for this situation: the bleak sobriety with which science fiction—filled with admiration for Kinsey and Freud —approaches the wide subject of sex: the desire to get as far away as possible from Earth; and natural asceticism.

Woman represents one of the strongest—if most attractive—chains that bind man to contemporary life. As mothers, wives, or sweethearts women involve men in the kind of complexities from which the male in his wishful thinking would like to escape, escape to what the science-fiction cult believes to be the more significant reality. In the old mythologies Mother Earth and woman were synonymous. Men pass while the earth remains. Woman, like the earth, forms the fixed substrate of society. To break man's dependence on either woman or earth is not now feasible. After all, we are still earthmen —or *terrans*, in science-fiction terminology.

But in SF the attempt is made, however, to minimize his dependence socially, psychologically, and physically. SF has little overt sexuality; instead there is intellectualized feeling *à la* Plato, who declared that the highest type of friendship can exist only between men. This aspect of the cult contains an obvious element of latent homosexuality, dramatized in the emotionless and humorless relationship between the senior and the junior male characters in SF. Incorporated here is the dangerous—and unconquerable—delusion that "Greek love" was really little more than an agreeable companionship between man and boy; and that there is no reason why this simple relationship should not be transplanted independently into the future. In any case, by rejecting glandular sexuality the SFer feels that he rises saintlike above mundane distractions and achieves a scientific objectivity dominated by reason and intellect alone. This new man—a coldly ascetic and intellectual creature—is the man who will be ready physically and mentally to cope with the unpredictable, soulless, and nerve-shattering bleaknesses of outer space.

Readers of science fiction are most attracted to seriousness and intellectual "rigor" of this kind. In a survey of science-fiction readers, John W. Campbell, Jr., comes up with the following average profile: "Technically trained, philosophically inclined, imaginative man between twenty and thirty-five." This means that we are not dealing with a crackpot audience seeking relief in fantasy. What are they seeking? One finds that a common denominator is the wish for a world where the scientist not only blueprints and supervises the production of guns and butter and satellite space-stations, but also possesses the political power that determines their use. We are reminded of the moral conflicts in men like Oppenheimer, who seem to feel that the scientist is responsible for the use of his gadgets over and above the normal channels of political government. But how to make this "responsibility" effective in a constitutional state is a problem which eludes Dr. Oppenheimer as well as the SFer.

When all is said and done, the SF cult carries forward an age-old tradition. Whenever and wherever man finds himself consciously alone with the universe he has resorted to "image making," peopling the earth and the heavens with creatures from the realm of his imagination. History has seen the rise and atrophy of mythologies from the time of the Sumerians to the Kremlinites. Today, with the new era of atomic science unlocking a vast realm of secrets, man again is asking himself the traditional questions about the universe. Old shapes in a new mythology are the answer.

In the old mythologies the creation of gods in the likeness of men was dominant. In the new mythology the stress has shifted away from an anthropomorphic image. The criterion is an abstract: Intelligence. After all, science fiction is in part an intellectual speculation of how techniques and apparatus can establish contact with outer space creatures—animal, mineral, or vegetable—that also possess intelligence, or how human intelligence can conquer the very inhospitable conditions of outer space. The old means of establishing contact with seen or unseen astral agents through rituals and magic has given way to visions of telegraphic and electronic communication. In primitive societies towering respect is given to the leader possessing magical powers. Why, ask science fictioners, should not the same attitude exist in our society toward scientists?

But while some of the science-fiction literature uses sound scientific information in speculating or meticulously describing the orbital workings of the universe and the possible flora and fauna of these planets we communicate with, the SF approach to politics and government is absurd. The assumption that the scientist would rule the world with paternal wisdom—and that laymen would acquiesce in this Big Fatherhood—is as historically silly as Plato's philosopher-kings, who turn out to be no more than dictators in disguise enforcing the "harmony" of the state through thought-control and the police. It is ridiculous to think that a scientist-dictator clique ruling the world or the universe would avoid the common human traits of jealously and ambition. Nevertheless, the SFer fancies the universe run by a sort of lofty, technocratic Signory, without considering that the real members of the real Venetian Signory assassinated their own grandmothers to keep office. Of the highest sort of real political intelligence, the compromises, ingenuity, and deceptions by means of which Elizabeth I (or Abraham Lincoln, for that matter) managed her situations, there is no hint in science fiction.

States in SF literature display an anatomy of power consisting of monolithic rule by a cabinet of scientific elders, plus an automatic citizenry. Station in life is usually determined from birth. If a person's character is found incompatible with the ideals of the SF state he is simply regenerated through psycho-physical treatments. Rarely do SF writers and believers think through to the ultimate, catastrophic socio-political consequences of their projected Utopia.

The scientist-leader ranks very high in the new mythology. Trained to be intellectually ascetic, the ideal SF hero also embodies humanistic and prophetic strains. Quite frequently in science-fiction literature there appears the "last man on earth" motif. Usually before cataclysms which threaten the world, or before destruction from outer space is threatened, some scientist with four-dimensional sense broadcasts prophetic warnings. Once this prophetic obligation is discharged—though ignored by most—a select band of believers heeds the call and makes appropriate provisions to survive. They usually wind up being the last men on earth. Or they determinedly take flight into the beyond. Then the last earthmen or the space-officers heave a sigh of relief at being alone at last, and out of the subway tube of the modern world. Why they care about life at all is not easy to understand; but their lack of *joie de vivre* is compensated for by manly courage and the grim resolution which makes it possible to bear the immense isolation of space.

Many basic humanistic doctrines underlie science-fiction thinking and can be summed up in this fashion: let us erase all social ills and ban wars since it is imperative that we create a worldwide front to deal with extraterrestrial powers, either through conflict or coming to terms by means of negotiation, when that occasion arises. All this explains the conclaves of international scientists who so often come together in science fiction and sound Messianic warnings to the tune of "It's later than you think; the end of the world is just around the corner." From this point of view Gerald Heard seems justified

in saying, "Science fiction is the prophetic . . . the apocalyptic literature of our particular and culminating epoch of crisis." But the
SFer has no reason to despair or turn religious (*i.e.*, superstitious)
for scientists can explain, if not control, all things, and hypothetical
theories of "group dynamics" even make all social and political
quandaries a thing of the past.

Yet a sense of urgency inspires the SFer. In the first place there
is that uncomfortable feeling that pervades science fiction, the
feeling that we are not alone in the universe, but are being constantly observed. Second, there is that feeling of time running out.
The awareness of life's brevity in the face of the vast and limitless
past and future urges the SFers to crash astral barriers *during*
their own lifetime. SF attempts to go beyond the hope offered by
most religions, which offer salvation and life eternal *after* death.
Of course, modern atomic experiments enhance certain dire speculations.

Like the Apostles' warnings to the ancient world, the science-
fiction scientists' forecasts fall on deaf ears and even gather ridi-
cule. But, far from being discouraged, an idealistic band of scientists
continues work on interstellar vessels designed to head for greener
pastures beyond our sphere. Their work, however, is shielded by
the protective secrecy of their laboratory, even as religious sects
sought the safety of the catacombs in warding off persecution. All
this encourages a kind of natural selectivity. Scoffers and disbe-
lievers remain outside of the circle of those who are worthy of the
great dream. Salvation is ultimately promised to those believers who
make up a "community of saints" sharing the basic SF tenets. Most
often space-ship building becomes a race against time, not a hobby
which would allow mere adventurers to satisfy idle curiosity about
the secrets and oddities to be found in the universe. Science fic-
tioneers' aims consist of beating out impending world disaster and
overcoming the limitations of a mortal life-span.

In mythologies of old, gods visiting humans assumed various
forms—a shower of gold, a swan, pilgrims, angels. Neither these
nor Hamlet's ancestral ghost appear in science fiction. Leda's swan,
allegorical pilgrims, and leprechauns have been displaced by aliens
from other planets who either maintain their own peculiar shapes
or for the sake of convenient inconspicuousness assume earthly
forms. But the things these ambassadors from outer space have in
common with the visitors of old are superhuman wisdom and superior knowledge and power.

Compared with the dangers and incalculable vistas lurking in the vast stretches of an unknown universe, earthly problems shrink to insignificance in the eyes of science fiction. Who can bother with a new suit, union negotiations, or even international politics? Such petty concerns. Instead, "psychokinesis!" (a favorite concept in science fiction which ascribes to the mind the ability to exert significant mastery over matter.) Specifically, SF holds that scientific insight gives man the "ability to manipulate the physical world by means of an advanced knowledge of the mathematical nature of the universe" (a definition given by Judith Merril in "Beyond the Barriers of Space and Time"). This idea goes back to the Greek circle of Pythagoras of the sixth century B.C., which regarded numbers as the mystical base and heart of the universe.

We see that the new mythology is a subtle point-for-point exchange of traditional religious doctrines for "modern" concepts. First of all, the scientist replaces the priest; the unknown replaces God; the spaceship, like the Egyptian solar boat, displaces the church as a vessel of salvation (interestingly enough, the church was always likened to a ship—*navis*); the saved ones in a spaceship assume the characteristics of superior men or saints casting off earthly chains; the new planet idyllically becomes the heavenly Jerusalem; the pilot or astrogator leads his community of saints like a savior; visitors from outer space take on the terror and sublimity of angels; the dashboard paraphernalia and control dials become as potent and dominant as icons and sacraments—faith is placed in technical efficiency; finally, the breakthrough into space, the bursting through gravitational pulls, constitutes a baptism or a climactic initiation into the heavenly mysteries. And once the universe is reduced to technology it becomes predictable and manageable. When the universe is stripped of spiritual content and is interpreted as a machine scientists assume the license of tinkering with it.

Unfortunately, for most of us the "machine of the universe" is so complex that it must remain as much a mystery as the Eleusinian rites were to the average Athenian, *unless* one becomes a dedicated disciple of the circle dominated by the scientists and space officers —the new priests!

All this does not mean that the universe loses its beauty. In fact, precise and machinelike motion and behavior are the esthetic zenith for an SF enthusiast. But if this sere universe is still "beautiful," it is a little less real. If science fiction has become a successful literature of escape, it has not become a literature of force and emotion. It is not that the science-fiction world does not correspond to the physical probabilities of the Future; for no doubt the real world of 5000 A.D. would seem far more bizarre to a contemporary invader than any present-day SFer has dreamed it to be. It is that science-fiction literature does not correspond to the normal aspirations of the human spirit. The science-fiction future is not one which strikes the average man as an age of promise; it is not—as were Cicero's Isles of the Blessed or Columbus's equal fanciful "Indies" —a world where most of us would care to abide. When Philip Wylie called science fiction "a symptom of our general mental disorder" he missed its dimensions. Is not science fiction only one more vain attempt—with new vocabulary and grandiose new symbolism—to loose the fetters of life, rather than understand them?

QUOTATIONS FROM SAMPLES OF SCIENCE FICTION

THE FEDERATION, on the other hand, looked back with a kind of affectionate contempt upon the world from which it had sprung. It had lured to Mars, Venus, and the satellites of the giant planets some of the finest intellects and the most adventurous spirits of the human race. Here was the new frontier, one that would expand forever toward the stars. It was the greatest challenge mankind had ever faced, it could be met only by supreme scientific skill and unyielding determination. *Arthur C. Clarke, "Earthlight" (Ballantine Books).*

ZEKE LOOKED UP at the four men, and then out toward the pylon again—all that was left of a race that had searched the stars in its need to find new frontiers. It must have been a hardy race, since it had dared to set up a colony across all those innumerable parsecs of space, without even the inspiration of other life. Then, when that colony had failed, the race had returned to the loneliness of its own little world, where the stars looked down grimly, no longer promising anything. Now Mars had been dead 10,000,-000 years, and the pylon stood as the final tombstone on the world which had become a prison. *Lester del Rey, "The Years Draw Night,"* Astounding Science Fiction (*October 1951*).

"MANY, VERY MANY, say that because of Man's machines and his science he shall sink back into oblivion, die the death of a race. But do not his machines make more efficient his control of energy, enlarge his store limitlessly, enable him to mold the universe into a likeness of the Purpose that includes all things? There are differences, Hecktor, that make men deny life for what it is. We are not as an amoeba, nor as a sea-worm, nor a flower: These vapor folk [certain outer-space creatures] are not as we. But, to my mind, the difference is a simple one. *All things differ in life.* We are more alive, far more alive than the bacillus or the worm. And these vapor creatures are more alive than we. Any race, any entity that is able to control the energy of the world about him, unify, and move steadily toward the Purpose that lies behind everything, and who can do these more intelligently, more efficiently than we, *must be more alive than we.*" P. Schuyler Miller, *"Cleon of Yzdral,"* Amazing Stories (*July 1931*).

"HOW IN THE NAME of all the hells can anything live in intergalactic space?"

The voice, strained and unrecognizable, came through the communicator of Grosvenor's space suit as he stood with the others near the air lock. It seemed to him that the question made the little group of men crowd closer together. For him, the proximity of the others was not quite enough. He was too aware of the impalpable yet inconceivable night that coiled about them, pressing down to the very blazing portholes.

Almost for the first time since the voyage had begun the immensity of that darkness struck home to Grosvenor. He had looked at it so often from the ship that he had become indifferent. But now he was suddenly aware that man's farthest stellar frontiers were but a pin point in this blackness that reached billions of light-years in every direction. A. E. Van Vogt, *"The Voyage of the Space Beagle"* (*Simon and Schuster*).

IT WAS ALL VERY WELL for the Senior Judge to tell him to seek adventure in interplanetary exploration, but only engineers and technicians were eligible for such billets. Perhaps he should have gone in for science, or engineering, instead of literature; then he might now be on Venus, contending against the forces of nature. . . .

The Covenant was the first scientific social document ever drawn up by man, and due credit must be given to its principal author, Dr. Micah [the name of the prophet who heralded the coming judgment] Novak, the same Novak who served as staff psychologist in the Revolution. The Revolutionists wished to establish maximum personal liberty. How could they accomplish that to a degree of high mathematical probability?

First they junked the concept of "justice." Examined semantically "justice" has no referent—there is no observable phenomenon in the space-time-matter continuum to which one can point, and say, "This is justice." Science can deal only with that which can be observed and measured. . . . . But damage, physical or economic, can be pointed to and measured. Citizens were forbidden by the Covenant to damage another. Any act not leading to damage, physical or economic, to some particular person, they declared to be lawful. *Robert A. Heinlein, "Revolt in 2100" (Shasta Publishers).*

QUESTIONS ON CONTENT

1. Do you feel that the authors approach their subject objectively? Cite passages to show that they do or do not.
2. How do the authors account for the distant view of women taken by SFers?
3. Who is the average reader of science fiction? Do you read it?
4. Why do the authors refer to the physicist, Dr. Oppenheimer? Discuss the meaning of this reference.
5. What parallels do the authors find between old mythologies and the new mythology being created in science fiction? In what paragraph are these parallels summarized?
6. *Brave New World* by Aldous Huxley (see excerpt, pp. 519–527) is science fiction, but how does it differ from the sort being described in this article?
7. What would keep a scientist from being a benevolent dictator?
8. Why does a "sense of urgency" inspire the SFer?
9. How new is the idea that numbers hold the secret of the universe?
10. Who are the "new priests"?
11. "Science-fiction literature does not correspond to the normal aspirations of the human spirit." Comment.
12. Which points in this article do the five excerpts from recent science fiction illustrate?

SUGGESTIONS FOR PAPERS

For a nonscientist to write about science or scientists is, admittedly, a tricky assignment. It is easy to be worshipful. It is even easier to be foolishly critical. You should try in your paper to avoid these extremes, unless, of course, you wish to be satirical. The selections in this section point up not only what science may do *for* man but also what science may do *to* man. Your paper should take into account this dual nature of science.

1. Huxley says that we act daily on inductive principles. Define induction; then show how the following hypotheses are a result of inductive reasoning: proficiency in your college work is denoted by the letter A; lack of proficiency is denoted by the letter F. Now define syllogism and draw up two syllogisms to fit your two inductions.

2. Look up a work on pomology (the science of apples) and test Huxley's illustrative induction that all green, hard apples are sour. Now comment on the fallacy of jumping to conclusions.

3. "The exception proves the rule" is a saying which is seldom understood in its correct sense. Give the ordinary interpretation of this saying. Can such an interpretation be squared with Huxley's statement: "in a scientific inquiry, a fallacy . . . is . . . sure to be in the long run constantly productive of mischievous if not fatal results"? End your paper with the correct meaning of the saying.

4. How does Huxley in "On a Piece of Chalk" practise what he recommends in "The Scientific Method"? Jot down what is said about the scientific method; then apply to "On a Piece of Chalk."

5. Do you see any reason why this piece of Huxley's ("On a Piece of Chalk") should have caused concern among religious leaders? If you do, indicate in your paper how much or how little times have changed since religion and science were regarded as incompatible. Be sure to cite the portion of Huxley's essay which would disturb nineteenth-century (and some twentieth-century) theologians.

6. Science attempts to control its experiments, to see to it that a supposed law is intentionally subjected to every sort of test which may upset the law. Do you find in this phase of the scientific method something different from "the necessary mode of working of the human mind"? Do most minds resist or shy away from facts which

may upset their pet ideas? Discuss your answers and use specific illustrations.

7. Someone has said that success in science rests upon the ability to ask questions that can be answered. This implies that scientists dodge the hard questions and devote themselves to things that can be weighed and measured. What are some of the questions which science avoids? Why are many scientists agnostics (not-knowers) in matters of religion? Does the method of scientific investigation have something to do with this? Discuss carefully.

8. The poet Browning has said that a scientific faith is an impossibility. What did he mean? Did he probably have in mind the method of scientific investigation? Show how faith and science are different modes of the working of the human mind.

9. Would you want all persons to think as you do? To find out how you think, choose a particular controversial subject—say, gambling—and examine your attitude on this subject. Suppose science could make your point of view the point of view of all men. Would you call in science to do so? Why, or why not? (Gambling, of course, does not have to be the topic.)

10. The next time that you attend church jot down notes on the sort of conduct recommended by the pastor. Arrange these notes in the form of a monologue which could be recorded and be re-produced on one of Sherover's "sleep-teaching sets" (see "Learn While You Sleep"). Would you accept this help from science in try-ing to convert the world to this sort of conduct? Why, or why not?

11. If you had one of the "sleep-teaching sets" to what specific use would you put it? What, in other words, would you like most to learn? Give a specific example or examples of recordings which you would want murmured to you while you sleep. You will have to compose the words for your ideal lessons, but you may, of course, quote from any source you like.

12. Society is unstable because of the struggle between classes of people, say Communist thinkers. Huxley has imagined one way of getting rid of the class struggle (see "A Stable Society"). Does the method he suggests appeal to you? Discuss your point of view.

13. In Huxley's *Brave New World*, the processes of birth and edu-cation are completely under the control of the state. The state sets quotas of so many infants to be produced in each class of society. The mentality of the infants is carefully controlled. At "decanting time" the conditioning of the infants begins. Thereafter no dis-satisfaction is possible. Is there anything basically wrong with this

process? What balance, if any, is there between what such a civilization would gain or lose? You will have to do some careful thinking here!

14. You have some sort of ideal for life. Suppose you were a dictator and had at your command all the world's top scientists. Upon what would you *first* put them to work? Be specific. Choose something which you consider to be fundamental.

15. "Man does not live by bread alone." What is the full meaning of this statement? Is there a clear distinction in your mind between what is "bread" and what is "not bread"? Do the things which science does *for* man all fall under the classification of "bread"? Are the things which science may do *to* man likely to destroy all but bread? Offer specific examples to illustrate any general statement which you may make.

16. Discuss lie detectors and truth drugs. Lie detectors are devices which indicate an emotional disturbance when a person tells an untruth. Truth drugs are supposed to render a person incapable of telling a lie—incapable of even refusing to talk. These scientific devices appear to be good things for society. Are there any dangers involved? Suppose an all-powerful, unscrupulous state had at its disposal both the sleep-teaching sets (see "Learn While You Sleep") and lie detectors or truth drugs. How could such a state capture the will of an individual who opposed it? Dramatize your paper, if you like.

17. Is there any close connection between democracy and science? Do you think science flourishes best in a democracy, or is science indifferent to politics? Which form of government is likely to emphasize what science may do *to* men? Use both real and imagined examples.

18. "An Outline of Scientists" expresses delightfully a layman's skepticism concerning what scientists say they know. What is *your* private opinion on this subject? Have you some specific doubts about some of the claims of scientists? Write about two or three "scientific facts" which you regard with suspicion.

19. It has been said that scientists have the highest respect for averages. What is good about this attitude? What is bad? Is your life being constantly averaged? Your weight? Your grades? Your life expectancy? Your intelligence? Is it a tendency of science to aim at the average?

20. If you are a reader of science fiction, test according to your experience with such writing the truth of "The Myth of Science

Fiction." List the characteristics as given in this article and offer illustrations from your reading.

21. "Science-fiction literature does not correspond to the normal aspirations of the human spirit." ("The Myth of Science Fiction.") What are the "normal aspirations of the human spirit"? What are the ideals emphasized by science fiction? Compare.

SOME TITLES FOR PAPERS

1. Daily Hypotheses
2. Some Sample Deductions
3. Deduction and Induction with Examples of Each
4. Science Is Measurement
5. Some Things Can't Be Measured
6. Description and Measurement in "On a Piece of Chalk"
7. Has Science Produced Leisure?
8. Education as Scientific Conditioning
9. The Great God Average
10. Advantages of Hit-and-Miss Education
11. Who Wants a Stable Society?
12. Sleep-taught Robots
13. Could Science Produce Men of Good Will?
14. Science Will Serve Any Master
15. Are Scientists Amoral?
16. If Everybody Made A
17. Why I Trust Science
18. Can Science Make Me Happy?
19. Men Are the Best Guinea Pigs
20. Truth Drugs and Lie Detectors
21. Science Can Undress Your Mind
22. Are Popular Polls Scientific?
23. Science and Dictators
24. Myths: Old and New
25. Better Outer Worlds?
26. Science and the Natural Aspirations of Men
27. The Dual Nature of Science
28. Inductions from My Readings in Science Fiction
29. Where Science Leaves Off
30. Analysis and Criticism of— (Choose any one of the selections in this chapter for analysis and criticism.)

❧ *LOVE AND MARRIAGE*

MARRIAGE IS A SIMPLE TERM meaning the legal union of a man with a woman. Love, on the other hand, is a complex emotion which, like poetry, can be felt but not defined. Unless the word *marriage* is otherwise qualified (as in *marriage of convenience*), it is assumed that *love* is the qualifier. As a result, marriage loses its simplicity in the combination *love-marriage*. Just what love has to do with marriage is the subject of a library of books and the staple of periodicals. Love and marriage, separately or in combination, concern everyone.

Stevenson in "On Marriage" is dubious that the high passion of love as described by the poets is suited to the calm and comfortable estate of marriage. All his recommendations are directed toward achieving peace in a relationship which otherwise offers unlimited opportunity for perpetual battle. Housman's little poem, "When I was One-and-Twenty," may be regarded as a regretful comment upon the wisdom of Stevenson's advice.

The third selection, "Love in America," contains a Frenchman's view of love and marriage in the United States. The author observes that Americans make a fetish of success in everything, including love-marriages. If the love-marriage does not work, the ingredients have been wrong or inaccurately measured. Success must be possible. Couples try to find the trouble with their recipe and in seeking for it have frank discussions of their respective faults. They tell each other home truths and thereby, observes de Roussy de Sales, jeopardize further their marriage.

The final selection, James Thurber's "Courtship Through the Ages," gives a humorous turn to the relationship of the sexes. Taking his cue from a scientific article on animal courtship, Thurber describes by analogy—and without saying so—the courting habits of American males and the coyness of American females.

❧ *On Marriage*

Robert Louis Stevenson

. . . The fact is, we are much more afraid of life than our ancestors, and cannot find it in our hearts either to marry or not to marry. Marriage is terrifying, but so is a cold and forlorn old age. The friendships of men are vastly agreeable, but they are insecure. You know all the time that one friend will marry and put you to the door; a second accept a situation in China, and become no more to you than a name, a reminiscence, and an occasional crossed letter, very laborious to read; a third will take up with some religious crotchet and treat you to sour looks thenceforward. So, in one way or another, life forces men apart and breaks up the goodly fellowships forever. The very flexibility and ease which make men's friendships so agreeable while they endure, make them the easier to destroy and forget. And a man who has a few friends, or one who has a dozen (if there be any one so wealthy on this earth), cannot forget on how precarious a base his happiness reposes; and how by a stroke or two of fate—a death, a few light words, a piece of stamped paper, a woman's bright eyes—he may be left, in a month, destitute of all. Marriage is certainly a perilous remedy. Instead of on two or three, you stake your happiness on one life only. But still, as the bargain is more explicit and complete on your part, it is more so on the other; and you have not to fear so many contingencies; it is not every wind that can blow you from your anchorage; and so long as Death withholds his sickle, you will always have a friend at home. People who share a cell in the Bastille, or are thrown together on an uninhabited island, if they do not immediately fall to fisticuffs, will find some possible ground of compromise.

From *Virginibus Puerisque* (1881).

They will learn each other's ways and humors, so as to know where they must go warily, and where they may lean their whole weight. The discretion of the first years becomes the settled habit of the last; and so, with wisdom and patience, two lives may grow indissolubly into one.

But marriage, if comfortable, is not at all heroic. It certainly narrows and damps the spirits of generous men. In marriage, a man becomes slack and selfish, and undergoes a fatty degeneration of his moral being. It is not only when Lydgate misallies himself with Rosamond Vincy, but when Ladislaw marries above him with Dorothea, that this may be exemplified. The air of the fireside withers out all the fine wildings of the husband's heart. He is so comfortable and happy that he begins to prefer comfort and happiness to everything else on earth, his wife included. Yesterday he would have shared his last shilling; to-day "his first duty is to his family," and is fulfilled in large measure by laying down vintages and husbanding the health of an invaluable parent. Twenty years ago this man was equally capable of crime or heroism; now he is fit for neither. His soul is asleep, and you may speak without constraint; you will not wake him. It is not for nothing that Don Quixote was a bachelor and Marcus Aurelius married ill. For women, there is less of this danger. Marriage is of so much use to a woman, opens out to her so much more of life, and puts her in the way of so much more freedom and usefulness, that, whether she marry ill or well, she can hardly miss some benefit. It is true, however, that some of the merriest and most genuine of women are old maids; and that those old maids, and wives who are unhappily married, have often most of the true motherly touch. And this would seem to show, even for women, some narrowing influence in comfortable married life. But the rule is none the less certain: if you wish the pick of men and women, take a good bachelor and a good wife.

I am often filled with wonder that so many marriages are passably successful, and so few come to open failure, the more so as I fail to understand the principle on which people regulate their choice. I see women marrying indiscriminately with staring burgesses and ferret-faced, white-eyed boys, and men dwelling in contentment with noisy scullions, or taking into their lives acidulous vestals. It is a common answer to say the good people marry because they fall in love; and of course you may use and misuse a word as much as you please, if you have the world along with you. But love is at least a somewhat hyperbolical expression for such lukewarm preference. It is not here, anyway, that Love employs his golden shafts; he cannot be said, with any fitness of language, to reign here and revel. Indeed, if this be love at all, it is plain the poets have been fooling with mankind since the foundation of the world. And you have only to look these happy couples in the face, to see they have never been in love, or in hate, or in any other high passion, all their days. When you see a dish of fruit at dessert, you sometimes set your affections upon one particular peach or nectarine, watch it with some anxiety as it comes round the table, and feel quite a sensible disappointment when it is taken by some one else. I have used the phrase "high passion." Well, I should say this was about as high a passion as generally leads to marriage. One husband hears after marriage that some poor fellow is dying of his wife's love. "What a pity!" he exclaims; "you know I could so easily have got another!" And yet that is a very happy union. Or again: A young man was telling me the sweet story of his love. "I like it well enough as long as her sisters are there," said this amorous swain; "but I don't know what to do when we're alone." Once more: A married lady was debating the subject with another lady. "You know dear," said the first, "after ten years of marriage, if he is nothing else, your husband is always an old friend." "I have many old friends," returned the other, "but I prefer them to be nothing more." "Oh, perhaps I might *prefer* that also!" There is a common note in these three illustrations of the modern idyll; and it must be owned the god goes among us with a limping gait and blear eyes. You wonder whether it was so always; whether desire was always equally dull and spiritless, and possession equally cold. I cannot help fancying most people make, ere they marry, some such table of recommendations as Hannah Godwin wrote to her brother William anent her friend, Miss Gay. It is so charmingly comical, and so pat to the occasion, that I must quote a few phrases. "The young lady is in every sense formed to make one of your disposition really happy. She has a pleasing voice, with which she accompanies her musical instrument with judgment. She has an easy politeness in her manners, neither free nor reserved. She is a good housekeeper and a good economist, and yet of a generous disposition. As to her internal accomplishments, I have reason to speak still more highly of them; good sense without vanity, a penetrating judgment without a disposition to satire, with about as much religion as my William likes, struck me with a wish that she was my William's wife." That is about the tune: pleasing voice, moderate good looks, unimpeachable internal accomplishments after the style of the copy-book, with about as much religion as my William likes; and then, with all speed, to church.

To deal plainly, if they only married when they fell in love, most people would die unwed; and among the others, there would be not a few tumultuous households. The Lion is the King of Beasts, but he is scarcely suitable for a domestic pet. In the same way, I suspect love is rather too violent a passion to make, in all cases, a good domestic sentiment. Like other violent excitements, it throws up not only what is best, but what is worst and smallest, in men's characters. Just as some people are malicious in drink, or brawling and virulent under the influence of religious feeling, some are moody, jealous, and exacting when they are in love, who are honest, downright, good-hearted fellows enough in the everyday affairs and humors of the world.

How then, seeing we are driven to the hypothesis that people choose in comparatively cold blood, how is it they choose so well? One is almost tempted to hint that it does not much matter whom you marry; that, in fact, marriage is a subjective affection, and if you have made up your mind to it, and once talked yourself fairly over, you could "pull it through" with anybody. But even if we take matrimony at its lowest, even if we regard it as no more than a sort of friendship recognized by the police, there must be degrees in the freedom and sympathy realized, and some principle to guide simple folk in their selection. Now what should this principle be? Are there no more definite rules than are to be found in the Prayer-book? Law and religion forbid the bans on the grounds of propinquity or consanguinity; society steps in to separate classes; and in all this, most critical matter, has common-sense, has wisdom, never a word to say? In the absence of more magisterial teaching, let us talk it over between friends: even a few guesses may be of interest to youths and maidens.

In all that concerns eating and drinking, company, climate, and ways of life, community of taste is to be sought for. It would be trying, for instance, to keep bed and board with an early riser or a vegetarian. In matters of art and intellect, I believe it is of no consequence. Certainly it is of none in the companionships of men, who will dine more readily with one who has a good heart, a good cellar, and a humorous tongue, than with another who shares all their favorite hobbies and is melancholy withal. If your wife likes Tupper, that is no reason why you should hang your head. She thinks with the majority, and has the courage of her opinions. I have always suspected public taste to be a mongrel product out of affectation by dogmatist; and felt sure, if you could only find an honest man of no special literary bent, he would tell you he thought much of Shakespeare bombastic and most absurd, and all of him written in very obscure English and wearisome to read. And not long ago I was able to lay by my lantern in content, for I found the honest man. He was a fellow of parts, quick, humorous, a clever painter, and with an eye for certain poetical effects of sea and ships. I am not much of a judge of that kind of thing, but a sketch of his comes before me sometimes at night. How strong, supple, and living the ship seems upon the billows! With what a dip and rake she shears the flying sea! I cannot fancy the man who saw this effect, and took it on the wing with so much force and spirit, was what you call commonplace in the last recesses of the heart. And yet he thought, and was not ashamed to have it known of him, that Ouida was better in every way than William Shakespeare. If there were more people of his honesty, this would be about the staple of lay criticism. It is not taste that is plentiful, but courage that is rare. And what have we in place? How many, who think no otherwise than the young painter, have we not heard disbursing second-hand hyperboles? Have you never turned sick at heart, O best of critics! when some of your own sweet adjectives were returned on you before a gaping audience? Enthusiasm about art is become a function of the average female being, which she performs with precision and a sort of haunting sprightliness, like an ingenious and well-regulated machine. Sometimes, alas! the calmest man is carried away in the torrent, bandies adjectives with the best, and out-Herods Herod for some shameful moments. When you remember that, you will be tempted to put things strongly, and say you will marry no one who is not like George the Second, and cannot state openly a distaste for poetry and painting.

The word "facts" is, in some ways, crucial. I have spoken with Jesuits and Plymouth Brethren, mathematicians and poets, dogmatic republicans and dear old gentlemen in bird's-eye neckcloths; and each understood the word "facts" in an occult sense of his own. Try as I might, I could get no nearer the principle of their division. What was essential to them, seemed to me trivial or untrue. We could come to no compromise as to what was, or what was not, important in the life of man. Turn as we pleased, we all stood back to back in a big ring, and saw another quarter of the heavens, with different mountain-tops along the sky-line and different constellations overhead. We had each of us some whimsy in the brain, which we believed more than anything else, and which discolored all experience to its own shade. How would you have people agree, when one is deaf and the other blind? Now this is where there should be community between man and wife. They should be agreed on their catchword in *"facts of religion,"* or *"facts of science,"* or *"society, my dear";* for without such an agreement all intercourse is a painful strain upon the mind. "About as much religion as my William likes," in short that is what is necessary to make a happy couple of any William and his spouse. For there are differences which no habit nor affection can reconcile, and the Bohemian must not intermarry with the Pharisee. Imagine Consuelo as Mrs. Samuel Budgett, the wife of a successful merchant! The best of men and the best of women may sometimes live together all their lives, and for want of some consent on fundamental questions, hold each other lost spirits to the end.

A certain sort of talent is almost indispensable for people who would spend years together and not bore themselves to death. But the talent, like the agreement, must be for and about life. To dwell happily together, they should be versed in the niceties of the heart, and born with a faculty for willing compromise. The woman must be talented as a woman, and it will not much matter although she is talented in nothing else. She must know her *métier de femme,* and have a fine touch for the affections. And it is more important that a person should be a good gossip, and talk pleasantly and smartly of common friends and the thousand and one nothings of the day and hour, than that she should speak with the tongues of men and angels; for awhile together by the fire, happens more frequently in marriage than the presence of a distinguished foreigner to dinner. That people should laugh over the same sort of jests, and have many a story of "grouse in the gun-room," many an old joke between them which time cannot wither nor custom stale, is a better preparation for life, by your leave, than many other things higher and better sounding in the world's ears. You could read Kant by yourself, if you wanted; but you must share a joke with some one else. You can forgive people who do not follow you through a philosophical disquisition; but to find your wife laughing when you had tears in your eyes, or staring when you were in a fit of laughter, would go some way toward a dissolution of the marriage.

I know a woman, who, from distaste or disability, could never so much as understand the meaning of the word *politics,* and has given up trying to distinguish Whigs from Tories; but take her on her own politics, ask her about other men or women and the chicanery of everyday existence—the rubs, the tricks, the vanities on which life turns—and you will not find many more shrewd, trenchant, and humorous. Nay, to make plainer what I have in mind, this same woman has a share of the higher more poetical understanding, frank interest in things for their own sake, and enduring astonishment at the most common. She is not to be deceived by custom, or made to think a mystery solved when it is repeated. I have heard her say she could wonder herself crazy over the human eyebrow. Now in a world where most of us walk very contentedly in the little lit circle of their own reason, and have to be reminded of what lies without by specious and clamant exceptions—earthquakes, eruptions of Vesuvius, banjos floating in mid-air at a *séance,* and the like—a mind so fresh and unsophisticated is no despicable gift. I will own I think it a better sort of mind than goes necesarily with the clearest views on public business. It will wash. It will find something to say at an odd moment. It has in it the spring of pleasant and quaint fancies. Whereas I can imagine myself yawning all night long until my jaws ached and the tears came into my eyes, although my companion on the other side of the hearth held the most enlightened opinions on the franchise or the ballot.

The question of professions, in as far as they regard marriage, was only interesting to women until of late days, but it touches all of us now. Certainly, if I could help it, I would never marry a wife who wrote. The practice of letters is miserably harassing to the mind; and after an hour or two's work, all the most human portion of the author is extinct; he will bully, backbite, and speak daggers. Music, I hear, is not much better. But painting, on the contrary, is often highly sedative; because so much of the labor, after your picture is once begun, is almost entirely manual, and of that skilled sort of manual labor which offers a continual series of successes, and so tickles a man, through his vanity, into good-humor. Alas! in letters there is nothing of this sort. You may write as beautiful a hand as you will, you have always something else to think of, and cannot pause to notice your loops and flourishes; they are beside the mark, and the first law stationer could put you to the blush. Rousseau, indeed, made some account of penmanship, even made it a source of livelihood, when he copied out the *Héloise* for *dilettante* ladies; and therein showed that strange eccentric prudence which guided him among so many thousand follies and insanities. It would be well for all of the *genus irritabile* thus to add something of skilled labor to intangible brain-work. To find the right word is so doubtful a success and lies so near to failure, that there is no satisfaction in a year of it; but we all know when we have formed a letter perfectly; and a stupid artist, right or wrong, is almost equally certain he has found a right tone or a right color, or made a dexterous stroke with his brush. And, again, painters may work out of doors; and the fresh air, the deliberate seasons and the "tranquillizing influence" of the green earth, counterbalance the fever of thought, and keep them cool, placable, and prosaic.

A ship captain is a good man to marry if it is a marriage of love, for absences are a good influence in love and keep it bright and delicate; but he is just the worst man if the feeling is more pedestrian, as habit is too frequently torn open and the solder has never time to set. Men who fish, botanize, work with the turning-lathe, or gather sea-weeds, will make admirable husbands; and a little amateur painting in water-color shows the innnocent and quiet mind. Those who have a few intimates are to be avoided; while those who swim loose, who have their hat in their hand all along the street, who can number an infinity of acquaintances and are not chargeable with any one friend, promise an easy disposition and no rival to the wife's influence. I will not say they are the best of men, but they are the stuff out of which adroit and capable women manufacture the best of husbands. It is to be noticed that those who have loved once or twice already are so much the better educated to a woman's hand; the bright boy of fiction is an odd and most uncomfortable mixture of shyness and coarseness, and needs a deal of civilizing. Lastly (and this is, perhaps, the golden rule), no woman should marry a teetotaller, or a man who does not smoke. It is not for nothing that this "ignoble tabagie," as Michelet calls it, spreads over all the world. Michelet rails against it because it renders you happy apart from thought or work; to provident women this will seem no evil influence in married life. Whatever keeps a man in the front garden, whatever checks wandering fancy and all inordinate ambition, whatever makes for lounging and contentment, makes just so surely for domestic happiness.

These notes, if they amuse the reader at all, will probably amuse him more when he differs than when he agrees with them; at least they will do no harm, for nobody will follow my advice. But the last word is of more concern. Marriage is a step so grave and decisive that it attracts light-headed, variable men by its very awfulness. They have been so tried among the constant squalls and currents, so often sailed for islands in the air or lain becalmed with burning heart, that they will risk all for solid ground below their feet. Desperate pilots, they run their sea-sick, weary bark upon the dashing rocks. It seems as if marriage were the royal road through life, and realized, on the instant, what we have all dreamed on summer Sundays when the bells ring, or at night when we cannot sleep for the desire of living. They think it will sober and change them. Like those who join a brotherhood, they fancy it needs but an act to be out of the coil and clamor forever. But this is a wile of the devil's. To the end, spring winds will sow disquietude, passing faces leave a regret behind them, and the whole world keep calling and calling in their ears. For marriage is like life in this—that it is a field of battle, and not a bed of roses.

QUESTIONS ON CONTENT

1. What is the chief advantage of marriage? The chief disadvantage? How does the first affect the second?
2. Why is marriage more advantageous to a woman than to a man?
3. The figure of passing the fruit at dessert is used to illustrate what?
4. Which god "goes among us with a limping gait"?
5. What does love have to do with marriage? Why is love compared to a lion?
6. What community of tastes, does the author think, should be shared by couples who are to marry?
7. Discuss Stevenson's opinion that public taste is "a mongrel product out of affectation by dogmatism." What has this observation to do with the task of choosing a wife?
8. Look up Tupper, Ouida, and George the Second in a biographical dictionary; then explain the references to them.
9. Explain the contrasts on p. 550. In what way does Stevenson consider "facts" relative?
10. In which of the arts—literature, music, composition, or painting—does Stevenson think it safe for a wife to indulge?

11. What is the "golden rule" for women in the choice of a husband? Comment.

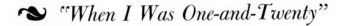

"When I Was One-and-Twenty"

A. E. HOUSMAN

When I was one-and-twenty
  I heard a wise man say,
'Give crowns and pounds and guineas
  But not your heart away;
Give pearls away and rubies   5
  But keep your fancy free.'
But I was one-and-twenty,
  No use to talk to me.

When I was one-and-twenty
  I heard him say again,   10
'The heart out of the bosom
  Was never given in vain;
'Tis paid with sighs a plenty
  And sold for endless rue.'
And I am two-and-twenty,   15
  And oh, 'tis true, 'tis true.

QUESTIONS ON CONTENT

1. Compare Stevenson's warning and that given by the "wise man" in this poem.
2. Explain line 14.

From *A Shropshire Lad* by A. E. Housman. Reprinted by permission of Henry Holt and Company, Inc.

❧ Love in America

RAOUL DE ROUSSY DE SALES

I

America appears to be the only country in the world where love
is a national problem.

Nowhere else can one find a people devoting so much time and
so much study to the question of the relationship between men and
women. Nowhere else is there such concern about the fact that this
relationship does not always make for perfect happiness. The great
majority of the Americans of both sexes seem to be in a state of
chronic bewilderment in the face of a problem which they are certainly not the first to confront, but which—unlike other people—
they still refuse to accept as one of those gifts of the gods which one
might just as well take as it is: a mixed blessing at times, and at
other times a curse or merely a nuisance.

The prevailing conception of love, in America, is similar to the
idea of democracy. It is fine in theory. It is the grandest system ever
evolved by man to differentiate him from his ancestors, the poor
brutes who lived in caverns, or from the apes. Love is perfect, in
fact, and there is nothing better. But, like democracy, it does not
work, and the Americans feel that something should be done about
it. President Roosevelt is intent on making democracy work. Everybody is trying to make love work, too.

In either case the result is not very satisfactory. The probable
reason is that democracy and love are products of a long and complicated series of compromises between the desires of the heart and
the exactions of reason. They have a peculiar way of crumbling into
ashes as soon as one tries too hard to organize them too well.

The secret of making a success out of democracy and love in their
practical applications is to allow for a fairly wide margin of errors,
and not to forget that human beings are absolutely unable to submit
to a uniform rule for any length of time. But this does not satisfy a

Reprinted from *The Atlantic Monthly*, CLXI (May 1938), 645–651, by permission of Mrs. de Roussy de Sales.

nation that, in spite of its devotion to pragmatism, also believes in perfection.

For a foreigner to speak of the difficulties that the Americans encounter in such an intimate aspect of their mutual relationship may appear as an impertinence. But the truth is that no foreigner would ever think of bringing up such a subject of his own accord. In fact, foreigners who come to these shores are quite unsuspecting of the existence of such a national problem. It is their initial observation that the percentage of good-looking women and handsome men is high on this continent, that they are youthful and healthy in mind and body, and that their outlook on life is rather optimistic.

If the newcomers have seen enough American moving pictures before landing here—and they usually have—they must have gathered the impression that love in America is normally triumphant, and that, in spite of many unfortunate accidents, a love story cannot but end very well indeed. They will have noticed that these love stories which are acted in Hollywood may portray quite regrettable situations at times and that blissful unions get wrecked by all sorts of misfortunes. But they never remain wrecked: even when the happy couple is compelled to divorce, this is not the end of everything. In most cases it is only the beginning. Very soon they will remarry, sometimes with one another, and always—without ever an exception—for love.

The observant foreigner knows, of course, that he cannot trust the movies to give him a really reliable picture of the American attitude towards love, marriage, divorce, and remarriage. But they nevertheless indicate that in such matters the popular mind likes to be entertained by the idea (1) that love is the only reason why a man and a woman should get married; (2) that love is always wholesome, genuine, uplifting, and fresh, like a glass of Grade A milk; (3) that when, for some reason or other, it fails to keep you uplifted, wholesome, and fresh, the only thing to do is to begin all over again with another partner.

Thus forewarned, the foreigner who lands on these shores would be very tactless indeed if he started questioning the validity of these premises. Besides, it is much more likely that he himself will feel thoroughly transformed the moment he takes his first stroll in the streets of New York. His European skepticism will evaporate a little more at each step, and if he considers himself not very young any more he will be immensely gratified to find that maturity and

even old age are merely European habits of thought, and that he
might just as well adopt the American method, which is to be young
and act young for the rest of his life—or at least until the expira-
tion of his visa.

If his hotel room is equipped with a radio, his impression that
he has at last reached the land of eternal youth and perfect love
will be confirmed at any hour of the day and on any point of the
dial. No country in the world consumes such a fabulous amount of
love songs. Whether the song is gay or nostalgic, the tune catchy or
banal, the verses clever or silly, the theme is always love and nothing
but love.

Whenever I go back to France and listen to the radio, I am
always surprised to find that so many songs can be written on other
subjects. I have no statistics on hand, but I think that a good 75
per cent of the songs one hears on the French radio programmes
deal with politics. There are love songs, of course, but most of
them are far from romantic, and this is quite in keeping with the
French point of view that love is very often an exceedingly comical
affair.

In America the idea seems to be that love, like so much else,
should be sold to the public, because it is a good thing. The very
word, when heard indefinitely, becomes an obsession. It penetrates
one's subconsciousness like the name of some unguent to cure heart-
aches or athlete's foot. It fits in with the other advertisements, and
one feels tempted to write to the broadcasting station for a free
sample of this thing called Love.

Thus the visitor from Europe is rapidly permeated with a delightful atmosphere of romanticism and sweetness. He wonders
why Italy and Spain ever acquired their reputation of being the
lands of romance. This, he says to himself, is the home of poetry
and passion. The Americans are the real heirs of the troubadours,
and station WXZQ is their love court.

To discover that all this ballyhoo about love (which is not confined to the radio or the movies) is nothing but an aspect of the
national optimistic outlook on life does not take very long. It
usually becomes evident when the foreign visitor receives the con-
fidences of one or more of the charming American women he will
chance to meet. This normally happens after the first or second
cocktail party to which he has been invited.

II

I wish at this point to enter a plea in defense of the foreign visitor, against whom a great many accusations are often made either in print or in conversation. These accusations fall under two heads. If the foreigner seems to have no definite objective in visiting America, he is strongly suspected of trying to marry an heiress. If for any reason he cannot be suspected of this intention, then his alleged motives are considerably more sinister. Many American men, and quite a few women, believe that the art of wrecking a happy home is not indigenous to this continent, and that in Europe it has been perfected to such a point that to practise it has become a reflex with the visitors from abroad.

It is very true that some foreign visitors come over here to marry for money in exchange for a title or for some sort of glamour. But there are many more foreigners who marry American women for other reasons besides money, and I know quite a few who have become so Americanized that they actually have married for love and for nothing else.

As for the charge that the Europeans are more expert than the Americans in spoiling someone else's marital happiness, it seems to me an unfair accusation. In most cases the initiative of spoiling whatever it is that remains to be spoiled in a shaky marriage is normally taken by one of the married pair, and the wrecker of happiness does not need any special talent to finish the job.

What is quite true, however, is that American woman entertains the delightful illusion that there *must* be some man on this earth who can understand her. It seems incredible to her that love, within legal bonds or outside of them, should not work out as advertised. From her earliest years she has been told that success is the ultimate aim of life. Her father and mother made an obvious success of their lives by creating her. Her husband is, or wants to be, a successful business man. Every day 130,000,000 people are panting and sweating to make a success of something or other. Success—the constant effort to make things work perfectly and the conviction that they can be made to—is the great national preoccupation.

And what does one do to make a success?

Well, the answer is very simple: one learns how, or one consults an expert.

That is what her husband does when he wants to invest his money or improve the efficiency of his business. That is what she did herself when she decided to "decorate" her house. In the American way of life there are no insoluble problems. You may not know the answer yourself, but nobody doubts that the answer exists—that there is some method or perhaps some trick by which all riddles can be solved and success achieved.

And so the European visitor is put to the task on the presumption that the accumulation of experience which he brings with him may qualify him as an expert in questions of sentiment.

The American woman does not want to be understood for the mere fun of it. What she actually wishes is to be helped to solve certain difficulties which, in her judgment, impede the successful development of her inner self. She seldom accepts the idea that maladjustments and misunderstandings are not only normal but bearable once you have made up your mind that, whatever may be the ultimate aim of our earthly existence, perfect happiness through love or any other form of expression is not part of the programme.

III

One of the greatest moral revolutions that ever happened in America was the popularization of Freud's works.

Up to the time that occurred, as far as I am able to judge, America lived in a blissful state of puritanical repression. Love, as a sentiment, was glorified and sanctified by marriage. There was a general impression that some sort of connection existed between the sexual impulses and the vagaries of the heart, but this connection was not emphasized, and the consensus was that the less said about it the better. The way certain nations, and particularly the French, correlated the physical manifestations of love and its more spiritual aspects was considered particularly objectionable. Love, in other words,—and that was not very long ago,—had not changed since the contrary efforts of the puritanically-minded and the romantic had finally stabilized it midway between the sublime and the parlor game.

The important point is that up to then (and ever since the first Pilgrims set foot on this continent) love had been set aside in the general scheme of American life as the one thing which could not be made to work better than it did. Each one had to cope with his own difficulties in his own way and solve them as privately as he could. It was not a national problem.

Whether or not people were happier under that system is beside the point. It probably does not matter very much whether we live and die with or without a full set of childish complexes and repressions. My own view is that most people are neither complex nor repressed enough as a rule; I wish sometimes for the coming of the Anti-Freud who will complicate and obscure everything again.

But the fact is that the revelations of psychoanalysis were greeted in America as the one missing link in the general programme of universal improvement.

Here was a system, at last, that explained fully why love remained so imperfect. It reduced the whole dilemma of happiness to sexual maladjustments, which in turn were only the result of the mistakes made by one's father, mother, or nurse, at an age when one could certainly not be expected to foresee the consequences. Psychoanalysis integrated human emotions into a set of mechanistic formulas. One learned with great relief that the failure to find happiness was not irreparable. Love, as a sublime communion of souls and bodies, was not a legend, nor the mere fancy of the poets. It was real, and—more important still—practically attainable. Anybody could have it, merely by removing a few obstructions which had been growing within himself since childhood like mushrooms in a dark cellar. Love could be made to work like anything else.

It is true that not many people are interested in psychoanalysis any more. As a fad or a parlor game, it is dead. Modern debutantes will not know what you are talking about if you mention the Œdipus complex or refer to the symbolic meaning of umbrellas and top hats in dreams. Traditions die young these days. But the profound effect of the Freudian revelation has lasted. From its materialistic interpretation of sexual impulses, coupled with the American longing for moral perfection, a new science has been born: the dialectics of love; and also a new urge for the American people—they want to turn out, eventually, a perfect product. They want to get out of love as much enjoyment, comfort, safety, and general sense of satisfaction, as one gets out of a well-balanced diet or a good plumbing installation.

IV

Curiously enough, this fairly new point of view which implies that human relationships are governed by scientific laws has not destroyed the romantic ideal of love. Quite the contrary. Malad-

justments, now that they are supposed to be scientifically determined, have become much more unbearable than in the horse-and-
buggy age of love. Husbands and wives and lovers have no patience
with their troubles. They want to be cured, and when they think
they are incurable they become very intolerant. Reformers always
are.

Usually, however, various attempts at readjustment are made
with devastating candor. Married couples seem to spend many
precious hours of the day and night discussing what is wrong
with their relationship. The general idea is that—according to the
teachings of most modern psychologists and pedagogues—one
should face the truth fearlessly. Husbands and wives should be
absolutely frank with one another, on the assumption that if love
between them is real it will be made stronger and more real still if
submitted, at frequent intervals, to the test of complete sincerity
on both sides.

This is a fine theory, but it has seldom been practised without
disastrous results. There are several reasons why this should be so.
First of all, truth is an explosive, and it should be handled with
care, especially in marital life. It is not necessary to lie, but there
is little profit in juggling with hand grenades just to show how
brave one is. Secondly, the theory of absolute sincerity presupposes
that, if love cannot withstand continuous blasting, then it is not
worth saving anyway. Some people want their love life to be a
permanent battle of Verdun. When the system of defense is destroyed beyond repair, then the clause of hopeless maladjustment
is invoked by one side, or by both. The next thing to do is to divorce,
and find someone else to be recklessly frank with for a season.

Another reason why the method of adjustment through truth-
telling is not always wise is that it develops fiendish traits of character which might otherwise remain dormant.

I know a woman whose eyes glitter with virtuous self-satisfaction
every time she has had a "real heart-to-heart talk" with her husband, which means that she has spent several hours torturing him,
or at best boring him to distraction, with a ruthless exposure of
the deplorable status of their mutual relationship to date. She is
usually so pleased with herself after these periodical inquests that
she tells most of her friends, and also her coiffeur, about it. "Dick
and I had such a wonderful time last evening. We made a real effort
to find out the real truth about each other—or, at least, I certainly

did. I honestly believe we have found a new basis of adjustment for ourselves. What a marvelous feeling that is—don't you think so?"

Dick, of course, if he happens to be present, looks rather nervous or glum, but that is not the point. The point is that Dick's wife feels all aglow because she has done her bit in the general campaign for the improvement of marital happiness through truth. She has been a good girl scout.

A man of my acquaintance, who believes in experimenting outside of wedlock, is unable to understand why his wife would rather ignore his experiments. "If I did not love her and if she did not love me," he argues, "I could accept her point of view. But why can't she see that the very fact that I want her to know everything I do is proof that I love her? If I have to deceive her or conceal things from her, what is the use of being married to her?"

Be it said, in passing, that this unfortunate husband believes that these extra-marital "experiments" are absolutely necessary to prevent him from developing a sense of inferiority, which, if allowed to grow, would destroy not only the love he has for his wife, but also his general ability in his dealings with the outside world.

V

The difference between an American cookbook and a French one is that the former is very accurate and the second exceedingly vague. A French recipe seldom tells you how many ounces of butter to use to make *crêpes Suzette,* or how many spoonfuls of oil should go into a salad dressing. French cookbooks are full of esoteric measurements such as a *pinch* of pepper, a *suspicion* of garlic, or a *generous sprinkling* of brandy. There are constant references to seasoning to *taste,* as if the recipe were merely intended to give a general direction, relying on the experience and innate art of the cook to make the dish turn out right.

American recipes look like doctors' prescriptions. Perfect cooking seems to depend on perfect dosage. Some of these books give you a table of calories and vitamins—as if that had anything to do with the problem of eating well!

In the same way, there is now flourishing in America a great crop of books which offer precise recipes for the things you should do, or avoid doing, in order to achieve happiness and keep the fires of love at a constant temperature. In a recent issue of *Time* maga-

zine, four such books were reviewed together. Their titles are descriptive enough of the purpose of the authors as well as the state
of mind of the readers: *Love and Happiness, So You're Going to
Get Married, Marriages Are Made at Home, Getting Along Together.*

I have not read all these books, but, according to the reviewer,
they all tend to give practical answers to the same mysterious problem of living with someone of the opposite sex. They try to establish sets of little rules and little tricks which will guarantee marital
bliss if carefully followed, in the same way that cookbooks guarantee
that you will obtain pumpkin pie if you use the proper ingredients
properly measured.

As the publisher of one of these books says on the jacket: "There
is nothing in this book about the complicated psychological problems
that send men and women to psychoanalysts, but there is a lot in it
about the little incidents of daily married life—the things that happen in the parlor, bedroom and bath—that handled one way enable people to live together happily forever after, and handled another way lead to Reno."

Time's review of these books is very gloomy in its conclusion:
"Despite their optimistic tone," it says, "the four volumes give a
troubled picture of United States domestic life—a world in which
husbands are amorous when wives are not, and vice versa; where
conflicts spring up over reading in bed or rumpling the evening
paper . . . the whole grim panorama giving the impression that
Americans are irritable, aggravated, dissatisfied people for whom
marriage is an ordeal that only heroes and heroines can bear."

But I believe that the editors of *Time* would be just as dejected
if they were reviewing four volumes about American cooking, and
for the same reasons. You cannot possibly feel cheerful when you
see the art of love or the art of eating thus reduced to such automatic formulas, even if the experts in these matters are themselves
cheerful and optimistic. Good food, the pleasures of love, and those
of marriage depend on imponderables, individual taste, and no
small amount of luck.

VI

Thus the problem of love in America seems to be the resultant
of conflicting and rather unrealistic ways of approaching it. Too
many songs, too many stories, too many pictures, and too much
romance on the one hand, and too much practical advice on the

other. It is as if the experience of being in love could only be one of two things: a superhuman ecstasy, the way of reaching heaven on earth and in pairs; or a psychopathic condition to be treated by specialists.

Between these two extremes there is little room for compromise. That the relationship between men and women offers a wide scale of variations seldom occurs to the experts. It is not necessarily true that there is but one form of love worth bothering about, and that if you cannot get the de luxe model, with a life guarantee of perfect functioning, nothing else is worth-while. It is not true either that you can indefinitely pursue the same quest for perfection, or that if a man and a woman have not found ideal happiness together they will certainly find it with somebody else. Life unfortunately does not begin at forty, and when you reach that age, in America or anywhere else, to go on complaining about your sentimental or physiological maladjustments becomes slightly farcical.

It is not easy, nor perhaps of any use, to draw any conclusion from all this, especially for a European who has lost the fresh point of view of the visitor because he lives here, and who is not quite sure of what it means to be a European any more. I sometimes wonder if there is any real difference between the way men and women get along—or do not get along—together on this side of the Atlantic and on the other. There are probably no more real troubles here than anywhere else. Human nature being quite remarkably stable, why should there be? But there is no doubt that the revolt against this type of human inadequacy is very strong indeed here, especially among the woman who imagine that the Europeans have found better ways of managing their heart and their senses than the Americans.

If this is at all true, I believe the reason is to be found in a more philosophical attitude on the part of the Europeans towards such matters. There are no theories about marital bliss, no recipes to teach you how to solve difficulties which, in the Old World, are accepted as part of the common inheritance.

Men and women naturally want to be happy over there, and, if possible, with the help of one another; but they learn very young that compromise is not synonymous with defeat. Even in school (I am speaking more particularly of France now) they are taught, through the literature of centuries, that love is a phenomenon susceptible of innumerable variations, but that—even under the best circumstances—it is so intertwined with the other experiences of each individual life that to be overromantic or too dogmatic about it is of little practical use. *"La vérité est dans les nuances,"* wrote Benjamin Constant, who knew a good deal about such matters.

And, speaking of the truly practical and realistic nature of love, it is a very strange thing that American literature contains no work of any note, nor even essays, on love as a psychological phenomenon. I know of no good study of the process of falling in and out of love, an analytical description of jealousy, coquettishness, or the development of tediousness. No classification of the various brands of love such as La Rochefoucauld, Pascal, Stendhal, Proust, and many others have elaborated has been attempted from the American angle. The interesting combinations of such passions as ambition, jealousy, religious fervor, and so forth, with love are only dimly perceived by most people and even by the novelists, who, with very few exceptions, seem to ignore or scorn these complicated patterns. These fine studies have been left to the psychiatrists, the charlatans, or the manufacturers of naïve recipes.

The reason for this neglect on the part of real thinkers and essayists may be that for a long time the standards imposed by the puritanical point of view made the whole study more or less taboo with respectable authors. And then the Freudian wave came along and carried the whole problem out of reach of the amateur observer and the artist. In other words, conditions have been such that there has been no occasion to fill this curious gap in American literature.

Of course, nothing is lost. The field remains open, and there is no reason to suppose that love in America will not cease to be a national problem, a hunting ground for the reformer, and that it will not become, as everywhere else, a personal affair very much worth the effort it takes to examine it as such. All that is necessary is for someone to forget for a while love as Hollywood—or the professor—sees it, and sit down and think about it as an eternally fascinating subject for purely human observation.

QUESTIONS ON CONTENT

1. What similarity does the author find between love and democracy?
2. Hollywood taught the author what lessons about love in America?
3. Are his observations concerning Hollywood's three teachings on the subject of love and marriage correct? Explain.

4. How do the French and Americans differ in the amount and kind of love put into songs?
5. What connection does the author find between the American belief in success and the problem of making love work?
6. Explain the last sentence of the second paragraph of section III.
7. Why does the author think Freud is responsible for the shift in America's attitude toward love (section III)?
8. Does the author recommend that married couples be utterly frank with each other? Discuss.
9. Is there any significance in the difference between a French and an American cookbook? How does the author apply this analogy?
10. What is the author's chief recommendation about making love work?

❧ Courtship Through the Ages

JAMES THURBER

Surely nothing in the astonishing scheme of life can have nonplussed Nature so much as the fact that none of the females of any of the species she created really cared very much for the male, as such. For the past ten million years Nature has been busily inventing ways to make the male attractive to the female, but the whole business of courtship, from the marine annelids up to man, still lumbers heavily along, like a complicated musical comedy. I have been reading the sad and absorbing story in Volume 6 (Cole to Dama) of the *Encyclopedia Britannica*. In this volume you can learn all about cricket, cotton, costume designing, crocodiles, crown jewels, and Coleridge, but none of these subjects is so interesting as the Courtship of Animals, which recounts the sorrowful lengths to which all males must go to arouse the interest of a lady.

We all know, I think, that Nature gave man whiskers and a mustache with the quaint idea in mind that these would prove attractive to the female. We all know that, far from attracting her, whiskers and mustaches only made her nervous and gloomy, so that man had to go in for somersaults, tilting with lances, and performing feats of parlor magic to win her attention; he also had to bring

Permission the author. © 1939 James Thurber. Originally in *The New Yorker*.

her candy, flowers and the fur of animals. It is common knowledge that in spite of all these "love displays" the male is constantly being turned down, insulted, or thrown out of the house. It is rather comforting, then, to discover that the peacock, for all his gorgeous plumage, does not have a particularly easy time in courtship; none of the males in the world do. The first peahen, it turned out, was only faintly stirred by her suitor's beautiful train. She would often go quietly to sleep while he was whisking it around. The *Britannica* tells us that the peacock actually had to learn a certain little trick to wake her up and revive her interest: he had to learn to vibrate his quills so as to make a rustling sound. In ancient times man himself, observing the ways of the peacock, probably tried vibrating his whiskers to make a rustling sound; if so, it didn't get him anywhere. He had to go in for something else; so, among other things, he went in for gifts. It is not unlikely that he got this idea from certain flies and birds who were making no headway at all with rustling sounds.

One of the flies of the family Empidae, who had tried everything, finally hit on something pretty special. He contrived to make a glistening transparent balloon which was even larger than himself. Into this he would put sweetmeats and tidbits and he would carry the whole elaborate envelope through the air to the lady of his choice. This amused her for a time, but she finally got bored with it. She demanded silly little colorful presents, something that you couldn't eat but that would look nice around the house. So the male Empis had to go around gathering flower petals and pieces of bright paper to put into his balloon. On a courtship flight a male Empis cuts quite a figure now, but he can hardly be said to be happy. He never knows how soon the female will demand heavier presents, such as Roman coins and gold collar buttons. It seems probable that one day the courtship of the Empidae will fall down, as man's occasionally does, of it own weight.

The bowerbird is another creature that spends so much time courting the female that he never gets any work done. If all the male bowerbirds became nervous wrecks within the next ten or fifteen years, it would not surprise me. The female bowerbird insists that a playground be built for her with a specially constructed bower at the entrance. This bower is much more elaborate than an ordinary nest and is harder to build; it costs a lot more, too. The female will not come to the playground until the male has filled it up with a great many gifts: silvery leaves, red leaves, rose petals, shells, beads, berries, bones, dice, buttons, cigar bands, Christmas seals, and the

Lord knows what else. When the female finally condescends to visit the playground, she is in a coy and silly mood and has to be chased in and out of the bower and up and down the playground before she will quit giggling and stand still long enough even to shake hands. The male bird is, of course, pretty well done in before the chase starts, because he has worn himself out hunting for eye glass lenses and begonia blossoms. I imagine that many a bowerbird, after chasing a female for two or three hours, says the hell with it and goes home to bed. Next day, of course, he telephones someone else and the same trying ritual is gone through with again. A male bowerbird is as exhausted as a night-club habitué before he is out of his twenties.

The male fiddler crab has a somewhat easier time, but it can hardly be said that he is sitting pretty. He has one enormously large and powerful claw, usually brilliantly colored, and you might suppose that all he had to do was reach out and grab some passing cutie. The very earliest fiddler crabs may have tried this, but, if so, they got slapped for their pains. A female fiddler crab will not tolerate any cave-man stuff; she never has and she doesn't intend to start now. To attract a female, a fiddler crab has to stand on tiptoe and brandish his claw in the air. If any female in the neighborhood is interested—and you'd be surprised how many are not—she comes over and engages him in light badinage, for which he is not in the mood. As many as a hundred females may pass the time of day with him and go on about their business. By nightfall of an average courting day, a fiddler crab who has been standing on tiptoe for eight or ten hours waving a heavy claw in the air is in pretty sad shape. As in the case of the males of all species, however, he gets out of bed next morning, dashes some water on his face, and tries again.

The next time you encounter a male web-spinning spider, stop and reflect that he is too busy worrying about his love life to have any desire to bite you. Male web-spinning spiders have a tougher life than any other males in the animal kingdom. This is because the female web-spinning spiders have very poor eyesight. If a male lands on a female's web, she kills him before he has time to lay down his cane and gloves, mistaking him for a fly or a bumblebee who has stumbled into her trap. Before the species figured out what to do about this, millions of males were murdered by ladies they called on. It is the nature of spiders to perform a little dance in front of the female, but before a male spinner could get near enough for the female to see who he was and what he was up to, she would lash out at him with a flat-iron or a pair of garden shears. One night, nobody knows when, a very bright male spinner lay awake worrying about calling on a lady who had been killing suitors right and left. It came to him that this business of dancing as a love display wasn't getting anybody anywhere except the grave. He decided to go in for web-twitching, or strand-vibrating. The next day he tried it on one of the nearsighted girls. Instead of dropping in on her suddenly, he stayed outside the web and began monkeying with one of its strands. He twitched it up and down and in and out with such a lilting rhythm that the female was charmed. The serenade worked beautifully; the female let him live. The *Britannica's* spider-watchers, however, report that this system is not always successful. Once in a while, even now, a female will fire three bullets into a suitor or run him through with a kitchen knife. She keeps threatening him from the moment he strikes the first low notes on the outside strings, but usually by the time he has got up to the high notes played around the center of the web, he is going to town and she spares his life.

Even the butterfly, as handsome a fellow as he is, can't always win a mate merely by fluttering around and showing off. Many butterflies have to have scent scales on their wings. Hepialus carries a powder puff in a perfumed pouch. He throws perfume at the ladies when they pass. The male tree cricket, Oecanthus, goes Hepialus one better by carrying a tiny bottle of wine with him and giving drinks to such doxies as he has designs on. One of the male snails throws darts to entertain the girls. So it goes, through the long list of animals, from the bristle worm and his rudimentary dance steps to man and his gift of diamonds and sapphires. The golden-eye drake raises a jet of water with his feet as he flies over a lake; Hepialus has his powder puff, Oecanthus his wine bottle, man his etchings. It is a bright and melancholy story, the age-old desire of the male for the female, the age-old desire of the female to be amused and entertained. Of all the creatures on earth, the only males who could be figured as putting any irony into their courtship are the grebes and certain other diving birds. Every now and then a courting grebe slips quietly down to the bottom of a lake and then, with a mighty "Whoosh!", pops out suddenly a few feet from his girl friend, splashing water all over her. She seems to be persuaded that this is a purely loving display, but I like to think that the grebe always has a faint hope of drowning her or scaring her to death.

I will close this investigation into the mournful burdens of the male with the *Britannica's* story about a certain Argus pheasant. It appears that the Argus displays himself in front of a female who stands perfectly still without moving a feather. (If you saw "June Moon" some years ago and remember the scene in which the song-writer sang "Montana Moon" to his grim and motionless wife, you have some idea what the female Argus probably thinks of her mate's display.) The male Argus the *Britannica* tells about was confined in a cage with a female of another species, a female who kept moving around, emptying ash-trays and fussing with lampshades all the time the male was showing off his talents. Finally, in disgust, he stalked away and began displaying in front of his water trough. He reminds me of a certain male (Homo sapiens) of my acquaintance who one night after dinner asked his wife to put down her detective magazine so that he could read her a poem of which he was very fond. She sat quietly enough until he was well into the middle of the thing, in-toning with great ardor and intensity. Then suddenly there came a sharp, disconcerting *slap!* It turned out that all during the male's dis-play, the female had been intent on a circling mosquito and had finally trapped it between the palms of her hands. The male in this case did not stalk away and display in front of a water trough; he went over to Tim's and had a flock of drinks and recited the poem to the fellas. I am sure they all told bitter stories of their own about how their displays had been interrupted by females. I am also sure that they all ended up singing "Honey, Honey, Bless Your Heart."

QUESTIONS ON CONTENT

1. Although this piece is concerned with animals, how can it be proved that the author is constantly thinking of men and women? Cite passages to prove that this is so.
2. What is the one thing apparently held in common by male ani-mals? By female animals? To what extent are these characteristics those of men and women, too?
3. How much use is made of exaggeration? Of understatement? Cite examples of both.
4. Is it apparent with which sex the author sympathizes? Explain.

SUGGESTIONS FOR PAPERS

You may already be a partner in a marriage enterprise. The chances are, however, that so far you are still a bystander, one who has observed at least one marriage at close range and who has already developed some rather definite ideas about alliances between males and females. Whatever your status, you cannot very well avoid this ubiquitous concern of all human beings. Your views will take shape from contact with what others in the selections of this chapter have to say on the subject of love and marriage.

1. What sort of person would fit your ideal as a partner in marriage? Consider the relative importance of the following ingredients: beauty, intelligence, disposition, social position, money, community of tastes (in what specific things?). Now, where do you place *love*? Does it affect your other demands?

2. Stevenson believes that marriage is less beneficial to men than to women. What are his reasons for thinking so? State your reasons for agreeing or disagreeing with him.

3. Stevenson says that the chief advantage of marriage is comfort and the chief disadvantage the quelling of "the fine wildings in the husband's heart." Examine this point of view; admit or attack the truth of it. Agreement may be qualified by skepticism concerning the fineness of the "wildings" in a husband's heart.

4. Stevenson apparently feels that marriage is an attitude and that "if you have made up your mind to it, and once talked yourself fairly over, you could 'pull it through' with anybody." Upon what would "pulling it through" depend?

5. Make a list of all Stevenson's recommendations concerning marriage requirements. Are they all related to undisturbed comfort? Which items on the list seem most important? Less and least important?

6. What kind of person is the speaker in "When I Was One-and-Twenty"? What kind of person did he marry? Did he marry for love? Or, do you believe that he was jilted? Why, perhaps, did he fail to "pull through"? All your answers will depend partly upon imagination and partly upon a close reading of the poem.

7. Compare "On Marriage" and "Love in America" on the following points concerning marriage: love as a necessary ingredient; the value of compromise; the need for community of interests.

8. Analyze "Courtship Through the Ages." What is the author's central point? How does he make this point clear through examples? Cite several. How does he make clear the analogy he has in mind between the courtship of animals and the courtship of men and women?

9. Look up the article in the *Encyclopedia Brittanica* from which

Thurber took his facts. Compare a half dozen of these facts as stated in the scientific article with the same facts as treated by Thurber. Now, refer to De Quincey's "The Literature of Knowledge and the Literature of Power," and show how this sort of comparison bears out De Quincey's distinction.

10. Show how apropos is the analogy in "Love in America" between French ideas of cooking and French ideas of love and marriage on the one hand and American ideas of cooking and American ideas of love and marriage on the other.

SOME TITLES FOR PAPERS

1. Ideal Marriage
2. Relative Success in Marriage
3. Can Love Survive Marriage?
4. Comfort Versus the Heroic
5. Some Advice about Marriage
6. Marriage Is an Attitude
7. Curious Combinations in Marriage
8. Some Observations on the Marriage I Know Best
9. Why I Choose Single Blessedness
10. Old Maids and Old Bachelors: A Comparison
11. Compromise: The Key to Successful Marriage
12. Can Love Always Survive the Truth?
13. Marriage Demands Rose-tinted Glasses
14. Nobody Listens to Advice about Marriage
15. The French Idea of Marriage as Gleaned from "Love in America"
16. The Hollywood Conception of Love and Marriage (with current examples)
17. An Analysis of Love as Seen by Popular Song Writers (with current examples)
18. Advice to the Lovelorn (with current examples)
19. Demand for Success Makes Many Marriages Fail
20. Married Couples I Have Known

❧ WOMEN AND MEN

IT HAS BEEN REPORTED that the New York Public Library contains more than ten thousand titles of books about women. The male as a male, and not as the generic representative of mankind, has been the subject of only a few hundred books. Most of the literature about women (1) is written by men and (2) is concerned with the mystery of feminine thinking and acting. That the mystery persists is perhaps a compliment to the adroitness of women. One part of this adroitness may doubtless be attributed to a selective reticence: women seldom indulge in autobiography and never in one so revealing as that of, say, Rousseau. Moreover, women never seem to find men a mystery and therefore are credited with intuition, a mysterious power!

The attitude of male writers on women ranges from the adoration of the poets (with notable exceptions) to the acidity of the philosophers. Schopenhauer represents the latter in his opinions "On Women." In the first paragraph of this essay, he quickly disposes of women's virtues and then devotes himself to the thesis that women "form the *sexus sequior*—the second sex, inferior in every respect to the first." He stresses the inability of women to be "perfectly truthful." John Donne in "Go and Catch a Falling Star" vigorously supports a corollary of this view by naming a number of impossible exploits, the least possible of which would be the discovery of "a woman true, and fair."

Schopenhauer was a German philosopher and Donne an English

poet. Both were concerned with what they assumed to be the characteristics of all members of the female sex. At this point, it is time for someone to take up the defense of women. A transplanted Englishman, now an American citizen, Ashley Montagu, does this in his article, "The Natural Superiority of Women." You will decide whether or not the author has successfully changed the standards which in the past have been used to support the claims of male superiority.

Thomas Hardy, with a fine impartiality, first condemns the hypocrisy of a male ("In Church") and then the vanity and callousness of the female ("At the Draper's"). Is it inaccurate to say that Hardy "condemns"? What would be a better word?

 # On Women

Arthur Schopenhauer

Schiller's poem in honour of women, *Würde der Frauen,* is the result of much careful thought, and it appeals to the reader by its antithetic style and its use of contrast; but as an expression of the true praise which should be accorded to them, it is, I think, inferior to these few words of Jouy's: *Without women the beginning of our life would be helpless; the middle, devoid of pleasure; and the end, of consolation.* The same thing is more feelingly expressed by Byron in *Sardanapalus:—*

> The very first
> Of human life must spring from woman's breast,
> Your first small words are taught you from her lips,
> Your first tears quench'd by her, and your last sighs
> Too often breathed out in a woman's hearing,
> When men have shrunk from the ignoble care
> Of watching the last hour of him who led them.
> (Act I, Scene 2.)

These two passages indicate the right standpoint for the appreciation of women.

You need only look at the way in which she is formed to see that

Reprinted from *Schopenhauer Selections,* edited by DeWitt H. Parker; copyright 1928 by Charles Scribner's Sons; used by permission of the publisher.

woman is not meant to undergo great labour, whether of the mind or of the body. She pays the debt of life not by what she does but by what she suffers; by the pains of childbearing and care for the child, and by submission to her husband, to whom she should be a patient and cheering companion. The keenest sorrows and joys are not for her, nor is she called upon to display a great deal of strength. The current of her life should be more gentle, peaceful and trivial than man's, without being essentially happier or unhappier.

Women are directly fitted for acting as the nurses and teachers of our early childhood by the fact that they are themselves childish, frivolous and short-sighted; in a word, they are big children all their life long—a kind of intermediate stage between the child and the full-grown man, who is man in the strict sense of the word. See how a girl will fondle a child for days together, dance with it and sing to it; and then think what a man, with the best will in the world, could do if he were put in her place.

With young girls Nature seems to have had in view what, in the language of the drama, is called *a coup de théâtre*. For a few years she dowers them with a wealth of beauty and is lavish in her gift of charm, at the expense of the rest of their life, in order that during those years they may capture the fantasy of some man to such a degree that he is hurried into undertaking the honourable care of them, in some form or other, as long as they live—a step for which there would not appear to be any sufficient warranty if reason only directed his thoughts. Accordingly Nature has equipped woman, as she does all her creatures, with the weapons and implements requisite for the safeguarding of her existence, and for just as long as it is necessary for her to have them. Here, as elsewhere, Nature proceeds with her usual economy; for just as the female ant, after fecundation, loses her wings, which are then superfluous, nay, actually a danger to the business of breeding; so, after giving birth to one or two children, a woman generally loses her beauty; probably, indeed, for similar reasons.

And so we find that young girls, in their hearts, look upon domestic affairs or work of any kind as of secondary importance, if not actually as a mere jest. The only business that really claims their attention is love, making conquests, and everything connected with this—dress, dancing, and so on.

The nobler and more perfect a thing is, the later and slower it is in arriving at maturity. A man reaches the maturity of his reasoning powers and mental faculties hardly before the age of twenty-eight; a woman, at eighteen. And then, too, in the case of woman, it is only reason of a sort—very niggard in its dimensions. That is why women remain children their whole life long; never seeing anything but what is quite close to them, cleaving to the present moment, taking appearance for reality, and preferring trifles to matters of the first importance. For it is by virtue of his reasoning faculty that man does not live in the present only, like the brute, but looks about him and considers the past and the future; and this is the origin of prudence, as well as of that care and anxiety which so many people exhibit. Both the advantages and the disadvantages which this involves, are shared in by the woman to a smaller extent because of her weaker power of reasoning. She may, in fact, be described as intellectually shortsighted, because, while she has an intuitive understanding of what lies quite close to her, her field of vision is narrow and does not reach to what is remote: so that things which are absent or past or to come have much less effect upon women than upon men. This is the reason why women are more often inclined to be extravagant, and sometimes carry their inclination to a length that borders upon madness. In their hearts women think that it is men's business to earn money and theirs to spend it—if possible during their husband's life, but, at any rate, after his death. The very fact that their husband hands them over his earnings for purposes of housekeeping strengthens them in this belief.

However many disadvantages all this may involve, there is at least this to be said in its favour: that the woman lives more in the present than the man, and that, if the present is at all tolerable, she enjoys it more eagerly. This is the source of that cheerfulness which is peculiar to woman, fitting her to amuse man in his hours of recreation, and, in case of need, to console him when he is borne down by the weight of his cares.

It is by no means a bad plan to consult women in matters of difficulty, as the Germans used to do in ancient times; for their way of looking at things is quite different from ours, chiefly in the fact that they like to take the shortest way to their goal, and, in general, manage to fix their eyes upon what lies before them; while we, as a rule, see far beyond it, just because it is in front of our noses. In cases like this, we need to be brought back to the right standpoint, so as to recover the near and simple view.

Then, again, women are decidedly more sober in their judgment than we are, so that they do not see more in things than is really there; whilst, if our passions are aroused, we are apt to see things in an exaggerated way, or imagine what does not exist.

The weakness of their reasoning faculty also explains why it is that women show more sympathy for the unfortunate than men do, and so treat them with more kindness and interest; and why it is that, on the contrary, they are inferior to men in point of justice, and less honourable and conscientious. For it is just because their reasoning power is weak that present circumstances have such a hold over them, and those concrete things which lie directly before their eyes exercise a power which is seldom counteracted to any extent by abstract principles of thought, by fixed rules of conduct, firm resolutions, or, in general, by consideration for the past and the future, or regard for what is absent and remote. Accordingly, they possess the first and main elements that go to make a virtuous character, but they are deficient in those secondary qualities which are often a necessary instrument in the formation of it.

Hence it will be found that the fundamental fault of the female character is that it has *no sense of justice*. This is mainly due to the fact, already mentioned, that women are defective in the powers of reasoning and deliberation; but it is also traceable to the position which Nature has assigned to them as the weaker sex. They are dependent, not upon strength, but upon craft; and hence their instinctive capacity for cunning, and their ineradicable tendency to say what is not true. For as lions are provided with claws and teeth, and elephants and boars with tusks, bulls with horns, and the cuttle fish with its cloud of inky fluid, so Nature has equipped woman, for her defence and protection, with the arts of dissimulation; and all the power which Nature has conferred upon man in the shape of physical strength and reason has been bestowed upon women in this form. Hence dissimulation is innate in woman, and almost as much a quality of the stupid as of the clever. It is as natural for them to make use of it on every occasion as it is for animals to employ their means of defence when they are attacked; they have a feeling that in doing so they are only within their rights. Therefore a woman who is perfectly truthful and not given to dissimulation is perhaps an impossibility, and for this very reason they are so quick at seeing through dissimulation in others that it is not a wise thing to attempt it with them. But this fundamental defect which I have stated, with all that it entails, gives rise to falsity, faithlessness, treachery, ingratitude, and so on. Perjury in a court of justice is more often committed by women than by men. It may, indeed, be generally questioned whether women ought to be sworn at all. From time to time one finds repeated cases everywhere of ladies, who want for nothing, taking things from shop-counters when no one is looking and making off with them.

Nature has appointed that the propagation of the species shall be the business of men who are young, strong and handsome; so that the race may not degenerate. This is the firm will and purpose of Nature in regard to the species, and it finds its expression in the passions of women. There is no law that is older or more powerful than this. Woe, then, to the man who sets up claims and interests that will conflict with it; whatever he may say and do, they will be unmercifully crushed at the first serious encounter. For the innate rule that governs women's conduct, though it is secret and unformulated, nay, unconscious in its working, is this: *We are justified in deceiving those who think they have acquired rights over the species by paying little attention to the individual, that is, to us. The constitution and, therefore, the welfare of the species have been placed in our hands and committed to our care, through the control we obtain over the next generation, which proceeds from us; let us discharge our duties conscientiously.* But women have no abstract knowledge of this leading principle; they are conscious of it only as a concrete fact; and they have no other method of giving expression to it than the way in which they act when the opportunity arrives. And then their conscience does not trouble them so much as we fancy; for in the darkest recesses of their heart they are aware that, in committing a breach of their duty towards the individual, they have all the better fulfilled their duty towards the species, which is infinitely greater.

And since women exist in the main solely for the propagation of the species, and are not destined for anything else, they live, as a rule, more for the species than for the individual, and in their hearts take the affairs of the species more seriously than those of the individual. This gives their whole life and being a certain levity; the general bent of their character is in a direction fundamentally different from that of man; and it is this which produces that discord in married life which is so frequent, and almost the normal state.

The natural feeling between men is mere indifference, but between women it is actual enmity. The reason of this is that trade-jealousy which, in the case of men, does not go beyond the confines of their own particular pursuit but with women embraces the whole sex; since they have only one kind of business. Even when they meet in the street women look at one another like Guelphs and Ghibellines. And it is a patent fact that when two women make first acquaintance with each other they behave with more constraint and dissimulation than two men would show in a like case; and hence it is that an exchange of compliments between two women is a much more ridiculous proceeding than between two men. Further, whilst a man will, as a general rule, always preserve a certain amount of consideration and humanity in speaking to others, even to those who are in a very inferior position, it is intolerable to see how proudly and disdainfully a fine lady will generally behave towards one who is in a lower social rank (I do not mean a woman who is in her service), whenever she speaks to her. The reason of this may be that, with women, differences of rank are much more precarious than with us; because, while a hundred considerations carry weight in our case, in theirs there is only one, namely, with which man they have found favour; as also that they stand in much nearer relations with one another than men do, in consequence of the one-sided nature of their calling. This makes them endeavour to lay stress upon differences of rank.

It is only the man whose intellect is clouded by his sexual impulses that could give the name of *the fair sex* to that undersized, narrow-shouldered, broad-hipped, and short-legged race: for the whole beauty of the sex is bound up with this impulse. Instead of calling them beautiful, there would be more warrant for describing women as the unæsthetic sex. Neither for music, nor for poetry, nor for fine art, have they really and truly any sense or susceptibility; it is a mere mockery if they make a pretence of it in order to assist their endeavour to please. Hence, as a result of this, they are incapable of taking a *purely objective interest* in anything; and the reason of it seems to me to be as follows. A man tries to acquire *direct* mastery over things, either by understanding them or by forcing them to do his will. But a woman is always and everywhere reduced to obtaining this mastery *indirectly*, namely through a man; and whatever direct mastery she may have is entirely confined to him. And so it lies in woman's nature to look upon everything only as a means for conquering man; and if she takes an interest in anything else it is simulated—a mere roundabout way of gaining her ends by coquetry and feigning what she does not feel. Hence even Rousseau declared: *Women have, in general, no love of any art; they have no proper knowledge of any; and they have no genius.*

No one who sees at all below the surface can have failed to remark the same thing. You need only observe the kind of attention
women bestow upon a concert, an opera, or a play—the childish
simplicity, for example, with which they keep on chattering during
the finest passages in the greatest masterpieces. If it is true that the
Greeks excluded women from their theatres, they were quite right
in what they did; at any rate you would have been able to hear what
was said upon the stage. In our day, besides, or in lieu of saying,
Let a woman keep silence in the church, it would be much to the
point to say, *Let a woman keep silence in the theatre.* This might,
perhaps, be put up in big letters on the curtain.

And you cannot expect anything else of women if you consider
that the most distinguished intellects among the whole sex have
never managed to produce a single achievement in the fine arts that
is really great, genuine, and original; or given to the world any work
of permanent value in any sphere. This is most strikingly shown in
regard to painting, where mastery of technique is at least as much
within their power as within ours—and hence they are diligent in
cultivating it; but still, they have not a single great painting to boast
of, just because they are deficient in that objectivity of mind which
is so directly indispensable in painting. They never get beyond a
subjective point of view. It is quite in keeping with this that ordinary
women have no real susceptibility for art at all; for Nature proceeds
in strict sequence—*non facit saltum.* The case is not altered by particular and partial exceptions; taken as a whole, women are, and remain, thorough-going philistines, and quite incurable. Hence, with
that absurd arrangement which allows them to share the rank and
title of their husbands, they are a constant stimulus to his ignoble
ambitions. And, further, it is just because they are philistines that
modern society, where they take the lead and set the tone, is in such
a bad way. Napoleon's saying—that *women have no rank*—should
be adopted as the right standpoint in determining their position in
society; and as regards their other qualities Chamfort makes the
very true remark: *They are made to trade with our own weaknesses
and our follies, but not with our reason. The sympathies that exist
between them and men are skin-deep only, and do not touch the
mind or the feelings or the character.* They form the *sexus sequior*—
the second sex, inferior in every respect to the first; their infirmities
should be treated with consideration; but to show them great reverence is extremely ridiculous, and lowers us in their eyes. When
nature made two divisions of the human race, she did not draw the

line exactly through the middle. These divisions are polar and opposed to each other, it is true; but the difference between them is not qualitative merely, it is also quantitative.

This is just the view which the ancients took of woman, and the view which people in the East take now; and their judgment as to her proper position is much more correct than ours, with our old French notions of gallantry and our preposterous system of reverence—that highest product of Teutonico-Christian stupidity. These notions have served only to make women more arrogant and overbearing; so that one is occasionally reminded of the holy apes of Benares, who in consciousness of their sanctity and inviolable position think they can do exactly as they please.

But in the West the woman, and especially the *lady*, finds herself in a false position; for woman, rightly called by the ancients *sexus sequior,* is by no means fit to be the object of our honour and veneration, or to hold her head higher than man and be on equal terms with him. The consequences of this false position are sufficiently obvious. Accordingly it would be a very desirable thing if this Number Two of the human race were in Europe also relegated to her natural place, and an end put to that lady-nuisance, which not only moves all Asia to laughter but would have been ridiculed by Greece and Rome as well. It is impossible to calculate the good effects which such a change would bring about in our social, civil and political arrangements. There would be no necessity for the Salic law: it would be a superfluous truism. In Europe the *lady*, strictly so-called, is a being who should not exist at all; she should be either a housewife or a girl who hopes to become one; and she should be brought up, not to be arrogant, but to be thrifty and submissive. It is just because there are such people as *ladies* in Europe that the women of the lower classes, that is to say, the great majority of the sex, are much more unhappy than they are in the East. And even Lord Byron says: *Thought of the state of women under the ancient Greeks —convenient enough. Present state, a remnant of the barbarism of the chivalric and the feudal ages—artificial and unnatural. They ought to mind home—and be well fed and clothed—but not mixed in society. Well educated, too, in religion—but to read neither poetry nor politics—nothing but books of piety and cookery. Music—drawing—dancing—also a little gardening and ploughing now and then. I have seen them mending the roads in Epirus with good success. Why not, as well as hay-making and milking?*

The laws of marriage prevailing in Europe consider the woman as the equivalent of the man—start, that is to say, from a wrong position. In our part of the world where monogamy is the rule, to marry means to halve one's rights and double one's duties. Now when the laws gave women equal rights with man, they ought to have also endowed her with a masculine intellect. But the fact is that, just in proportion as the honours and privileges which the laws accord to women exceed the amount which Nature gives, there is a diminution in the number of women who really participate in these privileges; and all the remainder are deprived of their natural rights by just so much as is given to the others over and above their share. For the institution of monogamy, and the laws of marriage which it entails, bestow upon the woman an unnatural position of privilege, by considering her throughout as the full equivalent of the man, which is by no means the case; and seeing this men who are shrewd and prudent very often scruple to make so great a sacrifice and to acquiesce in so unfair an arrangement.

Moreover, the bestowal of unnatural rights upon women has imposed upon them unnatural duties, and nevertheless a breach of these duties makes them unhappy. Let me explain. A man may often think that his social or financial position will suffer if he marries, unless he makes some brilliant alliance. His desire will then be to win a woman of his own choice under conditions other than those of marriage, such as will secure her position and that of the children. However fair, reasonable, fit and proper these conditions may be, if the woman consents by foregoing that undue amount of privilege which marriage alone can bestow, she to some extent loses her honour, because marriage is the basis of civic society; and she will lead an unhappy life, since human nature is so constituted that we pay an attention to the opinion of other people which is out of all proportion to its value. On the other hand, if she does not consent, she runs the risk either of having to be given in marriage to a man whom she does not like, or of being landed high and dry as an old maid; for the period during which she has a chance of being settled for life is very short. And in view of this aspect of the institution of monogamy, Thomasius' profoundly learned treatise *On Concubinage* is well worth reading; for it shows that, amongst all nations and in all ages, down to the Lutheran Reformation, concubinage was permitted; nay, that it was an institution which was to a certain extent actually recognized by law, and attended with no dishonour. It was only the Lutheran Reformation that degraded it from this position. It was seen to be a further justification for the marriage of the clergy; and then, after that, the Catholic Church did not dare to remain behindhand in the matter.

The first love of a mother for her child is, with the lower animals as with men, of a purely *instinctive* character, and so it ceases when the child is no longer in a physically helpless condition. After that, the first love should give way to one that is based on habit and reason; but this often fails to make its appearance, especially where the mother did not love the father. The love of a father for his child is of a different order, and more likely to last; because it has its foundation in the fact that in the child he recognizes his own inner self; that is to say, his love for it is metaphysical in its origin.

In almost all nations, whether of the ancient or the modern world, even amongst the Hottentots, property is inherited by the male descendants alone; it is only in Europe that a departure has taken place; but not amongst the nobility, however. That the property which has cost men long years of toil and effort, and been won with so much difficulty, should afterwards come into the hands of women, who then, in their lack of reason, squander it in a short time, or otherwise fool it away, is a grievance and a wrong, as serious as it is common, which should be prevented by limiting the right of women to inherit. In my opinion the best arrangement would be that by which women, whether widows or daughters, should never receive anything beyond the interest for life on property secured by mortgage, and in no case the property itself, or the capital, except where all male descendants fail. The people who make money are men, not women; and it follows from this that women are neither justified in having unconditional possession of it, nor fit persons to be entrusted with its administration. When wealth, in any true sense of the word, that is to say, funds, houses or land, is to go to them as an inheritance, they should never be allowed the free disposition of it. In their case a guardian should always be appointed; and hence they should never be given the free control of their own children, wherever it can be avoided. The vanity of women, even though it should not prove to be greater than that of men, has this much danger in it that it takes an entirely material direction. They are vain, I mean, of their personal beauty, and then of finery, show and magnificence. That is just why they are so much in their element in society. It is this, too, which makes them so inclined to be extravagant, all the more as their reasoning power is low. But with men vanity often takes the direction of non-material advantages, such as intellect, learning, courage.

That woman is by nature meant to obey may be seen by the fact that every woman who is placed in the unnatural position of complete independence, immediately attaches herself to some man, by whom she allows herself to be guided and ruled. It is because she needs a lord and master. If she is young, it will be a lover; if she is old, a priest.

QUESTIONS ON CONTENT

1. What constitutes man's debt to women in each part of his life?
2. Does the author justify the assertion that women are not formed for great labor of the mind?
3. In what way are women fitted to be nurses and teachers of the young?
4. How does the author illustrate Nature's *coup de théâtre* with women?
5. To what use does the author put this assertion: "The nobler and more perfect a thing is, the later and slower it is in arriving at maturity"? What can be objected to in this "reasoning"?
6. What are the advantages of woman's tendency to live in the present?
7. How do men and women stand in their approach to the abstractions: mercy and justice? What is woman's greatest protective weapon? What does this have to do with her sense of justice?
8. How do women in the "darkest recesses of their heart" justify dissimulation?
9. Compare the description of women (on p. 580) with the previous statement about the appearance of girls. Are the statements consistent?
10. What accounts for women's lack of objectivity?
11. In what sense does the author use the word *philistine*? Guess the meaning of the word from the context; then look it up in a dictionary.
12. Does the author make a distinction between the vanity of men and of women? Explain.
13. How much property do the women of the United States own? Do you regard a woman's right to inherit property as a good or a bad thing?
14. Debate each point made by the author.

❧ *"Go and Catch a Falling Star"*

John Donne

Go and catch a falling star,
   Get with child a mandrake root,
Tell me where all past years are,
   Or who cleft the devil's foot,
Teach me to hear mermaids singing,   5
   Or to keep off envy's stinging,
       And find
       What wind
Serves to advance an honest mind.

If thou be'st born to strange sights,   10
   Things invisible to see,
Ride ten thousand days and nights,
   Till age snow white hairs on thee,
Thou, when thou return'st, wilt tell me
   All strange wonders that befell thee,   15
       And swear
       No where
Lives a woman true, and fair.

If thou find'st one, let me know,
   Such a pilgrimage were sweet;   20
Yet do not, I would not go,
   Though at next door we might meet;
Though she were true when you met her,
   And till last you write your letter,
       Yet she   25
       Will be
False, ere I come, to two or three.

First published in 1633.

QUESTIONS ON CONTENT

1. What is the theme of this poem?
2. How does the poet emphasize the impossibility of succeeding in the quest for a constant woman? Compare Schopenhauer on this point.
3. Why does the poet lose interest in the sight of "a woman true, and fair"?

ᔆ *The Case against Women*

JAMES THURBER

A bright-eyed woman, whose sparkle was rather more of eagerness than of intelligence, approached me at a party one afternoon and said, "Why do you hate women, Mr. Thurber?" I quickly adjusted my fixed grin and denied that I hated women; I said I did not hate women at all. But the question remained with me, and I discovered when I went to bed that night that I had been subconsciously listing a number of reasons why I do hate women. It might be interesting—at least it will help pass the time—to set down these reasons, just as they came up out of my subconscious.

In the first place, I hate women because they always know where things are. At first blush, you might think that a perverse and merely churlish reason for hating women, but it is not. Naturally, every man enjoys having a woman around the house who knows where his shirt studs and his briefcase are, and things like that, but he detests having a woman around who knows where *everything* is, even things that are of no importance at all, such as, say, the snapshots her husband took three years ago at Elbow Beach. The husband has never known where these snapshots were since the day they were developed and printed; he hopes, in a vague way, if he thinks about them at all, that after three years they have been thrown out. But his wife knows where they are, and so do his mother, his grandmother, his greatgrandmother, his daughter, and the maid. They could put their fingers on them in a moment, with that quiet air of superior

From *Let Your Mind Alone!* by James Thurber, Harper & Brothers (1937). Reprinted by permission. Copyright, 1936 by James Thurber. Originally published in *The New Yorker*.

knowledge which makes a man feel that he is out of touch with all the things that count in life.

A man's interest in old snapshots, unless they are snapshots of himself in action with a gun, a fishing rod, or a tennis racquet, languishes in about two hours. A woman's interest in old snapshots, particularly of groups of people, never languishes; it is always there, as the years roll on, as strong and vivid as it was right at the start. She remembers the snapshots when people come to call, and just as the husband, having mixed drinks for everybody, sits down to sip his own, she will say, "George, I wish you would go and get those snapshots we took at Elbow Beach and show them to the Murphys." The husband, as I have said, doesn't know where the snapshots are; all he knows is that Harry Murphy doesn't want to see them; Harry Murphy wants to talk, just as he himself wants to talk. But Grace Murphy says that she wants to see the pictures; she is crazy to see the pictures; for one thing, the wife, who has brought the subject up, wants Mrs. Murphy to see the photo of a certain costume that the wife wore at Elbow Beach in 1933. The husband finally puts down his drink and snarls, "Well, where are they, then?" The wife, depending on her mood, gives him either the look she reserves for spoiled children or the one she reserves for drunken workmen, and tells him he knows perfectly well where they are. It turns out, after a lot of give and take, the slightly bitter edge of which is covered by forced laughs, that the snapshots are in the upper right-hand drawer of a certain desk, and the husband goes out of the room to get them. He comes back in three minutes with the news that the snapshots are not in the upper right-hand drawer of the certain desk. Without stirring from her chair, the wife favors her husband with a faint smile (the one that annoys him most of all her smiles) and reiterates that the snapshots *are* in the upper right-hand drawer of the desk. He simply didn't look, that's all. The husband knows that he looked; he knows that he prodded and dug and excavated in that drawer and that the snapshots simply are not there. The wife tells him to go look again and he will find them. The husband goes back and looks again—the guests can hear him growling and cursing and rattling papers. Then he shouts out from the next room. "They are *not* in this *drawer,* just as I told you, Ruth!" The wife quietly excuses herself and leaves the guests and goes into the room where her husband stands, hot, miserable, and defiant—and with a certain nameless fear in his heart. He has pulled the desk drawer out so far that it is about to fall on the floor, and he points at the disarray of the drawer with bitter triumph (still mixed with that nameless fear). "Look for yourself!" he snarls. The wife does not look. She says with quiet coldness, "What is that you have in your hand?" What he has in his hand turns out to be an insurance policy and an old bankbook —and the snapshots. The wife gets off the old line about what it would have done if it had been a snake, and the husband is upset for the rest of the evening; in some cases he cannot keep anything on his stomach for twenty-four hours.

Another reason I hate women (and I am speaking, I believe, for the American male generally) is that in almost every case where there is a sign reading "Please have exact change ready," a woman never has anything smaller than a ten-dollar bill. She gives ten-dollar bills to bus conductors and change men in subways and other such persons who deal in nickels and dimes and quarters. Recently, in Bermuda, I saw a woman hand the conductor on the little railway there a bill of such huge denomination that I was utterly unfamiliar with it. I was sitting too far away to see exactly what it was, but I had the feeling that it was a five-hundred-dollar bill. The conductor merely ignored it and stood there waiting—the fare was just one shilling. Eventually, scrabbling around in her handbag, the woman found a shilling. All the men on the train who witnessed the transaction tightened up inside; that's what a woman with a ten-dollar bill or a twenty or a five-hundred does to a man in such situations—she tightens him up inside. The episode gives him the feeling that some monstrous triviality is threatening the whole structure of civilization. It is difficult to analyze this feeling, but there it is.

Another spectacle that depresses the male and makes him fear women, and therefore hate them, is that of a woman looking another woman up and down, to see what she is wearing. The cold, flat look that comes into a woman's eyes when she does this, the swift coarsening of her countenance, and the immediate evaporation from it of all humane quality make the male shudder. He is likely to go to his stateroom or his den or his private office and lock himself in for hours. I know one man who surprised that look in his wife's eyes and never afterward would let her come near him. If she started toward him, he would dodge behind a table or a sofa, as if he were engaging in some unholy game of tag. That look, I believe, is one reason men disappear, and turn up in Tahiti or the Arctic or the United States Navy.

I (to quit hiding behind the generalization of "the male") hate women because they almost never get anything exactly right. They say, "I have been faithful to thee, Cynara, after my fashion" instead of "in my fashion." They will bet you that Alfred Smith's middle name is Aloysius, instead of Emanuel. They will tell you to take the 2:57 train, on a day that the 2:57 does not run, or, if it does run, does not stop at the station where you are supposed to get off. Many men, separated from a woman by this particular form of imprecision, have never showed up in her life again. Nothing so embitters a man as to end up in Bridgeport when he was supposed to get off at Westport.

I hate women because they have brought into the currency of our language such expressions as "all righty" and "yes indeedy" and hundreds of others. I hate women because they throw baseballs (or plates or vases) with the wrong foot advanced. I marvel that more of them have not broken their backs. I marvel that women, who coordinate so well in languorous motion, look uglier and sillier than a goose-stepper when they attempt any form of violent activity.

I have a lot of other notes jotted down about why I hate women, but I seem to have lost them all, except one. That one is to the effect that I hate women because, while they never lose old snapshots or anything of that sort, they invariably lose one glove. I believe that I have never gone anywhere with any woman in my whole life who did not lose one glove. I have searched for single gloves under tables in crowded restaurants and under the feet of people in darkened movie theatres. I have spent some part of every day or night hunting for a woman's glove. If there were no other reason in the world for hating women, that one would be enough. In fact, you can leave all the others out.

QUESTIONS ON CONTENT

1. Which of Thurber's charges against women fit Schopenhauer's observations on women?
2. How does Thurber's mood compare with Schopenhauer's? Donne's? (See previous selections in this chapter.)
3. How many of Thurber's charges are justified?
4. What other charges, of the same trivial sort, may be brought against women?
5. To balance the scales, draw up a list of those things men do which are irritating to women.
6. Why, in general, are women more reticent in their attacks on men? Or are they?

❧ *The Natural Superiority of Women*

ASHLEY MONTAGU

Oh, no! I can hear it said, *not* superior. Equal, partners, complementary, different, but *not* superior. I can even foresee that men will mostly smile, while women, alarmed, will rise to the defense of men—women always have, and always will. I hope that what I shall have to say in this article will make them even more willing to do so, for men need their help more than they as yet, mostly, consciously realize.

Women superior to men? This is a new idea. There have been people who have cogently, but apparently not convincingly, argued that women were as good as men, but I do not recall anyone who has publicly provided the evidence or even argued that women were better than or superior to men. How, indeed, could one argue such a case in the face of all the evidence to the contrary? Is it not a fact that by far the largest number of geniuses, great painters, poets, philosophers, scientists, etc., etc., have been men, and that women have made, by comparison, a very poor showing? Clearly the superiority is with men. Where are the Leonardos, the Michelangelos, the Shakespeares, the Donnes, the Galileos, the Whiteheads, the Kants, the Bachs, *et al.*, of the feminine sex? In fields in which women have excelled, in poetry and the novel, how many poets and novelists of the really first rank have there been? Haven't well-bred young women been educated for centuries in music? And how many among them have been great composers or instrumentalists? Composers—none of the first rank. Instrumentalists—well, in the recent period there have been such accomplished artists as Myra Hess and Wanda Landowska. Possibly there is a clue here to the answer to the question asked. May it not be that women are just about to emerge from the period of subjection during which they were the "niggers" of the masculine world?

The Royal Society of London has at last opened its doors and admitted women to the highest honor which it is in the power of the English scientific world to bestow—the Fellowship of the Royal

From *The Saturday Review*, March 1, 1952. Copyright, 1952, 1953, by Ashley Montagu. Reprinted by permission of The Macmillan Company.

Society. I well remember that when I was a youth—less than a quarter of a century ago—it was considered inconceivable that any woman would ever have brains enough to attain great distinction in science. Mme. Curie was an exception. But the half dozen women Fellows of the Royal Society in England are not. Nor is Lise Meitner. And Mme. Curie no longer remains the only woman to share in the Nobel Prize award for science. There is Marie Curie's daughter, Irene Joliot-Curie, and there is Gerty Cory (1947) for physiology and medicine. Nobel prizes in literature have gone to Selma Lagerlof, Grazia Deledda, Sigrid Undset, Pearl Buck, and Gabriela Mistral. As an artist Mary Cassatt (1845–1926) was every bit as good as her great French friends Degas and Manet considered her to be, but it has taken the rest of the world another fifty years grudgingly to admit it. Among contemporaries Georgia O'Keeffe can hold her own with the best.

It is not, however, going to be any part of this article to show that women are about to emerge as superior scientists, musicians, painters, or the like. I believe that in these fields they may emerge as equally good, and possibly not in as large numbers as men, largely because the motivations and aspirations of most women will continue to be directed elsewhere. But what must be pointed out is that women are, in fact, just beginning to emerge from the period of subjection when they were treated in a manner not unlike that which is still meted out to the Negro in the Western world. The women of the nineteenth century were the "niggers" of the male-dominated world. All the traits that are mythically attributed to the Negro at the present time were for many generations saddled upon women. Women had smaller brains than men and less intelligence, they were more emotional and unstable, in a crisis you could always rely upon them to swoon or become otherwise helpless, they were weak and sickly creatures, they had little judgment and less sense, could not be relied upon to handle money, and as for the world outside, there they could be employed only at the most menial and routine tasks.

The biggest dent in this series of myths was made by World War I, when women were for the first time called upon to replace men in occupations which were formerly the exclusive preserve of men. They became bus drivers, conductors, factory workers, farm workers, laborers, supervisors, executive officers, and a great many other things at which many had believed they could never work. At first it was said that they didn't do as well as men, then it was grudgingly admitted that they weren't so bad, and by the time the war was over many employers were reluctant to exchange their women employees for men! But the truth was out—women could do as well as men in most of the fields which had been considered forever closed to them because of their alleged natural incapacities, and in many fields, particularly where delicate precision work was involved, they had proved themselves superior to men. From 1918 to 1939 the period for women was one essentially of consolidation of gains, so that by the time that World War II broke out there was no hesitation on the part of anyone in calling upon women to serve in the civilian roles of men and in many cases also in the armed services.

But women have a long way to go before they reach full emancipation—emancipation from the myths from which they themselves suffer. It is, of course, untrue that women have smaller brains than men. The fact is that in proportion to body weight they have larger brains than men; but this fact is in itself of no importance because within the limits of normal variation of brain size and weight there exists no relation between these factors and intelligence. Women have been conditioned to believe that they are inferior to men, and they have assumed that what everyone believes is a fact of nature; and as men occupy the superior positions in almost all societies, this superiority is taken to be a natural one. "Woman's place is in the home" and man's place is in the counting house and on the board of directors. "Women should not meddle in men's affairs." And yet the world does move. Some women have become Members of Parliament and even attained Cabinet rank. In the United States they have even gotten as far as the Senate. They have participated in peace conferences, but it is still inconceivable to most persons that there should ever be a woman Prime Minister or President. And yet that day, too, will come. *Eppure si muove* [nevertheless it moves]!

Woman has successfully passed through the abolition period, the abolition of her thraldom to man; she has now to pass successfully through the period of emancipation, the freeing of herself from the myth of inferiority, and the realization of her potentialities to the fullest.

And now for the evidence which proves the superiority of woman to man. But first, one word in explanation of the use of the word "superiority." The word is used in its common sense as being of better quality than, or of higher nature or character. Let us begin at the very beginning. What about the structure of the sexes? Does one show any superiority over the other? The answer is a resounding "Yes!" And I should like this "Yes" to resound all over the world, for no one has made anything of this key fact which lies at the base of all the differences between the sexes and the superiority of the female to the male. I refer to the chromosomal structure of the sexes. The chromosomes, those small cellular bodies which contain the hereditary particles, the genes, which so substantially influence one's development and fate as an organism, provide us with our basic facts.

In the sex cells there are twenty-four chromosomes, but only one of these is a sex chromosome. There are two kinds of sex chromosomes, X and Y. Half the sperm cells carry X and half carry Y chromosomes. All the female ova are made up of X-chromosomes. When an X-bearing sperm fertilizes an ovum the offspring is always female. When a Y-bearing chromosome fertilizes an ovum the offspring is always male. And this is what makes the difference between the sexes. So what? Well, the sad fact is that the Y-chromosome is but an iota, the merest bit of a remnant of an X-chromosome; it is a crippled X-chromosome. The X-chromosomes are fully developed structures; the Y-chromosome is the merest comma. It is as if in the evolution of sex a particle one day broke away from an X-chromosome, and thereafter in relation to X-chromosomes could produce only an incomplete female—the creature we now call the male! It is to this original chromosomal deficiency that all the various troubles to which the male falls heir can be traced.

In the first place the chromosomal deficiency of the male determines his incapacity to have babies. This has always been a sore point with men, though consciously they would be the last to admit it, although in some primitive societies, as among the Australian aborigines, it is the male who conceives a child by dreaming it, and then telling his wife. In this way a child is eventually born to them, the wife being merely the incubator who hatches the egg placed there through the grace of her husband.

The fact that men cannot have babies and suckle them nor remain in association with their children as closely as the wife has an enormous effect upon their subsequent psychological development. Omitting altogether from consideration the psychologic influences exercised by the differences in the hormonal secretions of the sexes, one can safely say that the mother-child relationship confers enormous benefits upon the mother which are not nearly so substantively operative in the necessary absence of such a relationship between father and child. The maternalizing influences of being a mother in addition to the fact of being a woman has from the very beginning of the human species—about a million years ago—made the female the more humane of the sexes. The love of a mother for her child is the basic patent and the model for *all* human relationships. Indeed, to the extent to which men approximate in their relationships with their fellow men to the love of the mother for her child, to that extent do they move more closely to the attainment of perfect human relations. The mother-child relationship is a dependent-interdependent one. The interstimulation between mother and child is something which the father misses, and to that extent suffers from the want of. In short, the female in the mother-child relationship has the advantage of having to be more considerate, more self-sacrificing, more cooperative, and more altruistic than usually falls to the lot of the male.

The female thus acquires, in addition to whatever natural biological advantages she starts with, a competence in social understanding which is usually denied the male. This, I take it, is one of the reasons why women are usually so much more able to perceive the nuances and pick up the subliminal signs in human behavior which almost invariably pass men by. It was, I believe, George Jean Nathan who called woman's intuition merely man's transparency. With all due deference to Mr. Nathan and sympathy for his lot as a mere male, I would suggest that man's opacity would be nearer the mark. It is because women have had to be so unselfish and forbearing and self-sacrificing and maternal that they possess a deeper understanding than men of what it is to be human. What is so frequently termed feminine indecision, the inability of women to make up their minds, is in fact an inverse reflection of the trigger-thinking of men. Every salesgirl prefers the male customer because women take time to think about what they are buying, and the male usually hasn't the sense enough to do so. Women don't think in terms of "Yes" or "No." Life isn't as simple as all that—except to males. Men tend to think in terms of the all-or-none principle, in terms of black and white.

By comparison with the deep involvement of women in living, men appear to be only superficially so. Compare the love of a male for a female with the love of the female for the male. It is the difference between a rivulet and a great deep ocean. Women love the human race; men are, on the whole, hostile to it. Men act as if they haven't been adequately loved, as if they had been frustrated and rendered hostile, and becoming aggressive they say that aggressiveness is natural and women are inferior in this respect because they tend to be gentle and unaggressive! But it is precisely in this capacity to love and unaggressiveness that the superiority of women to men is demonstrated, for whether it be natural to be loving and cooperative or not, so far as the human species is concerned, its evolutionary destiny, its very survival is more closely tied to this capacity for love and cooperation than with any other. So that unless men learn from women how to be more loving and cooperative they will go on making the kind of mess of the world which they have so effectively achieved thus far.

And this is, of course, where women can realize their power for good in the world, and make their greatest gains. *It is the function of women to teach men how to be human.* Women must not permit themselves to be deviated from this function by those who tell them that their place is in the home in subservient relation to man. It is, indeed, in the home that the foundations of the kind of world in which we live are laid, and in this sense it will always remain true that the hand that rocks the cradle is the hand that rules the world. And it is in this sense that women must assume the job of making men who will know how to make a world fit for human beings to live in. The greatest single step forward in this direction will be made when women consciously assume this task—the task of teaching their children to be like themselves, loving and cooperative.

As for geniuses, I think that almost everyone will agree that there have been more geniuses for being human among women than there have among men. This, after all, is the true genius of women, and it is because we have not valued the qualities for being human anywhere nearly as highly as we have valued those for accomplishment in the arts and sciences that we have out-of-focusedly almost forgotten them. Surely, the most valuable quality in any human being is his capacity for being loving and cooperative. We have been placing our emphases on the wrong values—it is time we recognized what every man and every woman at the very least subconsciously knows—the value of being loving, and the value of those who can teach this better than anyone else.

Physically and psychically women are by far the superiors of men. The old chestnut about women being more emotional than men has been forever destroyed by the facts of two great wars. Women under blockade, heavy bombardment, concentration camp confinement, and similar rigors withstand them vastly more successfully than men. The psychiatric casualties of civilian populations under such conditions are mostly masculine, and there are more men in our mental hospitals than there are women. The steady hand at the helm is the hand that has had the practice at rocking the cradle. Because of their greater size and weight men are physically more powerful than women—which is not the same thing as saying that they are stronger. A man of the same size and weight as a woman of comparable background and occupational status would probably not be any more powerful than a woman. As far as constitutional strength is concerned women are stronger than men. Many diseases from which men suffer can be shown to be largely influenced by their relation to the male Y-chromosome. From fertilization on more males die than females. Deaths from almost all causes are more frequent in males at all ages. Though women are more frequently ill than men, they recover from illness more easily and more frequently than men.

Women, in short, are fundamentally more resistant than men. With the exception of the organ systems subserving the functions of reproduction women suffer much less frequently than men from the serious disorders which affect mankind. With the exception of India women everywhere live longer than men. For example, the expectation of life of the female child of white parentage in the United States at the present time is over seventy-one years, whereas for the male it is only sixty-five and a half years. Women are both biologically stronger and emotionally better shock absorbers than men. The myth of masculine superiority once played such havoc with the facts that in the nineteenth century it was frequently denied by psychiatrists that the superior male could ever suffer from hysteria. Today it is fairly well known that males suffer from hysteria and hysteriform conditions with a preponderance over the female of seven to one! Epilepsy is much more frequent in males, and stuttering has an incidence of eight males to one female.

At least four disorders are now definitely known to be due to genes carried in the Y-chromosomes, and hence are disorders which can appear only in males. These are barklike skin (ichthyosis hystrix gravior), dense hairy growth on the ears (hypertrichosis), nonpainful hard lesions of the hands and feet (keratoma dissapatum), and a form of webbing of the toes. It is, however, probable that the disadvantages accruing to the male are not so much due to what is in the Y-chromosome as to what is wanting in it. This is well shown in such serious disorders as hemophilia or bleeder's disease. Hemophilia is inherited as a single sex-linked recessive gene. The gene, or hereditary particle, determining hemophilia is linked to the X-chromosome. When, then, an X-chromosome which carries the hemophilia gene is transmitted to a female it is highly improbable that it will encounter another X-chromosome carrying such a gene; hence, while not impossible, hemophilia has never been described in a female. Females are the most usual transmitters of the hemophilia gene, but it is only the males who are affected, and they are affected because they don't have any properties in their Y-chromosome capable of suppressing the action of the hemophilia gene. The mechanism of and the explanation for (red-green) color blindness is the same. About 8 per cent of all white males are color blind, but only half of one per cent of females are so affected.

Need one go on? Here, in fact, we have the explanation of the greater constitutional strength of the female as compared with the male. This may not be, and probably is not, the complete explanation of the physical inferiorities of the male as compared with the female, but it is certainly physiologically the most demonstrable and least questionable one. To the unbiased student of the facts there can no longer remain any doubt of the constitutional superiority of the female. I hope that I have removed any remaining doubts about her psychological superiority where psychological superiority most counts, namely, in a human being's capacity for loving other human beings.

I think we have overemphasized the value of intellectual qualities and grossly underemphasized the value of the qualities of humanity which women possess to such a high degree. I hope I shall not be taken for an anti-intellectual when I say that intellect without humanity is not good enough, and that what the world is suffering from at the present time is not so much an overabundance of intellect as an insufficiency of humanity. Consider men like Lenin, Stalin, and Hitler. These are the extreme cases. What these men lacked was the capacity to love. What they possessed in so eminent a degree was the capacity to hate. It is not for nothing that the Bolsheviks attempted to abolish the family and masculinize women, while the Nazis made informers of children against their parents and put the state so much before the family that it became a behemoth which has wellnigh destroyed everyone who was victimized by it.

What the world stands so much in need of at the present time, and what it will continue to need if it is to endure and increase in happiness, is more of the maternal spirit and less of the masculine. We need more persons who will love and less who will hate, and we need to understand how we can produce them; for if we don't try to understand how we may do so we shall continue to flounder in the morass of misunderstanding which frustrated love creates. For frustrated love, the frustration of the tendencies to love with which the infant is born, constitutes hostility. Hatred is love frustrated. This is what too many men suffer from and an insufficient number of women recognize, or at least too many women behave as if they didn't recognize it. What most women have learned to recognize is that the much-bruited superiority of the male isn't all that it's cracked up to be. The male doesn't seem to be as wise and as steady as they were taught to believe. But there appears to be a conspiracy of silence on this subject. Perhaps women feel that men ought to be maintained in the illusion of their superiority because it might not be good for them or the world to learn the truth. In this sense this article, perhaps, should have been entitled "What Every Woman Knows." But I'm not sure that every woman knows it. What I am sure of is that many women don't appear to know it, and that there are even many women who are horrified at the thought that anyone can entertain the idea that women are anything but inferior to men. This sort of childishness does no one any good. The world is in a mess. Men, without any assistance from women, have created it, and they have created it not because they have been failed by women, but because men have never really given women a chance to serve them as they are best equipped to do—by teaching men how to love their fellow men.

Women must cease supporting men for the wrong reasons in the wrong sort of way, and thus cease causing men to marry them for the wrong reasons, too. "That's what a man wants in a wife, mostly," says Mrs. Poyser (in *Adam Bede*), "he wants to make sure o' one fool as 'ull tell him he's wise." Well, it's time that men learned the truth, and perhaps they are likely to take it more gracefully from another male than from their unacknowledged betters. It is equally important that women learn the truth, too, for it is to them that the most important part, the more fundamental part, of the task of remaking the world will fall, for the world will be remade only by remaking, or rather helping, human beings to realize themselves more fully in terms of what their mothers have to give them. Without adequate mothers life becomes inadequate, nasty, and unsatisfactory, and Mother Earth becomes a battlefield on which fathers slay their young and are themselves slain.

Men have had a long run for their money in running the affairs of the world. It is time that women realized that men will continue to run the world for some time yet, and that they can best assist them to run it more humanely by teaching them, when young, what humanity means. Men will thus not feel that they are being demoted, but rather that their potentialities for good are so much more increased, and what is more important, instead of feeling hostile toward women they will for the first time learn to appreciate them at their proper worth. There is an old Spanish proverb which has it that a good wife is the workmanship of a good husband. Maybe. But of one thing we can be certain: a good husband is the workmanship of a good mother. The best of all ways in which men can help themselves is to help women realize themselves. This way both sexes will come for the first time fully into their own, and the world of mankind may then look forward to a happier history than it has thus far enjoyed.

QUESTIONS ON CONTENT

1. What is the purpose of the first seven paragraphs? Why does the author spend so much time on this aspect of his subject?
2. What does the author consider his basic fact in proving the superiority of women? What are the points which depend upon this basic fact?
3. *"It is the function of women to teach men how to be human."* Why does the author italicize this sentence and no other in his article?
4. What point is made concerning the older standards of judging the relative merits of men and women? In what way does the author shift away from these standards?
5. What is said concerning longevity of men and women? Of the incidence of disease in men and women?
6. Compare Montagu's method with Schopenhauer's; with Thurber's; with Donne's.
7. Is the superiority of women proved to your satisfaction? Discuss.

❧ *In Church*

THOMAS HARDY

"And now to God the Father," he ends,
And his voice thrills up to the topmost tiles:
Each listener chokes as he bows and bends,
And emotion pervades the crowded aisles.
Then the preacher glides to the vestry-door   5
And shuts it, and thinks he is seen no more.

The door swings softly ajar meanwhile,
And a pupil of his in the Bible class,
Who adores him as one without gloss or guile,
Sees her idol stand with a satisfied smile   10
And re-enact at the vestry-glass
Each pulpit gesture in deft dumb-show
That had moved the congregation so.

QUESTIONS ON CONTENT

1. Could this poem be called "Hypocrisy"?
2. Speculate on what difference the discovery of the preacher's dumb show should make to the Bible class pupil's opinion of her idol.

❧ *At the Draper's*

THOMAS HARDY

"I stood at the back of the shop, my dear,
    But you did not perceive me.
Well, when they deliver what you were shown
    I shall know nothing of it, believe me!"

From Thomas Hardy, *Collected Poems*. Copyright 1925 by The Macmillan Company and used with their permission.

And he coughed and coughed as she paled and said,   5
  "O, I didn't see you come in there—
Why couldn't you speak?"—"Well, I didn't. I left
  That you should not notice I'd been there.

"You were viewing some lovely things. *'Soon required
  For a widow, of latest fashion';*   10
And I knew 'twould upset you to meet the man
  Who had to be cold and ashen

"And screwed in a box before they could dress you
  'In the last new note in mourning,'
As they defined it. So, not to distress you,   15
  I left you to your adorning."

QUESTIONS ON CONTENT

1. Of what disease, probably, is the husband dying?
2. In what essential respect is this poem like "In Church"?

SUGGESTIONS FOR PAPERS

Indispensable as they are to each other, nevertheless there is an abiding conflict between men and women. As a result, any analysis of one sex always involves comparisons with the other sex. Whether you are male or female, you will want to have a part in this argument and to set down on paper your best thinking on the subject.

1. Examine Schopenhauer's reasons in "On Women" for saying that "the fundamental fault of the female character is that it *has no sense of justice.*" Rephrase his reasons, then offer illustrations which support or refute these arguments.

2. Glean from the essay "On Women" all the *favorable* statements about women. Do these, added together, justify the conclusion that women are different from men but not necessarily inferior to men? (Example: women are shortsighted; men farsighted. Does not each way of seeing have its advantages? Schopenhauer says yes to this, but should he not also see the advantages in other differences?)

3. What in "On Women" is meant by the "lady-nuisance"? (*Lady* is not a synonym for *woman.*) Schopenhauer was thinking of Euro-

pean class distinctions, but does the United States have a "lady-nuisance" of its own? What are your own observations on the status of "ladies" in our country? Has there been a decline in "lady-prerogatives"? If so, why?

4. Do you believe that women practice untruth and deception more than men do? What is said on this subject in each of the selections in this chapter? Discuss the accusation in the light of your own observation and experience.

5. Thurber's "Case against Women" differs from "On Women" in what respects? Show how Schopenhauer would have treated Thurber's specific objections to certain of women's actions. What philosophic reasons—or reasons in Nature—might he have named to account for such things as a woman's knowing where everything is, her undying interest in snapshots, her refusal to have the exact change ready, her "cold, flat look" at other women's clothes, her inability to get anything right, her awkwardness in any form of violent activity, and her persistence in losing one glove?

6. Write an essay on "My Case against Men." Select three or four irritating male qualities for which you can find illustrations. Be as specific as Thurber is in his "Case against Women."

7. Why do women outlive men? Does this in itself prove that they are the stronger sex? If so, how? A paper on this subject can be in agreement or disagreement with the contentions of "The Natural Superiority of Women."

8. Analyze the case Ashley Montagu in "The Natural Superiority of Women" makes for women. Does he give his case away in the first seven paragraphs? How does he proceed with his argument after having granted so much? Is his chief point against men and for women conclusively argued? Cite passages to prove *your* argument.

9. Contrast the methods used by Thurber and by Montagu. How specific is each? How do the facts presented by each author differ? Which author is more personal? Is Thurber serious in his charges? Is Montagu in his defense of women? In answering these questions, cite appropriate passages.

10. Base your paper on any one of the following quotations:

(*a*) "Women are directly fitted for acting as the nurses and teachers of our early childhood by the fact that they are themselves childish, frivolous and short-sighted."

(*b*) "The nobler and more perfect a thing is, the later and slower it is in arriving at maturity."

(*c*) "It is by no means a bad plan to consult women in matters of difficulty."

(*d*) "Women are decidedly more sober in their judgment than we are."

(*e*) "The woman lives more in the present than the man."

(*f*) "Women show more sympathy for the unfortunate than men do."

(*g*) "The fundamental fault of the female character is that it has *no sense of justice.*"

(*h*) "Dissimulation is innate in women, and almost as much a quality of the stupid as of the clever."

(*i*) "The natural feeling between men is mere indifference, but between women it is actual enmity."

(*j*) "The most distinguished feminine intellects . . . have never . . . given to the world any work of permanent value in any sphere."

(*k*) "To marry means to halve one's rights and double one's duties."

(*l*) "Woman has successfully passed through the abolition period, the abolition of her thraldom to man."

(*m*) "Women love the human race; men are, on the whole, hostile to it."

(*n*) *"It is the function of women to teach men how to be human."*

(*o*) "A good husband is the workmanship of a good mother."

11. If you had nothing to go on except Hardy's two poems, what would you conclude about this poet's attitude towards women and men? Consider the implications of each poem and then write your conclusion.

SOME TITLES FOR PAPERS

1. Male versus Female
2. My Idea of Woman's Place
3. What Is Man's Place?
4. Do Women Want to Be Like Men?
5. Men and Women Are Alike But Different
6. The Truth Is (Not) in Them
7. Advantages of Being a Lady
8. Advantages of the Feminine Short View
9. My Case Against Men
10. My Case Against Women
11. Women Control Men Who Control Everything Else
12. Women Love a Pedestal
13. The New Status of Women
14. Courtship—and After?

15. A Woman's Sense of Justice
16. Women Live in the Present
17. Differences in Male and Female Vanity
18. Schopenhauer and Montagu: A Contrast
19. How to Argue a Point (Consider the methods used by Schopenhauer, Thurber, and Montagu.)

∿ *ABOUT EDUCATION*

THERE ARE THREE MAJOR CONTENTIONS about the function of education: (1) it should directly prepare students to earn a living; (2) it should directly prepare students to live but not to earn a living; (3) it should do some of both. Each of these contentions has strong adherents who offer a variety of proposals for achieving the aim of education which they support. The chief cleavage among educators of whatever stamp is over the question of method versus content. The extremists on the side of content say that what is taught is of far more importance than how it is taught. Probably the consensus among informed educators is that some method is desirable but that content is obviously the core of the educational process.

The selections in this chapter begin with "A Liberal Education Defined" by Thomas Henry Huxley. Huxley recognizes a natural and an artificial education. The first is inescapable, as Nature (with society as one of its products and colleagues) ceaselessly educates each individual. Artificial education supplements the teachings of Nature and seeks to bring man into full adjustment with his environment. A modern theory of education calls itself "progressive" and seeks to interfere as little as possible with natural education. The article "What about Progressive Education?" discusses four broad aims of progressive education. Development of the whole child is the center of the program. The child is placed in a miniature world which apes the adult world, and then is allowed to unfold his personality. He is supposed to acquire "whatever knowledge and skill he needs for taking his part in the world," but even this vague aim is subordinate to the child's "emotional adjustment" and to his "self-fulfillment as a unique individual." Obviously, method is almost the sole concern of the progressive educator.

For the past twenty years this theory of education has gained widespread acceptance among professional educators, with the result that more and more school systems have adopted, to a greater or lesser degree, the basic tenets of "progressive" education. Moreover, enough time has elapsed to allow an appraisal of the results produced by "life adjustment" programs. Strong protests are now being registered from many quarters. Mortimer Smith in "Adjustment Replaces Education" speaks for those who believe that "adjustment" is the negative of "education," for adjustment requires acceptance of things as they are, whereas education requires a critical examination of the *status quo* along with a willingness to advocate changes.

In "The Disadvantages of Being Educated," Albert J. Nock recognizes what education does to the "spirit of adapting" when he says: "Education deprives a young person of one of his most precious possessions, the sense of co-operation with his fellows." Clearly a society which has adjustment as its ideal will be a static society.

❧ A Liberal Education Defined

Thomas Henry Huxley

. . . Suppose it were perfectly certain that the life and fortune of every one of us would, one day or other, depend upon his winning or losing a game at chess. Don't you think that we should all consider it to be a primary duty to learn at least the names and the moves of the pieces; to have a notion of a gambit, and a keen eye for all the means of giving and getting out of check? Do you not think that we should look with a disapprobation amounting to scorn upon the father who allowed his son, or the state which allowed its members to grow up without knowing a pawn from a knight?

Yet, it is a very plain and elementary truth that the life, the fortune, and the happiness of every one of us, and, more or less, of

From "A Liberal Education; and Where to Find It," *Lay Sermons* (1868).

those who are connected with us, do depend upon our knowing something of the rules of a game infinitely more difficult and complicated than chess. It is a game which has been played for untold ages, every man and woman of us being one of the two players in a game of his or her own. The chess-board is the world, the pieces are the phenomena of the universe, the rules of the game are what we call the laws of nature. The player on the other side is hidden from us. We know that his play is always fair, just and patient. But also we know, to our cost, that he never overlooks a mistake, or makes the smallest allowance for ignorance. To the man who plays well, the highest stakes are paid, with that sort of overflowing generosity with which the strong shows delight in strength. And one who plays ill is checkmated—without haste, but without remorse.

My metaphor will remind some of you of the famous picture in which Retztch has depicted Satan playing at chess with man for his soul. Substitute for the mocking fiend in that picture a calm, strong angel who is playing for love, as we say, and would rather lose than win—and I should accept it as an image of human life.

Well, what I mean by Education is learning the rules of this mighty game. In other words, education is the instruction of the intellect in the laws of nature, under which name I include not merely things and their forces, but men and their ways; and the fashioning of the affections and of the will into an earnest and loving desire to move in harmony with those laws. For me, education means neither more nor less than this. Anything which professes to call itself education must be tried by this standard, and if it fails to stand the test, I will not call it education whatever may be the force of authority or of numbers upon the other side.

It is important to remember that, in strictness, there is no such thing as an uneducated man. Take an extreme case. Suppose that an adult man, in the full vigor of his faculties, could be suddenly placed in the world, as Adam is said to have been, and then left to do as he best might. How long would he be left uneducated? Not five minutes. Nature would begin to teach him, through the eye, the ear, the touch, the properties of objects. Pain and pleasure would be at his elbow telling him to do this and avoid that; and by slow degrees the man would receive an education which, if narrow, would be thorough, real, and adequate to his circumstances, though there would be no extras and very few accomplishments.

And if to this solitary man entered a second Adam, or, better still, an Eve, a new and greater world, that of social and moral phenomena, would be revealed. Joys and woes, compared with which all others might seem but faint shadows, would spring from the new relations. Happiness and sorrow would take the place of the coarser monitors, pleasure and pain; but conduct would still be shaped by the observation of the natural consequences of actions; or, in other words, by the laws of the nature of man.

To every one of us the world was once as fresh and new as to Adam. And then, long before we were susceptible of any other mode of instruction, nature took us in hand, and every minute of waking life brought its educational influence, shaping our actions into rough accordance with nature's laws, so that we might not be ended untimely by too gross disobedience. Nor should I speak of this process of education as past for anyone, be he as old as he may. For every man the world is as fresh as it was at the first day, and as full of untold novelties for him who has the eyes to see them. And nature is still continuing her patient education of us in that great university, the universe, of which we are all members—nature having no Test-Acts.

Those who take honours in nature's university, who learn the laws which govern men and things and obey them, are the really great and successful men in this world. The great mass of mankind are the "Poll," who pick up just enough to get through without much discredit. Those who won't learn at all are plucked; and then you can't come up again. Nature's pluck means extermination.

Thus the question of compulsory education is settled so far as nature is concerned. Her bill on that question was framed and passed long ago. But, like all compulsory legislation, that of nature is harsh and wasteful in its operation. Ignorance is visited as sharply as wilful disobedience—incapacity meets with the same punishment as crime. Nature's discipline is not even a word and a blow, and the blow first; but the blow without the word. It is left to you to find out why your ears are boxed.

The object of what we commonly call education—that education in which man intervenes and which I shall distinguish as artificial education—is to make good these defects in nature's methods; to prepare the child to receive nature's education, neither incapably nor ignorantly, nor with wilful disobedience; and to understand the preliminary symptoms of her pleasure, without waiting for the box on the ear. In short, all artificial education ought to be an anticipation of natural education. And a liberal education is an artificial education—which has not only prepared a man to escape the great evils of disobedience to natural laws, but has trained him to appreciate and to seize upon the rewards which nature scatters with as free a hand as her penalties.

That man, I think, has had a liberal education who has been so trained in youth that his body is the ready servant of his will, and does with ease and pleasure all the work that, as a mechanism, it is capable of; whose intellect is a clear, cold, logic engine, with all its parts of equal strength, and in smooth working order; ready, like a steam engine, to be turned to any kind of work, and spin the gossamers as well as forge the anchors of the mind; whose mind is stored with a knowledge of the great and fundamental truths of nature and of the laws of her operations; one who, no stunted ascetic, is full of life and fire, but whose passions are trained to come to heel by a vigorous will, the servant of a tender conscience; who has learned to love all beauty, whether of nature or of art, to hate all vileness, and to respect others as himself.

Such an one and no other, I conceive, has had a liberal education; for he is, as completely as a man can be, in harmony with nature. He will make the best of her, and she of him. They will get on together rarely; she as his ever-beneficent mother; he as her mouthpiece, her conscious self, her minister and interpreter.

QUESTIONS ON CONTENT

1. When does Huxley first define education? Is this his complete definition?
2. Why is "there no such thing as an uneducated man"?
3. What new monitors besides pleasure and pain would be added to a solitary Adam by the appearance of an Eve? Why?
4. The term "Poll" is used at Cambridge University to describe students who read for a pass instead of an honors degree. "Pluck" is the English term for "fail" or "flunk." How does Huxley use these terms?
5. Discuss the difference between natural and artificial education. Of which sort is a liberal education?
6. What do you deduce from the fact that Huxley does not prescribe how a liberal education is to be obtained? Read carefully his full description of a liberally educated man before you answer this question.

❧ *What about Progressive Education?*

CARLETON WASHBURNE

What is "progressive education" and what are its results? A few years ago only the initiated were familiar with the term. Now even people who know little or nothing about it write articles on it, blame the ill manners of youth upon it, fear that it undermines patriotism, wonder if it will prepare children for college, question whether it fits them for the rigors of real life.

In the minds of many parents, and some educators, a "progressive" school is one where there is no discipline—the children are rude and do as they please; where the three R's are neglected and, on the higher levels, there is no scholarship; where what learning there is is so sugar-coated that children are not prepared either for higher education or the rigors of life; and where an atmosphere of radicalism prevails.

Maybe there is such a school somewhere. If so, it would be disowned by every progressive educator. Yet these misconceptions are so widespread that they must have some origin. As we discuss what progressive education really is, perhaps we shall see why otherwise intelligent people have such fears and beliefs in regard to it.

Right at the start, however, we are confronted with one cause of confusion: there is no definitive statement of exactly what progressive education is. It is elusive. This is because it is not a set method, plan, or technique, but an attitude, an implicit philosophy, a point of view. No two progressive educators describe it in the same terms; no two schools practice it in identical ways.

Yet there are certain common elements in the thought and practice of most people who consider themselves or their schools progressive. These can be very simply stated. Progressive education is always concerned with the whole child—both as an individual and as a member of society. It is therefore concerned (1) with his health and his emotional adjustment; (2) with his self-fulfillment as a unique individual, having initiative and creativeness; (3) with his acquisition of whatever knowledge and skill he needs for taking

Reprinted from *Parents' Magazine*, XVI (June 1941), 34 ff., by permission of the author and the publisher.

his part in the world; and (4) with his development as a socially conscious, participating citizen of a democracy.

Let us look at these four aspects of education more closely.

The first evidently subdivides into two parts—physical health and emotional adjustment. The progressive school considers both as vital parts of education. On the physical side it tries to provide hygienic surroundings; an adequate physical education program; a program of physical examinations followed up by conferences with parents to see that defects are remedied; care that contagion does not spread; and adequate emphasis on health and safety in the curriculum.

This phase of modern education is characteristic not only of progressive schools but of many good schools which are in other ways traditional. The only opposition it meets is from those who want to keep taxes down and who think of education as mere book-learning.

The emotional adjustment of the child, however—mental hygiene —is much less understood, much less characteristic of even good traditional schools, but is considered basic in progressive education. The best progressive schools try to get down to the roots of behavior, to analyze the deep-seated causes of a child's lying, bullying, teasing, showing off, laziness, day dreaming, recalcitrance, over-concern with sex, or over-compliance. These forms of behavior are recognized as symptoms of something the child lacks in satisfying his basic emotional needs. The cure for these undesirable forms of behavior is obviously not in repressive discipline, or even in reasoning with the child. It lies in finding wherein the child is not getting the deep satisfactions necessary for his wholesome development, and then helping him to find acceptable ways of satisfying these needs.

And right here is a cause of one of the misconceptions regarding progressive education. The teacher who understands mental hygiene represses as little as possible, tries to give children a chance to work out their own characteristic design of growth in acceptable ways, tries to give them a sense of belonging, of being appreciated and loved, tries to help them to participate in the planning of their own lives and to co-operate with their fellows in group enterprises. This does not lead to the kind of order where you can hear the clock tick —a kind which we adults seldom have in our own lives. But, rightly conceived, it does not lead to chaos. It is not *laissez-faire*. A child's right to freedom is always limited by the equal right of his fellows. A child does not get the sense of belonging by a form of behavior that alienates him from his fellows. And co-operation with others necessarily calls for self-discipline and at times for subordination. The wise teacher leads children to see this for themselves and to behave acceptably, not through fear or because told to do so by a person in authority, but because they themselves see the desirability of such behavior. This is a slower process and requires skill, understanding, and patience. But it is a far surer, more permanent, and more socially useful type of discipline.

There are, of course, situations where one must obey a person in authority. In adult life such situations occur when we obey a traffic officer, or a superior in our work. Almost always, however, we see the reason for the obedience. And most of the time we work toward an end which we want to accomplish, and discipline ourselves. The worker who works only when the foreman's eye is on him is not worth his salt. Training in self-discipline toward ends one accepts as one's own is therefore much better training for actual life than training in blind obedience to authority.

The second aspect of progressive education is the development of the child's individuality—his self-fulfillment in accordance with his own characteristic design of growth. We have already seen that this is a basic need in his emotional life—that he must have a chance for self-expression. But it is also a necessity for his choice of wholesome use of leisure, for his choice of a vocation in which he will have both interest and skill, and for his own unique contribution to the growth of society.

The progressive school therefore encourages spontaneity, variation, initiative, creative work, and independent thinking. Many of the activities in the progressive school look to the outsider like mere play—painting, drawing, modeling, woodworking, issuing school papers, dramatizing, writing stories and verses, making and playing musical instruments, to name only a few. Yet these are among the most effective means of education. Through them the child not only gets needed emotional satisfaction, but discovers his own bents and his own limitations, which of his interests are passing impulses and which are lasting. Through them he finds where he can appreciate and enrich the culture in which he lives, and how he can best contribute to the work of society.

There is discipline, however, in each of these things. One has to learn to use tools—brush, or saw, or flute, or pen—and to use them well if one is to get satisfaction from them. The discipline of creative

work is incomparable discipline which does not disappear when the
eye of authority turns away, but which abides throughout life. It is
this discipline toward which progressive education strives.

The third aspect of progressive education has to do with the three
R's and scholarship—helping children and youth to acquire the skills
and knowledge which are necessary for participation in the work and
play of the world. Progressive education is very much concerned
with this responsibility. But it considers it as only part of education,
not as the whole. Its emphasis upon physical health and mental
hygiene, upon creative self-expression, and upon learning citizenship
through democratic participation in activities, makes the emphasis
upon learning arithmetic, reading, spelling, history, geography, and
science seem subordinate. But it is no less real. Progressive education insists, however, that learning shall be functional—not the
memorizing of dry facts, or drill in little-needed skills, on the supposition that someday one might need them, but live knowledge
applied to everyday problems. This is sound psychology. Such
learning is much more efficient and permanent than the endless drill
of the old school. But functional learning is pleasant, so some parents
feel that their children are not working as hard as they once did.
Many still adhere to the long discredited psychological notion of
mental training through mere intellectual effort and grind. What
they fail to realize is that one always works hardest on a job which
is interesting. It is not the work that seems like work which is most
efficient, but work that is done with the zest of play.

Does this unfit one for the drudgery of adult life? Maybe. But the
converse of this is that perhaps a generation that knows work can be
fun will try to make adult work more interesting.

Parents are often distressed by the tendency of progressive schools
to postpone formal learning—to have children begin reading at the
age of seven instead of six, or learn long division in the sixth grade
instead of fourth. But this, too, is sound psychology, and of proved
efficiency. Learning, to be effective, must be based on experience.
The progressive school seeks to give children experience first, the
symbols of reading, spelling, and number only when experience has
made these symbols meaningful. As will be shown later, this results
in no ultimate loss in time or quality of learning, but tends rather to
save time for the other aspects of education.

One other objection is raised: The children do not learn as many
facts—capitals and boundaries of states, dates of battles, and so on,
as did children in the old schools. No, they don't. To cram children's

heads with masses of memorized material is as painful as it is futile. What they learn instead, far better than under the old system, is a general orientation in the world and skill in using libraries and books of reference to find details as they need them. This is the way of the scholar.

Finally, the fourth aspect of progressive education is education for citizenship. This includes, first of all, direct experience with democratic living. The progressive school is a democratic school in which the superintendent and principals are chairmen of teachers' groups, executive officers and stimulating leaders, but not autocrats, and in which the teacher in the classroom exerts her authority as seldom as possible and acts far more often as the wise guide and arbiter, allowing the children, as far as they are able, to think and plan co-operatively. She even lets them learn by their mistakes when this can be done without serious harm. Only so can they feel responsibility.

Besides innumerable experiences in living democratically within the school the children have much more contact with the world outside than do those who have the traditional bookish schooling. They go on many field trips to get first-hand knowledge of their community and its environs. They see the interdependence of people, they become aware of the human and material resources of their surroundings, and, as they approach and go through adolescence, they see some of the many unsolved problems of our life today. Under good teaching they reach an appreciation of the ideals and accomplishments of our society, and a keen desire to play their part, as they grow up, in helping it to realize its ideals more fully. But while they are still children they participate directly in local improvements—clean-up campaigns, wild-flower planting and preservation, safety, and the like. They must learn citizenship by practicing it.

Direct experience is extended through pictures—mounted pictures from such magazines as the *National Geographic;* stereopticon slides, and movies. The children learn to know their own country— and through knowledge come respect and devotion. And they learn to know other peoples as fellow human beings.

Discussions, talks in assembly, and radio, broaden indirect experience further. And books—many books, far more than are used in traditional schools—extend experience indefinitely.

Youngsters—particularly adolescents and post-adolescents—get a keen sense of the controversial issues of the day and awake to a determination to help right the wrongs of society. And this is why progressive education is sometimes accused of radicalism. The young people are taught to look honestly at the evils that exist—war, class struggle, slums, corruptions, race prejudice—and to examine fearlessly all proposed solutions. If the parents have a strong emotional prejudice on one side of a controversial issue, their children are likely to take the opposite side in discussions at home. And parents don't like to hear their children espousing a point of view which differs from their own. Yet therein lies thought and progress.

Progressive education does not indoctrinate children with any particular solution to our problems, but instils in them a desire to examine all proposals, to get beneath propaganda and prejudice, to seek facts and reasons, and to think boldly. This is radicalism only in the best sense—getting at the roots of problems.

A patriotism based on understanding rather than shibboleths, a patriotism that is not afraid to acknowledge weaknesses in one's country and is determined to seek ways of overcoming them, is the only true patriotism.

So much for the theory and practice of progressive education. Does it work? Does it accomplish its aims?

This question cannot yet be answered categorically. We have no adequate measures for emotional adjustment, for creativeness, initiative, and development of individuality; or even for the various phases of citizenship, although some of these have been at least partially measured. But we can measure whether children educated in progressive schools do as well in the academic parts of education as do those in traditional schools, and this has been done.

For the past thirty years American schools of all kinds have been using standardized tests in reading, spelling, arithmetic, geography, history, and so on. Sheer knowledge and skill in these fields are accurately measured. Such tests have been used for comparing children's accomplishment, along academic lines, in progressive and traditional schools.

In terms of the broader objectives of progressive education J. Wayne Wrightstone, Director of the Division of Research of the New York City Schools, has made the most extensive comparison between traditional and progressive schools. He shows that in working skills, skill in organization, ability to interpret facts, ability to apply generalizations, civic beliefs, initiative, work spirit, reliability, courtesy (yes!), co-operation, critical thinking, children in progressive schools excelled those in traditional schools.

But do progressive schools prepare children for college? This is not properly a basic objective—each school should give students the best possible education on its own level, and the school that follows should adapt its course to the students. Nevertheless to many parents the question of whether the students can fit into college is crucial. On this point we have the most thorough study yet made of the results of progressive education.

Several years ago, with grants from the Carnegie Corporation and the General Education Board, and the co-operation of most of the leading colleges and universities of the United States, a commission of the Progressive Education Association selected thirty high schools which agreed to carry out an eight-year experiment. These high schools were told that all usual examinations and requirements for college entrance would be waived for their graduates for a period of five years, beginning when they had carried out an experimental program for three years. Each school was allowed to work out its own program. Some changed little, some changed to a really progressive kind of education. The graduates entered the various colleges as had been agreed, and then were meticulously compared with students of equal intelligence and similar home and community background in the same colleges.

Taken as a whole, the students from the thirty schools were equal or slightly superior to their peers from other schools in the college grades they made in almost every subject.

But some of the schools in the thirty had made very little change from traditional methods, while others had departed widely. The graduates of the six which were most traditional were compared with their matched pairs, and those from the schools which had made fullest use of their freedom to carry out a progressive program were compared with their own pairs. The results were striking. The students from the more traditional six schools were just equal to those with whom they were compared. But the students from the six most progressive high schools got higher grades in college than their peers in every subject but one. They spent more time on study, were more critical of their educational experiences, were more active in student social life, took more part in student government, dramatics, publications, and clubs, and attended more lectures, concerts, and plays.

Progressive education appears to be the best preparation for college.

It would be strange if the results of all these studies were not what we have found them to be—better than the results of traditional schooling. For the curriculum and methods of the old-type school are based upon a tradition that had its origin before we had begun any scientific study of how children develop, and it was planned, however inadequately, for a society which since then has undergone drastic changes. Progressive education, on the other hand, is simply modern psychology and social science applied to the all-round education of the child; an attempt, in the light of our best scientific findings and practical experience, to help each child to find self-fulfillment as an individual and as a participating member of a democratic society.

QUESTIONS ON CONTENT

1. What is the purpose of paragraphs 2 and 3?
2. Have you heard—or made—all the charges against progressive education listed in paragraph 2?
3. Why does the author say that progressive education is an "attitude"?
4. Is the description of the aims of progressive education similar to Huxley's description of a liberal education ("A Liberal Education Defined")?
5. Do you consider the emphasis upon "emotional adjustment" deserving of a central place in any system of education? Comment upon progressive educators' attitude toward "repressive discipline" or "reasoning with the child."
6. Comment upon "self-discipline" which is taught in the place of traditionally imposed discipline.
7. How do the progressive schools develop the child's personality?
8. What is the progressive attitude toward the "three R's"? Can you detect in these paragraphs any "card stacking" in favor of the progressive method? How does the progressive educator know, for example, what is "functional"? Why is it assumed that all facts are "dry"? *Who* has discredited the idea of "mental training through *mere* intellectual effort and grind"? Is progressive education "the way of the scholar"?
9. Do you get the impression that children in the traditional schools have little opportunity to become good citizens?
10. How does the author attempt to answer the question of whether or not progressive education works? Examine the evidence and decide whether it seems convincing.

❧ *Adjustment Replaces Education*

MORTIMER SMITH

The Life Adjustment movement is not new, it is but an old acquaintance going under a newly assumed name. It is the latest manifestation of the idea that the school's task is only incidentally to train the intelligence and impart knowledge, that its real function is to serve as a gigantic bureau of social services where the attempt will be made to adjust the student to all "real life problems." Its importance derives from two factors: it echoes and in a sense sums up what public school educators have been advocating for twenty years; and it has semiofficial, even quasi-governmental sanction.

One dedicated advocate of Life Adjustment asks, "Who does not thrill to see the leaders who marched in the vanguard of this crusade?" Apparently Quintilian, Luther, Rousseau, Jefferson, Ben Franklin, Horace Mann, and Henry Barnard, among others, were practicing Life Adjusters. He then makes what seems to be an accurate statement regarding its present standing among schemes of educational "reform":

> In its present form this movement has outgrown every other movement of educational discontent; it out-heralds any other movement ever conceived; it is the first movement which has at one and the same time enlisted the energy, faith, and encouragement of educators at all levels; national, state, and local. This is different from what happened with the work of the NEA Committees, with the pronouncements of colleges and professors, or of professional groups. It has strength; its organization is well conceived; its possibilities are great enough to challenge all professional persons at all levels.[1]

The movement originated on the highest "level," in the United States Office of Education, which office was then part of the Federal Security Agency and is now a division of the Department of Health,

From *The Diminished Mind*, 1954. Reprinted by permission of the author and by permission of Henry Regnery Co., Chicago.

[1] Adolph Unruh, "Life Adjustment Education—A Definition," *Progressive Education*, February, 1952.

Education, and Welfare. In 1947 the Commissioner of Education appointed a Commission on Life Adjustment Education for Youth, and eventually this body came forth with a statement of purpose. Incidentally, one could hardly get a better illustration of the isolation of public school education from the world of learning and scholarship than the membership composition of this Commission. When the (then) Commissioner of Education, presumably the moral if not the official leader of American education, decides that the time has arrived "to effect major improvements in the programs and processes of secondary education" one might reasonably suppose that the commission appointed for studying the problem would include some outstanding scholars and authorities in subject fields. A careful perusal of the ninety names comprising the list of "educational leaders" attending the original conference reveals administrators, professors of education, vocational, home economics, and agriculture specialists, and various educational bureaucrats, but not a single representative of the liberal arts. This would seem to indicate quite clearly what the U.S. Office of Education thinks of the place of the liberal arts in effecting "major improvements" in secondary education.[2]

The Commission's statement of purpose is in most regards a far from revolutionary document for it simply restates the aims of education as they have appeared in the "statement of purposes" of innumerable other commissions and committees issued during the past few years. The Commission wants an education which will equip all American youth to live democratically as home members, workers, and citizens; it is concerned with ethical and moral living, mental and emotional health, wholesome recreational interests; it believes in the dignity of work and the importance of personal satisfactions and achievements; and it makes the regulation bow to "the importance of fundamental skills."[3] In other words, it is the usual hotchpotch of unexceptionable, vague clichés, and has the usual weakness of such statements in trying to be all inclusive, as well as expressing an apparent unawareness that some purposes of the school are primary and others subsidiary.

But in one respect the statement of the Commission is a milestone in the history of American education for it implies baldly that the majority of American high school students are incapable either of being prepared for college or trained for vocations. The original

[2] U.S. Office of Education, *Life Adjustment Education for Every Youth,* Bulletin No. 22, 1951.

[3] *Ibid.*, pp. 9–10.

resolution which suggested a life adjustment program states that twenty per cent of the high school population can be prepared for college and another twenty per cent trained vocationally but for the remaining sixty per cent administrators must devise a new program. "College preparation or training for skilled occupations is neither feasible nor appropriate" for this group, says the Commission.[4]

This is pretty revolutionary doctrine and would seem to imply that the majority of American youth—sixty per cent—are so dull that all the school can attempt to do is to adjust them to their environment. Arthur Bestor has said that this statement, if true, invalidates most of the assumptions that have underlain American democracy, and "enthrones once again the ancient doctrine that a clear majority of the people are destined from birth to be hewers of wood and drawers of water."[5] That some advocates of Life Adjustment have faced up to this implication is shown by this reference from a professor of education: "The neglected group . . . lacking aroused interests or pronounced aptitudes (which is probably fortunate for a society having a large number of jobs to be done requiring no unusual aptitudes or interests) also lacks the drives which allow us to serve their brothers and sisters more easily."[6]

Just what is it that Life Adjustment is going to do for the sixty per cent which apparently fared so ill under more traditional school programs? The report, *Life Adjustment Education for Every Youth*, gives no indication that anything is going to be done to devise more efficient techniques for reaching this group with the values inherent in traditional subject matter, or that the Commission even believes there *are* any such values. The theme of the low educational aptitude of the majority is driven home throughout the report: Only a small minority can have any real understanding of abstract mathematics; few students will have either the ability or the need to write and speak with accuracy; and the report of a National Education Association subsidiary is quoted, with approval, to the effect that "reading to comprehend newspapers and magazines reasonably well" is a worthy aim in teaching "the educationally neglected student."[7] The Commission feels that "teachers are enthusiastic about the subjects they teach . . . more interested in securing greater enrollments

---

[4] *Ibid.*, p. 16, p. 19.

[5] Arthur E. Bestor, *Educational Wastelands*, (Urbana; The University of Illinois Press, 1953), p. 82.

[6] Edward K. Hankin, "The Crux of Life Adjustment Education," *Bulletin* of the National Association of Secondary-School Principals, November, 1953, p. 72.

[7] *Life Adjustment Education for Every Youth*, pp. 80–82.

for their subjects than in adjusting subjects to meet the needs of girls and boys. . . . There are enormous pressures for teachers and principals to continue doing the things they do well even though these practices fail to meet the needs of many pupils." [8] All this would seem to be a backhanded way of saying that even though teachers are enthusiastic about their subjects and competent in teaching them, they might as well give up the effort as far as the sixty per cent is concerned for they can't take it.

What the Commission is interested in for the sixty per cent, and what is heavily emphasized throughout the report are "the general areas" of citizenship, family life, conservation, general occupational adjustment, consumer education, leisure time, and health. These are undeniably worthy things many of which in former, less enlightened times, would come up incidentally in teaching the various subjects, but the unmistakable implication is that they are now largely to replace the subjects and become the curriculum itself. The Life Adjuster quoted earlier says the new curriculum is going to consist of nine items: education for family living, consumer economics, citizenship, job information, ethical and moral living, physical and emotional health, training for world citizenship and statesmanship, and —bringing up the rear of the procession as usual—training in fundamental skills. [9]

If one is to judge by the amount of discussion it gets in professional journals, and the number of influential educators who have paid homage to it, Life Adjustment is here to stay. Actually, as I have said, it's been here for a long time under various aliases such as Core Curriculum, General Education, Common Learnings, and Social Living, and is substantially the same program the Educational Policies Commission and other commissions affiliated with the National Education Association have been turning up periodically for the last twenty years. Whatever the nomenclature, these "programs" are similar in aim in that they all abandon formal subject matter in favor of integration of all subject matter towards an over-all objective, towards what the educators like to call "dynamic, functional learning." Perhaps it may be salutary to examine some of these programs which are springing up in junior and senior high schools all over the country. Many educators feel they represent an inevitable trend in public education. If so, one must shudder for the future of American youth, for these programs, no matter how much

[8] *Ibid.*, p. 11.
[9] "Life Adjustment Education—A Definition."

good will and sincerity may be behind them, are unfortunately almost unfailingly anti-intellectual, trivial and a caricature of genuine education.

Here, for example, is the report of a core program as carried on in the ninth grade in a Maryland high school.[10] The day is divided into six periods; in the morning the students study home economics (for the girls), shop (for the boys), physical education for three days of the week and music for the other two, and general mathematics and general science. (This program is probably even more meagre than it sounds for "general" mathematics and science are usually watered-down courses containing little real nourishment.) The two afternoon periods, totaling about 104 minutes, are devoted to "core," this particular program revolving around the topic "What Makes Us Tick," a unit for "study of human behavior and relationships." (Other units used in the same school have such titles as Life Can Be Beautiful, There Are No Robinson Crusoes, Am I Getting My Money's Worth?) This being a modern school everything is, of course, very democratic and involved with group dynamics—before anything can be done there must be "organization of personnel." Accordingly the class elects a steering committee, consisting of a chairman, vice-chairman, and secretary, and six subcommittees, these latter to be responsible for each "problem area" to be discussed. These problem areas (if you are still following me) were selected by the class and are as follows:

What parents should expect of us and what we desire and expect of our parents.

How we can get started in social activities in our own age groups.

How to have a successful "date."

What to do, according to the rules of etiquette, in certain embarrassing situations.

When we should give gifts on our own, separate from "the family" giving.

How to entertain at parties and other social activities.

Most of the class activity seemed to be involved with item number three—how to have a successful date. Listed among the "outstanding examples" of the students' activities in exploring this subject were a dramatization of how to make a date, a poll on "controversial date problems" which was given to a group starting with the seventh grade and extending up to the faculty, a group study of the cost of

[10] This is reported in Harold Alberty, *Reorganizing the High-School Curriculum* (New York; Macmillan, Revised Edition, 1953).

corsages which involved practicing telephone calls and personal interviews in the class, and a study of how to have "party fun."

This program was "democratically evaluated" by the class itself; with the members deciding that "outcomes actually covered more growth than the objectives included"; among these outcomes was learning to work better in a group, appreciating the other fellow's contribution, learning to write a script, learning good telephone etiquette. The teacher felt the unit had resulted in sincere interest in improving oral and written skills, increased poise in and respect for proper boy-girl social relationships, and excellent growth in group cooperation.

This core program must not be thought to be atypical; on the contrary it is representative in spirit and method of programs being carried on in schools over the country. The book which reports it, *Reorganizing the High-School Curriculum*, gives the details of many others "based upon the persistent common needs, problems and interests of youth." The "units" range from the sublime (studies of human rights and world peace) to the ridiculous (studies of "growing up" in which such items as these are considered: "How often should I change my clothing?" "What can I do to keep my teeth white and my skin soft?" "What can I do with my old-fashioned parents?" "What should I talk about on a date?" and, my favorite among these problems, "May I show how I feel with my water colors?") [11]

Another educationist tells us that Los Angeles County has developed a course (a course, no less!) in which personal problems are "outlined carefully" including the problem of *How to be Attractive and Well Groomed*. Under this heading are discussed such matters as how to banish unwanted hair, and how to bathe for health and cleanliness. (What else one bathes for, deponent saith not.) Among further questions which come up for consideration in this "course" (and I'm not making this up) are the following: How do you pick up a handkerchief? How do you sit down properly at various occasions? How can you improve your stride and still maintain poise? [12] Thus is "real life education" carried on.

Another document, *Improving School Holding Power*, shows that

[11] My favorite core unit is one used in the 10th grade in a Denver high school, "Orientation to the school building." One would suppose that this course would consist of a half-hour tour of the washrooms, laboratories, gymnasium, etc., but then one would be underestimating the ability of educators to inflate the simple into the complex.

[12] Leonard, *op. cit.*, pp. 342–43.

in various cities, such as Rochester, St. Louis, St. Paul, Minneapolis, and Detroit, programs have been introduced in the schools which follow closely the reasoning of the Life Adjustment advocates. It is interesting to learn from this booklet how St. Paul has increased the holding power of its high schools; among other devices it has adjusted school work to individual differences, reduced drastically the percentage of failures, abandoned grade standards on report cards in favor of individual standards, and eliminated the practice of making satisfactory scholastic accomplishment a requirement for athletic and club activities. This fairly complete abandonment of all educational standards may help to keep young people in school; it is difficult to see how any reasonable person could claim that it comprises sound preparation for maturity.[13]

What the core and similar programs amount to is a sort of juvenile bull session. Conceivably many of the items discussed are of real concern to the students but to make the discussion of them the whole curriculum, or a major part of it, with the consequent necessary neglect of real subject matter, is to cheat the youth by neglecting the basic facts and disciplines which alone will enable him to arrive at mature judgments about his concerns. Many of the items could probably be more advantageously discussed in private conversation with the teacher or school counselor than in a group. Not the least unfortunate aspect of these programs is just this emphasis on the group and belittling of individuality. (The youth who wants to discuss with a committee what he should talk about on a date doesn't deserve to have a date.)

Reading such a book as *Reorganizing the High-School Curriculum* (which is considered authoritative in the field) one gets the impression that none of the reorganizing is going to be in the direction of improved teaching of subject matter but entirely in the direction of finding ways of undermining subject matter. Although the author laments the sparsity of core programs in American schools, another advocate assures us that "procedures involving at least something of these principles and their applications will be found not many years hence in practically all but the very small, weak high schools

---

[13] *Improving School Holding Power,* Circular No. 291, U.S. Office of Education, 1951. In the matter of holding power, I have long suspected that changing the curriculum has little to do with keeping young people in school, and am glad to have my suspicion confirmed by an educationist who says that "only about one-fourth of those who discontinue say they do so because of the curriculum." See *The American Secondary School,* edited by Paul B. Jacobson (New York; Prentice-Hall, 1952), p. 120.

and the very large conservative ones." [14] Harl R. Douglass, who makes this prediction, states that progress will be slow for a number of reasons including the fact that parents (those notorious stumbling blocks) are confused and have a tendency to believe that the new program is less valuable than "the good old-fashioned authoritarian, fear-motivated program that they followed in school." [15] (Modern educators like to pretend that all American schools of twenty or more years ago were modeled on Mr. Squeers' Dotheboys Hall.)

The anti-intellectual bias which animates advocates of these programs is expressed with unusual bluntness in a book called *New Schools for a New Culture* which is a report of another core program, this one carried on since 1937 at the Evanston Township High School, Evanston, Illinois.

> In the school of tomorrow [say the authors of this report] the aristocratic, cultural tradition of education must be completely and finally abandoned. Scholarship must become functional. This does not mean that it will be concerned only with the material wants of man or that it will lack creativeness or intellectual stimulation, but it *will* cease to rattle the bones of the dead past solely for pleasure or, worse, out of a sense of academic duty. . . .
>
> Any help we can give them (those who possess unusual intellectual curiosity) should be theirs, but such favored people learn directly from their surroundings. Our efforts to teach them are quite incidental in their development. It is therefore unnecessary and futile for the schools to attempt to gear their programs to the needs of unusual people. . . .
>
> Teachers have thought they must clothe themselves with the robes of the scholar and perpetuate the scholarly tradition so far as possible in every one of their pupils.
>
> The school of tomorrow must accept in fact that general education in a democracy must be for the masses.[16]

Some of the argument in this statement is hard to follow, possibly because the authors have themselves abandoned that part of the cultural tradition which emphasizes lucid expression. Do they mean that any large part of scholarship is concerned with rattling the bones of the dead past, and if they do mean this, is it true? What do they mean by the airy reference to the "dead" past—isn't all the past

[14] Harl R. Douglass, *Secondary Education for Life Adjustment of American Youth* (New York; Ronald Press, 1952), p. 184.

[15] *Ibid.*, p. 185.

[16] Charles M. MacConnell, Ernest O. Melby, Christian O. Arndt, Leslee J. Bishop, *New Schools for a New Culture* (New York; Harper and Brothers, Revised Edition, 1953), pp. 154–55.

alive as it illumines the present? And if scholars get pleasure out of rattling the bones, isn't that functional? In the long run isn't the function and purpose of all education to increase man's pleasure by increasing his knowledge and understanding? And do they really mean to say that unusual people learn directly from their surroundings but that it is futile for the schools to provide the surroundings that will aid them in their development?

Aside from these ambiguities, it seems clear enough that they have a strong animus against education as a means of transmitting the intellectual and cultural tradition of the race, that they think it is foolish for a teacher of the masses to attempt to be a scholar, and that it is also foolish for a teacher to try to hold all students to some standard of scholarship.

A few pages further on in their book the authors strike another blow for the new schools in a new culture:

> It is well that the schoolmaster's efforts to make scholars of all who come to him have never met with conspicuous success. The world's work is not done from an armchair. . . . The work of the world is accomplished through intelligent and skillful action. The school of tomorrow must recognize this both by its emphasis and by its acceptances. Scholarship, we repeat, must become functional in human affairs, even though a place may be allowed a few scholars who concern themselves with what they call "pure learning." [17]

One fears that that implied sneer in their reference to pure learning bodes ill for those poor scholars who are going to apply to the educational commissars of the future to be "allowed" to pursue their armchair specialties. And one might well ask whether intelligent and skillful action appears full-blown out of the void or does it have its wellsprings in the discipline of intellectual and scholarly preparation? One would suppose that some armchair thinking would have to precede action, even in the new schools and the new culture.

It is interesting to see how the authors' anti-intellectual bias applies to a concrete subject such as written expression. They want, of course, the "simpler type" of writing "which meets the needs of the average citizen." It turns out that "writing is not learned through previous instruction. It is learned functionally *by writing when and what* one needs to write." But there are two nasty enemies lying in wait for the student, the professor in college and the future employer; the former sets artificial standards which students have to

[17] *Ibid.*, p. 162.

meet for college entrance, and the latter, being a good deal of a snob, foolishly accepts the professor's standards and demands them in his employees. "Such," sigh our authors, "are the values established by the intellectual aristocracy in America." [18]

One can imagine the difficulties the good student in the academic sense is going to have in the schools of tomorrow. Our authors say that the child who has learned to follow rules at home is often an honor student in school "that has for its chief objective the preparation of assigned lessons" so he is naturally going to be ill at ease when he goes to a school which abjures this objective. They readily admit he is going to be confused, and faced with the necessity of "remaking in four years a whole habit pattern" in which he has had years of conditioning, but fortunately the new teachers in the new school are willing to take on this "discouraging assignment" and "do with it as much as we are able." [19] In other words, although they can't guarantee anything, they will do their best to undermine any tendencies in new students towards academic accomplishment. This is a logical position for such determined equalitarians as the authors; an aristocracy of the intellect cannot be tolerated where intellectual matters are themselves held in contempt.

The casual reader wading through the involuted prose of *New Schools for a New Culture,* especially the reader who is out of touch with public school matters, may be inclined to think that the dreary viewpoint expressed therein is that of a small minority, or lunatic fringe, and in any case is only presentation of theory. To speak of the last supposition first, it should be borne in mind that the objectives are now being carried out in the core program of the Evanston Township High School which removes the authors' ideas from the realm of the merely theoretical. Secondly, far from being a scheme of a fringe group, it is sponsored by high priests in the hierarchy of American education. One of the authors of the book, Ernest O. Melby, was formerly dean of the School of Education at New York University, one of the largest and most influential such schools in the country. Dean Melby is an important figure in education by virtue of his position alone but his importance is further emphasized by the frequency with which he manages to get his viewpoint expressed not only in professional but also in lay journals. The point of view expounded in *New Schools for a New Culture* may be nonsense, dangerous nonsense, but it is not inconsequential for it is uttered by

[18] *Ibid.,* pp. 39–40.
[19] *Ibid.,* pp. 122–123.

respected and influential men in the educational world and has been translated into a going experiment in an actual public school.

The revolt against "intellectual aristocracy" reached its logical end when a principal of a junior high school publicly advocated abandoning the attempt to teach everyone to read. This quotation, from a paper written in 1951, has appeared widely but deserves reiteration as a warning of what American public school education may come to:

> Through the years we've built a sort of halo around reading, writing, and arithmetic. We've said they were for everybody . . . rich and poor, brilliant and not-so-mentally endowed, ones who liked them and those who failed to go for them. Teacher has said that these were something "everyone should learn." The principal has remarked, "All educated people know how to write, spell and read." When some child declared a dislike for a sacred subject, he was warned that, if he failed to master it, he would grow up to be a so-and-so.
>
> The Three R's for All Children, and All Children for the Three R's. That was it.
>
> We've made some progress in getting rid of that slogan. But every now and then some mother with a Phi Beta Kappa award or some employer who has hired a girl who can't spell stirs up a fuss about the schools . . . and ground is lost. . . .
>
> When we come to the realization that not every child has to read, figure, write and spell . . . that many of them either cannot or will not master these chores . . . then we shall be on the road to improving the junior high curriculum.
>
> Between this day and that a lot of selling must take place. But it's coming. We shall some day accept the thought that it is no more reasonable to require that each girl shall spell well than it is that each shall bake a good cherry pie. . . .
>
> If and when we are able to convince a few folks that mastery of reading, writing and arithmetic is not the one road leading to happy, successful living, and the next step is to cut down the amount of time and attention devoted to these areas in general junior high-school courses. . . .[20]

Here again, this blithe, and one might say frightening, contempt for learning cannot be dismissed as isolated, personal eccentricity. The paper from which these quotations are taken was read before the country's largest professional association of public high school

[20] A. H. Lauchner, "How Can the Junior High School Curriculum Be Improved?" *Bulletin* of the National Association of Secondary-School Principals, March 1951, pp. 299–300.

principals and was published in that association's official journal, and not as a horrible example, either. It would be absurd to suggest that all educationists subscribe to these views but the fact that they could be delivered to a professional association charged with the education of American youth and go unrebuked confirms one's suspicions that the educationists are more concerned with decrying the critics who accuse education of being anti-intellectual than they are with rebuking their own members whose remarks are flagrant proof of the charge.

The life–adjustment core–curriculum common–learnings people continue their efforts to undermine those colleges which still demand that a student who seeks entrance should present some evidence of exposure to the intellectual disciplines in high school. The U.S. Office of Education reports, with satisfaction, that in one state 121 high schools and thirty-eight colleges have signed an agreement according to which the colleges will "disregard the pattern of subjects of high-school graduates who are recommended for college entrance." The high schools' part of the agreement consists of a vague promise to improve "guidance procedures" and "to carry on continuous efforts to improve curriculum programs." [21] In some educationist circles the argument is no longer over the amount or quality of intellectual training; the question has been resolved by frank proposals to abandon entirely intellectual disciplines as such in high school. Here is a quotation from Harl R. Douglass, an influential and prolific Life Adjuster who is also director of the College of Education at the University of Colorado:

> In the early days of secondary and higher education in the United States, Latin and Greek were the subjects required for college entrance. A little later, mathematics, including arithmetic, was required. Still later, instruction in English and in science was added, and, in the latter part of the nineteenth century, a year of history. However valuable the study of these preferred subjects was for the purpose of preparing pupils for college curricula and college teaching as it existed in the seventeenth and eighteenth centuries or perhaps in the early part of the nineteenth century, it became increasingly questionable that the subjects most commonly required for college entrance made any unique or greatly superior contribution to the work of young people in college.[22]

[21] *Vitalizing Secondary Education*, Bulletin No. 3, Report of the First Commission on Life Adjustment Education for Youth, Reprinted 1954, U.S. Department of Health, Education and Welfare, p. 58.

[22] Douglass, *op. cit.*, p. 531.

I have read over this quotation several times and have come to the conclusion that, incredible as it may seem, the author means what he says, viz., that though, for entrance, colleges require preparation in mathematics, English, science, and history, such preparation is of no value to the student when he gets to college. That this interpretation is the correct one seems to be confirmed by another remark of the author's:

> An increasing number of theorists and administrators are advocating that, except possibly for a very few bright students, the study of foreign languages should be postponed to the college years. There are also some, and their number is slowly increasing, who hold a similar position with respect to the traditional courses in mathematics. These hold that algebra, geometry, and trigonometry have relatively little value except as college preparation or except for a few college curricula, and that therefore most of the instruction in those fields should be postponed until college.[23]

Because of the forces of reaction and entrenched custom, Dr. Douglass realizes that the happy day when the main body of subject matter may be dispensed with must be postponed, but in the meantime he has some practical suggestions for emasculating the content of subject matter. In the interests of making English "more meaningful" than in the past he suggests that it be organized into "idea-centered" units where the pupils "would be thrown into active language situations that would force them to discuss, to report findings, to interview, to take part in conversations, to write letters, to summarize reports, to take notes, and to write imaginatively about their own experiences." One would suppose that pupils would need some knowledge of the rules and structure of language to perform these tasks but Dr. Douglass assures us that just *doing* them does more to "establish comfort and proficiency in language than the work in grammar and usage that formerly dominated our courses of study." He does admit that the teacher may have to give some initial help so the pupils may "avoid language difficulties that they may get into," but such help may be given "through a nontechnical, thought approach to language problems not based on formal grammatical terminology." One may be puzzled as to what a "nontechnical, thought approach" may be but we are informed that three other professors of education have found it not only more "efficient" but

[23] *Ibid.*, p. 598.

"more economical in time" than traditional training in English usage.[24]

One of the professors to whom Dr. Douglass refers, John DeBoer of the University of Illinois, suggests that the school should make the effort to "cultivate more than one kind of English—the kind which is natural and comfortable and intelligible in the students' own group, and the kind which may have a much wider range of acceptability in English-speaking countries." These "levels of usage" are to be learned through "abundant uses" and through instruction based on "grounds of social practice" rather than through "systematic study *about* language." "Grammar is for editorial use by the advanced student." [25] I have not seen *Teaching Secondary English,* a volume of which Professor DeBoer is coauthor, but can imagine it must be a novel treatment of the subject.

Three more professors of education who look kindly on Life Adjustment and have written an influential textbook for teachers, find a new reason for belittling spelling and grammar:

> The teaching of spelling and grammar may contribute very little if anything, to the realization of democratic ideals—except as these skills may be required by a few persons for vocational purposes and thus for their well-being in society, as in the case of teachers and clerical workers. On the other hand, mastery of the habits of effective thinking and critical reading and listening is to be rated high on the scale of objectives that satisfy the democratic ideals. For democracy is based on the principle that the common man can manage public, as well as private, affairs if he has a chance to acquire information and to learn to think for himself.[26]

How the common man is going to manage his "critical reading" without benefit of spelling or the rules of the English language, or where he is going to acquire habits of effective thinking, or the literacy, that will enable him to manage public affairs, the authors do not state; nor, for that matter, do they tell us why the teacher should bother to learn spelling and the rules of grammar if she is only to teach them to other teachers, and clerks. In this connection, they set up a stern test to measure the usefulness of written expression. (Personal satisfaction and pleasure therein, of course, has nothing to do with it.)

[24] *Ibid.,* pp. 343, 344.

[25] John DeBoer, "The Teaching of Communication," *Progressive Education,* May, 1952.

[26] B. Othanel Smith, William O. Stanley, J. Harlan Shores, *Fundamentals of Curriculum Development* (Yonkers; World Book Company, 1950), p. 265.

No amount of past usefulness . . . can assure the value of subject matter for today. . . . Persons who believe that more emphasis should now be placed upon the study of grammar—on the ground that in the past such study has produced better written expression—must show that the social importance of good written expression is as great today as in the past century, when grammar played a dominant role in the school's program.[27]

Perhaps the people of the British Isles might testify to the social importance of Winston Churchill's written and spoken expression during the dark days of World War II. Churchill was not a brilliant student but he has spoken many times of his gratefulness to his schoolmasters in the English language for their persistency in keeping him to a task he disliked. I doubt if they, or any good teacher of any subject at any time, gave too much thought to the "social importance" of the subject but were content to believe that if education can produce a good *man* the social will take care of itself.

But let us return to Dr. Douglass and see what he has to say about the teaching of foreign languages. Here he is aware of the complications arising from lack of training in formal grammar but his ideal seems to be a "more functional, immediately practical" knowledge of a foreign language—which apparently does not include the ability to speak it correctly. Some of the "offerings" in foreign language courses which he approves are courses in world literature (in translation), special commercial courses, and short-unit courses in "traveler's Spanish."[28] (One may be permitted to feel for the traveler when he discovers that Spanish-speaking people don't speak traveler's Spanish.)

Dr. Douglass, of course, is against "verbalism." He claims that the high school education of the past was largely a matter of learning words and that the teacher accepted as evidence of learning the pupil's ability to repeat words found in the textbooks. (What good teacher in any age ever adopted such a method?) The educators are slowly solving the problem of providing "more meaningful and more vividly interesting experiences" but Dr. Douglass feels that "the problem has become somewhat accentuated . . . by increased dependence of young people upon pictures in comics, in movies, and in television." Then he adds that "the solution to this problem may be accelerated" by more training of teachers "with respect to the

[27] *Ibid.*, p. 287.
[28] Douglass, *op. cit.*, pp. 352, 353, 354.

use of audio-visual aids and community research."[29] I think this means that now that we have given up reading, the job of the teacher is to find superior pictures for the pupils to look at. The "community research" part of it, I suspect, would be good old Field Trips to the mayor's office and the county courthouse, interviewing merchants and social workers, etc.

Throughout his long book the author shows only impatience or scorn for those who insist that education must continue to be concerned with matters of the intellect and that it ought to have a body of subject content. He also consistently caricatures and misrepresents traditional schools to the point where the reader wonders how anybody who went to school before the coming of Life Adjustment managed to learn anything or survived the barbaric procedures of those schools. (Here is one horrible example of the evils of the schools of yesterday: "Such procedures as learning to obey the teacher and trying to learn things which were not understood and difficult were considered good mental and moral training."[30] Just think of anybody ever having had the idea that obeying the teacher and trying to learn something difficult was good training! It's hard to remember how antediluvian schools used to be before the educationists took over.)

Again, I feel the necessity of pointing out that Dr. Douglass is hardly an isolated phenomenon. He is the director of a teacher training institution and exerts influence far beyond his school and small state by the great number of education textbooks he has written, books used widely in the education of future teachers. He was also one of the chosen ninety who attended the original conference, called by the Commissioner of Education, which set up the Life Adjustment program.

If you are appalled by the picture he draws of the new and meaningful curriculum of the future you may be cheered by a couple of regretful admissions he has to make. You may be glad to know that "how to get rid of the conventional report card" and substitute one "less likely to stimulate parents to unwise attempts to provide incentives to better efforts" remains an unsolved problem.[31] Perhaps even more hopeful is his rueful admission that, despite all the advances we have made towards "a modern concept of objectives" and despite the professed theory of teachers and principals, "visits to the

[29] *Ibid.*, p. 603.
[30] *Ibid.*, p. 476.
[31] *Ibid.*, p. 608.

classrooms unmistakably reveal practices based on the assumption that there is subject matter to be taught." [32]

If enough teachers can maintain such an idiosyncrasy perhaps public school education may yet survive the onslaught of the Life Adjusters.

Perhaps the reader unversed in current educational philosophy will feel that in the foregoing pages I have, for the sake of making my point about the deleterious effect of Life Adjustment, been highly selective in my quotations. I assure him that I have not. Almost any of the books on curriculum revision which have appeared in the past fifteen or twenty years advocate the same "reforms" as these authors from whom I have been quoting. So do members of departments of education in the various states. [33] During the past twenty years many educational commissions have presented reports on secondary education; most of them—the Harvard report was a notable exception —explicitly or implicitly state the same conclusions that are now reached by the Commission on Life Adjustment Education for Youth. Stripped of their usual verbiage these reports seem more or less in agreement on two points: (1) a large segment of American youth, probably the majority, is incapable of absorbing education as we have known it in the past, and (2) a program of "adjustment" must be devised which will keep this large segment contented for four years in high school. Dr. Douglass, our Life Adjuster from the last chapter, goes even further and states that this program should be for everyone, not only for those who can't take something better:

> While the movement [Life Adjustment movement] was aimed especially at the development of a modern functional program of secondary education for those who will not go either (1) to college or (2) into occupations for which they can be trained specifically in high school, estimated to consist nationally of 60 per cent of high school boys and girls, it is coming to be believed by more and more people that a good program for that 60 per cent *might well be an excellent program for all American youth.* [Italics mine.] [34]

[32] *Ibid.*, p. 597.

[33] See, for example, the pamphlet "The Redirection, Reorganization, and Retooling of Secondary Education," issued by the Connecticut State Department of Education (1944). As this is a pioneer statement of the principles and aims of Life Adjustment it is not surprising that its author, Paul D. Collier, became first chairman of the Commission on Life Adjustment Education for Youth.

[34] Douglass, *op. cit.*, p. 170.

There's a noble ideal to aim at—mediocrity, or worse, for all. Instead of trying to reduce the ranks of the sixty per cent, let's be democratic and bring the other forty per cent down to the same level. The Commission on Life Adjustment Education for Youth seems to agree with Dr. Douglass for it states that "life adjustment education is for all, even though there is a special concern for the so-called sixty per cent." [35]

It is ironic that the current skepticism of the ability of the majority to "take" education comes not from those who are supposed to believe in an "aristocratic" education but from professional educators who are apt to make a fetish of democracy and equalitarianism. There is an old tradition that the majority of Americans aren't very bright—H. L. Menken called them "boobs" and "yokels," Albert Jay Nock thought them "subhuman," and the advertising agencies seem to put them at about the high-grade moron level—but it is somewhat surprising to observe this assumption becoming a plank in the reform platform of educators. Watching Americans at their devotions, reading comics or looking at television, or observing how easily they can be sold a product or a fad or how susceptible they are to propaganda, one would perhaps be foolhardy to defend their collective intelligence; but the folly of overestimating it seems to me to be less dangerous than the results of assuming its low quality.

I will return to the problem of what are apt to be the consequences when we assume the majority of our fellows to be fools or dullards, but for the moment perhaps we might look at the American intelligence when measured by the tests educators have themselves devised. According to an article by the Parent and Child Editor of the *New York Times,* only 16 per cent of American children between the ages of 3–14 are below average in intelligence, that is, with I.Q.'s below 90. Sixty-eight per cent are in the I.Q. range of 90–110 (called normal or average) and 15 per cent are in the above-average range of 110–135, while one per cent are in the gifted category of over 135. [36] If these figures are at all accurate (and if we accept intelligence tests as a not infallible but rough indication of native

---

[35] *Vitalizing Secondary Education,* p. 35.

[36] Dorothy Barclay, "Handling High I.Q.'s, *The New York Times Magazine,* November 22, 1953. While there is not precise agreement among psychologists and testers in regard to national intelligence averages there does seem to be general agreement that at least 60 per cent fall in the average (90–110) category. This is the figure, for instance, given in "The Concept of Intelligence," by Albert R. Lang, in the volume *Twentieth Century Education* (New York; Philosophical Library, 1946), p. 240.

intelligence) there is little justification for the contention of the Life Adjusters that 60 per cent of American youth are incapable of either college preparation or learning a trade. Before they released their figures they should have consulted the report of another government-sponsored body, the President's Commission on Higher Education, which estimated that 49 per cent of the population has the mental ability to complete fourteen years of schooling in general, and vocational, studies and that at least 32 per cent has the ability to complete advanced liberal or specialized education.[37]

There is no doubt that in any one classroom there will be a wide range of intelligence among the pupils, presenting to the teacher perplexing problems in method, but nothing will be solved by the device of abandoning real education for those who are less facile with ideas. Certainly the high school curriculum needs to be reorganized and improved but the efforts of the professional educators in this direction never seem to touch the great major problem, viz., how to reach the less gifted with the values inherent in subject matter, especially English and history. Their efforts all seem bent on doing away with these subjects or "integrating" and watering them down to the point where all substance and value is squeezed out. I don't know how this major problem is going to be solved but certainly the teaching profession as a whole ought to be addressing themselves to its solution. If we expect the boy with an I.Q. of 90 to become a citizen and make the judgments required of a citizen we ought to be busy devising ways of making him understand the ideas which have shaped his country and world and we ought to be teaching him how to "communicate" intelligibly. Perhaps if we succeed in inculcating these major learnings we can trust him to find out for himself what to talk about on a date and how often to change his clothing.

But to return to the basic assumption of the educators that the majority of Americans aren't very bright and therefore cannot be educated in the traditional sense but need to be adjusted to the group, we ought to ask ourselves what are the practical results of

[37] *Higher Education for American Democracy,* A Report of the President's Commission on Higher Education, 1948, p. 41. This Commission had its own anti-intellectual bias. See p. 32: "We shall be denying educational opportunity to many young people as long as we maintain the present orientation of higher education toward verbal skills and intellectual interests." What kind of higher education would be devoid of intellectual interests? Perhaps the Commission is using the term higher in the simple sense of being above the elementary and high schools.

such an assumption. One of the immediately recognizable results is that such an assumption tends to turn the educative process into primarily a group rather than an individual affair; it is not the person who matters but the team and its welfare. As the authors of *New Schools for a New Culture,* quoted earlier, have said, "it is futile for the schools to attempt to gear their programs to the needs of unusual people"; education in a democracy "must be for the masses." The "unusual people" are left to shift for themselves, or as Harl Douglass suggests, the program for the masses "might well be an excellent program for all American youth."

American educational theory tends more and more towards this mass conception, towards a system where the ideal is identical experience, where deviation from the commonalty is frowned upon. In this connection, I have seen a letter from the state department of education in one of our large states, informing parents who planned to teach their child at home that they would not under the law be permitted to do so, even though there was no question of the competency of the parent to teach. The department's reason for this decision is interesting:

> No matter how competent the parents may be, the child who obtains his schooling at home is not having an experience equivalent to that of the child who goes to an authorized school. The school program does not consist only of mastering the 3 R's and the various content subjects. Perhaps the most important part of the school program is the association in a group. . . . Practically all American living today is a co-operative affair. Children have to learn to take turns and to share. Group discipline and group loyalties have to be developed.

No one would argue that the state does not have the right to hold parents responsible for seeing that their children receive an education, but this statement advances an entirely novel conception in American law in relation to education, i.e., that the state has the right to demand that children be educated in groups and conditioned to group discipline and group loyalties. That this could be adopted as the official stand of one of our large states shows how easily and complacently we are drifting into a rigid educational conformity.

Another example of the growing impatience among educators with nonconformity is the opposition to private schools, even though only roughly eight per cent of youth attend private and parochial schools in this country. I would like to consider this opposition for a moment for it is bound up with the present ideological conflict in American education.

Parents send their children to private schools for a variety of reasons. Some do so because they feel there is social prestige attached to private school attendance; some think the chances of inculcating manners and the social graces are greater; some have religious reasons; some feel the private school educates better than the available public school. In some cases probably a combination of these reasons applies but there would seem to be small doubt that the last reason is in most cases the decisive one; in the vast majority of cases parents are motivated by the desire to secure for their children what they consider a superior education.

In any case, one would suppose that the principle of the right of parents to send their children to the school of their choice was well established, especially among those who like to lecture the rest of us about the "dynamics of democracy," but it is sometimes surprising how reluctantly this principle is accepted. Occasionally a voice is raised which suggests that maybe private schools are all right but they had better watch their step. How else is one to interpret Professor Sidney Hook's statement that the right to receive education in *addition* to that provided by the public schools is essential to democratic educational policy but that the "right to receive education in private schools from partisan agencies as a *substitute* for public education" may be, under certain instances, "an overt threat to democracy?" [38] Does this mean that a democratic educational policy will only sanction ancillary private schools or will full-time private schools be permitted which have proved themselves—and to what body?—non-partisan? Mr. Hook does not explain what he means by "partisan agencies" or under what circumstances they constitute an "overt threat" but in view of his well-known antipathy to all religion save the religion of democracy, perhaps one is justified in suspecting that his partisan agencies might turn out to be church schools, or even nondenominational schools which cannot bring themselves to the complete divorce of education and religion which seems to be Mr. Hook's ideal. I think that what Mr. Hook is really saying is that you can do whatever you want with your child, educationally, as long as he puts in full time in official, state-sponsored schools.

Former President James Bryant Conant of Harvard, who has become a vigorous opponent of the expansion of private schools, is con-

[38] *Education for Modern Man* (New York; Dial Press, 1946), p. 39.

vinced that they are a threat to unity in our American life. Says he: "The greater the proportion of our youth who fail to attend our public schools and who receive their education elsewhere, the greater the threat to democratic unity." "If one wished generation after generation to perpetuate class distinction based on hereditary status in a given society, one would certainly demand a dual system of schools. . . . A dual system serves and helps to maintain group cleavages, the absence of a dual system does the reverse. This is particularly true of secondary schools." [39]

Mr. Conant is so convinced of the importance of the American public school "as an instrument for strengthening the spirit of national unity" he is willing to argue with parents that this social function outweighs any possible drawbacks arising from the school's inefficiency in carrying out its primary function of promoting moral values and providing a good education.

> If they [parents] have doubts about the ability of secular schools to promote the growth of moral and spiritual values, then these doubts must be weighed against the advantages of a pupil's attending a free school for all denominations. Similarly, if a family questions the ability of the local high school to prepare a gifted boy or girl adequately for university work (and the question unfortunately must be raised in many communities today), the family will have to balance these misgivings against the advantage of mixing with all sorts of people while at school. [40]

In other words, parents whose son's sense of moral values may be blunted can say to each other, "Ah, yes, but it's nondenominational, democratic blunting, free for all"; and parents whose daughter may not be learning anything in school can always console each other by saying, "But how nice that she can mix with all sorts of people." This attitude of Mr. Conant's betrays a wholly social conception of education; it implies that the purpose of education is not cultivation of the individual's moral and ethical and intellectual perceptions but adjustment to the group in the interests of an undefined "unity." It is one more piece of evidence, and from an influential source, of the modern educator's preoccupation with the person not as a person, but as a sociological specimen.

One might well ask what is this "unity" on behalf of which Mr. Conant is willing to sacrifice youth? Why isn't the healthy system to

[39] *Education and Liberty* (Cambridge; Harvard University Press, 1952), pp. 81–82.
[40] *Ibid.*, p. 83.

have diversity in our unity? Don't adults who have gone to both private and public schools quite frequently manage to cooperate in public service, both locally and nationally? Anyone who has ever served on a committee or engaged in a community activity (and this must include just about every adult American) knows that the answer to that last question is in the affirmative. It is perhaps not unity we need, or certainly not unity based on the artificial criterion of attendance at the same school; this kind of test supposes erroneously that just being together produces unity. What we need is a sense of community and we get that only when persons associating together, whether they be from public or private schools, have learned some of the things appropriate to all men. To think you can balance "the growth of moral and spiritual values" and adequate preparation for university work against "the advantage of mixing with all sorts of people" and grant the edge to the latter is simply to "make a strong pull and a long pull and a pull all together for the sake of togetherness," as Santayana thought Billy Phelps' Yale was doing.

Both Mr. Conant and Mr. Hook think we are getting diversity in our public education because politically we are still committed to the concept of local responsibility for our schools. As far as boards of education are concerned I think this concept of local responsibility is fast becoming a myth; the boards may still exercise responsibility as plant managers but it is becoming increasingly clear that the American public school is rapidly becoming a monolithic structure as far as what goes on in the schools in the way of learning is concerned. This is no longer, in the large sense, being decided at the local level at all but by the professors of education and their satellites in the state departments of education as I shall try to show in a later chapter.

At best a sociological theory of the aims of education is apt to produce docile individuals animated by a desire for group conformity and social solidarity, qualities admirable, perhaps, in an army but considerably less admirable in potentially free human beings. But the sociological theory of education can turn in another direction than acceptance of and adjustment to current social mores —in quite the opposite direction, as a matter of fact. If the majority of American youth is dull and hence malleable, why can't doctrinaires, if they can achieve strategic positions, mold youths in any desired shape, towards any ideology? The twentieth century, which has witnessed an increasing disregard for the individual, has been the great period of human manipulation when diabolical, or merely

clever men, have devised ways of inducing the masses to accept a
new ideology, or a new commercial product. It is unreasonable to
expect that organized education should escape this itch for manipulation, nor has it, as we shall now see when we turn to consideration
of the school of thought in education known as Social Reconstruction.

QUESTIONS ON CONTENT

1. What are some basic statistics upon which the Life-Adjustment
   program of education is based? For example, what percentage of
   high school students can be prepared for a college education?
   For a vocation? For neither? (What percentage of high school
   students now enter college, whether they are prepared for it or
   not?)
2. Comment on the course of study in the ninth grade of a Maryland high school (see p. 623). Were such projects a part of your
   high school experience? If so, try to recall how you felt about the
   experience then and how you feel about it now.
3. "The youth who wants to discuss with a committee what he
   should talk about on a date doesn't deserve to have a date."
   Comment.
4. What is the steady tone of this selection? Cite passages indicating scorn, sarcasm? Is there any name-calling?
5. In what way does the author use the pattern of I.Q.'s in the
   United States to refute the arguments of the Life-Adjusters?
6. What becomes of the individual in a Life-Adjustment program?
7. Explain the author's attitude towards private schools? How does
   it go counter to Sidney Hook's and to Conant's attitudes? What
   is your attitude?
8. State your own understanding of what this argument on theories
   of education is about.

❧ The Disadvantages of Being Educated

ALBERT J. NOCK

I

My interest in education had been comfortably asleep since my late youth, when circumstances waked it up again about six years ago. I then discovered that in the meantime our educational system had changed its aim. It was no longer driving at the same thing as formerly, and no longer contemplated the same kind of product. When I examined it I was as far "out" on what I expected to find as if I had gone back to one of the sawmills familiar to my boyhood in Michigan, and found it turning out boots and shoes.

The difference seemed to be that while education was still spoken of as a "preparation for life," the preparation was of a kind which bore less directly on intellect and character than in former times, and more directly on proficiency. It aimed at what we used to call training rather than education; and it not only did very little with education, but seemed to assume that training *was* education, thus overriding a distinction that formerly was quite clear. Forty years ago a man trained to proficiency in anything was respected accordingly, but was not regarded as an educated man, or "just as good," on the strength of it. A trained mechanic, banker, dentist or man of business got all due credit for his proficiency, but his education, if he had any, lay behind that and was not confused with it. His training, in a word, bore directly upon what he could do or get, while his education bore directly on neither; it bore upon what he could become and be.

Curiosity led me to look into the matter a little more closely, and my observations confirmed the impression that the distinction between training and education was practically wiped out. I noticed, too, that there was a good deal of complaint about this: even professional educators, many of them, were dissatisfied with it. Their complaints, when boiled down, seemed to be that education is too little regarded as an end in itself, and that most of the country's student-population take a too strictly vocational view of what they

From *Free Speech and Plain Language*, 1937. Reprinted by permission of William Morrow and Co., Inc.

are doing, while the remainder look at it as a social experience, encouraged largely in order to keep the cubs from being underfoot at home, and reciprocally appreciated mostly because it puts off the evil day when they must go to work; and that our institutions show too much complacency in accommodating themselves to these views.

These complaints, I observed, were not confined to educators; one heard them from laymen as well, and the laymen seemed to be as clear in their minds about the difference between education and training as the professional educators were. For example, one of America's most distinguished artists (whom I am not authorized to quote, and I, therefore, call him Richard Roe) told a friend of mine that when his ship came in he proposed to give magnificent endowments to Columbia, Harvard, Princeton and Yale on the sole condition that they should shut up shop and go out of business forever. Then he proposed to put up a bronze plate over the main entrance to each of these institutions, bearing this legend:

CLOSED

THROUGH THE BENEFACTION

OF

RICHARD ROE

AN HUMBLE PAINTER

IN BEHALF OF EDUCATION

As I saw the situation at the moment, these complaints seemed reasonable. Training is excellent, it can not be too well done, and opportunity for it can not be too cheap and abundant. Probably a glorified crèche for delayed adolescents here and there is a good thing, too; no great harm in it anyway. Yet it struck me as apparently it struck others, that there should also be a little education going on. Something should be done to mature the national resources of intellect and character as well as the resources of proficiency; and, moreover, something should be done to rehabilitate a respect for these resources as a social asset. Full of this idea, I rushed into print with the suggestion that in addition to our present system of schools, colleges and universities which are doing first-class work as training-schools, we ought to have a few educational institutions. My notion was that the educable person ought to have something like an even chance with the ineducable, because he is socially useful. I thought that even a society composed of well-trained ineducables might be improved by having a handful of educated persons sifted around in it every now and then. I, therefore, offered the suggestion, which did not seem exorbitant, that in a population of a hundred and twenty-odd million there should be at least one set of institutions, consisting of a grade-school, a secondary school, and an undergraduate college, which should be strictly and rigorously educational, kept in perpetual quarantine against the contagion of training.

II

This was five years ago, and about eighteen months ago I repeated the suggestion. My modest proposal was hardly in print before I received a letter from a friend in the University of Oxford, propounding a point which—believe it or not—had never occurred to me.

But think of the poor devils who shall have gone through your mill! It seems a cold-blooded thing . . . to turn out a lot of people who simply can't live at home. Vivisection is nothing to it. As I understand your scheme, you are planning to breed a batch of cultivated, sensitive beings who would all die six months after they were exposed to your actual civilization. This is not Oxford's superciliousness, I assure you, for things nowadays are precious little better with us. I agree that such people are the salt of the earth, and England used to make some kind of place for them. . . . But now—well, I hardly know. It seems as though some parts of the earth were jolly well salt-proof. The salt melts and disappears, and nothing comes of it.

As I say, I had never thought of that. It had never occurred to me that there might be disadvantages in being educated. I saw at once where my mistake lay. I had been looking at the matter from the point of view of an elderly person to whom such education as he had was just so much clear gain, not from the point of view of a youth who is about to make his start in the world. I saw at once that circumstances, which had been more or less in favour of my educated contemporaries, were all dead against the educated youngster of today. Therefore, last year, when I was appointed to deal again with the subject in a public way, I went back on all I had said, and ate my ration of humble-pie with the best grace I could muster.

Every shift in the social order, however slight, puts certain classes irrevocably out of luck, as our vulgarism goes. At the beginning of the sixteenth century the French feudal nobility were out of luck. They could do nothing about it, nobody could do anything about it, they were simply out of luck. Since the middle of the last century, monarchs and a hereditary aristocracy are out of luck. The *Zeitgeist* seems always arbitrarily to be picking out one or another social institution, breathing on it with the devouring breath of a dragon; it decays and dissolves, and those who represent it are out of luck. Up to a few years ago an educated person, even in the United States, was not wholly out of luck; since then, however, an educated young man's chance, or an educated young woman's, is slim. I do not here refer exclusively to the mere matter of picking up a living, although, as I shall show, education is a good bit of hindrance even to that; but also to conditions which make any sort of living enjoyable and worth while.

So in regard to my championship of education it turned out again that everybody is wiser than anybody, at least from the short-time point of view, which is the one that human society invariably takes. Some philosophers think that society is an organism, moving instinctively always towards the immediate good thing, as certain blind worms of a very low order of sensibility move toward food. From the long-time point of view, this may often be a bad thing for the worm; it may get itself stepped on or run over or picked up by a boy looking for fish-bait. Nothing can be done about it, however, for the worm's instinct works that way, and, according to these philosophers, so does society's, and the individual member of society has little practical choice but to go along.

Hence our institutions which profess and call themselves educational, have probably done the right thing—the immediate right thing, at any rate—in converting themselves, as our drugstores have done, into something that corresponds only very loosely to their profession. No doubt the lay and professional complaint against this tendency is wrong; no doubt the artist Richard Roe's proposal to close up our four great training-schools is wrong. No doubt, too, our young people are right in instinctively going at education, in the traditional sense of the term, with very long teeth. If I were in their place, I now think I should do as they do; and since I am in the way of recantation, as an old offender who has at last seen the light of grace, I may be allowed to say why I should do so—to show what I now plainly see to be the disadvantages of being educated.

III

Education deprives a young person of one of his most precious possessions, the sense of co-operation with his fellows. He is like a pacifist in 1917, alone in spirit—a depressing situation, and especially, almost unbearably, depressing to youth. "After all," says Dumas's hero, "man is man's brother," and youth especially needs a free play of the fraternal sense; it needs the stimulus and support of association in common endeavour. The survivor of an older generation in America has had these benefits in some degree; he is more or less established and matured and can rub along fairly comfortably on his spiritual accumulations; and besides, as age comes on, emotions weaken and sensitiveness is dulled. In his day, from the spiritual and social point of view, one could afford to be educated—barely and with difficulty afford it perhaps, but education was not a flat liability. It netted enough to be worth its price. At present one can afford only to be trained. The young person's fellows are turning all their energy into a single narrow channel of interest; they have set the whole current of their being in one direction. Education is all against his doing that, while training is all for it; hence training puts him in step with his fellows, while education tends to leave him a solitary figure, spiritually disqualified.

For these reasons: education, in the first place, discloses other channels of interest and makes them look inviting. In the second place, it gives rise to the view that the interest which absorbs his fellows is not worth mortgaging one's whole self, body, mind and spirit, to carry on. In the third place, it shows what sort of people one's fellows inevitably become, through their exclusive absorption in this one interest, and makes it hard to reconcile oneself to the thought of becoming like them. Training, on the other hand, raises no such disturbances; it lets one go on one's chosen way, with no uncertainty, no loss of confidence, as a man of the crowd. Education is divisive, separatist; training induces the exhilarating sense that one is doing with others what others do and thinking the thoughts that others think.

Education, in a word, leads a person on to ask a great deal more of life than life, as at present organized, is willing to give him; and it begets dissatisfaction with the rewards that life holds out. Training tends to satisfy him with very moderate and simple returns. A good income, a home and family, the usual run of comforts and conveniences, diversions addressed only to the competitive or sporting spirit or else to raw sensation—training not only makes directly for getting these, but also for an inert and comfortable contentment with them. Well, these are all that our present society has to offer, so it is undeniably the best thing all round to keep people satisfied with them, which training does, and not to inject a subversive influence, like education, into this easy complacency. Politicians understand this—it is their business to understand it—and hence they hold up "a chicken in every pot and two cars in every garage" as a satisfying social ideal. But the mischief of education is its exorbitance. The educated lad may like stewed chicken and motor-cars as well as anybody, but his education has bred a liking for other things too, things that the society around him does not care for and will not countenance. It has bred tastes which society resents as culpably luxurious, and will not connive at gratifying. Paraphrasing the old saying, education sends him out to shift for himself with a champagne appetite amidst a gin-guzzling society.

Training, on the other hand, breeds no such tastes; it keeps him so well content with synthetic gin that a mention of champagne merely causes him to make a wry face. Not long ago I met a young acquaintance from the Middle West who has done well by himself in a business way and is fairly rich. He looked jaded and seedy, evidently from overwork, and as I was headed for Munich at the moment, I suggested he should take a holiday and go along. He replied, "Why, I couldn't sell anything in Munich—I'm a business man." For a moment or two I was rather taken aback by his attitude, but I presently recognized it as the characteristic attitude of trained proficiency, and I saw that as things are it was right. Training had kept his demands on life down to a strictly rudimentary order and never tended to muddle up their clear simplicity or shift their direction. Education would have done both; he was lucky to have had none.

It may be plainly seen, I think, that in speaking as he did, my friend enjoyed the sustaining sense of co-operation with his fellows. In his intense concentration, his singleness of purpose, and in the extremely primitive simplicity of his desires and satisfactions, he was completely in the essential movement of the society surrounding him, indeed, if his health and strength hold out, he may yet become one of those representative men like Mr. Ford, the late Mr. Eastman or Mr. Hoover, who take their tone from society in the first instance and in turn give back that tone with interest. Ever since the first westward emigration from the Atlantic seaboard, American civilization may be summed up as a free-for-all scuffle to get rich quickly and by any means. In so far as a person was prepared to accept the terms of this free-for-all and engage in it, so far he was sustained by the exhilaration of what Mr. Dooley called "th' com-

mon impulse f'r th' same money." In so far as he was not so prepared, he was deprived of this encouragement.

To mark the tendency of education in these circumstances, we
need consider but one piece of testimony. The late Charles Francis
Adams was an educated man who overlived the very fag-end of the
period when an American youth could afford, more or less hardly,
to be educated. He was a man of large affairs, in close relations
with those whom the clear consenting voice of American society acclaimed as its representative men, and whose ideals of life were
acclaimed as adequate and satisfying; they were the Fords, East-
mans, Owen Youngs, Hoovers, of the period. At the close of his
career he wrote this:

> As I approach the end, I am more than a little puzzled to ac-
> count for the instances I have seen of business success—money-
> getting. It comes from rather a low instinct. Certainly, as far as my
> observation goes, it is rarely met in combination with the finer
> or more interesting traits of character. I have known, and known
> tolerably well, a good many "successful" men—"big" financially—
> men famous during the last half-century; and a less interesting
> crowd I do not care to encounter. Not one that I have ever known
> would I care to meet again, either in this world or in the next; nor
> is one of them associated in my mind with the idea of humour,
> thought or refinement. A set of mere money-getters and traders,
> they were essentially unattractive and uninteresting. The fact is
> that money-getting, like everything else, calls for a special aptitude
> and great concentration; and for it I did not have the first to any
> marked degree, and to it I never gave the last. So, in now summing
> up, I may account myself fortunate in having got out of my ven-
> tures as well as I did.

This is by no means the language of a man who, like my acquaintance from the Middle West, is sustained and emboldened
by the consciousness of being in co-operation with his fellows—
far from it. It will be enough, I think, to intimate pretty clearly the
divisive and separatist tendency of education, and to show the serious risk that a young person of the present day incurs in acquiring
an education. As matters now stand, I believe that he should not take
that risk, and that any one advising or tempting him to take it is
doing him a great disservice.

IV

An educated young man likes to think; he likes ideas for their own sake and likes to deal with them disinterestedly and objectively. He will find this taste an expensive one, much beyond his means, because the society around him is thoroughly indisposed towards anything of the kind. It is preëminently a society, as John Stuart Mill said, in which the test of a great mind is agreeing in the opinions of small minds. In any department of American life this is indeed the only final test; and this fact is in turn a fair measure of the extent to which our society is inimical to thought. The president of Columbia University is reported in the press as having said the other day that "thinking is one of the most unpopular amusements of the human race. Men hate it largely because they cannot do it. They hate it because if they enter upon it as a vocation or avocation it is likely to interfere with what they are doing." This is an interesting admission for the president of Columbia to make—interesting and striking. Circumstances have enabled our society to get along rather prosperously, though by no means creditably, without thought and without regard for thought, proceeding merely by a series of improvisations; hence it has always instinctively resented thought, as likely to interfere with what it is doing. Therefore, the young person who has cultivated the ability to think and the taste for thinking is at a decided disadvantage, for this resentment is now stronger and more heavily concentrated than it ever was. Any doubt on this point may be easily resolved by an examination of our current literature, especially our journalistic and periodical literature.

The educated lad also likes to cultivate a sense of history. He likes to know how the human mind has worked in the past, and upon this knowledge he instinctively bases his expectations of its present and future workings. This tends automatically to withdraw him from many popular movements and associations because he knows their like of old, and knows to a certainty how they will turn out. In the realm of public affairs, for instance, it shapes his judgment of this-or-that humbugging political nostrum that the crowd is running eagerly to swallow; he can match it all the way back to the politics of Rome and Athens, and knows it for precisely what it is. He can not get into a ferment over this-or-that exposure of the almost incredible degradation of our political, social and cultural character; over any investigation of Tammany's misdoings; over the Federal Government's flagitious employment of the income-tax law to establish a sleeping-partnership in the enterprises of gamblers, gangsters, assassins and racketeers; over the wholesale looting of public property through official connivance; over the crushing burden which an ever-increasing bureaucratic rapacity puts upon production. He knows too much about the origin and nature of government not to know that all these matters are representative, and that nothing significant can be done about them except by a self-sprung change of character in the people represented. He is aware, with Edmund Burke, that "there never was for any long time a corrupt representation of a virtuous people, or a mean, sluggish, careless people that ever had a good government of any form." He perceives, with Ibsen, that "men still call for special revolutions, for revolutions in politics, in externals. But all that sort of thing is trumpery. It is the soul of man that must revolt."

Thus in these important directions, and in others more or less like them, the educated youth starts under disadvantages from which trained youth is free. The trained youth has no incentive to regard these matters except as one or another of them may bear upon his immediate personal interest. Again, while education does not make a gentleman, it tends to inculcate certain partialities and repugnances which training does not tend to inculcate, and which are often embarrassing and retarding. They set up a sense of self-respect and dignity as an arbiter of conduct, with a jurisdiction far outreaching that of law and morals; and this is most disadvantageous. Formerly this disadvantage was not so pressing, but now it is of grave weight. At the close of Mr. Jefferson's first term, some of his political advisers thought it would be a good move for him to make a little tour in the North and let the people see him. He replied, with what now seems an incomprehensible austerity, that he was "not reconciled to the idea of a chief magistrate parading himself through the several States as an object of public gaze, and in quest of an applause which, to be valuable, should be purely voluntary." In his day a chief magistrate could say that and not lose by it; Mr. Jefferson carried every northern State except Connecticut and every southern State except Maryland. At the present time, as we have lately been reminded, the exigencies of politics have converted candidacy for public office into an exact synonym for an obscene and repulsive exhibitionism.

Again, education tends towards a certain reluctance about pushing oneself forward; and in a society so notoriously based on the principle of each man for himself, this is a disadvantage. Charles

Francis Adams's younger brother, Henry, in his remarkable book called *The Education of Henry Adams,* makes some striking observations on this point. Henry Adams was no doubt the most accomplished man in America, probably the ablest member of the family which as a whole has been the most notable in American public service since 1776. His youth was spent in acquiring an uncommonly large experience of men and affairs. Yet he says that his native land never offered him but one opportunity in the whole course of his life, and that was an assistant-professorship of history at Harvard, at four dollars a day; and he says further that he "could have wept on President Eliot's shoulder in hysterics, so grateful was he for the rare good-will that inspired the compliment." He recalls that at the age of thirty:

> No young man had a larger acquaintance and relationship than Henry Adams, yet he knew no one who could help him. He was for sale, in the open market. So were many of his friends. All the world knew it, and knew too that they were cheap; to be bought at the price of a mechanic. There was no concealment, no delicacy and no illusion about it. Neither he nor his friends complained; but he felt sometimes a little surprised that, as far as he knew, no one seeking in the labour-market even so much as inquired about their fitness. . . . The young man was required to impose himself, by the usual business methods, as a necessity on his elders, in order to compel them to buy him as an investment. As Adams felt it, he was in a manner expected to blackmail.

Such were the disabilities imposed upon the educated person fifty years ago, when as Adams says, "the American character showed singular limitations which sometimes drove the student of civilized man to despair." Owing to increased tension of the economic system, they are now much heavier. Even more than then, the educated youth emerges, as Adams and his friends did, to find himself "jostled of a sudden by a crowd of men who seem to him ignorant that there is a thing called ignorance; who have forgotten how to amuse themselves; who can not even understand that they are bored."

One might add a few more items to the foregoing, chiefly in the way of spiritual wear and tear—specific discouragements, irritations, disappointments—which in these days fall to the lot of the educated youth, and which the trained youth escapes; but I have mentioned enough for the purpose. Now, it is quite proper to say that the joys and satisfactions of being educated should be brought out as an offset. One can not get something for nothing, nor can one "have it going and coming." If an education is in itself as rewarding a thing as it is supposed to be, it is worth some sacrifice. It is unreasonable to court the joy of making oneself at home in the world's culture, and at the same time expect to get Standard Oil dividends out of it. Granted that your educated lad is out of step, lonesome, short on business acumen and concentration, and all the rest of it—well, he has his education; nobody can get it away from him; his treasure is of the sort that moth and rust do not corrupt, and stockmarket operators can not break through and mark down quotations on it. Agreed that if Charles Francis Adams had not been an educated gentleman he might have become another Gould, Fisk, Harriman, Rockefeller, Huntington, Morgan; but given his choice, would he have swapped off his education and its satisfactions for the chance to change places with any of them? Certainly not.

Certainly not; but times have changed. If economic opportunity were now what it was even in Henry Adams's day, a young person just starting out might think twice about balancing the advantages of an education against its disadvantages. In that day, by a little stretching and with a little luck, a young person might come to some sort of compromise with society, but the chance of this is now so remote that no one should take it. Since the closing of the frontier, in or about 1890, economic exploitation has tightened up at such a rate that compromise is hardly possible. It takes every jot of a young person's attention and energy merely to catch on and hang on; and as we have been noticing these last two years, he does not keep going any too well, even at that. The question is not one of being willing to make reasonable sacrifices; it is one of accepting every reasonable prospect of utter destitution. The joys and satisfactions of an education are all that Commencement orators say they are, and more; yet there is force in the Irishman's question, "What's the world to a man when his wife's a widdy?"

V

Things may change for the better, in time; no doubt they will. Economic opportunity may, by some means unforeseen at present, be released from the hold of its present close monopoly. The social value of intellect and character may some day be rediscovered, and the means of their development may be rehabilitated. Were I to be alive when all this happens, I should take up my parable of five years ago, and speak as strongly for education as I did then. But I shall not be alive, and I suspect also that none of the young persons now going out into the world from our training-schools will be alive; so there is no practical point to considering this prospect at present. Hence I can only raise my voice in recantation from the mourner's bench, a convert by force of expediency if not precisely in principle—rice-Christian style, perhaps, and yet, what is one to say? I belong to an earlier time, and for one reason or another the matter of rice does not present itself as an over-importunate problem, but nevertheless I see that the Christians have now "cornered" all the rice, so I can not advise young persons to do as I and my contemporaries did. No, they are right, their training-schools are right; Richard Roe and I are wrong. Let them be honest Christians if they can possibly manage the will-to-believe—one can make astonishing success with that sometimes by hard trying—but if not, let them be rice-Christians, they can do no better.

QUESTIONS ON CONTENT

1. What distinction is made between training and education?
2. What convinced the author that education is a disadvantage to modern youth?
3. Explain the comparison between society and "certain blind worms of a very low order of sensibility."
4. What sort of disturbances in the minds of young people does education create which training does not?
5. "Education is divisive, separatist; training induces the exhilarating sense that one is doing with others what others do and thinking the thoughts that others think." Comment. Compare "training" as defined here with "adjustment" as defined in "Adjustment Replaces Education."
6. Explain what is meant by "rice-Christians."
7. What is the purpose of each section of this article?

SUGGESTIONS FOR PAPERS

The concerns of professional educators are very vitally the concerns of the students who are the willing or unwilling recipients of whatever the educators decide to give them. You have now had a fair sample of what your college has to offer, but you may feel that you are caught up in a system which urges you along through a sort of educational gantlet. You have now an opportunity to examine the direction in which you are going and the forces which are pushing you along. What *are* your ideas about education? What is it and, in your opinion, what should it be? All the suggestions below offer you an opportunity to express yourself on this subject.

1. Write your paper on the limitations of natural education as defined by Huxley. How much could one learn from Nature if he were alone on earth? What complications would set in the moment a companion joined him? Limit your consideration to the one problem of survival in a hostile world.

2. "A Liberal Education Defined" describes in detail the acquirements of a liberally educated man. Itemize the analysis; then indicate what your college is doing to give you a liberal education. What does it do about your body? What does it do toward shaping your intellect into "a clear, cold, logic engine"? How does it present the "fundamental truths of nature"? Is it concerned with whether you love all beauty?

3. Consider carefully the first aim of progressive education: concern with the child's emotional adjustment. Is the aim different in traditional schools? Is the emphasis different? Is the method of attaining the adjustment different? In traditional and progressive schools children present the same complex of good and bad behavior. The latter, in both schools, consists of "lying, bullying, teasing, showing off, laziness, day dreaming, recalcitrance, overconcern with sex, or over-compliance." Select three of the bad traits and show how the traditional and the progressive teacher, respectively, handle the guilty child. Which method seems preferable to you?

4. The second aim of progressive education is concerned with the child's "self-fulfillment." Compare the traditional and the progressive approach toward achieving this goal.

5. Examine the attitude of progressive education toward content courses such as arithmetic, reading, spelling, history, geography, and science. What is meant by the statement that "learning shall be functional" ("What about Progressive Education?"). What is meant by "live knowledge applied to every day problems"? Does this imply that the child does not live except in the schoolroom? What do the progressive educators propose to do about drudgery? Is there no basis for believing that one may learn to like what at first seemed dull to him? Is there evidence of a complete misunderstanding of

the "way of the scholar"? Is there any such thing as a completely nondrudging scholar?

6. Compare the fourth aim of progressive education—education for citizenship—with the traditional aim toward this goal. Are the methods radically different?

7. What do you consider to be the chief fault with the training you received in high school? Was the discipline traditional or progressive? Were athletics harmfully overstressed? Did you learn enough? If not, was the fault yours or the school's? What would you recommend to improve your high school?

8. What do you consider to be the chief fault with the training you are receiving in college? Does your curriculum favor the practical, the impractical, or a smattering of both? Is the emphasis about right or is it, for your purposes, unbalanced? Whatever you choose as your central complaint, be sure to offer a constructive suggestion for improvement.

9. Define "adjustment" as used by modern professional educators. Upon what supposed facts is the theory of adjustment based? If this theory becomes the basis of training for all, what is certain to happen to society? Use "Adjustment Replaces Education" for references.

10. "What About Progressive Education?" presents the theory of adjustment as a basic training. "Adjustment Replaces Education" attacks this theory. State the case for the Adjustment Theory along with passages supporting the idea. State the case against this theory along with supporting quotations. In the conclusion to your paper choose the winner of this debate and offer reasons for your verdict.

11. Analyze "The Disadvantages of Being Educated." First, indicate the characteristics of the educated person; then list those of the trained person. Now, show how the trained person has, or has not, an advantage in present-day society.

12. Show how the selections in this chapter form a closely knit sequence. "A Liberal Education Defined" comes first. Why? What happens to this definition in "What About Progressive Education?" How is "Adjustment Replaces Education" related to the two previous selections? Finally, in what way is "The Disadvantages of Being Educated" a comment on the three previous selections?

13. Choose a quotable passage from any of the selections and use it as the springboard for your paper.

SOME TITLES FOR PAPERS

1. Nature's School
2. The School of Hard Knocks
3. My Idea of a Liberal Education
4. Education for Living
5. Education for Earning a Living
6. Method versus Content, with Examples
7. What Is Functional Education?
8. The Schools and Emotional Adjustment
9. Learning to Avoid Drudgery
10. Do You Know What You Like or Like What You Know?
11. The Way of the Scholar
12. Training for Citizenship
13. One Man's Dry Facts Are Another Man's Passion
14. Putting Away Childish Things
15. Should a Child's Whims Direct His Education?
16. Freshman Week in Retrospect
17. To Work or Not to Work One's Way Through College
18. One Way to Improve My College
19. Silly Projects in High School
20. Life-Adjustment Training: Pro and Con
21. Ignorance Is Bliss
22. Schools Should Teach What Cannot Be Learned Elsewhere
23. Adjustment Means Stagnation

❧ *SOME ESSENTIALS OF THE POETIC EXPERIENCE*

As you have observed, poems are an integral part of this book. You have been asked to read poems along with the prose selections, and no attempt has been made to emphasize a distinction between poetry and prose. The poems through contributing to the idea under discussion have earned the right to space. Furthermore, you may feel that at least some poets in some poems are concerned with ideas and not exclusively with sensation. You may recognize that a poet's "fundamental brainwork"—Rossetti's phrase—is very similar to the brainwork of any other writer. Since most people shy away from poetry as poetry, it has been at least a minor purpose in this book to neutralize this tendency by presenting poetry as idea.

In this chapter, some of the essentials of a full poetic experience are discussed. De Quincey, in the first selection, offers his classic distinction between the literature of knowledge and the literature of power. The former would include all scientific writing; the latter all poetry, along with other forms of imaginative literature. The second selection, Max Eastman's "Poetic People," makes a distinction similar to De Quincey's. Eastman contrasts practical people with poetic people. Practical people, in a "pure" state, would be the writers and the readers of the literature of knowledge; poetic people, also in a "pure" state, would be the writers and the readers of the literature of power. Both selections are concerned with broad classifications; both emphasize the physical use of knowledge to the practical man and the spiritual uses of power to the impractical man. That most persons straddle these classifications will be apparent.

In the third selection, "Obscurity in Poetry," E. B. White pays his tribute to poetry and lists various kinds of obscurity which make some poems difficult to understand. Legitimate difficulty arises out of a need for indirection. This need for indirection is more fully discussed in the final selection, "On Reading Poetry." Also in this selection is presented the reasonable view that a poem is a unique attempt to communicate an experience and that it should not be prejudged because of authorship or the fact that it is poetry or for any other reason. With the honesty of good critics, the authors, Wright Thomas and S. G. Brown, then proceed to show in illuminating detail how a poem should be read. Obviously they believe that reading poetry can be exquisite fun.

❧ Literature of Knowledge and Literature of Power

Thomas De Quincey

What is it that we mean by *literature?* Popularly, and amongst the thoughtless, it is held to include everything that is printed in a book. Little logic is required to disturb *that* definition. . . .

In that great social organ which, collectively, we call literature, there may be distinguished two separate offices, that may blend and often *do* so, but capable, severally, of a severe insulation, and naturally fitted for reciprocal repulsion. There is first, the literature of *knowledge*, and secondly, the literature of *power*. The function of the first is to *teach;* the function of the second is to *move:* the first is a rudder, the second an oar or a sail. The first speaks to the *mere* discursive understanding; the second speaks ultimately, it may happen, to the higher understanding, or reason, but always *through* affections of pleasure and sympathy. . . . Men have so little reflected on the higher functions of literature as to find it a paradox if one should

From *The Poetry of Pope* (1848).

describe it as a mean or subordinate purpose of books to give information. But this is a paradox only in the sense which makes it honorable to be paradoxical. Whenever we talk in ordinary language of seeking information or gaining knowledge, we understand the words as connected with something of absolute novelty. But it is the grandeur of all truth which *can* occupy a very high place in human interests that it is never absolutely novel to the meanest of minds: it exists eternally by way of germ or latent principle, in the lowest as in the highest, needing to be developed but never to be planted. To be capable of transplantation is the immediate criterion of a truth that ranges on a lower scale. Besides which, there is a rarer thing than truth, namely, *power*, or deep sympathy with truth. What is the effect, for instance, upon society, of children? By the pity, by the tenderness, and by the peculiar modes of admiration, which connect themselves with the helplessness, with the innocence, and with the simplicity of children, not only are the primal affections strengthened and continually renewed, but the qualities which are dearest in the sight of heaven— the frailty, for instance, which appeals to forbearance, the innocence which symbolizes the heavenly, and the simplicity which is most alien from the worldly—are kept up in perpetual remembrance, and their ideals are continually refreshed. A purpose of the same nature is answered by the higher literature, *viz.*, the literature of power. What do you learn from *Paradise Lost?* Nothing at all. What do you learn from a cookery-book? Something new, something that you did not know before, in every paragraph. But would you therefore put the wretched cookery-book on a higher level of estimation than the divine poem? What you owe to Milton is not any knowledge, of which a million separate items are still but a million of advancing steps on the same earthly level; what you owe is *power*, that is, exercise and expansion to your own latent capacity of sympathy with the infinite, where every pulse and each separate influx is a step upwards, a step ascending as upon a Jacob's ladder from earth to mysterious altitudes above the earth. *All* the steps of knowledge, from first to last, carry you further on the same plane, but could never raise you one foot above your ancient level of earth; whereas the very *first* step in power is a flight, is an ascending movement into another element where earth is forgotten.

Were it not that human sensibilities are ventilated and continually called out into exercise by the great phenomena of infancy, or of real life as it moves through chance and change, or of literature as it recombines these elements in the mimicries of poetry, romance, etc., it is certain that, like any animal power or muscular energy falling into disuse, all such sensibilities would gradually droop and dwindle. It is in relation to these great *moral* capacities of man that the literature of power, as contra-distinguished from that of knowledge, lives and has its field of action. It is concerned with what is highest in man; for the Scriptures themselves never condescended to deal by suggestion or cooperation with the mere discursive understanding: when speaking of man in his intellectual capacity, the Scriptures speak, not of the understanding, but of *"the understanding heart,"* making the heart,— that is, the great *intuitive* (or nondiscursive) organ, to be the inter-changeable formula for man in his highest state of capacity for the infinite. Tragedy, romance, fairy tale, or epopee, all alike restore to man's mind the ideals of justice, of hope, of truth, of mercy, of retribution, which else (left to the support of daily life in its realities) would languish for want of sufficient illustration. . . . It is certain that, were it not for the literature of power, these ideals would often remain amongst us as mere arid notional forms; whereas, by the creative forces of man put forth in literature, they gain a vernal life of restoration and germinate into vital activities. The commonest novel, by moving in alliance with human fears and hopes, with human instincts of wrong and right, sustains and quickens those affec-tions. Calling them into action, it rescues them from torpor. And hence the pre-eminency, over all authors that merely *teach,* of the meanest that moves, or that teaches, if at all, indirectly *by* moving. The very highest work that has ever existed in the literature of knowl-edge is but a provisional work, a book upon trial and sufferance. . . . Let its teaching be even partially revised, let it be but expanded, nay, even let its teaching be but placed in a better order, and instantly it is superseded. Whereas the feeblest works in literature of power, sur-viving at all, survive as finished and unalterable among men. For in-stance, the *Principia* of Sir Isaac Newton was a book *militant* on earth from the first. In all stages of its progress it would have to fight for its existence: first, as regards absolute truth; secondly, when that combat was over, as regards its form, or mode of presenting the truth. And as soon as a La Place, or anybody else, builds higher upon the founda-tions laid by this book, effectually he throws it out of the sunshine into decay and darkness; by weapons won from this book he superan-nuates and destroys this book, so that soon the name of Newton re-mains as a mere *nominis umbra,* but his book, as a living power, has transmigrated into other forms. Now, on the contrary, the *Iliad,* the *Prometheus* of Æschylus, the *Othello* or *King Lear,* the *Hamlet* or

Macbeth, and the *Paradise Lost* are not militant but triumphant forever, as long as the languages exist in which they speak or can be
taught to speak. They never *can* transmigrate into new incarnations.
To reproduce these in new forms or variations, even if in some things
they should be improved, would be to plagiarize. A good steam-
engine is properly superseded by a better. But one lovely pastoral
valley is not superseded by another, nor a statue of Praxiteles by a
statue of Michael Angelo. These things are separated, not by imparity,
but by disparity. They are not thought of as unequal under the same
standard, but as different in *kind,* and, if otherwise equal, as equal
under a different standard. Human works of immortal beauty and
works of nature in one respect stand on the same footing: they never
absolutely repeat each other, never approach so near as not to differ;
and they differ not as better and worse, or simply by more and less;
they differ by undecipherable and incommunicable differences, that
cannot be caught by mimicries, that cannot be reflected in the mirror
of copies, that cannot become ponderable in the scales of vulgar comparison.

QUESTIONS ON CONTENT

1. Literature's one essential element, according to De Quincey, is
   "some relation to a general and common interest of man." Discuss.
2. Why does the author call the literature of knowledge a "rudder"
   and the literature of power "an oar or a sail"?
3. What does the author mean when he says that all truth "is never
   absolutely novel [new] to the meanest mind"?
4. The author defines *power* as "deep sympathy with truth." How
   does he illustrate this definition?
5. Knowledge, says the author, consists of "a million separate items
   . . . a million of advancing steps on the same earthly level." Explain.
6. "The very highest work . . . in the literature of knowledge is
   but . . . a book upon trial and sufferance." Explain. What difference, for example, would one find in the Eleventh and the
   Fourteenth Editions of the *Encyclopædia Britannica?*
7. Explain the contrasting qualities of "a good steam-engine" and
   "a lovely pastoral valley."
8. From the examples given of the literature of power, would you
   gather that De Quincey regards poetry as the highest form of the
   literature of power?

❧ *Poetic People*

M<small>AX</small> E<small>ASTMAN</small>

A simple experiment will distinguish two types of human nature. Gather a throng of people and pour them into a ferryboat. By the time the boat has swung into the river you will find that a certain proportion have taken the trouble to climb upstairs, in order to be out on deck and see what is to be seen as they cross over. The rest have settled indoors, to think what they will do upon reaching the other side, or perhaps lose themselves, in apathy and tobacco smoke. But leaving out those apathetic, or addicted to a single enjoyment, we may divide all the alert passengers on the boat into two classes— those who are interested in crossing the river, and those who are merely interested in getting across.

And we may divide all the people of the earth, or all the moods of people, in the same way. Some of them are chiefly occupied with attaining ends, and some with receiving experiences. The distinction of the two will be more marked when we name the first mind practical, and the second poetic, for common knowledge recognizes that a person poetic or in a poetic mood is impractical, and a practical person is intolerant of poetry.

We can see the force of this intolerance too, and how deeply it is justified, if we make clear to our minds just what it means to be practical, and what a great thing it is. It means to be controlled in your doings by the consideration of ends yet unattained. The practical man is never distracted by things or aspects of things, which have no bearing on his purpose, but, ever seizing the significant he moves with a single mind and a single emotion toward the goal. And even when the goal is achieved you will hardly see him pause to rejoice in it; he is already on his way to another achievement. For this is the irony of his nature. His joy is not in any conquest or destination, but his joy is in getting toward it. To which joy he adds the pleasure of being praised as a practical man, and a man who will arrive.

In a more usual sense, perhaps, a practical man is a man occupied

Reprinted from *The Enjoyment of Poetry* by Max Eastman; copyright 1913 by Charles Scribner's Sons, 1941 by Max Eastman; used by permission of the publishers.

with attaining certain ends that people consider important. He must stick pretty close to the business of feeding and preserving life. Nourishment and shelter, money-making, maintaining respectability, and if possible a family—these are the things that give its meaning to the common word "practical." An acute regard for such features of the scenery, and the universe, as contribute or can be made to contribute to these ends, and a systematic neglect of all other features, are the traits of mind which this word popularly suggests. And it is because of the vital importance of these things to almost all people that the word "practical" is a eulogy, and is able to be so scornful of the word "poetic."

"It is an earnest thing to be alive in this world. With competition, with war, with disease and poverty and oppression, misfortune and death on-coming, who but fools will give serious attention to what is not significant to the business."

"Yes—but what is the *use* of being alive in the world, if life is so oppressive in its moral character that we must always be busy getting somewhere, and never simply realizing where we are? What were the value of your eternal achieving, if we were not here on our holiday to appreciate, among other things, some of the things you have achieved?"

Thus, if we could discover a purely poetic and purely practical person, might they reason together. But we can discover nothing so satisfactory to our definitions, and therefore let us conclude the discussion of the difference between them. It has led us to our own end —a clearer understanding of the nature of poetic people, and of all people when they are in the poetic mood. They are lovers of the qualities of things. They are not engaged, as the learned say that all life is, in becoming adjusted to an environment; but they are engaged in becoming acquainted with it. They are possessed by the impulse to realize, an impulse as deep, and arbitrary, and unexplained as that "will to live" which lies at the bottom of all explanations. It seems but the manifestation, indeed, of that will itself in a concrete and positive form. It is a wish to experience life and the world. That is the essence of the poetic temper.

QUESTIONS ON CONTENT

1. Is the distinction between practical and poetic people in this essay similar to the distinction between knowledge and power of the

previous essay? Discuss. Which type of literature do the practical people read? The poetic people?
2. What class of persons does the author exclude from consideration as either practical or poetic?
3. Are pure types of practical or of poetic persons rare? Which is rarer?
4. Does the chief power of the practical person consist of his ability to *exclude* from his attention the "non-essentials"? Explain.
5. "A person poetic or in a poetic mood is impractical." Why?

❧ *Obscurity in Poetry*

E. B. WHITE

"I wish poets could be clearer," shouted my wife angrily from the next room.

Hers is a universal longing. We would all like it if the bards would make themselves plain, or we think we would. The poets, however, are not easily diverted from their high mysterious ways. A poet dares be just so clear and no clearer; he approaches lucid ground warily, like a mariner who is determined not to scrape his bottom on anything solid. A poet's pleasure is to withhold a little of his meaning, to intensify by mystification. He unzips the veil from beauty, but does not remove it. A poet utterly clear is a trifle glaring.

The subject is a fascinating one. I think poetry is the greatest of the arts. It combines music and painting and storytelling and prophecy and the dance. It is religious in tone, scientific in attitude. A true poem contains the seed of wonder; but a bad poem, egg-fashion, stinks. I think there is no such thing as a long poem. If it is long it isn't a poem; it is something else. A book like *John Brown's Body*, for instance, is not a poem—it is a series of poems tied together with cord. Poetry is intensity, and nothing is intense for long.

Some poets are naturally clearer than others. To achieve greater popularity or great fame it is of some advantage to be either extremely clear (like Edgar Guest) or thoroughly opaque (like Gertrude Stein). The first poet in the land—if I may use the word poet loosely

From *One Man's Meat* by E. B. White. Copyright 1939 by E. B. White. Used by permission of the publishers, Harper & Brothers.

—is Edgar Guest. He is the singer who, more than any other, gives to Americans the enjoyment of rhyme and meter. Whether he gives also to any of his satisfied readers that blinding, aching emotion which I get from reading certain verses by other writers is a question which interests me very much. Being democratic, I am content to have the majority rule in everything, it would seem, but literature.

There are many types of poetical obscurity. There is the obscurity which results from the poet's being mad. This is rare. Madness in poets is as uncommon as madness in dogs. A discouraging number of reputable poets are sane beyond recall. There is also the obscurity which is the result of the poet's wishing to appear mad, even if only a little mad. This is rather common and rather dreadful. I know of nothing more distasteful than the work of a poet who has taken leave of his reason deliberately, as a commuter might of his wife.

Then there is the unintentional obscurity, or muddiness, which comes from the inability of some writers to express even a simple idea without stirring up the bottom. And there is the obscurity which results when a fairly large thought is crammed into a three- or four-foot line. The function of poetry is to concentrate; but sometimes over-concentration occurs, and there is no more comfort in such a poem than there is in the subway at the peak hour.

Sometimes a poet becomes so completely absorbed in the lyrical possibilities of certain combinations of sounds that he forgets what he started out to say, if anything, and here again a nasty tangle results. This type of obscurity is one which I have great sympathy for: I know that quite frequently in the course of delivering himself of a poem a poet will find himself in possession of a lyric bauble—a line as smooth as velvet to the ear, as pretty as a feather to the eye, yet a line definitely out of plumb with the frame of the poem. What to do with a trinket like this is always troubling to a poet, who is naturally grateful to his Muse for small favors. Usually he just drops the shining object into the body of the poem somewhere and hopes it won't look too giddy. (I sound as though I were contemptuous of poets; the fact is I am jealous of them. I would rather be one than anything.)

My quarrel with poets (who will be surprised to learn that a quarrel is going on) is not that they are unclear but that they are too diligent. Diligence in a poet is the same as dishonesty in a bookkeeper. There are rafts of bards who are writing too much, too diligently, and too slyly. Few poets are willing to wait out their pregnancy—they prefer to have a premature baby and allow it to incubate after being safely laid in Caslon Old Style.

I think Americans, perhaps more than other people, are impressed by what they don't understand, and the poets take advantage of this. Gertrude Stein has had an amazing amount of newspaper space, out of all proportion to the pleasure she has given people by her writings, it seems to me, although I am just guessing. Miss Stein is preoccupied with an experimental sort of writing which she finds diverting and exciting and which is all right by me. Her deep interest in the sound that words make is laudable; too little attention is paid by most writers to sound, and too many writers are completely tone-deaf. But on the other hand I am not ready to believe that any writer, except with dogged premeditation, would always work in so elegantly obscure and elliptical a fashion as the author of "A rose is a rose"— never in a more conventional manner. To be one hundred per cent roundabout one must be pure genius—and nobody is that good.

On the whole, I think my wife is right: the poets could be a little clearer and still not get over on to ground which is unsuitably solid. I am surprised that I have gone on this way about them. I too am cursed with diligence. I bite my pencil and stare at a marked calendar.

QUESTIONS ON CONTENT

1. "Poetry is intensity, and nothing is intense for long." Explain.
2. List the causes of poetical obscurity. Can you name poets or poems to illustrate each type of obscurity?
3. Why is "extremely clear" poetry avoided by most poets? Is pleasure in rhyme and meter the limit of most people's enjoyment of poetry?
4. What meaning has the word *diligence* on p. 666? Why is diligence in a poet compared to dishonesty in a bookkeeper?

❧ On Reading Poems

WRIGHT THOMAS AND S. G. BROWN

I

In certain ways the art of reading poetry is like the art of listening to music: a trained listener, for example, listens to a Mozart Concerto

From *Reading Poems* by Wright Thomas and S. G. Brown. Copyright 1941 by Oxford University Press, Inc.

or a Brahms Symphony with very great pleasure; but if we should ask him whether he likes "music" he would reply that he likes Mozart and Brahms, not simply "music." There is, for him, no such thing as music; there are only musical compositions of which he likes many and dislikes others, even though he may have mastered the art of listening to most of them. And it is so with reading poetry. Before we set out to read a poem we ought to realize that there is really no such thing as "poetry"; there are only poems, of which we shall like many and dislike others. "Poetry" is a word which stands for our generalized idea of *all* poems, for our abstract notion, for our summary of all the poems we know anything about and those we do not know about. As such it is a useful word, but it is *only a word*. And it is not a word which stands for any *thing* that we can point to and say "There it is." We may say that *Hamlet, Paradise Lost,* the *Iliad* of Homer, and Sandburg's *Fog* are poetry, and this is often a useful convenience; but the poems are obviously so very different that we are not helped in reading them by knowing that they are "poetry." "Poetry," this is to say, stands for something in the subjective world, the world of our minds; it is an idea in our minds. If we start to read a *particular poem* as "poetry" we shall expect *this* poem to be whatever our notion of poetry happens to be. When we say "I don't like poetry," we are describing the general effect of displeasure left in our recollection by reading poems. And if we "do not like poetry" we shall not like *this* poem. Our position is hopeless; we shall never learn to like poems and one of the highest pleasures of the human mind will be permanently cut off from us. On the other hand, we shall get into the same sort of difficulty if we are satisfied to say that we "like poetry"; for in that case we shall in all probability read the particular poem with our minds only partly awake, assuming that we like it because we like "poetry." We may never actually come to a full comprehension of the poem at all, and hence never fully enjoy it.

If our notion of poetry is clear and strong, it will try to force the particular poem we are reading to conform to it. For example, "poetry is all emotion"; therefore this poem will be all emotion. Or, "poetry is smooth in sound"; therefore this poem should be smooth in sound. "Poetry is all right for women but not for men." "Poetry is written by long-haired dreamers." "Poetry is good because it is cultural." "Poetry is ruined by careful study." These notions, and dozens of others, are created by our actual reading of poems, or by what we read about poetry, or by the notions about poetry that we hear from our friends or teachers, etc. Our notion may be pleasant or distasteful, adequate or narrow, justified or unjustified, but whatever it is it sets up expectations that are not useful to us in reading a particular poem—but, in fact, quite the opposite. Even when we expect to enjoy the poem in *certain ways* our reading of the poem will be distorted. For if it cannot be forced to fit these ways, we may even say "This isn't poetry."

The danger of bringing abstract notions to the reading of a poem is never greater than when it is a question of notions about a particular author. For example, "Tennyson was a Victorian sentimentalist"; therefore this poem will be sentimental. Or, "Shakespeare was a great genius"; therefore this poem is perfect, wonderful, and probably beyond my powers of comprehension. Or again, "modern poetry is always very difficult and obscure"; therefore I shall not be able to understand this poem of W. H. Auden. The truth of the matter is that the only really useful expectation that a reader can bring to a poem is that it will be in certain ways unique, a thing in itself, and will provide him with a new experience. We might even make a parody of Gertrude Stein, "a poem is a poem is a poem is a poem."

Reading a poem is an activity, not a passive reception. The reader must create; he must, in fact, *create a poem* where none existed before—that is, in his own consciousness. No one can do this for him. That this is true is clear if we ask the question: where is a poem? Is it in the mind of the poet? It *was*, but whether it is now or not is of no concern to us—the poet may well be dead. Is the poem in the ink marks on a page of this book? Obviously not. Is it in the sound waves made by someone speaking? No—these are just a succession of condensed and rarefied states of air. The fact is that a poem is not in existence at all until we create it in our consciousness; and this is the true meaning of "reading" a poem. In this essay . . . *when we speak of a "poem" we mean the experience which the reader creates in his mind by using the words of the poet, and by "reading" we mean the process by which he creates the poem.*

II

It is obvious that the reader of a poem needs certain skills which are used in the creation of a poem. These skills are the special talents of the poet, but they are also possessed, in lesser degree, by everybody else. And, fortunately, they can be increased, like other skills, by training and exercise, and by understanding something of their nature and of the activities in which they are used. The most important of these activities is in *using language*. The reader, as well as the poet, must have skill in using the medium of communication between them. The poet is conscious of an experience; to him, from the point at which he starts to write, the poem is not the original experience but the experience which *these words* "mean" to him. The reader must use these words, in reverse order so to speak, to create in himself an experience. The first aim of the good reader, it follows, is to use the words of the poet to create in himself an experience which resembles as nearly as possible the experience which the words "meant" to the poet, to *re-create* the experience of the poet. This resemblance, of course, can never be complete; that fact must be accepted. But we ought not therefore to conclude that the reader should rest content with creating an experience vaguely like that of the poet. Nor does it follow that a number of readers cannot reach a reasonably close agreement on what the poem "means." We should *conclude*, on the other hand, that our comprehension of the poem is tentative, that we can come to a closer comprehension if we can know what it "means" to others, and that careful study of a poem will not tear it to pieces but will, rather, enable us to create an experience more nearly like that of the poet and hence to enjoy it more fully (or to dislike it for honest reasons). Above all, we should conclude that skill in the use of language is of first importance to the reader as well as to the poet.

Most of us assume that we have a good deal of this skill in language, at least as readers. But the truth is not so flattering. Nearly everyone needs to use language much more effectively if he wishes to become a good reader. We can increase our efficiency by observing what happens when we read a poem, that is, when we create an experience by using the words of a poet. Here are words for us to use in creating a poetic experience:

1. *That time of year thou mayst in me behold*
2. *When yellow leaves, or none, or few, do hang*
3. *Upon those boughs which shake against the cold,*
4. *Bare ruin'd choirs, where late the sweet birds sang.*
5. *In me thou see'st the twilight of such day*
6. *As after sunset fadeth in the west,*
7. *Which by and by black night doth take away,*
8. *Death's second self, that seals up all in rest.*
9. *In me thou see'st the glowing of such fire,*
10. *That on the ashes of his youth doth lie,*
11. *As the death-bed whereon it must expire,*
12. *Consum'd with that which it was nourish'd by.*

13. *This thou perceiv'st, which makes thy love more strong,*
14. *To love that well which thou must leave ere long.*

An element of the experience of this poem is what we may call its *plain sense*, that part of its total meaning which can be summarized in prose: "You know that I am growing old; therefore you love me more, since you must soon leave me." We can call this plain sense the skeleton of the experience. The skeleton has an important function in any structure: it holds the other parts together. And it is by understanding the skeleton that we understand the general shape of the structure. In most poems (not in all) this plain sense meaning is of considerable importance; but it is never more than the skeleton of the experience. A person, as we see him, is not that particular person because of his bone-frame; his individuality, to us, is his whole appearance. So the plain sense of this poem might be the skeleton of a hundred poems, each different. The poem is itself unique, because of the flesh and blood (so to speak) on its skeleton—that is, the meaning of all the words working together as a whole. In our discussion of this experience, however, we can for convenience notice separately other elements of the whole.

The plain sense of the first twelve lines is "You know that I am growing old." It is said three different times, ll. 1–4, 5–8, and 9–12. But the whole meaning of ll. 1–4 is not the same as that of the other lines. What are the elements of the whole meaning of ll. 1–4? One is the sight of trees in early winter shaken by cold winds. This is the sight of the year growing old, as I am growing old. You remember that in the summer sweet birds sang in these branches, now bare, ruined —like the ruins of a cathedral, the broken arches of its choir, under which sweet voices once sang. This remembering and these sights of the dying year may make you feel as you feel when you know that I am growing old. I do not say what you feel: I say I am that time of year—those yellow leaves, or none, or few—hanging leaves—boughs shaking in the cold wind, bare, ruined—bare, ruined choirs—once the leaves of summer, sweet songs in trees and choir. The meaning of ll. 1–4 is the whole experience—plain sense, the sights, the sounds, the feelings. All these are present simultaneously in our consciousness as a unified experience; and our responses to them are continuously interacting—the aging man, the leaves, the boughs, the wind, the cold, the ruined choirs, and the remembrance of summer, birds, singing voices. This interaction is especially effective when the desolation of the cathedral is added, together with the contrasting joyousness of song both of the birds in summer and of the cathedral singers. This is brought about rapidly (in one line) so that the compression and condensation of a new sight (ruined choir) of desolation suddenly set against an earlier happiness, and the mental task of understanding "sweet birds" as both birds and choir singers, force into intense activity our creative ability, our power to fuse all these elements together into a unified experience of plain sense, sights, sounds, and feeling. Of these elements the first three, while they are important and necessary, are functioning here chiefly for the sake of the *feeling*. The feeling is not stated, named, or described. The reader must *create* it through his response to the plain sense, sights, and sounds. This is a typical occurrence in a poem.

It is so typical and important that it deserves special consideration for a moment. We all know, in our everyday lives, how difficult it is to tell someone just what emotion or feeling we had at a certain moment yesterday. We can describe it directly only in very crude terms, by stating or naming it—"I was happy, joyous, cheerful, ecstatic, merry, etc." Dozens of such words fail to express the emotion; the person to whom we are talking hardly understands at all, and certainly does not himself feel the emotion. To put the matter in the terms of this essay, he could not use our words to create in himself a similar experience. And this is what a poet wishes his words to be used for; he wishes his words to *communicate* his experience to the reader. Now, in everyday life, if we really wish our hearer to share our emotion, we quite naturally (with no thought of being a poet) do one of two things, or both. We may say "I felt like a million dollars—I had that wonderful feeling you get when the pain of a terrible headache suddenly leaves—I felt like writing a poem." Or we may set about describing all the circumstances of yesterday's moment—the things about us, the events, what she looked like, what she said, what we said. Or we may use both methods. What we are forced to do to communicate our feelings is what the poet is forced to do. In this poem the feeling of growing old is not stated or described; to communicate the feeling to us the poet describes *things* that arouse in us this feeling—leaves, branches; and then, to reinforce our feeling about these things, he shows us other *things*—choirs, birds. The feeling about the aging man is communicated through wintry branches which are communicated (in part) by choirs and birds. Here is the answer to a question often asked in all good faith by inexperienced readers, "Why doesn't the poet just say that his friend should feel sad because the poet is growing old, instead of beating about the bush and puzzling me with talk about branches, choirs and birds?" *Neither we nor the*

poet can communicate feeling directly. Mr. T. S. Eliot has said this
excellently, and given us a useful term for the *things* in a poem.

> The only way of expressing emotion in the form of art [for ex-
> ample the art of poetry] is by finding an "objective correlative";
> in other words, a set of objects, a situation, a chain of events which
> shall be the formula of that *particular* emotion; such that when the
> external facts, which must terminate in sensory experience, are
> given, the emotion is immediately evoked. [*Selected Essays,* Har-
> court, Brace and Co., 1932, p. 124.]

In ll. 1–4 of this poem the branches, choirs, and birds are the objective correlatives of the emotion.

We have said that in these lines the plain sense, sights, and sounds
are functioning chiefly for the sake of the feeling. Earlier we said that
the skeleton of the whole poem was the plain sense and that the sense
of ll. 1–4 was "You know I am growing old." We can now see that
this plain sense is not the skeleton of the whole poem, or the most
important part, or even the most important part of ll. 1–4. Notice
the plain sense of the whole poem: "You know that I am growing
old; therefore you love me more, since you must soon leave me." The
word "therefore" means that greater love (in the person addressed
by the poet) is aroused by his knowing that the poet is growing old;
but this result is not likely unless the "knowing" first arouses *feelings*
in him—the feelings that are in ll. 1–4. These feelings are therefore
an even more important part of the experience of ll. 1–4 than is the
plain sense. And this, too, is typical of a great many poems: although
the plain sense meaning is important, it often functions chiefly for the
sake of the feeling that accompanies it. A poet may even make statements whose plain sense is nonsense to many readers (or to all): if
the reader understands that the statement is not made for its own
sake (that is, to assert its truth) but for the sake of expressing feeling,
the poet may succeed excellently in his purpose, which is to communicate an experience. Hyperbole is an example of this. Robert
Burns, trying to communicate to his sweetheart his feeling of love,
wrote:

> And I will luve thee still, my dear,
> Till a' the seas gang dry.

No one doubts that his sweetheart understood the meaning of that
nonsense.

The function of ll. 5–8 is to sharpen and focus still more immediately the experience which the reader has already had from ll. 1–4.

The plain sense is "You see that I am approaching death," but this is very far from the whole meaning of the lines. Upon this skeleton the poet builds two comparisons, one immediate and the other implied. He is not only like the dying year, as he had already said, but like the "twilight" of day, that ambiguous period just before the blackness of night hides the day forever. But the blackness of night suggests that other blackness which engulfs everyone in the end, death itself. The reader is now forced to intensify his imaginative activity of re-creation by moving rapidly from the larger conception of the year to the narrower image of day, while, in addition, he must recollect that night is like death because it swallows up light (which is like life) in blackness.

The plain sense of ll. 9–12 is simply a more emphatic statement of the plain sense of the previous four lines. But here the plain sense is of almost no importance at all. The purport of the lines is to bring the whole experience into final and complete focus upon an image of fire: for a fire is "Consumed with that which it was nourished by." A dying fire lies upon the ashes of its youth, yet it still glows, preserving light and life; and so too the poet still retains within himself the spent energies of his youth, yet retains light and life. But the inevitability of a fire's dying out brings almost unendurably to the reader the experience of the inevitability of the life of a man dying out of his body.

The experience is now complete and it remains only to draw the conclusion, to interpret its meaning. And the concluding couplet performs just that function: it makes a direct statement which does not need to be translated into prose. But after reading the poem with this thoroughness we do not make the mistake of supposing that it performs any *other function*. The couplet is not a statement of the "meaning" of the whole poem; it is a statement of the "meaning" of the *experience* of the poem. It has no meaning at all until the experience of ll. 1–12 has been fully re-created in the consciousness of the reader.

QUESTIONS ON CONTENT

1. Is the comparison between "music" as a general term and "poetry" as a general term helpful? Are there many other such terms, such as sports, radio, food, etc.?
2. What two attitudes toward poetry make "our position hopeless" so far as appreciation of poetry is concerned?
3. Summarize the argument in paragraph 2 against a clear, strong

notion of poetry. Can such a contention be carried too far? Can the notion *against* strong opinions about the notion of poetry be detrimental too?

4. Do you share any of these notions of poetry?
5. Is pigeonholing authors a danger?
6. Much is said of wrong approaches to poetry. What is the right approach?
7. If one can legitimately ask "Where is a poem?" should he also ask the same question of a painting, a statue, or a radio program? Discuss.
8. Have the authors created a sort of mathematical formula for the approach to a poem? Poet A has experience X which he attempts to communicate as poem Y. Reader-poet B peruses poem Y in order to participate in experience X. Y is an approximation of X even for poet A. Reader-poet B in getting at the full flavor of X through Y requires a maximum of sympathetic effort.
9. The authors associate a cathedral with the word "choirs" in their interpretation of lines 1–4. Is this justified? Explain.
10. The author of "Obscurity in Poetry" observes that a certain amount of obscurity is essential to good poetry. He does not say why. What is said on this point in this essay? Is "objective correlative" a useful term? Why? Is it more inclusive than "metaphor"?
11. Do all poems have to have a sensible meaning?
12. The authors say that in lines 9–12 of Shakespeare's sonnet "the plain sense is of almost no importance at all." Do you agree?
13. Why do the authors withhold the information that the sonnet which they analyze was written by Shakespeare? Would knowledge of the authorship help in any way? See question 9, above, for example.

SUGGESTIONS FOR PAPERS

You have acquired some sort of attitude toward the word *poetry* and perhaps toward a few poems. In reading the selections in this chapter, you have had the opportunity to decide what place poetry should have in your life. Poetry, of course, is not the life business of anyone except the professional poets. Therefore, your thinking on the subject of poetry and you should keep perspective. You should know something of science, of warfare, of democracy, of communism —how much should you know of poetry?

1. Explain why the literature of knowledge is always provisional. How many natural *laws* are there? Consider, too, the vast number of *hypotheses* which never attain the dignity of *theories*. Select one or two striking examples to illustrate the constant shifting and adjustment in the field of knowledge.

2. When, where, and by whom were you first introduced to poetry? Describe as accurately as you can this first experience. Next, what has been your subsequent experience with poetry? Finally, how do you now feel about it?

3. You have read a few poems in the preceding chapters. Look back at several of those poems and then write about their effectiveness in relation to the idea of the chapter in which they appeared. Were they more or less effective than the prose selections in the same chapters? Why or why not?

4. Do you classify yourself as one of Eastman's practical or one of his poetic people? What would you be doing while crossing water on a ferry? Substitute if possible an actual experience of your own that will help to classify you as practical or poetic. It is unlikely, of course, that you will fall completely into either category.

5. Do you agree with the wife of E. B. White ("Obscurity in Poetry") that poets should be clearer? Is there any limit to the clearness which you desire? Select one of the poems in an earlier chapter and show just what you mean by objectionable obscurity; then suggest a clearer statement. Finally, decide whether or not the added clearness has spoiled the poem.

6. Edgar Guest and Gertrude Stein may represent the extremes of simpleness and unintelligibility in poetry. Which commits the greater crime? Show the limits to the enjoyment of simpleness; then examine the same limits with respect to unintelligibility. If you can find samples of Guest and Gertrude Stein for use as examples, so much the better.

7. Apply the reasoning about the term *poetry* ("On Reading Poems," paragraphs 1–2) to several other general terms: sports, Jews, Negroes, Southern cooking, painting, sculpture. Add to the list; then choose three or four terms for analysis with examples. Is this kind of reasoning essentially "democratic"? Why?

8. What are the disadvantages of a clear, strong opinion about the term *poetry*? "On Reading Poems" contains a representative list of generalizations about poetry. Have you used some of these generalizations? Which ones? Is the case against their use sufficiently strong for you to abandon them? If not, defend them.

9. Select a short poem for the kind of analysis that Thomas and Brown applied to the sonnet in "On Reading Poetry." Several poems from the preceding or succeeding chapters are suitable for this purpose. (If you follow this suggestion now, perhaps your instructor will approve of your doing another similar paper in connection with the selections in the next chapter.)

10. Base your paper on one of the following quotations:

(*a*) "*All* the steps of knowledge, from first to last, carry you further on the same plane, but could never raise you one foot above your ancient level of earth."

(*b*) "Human works of immortal beauty and works of nature in one respect stand on the same footing: they never absolutely repeat each other."

(*c*) "A person poetic or in a poetic mood is impractical, and a practical person is intolerant of poetry."

(*d*) "A poet dares to be just so clear and no clearer."

(*e*) "I think there is no such thing as a long poem."

(*f*) "To be one hundred per cent roundabout one must be pure genius—and nobody is that good."

(*g*) "Reading a poem is an activity, not a passive reception."

SOME TITLES FOR PAPERS

1. My Experience with Poetry
2. Facts May Change but Wisdom Lingers
3. Literary and Scientific Plagiarism: The Difference
4. The Practical *vs.* the Poetic
5. The Challenge of Obscure Poems
6. Meeting Poems Halfway
7. The Poet Creates; the Reader Re-creates
8. The Poet and the Scientist: A Contrast
9. Simpleness in Poetry
10. Objective Correlatives Illustrated
11. The Whole Meaning of a Short Poem
12. My Favorite Poem and Why
13. Poetry Requires a Mind Alive
14. The Plain Sense of Poems

CHAPTER 19

❧ *POEMS AND IDEAS*

MANY ARE THE MOODS of man, and poets are aware of this. But the characteristic mood of the poets themselves is not gay. It is a mood sometimes lightly touched with sadness, sometimes deep dyed in melancholy. Perhaps this is so because gaiety is essentially active and its moments pass away in an explosion of energy. If one recollects these active moments of high spirits, he must do so in quiet reflectiveness, and the very gaiety of the past becomes the occasion for sadness. If gaiety is thus transmuted, the memory of pain, disappointments, frustrations is doubly melancholy. The consequence is a poetic literature filled with shadows and darkness. Most of us respond pleasurably to these lamentations because they provide companionship in our own fits of melancholy.

The selections in this chapter are all more or less dark in mood. They were chosen as representing some of the everlasting reasons man has for dejection. They were chosen, too, as illustrations of the thesis that poetic writing, though it repeat the plain sense of other pieces of poetic writing, remains in its whole meaning a unique record of an experience. (See "On Reading Poems" Chapter 18.)

The experiences represented in the following poems are varied. Some of them refer to love unwon ("To His Coy Mistress") or to love a-winning ("Love Among the Ruins") or to love lost ("Love's Immortality," "Tragic Memory," "Earth's Immortalities: Love") or love gained ("Dover Beach"). They treat of fame and glory ("Ozymandias," "Earth's Immortalities: Fame," "Cool Tombs"), of loneliness ("Mr. Flood's Party"), of life's preponderant ills ("Terence, This Is Stupid Stuff"), of the evil of the large world ("The World Is Too Much With Us"), and the evil of the small world ("Soliloquy of the Spanish Cloister"); of the dashing heroism of war ("The Charge of the Light Brigade") and of the dismal horrors of war (*"Dulce et Decorum Est"*).

❧ *To His Coy Mistress*

ANDREW MARVELL

Had we but world enough, and time,
This coyness, Lady, were no crime.
We would sit down and think which way
To walk and pass our long love's day.
Thou by the Indian Ganges' side   5
Shouldst rubies find; I by the tide
Of Humber would complain. I would
Love you ten years before the Flood,
And you should, if you please, refuse
Till the conversion of the Jews.   10
My vegetable love should grow
Vaster than empires, and more slow;
An hundred years should go to praise
Thine eyes and on thy forehead gaze;
Two hundred to adore each breast,   15
But thirty thousand to the rest;
An age at least to every part,
And the last age should show your heart.
For, Lady, you deserve this state,
Nor would I love at lower rate.   20
   But at my back I always hear
Time's wingèd chariot hurrying near;
And yonder all before us lie
Deserts of vast eternity.
Thy beauty shall no more be found,   25
Nor in thy marble vault shall sound

First published in 1681.

My echoing song; then worms shall try
That long preserved virginity,
And your quaint honor turn to dust,
And into ashes all my lust: 30
The grave's a fine and private place,
But none, I think, do there embrace.
　　Now therefore, while the youthful hue
Sits on thy skin like morning lew,
And while thy willing soul transpires   35
At every pore with instant fires,
Now let us sport us while we may,
And now, like amorous birds of prey,
Rather at once our time devour
Than languish in his slow-chapt power.   40
Let us roll all our strength and all
Our sweetness, up into one ball,
And tear our pleasures with rough strife
Thorough the iron gates of life:
Thus, though we cannot make our sun   45
Stand still, yet we will make him run.

QUESTIONS ON CONTENT

1. What constitutes the tinge of melancholy in this poem?
2. The first twenty lines seem light with a lover's hyperbole. Beginning with line 21 what becomes of the fretfulness?
3. What does the poet mean by "My vegetable love," line 11?
4. There is a question as to whether the rime word in line 34 should be "lew" or "dew." After determining the meaning of "lew" and the suggestiveness of "dew," argue for one or the other as the better word to express the poet's meaning.
5. "To His Coy Mistress" expresses the need for undelayed, passionate living because life is short. What other effect might thoughts about a short life produce? Explain.
6. State the plain sense of this poem, then, develop the poetic experience. (See "On Reading Poems.")
7. Is this a pagan poem? Discuss.
8. What do the final two lines of the poem mean?

❧ *Love's Immortality*

WILLIAM BYRD

Crowned with flowers I saw fair Amaryllis
  By Thyrsis sit, hard by a fount of crystal;
And with her hand, more white than snow or lilies,
  On sand she wrote, "My faith shall be immortal":
And suddenly a storm of wind and weather   5
Blew all her faith and sand away together.

From *Psalms, Sonnets, and Songs*, first published in 1588.

QUESTIONS ON CONTENT

1. Is the title a good example of irony?
2. How is capriciousness suggested?
3. Is time an element in this poem as it was in "To His Coy Mistress"?
4. Does the poem do more than record the fact of Amaryllis's fickleness? Is there any explanation? Is one justified in deducing that faithlessness is a characteristic of women?

❧ *Tragic Memory*

GEORGE MEREDITH

In our old shipwrecked days there was an hour,
When in the firelight steadily aglow,
Joined slackly, we beheld the red chasm grow
Among the clicking coals. Our library-bower
That eve was left to us: and hushed we sat   5
As lovers to whom Time is whispering.
From sudden-opened doors we heard them sing:
The nodding elders mixed good wine with chat.
Well knew we that Life's greatest treasure lay

From *Modern Love*, first published in 1862.

With us, and of it was our talk. "Ah, yes!   10
Love dies!" I said: I never thought it less.
She yearned to me that sentence to unsay.
Then when the fire domed blackening, I found
Her cheek was salt against my kiss, and swift
Up the sharp scale of sobs her breast did lift:—   15
Now am I haunted by that taste! that sound!

QUESTIONS ON CONTENT

1. Explain the title.
2. Does the final line illuminate the preceding fifteen lines?
3. Why does the lover say "Ah, yes!/ Love dies!" since he did not believe it?
4. What was Time whispering (line 6)? Compare "To His Coy Mistress" (line 21).
5. Is there any hint in this poem of what caused love's death? Compare "Love's Immortality."
6. Is there any symbolic relation between the "fire" of this poem and the "sand" in "Love's Immortality"?

❧ *Ozymandias*

PERCY BYSSHE SHELLEY

I met a traveler from an antique land
Who said: Two vast and trunkless legs of stone
Stand in the desert. Near them, on the sand,
Half sunk, a shattered visage lies, whose frown,
And wrinkled lip, and sneer of cold command,   5
Tell that its sculptor well those passions read
Which yet survive, stamped on these lifeless things,
The hand that mocked them and the heart that fed.
And on the pedestal these words appear:
"My name is Ozymandias, king of kings;   10
Look on my works, ye Mighty, and despair!"
Nothing beside remains. Round the decay

First published in *The Examiner*, January 11, 1819.

Of that colossal wreck, boundless and bare
The lone and level sands stretch far away.

QUESTIONS ON CONTENT

1. Why does the poet simply report the traveler's story without comment?
2. "The hand" (line 8) is the sculptor's. To what does *them* in the same line refer?
3. Compare this poem with each of the preceding selections.
4. Could this poem aptly bear the title: "On the Vanity and Shortness of Life"? Explain.

❧ *Earth's Immortalities*

ROBERT BROWNING

Fame

See, as the prettiest graves will do in time,
Our poet's wants the freshness of its prime;
Spite of the sexton's browsing horse, the sods
Have struggled through its binding osier rods;
Headstone and half-sunk footstones lean awry,   5
Wanting the brick-work promised by-and-by;
How the minute grey lichens, plate o'er plate,
Have softened down the crisp-cut name and date!

Love

So, the year's done with!
　　(*Love me for ever!*)
All March begun with,
　　April's endeavour;
May-wreaths that bound me   5
　　June needs must sever;
Now snows fall round me,
　　Quenching June's fever—
　　(*Love me for ever!*)

From *Dramatic Romances* (1845).

QUESTIONS ON CONTENT

1. The neglect of a poet's grave implies what?
2. Is there an extra measure of irony in lines 3–4 of "Fame"? Explain.
3. What kind of neglect is suggested by "the brick-work promised by-and-by" (line 6)?
4. Compare in detail "Ozymandias" and "Fame." Which poem comes nearer to a direct comment? Explain.
5. Discuss the arrangement of details in "Fame." How does this arrangement serve to relate the speaker to the poet's grave?
6. In "Love," explain the difference in tone of line 2 and the same words in line 9.
7. Compare "Love" and "Love's Immortality." Does either poem explain what caused love's decay?
8. Does it make any difference that the sex of the speaker in "Love" is not given? Do you think you know which it is?
9. What progress have the lovers made in each of the months?

❧ *Cool Tombs*

CARL SANDBURG

When Abraham Lincoln was shoveled into the tombs, he forgot the copperheads and the assassin . . . in the dust, in the cool tombs.

And Ulysses Grant lost all thought of con men and Wall Street, cash and collateral turned ashes . . . in the dust, in the cool tombs.

Pocahontas' body, lovely as a poplar, sweet as a red haw in November or a pawpaw in May—did she wonder? does she remember? . . . in the dust, in the cool tombs?

Take any streetful of people buying clothes and groceries, cheering a hero or throwing confetti and blowing tin horns . . . tell me if the lovers are losers . . . tell me if any get more than the lovers . . . in the dust . . . in the cool tombs.

From *Cornhuskers* by Carl Sandburg. Copyright, 1918, by Henry Holt and Company, Inc. Copyright, 1946, by Carl Sandburg. Used by permission of the publishers.

QUESTIONS ON CONTENT

1. Does this poem express a different view of love's immortality from that set forth in the previous poems on the subject?
2. Why did the poet choose Lincoln, Grant, and Pocahontas for examples of those who occupy the "cool tombs"?
3. What are "copperheads"? Who was the "assassin"?
4. What is a "con man"? Why associate Grant with "con men and Wall Street, cash and collateral"?

❦ *Love among the Ruins*

ROBERT BROWNING

I

Where the quiet-coloured end of evening smiles
    Miles and miles
On the solitary pastures where our sheep
    Half-asleep
Tinkle homeward thro' the twilight, stray or stop   5
    As they crop—
Was the site once of a city great and gay,
    (So they say)
Of our country's very capital, its prince
    Ages since   10
Held his court in, gathered councils, wielding far
    Peace or war.

II

Now,—the country does not even boast a tree
    As you see,
To distinguish slopes of verdure, certain rills   15
    From the hills
Intersect and give a name to, (else they run
    Into one)
Where the domed and daring palace shot its spires
    Up like fires   20

From *Men and Women* (1855).

O'er the hundred-gated circuit of a wall
    Bounding all,
Made of marble, men might march on nor be pressed,
    Twelve abreast.

III

And such plenty and perfection, see, of grass   25
    Never was!
Such a carpet as, this summer-time, o'erspreads
    And embeds
Every vestige of the city, guessed alone,
    Stock or stone—   30
Where a multitude of men breathed joy and woe
    Long ago;
Lust of glory pricked their hearts up, dread of shame
    Struck them tame;
And that glory and that shame alike, the gold   35
    Bought and sold.

IV

Now,—the single little turret that remains
    On the plains,
By the caper overrooted, by the gourd
    Overscored,   40
While the patching houseleek's head of blossom winks
    Through the chinks—
Marks the basement whence a tower in ancient time
    Sprang sublime,
And a burning ring, all round, the chariots traced   45
    As they raced,
And the monarch and his minions and his dames
    Viewed the games.

V

And I know, while thus the quiet-coloured eve
    Smiles to leave   50
To their folding, all our many-tinkling fleece
    In such peace,
And the slopes and rills in undistinguished grey
    Melt away—
That a girl with eager eyes and yellow hair   55
    Waits me there

In the turret whence the charioteers caught soul
   For the goal,
When the king looked, where she looks now, breathless, dumb
   Till I come.   60

VI

But he looked upon the city, every side,
   Far and wide,
All the mountains topped with temples, all the glades'
   Colonnades,
All the causeys, bridges, aqueducts,—and then, 65
   All the men!
When I do come, she will speak not, she will stand,
   Either hand
On my shoulder, give her eyes the first embrace
   Of my face,   70
Ere we rush, ere we extinguish sight and speech
   Each on each.

VII

In one year they sent a million fighters forth
   South and North,
And they built their gods a brazen pillar high   75
   As the sky,
Yet reserved a thousand chariots in full force—
   Gold, of course.
Oh heart! oh blood that freezes, blood that burns!
   Earth's returns   80
For whole centuries of folly, noise and sin!
   Shut them in,
With their triumphs and their glories and the rest!
   Love is best.

QUESTIONS ON CONTENT

1. Is this poem an extension of the theme in "Ozymandias"? Discuss.
2. What caused the fall of the "city great and gay"?
3. What is the occupation of the speaker?
4. Compare this poem and "Cool Tombs." What part does love play in each?

❧ *Dover Beach*

Matthew Arnold

The sea is calm tonight,
The tide is full, the moon lies fair
Upon the Straits—on the French coast the light
Gleams and is gone; the cliffs of England stand,
Glimmering and vast, out in the tranquil bay.   5
Come to the window; sweet is the night-air!
Only, from the long line of spray
Where the sea meets the moon-blanched land,
Listen! you hear the grating roar
Of pebbles which the waves draw back, and fling,   10
At their return, up the high strand,
Begin, and cease, and then again begin,
With tremulous cadence slow, and bring
The eternal note of sadness in.

Sophocles long ago   15
Heard it on the Aegean, and it brought
Into his mind the turbid ebb and flow
Of human misery; we
Find also in the sound a thought,
Hearing it by this distant northern sea.   20
The Sea of Faith
Was once, too, at the full, and round earth's shore
Lay like the folds of a bright girdle furled.
But now I only hear
Its melancholy, long, withdrawing roar,   25
Retreating, to the breath
Of the night-wind, down the vast edges drear
And naked shingles of the world.

Ah, love, let us be true
To one another! for the world, which seems   30
To lie before us like a land of dreams,

From *New Poems* (1867).

So various, so beautiful, so new,
Hath really neither joy, nor love, nor light,
Nor certitude, nor peace, nor help for pain;
And we are here as on a darkling plain   35
Swept with confused alarms of struggle and flight,
Where ignorant armies clash by night.

QUESTIONS ON CONTENT

1. To whom does the speaker say, "Come to the window" (line 6)?
2. What is the "eternal note of sadness" (line 14)? Upon what train
   of thought does this "note" set the speaker?
3. Can you follow the sequence of the poet's thinking? The scene of
   quiet beauty, the low cadence of the sea with its sad undertones
   remind the poet of Sophocles, who had lived over two thousand
   years before and had brooded over the suggestive sadness of the
   sea's rhythm. Complete the sequence.
4. When did the Sea of Faith engirdle the earth? Is this an exaggeration?
5. What are the different meanings of *love* as used in line 29 and in
   line 33?
6. This poem is a love poem, but the love element is unobtrusive.
   Why?
7. Compare "Dover Beach" and "Love among the Ruins."

❧ *Ode to a Nightingale*

JOHN KEATS

My heart aches, and a drowsy numbness pains
   My sense, as though of hemlock I had drunk,
Or emptied some dull opiate to the drains
   One minute past, and Lethe-wards had sunk:
'Tis not through envy of thy happy lot,   5
   But being too happy in thine happiness,—
      That thou, light-wingèd Dryad of the trees,
         In some melodious plot
Of beechen green, and shadows numberless,
   Singest of summer in full-throated ease.   10

First published in 1820.

O for a draught of vintage! that hath been
  Cool'd a long age in the deep-delvèd earth,
Tasting of Flora and the country green,
Dance, and Provençal song, and sunburnt mirth!
O for a beaker full of the warm South!   15
  Full of the true, the blushful Hippocrene,
    With beaded bubbles winking at the brim,
      And purple-stainèd mouth;
That I might drink, and leave the world unseen,
  And with thee fade away into the forest dim: 20

Fade far away, dissolve, and quite forget
  What thou among the leaves hast never known,
The weariness, the fever, and the fret
  Here, where men sit and hear each other groan;
Where palsy shakes a few, sad, last gray hairs,   25
  Where youth grows pale, and spectre-thin, and dies;
    Where but to think is to be full of sorrow
      And leaden-eyed despairs;
Where Beauty cannot keep her lustrous eyes,
  Or new Love pine at them beyond to-morrow.   30

Away! away! for I will fly to thee,
  Not charioted by Bacchus and his pards,
But on the viewless wings of Poesy,
  Though the dull brain perplexes and retards:
Already with thee! tender is the night,   35
  And haply the Queen-Moon is on her throne,
    Cluster'd around by all her starry fays;
      But here there is no light,
Save what from heaven is with the breezes blown
  Through verdurous glooms and winding mossy ways.   40

I cannot see what flowers are at my feet,
  Nor what soft incense hangs upon the boughs,
But, in embalmèd darkness, guess each sweet
  Wherewith the seasonable month endows
The grass, the thicket, and the fruit-tree wild;   45
  White hawthorne, and the pastoral eglantine;
    Fast fading violets cover'd up in leaves;
      And mid-May's eldest child,

The coming musk-rose, full of dewy wine,
   The murmurous haunt of flies on summer eves.   50

Darkling I listen: and, for many a time
   I have been half in love with easeful Death,
Call'd him soft names in many a musèd rhyme,
   To take into the air my quiet breath;
Now more than ever seems it rich to die,   55
   To cease upon the midnight with no pain,
      While thou art pouring forth thy soul abroad
         In such an ecstasy!
Still wouldst thou sing, and I have ears in vain—
   To thy high requiem become a sod.   60

Thou wast not born for death, immortal bird!
   No hungry generations tread thee down;
The voice I hear this passing night was heard
   In ancient days by emperor and clown:
Perhaps the self-same song that found a path   65
   Through the sad heart of Ruth, when, sick for home,
      She stood in tears amid the alien corn;
         The same that oft-times hath
Charm'd magic casements, opening on the foam
   Of perilous seas, in faery lands forlorn.   70

Forlorn! the very word is like a bell
   To toll me back from thee to my sole self!
Adieu! the fancy cannot cheat so well
   As she is famed to do, deceiving elf.
Adieu! adieu! thy plaintive anthem fades   75
   Past the near meadows, over the still stream,
      Up the hill-side; and now 'tis buried deep
         In the next valley-glades:
Was it a vision, or a waking dream?
   Fled is that music:—do I wake or sleep?   80

QUESTIONS ON CONTENT

1. Is the nightingale related to Keats's thoughts in the same way
   that the sea is related to Arnold's thoughts in "Dover Beach"?
   Discuss.

2. How does the listener to the nightingale interpret the song? Is it to him the essence of carefree happiness? Then, does this essence suggest other concentrations, such as "a beaker full of the warm South"?
3. If in lines 11–20 the poet longs for wine to lift him from his sorrow, what does he turn to in lines 31–40?
4. In lines 21–30 is the essential theme the shortness of time? Or is it that misery and suffering are man's unavoidable lot? Or is it simply a personal complaint? Do the last two lines recall the warning in "To His Coy Mistress"?
5. Since it is dark, how does the poet know so well his surroundings?
6. Explain lines 51–60. Is this the third idea the poet has had for ridding himself of the intolerable present? What were the other two?

❧ *Mr. Flood's Party*

EDWIN ARLINGTON ROBINSON

Old Eben Flood, climbing alone one night
Over the hill between the town below
And the forsaken upland hermitage
That held as much as he should ever know
On earth again of home, paused wearily.   5
The road was his with not a native near;
And Eben, having leisure, said aloud,
For no man else in Tilbury Town to hear:

"Well, Mr. Flood, we have the harvest moon
Again, and we may not have many more;   10
The bird is on the wing, the poet says,
And you and I have said it here before.
Drink to the bird." He raised up to the light
The jug that he had gone so far to fill,
And answered huskily: "Well, Mr. Flood,   15
Since you propose it, I believe I will."

Collected Poems, 1935. Reprinted by permission of The Macmillan Company.

Alone, as if enduring to the end
A valiant armor of scarred hopes outworn,
He stood there in the middle of the road
Like Roland's ghost winding a silent horn.   20
Below him, in the town among the trees,
Where friends of other days had honored him,
A phantom salutation of the dead
Rang thinly till old Eben's eyes were dim.

Then, as a mother lays her sleeping child   25
Down tenderly, fearing it may awake,
He set the jug down slowly at his feet
With trembling care, knowing that most things break;
And only when assured that on firm earth
It stood, as the uncertain lives of men   30
Assuredly did not, he paced away,
And with his hands extended paused again:

"Well, Mr. Flood, we have not met like this
In a long time; and many a change has come
To both of us, I fear, since last it was   35
We had a drop together. Welcome home!"
Convivially returning with himself,
Again he raised the jug up to the light;
And with an acquiescent quaver said:
"Well, Mr. Flood, if you insist, I might.   40

"Only a very little, Mr. Flood—
For auld lang syne. No more, sir; that will do."
So, for the time, apparently it did,
And Eben evidently thought so too;
For soon amid the silver loneliness   45
Of night he lifted up his voice and sang,
Secure, with only two moons listening,
Until the whole harmonious landscape rang—

"For auld lang syne." The weary throat gave out,
The last word wavered; and the song being done,
He raised again the jug regretfully   50
And shook his head, and was again alone.

There was not much that was ahead of him,
And there was nothing in the town below,
Where strangers would have shut the many doors   55
That many friends had opened long ago.

QUESTIONS ON CONTENT

1. How much are we told of Eben Flood's past? How much can we legitimately surmise?
2. Is Eben Flood a drunkard? Give reasons for your answer.
3. Define "pathos." Does this poem contain pathos? Explain.
4. What is meant by "The bird is on the wing"? Compare "Time's wingèd chariot" ("To His Coy Mistress").
5. Who was Roland and what picture do you see in the phrase, "winding a silent horn"?
6. What figure of speech describes Eben Flood's care in handling his jug? Why is it effective?

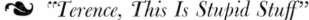 *"Terence, This Is Stupid Stuff"*

A. E. HOUSMAN

"Terence, this is stupid stuff:
You eat your victuals fast enough;
There can't be much amiss, 'tis clear,
To see the rate you drink your beer.
But oh, good Lord, the verse you make,   5
It gives a chap the belly-ache.
The cow, the old cow, she is dead;
It sleeps well, the hornèd head:
We poor lads, 'tis our turn now
To hear such tunes as killed the cow.   10
Pretty friendship 'tis to rhyme
Your friends to death before their time
Moping melancholy mad:
Come, pipe a tune to dance to, lad."

From A. E. Housman, *A Shropshire Lad*, Henry Holt and Company, Inc.

Why, if 'tis dancing you would be,   15
There's brisker pipes than poetry.
Say, for what were hop-yards meant,
Or why was Burton built on Trent?
Oh many a peer of England brews
Livelier liquor than the Muse,   20
And malt does more than Milton can
To justify God's ways to man.
Ale, man, ale's the stuff to drink
For fellows whom it hurts to think:
Look into the pewter pot   25
To see the world as the world's not.
And faith, 'tis pleasant till 'tis past:
The mischief is that 'twill not last.
Oh I have been to Ludlow fair
And left my necktie God knows where,   30
And carried half-way home, or near,
Pints and quarts of Ludlow beer:
Then the world seemed none so bad,
And I myself a sterling lad;
And down in lovely muck I've lain,   35
Happy till I woke again.
Then I saw the morning sky:
Heigho, the tale was all a lie;
The world, it was the old world yet,
I was I, my things were wet,   40
And nothing now remained to do
But begin the game anew.

Therefore, since the world has still
Much good, but much less good than ill,
And while the sun and moon endure   45
Luck's a chance, but trouble's sure,
I'd face it as a wise man would,
And train for ill and not for good.
'Tis true, the stuff I bring for sale
Is not so brisk a brew as ale: 50
Out of a stem that scored the hand
I wrung it in a weary land.
But take it: if the smack is sour,

The better for the embittered hour;
It should do good to heart and head   55
When your soul is in my soul's stead;
And I will friend you, if I may,
In the dark and cloudy day.

    There was a king reigned in the East:
There, when kings will sit to feast,   60
They get their fill before they think
With poisoned meat and poisoned drink.
He gathered all that springs to birth
From the many-venomed earth;
First a little, thence to more,   65
He sampled all her killing store;
And easy, smiling, seasoned sound,
Sate the king when healths went round.
They put arsenic in his meat
And stared aghast to watch him eat;   70
They poured strychnine in his cup
And shook to see him drink it up:
They shook, they stared as white's their shirt:
Them it was their poison hurt.
—I tell the tale that I heard told.   75
Mithridates, he died old.

QUESTIONS ON CONTENT

1. Who are the speakers? What is the complaint of the first speaker?
2. To what does "this" refer in the first line?
3. How close kin are Eben Flood and Terence? Discuss.
4. Put the following couplet into your own words: "Out of a stem that scored the hand/ I wrung it in a weary land."
5. Pick out three or four quotable couplets and explain their meaning.
6. What is the moral of the tale of Mithridates? Does it illustrate the central thought of the poem?
7. Define "pessimism." Would you classify this poem as pessimistic? Discuss.
8. How does the attitude in this poem differ from that expressed by Keats in "Ode to a Nightingale"?

❧ *"The World Is Too Much With Us"*

William Wordsworth

The world is too much with us: late and soon,
Getting and spending, we lay waste our powers:
Little we see in Nature that is ours;
We have given our hearts away, a sordid boon!
The sea that bares her bosom to the moon;   5
The winds that will be howling at all hours,
And are up-gathered now like sleeping flowers;
For this, for everything, we are out of tune;
It moves us not.—Great God! I'd rather be
A Pagan suckled in a creed outworn;   10
So might I, standing on this pleasant lea,
Have glimpses that would make me less forlorn;
Have sight of Proteus rising from the sea;
Or hear old Triton blow his wreathèd horn.

QUESTIONS ON CONTENT

1. Compare the views of Terence ("Terence, This Is Stupid Stuff")
   and Wordsworth as they consider the ills of the world. How
   different are their suggestions for mitigating these evils?
2. What is the relationship between "a creed outworn" and the
   references to "Proteus" and "old Triton"?
3. Compare this poem and "Dover Beach." Each describes something the world has lost. In each poem what is this?
4. What is the plain sense of this poem? Develop the poetic experience. Follow in detail the process used in "On Reading Poems."
5. Is the world still "too much with us"? Discuss.

First published in 1806.

❧ *Soliloquy of the Spanish Cloister*

ROBERT BROWNING

Gr-r-r—there go, my heart's abhorrence!
    Water your damned flower-pots, do!
If hate killed men, Brother Lawrence,
    God's blood, would not mine kill you!
What? your myrtle-bush wants trimming?   5
    Oh, that rose has prior claims—
Needs its leaden vase filled brimming?
    Hell dry you up with its flames!

At the meal we sit together:
    Salve tibi! I must hear   10
Wise talk of the kind of weather,
    Sort of season, time of year:
Not a plenteous cork-crop: scarcely
    Dare we hope oak-galls, I doubt:
What's the Latin name for "parsley"?   15
    What's the Greek name for Swine's Snout?

Whew! We'll have our platter burnished,
    Laid with care on our own shelf!
With a fire-new spoon we're furnished,
    And a goblet for ourself,   20
Rinsed like something sacrificial
    Ere 'tis fit to touch our chaps—
Marked with L for our initial!
    (He-he! There his lily snaps!)

Saint, forsooth! While brown Dolores   25
    Squats outside the Convent bank
With Sanchicha, telling stories,
    Steeping tresses in the tank,
Blue-black, lustrous, thick like horsehairs,
    —Can't I see his dead eye glow,   30

First published in 1842.

Bright as 'twere a Barbary corsair's?
  (That is, if he'd let it show!)

When he finishes refection,
  Knife and fork he never lays
Cross-wise, to my recollection,   35
  As do I, in Jesu's praise.
I the Trinity illustrate,
  Drinking watered orange-pulp—
In three sips the Arian frustrate;
  While he drains his at one gulp.   40

Oh, those melons! If he's able
  We're to have a feast! so nice!
One goes to the Abbot's table,
  All of us get each a slice.
How go on your flowers? None double?   45
  Not one fruit-sort can you spy?
Strange!—And I, too, at such trouble
  Keep them close-nipped on the sly!

There's a great text in Galatians,
  Once you trip on it, entails   50
Twenty-nine distinct damnations,
  One sure, if another fails:
If I trip him just a-dying,
  Sure of heaven as sure can be,
Spin him round and send him flying   55
  Off to hell, a Manichee?

Or, my scrofulous French novel
  On gray paper with blunt type!
Simply glance at it, you grovel
  Hand and foot in Belial's gripe: 60
If I double down its pages
  At the woeful sixteenth print,
When he gathers his greengages,
  Ope a sieve and slip it in't?

Or, there's Satan!—one might venture   65
  Pledge one's soul to him, yet leave

Such a flaw in the indenture
  As he'd miss till, past retrieve,
Blasted lay that rose-acacia
  We're so proud of! *Hy, Zy, Hine.* . . .   70
'St, there's Vespers! *Plena, gratiâ,*
  Ave, Virgo! Gr-r-r—you swine!

QUESTIONS ON CONTENT

1. There are many love poems but few hate poems. Why is this?
2. What is Brother Lawrence doing? Where is the speaker?
3. Why does the speaker hate Brother Lawrence? Describe the sort of person you think Brother Lawrence really is. Is he without fault?
4. Who is more outwardly pious, the speaker or Brother Lawrence? Cite proof.
5. What is the central irony of this poem?

✑ *The Charge of the Light Brigade*

ALFRED, LORD TENNYSON

I

Half a league, half a league,
Half a league onward,
All in the valley of Death
  Rode the six hundred.
"Forward the Light Brigade!   5
Charge for the guns!" he said.
Into the valley of Death
  Rode the six hundred.

II

"Forward, the Light Brigade!"
Was there a man dismay'd?   10
Not tho' the soldier knew
  Some one had blunder'd.

First published in 1854.

Theirs not to make reply,
Theirs not to reason why,
Theirs but to do and die.   15
Into the valley of Death
  Rode the six hundred.

III

Cannon to right of them,
Cannon to left of them,
Cannon in front of them   20
  Volley'd and thunder'd;
Storm'd at with shot and shell,
Boldly they rode and well,
Into the jaws of Death,
Into the mouth of hell   25
  Rode the six hundred.

IV

Flash'd all their sabres bare,
Flash'd as they turn'd in air,
Sabring the gunners there,
Charging an army, while   30
  All the world wonder'd.
Plunged in the battery-smoke
Right thro' the line they broke;
Cossack and Russian
Reel'd from the sabre-stroke   35
  Shatter'd and sunder'd.
Then they rode back, but not,
  Not the six hundred.

V

Cannon to right of them,
Cannon to left of them,   40
Cannon behind them
  Volley'd and thunder'd;
Storm'd at with shot and shell,
While horse and hero fell,
They that had fought so well   45
Came thro' the jaws of Death,
Back from the mouth of hell,

All that was left of them,
Left of six hundred.

VI

When can their glory fade?   50
O the wild charge they made!
   All the world wonder'd.
Honor the charge they made!
Honor the Light Brigade,
   Noble six hundred!

QUESTIONS ON CONTENT

1. Does this famous poem stir you? Why, or why not?
2. Comment on these lines: "Theirs not to make reply,/ Theirs not to reason why,/ Theirs but to do and die." Debate the military necessity of such an attitude.
3. In World War II it is alleged that the sending of troops across the Rapido River in Italy was a great blunder. Why was there no poem to celebrate this charge into death? Discuss.

❦ *Dulce et Decorum Est*

WILFRED OWEN

Bent double, like old beggars under sacks,
Knock-kneed, coughing like hags, we cursed through sludge,
Till on the haunting flares we turned our backs,
And towards our distant rest began to trudge.
Men marched asleep. Many had lost their boots,   5
But limped on, blood-shod. All went lame, all blind;
Drunk with fatigue; deaf even to the hoots
Of gas-shells dropping softly behind.

Gas! Gas! Quick, boys!—An ecstasy of fumbling,
Fitting the clumsy helmets just in time,   10

All rights reserved. Reprinted by permission of the publisher, New Directions.

But some one still was yelling out and stumbling
And floundering like a man in fire or lime.—
Dim through the misty panes and thick green light,
As under a green sea, I saw him drowning.

In all my dreams before my helpless sight   15
He plunges at me, guttering, choking, drowning.

If in some smothering dreams, you too could pace
Behind the wagon that we flung him in,
And watch the white eyes writhing in his face,
His hanging face, like a devil's sick of sin,   20
If you could hear, at every jolt, the blood
Come gargling from the froth-corrupted lungs
Bitten as the cud
Of vile, incurable sores on innocent tongues,—
My friend, you would not tell with such high zest   25
To children ardent for some desperate glory,
The old Lie: Dulce et decorum est
Pro patria mori.

QUESTIONS ON CONTENT

1. Examine the details of this poem, then contrast the total effect produced by "The Charge of the Light Brigade." How do you account for the difference?
2. Will Durant ("Why Men Fight") says that "Prejudice is fatal to philosophy but indispensable to a people." Apply this dictum to Wilfred Owen's poem; then to Tennyson's. Which poet is more philosophical?

SUGGESTIONS FOR PAPERS

The selections in this chapter suggest three general approaches to a writing assignment: (1) a personal approach in which you take a cue from the method of the poets but record your own experiences with the emotions of love, hate, bravery, cowardice or the like; (2) an impersonal one in which you analyze with care one or more of the poems; (3) a combination of the impersonal and the personal approaches, in which you start with analysis and then apply the analysis to your own experience.

1. What in life makes you saddest? Its shortness? Its apparent aimlessness? Its cruelty? Its coldness? Its inequalities? Its insecurity? Or what? If what makes you saddest is something more personal than the qualities suggested, can you link your gloom to some sort of generalization about life?

2. Discuss the word *fame*. First, define the word; then determine what fame implies. How does one achieve fame? Select two examples of famous men, one deserving and the other, in your opinion, undeserving of the honor. By definition, can the second of your examples be called famous? What word would better describe him? And, finally, is the uneven distribution of "fame" a proper cause for gloom?

3. Discuss the selections in this chapter which comment directly or indirectly on fame. You will find that the following poems, "Ozymandias," "Fame" from "Earth's Immortalities," and "Cool Tombs," will each yield material for this paper.

4. Discuss the range of experiences represented in the selections on love. Isolate the differences and then present what may be called a composite poetic view of love.

5. It has been said that a hundred poems may be written upon the same idea, yet each poem will be unique. (See "On Reading Poems," Chapter 18). Show the truth of this observation by analyzing the poems in this chapter that are alike in theme. How, for example, are "Ozymandias" and "Earth's Immortalities: Fame" alike? How are they unique?

6. Select a poem from this chapter for complete analysis with the object to reveal its whole meaning. (Review first the method demonstrated in "On Reading Poems," Chapter 18.)

7. Compare "Dover Beach" and "Ode to a Nightingale." What, in each instance, inspired the poet? Is Sophocles an extra element in "Dover Beach"? What makes the world an almost intolerable place to each poet? Keats mentions three possible escapes. What are they? Arnold mentions but one possible comfort. What is it? How do the figures of speech in each poem grow out of the original impetus for writing the poem?

8. Set up questions similar to those posed in Suggestion 7 above and compare any one of the following pairs of poems: "Mr. Flood's Party" and "The World Is Too Much With Us"; "Terence, This Is Stupid Stuff" and "The World Is Too Much with Us"; "The Charge of the Light Brigade" and "*Dulce et Decorum Est.*"

9. Examine closely the characterizations in "Soliloquy of the

Spanish Cloister." What do you know about the speaker from what he tells us? What do you know about Brother Lawrence? First take literally all the speaker says about Brother Lawrence and implies about himself; then interpret; that is, show the difference between what is said and implied and what is the truth.

10. Write about the point of view (the position of observer-poet or speaker) in each of the following poems: "Ozymandias," "Earth's Immortalities: Fame," "Dover Beach," "Ode to a Nightingale," "Mr. Flood's Party," "Soliloquy of the Spanish Cloister." For example, the observer-reader may follow the eyes of the speaker in "Earth's Immortalities: Fame" as they move from the whole appearance of the poet's grave to the details of his tombstone. Is there a similar process in other poems?

SOME TITLES FOR PAPERS

1. My Darkest Mood
2. A Tale Told by an Idiot
3. To Make Much of Time
4. Time's Wingèd Chariot
5. Fame Is Worth Having
6. Our Names Are Writ in Water
7. Judas Is Remembered Too
8. My Tragic Memory
9. Hitler: The Modern Ozymandias
10. Some Monuments Remain
11. Poems Alike but Unique
12. Down the Shingles of the World
13. The Whole Meaning of a Poem
14. Irony Defined and Illustrated
15. Metaphor Defined and Illustrated
16. Love's Many Meanings
17. Is It Better to Have Loved and Lost?
18. Getting and Spending
19. How To Banish Melancholy
20. Hatred in a Cloister
21. Patriotism and Philosophy
22. Two Poems Compared
23. Subjects Attractive to the Poets

❧ *FICTION AND IDEAS: FIVE STORIES FOR ANALYSIS*

THIS CHAPTER DOES NOT PROPOSE a technical treatment of the short story. Instead it invites attention to the ideas contained in five stories. These ideas are the themes about which the story-tellers have woven a fabric of narration. Although not a chapter built around one idea —as has been the practice in most of the previous chapters—this section offers one constant: each story-teller has used his tale to illustrate a theme.

George Milburn in "The Apostate" simply "records" an apology offered by a businessman for resigning from the Rotary Club. Unintentional self-revelation, including a blindness to the identity of what he believed in and what his college son believed in, reveals the theme, or controlling idea of the story. The story was invented to illustrate the idea.

Maupassant in "A Piece of String" also worked from a controlling idea. His central character, a peasant, is apparently a victim of circumstances but only apparently, as an analysis of the story will show. Although the speaker in "The Apostate" and the peasant in "A

Piece of String" are worlds apart in many respects, how are they alike? What makes each of them so eager to tell his story?

"The Lottery Ticket" by Chekhov sets forth in crisp, economical fashion another bit of irony. Again, the author invents a story to illustrate a theme: to show how the prospect of riches can throw a cruel light on the dark, unpleasant recesses of a man's (and a woman's) soul.

Shirley Jackson deals with a different sort of chance-taking in her provocative story, "The Lottery." If you are puzzled by this story, read it again after looking up the meaning of the word "scapegoat." You will note that the author has given us a sense of "villages" not a "village" and of "villagers" not individuals. Why? Does this method suggest that we have to be alert to levels of meaning beyond the literal?

"Young Goodman Brown" by Hawthorne is clearly an allegory; that is, each character stands for a whole class of persons and each action for a whole class of actions. Once more, as in the preceding stories, the narrative is invented to illustrate a theme.

❧ *The Apostate*

GEORGE MILBURN

Harry, you been jacking me up about how I been neglecting Rotary lately, so I'm just going to break down and tell you something. Now I don't want you to take this personal, Harry, because it's not meant personal at all. No siree! Not *a*-tall! But, just between you and I, Harry, I'm not going to be coming to Rotary lunches any more. I mean I'm quitting Rotary! . . .

Now whoa there! Whoa! Whoa just a minute and let me get in a word edgeways. Just let me finish my little say.

Don't you never take it into your head that I haven't been wrestling with this thing plenty. I mean I've argued it all out with myself. Now I'm going to tell you the whyfor and the whereof and the howcome about this, Harry, but kindly don't let what I say go no further. Please keep it strictly on the Q.T. Because I guess the rest of the

From *No More Trumpets*. Copyright 1933 by Harcourt, Brace and Company, Inc. Permission to reprint granted by Paul R. Reynolds & Son, 599 Fifth Avenue, New York 17, New York.

boys would suspicion that I was turning highbrow on them. But you've always been a buddy to me, Harry, you mangy old son of a hoss thief, you, so what I'm telling you is the straight dope.

Harry, like you no doubt remember, up till a few months ago Rotary was about "the most fondest thing I is of," as the nigger says. There wasn't nothing that stood higher for me than Rotary.

Well, here, about a year ago last fall I took a trip down to the university to visit my son and go to a football game. You know Hubert Junior, my boy. Sure. Well, this is his second year down at the university. Yes sir, that boy is getting a college education. I mean, I'm all for youth having a college education.

Of course I think there is such a thing as too much education working a detriment. Take, for instance, some of these longhairs running around knocking the country right now. But what I mean is, a good, sound, substantial college education. I don't mean a string of letters a yard long for a man to write after his John Henry. I just mean that I want my boy to have his sheepskin, they call it, before he starts out in the world. Like the fellow says, I want him to get his A.B. degree, and then he can go out and get his J.O.B.

Now, Harry, I always felt like a father has got certain responsibilities to his son. That's just good Rotary. That's all that is. You know that that's just good Rotary yourself, Harry. Well, I always wanted Hubert to think about me just like I was a pal to him, or say an older brother, maybe. Hubert always knew that all he had to do was come to me, and I would act like a big buddy to him, irregardless.

Well, like I was telling you, Harry, I started Hubert in to the university two years ago, and after he had been there about two months, I thought I would run down and see how he was getting along and go to a football game. So I and Mrs. T. drove over one Friday. We didn't know the town very well, so we stopped at a filling station, and I give Hubert a ring, and he come right on down to where we was to show us the way. Just as soon as he come up, I could see right then that he had something on his mind bothering him.

He called me aside and took me into the filling-station rest-room, and says: "For the love of God, Dad, take that Rotary button out of your coat lapel," he says to me.

Harry, that come as a big surprise to me, and I don't mind telling you that it just about took the wind out of my sails. But I wasn't going to let on to him, so I rared back on my dignity, and says, "Why, what do you mean, take that Rotary button out of my lapel, young man?" I says to him.

"Dad," Hubert says to me, serious, "any frat house has always got a few cynics in it. If you was to wear that Rotary button in your lapel out to the frat house, just as soon as you got out of sight, some of those boys at the house would razz the life out of me," he says.

"Hubert," I says, "there's not a thing that this lapel badge represents that any decent, moral person could afford to make fun of. If that's the kind of Reds you got out at your fraternity, the kind that would razz a what you might call sacred thing—yes sir, a sacred thing—like Rotary, well I and your mamma can just go somewheres else and put up. I don't guess the hotels have quit running," I says to him.

By now I was on my high horse right, see?

"Now, Dad," Hubert says, "it's not that. I mean, person'ly I'm awful proud of you. It's just that I haven't been pledged to this fraternity long, see, and when some of those older members found out you was a Rotarian they would deal me a lot of misery, and I couldn't say nothing. Person'ly I think Rotary is all right," he says to me.

"Well, you better, son," I says, "or I'm going to begin to think that you're sick in the head."

The way he explained it, though, Harry, that made it a horse of a different tail, as the saying goes, so I give in and took off my Rotary button right there. Stuck it in my pocket, see? So we went on out and visited at Hubert's fraternity house, and do you know that those boys just got around there and treated we folks like we was princes of the blood. I mean you would of thought that I was an old ex-graduate of that university. And we saw the big pigskin tussle the next day, fourteen to aught, favor us, and we had such a scrumptious time all around I forgot about what Hubert had said.

Ever'thing would of been all right, except for what happened later. I guess some of those older boys at the frat house begin using their form of psychology on Hubert. I mean they finely got his mind set against Rotary, because when he come home for the summer vacation that was about the size of things.

I mean all last summer, I thought Hubert never would let up. He just kept it up, making sarcastic remarks about Rotary, see? Even when we was on our vacation trip. You know we drove out to California and back last summer, Harry. Come back with the same air in the tires we started out with. Well, I thought it would be kind of nice to drop in and eat with the Hollywood Rotary—you know, just to be able to say I had. Well, do you know that that boy Hubert made so much fun of the idea I just had to give it up? That was the way it was the whole trip. He got his mother around on his side, too. Just to be frank with you, I never got so sick and tired of anything in all my born days.

Well, Harry, I had my dander up there for a while, and all the bickering in the world couldn't of shook me from my stand. But finely Hubert went back to college in September, and I thought I would have a little peace. Then I just got to thinking about it, and it all come over me. "Look here, Mister Man," I says to myself, "your faith and loyalty to Rotary may be a fine thing, and all that, but it's just costing you the fellowship of your own son." Now a man can't practice Rotary in the higher sense, and yet at the same time be letting his own son's fellowship get loose from him. So there it was. Blood's thicker than water, Harry. You'll have to admit that.

Right along in there, Harry, was the first time I begin to attending meetings irregular. I'll tell you—you might not think so—but it was a pretty tough struggle for me. I remember one Monday noon, Rotary-meeting day, I happened to walk past the Hotel Beckman just at lunch-time. The windows of the Venetian Room was open, and I could hear you boys singing a Rotary song. You know that one we sing set to the tune of "Last Night on the Back Porch." It goes:

> *I love the Lions in the morning,*
> *The Exchange Club at night,*
> *I love the Y's men in the evening,*
> *And Kiwanis are all right . . .*

Well, I couldn't carry a tune if I had it in a sack, but anyway that's the way it goes. So I just stopped in my tracks and stood there listening to that song coming out of the Hotel Beckman dining room. And when the boys come to the last verse,

> *I love the Optimists in the springtime,*
> *The Ad Club in the fall,*
> *But each day—and in every way—*
> *I love Rotary best of all. . . .*

I tell you, Harry, that just got me. I had a lump in my throat big enough to choke a cow. The tears begin coming up in my eyes, and it might sound ridiculous to hear me tell it now, but I could of broke down and bawled right there on the street. I got a grip on myself and walked on off, but right then I says to myself, "The hell with Hubert and his highbrow college-fraternity ideas; I'm going back to Rotary next week."

Well, I did go back the next week, and what happened decided me on taking the step I decided on. Here's what decided me. You know, I never got very well acquainted with Gay Harrison, the new secretary. I mean, of course, I know him all right, but he hasn't been in Rotary only but about a year. Well, on that particular day, I just happened to let my tongue slip and called him Mister Harrison, instead of by his nickname. Well, of course, the boys slapped a dollar fine on me right then and there. I haven't got no kick to make about that, but the point is, I had a letter from Hubert in my pocket right then, telling me that he had run short of money. So I just couldn't help but be struck by the idea "I wish I was giving Hubert this dollar." So that's what decided me on devoting my time and finances to another kind of fellowship, Harry.

I get down to the university to see Hubert more frequent now. I make it a point to. And the boys come to me, and I been helping them a little on their frat building fund. There's a fine spirit of fellowship in an organization like that. Some boys from the best families of the State are members, too. You might think from what I said that they'd be uppish, but they're not. No siree. Not a bit of it. I been down there enough for them to know me, now, and they all pound me on the back and call me H.T., just like I was one of them. And I do them, too. And I notice when they sit down to a meal, they have some songs they sing just as lively and jolly as any we had at Rotary. Of course, like Hubert said, a few of them might have some wild-haired ideas about Rotary, but they're young yet. And as far as I can see there's not a knocker nor a sourbelly among them. Absolutely democratic.

It puts me in mind of a little incidence that happened last month when the frat threw a big Dad's Day banquet for us down there. All the fathers of the boys from all over the State was there. Well, to promote the spirit of fellowship between dad and son, the fraternity boys all agreed to call their dads by their first name, just treating the dads like big buddies. So at the table Hubert happened to forget for a minute, and says to me "Dad" something. Well sir, the president of the frat flashed out, "All right, Hubie, we heard you call H.T. 'Dad.' So that'll cost you a dollar for the ice-cream fund." Ever'body had a good laugh at Hubert getting caught like that, but do you know, that boy of mine just forked right over without making a kick. That shows the stuff, don't it, Harry? Nothing wrong with a boy like that.

And the whole bunch is like that, ever'one of them. I'll tell you, Harry, the boys at that frat of Hubert's are the builders in the coming generation. Any man of vision can see that.

Well, that's that. Now what are you going to say?

QUESTIONS ON CONTENT

1. Define "irony," then show what is ironical about this story.
2. Why does the author allow the speaker to be semi-illiterate in his speech? Does this contribute to the story's realism?
3. What, if anything, prevented the father from seeing the parallel between the conduct of Rotarians and the conduct of Hubert's fraternity brothers? Is this sort of blindness convincing? Explain.
4. If you are a member of a fraternity, comment on the accuracy of the author's partial view of fraternity life.

~ *Piece of String*

GUY DE MAUPASSANT

It was market-day, and over all the roads round Goderville the peasants and their wives were coming towards the town. The men walked easily, lurching the whole body forward at every step. Their long legs were twisted and deformed by the slow, painful labors of the country:—by bending over to plough, which is also what makes their left shoulders too high and their figures crooked; and by reaping corn, which obliges them for steadiness' sake to spread their knees too wide. Their starched blue blouses, shining as though varnished, ornamented at collar and cuffs with little patterns of white stitchwork, and blown up big around their bony bodies, seemed exactly like balloons about to soar, but putting forth a head, two arms, and two feet.

Some of these fellows dragged a cow or a calf at the end of a rope. And just behind the animal, beating it over the back with a leaf-covered branch to hasten its pace, went their wives, carrying large baskets from which came forth the heads of chickens or the heads of ducks. These women walked with steps far shorter and quicker than the men; their figures, withered and upright, were adorned with scanty little shawls pinned over their flat bosoms; and they enveloped their heads each in a white cloth, close fastened round the hair and surmounted by a cap.

Now a char-à-banc passed by, drawn by a jerky-paced nag. It shook up strangely the two men on the seat. And the woman at the bottom of the cart held fast to its sides to lessen the hard joltings.

In the market-place at Goderville was a great crowd, a mingled multitude of men and beasts. The horns of cattle, the high and long-napped hats of wealthy peasants, the head-dresses of the women, came to the surface of that sea. And voices clamorous, sharp, shrill, made a continuous and savage din. Above it a huge burst of laughter from the sturdy lungs of a merry yokel would sometimes sound, and sometimes a long bellow from a cow tied fast to the wall of a house.

It all smelled of the stable, of milk, of hay, and of perspiration, giving off that half-human, half-animal odor which is peculiar to the men of the fields.

Maître Hauchecorne, of Bréauté, had just arrived at Goderville, and was taking his way towards the square, when he perceived on the ground a little piece of string. Maître Hauchecorne, economical, like all true Normans, reflected that everything was worth picking up which could be of any use; and he stooped down—but painfully, because he suffered from rheumatism. He took the bit of thin cord from the ground, and was carefully preparing to roll it up when he saw Maître Malandain, the harness-maker, on his door-step, looking at him. They had once had a quarrel about a halter, and they had remained angry, bearing malice on both sides. Maître Hauchecorne was overcome with a sort of shame at being seen by his enemy looking in the dirt so for a bit of string. He quickly hid his find beneath his blouse; then in the pocket of his breeches; then pretended to be still looking for something on the ground which he did not discover; and at last went off towards the market-place, with his head bent forward, and a body almost doubled in two by rheumatic pains.

He lost himself immediately in the crowd, which was clamorous, slow, and agitated by interminable bargains. The peasants examined the cows, went off, came back, always in great perplexity and fear of being cheated, never quite daring to decide, spying at the eye of the seller, trying ceaselessly to discover the tricks of the man and the defect in the beast.

The women, having placed their great baskets at their feet, had pulled out the poultry, which lay upon the ground, tied by the legs, with eyes scared, with combs scarlet.

They listened to propositions, maintaining their prices, with a dry manner, with an impassible face; or, suddenly, perhaps deciding to take the lower price which was offered, they cried out to the customer, who was departing slowly:

"All right, I'll let you have them, Maît' Anthime."

Then, little by little, the square became empty, and when the *Angelus* struck midday those who lived at a distance poured into the inns.

At Jourdain's the great room was filled with eaters, just as the vast court was filled with vehicles of every sort—wagons, gigs, char-à-bancs, tilburys, tilt-carts which have no name, yellow with mud, misshapen, pieced together, raising their shafts to heaven like two arms, or it may be with their nose in the dirt and their rear in the air.

Just opposite to where the diners were at table the huge fireplace, full of clear flame, threw a lively heat on the backs of those who sat along the right. Three spits were turning, loaded with chickens, with pigeons, and with joints of mutton; and a delectable odor of roast meat, and of gravy gushing over crisp brown skin, took wing from the hearth, kindled merriment, caused mouths to water.

All the aristocracy of the plough were eating there, at Maît' Jourdain's, the inn-keeper's, a dealer in horses also, and a sharp fellow who had made a pretty penny in his day.

The dishes were passed round, were emptied, with jugs of yellow cider. Every one told of his affairs, of his purchases and his sales. They asked news about the crops. The weather was good for green stuffs, but a little wet for wheat.

All of a sudden the drum rolled in the court before the house. Every one, except some of the most indifferent, was on his feet at once, and ran to the door, to the windows, with his mouth still full and his napkin in his hand.

When the public crier had finished his tattoo he called forth in a jerky voice, making his pauses out of time:

"Be it known to the inhabitants of Goderville, and in general to all—persons present at the market, that there has been lost this morning, on the Beuzeville road, between—nine and ten o'clock, a pocket-book of black leather, containing five hundred francs and business papers. You are requested to return it—to the mayor's office, at once, or to Maître Fortuné Houlbrèque, of Manneville. There will be twenty francs reward."

Then the man departed. They heard once more at a distance the dull beatings on the drum and the faint voice of the crier.

Then they began to talk of this event, reckoning up the chances which Maître Houlbrèque had of finding or of not finding his pocket-book again.

And the meal went on.

They were finishing their coffee when the corporal of gendarmes appeared on the threshold.

He asked:

"Is Maître Hauchecorne, of Bréauté, here?"

"Here I am."

And the corporal resumed:

"Maître Hauchecorne, will you have the kindness to come with me to the Mayor's office? M. le Maire would like to speak to you."

The peasant, surprised and uneasy, gulped down his little glass of cognac, got up, and, even worse bent over than in the morning, since the first steps after a rest were always particularly difficult, started off, repeating:

"Here I am, here I am."

And he followed the corporal.

The mayor was waiting for him, seated in an arm-chair. He was the notary of the place, a tall, grave man of pompous speech.

"Maître Hauchecorne," said he, "this morning on the Beuzeville road, you were seen to pick up the pocket-book lost by Maître Houlbrèque, of Manneville."

The countryman, speechless, regarded the mayor, frightened already by this suspicion which rested on him he knew not why.

"I, I picked up that pocket-book?"

"Yes, you."

"I swear I didn't even know nothing about it at all."

"You were seen."

"They saw me, me? Who is that who saw me?"

"M. Malandain, the harness-maker."

Then the old man remembered, understood, and, reddening with anger:

"Ah! he saw me, did he, the rascal? He saw me picking up this string here, M'sieu' le Maire."

And, fumbling at the bottom of his pocket, he pulled out of it the little end of string.

But the mayor incredulously shook his head:

"You will not make me believe, Maître Hauchecorne, that M. Malandain, who is a man worthy of credit, has mistaken this string for a pocket-book."

The peasant, furious, raised his hand and spit as if to attest his good faith, repeating:

"For all that, it is the truth of the good God, the blessed truth, M'sieu' le Maire. There! on my soul and my salvation I repeat it."

The mayor continued:

"After having picked up the thing in question, you even looked for some time in the mud to see if a piece of money had not dropped out of it."

The good man was suffocated with indignation and with fear.

"If they can say—if they can say . . . such lies as that to slander an honest man! If they can say!——"

He might protest, but he was not believed.

He was confronted with M. Malandain, who repeated and sustained his testimony. They abused one another for an hour. At his own request Maître Hauchecorne was searched. Nothing was found upon him.

At last, the mayor, much perplexed, sent him away, warning him that he would inform the public prosecutor, and ask for orders.

The news had spread. When he left the mayor's office, the old man was surrounded, interrogated with a curiosity which was serious or mocking as the case might be, but into which no indignation entered. And he began to tell the story of the string. They did not believe him. They laughed.

He passed on, button-holed by every one, himself button-holing his acquaintances, beginning over and over again his tale and his protestations, showing his pockets turned inside out to prove that he had nothing.

They said to him:

"You old rogue, *va!*"

And he grew angry, exasperated, feverish, in despair at not being believed, and always telling his story.

The night came. It was time to go home. He set out with three of his neighbors, to whom he pointed out the place where he had picked up the end of string; and all the way he talked of his adventure.

That evening he made the round in the village of Bréauté, so as to tell every one. He met only unbelievers.

He was ill of it all night long.

Guy de Maupassant717

The next day, about one in the afternoon, Marius Paumelle, a farm hand of Maître Breton, the market-gardener at Ymauville, returned the pocket-book and its contents to Maître Houlbrèque, of Manneville.

This man said, indeed, that he had found it on the road; but not knowing how to read, he had carried it home and given it to his master.

The news spread to the environs. Maître Hauchecorne was informed. He put himself at once upon the go, and began to relate his story as completed by the *dénouement*. He triumphed.

"What grieved me," said he, "was not the thing itself, do you understand; but it was the lies. There's nothing does you so much harm as being in disgrace for lying."

All day he talked of his adventure; he told it on the roads to the people who passed; at the cabaret to the people who drank; and the next Sunday, when they came out of church. He even stopped strangers to tell them about it. He was easy, now, and yet something worried him without his knowing exactly what it was. People had a joking manner while they listened. They did not seem convinced. He seemed to feel their tittle-tattle behind his back.

On Tuesday of the next week he went to market at Goderville, prompted entirely by the need of telling his story.

Malandain, standing on his door-step, began to laugh as he saw him pass. Why?

He accosted a farmer of Criquetot, who did not let him finish, and, giving him a punch in the pit of his stomach, cried in his face: "Oh, you great rogue, *va!*" Then turned his head upon him.

Maître Hauchecorne remained speechless, and grew more and more uneasy. Why had they called him "great rogue"?

When seated at table in Jourdain's tavern he began again to explain the whole affair.

A horse-dealer of Montivilliers shouted at him:

"Get out, get out, you old scamp; I know all about your string!"

Hauchecorne stammered:

"But since they found it again, the pocket-book!"

But the other continued:

"Hold your tongue, daddy; there's one who finds it and there's another who returns it. And no one the wiser."

The peasant was choked. He understood at last. They accused him of having had the pocket-book brought back by an accomplice, by a confederate.

He tried to protest. The whole table began to laugh.

He could not finish his dinner, and went away amid a chorus of jeers.

He went home, ashamed and indignant, choked with rage, with confusion, the more cast-down since from his Norman cunning, he was, perhaps, capable of having done what they accused him of, and even of boasting of it as a good trick. His innocence dimly seemed to him impossible to prove, his craftiness being so well known. And he felt himself struck to the heart by the injustice of the suspicion.

Then he began anew to tell of his adventure, lengthening his recital every day, each time adding new proofs, more energetic protestations, and more solemn oaths which he thought of, which he prepared in his hours of solitude, his mind being entirely occupied by the story of the string. The more complicated his defence, the more artful his arguments, the less he was believed.

"Those are liars' proofs," they said behind his back.

He felt this; it preyed upon his heart. He exhausted himself in useless efforts.

He was visibly wasting away.

The jokers now made him tell the story of "The Piece of String" to amuse them, just as you make a soldier who has been on a campaign tell his story of the battle. His mind, struck at the root, grew weak.

About the end of December he took to his bed.

He died early in January, and, in the delirium of the death-agony, he protested his innocence, repeating:

"A little bit of string—a little bit of string—see, here it is, M'sieu' le Maire."

QUESTIONS ON CONTENT

1. In what way do the first five paragraphs serve the author's purpose? Could they be omitted? Explain.
2. Characterize Maître Hauchecorne. In what respect was he innocent of the charge brought against him? In what respect was he not innocent?
3. Examine the passage describing the picking up of the piece of string. Are the motions of the peasant natural ones? Suppose a friend had been watching him instead of an enemy. What would have happened to the story? Is this part of the story a good example of coincidence?

4. Does this story have implications beyond its literal meaning? Is it simply the tale of an unfortunate peasant? What about the minds and the hearts of the people who would not believe him? *Why* didn't they believe him? (Compare the people in this story with the people in Shirley Jackson's "The Lottery.")

❧ *The Lottery Ticket*

Anton Chekhov

Ivan Dmitritch, a middle-class man who lived with his family on an income of twelve hundred a year and was very well satisfied with his lot, sat down on the sofa after supper and began reading the newspaper.

"I forgot to look at the newspaper today," his wife said to him as she cleared the table. "Look and see whether the list of drawings is there."

"Yes, it is," said Ivan Dmitritch; "but hasn't your ticket lapsed?"

"No; I took the interest on Tuesday."

"What is the number?"

"Series 9,499, number 26."

"All right . . . we will look . . . 9,499 and 26."

Ivan Dmitritch had no faith in lottery luck, and would not, as a rule, have consented to look at the lists of winning numbers, but now, as he had nothing else to do and as the newspaper was before his eyes, he passed his finger downwards along the column of numbers. And immediately, as though in mockery of his scepticism, no further than the second line from the top, his eye was caught by the figure 9,499! Unable to believe his eyes, he hurriedly dropped the paper on his knees without looking to see the number of the ticket, and, just as though some one had given him a douche of cold water, he felt an agreeable chill in the pit of the stomach; tingling and terrible and sweet!

"Masha, 9,499 is there!" he said in a hollow voice.

His wife looked at his astonished and panic-stricken face, and realized that he was not joking.

From *The Wife and Other Stories*, 1918. Published by permission of The Macmillan Company.

"9,499?" she asked, turning pale and dropping the folded table-cloth on the table.

"Yes, yes . . . it really is there!"

"And the number of the ticket?"

"Oh, yes! There's the number of the ticket too. But stay . . . wait! No! I say! Anyway, the number of our series is there! Anyway, you understand. . . ."

Looking at his wife, Ivan Dmitritch gave a broad, senseless smile, like a baby when a bright object is shown it. His wife smiled too; it was as pleasant to her as to him that he only mentioned the series, and did not try to find out the number of the winning ticket. To torment and tantalize oneself with hopes of possible fortune is so sweet, so thrilling!

"It is our series," said Ivan Dmitritch, after a long silence. "So there is a probability that we have won. It's only a probability, but there it is!"

"Well, now look!"

"Wait a little. We have plenty of time to be disappointed. It's on the second line from the top, so the prize is seventy-five thousand. That's not money, but power, capital! And in a minute I shall look at the list, and there—26! Eh? I say, what if we really have won?"

The husband and wife began laughing and staring at one another in silence. The possibility of winning bewildered them; they could not have said, could not have dreamed, what they both needed that seventy-five thousand for, what they would buy, where they would go. They thought only of the figures 9,499 and 75,000 and pictured them in their imagination, while somehow they could not think of the happiness itself which was so possible.

Ivan Dmitritch, holding the paper in his hand, walked several time from corner to corner, and only when he had recovered from the first impression began dreaming a little.

"And if we have won," he said—"why, it will be a new life, it will be transformation! The ticket is yours, but if it were mine I should, first of all, of course, spend twenty-five thousand on real property in the shape of an estate; ten thousand on immediate expenses, new furnishing . . . travelling . . . paying debts, and so on. . . . The other forty thousand I would put in the bank and get interest on it."

"Yes, an estate, that would be nice," said his wife, sitting down and dropping her hands in her lap.

"Somewhere in the Tula or Oryol provinces. . . . In the first place we shouldn't need a summer villa, and besides, it would always bring in an income."

And pictures came crowding on his imagination, each more gracious and poetical than the last. And in all these pictures he saw himself well-fed, serene, healthy, felt warm, even hot! Here, after eating a summer soup, cold as ice, he lay on his back on the burning sand close to a stream or in the garden under a lime-tree. . . . It is hot. . . . His little boy and girl are crawling about near him, digging in the sand or catching ladybirds in the grass. He dozes sweetly, thinking of nothing, and feeling all over that he need not go to the office today, tomorrow, or the day after. Or, tired of lying still, he goes to the hayfield, or to the forest for mushrooms, or watches the peasants catching fish with a net. When the sun sets he takes a towel and soap and saunters to the bathing-shed, where he undresses at his leisure, slowly rubs his bare chest with his hands, and goes into the water. And in the water, near the opaque soapy circles, little fish flit to and fro and green water-weeds nod their heads. After bathing there is tea with cream and milk rolls. . . . In the evening a walk or *vint* with the neighbors.

"Yes, it would be nice to buy an estate," said his wife, also dreaming, and from her face it was evident that she was enchanted by her thoughts.

Ivan Dmitritch pictured to himself autumn with its rains, its cold evenings, and its St. Martin's summer. At that season he would have to take longer walks about the garden and beside the river, so as to get thoroughly chilled, and then drink a big glass of vodka and eat a salted mushroom or a soused cucumber, and then—drink another. . . . The children would come running from the kitchen-garden, bringing a carrot and a radish smelling of fresh earth. . . . And then, he would lie stretched full length on the sofa, and in leisurely fashion turn over the pages of some illustrated magazine, or, covering his face with it and unbuttoning his waistcoat, give himself up to slumber.

The St. Martin's summer is followed by cloudy, gloomy weather. It rains day and night, the bare trees weep, the wind is damp and cold. The dogs, the horses, the fowls—all are wet, depressed, downcast. There is nowhere to walk; one can't go out for days together; one has to pace up and down the room, looking despondently at the grey window. It is dreary!

Ivan Dmitritch stopped and looked at his wife.

"I should go abroad, you know, Masha," he said.

And he began thinking how nice it would be in late autumn to go abroad somewhere to the South of France . . . to Italy . . . to India!

"I should certainly go abroad too," his wife said. "But look at the number of the ticket!"

"Wait, wait! . . ."

He walked about the room and went on thinking. It occurred to him: what if his wife really did go abroad? It is pleasant to travel alone, or in the society of light, careless women who live in the present, and not such as think and talk all the journey about nothing but their children, sigh, and tremble with dismay over every farthing. Ivan Dmitritch imagined his wife in the train with a multitude of parcels, baskets, and bags; she would be sighing over something, complaining that the train made her head ache, that she had spent so much money. . . . At the stations he would continually be having to run for boiling water, bread and butter. . . . She wouldn't have dinner because of its being too dear. . . .

"She would begrudge me every farthing," he thought, with a glance at his wife. "The lottery ticket is hers, not mine! Besides, what is the use of her going abroad? What does she want there? She would shut herself up in the hotel, and not let me out of her sight. . . . I know!"

And for the first time in his life his mind dwelt on the fact that his wife had grown elderly and plain, and that she was saturated through and through with the smell of cooking, while he was still young, fresh, and healthy, and might well have got married again.

"Of course, all that is silly nonsense," he thought; "but . . . why should she go abroad? What would she make of it? And yet she would go, of course. . . . I can fancy. . . . In reality it is all one to her, whether it is Naples or Klin. She would only be in my way. I should be dependent upon her. I can fancy how, like a regular woman, she will lock the money up as soon as she gets it. . . . She will look after her relations and grudge me every farthing."

Ivan Dmitritch thought of her relations. All those wretched brothers and sisters and aunts and uncles would come crawling about as soon as they heard of the winning ticket, would begin whining like beggars, and fawning upon them with oily, hypocritical smiles. Wretched, detestable people! If they were given anything, they would ask for more; while if they were refused, they would swear at them, slander them, and wish them every kind of misfortune.

Ivan Dmitritch remembered his own relations, and their faces, at which he had looked impartially in the past, struck him now as repulsive and hateful.

"They are such reptiles!" he thought.

And his wife's face, too, struck him as repulsive and hateful. Anger surged up in his heart against her, and he thought malignantly:

"She knows nothing about money, and so she is stingy. If she won it she would give me a hundred roubles, and put the rest away under lock and key."

And he looked at his wife, not with a smile now, but with hatred. She glanced at him too, and also with hatred and anger. She had her own daydreams, her own plans, her own reflections; she understood perfectly well what her husband's dreams were. She knew who would be the first to try to grab her winnings.

"It's very nice making daydreams at other people's expense!" is what her eyes expressed. "No, don't you dare!"

Her husband understood her look; hatred began stirring again in his breast, and in order to annoy his wife he glanced quickly, to spite her at the fourth page on the newspaper and read out triumphantly:

"Series 9,499, number 46! Not 26!"

Hatred and hope both disappeared at once, and it began immediately to seem to Ivan Dmitritch and his wife that their rooms were dark and small and low-pitched, that the supper they had been eating was not doing them good, but lying heavy on their stomachs, that the evenings were long and wearisome. . . .

"What the devil's the meaning of it?" said Ivan Dmitritch, beginning to be ill-humored. "Wherever one steps there are bits of paper under one's feet, crumbs, husks. The rooms are never swept! One is simply forced to go out. Damnation take my soul entirely! I shall go and hang myself on the first aspen-tree!"

QUESTIONS ON CONTENT

1. Piece together from the facts given in the story a picture of Ivan Dmitritch's household as the story opens. On the basis of this picture, do you consider believable the change which occurred? Explain.

2. Why doesn't Chekhov describe the inner workings of Masha's mind? Is she innocent?

3. What do you think would have happened if Masha had won the lottery? Since she did not win, will Ivan really hang himself? Discuss.

✎ *The Lottery*

SHIRLEY JACKSON

The morning of June 27th was clear and sunny, with the fresh warmth of a full-summer day; the flowers were blossoming profusely and the grass was richly green. The people of the village began to gather in the square, between the post office and the bank, around ten o'clock; in some towns there were so many people that the lottery took two days and had to be started on June 26th, but in this village, where there were only about three hundred people, the whole lottery took only about two hours, so it could begin at ten o'clock in the morning and still be through in time to allow the villagers to get home for noon dinner.

The children assembled first, of course. School was recently over for the summer, and the feeling of liberty sat uneasily on most of them; they tended to gather together quietly for a while before they broke into boisterous play, and their talk was still of the classroom and the teacher, of books and reprimands. Bobby Martin had already stuffed his pockets full of stones, and the other boys soon followed his example, selecting the smoothest and roundest stones; Bobby and Harry Jones and Dickie Delacroix—the villagers pronounced this name "Dellacroy"—eventually made a great pile of stones in one corner of the square and guarded it against the raids of the other boys. The girls stood aside, talking among themselves, looking over their shoulders at the boys, and the very small children rolled in the dust or clung to the hands of their older brothers or sisters.

Soon the men began to gather, surveying their own children, speaking of planting and rain, tractors and taxes. They stood together, away from the pile of stones in the corner, and their jokes were quiet and they smiled rather than laughed. The women, wearing faded house dresses and sweaters, came shortly after their menfolk. They greeted one another and exchanged bits of gossip as they went to join their husbands. Soon the women, standing by their

Reprinted by permission of the author. Copyright 1948 The New Yorker Magazine, Inc.

husbands, began to call to their children, and the children came reluctantly, having to be called four or five times. Bobby Martin ducked under his mother's grasping hand and ran, laughing, back to the pile of stones. His father spoke up sharply, and Bobby came quickly and took his place between his father and his oldest brother.

The lottery was conducted—as were the square dances, the teenage club, the Halloween program—by Mr. Summers, who had time and energy to devote to civic activities. He was a round-faced, jovial man and he ran the coal business, and people were sorry for him, because he had no children and his wife was a scold. When he arrived in the square, carrying the black wooden box, there was a murmur of conversation among the villagers, and he waved and called, "Little late today, folks." The postmaster, Mr. Graves, followed him, carrying a three-legged stool, and the stool was put in the center of the square and Mr. Summers set the black box down on it. The villagers kept their distance, leaving a space between themselves and the stool, and when Mr. Summers said, "Some of you fellows want to give me a hand?," there was a hesitation before two men, Mr. Martin and his oldest son, Baxter, came forward to hold the box steady on the stool while Mr. Summers stirred up the papers inside it.

The original paraphernalia for the lottery had been lost long ago, and the black box now resting on the stool had been put into use even before Old Man Warner, the oldest man in town, was born. Mr. Summers spoke frequently to the villagers about making a new box, but no one liked to upset even as much tradition as was represented by the black box. There was a story that the present box had been made with some pieces of the box that had preceded it, the one that had been constructed when the first people settled down to make a village here. Every year, after the lottery, Mr. Summers began talking again about a new box, but every year the subject was allowed to fade off without anything's being done. The black box grew shabbier each year; by now it was no longer completely black but splintered badly along one side to show the original wood color, and in some places faded or stained.

Mr. Martin and his oldest son, Baxter, held the black box securely on the stool until Mr. Summers had stirred the papers thoroughly with his hand. Because so much of the ritual had been forgotten or discarded, Mr. Summers had been successful in having slips of paper substituted for the chips of wood that had been used for generations. Chips of wood, Mr. Summers had argued, had been all very well when the village was tiny, but now that the population was more than three hundred and likely to keep growing, it was necessary to use something that would fit more easily into the black box. The night before the lottery, Mr. Summers and Mr. Graves made up the slips of paper and put them into the box, and it was then taken to the safe of Mr. Summers' coal company and locked up until Mr. Summers was ready to take it to the square next morning. The rest of the year, the box was put away, sometimes one place, sometimes another; it had spent one year in Mr. Graves' barn and another year underfoot in the post office, and sometimes it was set on a shelf in the Martin grocery and left there.

There was a great deal of fussing to be done before Mr. Summers declared the lottery open. There were the lists to make up—of heads of families, heads of households in each family, members of each household in each family. There was the proper swearing-in of Mr. Summers by the postmaster, as the official of the lottery; at one time, some people remembered, there had been a recital of some sort, performed by the official of the lottery, a perfunctory, tuneless chant that had been rattled off duly each year; some people believed that the official of the lottery used to stand just so when he said or sang it, others believed that he was supposed to walk among the people, but years and years ago this part of the ritual had been allowed to lapse. There had been, also, a ritual salute, which the official of the lottery had had to use in addressing each person who came up to draw from the box, but this also had changed with time, until now it was felt necessary only for the official to speak to each person approaching. Mr. Summers was very good at all this; in his clean white shirt and blue jeans, with one hand resting carelessly on the black box, he seemed very proper and important as he talked interminably to Mr. Graves and the Martins.

Just as Mr. Summers finally left off talking and turned to the assembled villagers, Mrs. Hutchinson came hurriedly along the path to the square, her sweater thrown over her shoulders, and slid into place in the back of the crowd. "Clean forgot what day it was," she said to Mrs. Delacroix, who stood next to her, and they both laughed softly. "Thought my old man was out back stacking wood," Mrs. Hutchinson went on, "and then I looked out the window and the kids was gone, and then I remembered it was the twenty-seventh and came a-running." She dried her hands on her apron, and Mrs. Delacroix said, "You're in time, though. They're still talking away up there."

Mrs. Hutchinson craned her neck to see through the crowd and found her husband and children standing near the front. She tapped Mrs. Delacroix on the arm as a farewell and began to make her way through the crowd. The people separated good-humoredly to let her through; two or three people said, in voices just loud enough to be heard across the crowd, "Here comes your Mrs., Hutchinson," and "Bill, she made it after all." Mrs. Hutchinson reached her husband, and Mr. Summers, who had been waiting, said cheerfully, "Thought we were going to have to get on without you, Tessie." Mrs. Hutchinson said, grinning, "Wouldn't have me leave m'dishes in the sink, now, would you, Joe?," and soft laughter ran through the crowd as the people stirred back into position after Mrs. Hutchinson's arrival.

"Well, now," Mr. Summers said soberly, "guess we better get started, get this over with, so's we can go back to work. Anybody ain' here?"

"Dunbar," several people said. "Dunbar, Dunbar."

Mr. Summers consulted his list. "Clyde Dunbar," he said. "That's right. He's broke his leg, hasn't he? Who's drawing for him?"

"Me, I guess," a woman said, and Mr. Summers turned to look at her. "Wife draws for her husband," Mr. Summers said. "Don't you have a grown boy to do it for you, Janey?" Although Mr. Summers and everyone else in the village knew the answer perfectly well, it was the business of the official of the lottery to ask such questions formally. Mr. Summers waited with an expression of polite interest while Mrs. Dunbar answered.

"Horace's not but sixteen yet," Mrs. Dunbar said regretfully. "Guess I gotta fill in for the old man this year."

"Right," Mr. Summers said. He made a note on the list he was holding. Then he asked, "Watson boy drawing this year?"

A tall boy in the crowd raised his hand. "Here," he said. "I'm drawing for m'mother and me." He blinked his eyes nervously and ducked his head as several voices in the crowd said things like "Good fellow, Jack," and "Glad to see your mother's got a man to do it."

"Well," Mr. Summers said, "guess that's everyone. Old Man Warner make it?"

"Here," a voice said, and Mr. Summers nodded.

A sudden hush fell on the crowd as Mr. Summers cleared his throat and looked at the list. "All ready?" he called. "Now, I'll read the names—heads of families first—and the men come up and take a paper out of the box. Keep the paper folded in your hand without looking at it until everyone has had a turn. Everything clear?"

The people had done it so many times that they only half listened to the directions; most of them were quiet, wetting their lips, not looking around. Then Mr. Summers raised one hand high and said, "Adams." A man disengaged himself from the crowd and came forward. "Hi, Steve," Mr. Summers said, and Mr. Adams said, "Hi, Joe." They grinned at one another humorlessly and nervously. Then Mr. Adams reached into the black box and took out a folded paper. He held it firmly by one corner as he turned and went hastily back to his place in the crowd, where he stood a little apart from his family, not looking down at his hand.

"Allen," Mr. Summers said. "Anderson. . . . Bentham."

"Seems like there's no time at all between lotteries any more," Mrs. Delacroix said to Mrs. Graves in the back row. "Seems like we got through with the last one only last week."

"Time sure goes fast," Mrs. Graves said.

"Clark. . . . Delacroix."

"There goes my old man," Mrs. Delacroix said. She held her breath while her husband went forward.

"Dunbar," Mr. Summers said, and Mrs. Dunbar went steadily to the box while one of the women said, "Go on, Janey," and another said, "There she goes."

"We're next," Mrs. Graves said. She watched while Mr. Graves came around from the side of the box, greeted Mr. Summers gravely, and selected a slip of paper from the box. By now, all through the crowd there were men holding the small folded papers in their large hands, turning them over and over nervously. Mrs. Dunbar and her two sons stood together, Mrs. Dunbar holding the slip of paper.

"Harburt. . . . Hutchinson."

"Get up there, Bill," Mrs. Hutchinson said, and the people near her laughed.

"Jones."

"They do say," Mr. Adams said to Old Man Warner, who stood next to him, "that over in the north village they're talking of giving up the lottery."

Old Man Warner snorted. "Pack of crazy fools," he said. "Listening to the young folks, nothin's good enough for *them*. Next thing you know, they'll be wanting to go back to living in caves, nobody work any more, live *that* way for a while. Used to be a saying about

'Lottery in June, corn be heavy soon.' First thing you know, we'd all be eating stewed chickweed and acorns. There's *always* been a lottery," he added petulantly. "Bad enough to see young Joe Summers up there joking with everybody."

"Some places have already quit lotteries," Mrs. Adams said.

"Nothing but trouble in *that*," Old Man Warner said stoutly. "Pack of young fools."

"Martin." And Bobby Martin watched his father go forward. "Overdyke. . . . Percy."

"I wish they'd hurry," Mrs. Dunbar said to her older son. "I wish they'd hurry."

"They're almost through," her son said.

"You get ready to run tell Dad," Mrs. Dunbar said.

Mr. Summers called his own name and then stepped forward precisely and selected a slip from the box. Then he called, "Warner."

"Seventy-seventh year I been in the lottery," Old Man Warner said as he went through the crowd. "Seventy-seventh time."

"Watson," The tall boy came awkwardly through the crowd. Someone said, "Don't be nervous, Jack," and Mr. Summers said, "Take your time, son."

"Zanini."

After that, there was a long pause, a breathless pause, until Mr. Summers, holding his slip of paper in the air, said, "All right, fellows." For a minute no one moved, and then all the slips of paper were opened. Suddenly, all the women began to speak at once, saying, "Who is it?," "Who's got it?," "Is it the Dunbars?," "Is it the Watsons?" Then voices began to say, "It's Hutchinson. It's Bill," "Bill Hutchinson's got it."

"Go tell your father," Mrs. Dunbar said to her older son.

People began to look around to see the Hutchinsons. Bill Hutchinson was standing quiet, staring down at the paper in his hand. Suddenly, Tessie Hutchinson shouted to Mr. Summers, "You didn't give him time enough to take any paper he wanted. I saw you. It wasn't fair!"

"Be a good sport, Tessie," Mrs. Delacroix called, and Mrs. Graves said, "All of us took the same chance."

"Shut up, Tessie," Bill Hutchinson said.

"Well, everyone," Mr. Summers said, "that was done pretty fast, and now we've got to be hurrying a little more to get done in time." He consulted his next list. "Bill," he said, "you draw for the Hutchinson family. You got any other households in the Hutchinsons?"

"There's Don and Eva," Mrs. Hutchinson yelled. "Make *them* take their chance!"

"Daughters draw with their husbands' families, Tessie," Mr. Summers said gently. "You know that as well as anyone else."

"It wasn't *fair*," Tessie said.

"I guess not, Joe," Bill Hutchinson said regretfully. "My daughter draws with her husband's family, that's only fair. And I've got no other family except the kids."

"Then, as far as drawing for families is concerned, it's you," Mr. Summers said in explanation, "and as far as drawing for households is concerned, that's you, too. Right?"

"Right," Bill Hutchinson said.

"How many kids, Bill?" Mr. Summers asked formally.

"Three," Bill Hutchinson said. "There's Bill, Jr., and Nancy, and little Dave. And Tessie and me."

"All right, then," Mr. Summers said. "Harry, you got their tickets back?"

Mr. Graves nodded and held up the slips of paper.

"Put them in the box, then," Mr. Summers directed. "Take Bill's and put it in."

"I think we ought to start over," Mrs. Hutchinson said, as quietly as she could. "I tell you it wasn't *fair*. You didn't give him time enough to choose. *Every*body saw that."

Mr. Graves had selected the five slips and put them in the box, and he dropped all the papers but those onto the ground, where the breeze caught them and lifted them off.

"Listen, everybody," Mrs. Hutchinson was saying to the people around her.

"Ready, Bill?" Mr. Summers asked, and Bill Hutchinson, with one quick glance around at his wife and children, nodded.

"Remember," Mr. Summers said, "take the slips and keep them folded until each person has taken one. Harry, you help little Dave." Mr. Graves took the hand of the little boy, who came willingly with him up to the box. "Take a paper out of the box, Davy," Mr. Summers said. Davy put his hand into the box and laughed. "Take just *one* paper," Mr. Summers said. "Harry, you hold it for him." Mr. Graves took the child's hand and removed the folded paper from the tight fist and held it while little Dave stood next to him and looked up at him wonderingly.

"Nancy next," Mr. Summers said. Nancy was twelve, and her school friends breathed heavily as she went forward, switching her skirt, and took a slip daintily from the box. "Bill, Jr.," Mr. Summers said, and Billy, his face red and his feet overlarge, nearly knocked the box over as he got a paper out. "Tessie," Mr. Summers said. She hesitated for a minute, looking around defiantly, and then set her lips and went up to the box. She snatched a paper out and held it behind her.

"Bill," Mr. Summers said, and Bill Hutchinson reached into the box and felt around, bringing his hand out at last with the slip of paper in it.

The crowd was quiet. A girl whispered, "I hope it's not Nancy," and the sound of the whisper reached the edges of the crowd.

"It's not the way it used to be," Old Man Warner said clearly. "People ain't the way they used to be."

"All right," Mr. Summers said. "Open the papers. Harry, you open little Dave's."

Mr. Graves opened the slip of paper and there was a general sigh through the crowd as he held it up and everyone could see that it was blank. Nancy and Bill, Jr., opened theirs at the same time, and both beamed and laughed, turning around to the crowd and holding their slips of paper above their heads.

"Tessie," Mr. Summers said. There was a pause, and then Mr. Summers looked at Bill Hutchinson, and Bill unfolded his paper and showed it. It was blank.

"It's Tessie," Mr. Summers said, and his voice was hushed. "Show us her paper, Bill."

Bill Hutchinson went over to his wife and forced the slip of paper out of her hand. It had a black spot on it, the black spot Mr. Summers had made the night before with the heavy pencil in the coalcompany office. Bill Hutchinson held it up, and there was a stir in the crowd.

"All right, folks," Mr. Summers said. "Let's finish quickly."

Although the villagers had forgotten the ritual and lost the original black box, they still remembered to use stones. The pile of stones the boys had made earlier was ready; there were stones on the ground with the blowing scraps of paper that had come out of the box. Mrs. Delacroix selected a stone so large she had to pick it up with both hands and turned to Mrs. Dunbar. "Come on," she said, "Hurry up."

Mrs. Dunbar had small stones in both hands, and she said gasping for breath, "I can't run at all. You'll have to go ahead and I'll catch up with you."

The children had stones already, and someone gave little Davy Hutchinson a few pebbles.

Tessie Hutchinson was in the center of a cleared space by now, and she held her hands out desperately as the villagers moved in on her. "It isn't fair," she said. A stone hit her on the side of the head.

Old Man Warner was saying, "Come on, come on, everyone." Steve Adams was in the front of the crowd of villagers, with Mrs. Graves beside him.

"It isn't fair, it isn't right," Mrs. Hutchinson screamed, and then they were upon her.

QUESTIONS ON CONTENT

1. Briefly summarize what happens in the story. When did you suspect that the story must have a meaning beyond the literal one?
2. Why does the story start so quietly? Why does it continue in muted fashion until nearly the end? In other words, does the tone help establish the meaning?
3. Does the author attempt to realize the characters as individuals? Does she tell us where the village of her story is located? Is she dealing with individuals and *a* village?
4. Why is so much attention devoted to the lottery box? And why is the tradition of the box emphasized?
5. What is significant about the fact that other villages are preparing to give up the lottery, if they have not already done so?
6. Does the tradition of the "scape-goat" help explain this story? Discuss.
7. Since Mrs. Delacroix has been so friendly with Tessie, why does she select so large a stone? What do you make of the fact that the villagers have all been in neighborly mood towards Tessie before the drawing and in hostile mood after the drawing?
8. Life as a lottery is a common metaphor. Ivan Dmitritch's wife ("The Lottery Ticket") failed to win, with disastrous results; yet it is implied that winning would have been just as disastrous. Tessie Hutchinson "won." What conclusions may one draw from the combined evidence of these two stories?
9. Define "allegory." Do all the details of this story fit into a consistent allegorical sequence? Try various interpretations. Which interpretation is best supported by the facts of the story?

❧ *Young Goodman Brown*

NATHANIEL HAWTHORNE

Young Goodman Brown came forth at sunset into the street at Salem village; but put his head back, after crossing the threshold, to exchange a parting kiss with his young wife. And Faith, as the wife was aptly named, thrust her own pretty head into the street, letting the wind play with the pink ribbons of her cap while she called to Goodman Brown.

"Dearest heart," whispered she, softly and rather sadly, when her lips were close to his ear, "prithee put off your journey until sunrise and sleep in your own bed to-night. A lone woman is troubled with such dreams and such thoughts that she's afeard of herself sometimes. Pray tarry with me this night, dear husband, of all nights in the year."

"My love and my Faith," replied young Goodman Brown, "of all nights in the year, this one night must I tarry away from thee. My journey, as thou callest it, forth and back again, must needs be done 'twixt now and sunrise. What, my sweet, pretty wife, dost thou doubt me already, and we but three months married?"

"Then God bless you!" said Faith, with the pink ribbons; "and may you find all well when you come back."

"Amen!" cried Goodman Brown. "Say thy prayers, dear Faith, and go to bed at dusk, and no harm will come to thee."

So they parted; and the young man pursued his way until, being about to turn the corner by the meeting-house, he looked back and saw the head of Faith still peeping after him with a melancholy air, in spite of her pink ribbons.

"Poor little Faith!" thought he, for his heart smote him. "What a wretch am I to leave her on such an errand! She talks of dreams, too. Methought as she spoke there was trouble in her face, as if a dream had warned her what work is to be done to-night. But no, no; 't would kill her to think it. Well, she's a blessed angel on earth; and after this one night I'll cling to her skirts and follow her to heaven."

With this excellent resolve for the future, Goodman Brown felt

First published in 1835.

himself justified in making more haste on his present evil purpose. He had taken a dreary road, darkened by all the gloomiest trees of the forest, which barely stood aside to let the narrow path creep through, and closed immediately behind. It was all as lonely as could be; and there is this peculiarity in such a solitude, that the traveller knows not who may be concealed by the innumerable trunks and the thick boughs overhead; so that with lonely footsteps he may yet be passing through an unseen multitude.

"There may be a devilish Indian behind every tree," said Goodman Brown to himself; and he glanced fearfully behind him as he added, "What if the devil himself should be at my very elbow!"

His head being turned back, he passed a crook of the road, and, looking forward again, beheld the figure of a man, in grave and decent attire, seated at the foot of an old tree. He arose at Goodman Brown's approach and walked onward side by side with him.

"You are late, Goodman Brown," said he. "The clock of the Old South was striking as I came through Boston, and that is full fifteen minutes agone."

"Faith kept me back a while," replied the young man, with a tremor in his voice, caused by the sudden appearance of his companion, though not wholly unexpected.

It was now deep dusk in the forest, and deepest in that part of it where these two were journeying. As nearly as could be discerned, the second traveller was about fifty years old, apparently in the same rank of life as Goodman Brown, and bearing a considerable resemblance to him, though perhaps more in expression than features. Still they might have been taken for father and son. And yet, though the elder person was as simply clad as the younger, and as simple in manner too, he had an indescribable air of one who knew the world, and who would not have felt abashed at the governor's dinner table or in King William's court, were it possible that his affairs should call him thither. But the only thing about him that could be fixed upon as remarkable was his staff, which bore the likeness of a great black snake, so curiously wrought that it might almost be seen to twist and wriggle itself like a living serpent. This, of course, must have been an ocular deception, assisted by the uncertain light.

"Come, Goodman Brown," cried his fellow-traveller, "this is a dull pace for the beginning of a journey. Take my staff, if you are so soon weary."

"Friend," said the other, exchanging his slow pace for a full stop, "having kept covenant by meeting thee here, it is my purpose now to return whence I came. I have scruples touching the matter thou wot'st of."

"Sayest thou so?" replied he of the serpent, smiling apart. "Let us walk on, nevertheless, reasoning as we go; and if I convince thee not thou shalt turn back. We are but a little way in the forest yet."

"Too far! too far!" exclaimed the goodman, unconsciously resuming his walk. "My father never went into the woods on such an errand, nor his father before him. We have been a race of honest men and good Christians since the days of the martyrs; and shall I be the first of the name of Brown that ever took this path and kept—"

"Such company, thou wouldst say," observed the elder person, interpreting his pause. "Well said, Goodman Brown! I have been as well acquainted with your family as with ever a one among the Puritans; and that's no trifle to say. I helped your grandfather, the constable, when he lashed the Quaker women so smartly through the streets of Salem; and it was I that brought your father a pitch-pine knot, kindled at my own hearth, to set fire to an Indian village, in King Philip's war. They were my good friends, both; and many a pleasant walk have we had along this path, and returned merrily after midnight. I would fain be friends with you for their sake."

"If it be as thou sayest," replied Goodman Brown, "I marvel they never spoke of these matters; or, verily, I marvel not, seeing that the least rumor of the sort would have driven them from New England. We are a people of prayer, and good works to boot, and abide no such wickedness."

"Wickedness or not," said the traveller with the twisted staff, "I have a very general acquaintance here in New England. The deacons of many a church have drunk the communion wine with me; the selectmen of divers towns make me their chairman; and a majority of the Great and General Court are firm supporters of my interest. The governor and I, too—But these are state secrets."

"Can this be so?" cried Goodman Brown, with a stare of amazement at his undisturbed companion. "Howbeit, I have nothing to do with the governor and council; they have their own ways, and are no rule for a simple husbandman like me. But, were I to go on with thee, how should I meet the eye of that good old man, our minister, at Salem village? Oh, his voice would make me tremble both Sabbath day and lecture day."

Thus far the elder traveller had listened with due gravity; but now burst into a fit of irrepressible mirth, shaking himself so violently that his snake-like staff actually seemed to wriggle in sympathy.

"Ha! ha! ha!" shouted he again and again; then composing himself, "Well, go on, Goodman Brown, go on; but, prithee, don't kill me with laughing."

"Well, then, to end the matter at once," said Goodman Brown, considerably nettled, "there is my wife, Faith. It would break her dear little heart; and I'd rather break my own."

"Nay, if that be the case," answered the other, "e'en go thy ways, Goodman Brown. I would not for twenty old women like to one hobbling before us that Faith should come to any harm."

As he spoke he pointed his staff at a female figure on the path, in whom Goodman Brown recognized a very pious and exemplary dame, who had taught him his catechism in youth, and was still his moral and spiritual adviser, jointly with the minister and Deacon Gookin.

"A marvel, truly, that Goody Cloyse should be so far in the wilderness at nightfall," said he. "But with your leave, friend, I shall take a cut through the woods until we have left this Christian woman behind. Being a stranger to you, she might ask whom I was consorting with and whither I was going."

"Be it so," said his fellow-traveller. "Betake you the woods, and let me keep the path."

Accordingly the young man turned aside, but took care to watch his companion, who advanced softly along the road until he had come within a staff's length of the old dame. She, meanwhile, was making the best of her way, with singular speed for so aged a woman, and mumbling some indistinct words—a prayer, doubtless—as she went. The traveller put forth his staff and touched her withered neck with what seemed the serpent's tail.

"The devil!" screamed the pious old lady.

"Then Goody Cloyse knows her old friend?" observed the traveller, confronting her and leaning on his writhing stick.

"Ah, forsooth, and it is your worship indeed?" cried the good dame. "Yea, truly, is it, and in the very image of my old gossip, Goodman Brown, the grandfather of the silly fellow that now is. But—would your worship believe it?—my broomstick hath strangely disappeared, stolen, as I suspect, by that unhanged witch, Goody Corey, and that, too, when I was all anointed with the juice of smallage, and cinquefoil, and wolf's bane—"

"Mingled with fine wheat and the fat of a new-born babe," said the shape of old Goodman Brown.

"Ah, your worship knows the recipe," cried the old lady, cackling aloud. "So, as I was saying, being all ready for the meeting, and no horse to ride on, I made up my mind to foot it; for they tell me there is a nice young man to be taken into communion to-night. But now your good worship will lend me your arm, and we shall be there in a twinkling."

"That can hardly be," answered her friend. "I may not spare you my arm, Goody Cloyse; but here is my staff, if you will."

So saying, he threw it down at her feet, where, perhaps, it assumed life, being one of the rods which its owner had formerly lent to the Egyptian magi. Of this fact, however, Goodman Brown could not take cognizance. He had cast up his eyes in astonishment, and, looking down again, beheld neither Goody Cloyse nor the serpentine staff, but this fellow-traveller alone, who waited for him as calmly as if nothing had happened.

"That old woman taught me my catechism," said the young man; and there was a world of meaning in this simple comment.

They continued to walk onward, while the elder traveller exhorted his companion to make good speed and persevere in the path, discoursing so aptly that his arguments seemed rather to spring up in the bosom of his auditor than to be suggested by himself. As they went, he plucked a branch of maple to serve for a walking stick, and began to strip it of the twigs and little boughs, which were wet with evening dew. The moment his fingers touched them they became strangely withered and dried up as with a week's sunshine. Thus the pair proceeded, at a good free pace, until suddenly, in a gloomy hollow of the road, Goodman Brown sat himself down on the stump of a tree and refused to go any farther.

"Friend," said he, stubbornly, "my mind is made up. Not another step will I budge on this errand. What if a wretched old woman do choose to go to the devil when I thought she was going to heaven: is that any reason why I should quit my dear Faith and go after her?"

"You will think better of this by and by," said his acquaintance, composedly. "Sit here and rest yourself a while; and when you feel like moving again, there is my staff to help you along."

Without more words, he threw his companion the maple stick, and was as speedily out of sight as if he had vanished into the deepening gloom. The young man sat a few moments by the roadside, applauding himself greatly, and thinking with how clear a con-science he should meet the minister in his morning walk, nor shrink from the eye of good old Deacon Gookin. And what calm sleep would be his that very night, which was to have been spent so wickedly, but so purely and sweetly now, in the arms of Faith! Amidst these pleasant and praiseworthy meditations, Goodman Brown heard the tramp of horses along the road, and deemed it advisable to conceal himself within the verge of the forest, con-scious of the guilty purpose that had brought him thither, though now so happily turned from it.

On came the hoof tramps and the voices of the riders, two grave old voices, conversing soberly as they drew near. These mingled sounds appeared to pass along the road, within a few yards of the young man's hiding-place; but, owing doubtless to the depth of the gloom at that particular spot, neither the travellers not their steeds were visible. Though their figures brushed the small boughs by the wayside, it could not be seen that they intercepted, even for a moment, the faint gleam from the strip of bright sky athwart which they must have passed. Goodman Brown alternately crouched and stood on tiptoe, pulling aside the branches and thrusting forth his head as far as he durst without discerning so much as a shadow. It vexed him the more, because he could have sworn, were such a thing possible, that he recognized the voices of the minister and Deacon Gookin, jogging along quietly, as they were wont to do, when bound to some ordination or ecclesiastical council. While yet within hearing, one of the riders stopped to pluck a switch.

"Of the two, reverend sir," said the voice like the deacon's, "I had rather miss an ordination dinner than to-night's meeting. They tell me that some of our community are to be here from Falmouth and beyond, and others from Connecticut and Rhode Island, besides several of the Indian powwows, who, after their fashion, know al-most as much deviltry as the best of us. Moreover, there is a goodly young woman to be taken into the communion."

"Mighty well, Deacon Gookin!" replied the solemn old tones of the minister. "Spur up, or we shall be late. Nothing can be done, you know, until I get on the ground."

The hoofs clattered again; and the voices, talking so strangely in the empty air, passed on through the forest, where no church had ever been gathered or solitary Christian prayed. Whither, then, could these holy men be journeying so deep into the heathen wilder-ness? Young Goodman Brown caught hold of a tree for support, being ready to sink down on the ground, faint and overburdened with the heavy sickness of his heart. He looked up to the sky, doubting whether there really was a heaven above him. Yet there was the blue arch, and the stars brightening in it.

"With heaven above and Faith below, I will yet stand firm against the devil!" cried Goodman Brown.

While he still gazed upward into the deep arch of the firmament and had lifted his hands to pray, a cloud, though no wind was stirring, hurried across the zenith and hid the brightening stars. The blue sky was still visible, except directly overhead, where this black mass of cloud was sweeping swiftly northward. Aloft in the air, as if from the depths of the cloud, came a confused and doubtful sound of voices. Once the listener fancied that he could distinguish the accents of towns-people of his own, men and women, both pious and ungodly, many of whom he had met at the communion table, and had seen others rioting at the tavern. The next moment, so indistinct were the sounds, he doubted whether he had heard aught but the murmur of the old forest, whispering without a wind. Then came a stronger swell of those familiar tones, heard daily in the sunshine at Salem village, but never until now from a cloud of night. There was one voice, of a young woman, uttering lamentations, yet with an uncertain sorrow, and entreating for some favor, which, perhaps, it would grieve her to obtain; and all the unseen multitude, both saints and sinners, seemed to encourage her onward.

"Faith!" shouted Goodman Brown, in a voice of agony and desperation; and the echoes of the forest mocked him, crying, "Faith! Faith!" as if bewildered wretches were seeking her all through the wilderness.

The cry of grief, rage, and terror was yet piercing the night, when the unhappy husband held his breath for a response. There was a scream, drowned immediately in a louder murmur of voices, fading into far-off laughter, as the dark cloud swept away, leaving the clear and silent sky above Goodman Brown. But something fluttered lightly down through the air and caught on the branch of a tree. The young man seized it, and beheld a pink ribbon.

"My Faith is gone!" cried he, after one stupefied moment. "There is no good on earth; and sin is but a name. Come, devil; for to thee is this world given."

And, maddened with despair, so that he laughed loud and long, did Goodman Brown grasp his staff and set forth again, at such a rate that he seemed to fly along the forest path rather than to walk or run. The road grew wilder and drearier and more faintly traced, and vanished at length, leaving him in the heart of the dark wilderness, still rushing onward with the instinct that guides mortal man to evil. The whole forest was peopled with frightened sounds—the creaking of the trees, the howling of wild beasts, and the yell of Indians; while sometimes the wind tolled like a distant church bell, and sometimes gave a broad roar around the traveller, as if all Nature were laughing him to scorn. But he was himself the chief horror of the scene, and shrank not from its other horrors.

"Ha! ha! ha!" roared Goodman Brown when the wind laughed at him. "Let us hear which will laugh loudest. Think not to frighten me with your deviltry. Come witch, come wizard, come Indian powwow, come devil himself, and here comes Goodman Brown. You may as well fear him as he fear you."

In truth, all through the haunted forest there could be nothing more frightful than the figure of Goodman Brown. On he flew among the black pines, brandishing his staff with frenzied gestures, now giving vent to an inspiration of horrid blasphemy, and now shouting forth such laughter as set all the echoes of the forest laughing like demons around him. The fiend in his own shape is less hideous than when he rages in the breast of man. Thus sped the demoniac on his course, until, quivering among the trees, he saw a red light before him, as when the felled trunks and branches of a clearing have been set on fire, and throw up their lurid blaze against the sky, at the hour of midnight. He paused, in a lull of the tempest that had driven him onward, and heard the swell of what seemed a hymn, rolling solemnly from a distance with the weight of many voices. He knew the tune; it was a familiar one in the choir of the village meeting-house. The verse died heavily away, and was lengthened by a chorus, not of human voices, but of all the sounds of the benighted wilderness pealing in awful harmony together. Goodman Brown cried out, and his cry was lost to his own ear by its unison with the cry of the desert.

In the interval of silence he stole forward until the light glared full upon his eyes. At one extremity of an open space, hemmed in by the dark wall of the forest, arose a rock, bearing some rude, natural resemblance either to an altar or a pulpit, and surrounded by four blazing pines, their tops aflame, their stems untouched, like candles at an evening meeting. The mass of foliage that had over-grown the summit of the rock was all on fire, blazing high into the night and fitfully illuminating the whole field. Each pendant twig and leafy festoon was in a blaze. As the red light arose and fell, a numerous congregation alternately shone forth, then disappeared in shadow, and again grew, as it were, out of the darkness, peopling the heart of the solitary woods at once.

"A grave and dark-clad company," quoth Goodman Brown.

In truth they were such. Among them, quivering to and fro between gloom and splendor, appeared faces that would be seen next day at the council board of the province, and others which, Sabbath after Sabbath, looked devoutly heavenward, and benignantly over the crowded pews, from the holiest pulpits in the land. Some affirm that the lady of the governor was there. At least there were high dames well known to her, and wives of honored husbands, and widows, a great multitude, and ancient maidens, all of excellent repute, and fair young girls, who trembled lest their mothers should espy them. Either the sudden gleams of light flashing over the obscure field bedazzled Goodman Brown, or he recognized a score of the church members of Salem village famous for their especial sanctity. Good old Deacon Gookin had arrived, and waited at the skirts of that venerable saint, his revered pastor. But, irreverently consorting with these grave, reputable, and pious people, these elders of the church, these chaste dames and dewy virgins, there were men of dissolute lives and women of spotted fame, wretches given over to all mean and filthy vice, and suspected even of horrid crimes. It was strange to see that the good shrank not from the wicked, nor were the sinners abashed by the saints. Scattered also among their pale-faced enemies were the Indian priests, or pow-wows, who had often scared their native forest with more hideous incantations than any known to English witchcraft.

"But where is Faith?" thought Goodman Brown; and, as hope came into his heart, he trembled.

Another verse of the hymn arose, a slow and mournful strain, such as the pious love, but joined to words which expressed all that our nature can conceive of sin, and darkly hinted at far more. Unfathomable to mere mortals is the lore of fiends. Verse after verse was sung; and still the chorus of the desert swelled between like the deepest tone of a mighty organ; and with the final peal of that dreadful anthem there came a sound, as if the roaring wind, the rushing streams, the howling beasts, and every other voice of the unconcerted wilderness were mingling and according with the voice of guilty man in homage to the prince of all. The four blazing pines threw up a loftier flame, and obscurely discovered shapes and visages of horror on the smoke wreaths above the impious assembly. At the same moment the fire on the rock shot redly forth and formed a glowing arch above its base, where now appeared a figure. With reverence be it spoken, the figure bore no slight similitude, both in garb and manner, to some grave divine of the New England churches.

"Bring forth the converts!" cried a voice that echoed through the field and rolled into the forest.

At the word, Goodman Brown stepped forth from the shadow of the trees and approached the congregation, with whom he felt a loathful brotherhood by the sympathy of all that was wicked in his heart. He could have well-nigh sworn that the shape of his own dead father beckoned him to advance, looking downward from a smoke wreath, while a woman, with dim features of despair, threw out her hand to warn him back. Was it his mother? But he had no power to retreat one step, nor to resist, even in thought, when the minister and good old Deacon Gookin seized his arms and led him to the blazing rock. Thither came also the slender form of a veiled female, led between Goody Cloyse, that pious teacher of the catechism, and Martha Carrier, who had received the devil's promise to be queen of hell. A rampant hag was she. And there stood the proselytes beneath the canopy of fire.

"Welcome, my children," said the dark figure, "to the communion of your race. Ye have found thus young your nature and your destiny. My children, look behind you!"

They turned; and flashing forth, as it were, in a sheet of flame, the fiend worshippers were seen; the smile of welcome gleamed darkly on every visage.

"There," resumed the sable form, "are all whom ye have reverenced from youth. Ye deemed them holier than yourselves, and shrank from your own sin, contrasting it with their lives of righteousness and prayerful aspirations heavenward. Yet here are they all in my worshipping assembly. This night it shall be granted you to know their secret deeds; how hoary-bearded elders of the church have whispered wanton words to the young maids of their households; how many a woman, eager for widow's weeds, had given her husband a drink at bedtime and let him sleep his last sleep in her bosom; how beardless youths have made haste to inherit their fathers' wealth; and how fair damsels—blush not, sweet ones—have dug little graves in the garden, and bidden me, the sole guest, to an infant's funeral. By the sympathy of your human hearts for sin ye shall scent out all the places—whether in church, bed-chamber, street, field, or forest—where crime has been committed, and shall exult to behold the whole earth one stain of guilt, one mighty blood spot. Far more than this. It shall be yours to penetrate, in every bosom, the deep mystery of sin, the fountain of all wicked arts, and which inexhaustibly supplies more evil impulses than human power —than my power at its utmost—can make manifest in deeds. And now, my children, look upon each other."

They did so; and, by the blaze of the hell-kindled torches, the wretched man beheld his Faith, and the wife her husband, trembling before that unhallowed altar.

"Lo, there ye stand, my children," said the figure, in a deep and solemn tone, almost sad with its despairing awfulness, as if his once angelic nature could yet mourn for our miserable race. "Depending upon one another's hearts, ye had still hoped that virtue were not all a dream. Now are ye undeceived. Evil is the nature of mankind. Evil must be your only happiness. Welcome again, my children, to the communion of your race."

"Welcome," repeated the fiend worshippers, in one cry of despair and triumph.

And there they stood, the only pair, as it seemed, who were yet hesitating on the verge of wickedness in this dark world. A basin was hollowed, naturally, in the rock. Did it contain water, reddened by the lurid light? or was it blood? or, perchance, a liquid flame? Herein did the shape of evil dip his hand and prepare to lay the mark of baptism upon their foreheads, that they might be partakers of the mystery of sin, more conscious of the secret guilt of others, both in deed and thought, than they could now be of their own. The husband cast one look at his pale wife, and Faith at him. What polluted wretches would the next glance show them to each other, shuddering alike at what they disclosed and what they saw!

"Faith! Faith!" cried the husband, "look up to heaven, and resist the wicked one."

Whether Faith obeyed he knew not. Hardly had he spoken when he found himself amid calm night and solitude, listening to a roar of the wind which died heavily away through the forest. He staggered against the rock, and left it chill and damp; while a hanging twig, that had been all on fire, besprinkled his cheek with the coldest dew.

The next morning young Goodman Brown came slowly into the

street of Salem village, staring around him like a bewildered man. The good old minister was taking a walk along the graveyard to get an appetite for breakfast and meditate his sermon, and bestowed a blessing, as he passed, on Goodman Brown. He shrank from the venerable saint as if to avoid an anathema. Old Deacon Gookin was at domestic worship, and the holy words of his prayer were heard through the open window. "What God doth the wizard pray to?" quoth Goodman Brown. Goody Cloyse, that excellent old Christian, stood in the early sunshine at her own lattice, catechizing a little girl who had brought her a pint of morning's milk. Goodman Brown snatched away the child as from the grasp of the fiend himself. Turning the corner by the meeting-house, he spied the head of Faith, with the pink ribbons, gazing anxiously forth, and bursting into such joy at sight of him that she skipped along the street and almost kissed her husband before the whole village. But Goodman Brown looked sternly and sadly into her face, and passed on without a greeting.

Had Goodman Brown fallen asleep in the forest and only dreamed a wild dream of a witch-meeting?

Be it so if you will; but, alas! it was a dream of evil omen for young Goodman Brown. A stern, a sad, a darkly meditative, a distrustful, if not a desperate man did he become from the night of that fearful dream. On the Sabbath day, when the congregation were singing a holy psalm, he could not listen because an anthem of sin rushed loudly upon his ear and drowned all the blessed strain. When the minister spoke from the pulpit with power and fervid eloquence, and, with his hand on the Bible, of the sacred truths of our religion, and of saint-like lives and triumphant deaths, and of future bliss or misery unutterable, then did Goodman Brown turn pale, dreading lest the roof should thunder down upon the gray blasphemer and his hearers. Often, awaking suddenly at midnight, he shrank from the bosom of Faith; and at morning or eventide, when the family knelt down at prayer, he scowled and muttered to himself, and gazed sternly at his wife, and turned away. And when he had lived long, and was borne to his grave a hoary corpse, followed by Faith, an aged woman, the children and grandchildren, a goodly procession, besides neighbors not a few, they carved no hopeful verse upon his tombstone, for his dying hour was gloom.

QUESTIONS ON CONTENT

1. Explain Goodman Brown's statement: "after this one night, I'll cling to her [Faith's] skirts and follow her to heaven."
2. Why did the staff of Brown's companion bear "the likeness of a great black snake"? And why was such a staff offered to Brown?
3. What sins of his forebears are revealed to Brown? Why?
4. Comment on the names given to the various persons who appear in the story.
5. What was the occasion for the conclave in the forest?
6. Explain each element in this story as part of an allegory. Does the allegory break down at the end? Explain.
7. Does Hawthorne ever in his own person as storyteller name the Devil as one of the characters? Does he say that the staff was a snake or even that it actually resembled a snake? Does he insist on a dream-solution for Young Goodman Brown's experience? Examine the text carefully for your answers, and then draw a conclusion from what you find.

SUGGESTIONS FOR PAPERS

All the stories in this section almost surely were invented as means of illustrating an idea or a theme. Your paper may be written about the way in which the narratives illuminate an idea. Since theme is dominant, you will have to look closely at the details used to make each theme clear.

1. Analyze any one of the stories by answering the following questions: (1) What is the theme (the controlling idea) of the story? (2) How does each detail help to develop the theme? (3) If there are any extraneous (non-contributing) details, can you justify their inclusion? (4) How effective, in your opinion, has the author been in presenting his thesis?

2. Examine the titles of the five stories. Open your paper with remarks on the significance of titles. Devote one paragraph to each title, discussing its appropriateness or lack of appropriateness.

3. Define irony and then discuss the element of irony as it appears in any three of the stories.

4. Define coincidence and then show what part it plays in the five stories.

5. Write your paper on one of the following characters; cite passages which will support your characterization. (1) H.T. in "The Apostate"; (2) Maître Hauchecorne in "A Piece of String"; (3) Ivan Dmitritch in "The Lottery Ticket"; (4) Tessie Hutchinson in "The Lottery"; (5) Young Goodman Brown in the story of that name.

6. Consider the function of some of the minor characters. For example, what kind of person was Hubie in "The Apostate"? Maître Malandain in "A Piece of String"? Masha in "The Lottery Ticket"? Mrs. Delacroix, or one of the other minor characters, in "The Lottery"? Is Faith in "Young Goodman Brown" a minor character? How does each contribute to the action of the story or to the development of the theme?

7. Compare "A Piece of String" and "The Lottery." The stories are unlike in many ways, but it will be a good test of close reading and careful thinking to search out at least one important respect in which the stories are alike.

8. Defend or attack the credibility of the transformations which take place in "The Lottery Ticket." Here you will have to examine every detail of the story and call on these details to support your judgment.

9. Set down the literal facts of "The Lottery." Have you ever heard of such lotteries? If not, what do you make of the story? Is it an allegory? Try out an allegorical interpretation to see whether the facts will justify this approach.

10. Consider "Young Goodman Brown" as an allegory. If the allegory is consistent, all elements in the story may be accounted for. For examples, what does Brown represent? His wife, Faith? Brown's fellow-traveller through the forest? Goody Cloyse? The old minister? Deacon Gookin? The forest? The walking staff? The dark cloud? Goodman Brown's journey? The singing? Cite other elements in the story which may be interpreted allegorically. Now, consider all the speeches of "the sable form." Does he tell the truth about the universal wickedness of mankind? What, finally, do you consider to be Hawthorne's real attitude towards evil?

SOME TITLES FOR PAPERS

1. Irony Defined and Illustrated

2. Coincidence Defined, with Examples

3. A Characterization of . . .
4. The Function of Minor Characters
5. An Analysis of Five Titles
6. Point of View
7. Is Ritual Ridiculous?
8. The Guilt of Maître Hauchecorne
9. The Problem of Sudden Wealth
10. Ivan Dmitritch, Before and After
11. Two Lotteries
12. Life Is a Lottery
13. The Meaning of "The Lottery"
14. "A Piece of String" and "The Lottery," a Comparison
15. The Allegory in "Young Goodman Brown"
16. Are All Men Secretly Wicked?
17. The Best of Five: An Opinion
18. The Worst of Five: An Opinion
19. Sin in These Five Stories: An Inductive Study

CHAPTER 21

∾ WRITING ABOUT BOOKS

As ONE READS, the experience of a book speeds through one's mind and, unless detained, vanishes with disconcerting promptness. To detain the experience, to give it a closer examination, to organize impressions, and then to state them are part of the discipline which leads to expert, pleasurable reading. Most courses in English offer students the opportunity to write about books, particularly—in the freshman year—about biographies and novels. Until you feel your delight in a book measurably intensified through closely examining it, you will continue to feel that assignments of papers about books are simply high hurdles to bark your shins on. Honestly take these hurdles and no one will have to insist on the exhilaration you have experienced.

The selections in this chapter demonstrate various accepted ways of writing about books. Crane Brinton in reviewing Carl Van Doren's prize-winning biography, *Benjamin Franklin,* avoids the well-known facts of Franklin's life and concentrates on describing the biographer's method of handling the facts. He calls his review, "A Dozen Men in One."

Novels present a different problem. Louis Kronenberger's "Hungry Caravan," a review of John Steinbeck's *The Grapes of Wrath,* follows the normal pattern of professional reviews. "With Grace under Pressure," Mark Schorer's review of Ernest Hemingway's *The Old Man and the Sea,* describes the special merits of the book and exhibits some of these merits through expertly chosen quotations. The techniques of these two reviews will give you some guidance in how to write about novels.

An editorial from *Life*, "Wanted: An American Novel," possibly heralds a shift in public taste, a shift from a liking for strong, raw drink to relieved acceptance of milder potions. The editorial may have been partly inspired by the appearance of a milder potion in the form of Herman Wouk's novel, *Marjorie Morningstar*. *Time* reviews this novel as part of an article on Wouk's spectacular career.

These last two selections suggest additional approaches to books. The editorial from *Life* seeks to summarize the chief characteristics of an era in novel-writing. The article in *Time* reviews a novel as part of an examination of the novelist's whole career.

∾ *A Dozen Men in One*

CRANE BRINTON

(A Review of *Benjamin Franklin* by Carl Van Doren. New York: The Viking Press. 1938.)

In these days of Freudians, Marxists, debunkers, Stracheyites, Guedallans, and other practitioners of the unsettled and unsettling art of the "new" biography, one does not often come across a book as clearly in the tradition of biography in the English language as Mr. Van Doren's *Franklin*. Or perhaps, since Mr. Granville Hicks has appropriated the phrase "the great tradition" for the Marxists, we had better say that Mr. Van Doren's book is near the central core of biography in English, that it is mined from the same vein that Boswell, Lockhart, Froude, and Morley worked.

This is not to say that Mr. Van Doren has unmistakably written an enduring book, a "classic" that will be enshrined in the textbooks a hundred years hence. He may well have done so. But the reviewer who ventures confidently on such long-range predictions is trespassing on ground properly left to posterity and to the blurb-writers. He had better not even attempt to guess at the possible sale of the book, for those more close to the trade are usually far better guessers than he. All the reviewer can safely do is describe the kind

The Saturday Review of Literature, October 8, 1938. Reprinted by permission of the *The Saturday Review*.

of book he is dealing with, its scope, its methods, its general flavor. Mr. Van Doren's book is clearly the kind of book men at the central core of biography in English have written; it is not the kind of book—good or bad as they may be—men like Mr. André Maurois, Mr. Stefan Zweig, or Mr. W. E. Woodward have written.

It is a long book, but barely long enough for the long, full life it records. Franklin was a dozen men, artisan, business man, inventor, scientist, philosopher (this last strictly in the eighteenth-century, not in the technical or academic, sense), moralist, man of letters, soldier, diplomatist, and statesman. He was the most Protean, the most Goethean, of Americans, and deserves all the space Mr. Van Doren's publishers have granted. Mr. Van Doren has room enough to let Franklin expand properly, and speak for himself in his autobiography, his letters, and his innumerable editorial writings, articles, pamphlets, from the "Silence Dogood" letters in his brother's *New England Courant* to *Poor Richard*, his little French verses, and those "surreptitious" writings which, like the even broader ones of Mark Twain, continue to circulate in a queer underworld of print. Yet Mr. Van Doren's preface, "in effect, Franklin's autobiography is here completed on his own scale, and in his own words," is misleading. The biographer of Swift and Peacock is not so false to the methods of his craft as to confuse autobiography with biography. He lets Franklin speak for himself, but he fills in the spaces, criticizes, arranges, explains as a good biographer must. You never feel that he is warping his subject to fit his own theories and sentiments, that he is stuffing out a dummy. He is a biographer, and not a ventriloquist. He admires and likes Franklin—indeed this is, like almost all lives in what we have ventured to call the central core of English biography, a "sympathetic" biography—but it is no mere hagiography. Anyway, Franklin was much too successful to tempt the lay canonizers. Those who want to make saints for this harsh world have rightly turned to such eternal witnesses to the discomforts of virtue as Paine and Marat.

Mr. Van Doren skillfully contrives to remain always on the right side of the uncertain boundary which divides biography from history. It would be easy to make Franklin an excuse for writing a history of the Western world in the eighteenth century. At one time or other his life touched almost everything of importance that was going on in America, England, and France for some eighty years. Mr. Van Doren does not leave his reader in ignorance of anything in Franklin's environment that is essential to understanding what he did and how he did it. When, for instance, he comes to that eternal historical puzzle centered around the early negotiations between the rebel Americans and the French, he untwists beautifully the tangle into which Arthur Lee, Silas Deane, Franklin, Beaumarchais, and Vergennes managed to get, to the despair of the historian. There are few short accounts of the "affair of Beaumarchais's million" as clear, as fair-minded as the one Mr. Van Doren gives here. If you want a neat example of the difference between careful, judicial writing and violently partisan writing, compare Mr. Van Doren's treatment of this affair and that of Mr. Frank Smith in his just-published life of Thomas Paine. Paine, at the American end, got up to his neck, and beyond, in the affair, and his recent biographer is sure that everyone else involved was either a grafter or a fool. Mr. Van Doren knows better, as Franklin himself knew better.

Mr. Van Doren, then, holds the difficult balance between "Life" and "Times" always in favor of Franklin the man, so that the reader understands what is going on, but is never swamped with unnecessary historical details. He also holds what is, in the present state of the publishing business, an even more difficult balance between the demands of the scholar and the demands of the general reader. The book is the October choice of the Book-of-the-Month Club, and will not disappoint the numerous readers such a choice guarantees it. It makes splendid, leisurely reading, following down all the highroads and all the little lanes of Franklin's varied life. It has none of the panting immediacy, the melodrama with which some biographers try to spice their books, nor is it "epic" in the cheap sense the word seems to have acquired. Mr. Van Doren even leaves the epigrams and the aphorisms to Franklin himself, who borrowed or invented enough to be read steadily and consecutively, and, something rarer and more difficult to bring off, it can be dipped into here and there, as you would dip into Boswell. But it is also a work of great erudition, one that will undoubtedly run successfully the gauntlet of the learned reviews. Mr. Van Doren's fifteen years of research have been incorporated in the work with the care of the artist and the scholar. They are not displayed with the pedant's glee, but neither have they been concealed as something supposedly detrimental to a wide circulation among the reading public. Simply from the point of view of the mechanics of book-making, the book is an admirable example of what to do with the necessary, but often clumsy, apparatus of learning. The footnotes are there, and the bibliography is there, but there so unobtrusively that no one need be bothered by them who doesn't want to be. The index, a vital matter too often skimped in new books nowadays, is a marvel of completeness.

This is certainly the Franklin book of our generation. Franklin had a tremendous press in his own day, and men have been writing about him ever since. Mr. Van Doren has mastered this great body of writing, got the best out of it, and put in much himself. He is scrupulously fair to his predecessors, though perhaps he passes over a bit lightly what the French, and notably M. Bernard Fay, have done for Franklin. It is true that in general the French have made him a bit too much of a Frenchman—it's a habit they have with those they like—and Mr. Van Doren has done well to insist that he was a Yankee transplanted to Philadelphia, and not the dream of eighteenth-century French *salons* made flesh. As one of the Founders, he was bound to become for many Americans something of a figure from the schoolbooks, a hero and a symbol, less and more than a man. But he has never been stuffed by the literary and pedagogical taxidermists as Washington has been stuffed, and it is not quite certain that Mr. Van Doren is altogether justified in complaining in his preface that "the dry, prim people" have really succeeded hitherto in monopolizing him as one of their own. Certainly ordinary folk have never forgotten the Franklin who gave such extraordinary advice to a young man on the choice of a mistress.

Franklin was indeed no romanticist, no heaven-storming seeker, nor even, as a Wordsworth or a Keats fixed the word on our language, a poet. He was a Yankee, but that kind of Yankee which utterly excludes the Bronson Alcotts, and even a good deal of the Thoreaus. He was a man of the eighteenth century, but of that eighteenth century which utterly excludes the Rousseaus, and even much of the Samuel Johnsons, and the Burkes. You cannot fairly make Franklin into anything like a Shelley or a Byron. But of course Mr. Van Doren does not try to, and by his "dry, prim people" does not seem to mean more than stupid, unimaginative people who shelter themselves from this world with a few neat formulas. Such people never had any real claim on Franklin, and, with Mr. Van Doren's work, will have even less claim on him.

QUESTIONS ON CONTENT

1. Does the title of this review accurately describe Franklin? (See the third paragraph.)

2. What is the purpose of the first paragraph? How many of the allusions can you identify?
3. At what point does the reviewer tell how he intends to write about this book? Does he follow his announced plan?
4. "He is a biographer, not a ventriloquist." Explain.
5. Why does the reviewer think Mr. Van Doren must have been tempted to write the history of Franklin's times?
6. What is the "difficult balance between the demands of the scholar and the demands of the general reader"?
7. What is the purpose of the final paragraph?
8. Why are we told almost nothing of the *contents* of this book?

❧ *Hungry Caravan: A Review of* The Grapes of Wrath *by John Steinbeck*

LOUIS KRONENBERGER

This is in many ways the most moving and disturbing social novel of our time. What is wrong with it, what is weak in it, what robs it of the stature it clearly attempts, are matters which must presently be pointed out; but not at once. First it should be pointed out that *The Grapes of Wrath* comes at a needed time in a powerful way. It comes, perhaps, as *The Drapier's Letters* or *Uncle Tom's Cabin* or some of the social novels of Zola came. It burns with no pure gemlike flame, but with hot and immediate fire. It is, from any point of view, Steinbeck's best novel, but it does not make one wonder whether, on the basis of it, Steinbeck is now a better novelist than Hemingway or Farrell or Dos Passos; it does not invoke comparisons; it simply makes one feel that Steinbeck is, in some way all his own, a force.

The publishers refer to the book as "perhaps the greatest single creative work that this country has produced." This is a foolish and extravagant statement, but unlike most publishers' statements, it seems the result of honest enthusiasm, and one may hope that the common reader will respond to the book with an enthusiasm of the same sort. And perhaps he will, for *The Grapes of Wrath* has, overwhelmingly, those two qualities vital to a work of social pro-

From *The Nation*, April 15, 1939. Reprinted by permission.

test: great indignation and great compassion. Its theme is large and tragic, and, on the whole, is largely and tragically felt. No novel of our day has been written out of a more genuine humanity, and none, I think, is better calculated to awaken the humanity of others.

Throughout the Southwest hundreds of thousands of small farmers and sharecroppers have been driven, by the banks and the big land-owners, from their farms—to move westward, with their families, in a dusty caravan of jalopies, to California. To California, because handbills lure them there with promises of work. But the real purpose of the handbills is to flood the California market with such a surplus of workers that the price of labor sinks to almost nothing. Hungry men, by accepting lower wages, oust ill-paid men from their jobs; then, in desperation, the ousted men snatch the jobs back at wages even lower. The result is a horde of the starving and homeless, living in filth and roadside camps, forever wandering, all thought of security ended.

In the fate of one such family—the Joads of Oklahoma—John Steinbeck has told the fate of all. Their fate is the theme of an angry and aroused propagandist, but the Joads themselves are the product of a lively novelist. A racy, picturesque, somewhat eccentric tribe, with certain resemblances to Erskine Caldwell's Georgia exhibits, the Joads—mean, merry, shameless Grandpa; brooding, conscience-stricken Uncle John; strong, tough, understanding Ma; Al, a squirt thinking only of women and cars; Tom, who has been in prison for killing a man in a brawl—the Joads, with their salty, slanting speech, their frank and boisterous opinions, their unrepressed, irrepressible appetites, would, in a stable world, be the stuff of rich folk-comedy. But suddenly uprooted and harassed, they are creatures forced to fight for their very existence. During the first half of Steinbeck's long book the Joads, both as people and as symbols, have tremendous vitality. Steinbeck's account of this one family leaving home and journeying forth in a rickety makeshift truck is like some night-lighted, rude Homeric chronicle of a great migration. It has a vigor, as of half-childlike, half-heroic adventuring, that almost blots out the sense of its desperate origins and painful forebodings.

But after the Joads reach California, something—a kind of inner life—disappears from the book. The economic outrage, the human tragedy are made brutally clear. The chronicle of the Joads remains vivid; the nature of their fate becomes ever more infuriating. As a tract, the book goes on piling up its indictment, conducting the reader on a sort of grand tour of exploitation and destitution. And all this has, emotionally at least, a very strong effect. But somehow the book ceases to grow, to maintain direction. It is truly enough a story of nomads; but from that it does not follow that the proletarian novel must fall into the loose pattern of the picaresque novel. Artistically speaking, the second half of *The Grapes of Wrath,* though it still has content and suspense, lacks form and intensity. The people simply go on and on, with Steinbeck left improvising and amplifying until—with a touch of new and final horror—he abruptly halts.

The Grapes of Wrath is a superb tract because it exposes something terrible and true with enormous vigor. It is a superb tract, moreover, by virtue of being thoroughly animated fiction, by virtue of living scenes and living characters (like Ma), not by virtue of discursive homilies and dead characters (like the socialistic preacher). One comes away moved, indignant, protesting, pitying. But one comes away dissatisfied, too, aware that *The Grapes of Wrath* is too unevenly weighted, too uneconomically proportioned, the work of a writer who is still self-indulgent, still undisciplined, still not altogether aware of the difference in value of various human emotions. The picturesqueness of the Joads, for example, is fine wherever it makes them live more abundantly, but false when simply laid on for effect. Steinbeck's sentimentalism is good in bringing him close to the lives of his people, but bad when it blurs his insight. Again, the chapters in which Steinbeck halts the story to editorialize about American life are sometimes useful, but oftener pretentious and flatulent.

But one does not take leave of a book like this in a captious spirit. One salutes it as a fiery document of protest and compassion, as a story that had to be told, as a book that must be read. It is, I think, one of those books—there are not very many—which really do some good.

QUESTIONS ON CONTENT

1. What does the author seek to do in the first paragraph?
2. What two great qualities does the reviewer find in the novel?
3. How is this review like the review of *Benjamin Franklin?* How does it differ?
4. What function does each paragraph in this review serve? Discuss.

❧ *With Grace Under Pressure*

Mark Schorer

(A Review of *The Old Man and the Sea* by Ernest Hemingway. New York: Scribner's. 1952.)

The only guts that are mentioned in this story are the veritable entrails of fish, but we are nevertheless reminded on every page that Hemingway once defined this favorite word, in its metaphorical use, as "grace under pressure." Grace, in the fullest sense, is the possession of this old man, just as grace was precisely what Colonel Cantwell, in *Across the River and Into the Trees,* was totally without. But here it is, complete and absolute, the very breath of this old man, so thoroughly his in his essence as in his *ambiente,* that it can only be there under pressure as at all other times, and indeed, even under the greatest pressure, he hardly alters. Grace, by which one means now not the old stiff upper lip (this old man's upper lip is not so very stiff) which came to some of the older heroes a little easily sometimes, a quality more nearly a manner of speaking than of being; not that now, but benignity, nothing less, and beautifully, masterfully presented, so that the satisfaction one has in this creation is plain happiness, and then, I suppose, gratitude.

The old man has a Franciscan quality that so pervades his habit of thought as to support and give the body of dramatic plausibility, even inevitability to the suggestion of Christian martyrdom which comes at the end. Early in the story, when the old man is being helped by the boy, he thanks him for the food he gives him. "He was too simple to wonder when he had attained it and he knew it was not disgraceful and it carried no loss of true pride." Humility—the assumption, without self-consciousness and therefore without sentimentality—is the old man's strength.

> He was very fond of flying fish as they were his principal friends on the ocean. He was sorry for the birds, especially the small delicate dark terns that were always flying and looking and almost never finding, and he thought, "The birds have a harder life than

New Republic, October 6, 1952. Reprinted by permission of the *New Republic.*

we do except for the robber birds and the heavy strong ones. Why did they make birds so delicate and fine as those sea swallows when the ocean can be so cruel? She is kind and very beautiful. But she can be so cruel and it comes so suddenly and such birds that fly, dipping and hunting, with their small sad voices are made too delicately for the sea."

And again, now of porpoises, and then of the marlin itself:

"They are good," he said. "They play and make jokes and love one another. They are our brothers like the flying fish."
Then he began to pity the great fish that he had hooked. He is wonderful and strange and who knows how old he is, he thought. Never have I had such a strong fish nor one who acted so strangely. Perhaps he is too wise to jump. He could ruin me by jumping or by a wild rush. But perhaps he has been hooked many times before and he knows that this is how he should make his fight. He cannot know that it is only one man against him, nor that it is an old man. But what a great fish he is. . . . I wonder if he has any plans or if he is just as desperate as I am?

And thus, with a kind of Biblical abstraction that always assumes the independence of all things in their own character, which is likewise independent and separate (in this recognition lie the true sources of brotherhood as of pity), he speaks to a bird, to his fish, and to the parts of his own body, his hands and his head. With a few wavering exceptions, Hemingway sustains the perilous poise of all this with great beauty over pits of possible bathos.

Everywhere the book is being called a classic. In at least one sense, the word cannot be applied, for here and there, where the writing wavers, its pure lucidity is muddled by all that hulking personality which, at his worst, Hemingway has made all too familiar. I do not have in mind the talk about baseball, which has bothered at least one reviewer. "The baseball" is a near obsession with most Caribbean natives, but we do not have to know this to accept the old man's interest as his own rather than as Hemingway's. (After all, DiMaggio's father *was* a fisherman, as the old man tells us, and the sword of the marlin is "as long as a baseball bat.") But a murky paragraph that has to do with "mysticism about turtles" is a case in point. Or a sentence such as this: "He did not truly feel good because the pain from the cord across his back had almost passed pain and gone into a dullness that he mistrusted"—is it a quibble to suggest that the word "truly" and its location spoil this sentence, jar us out of the mind of the old man whom we are coming to know into the reflection that we've read Hemingway before? Or a brief passage such as this:

> After he judged that his right hand had been in the water long enough he took it out and looked at it.
> "It is not bad," he said. "And pain does not matter to a man. . . .
> "You did not do so badly for something worthless," he said to his left hand. "But there was a moment when I could not find you."
> Why was I not born with two good hands? he thought. Perhaps it was my fault in not training that one properly. But God knows he has had enough chances to learn. He did not do so badly in the night, though, and he has only cramped once. If he cramps again let the line cut him off.

The last sentence tells us with dramatic concreteness what the generalization, "pain does not matter to a man," which is really Hemingway's, does not tell us at all. It should not have been written, precisely because what *is* written must make *us* speak that conclusion, it should be our generalization from his evidence.

But the old man seldom lapses into dramatic falseness. In his age, alone at sea, he has taken to speaking aloud, and instead of dialogue between characters by which most fiction moves, this story moves by little dialogues in the old man himself, the exchange of what is spoken and what is not spoken. This is almost a running drama between that which is only possible and that which is real:

> "Fish," he said, "I love you and respect you very much. But I will kill you dead before this day ends."
> Let us hope so, he thought.

The threat of over-generalization is almost always in the spoken words, which, then, are immediately rooted in actuality by the reservations of the unspoken. And of course, Hemingway's incredible gift for writing of the natural life serves the same function. Whether he is describing plankton, jelly fish, the sucking fish that swim in the shadow of the marlin, the gutting of a dolphin that contains two flying fish, or turtles, they are all always there before us, actualities, and the old man is an actuality among them.

The novel is nearly a fable. The best fiction, at its heart, always is, of course, but with his particular diction and syntax, Hemingway's stories approach fable more directly than most, and never so directly as here. It is the quality of his fiction at its very best, the marvelous simplicity of line. ("'Be calm and strong, old man', he said.") There has been another strain in his fiction, to be sure—his personal ambition to become a character in a tall tale, folklore as opposed to fable. That is the weaker man pushing aside the great novelist. The strain glimmers once in this story when we are told of the old man's feat of strength in his youth: "They had gone one day and one night with their elbows on a chalk line on the table and their forearms straight up and their hands gripped tight." Take it away.

The true quality of fable is first of all in the style, in the degree of abstraction, which is not only in some ways Biblical but is always tending toward the proverbial rhythm. ("The setting of the sun is a difficult time for fish.") Next, it is in the simplicity of the narrative, and in the beautiful proportion (about three-fourths to one-fourth) of its rise and fall. Finally, of course, it is in the moral significance of the narrative, this fine story of an ancient who goes too far out, "beyond the boundaries of permitted aspiration," as Conrad put it ("You violated your luck when you went too far outside," the old man thinks), and encounters his destiny:

> His choice had been to stay in the deep dark water far out beyond all snares and traps and treacheries. My choice was to go there to find him beyond all people. Beyond all people in the world. Now we are joined together and have been since noon. And no one to help either one of us.

In this isolation, he wins a Conradian victory, which means destruction and triumph. We permit his martyrdom because he has earned it. His sigh is "just a noise such as a man might make, involuntarily, feeling the nail go through his hands and into the wood." He stumbles under the weight of his mast when he carries it across his shoulder, up a hill. He sleeps, finally, "with his arms out straight and the palms of his hands up." There is more than this, and for those who, like this reviewer, believe that Hemingway's art, when it is art, is absolutely incomparable, and that he is unquestionably the greatest craftsman in the American novel in this century, something that is perhaps even more interesting. For this appears to be not only a moral fable, but a parable, and all the controlled passion in the story, all the taut excitement in the prose come, I believe, from the parable. It is an old man catching a fish, yes; but it is also a great artist in the act of mastering his subject, and, more than that, of actually writing about that struggle. Nothing is more important than his craft, and it is beloved; but because it must be struggled with and mastered, it is also a foe, enemy to all self-indulgence, to all looseness of feeling, all laxness of style, all soft pomposities.

> "I am a strange old man."
> "But are you strong enough now for a truly big fish?"
> "I think so. And there are many tricks."

Hemingway, who has always known the tricks, is strong enough now to have mastered his greatest subject. "I could not fail myself and die on a fish like this," the old man reflects. They win together, the great character, the big writer.

QUESTIONS ON CONTENT

1. Why does the reviewer carefully explain his title? What is metaphorical about calling courage "grace under pressure"?
2. Why is Hemingway's hero said to have a "Franciscan quality"? How does the reviewer demonstrate this quality?
3. Examine the passages cited to prove an occasional lapse into "dramatic falseness." Do you think the charge of dramatic falseness is proved? (Note how Mr. Schorer digs into these passages to release not only the sense but the tone. Such digging is the mark of sensitive reading.)
4. What is the difference between a fable and a parable? How are these terms applied to Hemingway's book?
5. Discuss fully the final sentence: "They win together, the great character, the big writer."

❧ *Wanted: An American Novel*

Editors of LIFE

Sloan Wilson, a young writer whose first novel (*The Man in the Gray Flannel Suit*) is moving up best-seller lists, recently made a statement in defense of his book's happy ending which is worth repeating: "The world's treated me awfully well," he said, "and I guess it's crept into my work. . . . These are, we forget, pretty

Editorial from LIFE Magazine, September 12, 1955. Copyright Time Inc.

good times. Yet too many novelists are still writing as if we were back in the Depression years."

Wilson put his finger on a strange contradiction. Ours is the most powerful nation in the world. It has had a decade of unparalleled prosperity. It has gone further than any other society in the history of man toward creating a truly classless society. Yet it is still producing a literature which sounds sometimes as if it were written by an unemployed homosexual living in a packing-box shanty on the city dump while awaiting admission to the county poorhouse.

This is doubly strange because past American eras have produced art which faithfully mirrored their times; *The Great Gatsby* still speaks eloquently of Prohibition's frauds and deceits, *Main Street* of the high tide of provincial self-satisfaction, *The Grapes of Wrath* with a just anger for the unnecessary humiliations of Depression, while *Look Homeward, Angel* may well speak for a timeless America. But who speaks for America today? One might argue, with some plausibility, that the fearful indecisions of an atomic age keep a representative literature from being born, but when has life ever been secure? Atomic fear or not, the incredible accomplishments of our day are surely the raw stuff of saga.

Wilson's uneven book may be flimsy art but it is at least affirmative. Happily there are a few other signs of a trend away from degeneracy and negation. For example, Lionel Shapiro's *Sixth of June,* though it revolves about a triangle, is not resolved by adultery. Herman Wouk's *Marjorie Morningstar* is a mutiny, says Time, against "three decades of U.S. fiction dominated by skeptical criticism, sexual emancipation, social protest and psychoanalytical sermonizing." Wouk's book even endorses premarital chastity. And there is visible in other work what Critic Maxwell Geismar calls "a return to the security of a religious universe."

A change is needed. Nobody wants Pollyanna literature. Poets have always had what Robert Frost admits is "a vested interest in human misery"; agony begets art. Maybe art mistrusts prosperity. But at least the breeches-busting Paul Bunyan of the U.S. today seems to deserve better literature than the papaya-smelly, overripe school of the Truman Capotes, or the obscenity-obsessed school of "new realism" exemplified by a parade of war novels which mostly read like the diary of a professional grievance collector with a dirty

mind and total recall. James Gould Cozzens' *Guard of Honor* was
one of the few military novels that rang true with dignity. In most
of the others the enemy is not the one shooting at us but our own
officers and Army.

Europeans are already prejudiced against America by savage
animadversions in their own classics against our "vulgar" democracy
("If I had remained another day in that horrible . . . United States,
where there is neither hope nor faith nor charity," wrote Balzac,
"I should have died without being sick"). Small wonder that our
own self-depreciation helps them enlarge the evil image to that
which France's Michel Mohrt describes in his new study of American novels: "a hypocritical society based on the power of money,
racial prejudice, sexual taboos. Exile, alcohol, suicide seem the only
escape." Such a onetime exile, Henry (*Tropic of Cancer*) Miller,
puts it more savagely in the current *Chicago Review*. The American
seen through the eyes of our leading writers, he asserts, is "a digit
in machine-made formulas . . . he has neither face nor name but
is shuffled about like the victim of a soulless society on an electronic
chessboard operated by a dummy hidden in the cells of a publisher's
diseased brain. . . ." The writing, he adds, "reeks of embalming
fluid."

It is understandable that American groups which feel the most
isolated should produce the most anguished writing, and that so
much of it should come from the South. Its ante bellum slave
society was in some ways similar to the feudal Russian system whose
injustices and tensions produced a Dostoevski and a Tolstoi. William
Faulkner has a patent kinship with Dostoevski and his preoccupation
with guilt. But Faulkner, for all his enormous gifts, can be searched
in vain for that quality of redemption, through love and brotherhood, which always shines amid Dostoevski's horrors. It shines also
amid the worst havoc of Tolstoi's overturned world (Moscow, too,
was burned, even if not by Sherman).

To find this redeeming quality of spiritual purpose today's reader
must turn not to novels but to nonfiction like Russel Davenport's
The Dignity of Man or to the British book, *The Conquest of Everest*.
That conquest held a deeper meaning than the achievement. The
European Hillary and the Asian Tenzing are a hopeful symbol for
a wider brotherhood yet to be achieved. Their final triumph expresses the unquenchable reaching of man's soul for a truth higher
than reality, for a good better than himself, the qualities which

modern literature so often deny. In every healthy man there is a wisdom deeper than his conscious mind, reaching beyond memory to the primeval rivers, a yea-saying to the goodness and joy of life. This is what is most missing from our hothouse literature—the joy of life itself.

QUESTIONS ON CONTENT

1. What is the central thesis of this editorial? Show how this thesis is supported.
2. Are novelists supposed to mirror faithfully their times? Discuss.
3. Is a "flimsy art" all right if "it is at least affirmative"? Explain.
4. What evidence is cited as pointing to a veering away from "degeneracy and negation"?
5. What is meant by "Pollyanna literature"? If one is to express "the joy of life," how is he to avoid the charge of being unrealistic? Discuss.

❧ *The Wouk Mutiny*

EDITORS OF TIME

The desk is bare except for a well-thumbed dictionary, a picture of the novelist's wife and an old-fashioned gold watch with Roman numerals and a heavy lid. For five years the watch has lain open on the desk while its owner listened to its ticking and wrote steadily, using the same aging desk pen and yellow lined pads. Says Herman Wouk (pronounced woke): "I reported in to my boss, the desk, five or six days a week, at least six hours a day." Out of this unflinching writing stint came some of the U.S.'s most successful fiction. Wouk's total output to date: three plays, a movie and four novels, including *The Caine Mutiny,* the biggest U.S. bestseller since *Gone With the Wind.*

Last week the gold watch (brought to the U.S. from Russia 27 years ago by Novelist Wouk's grandfather) was shut and resting in the desk drawer. Novelist Wouk was taking his first vacation in nearly a decade from the job of writing—"the loneliest job in the

Time, September 5, 1955. Reprinted by permission; copyright Time Inc., 1955.

world." Wouk, a tall, darkly handsome man of 40, was relaxing at his ocean-front home on New York's Fire Island, trying to fix a 30-year-old reading lamp, lolling on the sand, teaching his five-year-old son how to float. He was formidably calm about a D-day as unnerving as any faced by that old rust-bucket, U.S.S. *Caine*—the publication this week of his latest novel, *Marjorie Morningstar*. Months ago, Fellow Author J. P. Marquand warned: "The critics will be waiting for you with meat cleavers the next time around."

Much to Live Down. Wouk knows that he will have to live up to *The Caine Mutiny* before he can ever live its fame down. *The Caine's* total sales figures to date are of heroic proportions: in all editions, some 3,000,000 Americans bought the novel; it sold more than 2,000,000 copies in Britain, and it has been translated into 17 foreign languages. The play based on the book, *The Caine Mutiny Court-Martial,* packed in Broadway theatergoers for two seasons and grossed about $2,500,000. The movie piled up a box office take of $12 million and is still going. Like many a giant industry, the *Caine* even spawned byproducts, *e.g.,* the manufacture of "Queeg balls," modeled on the two steel bearings that the skipper of the *Caine* obsessively rolled in his left palm whenever his nerves were shaky.

To Herman Wouk himself, *The Caine Mutiny* brought the Pulitzer Prize (1951), nearly a million dollars in cash, countless autograph hunters (whom he loves), countless requests for speaking engagements (most of which he declines), and several thousand letters (all of which he answered). But to Novelist Wouk, a cool customer in a superheated profession, *The Caine* is simply "Novel No. 3" (No. 1 was *Aurora Dawn;* No. 2, *City Boy*), and he does not worry for an instant that *Marjorie* may be lost in the undertow of *The Caine's* popularity. This unique assurance is typical of Herman Wouk, a unique figure in American letters.

Chipless Shoulder. Wouk, a man of paradox, seems like an enigmatic character in search of an author. He is a devout Orthodox Jew who has achieved worldly success in worldly-wise Manhattan while adhering to dietary prohibitions and traditional rituals which many of his fellow Jews find embarrassing. He is an ex-radio gagwriter who severely judges his own work by the standards of the great English novelists. He is a Columbia-educated (class of '34), well-read intellectual with an abiding faith in "the common reader" ("They're good enough to elect our Presidents, aren't they?"). Although he is a highly sensitive member of a religious minority, he is one of the few living U.S. writers who carries no chip on his shoulder and who gives the U.S. straight A's in his fictional report cards.

In *The Caine Mutiny*, Wouk defied recent literary fashion and loosed some real shockers by declaring his belief in 1) decency— in language as well as deeds, 2) honor, 3) discipline, 4) authority, 5) hallowed institutions like the U.S. Navy. In *Marjorie Morningstar*, Wouk will set more teeth on edge by advocating chastity before marriage, suggesting that real happiness for a woman is found in a home and children, cheering loud and long for the American middle class and blasting Bohemia and Bohemians. Wouk is a Sinclair Lewis in reverse. His chief significance is that he spearheads a mutiny against the literary stereotypes of rebellion—against three decades of U.S. fiction dominated by skeptical criticism, sexual emancipation, social protest and psychoanalytic sermonizing.

Yet Wouk is no tractmonger. He is first and last a topnotch storyteller, and his readers know it. *Marjorie* seemed slated to be a runaway bestseller. It was the unanimous choice of the Book-of-the-Month Club judges for September, and the publishers, Doubleday, took the hard-headed gamble of an initial printing of 100,000 copies.

The Caine was a story of action and adventure; *Marjorie* is a love story, and beyond that, a girl's quest for her own identity. *The Caine* was a clear-eyed account of life aboard a destroyer-minesweeper in World War II; *Marjorie* is a clear-eyed and warmhearted account of Jewish family life in the 1930s. *Marjorie* is overlong, sometimes graceless, often plodding, but like *The Caine*, it has a compelling sense of reality, as if the novelist had planted hidden microphones in the house next door and poked a zoomar lens down the chimney.

Who is Marjorie? Marjorie Morgenstern is an American Everygirl who happens to be Jewish. She is, says her creator, "Betsy Jones, Hazel Klein, Sue Wilson." She is every girl who ever dreamed of seeing her name on a Broadway marquee, who fell in love and set out to land a man. She is every girl who ever pooh-poohed her parents' stodgy, old-fashioned precepts about life, who ever yearned for Don Juan and settled for Steady John.

From Hunter to Sodom. On the first of the book's 565 pages, Hoover is still President, Marjorie is 17, and the Morgenstern family has just made the great social leap from the Bronx Park East to Manhattan's Central Park West. Marjorie is a blue-eyed, brown-haired beauty who can scarcely see past her next prom date. But eagle-eyed Mama Morgenstern is already shopping in the marriage mart.

First, there is a holdover from Bronx days named George Drobes, who intrigues Margie because he has a jalopy named Penelope and his kisses tingle. But to Mama, George is just a snuffling auto mechanic. When the wealthy son of a department-store owner brings Margie home after a horseback-riding spill in Central Park, Mama lights up. But her social grasp exceeds the Morgenstern economic reach, and the new romance fades. Margie doesn't really care. Her destiny, she feels, is to be an actress. She has long since scribbled her stage name on a scrap of paper—MARJORIE MORNINGSTAR.

When she wants to talk about what is closest to her heart—the glorious career of Marjorie Morningstar—she goes to the West 90s brownstone flat of her dearest friend, a fat, good-natured girl with intellectual pretensions named Marsha Zelenko. Marsha lives with her parents in an apartment decorated with Mexican copper plates, Chinese screens and African masks. Papa Zelenko strums the balalaika; Mama Zelenko pounds out Bach on the piano. After Margie scores a hit in a Hunter College production of *The Mikado*, Marsha gets her a job as dramatic coach at a children's camp in the Adirondacks. Across the lake is an adult resort camp named South Wind, and South Wind, Mama Morgenstern snorts, is nothing less than Sodom.

Virgin on the Verge. To Sodom, of course, the girls surreptitiously go. There Marjorie meets Noel Airman (real name: Saul Erhmann), who has red hair, a handsome profile and the glamorous job of putting on revues at South Wind. To the despair of Noel's aspiring, pimply assistant, Wally Wronken, Airman is a triple-threat man—an artist, a libertine and an intellectual who can shred phony highbrows "like a flame thrower."

When Noel gets around to shredding Margie's shirtwaist in his cabin one cozy evening, Margie does a sudden uncooperative freeze. Noel turns eloquently nasty and, incidentally, states the main theme of the book: "Your name is Shirley," he tells Marjorie, "the respectable girl, the mother of the next generation, all tricked out to appear gay and girlish and carefree, but with a terrible threatening solid dullness jutting through, like the gray rocks under the spring grass in Central Park . . . What [Shirley] wants is what a woman should want . . . big diamond engagement ring, house in a good neighborhood, furniture, children, well-made clothes, furs—but she'll never say so. Because in our time those things are supposed to be stuffy and dull . . . She's Lady Brett Ashley,[1] with witty, devil-may-care whimsey and shocking looseness all over the place. A dismal caricature, you understand, and nothing but talk . . . To simulate Lady Brett, however, as long as she's in fashion, Shirley talks free and necks on a rigidly graduated scale . . . She can find no guidance anywhere . . . In literature her problem doesn't exist. The old novels are all about Jane Austen and Dickens heroines . . . And the new novels are all more or less about Brett Ashley, who sleeps with any guy who really insists, but is a poetic pure tortured soul at heart. This leaves Shirley squarely in the middle. What can she do . . . ?"

What indeed? For 417 pages, Margie is a virgin on the verge. Then, on the eve of Noel Airman's first Broadway opening, Lady Brett Ashley wins out over Shirley, in a Central Park South hotel room. This may well be the longest to-do over the loss of a girl's virginity since Richardson's *Pamela*. Says Wouk defensively: "Some people may get impatient and think, 'She's going to sleep with this guy, what's all the fuss?' But it's still a great suspense thing to a girl. If you don't think so, take a poll. The question may be more serious to Marjorie because of her Old Testament upbringing. But it is a key problem for any girl. It's a general American dilemma."

The "Gilded Ghetto." When Margie is not coping with her dilemma, she is occupied with shyster theatrical producers, a pedestrian suitor named Dr. Shapiro, and the diehard devotion of little Wally Wronken. A character who warms Marjorie's heart, and the reader's, is her uncle, Samson-Aaron, a robustious clown, a seamsplitting glutton, and a lovable deadbeat ("But a nickel, Modgerie, a nickel I alvays had, to buy you a Hershey bar ven I came to this house"). In his simple way, he shows Marjorie how close she really is to the faith she once brashly dismissed as a Stone Age relic.

Author Wouk is at his best when he pictures the rarely described world of Manhattan's Upper West Side, which one of his characters calls the "gilded ghetto." Wouk knows its customs, prejudices, social gradations, *e.g.*, West End Avenue is a worse address than Central Park West; mothers run a secret service on eligible suitors as efficiently as any conducted in Junior League territory. Most amusing and effective are Wouk's accounts of big family occasions, *e.g.*, the mammoth *bar mitzvah* [2] with its ostentatious but somehow touching

---

[1] The promiscuous heroine of Hemingway's "lost generation" novel *The Sun Also Rises*.

[2] The ceremony at which a boy of 13 assumes adult religious responsibility.

banquet that finds Marjorie's brother making a grand entrance to the
strains of *Pomp and Circumstance*, flanked by a cauldron of flaming
brandy for the grapefruit appetizers.

In such scenes Wouk gives his people a special tang and zest.
A Passover dinner at the Morgensterns' is turned into a hilarious
romp by a progressively raised brat named Neville ("The Devil")
Sapersteen, who bites little girls in the rump and needs 47 toy airplanes handy at all times in an open suitcase because, as the mother
explains, they're "a sort of security symbol." ("Morris, leave the
lid up or he'll get a trauma.")

On to Mamaroneck. When Noel's play and his affair with Margie
both turn out to be flops, he flees to Paris, but Margie follows him,
still determined to lasso the cad with a wedding ring. Aboard ship
she meets another charmer, Mike Eden, who has a bad case of
nerves, but for good cause: he is playing Scarlet Pimpernel in Nazi
Germany and smuggling out persecuted Jews. Still, Noel has a fatal
hold on her, and she finally catches up with him, only to find him
living with and off a lady photographer.

Noel as a brilliant, devastating heel—a West Side version of a
Scott Fitzgerald hero—rarely rings true. But his deterioration and
his ultimate meaning are convincing. "He takes the current myths for
solid facts," says one character about him. "It never occurs to him
that the Oedipus complex really doesn't exist, that it is a piece of
moralistic literature. He's as orthodox as your own father, Marjorie,
in his fashion . . . making a life's work out of being dogmatic,
clever, supercilious—and inwardly totally confused and wretched."

Author Wouk builds up real suspense about the question of whom
Marjorie will finally marry—a reformed Noel, a romantic Eden, a
successful Wally, or plain Dr. Shapiro. The last chapter finds her a
contented matron of Mamaroneck, who in her memory has revamped
the past to suit the present. As she gets a little high and waltzes
alone to the strains of *Falling in Love with Love*, she seems for a
moment like the dream girl of old. But the moment passes. An old
beau who is visiting her decides: "You couldn't write a play about
her that would run a week, or a novel that would sell a thousand
copies."

Island of Normalcy. Herman Wouk obviously disagrees. To him,
Marjorie is a story he felt he had to tell: "This person has haunted
me for years. It's not a girl I was in love with. It is a lot of girls
I knew, since I grew up in all this."

Like Marjorie, Wouk was born in The Bronx, the son of Abraham

Isaac and Esther Levine Wouk. Both parents came from Minsk,
Russia. Papa Wouk started washing clothes in a basement, rose
to be president of one of New York's largest power laundries. One of
Herman's earliest memories is playing hide and seek among the
machines. The Wouk family was "restless, like most New Yorkers,"
and while Herman was still a child, made four moves, from one
canyonlike apartment house to another, all within what Wouk calls
"that romantic, and much overcriticized borough," The Bronx.

Though he was later to toss a nostalgic valentine to his Bronx
boyhood in his novel, *City Boy*, little Herman got off to a depressing
start. He was the neighborhood fat boy, forever guzzling chocolate
milkshakes. In street fights, "I was clobbered." But he had two
powerful consolations: the Wouk home life and books. As soon as
he learned to read, he would sprawl on the floor for hours with a
tattered old dictionary, glorying in big words like anthropomor-
phism.

The love that Mama and Papa Wouk lavished on him, his sister
Irene and his brother Victor warms Herman to this day. Best of all
he liked the Sabbath. As a rabbi's daughter, "Mama was treated
rather like a princess around the house." But when Friday afternoon
came, "she scrubbed the kitchen on her hands and knees until the
place shone. The candles were lit, and we sang the joyful Sabbath
hymns and drank the sacramental wine; the children, too. My father
usually talked about the Bible." As in Marjorie Morgenstern's home,
the menu was always gefilte fish,[3] chicken noodle soup, roast chicken,
stewed prunes, tea and sponge cake. Those evenings, says Wouk,
made for "an island of normalcy. Home seemed to be the place
where everything happened as it should happen."

All Wouk & No Play. At school, says Wouk, he was "criminally
lazy," but he got good grades by cramming for exams.

When his grandfather, Rabbi Mendel Leib Levine, came to the
U.S. from Russia, he took over Herman's religious training. Rabbi
Levine, now an alert 90-year-old living in Tel Aviv, is one of the
two men who, Wouk believes, have most influenced his life (the
other: Columbia's late Philosopher Irwin Edman). "For 23 years,"
recalls Wouk, "my grandfather never ate any meat except fowl, because he insisted on personally seeing the slaughtering done according to the prescribed ritual."

At Columbia, Wouk worked for the college daily, edited the
humor magazine (sample humor: "Have you heard of the guy who

[3] Balls of chopped fish, egg, onion and seasoning, boiled with vegetables.

read Dante's *Inferno* just for the hell of it?"). He wrote two varsity shows (wrote a collegiate critic: "All Wouk and no play").

The Gag Factory. Wouk majored in comparative literature (like *The Caine's* Willie Keith) and in philosophy (like *Marjorie's* Noel Airman). This was the period of what Wouk now calls "the great sophomoric enlightenment . . . I discovered the 18th and 19th centuries, and, for a time, I didn't observe my religion very carefully." In time he went back to his faith. His return was not caused by any particular crisis, only "the crisis of living as an adult. I felt there's a wealth in Jewish tradition, a great inheritance. I'd be a jerk not to take advantage of it."

Before graduation, Wouk had announced that he was going to be a writer. His sister Irene still remembers the family powwows that ensued: "Father said if Herman wanted to write, why not write advertising copy for the Fox Square Laundry? Mother twisted her apron in anguish and insisted that he go to law school." (Years later proud Mama Wouk was seen carrying *The Caine Mutiny* almost everywhere she went.)

Herman found an out. A friend had landed a writing post at a resort camp, Copake, and Herman tagged along as his unpaid assistant. Copake was a less imposing facsimile of South Wind, the camp in *Marjorie Morningstar,* and Herman's was roughly the Wally Wronken post.

Next, Wouk went to work (at $15 a week) for a cigar-chomping "czar of gagwriters" who ran a joke factory supplying gags to Fanny Brice, Lou Holtz, Eddie Cantor *et al.* Wouk's job was to clip and card-index old jokes and to clean up the off-color items. Two years later he was hired as a radio gagwriter by Fred Allen. His special chore for the Allen program: the "People You Didn't Expect to Meet" interview, for which he unearthed weirdies, *e.g.,* a goldfish doctor, a worm salesman and "the man who inserts the cloves in the hams you see in Lindy's window." Allen also credits Wouk with such skits as "Detective One Long Pan Was Disguised as a Girdle So They Knew He Was Closing In."

The Greatest Experience. Though he was making $200 a week during the depths of The Depression, squiring showgirls around town and living in a swank apartment at Manhattan's Essex House, Wouk began to feel that "gags were not the answer to the riddle of existence." He talked to his grandfather, and put his probings into a diary (he still keeps it, so far has filled 20 volumes—6,000 pages). When Pearl Harbor came, Wouk enlisted in the Navy. At midshipman's school he graduated in the top 20 in a class of 500, further distinguished himself by writing a paper on "The Responsibilities of Naval Leadership" in verse and in the meter of a French ballade. At school and throughout his Navy career, Wouk held fast to Jewish law and custom. On the Liberty ship taking him to the Pacific in 1942, Wouk often ate nothing but bread and potatoes, because the ship's menu was dominated by pork. One day he posted a satirical poem on the bulletin board:

> *Of all God's creatures small and big*
> *We owe most to our friend, the pig . . .*
> *Yeoman, record this in the log:*
> *Twenty-one-gun salute—the hog!*

A senior officer saw the verse and issued an order: "Give this man something he can eat."

For Wouk, the wartime Navy was "the greatest experience of my life . . . I had known two worlds, the wise guys of Broadway and the wise guys of Columbia—two small worlds that sometimes take themselves for the whole world. In the Navy, I found out more than I ever had about people and about the United States. I had always been a word boy, and suddenly I had to cope with the peculiar, marvelous world of the machine."

In Love with the Boss. Unlike the *Caine*, the destroyer-minesweeper *Zane*, to which Wouk was assigned, swept mines aplenty —off the Marshalls, Kwajalein, Eniwetok, the Marianas, Guam, Saipan, Tinian. In two years Wouk was successively assistant communications officer, communications officer, ship's first lieutenant and navigator. Later he was reassigned to another minesweeper, the *Southard*, saw action in six Pacific campaigns. He rose to executive officer, had been recommended to become captain of his ship when it was wrecked in a typhoon at Okinawa.

One night late in 1944, when the *Zane* put in at San Pedro for repairs, Lieut. Wouk and a few fellow officers went out on the town. After all the bars had closed, one of the men remembered a birthday party being given for the boss of a file clerk he knew. "So we all barged in. I made a date with one of the file clerks for lunch the next day. All through lunch the girl raved about her boss, this beautiful, witty, talented creature. Naturally I went back to her office to take a second look, and I made a date with the boss."

The boss was Betty Brown, a trim, pretty redhead and a Phi Beta Kappa from the University of Southern California. For Wouk, it was a clear case of love at second sight. Betty was a Protestant, but not a practicing one. She thinks now that part of Herman's appeal for her was that he made her see "that one didn't have to be a stupe to be religious." When Herman went back to sea, Betty Brown began studying Judaism, and a year later, on her 25th birthday, became a Jewish convert. Betty's Hebrew name is Sarah Batya: Wouk picked Sarah, and Batya (chosen for its resemblance to Betty) means "daughter of God." When Herman broached the idea of marrying Sarah, "Mama thought the end of the world had come," but "Grandfather understood."

Through the years on shipboard, Wouk had been pecking away at a novel. *Aurora Dawn* was written in an 18th century style as quaint as a minuet, but it dealt with a 20th century subject, "the contrast between the rat-race values of the radio-advertising world and the stable values of an Old Testament hillbilly prophet who gets mixed up with it." Wouk thinks of it as "a compendium of first-novel errors," but the Book-of-the-Month Club grabbed it. From that day to this, Wouk has pursued "the hard, borderline trade" of writing with monastic dedication.

The Craftsman. His day does not begin at his desk, but in prayer, for which he dons the traditional black-and-white prayer shawl and straps phylacteries (small leather cases containing texts from the Pentateuch) to his left arm and his forehead. He prays twice more each day, just before and just after sundown. He also reads from the Pentateuch for an hour daily. He tries to start writing by 9 o'clock, takes a lunch break at 1, sometimes naps for a while, but gets back to his desk in time to turn out about 1,500 words a day. He rarely rewrites.

Wouk, a meticulous researcher,[4] tries for "plain style, clarity of expression, as I'm not a poet, and not a high stylist." He shuns obscenity in his books: "You don't use dirty language in someone's home. When a reader holds my book, we are in an even closer relationship than a guest's." Pinpointing his own faults, he says: "I overwrite. I fail to achieve the standard of excellence I strive for, and fall into mediocrity." He reads and rereads Shakespeare, but Dickens is his all-time favorite author ("He could create reality with a stroke").

At day's end Wouk relaxes with a martini and a long Havana

---

[4] While collecting weather data for the *Caine* in Washington, he stumbled on a movie idea about hurricane-hunting pilots; the movie (*Slattery's Hurricane*) netted him $85,000.

cigar ("They are like lollipops"), plays with his boys Nathaniel, 5, and Joseph, 17 months. The Wouks' first son, Abraham, was drowned in a Mexican swimming pool in 1951, when he slipped out of the house early one morning to sail a toy boat his father had given him.

Built-In Engine. One night a week Wouk gives a course in advanced rhetoric at New York's Yeshiva University to a class of rabbinical students. He owns no car and no boat ("Possessions are disastrous"), but he does own two homes. In addition to the Fire Island summer place, he has a fashionable cooperative apartment in Manhattan's East 60s. He and his wife are homebodies; they love to read and listen to records.

Somewhere inside Herman Wouk there plays a permanent recording of *The Little Engine That Could.* He has at various times doggedly tackled flying, boxing, aquaplaning, and taught himself to type, play the piano, and do the breast stroke. When Wouk saw Shaw's *Don Juan in Hell,* he went home in despair: "You worm! You thug!" he raged at himself. "Get out of this business!" But next morning he was still in business, lifting the court-martial sequence out of *The Caine.* He wrote the whole play in "three horrible weeks."

Accent on Form. From *Babbit,* to *The Grapes of Wrath,* to *The Naked and the Dead,* a generation of talented but angry men has been bending the ear of U.S. readers, almost suggesting that thinking men should secede from the U.S. Wouk is not an angry man. But there is more than artless optimism or patriotism beneath the surface of his stories. Wouk denies taking stands for or against anything, but the evidence of the books contradicts him. There is an indictment in *The Caine Mutiny*—not, ultimately, of Queeg, the maniacal martinet, but of Keefer, the phony intellectual. There is an indictment in *Marjorie Morningstar*—of Noel Airman, the restless Bohemian.

These characters are not indicted because they are intellectuals, but because they are irresponsible. What Wouk is saying, in effect, is that if everyone acted like Keefer, armies would fall apart, and wars would be lost. If everyone acted like Airman, marriages, families and society would crumble. These are platitudes, but they are the platitudes (as Wouk has Willie Keith say) of "growing up."

To Wouk, rebellion for rebellion's sake is an outmoded adolescent cliché. Friends find him a hard man to know, perhaps because he is without capacity for the sustained and often neurotic introspection in which writers often indulge. If all this makes him a conformist, he is willing to bear the tag, provided that the accent is on the second syllable. Says Wouk: "One must impose a form on life."

The critical meat cleavers may indeed be out for Herman Wouk this time around, but though they cut up the work, they will miss the man. Novels No. 5 and No. 6 are already in the mental blueprint stage ("I wouldn't even tell my wife what they're about"). Says Wouk earnestly: "I'm going to write novels for the rest of my life, each one better than the last."

QUESTIONS ON CONTENT

1. Why is Wouk called "a unique figure in American letters"? Name some of the paradoxes in which Wouk is involved.
2. Why are the five points of belief expressed in *The Caine Mutiny* called "real shockers"? (Compare the thesis of "Wanted: An American Novel.")
3. Explain: "Wouk is a Sinclair Lewis in reverse."
4. Does this review so thoroughly summarize this novel that the reader's curiosity is dampened? Explain.
5. Is interest in what Wouk has written stimulated by the attention given to his personal life? Discuss.

SUGGESTIONS FOR PAPERS

Writing about those who write about books may seem to be a distant sort of assignment. Your job, however, is chiefly to examine various methods used by those whose job it is to report books. If you can develop an approach to your own problem of reporting what you find in books, the purpose of this chapter will be realized.

1. Examine the titles of each review in this chapter. Why didn't the reviewers simply use the titles of the books which they were considering? Which titles exhibit the central idea of the review? Do they also isolate the central idea of the book being reviewed? What do you conclude concerning the importance of titles for this sort of article?

2. Examine the first paragraph in each review. What pattern do you discover about getting a review started? (I The function of beginnings; II Samples of beginnings; III Conclusions drawn from these samples.)

3. Examine last paragraphs of these reviews. What pattern do

you discover about ending reviews? (Same structure suggested for number 2.)

4. Isolate the body of each review. At what point does the body of the review start and end? What sort of material is treated in the body? What conclusions may be drawn concerning the middle sections ("the body") of these reviews?

5. Define "allusion." Look up all the allusions in one of the reviews or in the editorial from *Life* and show how identification of the allusions serves to illuminate what the writer has to say.

6. Read another review of one of the books considered in this chapter. (Consult the *Book Review Digest,* in which you will find a number of reviews of these books listed.) Compare the two reviews.

7. Consider carefully the thesis of the editorial, "Wanted: An American Novel." First, set down what you think the thesis is. Next, consider the implications of the thesis. Finally, attack or defend the thesis.

8. *Time* editors in "The Wouk Mutiny" list five beliefs of the novelist Wouk as exhibited in *The Caine Mutiny.* Examine these beliefs with the idea of showing that they are, or are not, good criteria for producing good novels.

9. Show how a usable formula may be worked out to guide one in writing about books. This formula may be deduced from the structure of the five reviews which you have read.

10. Select the review which best succeeds in introducing the book being reviewed to the reader. Closely analyze the reasons for making this selection. Does the reviewer consider impartially the strength and weakness of the book? Does he prove his points by *telling* or by *showing* (that is, by quoting appropriate passages)? Does he tell enough but not too much of the contents?

SOME TITLES FOR PAPERS

1. The Importance of Titles for Reviews
2. Beginnings Examined
3. Endings Examined
4. Between Beginning and Ending
5. Putting Books in Context
6. The Function of Allusions, with Examples
7. Scholarly Work for the General Reader
8. The Use of Quotations in Book Reviews

Index to Authors and Titles

777